ENCYCLOPEDIA OF
FEDERAL AGENCIES
AND COMMISSIONS

ENCYCLOPEDIA OF FEDERAL AGENCIES AND COMMISSIONS

Kathleen Thompson Hill
&
Gerald N. Hill

Facts On File, Inc.

Encyclopedia of Federal Agencies and Commissions

Facts On File, Inc.
132 West 31st Street
New York NY 10001

Library of Congress Cataloging-in-Publication Data
Hill, Kathleen, 1941–
Encyclopedia of federal agencies and commissions / by Kathleen Thompson Hill
& Gerald N. Hill.
p. cm.
Includes bibliographical references and index.
ISBN 0-8160-4843-6
1. Administrative agencies—United States—Encyclopedias.
2. Executive departments—United States—Encyclopedias. 3. Independent regulatory commissions—United States—Encyclopedias. 4. United States—Politics and government—Encyclopedias. I. Hill, Gerald N. II. Title.

JK9.H536 2004
351.73'03—dc222003061221

Text design by David Strelecky

Cover design by Cathy Rincon

Line illustrations by David Hodges

Printed in the United States of America

VB FOF 10 9 8 7 6 5 4 3 2 1

This book is printed on acid-free paper.

— CONTENTS —

~ INTRODUCTION ~

The United States bears little resemblance to the uncertain experiment in a democratic republic that was launched in 1789 with a population of almost 4 million. The Executive Branch was operated by three departments—State, Treasury, and War—and an attorney general. Secretary of State Thomas Jefferson had a total staff of five clerks. The entire armed forces—army and navy—consisted of 718 men. The budget was numbered in the thousands, not trillions, and the money came primarily from tariffs and some licensing, for an income tax would not be legalized for 125 years.

As the nation grew in size, population, and power, the government expanded and took on new functions to meet the needs and challenges of the changing world. The challenge of the American people to deal with the government has become more complex and difficult. The era when President Abraham Lincoln would set aside time each week to listen to the problems and requests of average citizens is just a quaint memory.

Government assistance has become commonplace—for business, for agriculture, or through available loans to make home purchase possible. The individual can greatly benefit from knowing where and how that federal aid can be obtained. In some cases, the federal government protects our society from foul air, contaminated water, or spreading disease.

The federal government occasionally steps in to guarantee individual rights against ethnic discrimination, vote fraud, or stock manipulation (or at least it tries to). Government regulation enters everyone's life, and the individual must know where to look to meet those standards or even be sure what they are.

For people to gain the full benefits of government programs, avoid difficulties of dealing with the government, and avoid the snares lurking among government bureaucracy and arcane regulations, clearly understood information must be readily available. The government and its programs are not a neat package. Often they were created by a historic chance to meet an emergency need and linger on (such as farm subsidies).

Constantly in the throes of creation and evolution of competing ideas, the federal government is rife with redundancies, often creating confusion even among the agencies themselves, with duplicated and overlapping offices and programs. For example, the "intelligence community" is scattered in a dozen locations, as if each agency wanted its own intelligence office. To sort these out, both public and private officials and businesses need roadmaps to find their way through the Cretan maze that is the U.S. government.

In the most powerful, far-reaching, and complex government in the history of the world, a single source that shows the public how to navigate through its complexities is essential. Our goal is to create that guide. The fledgling government of 1789 is a success, even with its uniquely American pitfalls. We hope to help readers and researchers find their way through the bureaucratic gridlock and enjoy the trip.

—Kathleen Thompson Hill
Gerald N. Hill

EXECUTIVE
BRANCH

EXECUTIVE OFFICE OF THE PRESIDENT

THE WHITE HOUSE

The White House is not only the residence of the president and his wife (and, possibly in the future, of a woman president and her husband), but is also the working hub of the executive branch of government. President George Washington selected the site for the mansion on June 29, 1791, on a visit to the newly designated District of Columbia. Plans for what is now the central element of the building were begun in 1792, and it was constructed in 1799 and 1800. Called the President's House at the time, it was the largest house in the United States. Although the plastering was not completed, the furniture inadequate, and there was no garden, President John Adams arrived on November 1, 1800, exactly a month before Washington City officially became the capital of the United States, and spent the night in an upstairs bedroom next to a room designated as his office. The next morning he wrote a letter to his wife, Abigail, still back at the Adams farm in Quincy, Massachusetts, in which he penned his famous benediction: "I pray to heaven to bestow the best of blessings on this house and all that shall hereafter inhabit. May none but honest and wise men ever rule under this roof."

Abigail Adams joined the president on November 16, 1800, and reported to friends back home that the house was beautifully situated above the Potomac River, and the country was "romantic but wild." (David McCullough, *John Adams*, 551–553) Indeed, the capitol building was incomplete, Washington City was only a scattering of boardinghouses and stores, the land swampy, and the roads not much better than rutted trails. The Adamses kept all 13 fireplaces blazing to ward off the cold and dry the rooms as they were plastered. Abigail hung her laundry out to dry in the large audience room on the ground floor. They held the first reception in the President's House on January 1, 1801. Adams ordered the planting of a garden, but his successor, Thomas Jefferson, who took office on March 4, 1801, changed the proposed design to one of his own, planted trees, and laid out a flower garden, walls, and fences.

During the War of 1812 against Great Britain, on August 24 and 25, 1814, British troops invaded Washington, D.C., and set fire to the President's House, the Capitol, and all other government buildings except the Patent Office, in retaliation for the burning of York (Toronto), Canada, in April 1813 by the American army. Just before President Madison and other government officials fled Washington, Dolley Madison, the president's wife, rescued paintings and artwork from the mansion, and had them hauled to safety in a wagon. The Madisons returned to Washington two days later, and stayed in the Octagon House while the badly damaged mansion was repaired and expanded. To cover the smoke stains on the outside walls the building was whitewashed in 1817. Soon it would be popularly referred to as the White House. In 1902 at the request of President Theodore Roosevelt it was officially designated the "White House."

Throughout the 19th century the second floor of the White House was employed both for the president's working offices and the residence of the presidential family, while the first floor was used for receptions, ceremonial events, state banquets, and festive occasions. On the day of President Andrew Jackson's inauguration, the chairs, carpets, walls, and draperies suffered substantial damage when the ground floor of the White House was opened to some 5,000 citizens celebrating the accession of a "people's president." Presidents James Monroe, John Quincy Adams, and Andrew Jackson all took an avid interest in the gardens, planting trees and completing Jefferson's garden plans. John Quincy Adams hired the first White House gardener. President Rutherford B. Hayes inaugurated a tradition of planting commemorative trees, of which there are almost 40 today.

In 1902 President Theodore Roosevelt attempted to solve the less-than-satisfactory second floor mix of executive offices with personal living quarters by urging a west wing and an east wing for presidential business, both reached by colonnades from the central mansion—concepts Jefferson had recommended a hundred years earlier. Construction of the West Wing was completed in 1906, but the East Wing was not added until 1942. In 1909 the Oval Office as the president's principal workspace was built in the center of the south side of the west wing, but in 1934 it was reconstructed at the southeast corner. President Franklin D. Roosevelt held his frequent press conferences in the Oval Office with the reporters standing and Roosevelt seated behind the large desk. The desk in the Oval Office, a gift from Queen Victoria of Great Britain in 1880, is called the *Resolute* desk because it was built of wood from a British navy ship that had once been salvaged by an American vessel and returned to Britain. Starting with President Rutherford B. Hayes, every president except Johnson, Nixon, and Ford has used this desk.

Ellen (Mrs. Woodrow) Wilson had a rose garden planted just outside the Oval Office. President John F. Kennedy had it redesigned so that it could be used for ceremonial occasions, a purpose it often serves. Lady Bird Johnson named it the Jacqueline Kennedy Rose Garden.

During the administration of President Calvin Coolidge a third floor was added to provide more living space in the main building. A portico on the second floor was built in 1948, a concept of President Harry Truman's opposed by architectural purists.

In late 1948 it was discovered that the main portion of the mansion was in extremely bad condition with floors in danger of collapsing and dryrot in many places, and the professional conclusion was that three interior floors of the residence had to be disassembled and rebuilt with modern infrastructure, new facilities, reformulated use of space—in short, a massive job to save the White House, which had not had a major structural improvement since 1817. The project took more than two and half years. The Trumans were required to move to the nearby Blair House (usually used as a residence for visiting dignitaries), and the president would walk to work each day to the West Wing accompanied by wary Secret Service agents.

On the first floor of the West Wing is the Oval Office, with nearby staff, secretaries, the cabinet room, the president's study, the Roosevelt Room available for meetings, and offices for the chief of staff, the vice president (first used by Vice President Walter Mondale), the National Security Advisor, the press secretary, and communications directors. Second-floor offices are occupied by the chair of the National Economic Council, White House counsel, directors of legislative affairs, political affairs, and public liaison, and other officials of the executive White House whom the president chooses to have under one roof rather than at the Eisenhower Executive Office Building.

The East Wing houses the offices of the first lady, the president's theater, the visitors' entrance, and miscellaneous offices. It is connected to the mansion by the east colonnade.

CONTACT Address: The White House, 1600 Pennsylvania Avenue NW, Washington, DC 20500; Phone: basic switchboard: (202) 456-1414, comments: (202) 456-1111; Fax: (202) 456-2461, for the hearing impaired: (202) 456-6213, for comments: (202) 395-0805 (equal employment opportunity office), (202) 456-2121 (visitors' office); E-mail: president: president@whitehouse.gov, vice president: vice.president@whitehouse.gov; Website: www.whitehouse.gov/contact.

VISITING AND TOURS

The White House Visitors Center located in the East Wing is open every day 7:30 A.M. to 4:00 P.M.

The center contains exhibits, a sales area, and the only restrooms available to the public. Tours and individuals must start here. The best way to guarantee getting tickets to a tour is to ask at the office of one's member of Congress, and is mandatory for school groups (grades 4 to 12 from the same school), hearing-impaired and visually-impaired groups, and veterans' groups. For visitors mobility-impaired and requiring a wheelchair, notify the officer at the visitors entrance to see if a wheelchair is available since the number is limited.

For visiting information, telephone (202) 456-7041 at any time of day or night.

OFFICE OF THE VICE PRESIDENT

The office of vice president was a remarkable invention of the Constitutional Convention in September 1787, reported back to the delegates by the "Committee on Postponed Matters." Prior to that time the office was unknown not only in government but in business. Faced with the issue of how to replace the president in case of his death, resignation, or impeachment, the Founding Fathers decided that by creating an office of an automatic successor in the case of a vacancy in the presidency the transition would be prompt and smooth. Since the person must be able to become president at any moment, the qualifications for vice president were the same as the chief executive: more than 35 years old native-born citizen of the United States.

On the theory that the vice president normally would be the second most popular man in the country, the delegates to the Constitutional Convention provided that the runner-up in electoral votes would be elected vice president. If the vice president did not get a majority, then the Senate would choose among the two leaders in electoral votes, which is still in effect. But the original election system gave each elector (until 1828 elected by the legislatures) two votes without distinguishing between president and vice president. The system was the one major error in Constitution drafting at the convention. The system allowed Alexander Hamilton to make a successful attempt to deny John Adams the presidency in favor of his vice presidential running mate in 1796, and in 1800 resulted in a tie between the two candidates on the Democratic-Republican ticket, Thomas Jefferson and Aaron Burr. It took 36 House ballots to break the deadlock, achieved when one Federalist congressman agreed to abstain, thus giving his state to Jefferson. By 1804 the Constitution had been amended to provide that the votes for president and vice president would be so specified, and the two-vote-per-elector method was scrapped.

CONSTITUTIONAL DUTIES

Having created the office, the framers of the Constitution had to give the vice president something to do, and they chose to make him president of the Senate, as presiding officer, only able to vote in the case of a tie. It soon became the practice that the vice president could not participate in debate, after the first vice president, John Adams, was rebuked for being partisan from the chair. Only on procedural matters could he speak, and for a century he has turned to the clerk of the Senate and the parliamentarian (dating from 1935) for prompt advice, who cue him on the rules. Thomas Jefferson, the second vice president, wrote a manual of Senate rules, much of which survives more than two centuries later. In 1884 the Senate adopted a set of detailed standing rules, 40 in number and often amended since, known as *Senate Procedures,* in which senior senators are well versed.

The vice president has another responsibility derivative from his constitutional duties, which is almost universally overlooked: presiding officer of the Senate when the Senate tries federal judges, including a justice of the Supreme Court, on impeachment charges. Thus, the vice president serves as the judge in such proceedings, while the senators are the jurors.

Urged by President Thomas Jefferson, who oftimes placed partisan politics over the independence of the three branches of government, his Democrat-Republicans in the House attempted in 1804 to curb the Federalist-dominated judiciary by bringing eight impeachment charges against Justice Samuel Chase, including that he had "bullied" attorneys, made anti- Democratic-Republican comments in a charge to a grand jury, and that he was temperamentally unfit. The 10-day impeachment trial opened on January 2, 1805, with Vice President Burr—fresh from having killed Federalist leader Alexander Hamilton in a duel (and hated by every Federalist senator), and previously shunned by Jefferson as well—sitting in the chair. Leading legal talent lined up on both sides. To the surprise of the Senate, Burr took complete charge, pointing out that this was a trial and the Senate sat as a jury, so he ordered the senators to keep their seats and listen to every word, and that they could not eat, drink, or wander in and out as was their common practice. The vice president displayed a keen knowledge of the rules of evidence and trial conduct, ruled promptly and with precision; but most of all he conducted this crucial trial with the utmost in dignity and fairness. If the vote was to be on party lines, Justice Chase would be dismissed from office and the independence of the judiciary envisioned by the framers of the Constitution would be crippled. Chase was acquitted, and Burr's tarnished reputation somewhat burnished. But most important the vice president had helped save the separation of power among the branches of government.

Nevertheless, until well into the 20th century the vice president had little to do and only then on the largesse of the president. Adams wrote his wife, Abigail, that "My country in its wisdom contrived for me the most insignificant office that ever the invention of man contrived or his imagination conceived."

Franklin D. Roosevelt's first vice president, John Nance Garner (1933–41), found he had less power than when he was Speaker of the House, and made the famous comment that the vice presidency "isn't worth a pitcher of warm spit" (and that's the clean version). America's funniest vice president, Thomas R. Marshall (1913–21) said that a vice president was like a man in "a catatonic state, who knows what's going on around him, but can't do anything about it." Vice presidents were seldom close to their presidents, with the exception of Van Buren, who was Jackson's closest adviser and chosen successor.

BACKGROUND OF VICE PRESIDENTS

Contrary to the public myth that the second place usually has been occupied by obscure figures or party hacks (epitomized by Vice President Throttlebottom in the 1930s musical *Of Thee I Sing,* who could visit the White House only on a guided tour), most of the vice presidents were substantial political figures at the time they were elected. John Adams (1789–97), the first vice president, Thomas Jefferson (1797–1801), and Theodore Roosevelt (1901) are still well known. Ironically, Adams arrived at New York, the first U.S. capital, on April 20, 1789, 10 days before President-elect Washington, and was inducted before the Senate (there was no specific oath for the vice president until Congress adopted one). Thus, for 10 days the United States had a vice president, but no president.

Among less familiar early vice presidents, George Clinton (1805–12) was seven times governor of New York, Elbridge Gerry (1813–14) signed the Declaration of Independence, was a diplomat and governor of Massachusetts, Daniel Tompkins (1817–25) was governor of New York, John C. Calhoun (1825–32), a congressional leader and secretary of war, and Martin Van Buren (1833–37) had been governor and secretary of state. John Tyler (1841), the first vice president to succeed to the presidency by death of the president, was a former senator and governor of Virginia. He set a vital precedent by insisting he was president and not just "acting" president upon the demise of President William Henry Harrison after only 30 days in office.

Richard Johnson (1837–41), George Dallas (1845–49), William R. King (1849, dying within less than two months), Hannibal Hamlin (1861–65), Andrew Johnson (1865), Henry Wilson (1873–75), Thomas Hendricks (1885), Charles Fairbanks (1905–09), Thomas Marshall (1913–21), Calvin Coolidge (1921–23), Charles Curtis (1929–33), Harry Truman (1945), Alben Barkley (1949–53), Richard Nixon (1953–61), Lyndon B. Johnson (1961–63), Hubert Humphrey (1965–69), Nelson Rockefeller (1974–77), Walter Mondale (1977–81), Dan Quayle (1989–93), and Al Gore (1993–2001) were all senators or governors or both. Schuyler Colfax (1869–73) and John Nance Garner (1933–41) were Speakers of the House; Charles Dawes (1925–29) won the Nobel Peace Prize; Henry Wallace (1941–45) was secretary of agriculture; Gerald Ford (1973–74) was Republican leader in the House; George H.W. Bush (1981–89) had a résumé of top-level government service of considerable length. Aaron Burr (1801–05), vilified for shooting Alexander Hamilton in a duel and his involvement in a filibustering scheme to create a nation of northern Mexico, had been a senator and political leader in New York, and even confessed bribe-taker Spiro Agnew (1969–73) was governor of Maryland.

NOMINATING VICE PRESIDENTIAL CANDIDATES

Nominees for vice president at national party conventions were traditionally intended to "balance" the ticket, based on factors of geography,

philosophy (conservative to balance a moderate, for example), age, or political experience. Dallas and Dawes were each hastily chosen after the proposed nominees rejected the honor. Ex-congressman and noted orator John C. Breckinridge (1857–61), the youngest vice president at age 35, and Coolidge were each nominated from the convention floor—Breckinridge as a moderate southerner to balance northerner James Buchanan and squeaky-clean Coolidge as the delegates' reaction to being bull-dozed by the party bosses in the "smoke-filled room" into accepting Warren Harding. Several nominees were selected to satisfy the perceived desires of key political bosses particularly from vote-heavy New York. Vice presidents from that state included Millard Fillmore (1849–50) only a state comptroller; William Wheeler (1877–81) was the rare honest New York congressman; Chester Alan Arthur (1881) had never been elected to office but seized on the offer to balance the ticket; millionaire Levi P. Morton (1889–93) had been ambassador to France; and James "Sunny Jim" Sherman (1909–12) was a pleasant technician from the House.

Adlai Stevenson (1893–97) from Illinois had been assistant postmaster general and was intended to balance independent-minded Grover Cleveland; Garret Hobart (1897–99) was a New Jersey Republican national committeeman and was nominated because McKinley's campaign manager, Mark Hanna, demanded it. In 1864 pro-Union Democrat Andrew Johnson was nominated (with behind-the-scenes nudging by President Lincoln) to create a pro-Union coalition ticket with Republican Lincoln. In 1932 House Speaker Garner was awarded the vice presidential nomination for releasing his delegates to Franklin D. Roosevelt in order to give FDR enough convention votes to reach the two-thirds majority he needed.

Governor Theodore Roosevelt was pushed for the vice presidential nomination by political boss Senator Thomas Platt in order to get Teddy out of New York, where he refused to make appointments of incompetents urged by the boss. McKinley's campaign manager, Mark Hanna, shouted at Platt: "Don't any of you realize that there is only one life between that madman [Roosevelt] and the presidency?" Hanna was right; five months into his second term McKinley was shot by a real madman, and Roosevelt was president.

Until 1940 the vice presidential candidates were chosen by party leaders with the presidential nominee having little input. That year Roosevelt demanded that his secretary of agriculture, Henry A. Wallace, be nominated by the Democratic convention if FDR agreed to run for an unprecedented third term. Four years later the Democrats staged the only 20th-century contentious floor fight for the vice president nomination and denied Wallace renomination in favor of Senator Harry S. Truman, in part because Wallace had embarrassed the Roosevelt administration by publicly feuding with the secretary of commerce over allocation of war resources. Nevertheless, Wallace campaigned vigorously for the Roosevelt-Truman ticket.

Since that time the conventions have generally awaited for the presidential nominee to name his choice for a running mate, sometimes after going through the motions of having a committee of party leaders make recommendations. John F. Kennedy's offer of the vice president slot to the runner-up for the nomination, Senate leader Texan Lyndon Johnson, was intended to heal wounds and gain the support of southern politicos. This proved to be the one time in presidential election history that the choice of the vice presidential nominee made a difference in the final result. In the tight 1960 race Johnson successfully campaigned to keep several southern states in the Democratic column, and helped hold some Protestants dubious about Catholic Kennedy. Reagan's selection of his major convention challenger, George H. W. Bush, brought the Republicans into the campaign as unified, despite Bush's

primary campaign crack that Reagan's supply side idea was "voodoo economics."

By the same token, 1972 Democratic nominee Senator George McGovern's hasty, late-night choice of Senator Thomas Eagleton—soon revealed to have had several bouts with mental depression and shock treatments in an institution—doomed the McGovern campaign from the start. Eagleton voluntarily left the ticket and the Democratic National Committee chose former Peace Corps director (and Kennedy in-law) Sargent Shriver, who proved an able campaigner, but it did no good.

Jimmy Carter systematically interviewed several potential vice presidents before selecting Walter Mondale. George H. W. Bush picked Senator Dan Quayle as a purely personal choice without informing any of his advisers. Al Gore as Bill Clinton's running mate was unusual in that Gore did not balance the ticket. Clinton and Gore were approximately the same age, came from neighboring southern states, and were of almost identical philosophies. Richard Cheney was chair of George W. Bush's search committee for a vice presidential nominee and eventually suggested himself. Since the Constitution provides that the president and vice president must be residents of different states, Cheney had to quickly move from Texas to his original home state of Wyoming, where he had a second residence and had served as a representative, and re-register.

MODERN VICE PRESIDENTS AND ADDED FUNCTIONS

Wallace (1941–45) was the first vice president given administrative duties, including chairing the wartime Board of Economic Warfare. Since that time most vice presidents have performed some functions other than presiding over the Senate, if only ceremonial, political, or diplomatic. During illnesses of President Eisenhower and the recovery of the seriously wounded President Reagan, Vice Presidents Nixon and

George Bush, respectively, called cabinet meetings, but were careful not to take any action without presidential approval and studiously avoided doing or saying anything that could be considered usurping presidential powers. Eisenhower was happy to have Nixon perform the dirty work of politics, attacking Democrats and touring the country in support of Republican members of Congress, and quite often accusing the opposition of being "soft on communism."

Vice Presidents Lyndon B. Johnson, Hubert Humphrey (1965–69), Walter Mondale (1977–81), George H. W. Bush (1981–89), Dan Quayle (1989–93), Al Gore (1993–2001), and Richard Cheney all performed significant tasks for the administrations they served. Gore headed up a task force on "Reinventing Government" to streamline and reduce the federal bureaucracy, and Cheney has been a powerful voice in policymaking, diplomacy, and public pronouncements—the most influential of any second man. By statute nowadays the vice president is a member of the National Security Council and on the Board of Regents of the Smithsonian Institution, as well as serving on various committees as the president directs.

VACANCY IN VICE PRESIDENCY OR DISABILITY OF THE PRESIDENT

Between the elections of 1789 and 1966, due to the death of either the president or the vice president (and Calhoun's resignation three months early to accept election to the Senate), there was no vice president for a total of almost 34 years. Based on various federal statutes determining presidential succession, the president pro tem of the Senate, the secretary of state, or the Speaker of the House would be next in line. Worse yet, for brief periods of time there was no Senate president pro tem. A further complication was the repeated situation when the president suffered life-threatening illnesses. George Washington, Grover Cleveland, Woodrow Wilson, Dwight D. Eisenhower, and Ronald Reagan (seriously wounded in an assassination attempt in 1981) were dangerously ill, but recovered. In the case of Wilson, who suffered two strokes that left him invalided and unable to function fully during the last 18 months of his administration, his wife, Edith, made many executive decisions in the president's name. She and Wilson's physician conspired to prevent Vice President Thomas Marshall from visiting the president.

With the sudden death of Franklin D. Roosevelt, the illnesses of Eisenhower, the assassination of John F. Kennedy, the two attempts on the life of Gerald Ford, and the near-fatal shooting of Reagan all in recent memory, Congress determined that it was necessary to find a permanent solution to prevent the gaps in succession or maintenance of government during potential periods of presidential disability. The Senate Judiciary Committee, chaired by Senator Birch Bayh, proposed what became the Twenty-fifth Amendment, which was adopted by Congress and ratified by the sufficient number of states in 1967. There are three key elements to the Amendment:

- In case of vacancy in the vice presidency "the President shall nominate a Vice President who shall take office upon confirmation by a majority vote of both House of Congress."

- In case the president believes he is unable to discharge his duties, he may notify the Speaker of the House and the president pro tempore of the Senate of that fact and the vice president shall be acting president until the president notifies them in writing that he is able to function. This has been used for brief periods when the president foresees being anesthetized for an operation or medical procedure, when the writing specifies the anticipated period of incapacity.

- When the vice president and a majority of the cabinet declare in writing submitted to the Speaker of the House and the president pro tempore of the Senate such a declaration, the vice president shall become acting president. When the president submits a declaration to the same officers that he is able to resume his duties, but the vice president and a majority of the cabinet disagree, they shall declare in writing to the Speaker and president pro tem that the disability still exists. In that case the House and Senate shall convene within 48 hours and within 21 days determine whether the disability exists, which can only be so judged by a two-thirds vote of each body. If Congress does not decide the disability exists, the president shall resume his duties.

Fortunately, the Twenty-fifth Amendment was in place in the 1970s, when Vice President Spiro Agnew was charged with taking bribes (payoffs for approving state contracts when governor and receiving a nickel kickback for every pack of cigarettes sold in Maryland state buildings) and tax evasion, forcing his resignation on October 10, 1973, as part of a plea bargain with the U.S. attorney to avoid a prison term, leaving the vice presidency vacant. President Nixon appointed Republican House leader Gerald Ford, who was approved by both houses of Congress after hearings and became vice president on December 26, 1973. When President Nixon was forced to resign on August 9, 1974, as a result of the evolving Watergate scandal, Ford became president. He, in turn, nominated former New York governor Nelson Rockefeller for vice president. After prolonged hearings, in which there was considerable objection from conservative witnesses, Rockefeller was confirmed on December 19, 1974. During the period of the hearings pending confirmation, the Speaker of the House was the legal successor to the presidency.

Fourteen vice presidents have subsequently become president. Adams, Jefferson, Van Buren, Nixon, and the first George Bush ran and were elected; Tyler, Fillmore, Andrew Johnson, Arthur, Theodore Roosevelt, Coolidge, Truman, and

Lyndon Johnson upon the death of the president, and Ford when Nixon resigned rather than face an impeachment trial he was sure to lose.

LOCATION Currently the vice president has three offices. The office that the public can visit is the so-called Ceremonial Office, which is an elegant suite in the Eisenhower Office Building, Washington, D.C. 20501, across the street from the West Wing, dating back to 1871, and served for many years as the office of the secretary of the navy. The first vice president to use the office was Lyndon B. Johnson, and with the exception of Hubert Humphrey it has been used by all vice presidents since. The key piece of furniture is a desk that was the president's desk in the Oval Office 1901–29 and used by President Truman. Vice President Johnson and all vice presidents since have used the desk. Above it hangs a century-old chandelier that began existence as a gas-lit Victorian fixture. Secondly, as modern vice presidents became integral members of presidential administrations, a working office in the West Wing was provided the vice president, starting with Walter Mondale, and continuing. Since the vice president is president of the Senate, there is an office for the vice president in the Senate wing of the Capitol, which some have used to good effect in monitoring legislation and entertaining senators. Woodrow Wilson's vice president Thomas Marshall, known for his Indiana witticisms, kept the office door open and said he felt like a monkey in the zoo waiting for passersby to throw him peanuts.

Beginning in 1975, as the result of legislation sponsored by Senator (and former vice president) Hubert Humphrey, the government has provided the vice president with an official residence. A 20-room Victorian, built in the 1890s as the house for the superintendent of the Naval Observatory, it stands on a hill off Massachusetts Avenue. Multimillionaire Nelson Rockefeller was the vice president when the home became available, but he preferred his own estate, which was much more spacious. He used the official residence only for entertaining. However, Walter and Joan Mondale, who moved there in January 1977, loved living in the residence, as have other vice presidents.

CONTACT Phone: (202) 456-2326; Website: www.whitehouse.gov.

OFFICE OF MANAGEMENT AND BUDGET

The Office of Management and Budget (OMB) was inaugurated as the Bureau of the Budget in 1921 by President Warren G. Harding, on the recommendation and urging of Charles G. Dawes, who became its initial director. Dawes, a successful lawyer, banker, and brigadier general in charge of the American Army's overseas supply procurement in World War I, believed that management of the budget was essential to a more businesslike and efficient federal executive. Under Dawes's dynamic leadership the bureau became a symbol of good government in the cloud of the corruption-riddled Harding administration. Dawes was elected vice president of the United States in 1924 and was awarded the Nobel Peace Prize in 1925 for restructuring the reparations plan for the defeated nations in World War I.

Originally located within the Treasury Department, under President Franklin D. Roosevelt it was transferred to the Executive Office of the President in 1939, where its staff had a direct involvement in the preparation of the budget proposed by the president. As its management responsibilities expanded, it was renamed the Office of Management and Budget (OMB) under President Richard Nixon.

FUNCTIONS

The chief functions of OMB are assisting the president in preparation and justifying the proposed budget and the interrelated task of recommending the proper allocation of resources and effective management of agencies consistent with the goals in the budget and the available resources. It continually monitors the activities of all government agencies, promoting consistent and improved management and coordination among agencies. While required to enforce caps on certain spending and strict fiscal responsibility, it tries to protect the goals and philosophy of the incumbent administration. All of these activities are conducted within an extensive web of statutes and regulations.

What the OMB does not do is significant. It conducts no programs, gives no grants, does not handle funds, and seldom issues regulations. It makes plans, sets goals, gives practical advice, gathers information and analyzes it dispassionately, and plans for the future (and adjusts those plans even after abrupt changes in circumstances). The president relies heavily upon the collective opinion of the staff.

Election of a new president with a different agenda or external circumstances often requires changes in the philosophy and emphasis of OMB. In short, OMB performs a balancing act in which the need to maintain businesslike professional management, political and entrenched bureaucratic pressures, policy demands of the administration, and economic reality are all juggled. For example, in the first year of the Reagan administration the office was directed by its director—an economic adviser to the new president—to adopt a policy grounded in so-called supply side economics, sharply different from those advocated by President Carter. After planning for five years based on an anticipated continuing budget surplus, suddenly before the end of 2001 the OMB faced an unexpected deficit.

ORGANIZATION

Resource Management Offices are each staffed by experts in a particular program. Each of these offices provides information, analysis, and evaluation of options, implementation, and basic budget concepts to federal agencies and members of Congress. In the case of the latter they assist in negotiating with relevant congressional committee leaders in regard to program, resources, and budget. Budget review is conducted on a continuing basis by these offices, including monitoring the status of legislative action.

The *Legislative Reference Division* coordinates the incumbent administration's legislative program, resolves differences among agency positions in regard to specific legislation, and prepares statements in support of legislation.

The *Office of Federal Financial Management* develops and directs financial management systems to be employed by executive departments and agencies.

The *Office of Federal Procurement Policy* works on improving procurement practices in regard to purchases of property, goods, and services by all federal agencies or when federally assisted.

The *Office of Information and Regulatory Affairs* adopts policies for management of statistics, information dissemination by federal entities, and adoption of regulations.

MANAGEMENT

The director and deputy director of the OMB are appointed by the president subject to confirmation by the Senate, as are four other top administrators. Thus, the upper echelon reflects the philosophy of the administration. Most of the remaining officials of the office are personal appointments by the president or the director not subject to confirmation. At the next level are specialists who provide a continuum of professionalism.

CONTACT Address: Office of Management and Budget, 725 17th Street NW, Washington, DC 20503; Phone: (202) 395-3080; Fax: (202) 395-3504; Website: www.whitehouse.gov/omb.

NATIONAL SECURITY COUNCIL

The National Security Council was established on July 26, 1947, as one element of the National Security Act, which was enacted during the administration of President Harry S. Truman. It was a key response of that administration to the increasing aggressiveness of the Soviet Union marking the onset of the cold war. Other elements of that act included formation of the Central Intelligence Agency, bringing the Departments of War (army and air force) and Navy together as the Defense Department headed by a secretary of defense, and establishment of a coordinated National Military Establishment and the National Resources Board.

While conceived as a means to develop foreign policy relating to security and defense, to encourage and implement cooperation between such departments as State and Defense, and as a conduit for information to the administration, the council's principal function became primarily as advisory to the president. Its chief, now entitled NATIONAL SECURITY ADVISOR, has near-cabinet status, a role not imagined in the early years of the NSC. The council's initial membership consisted of the president as nominal chair, the secretaries of defense and state, the chair of the National Security Resources Board, and the secretaries of army, navy, and air force—the latter three were soon replaced by secretary of the treasury and the vice president. While Truman was still president, he added the director of the Bureau of the Budget, the chairman of the Joint Chiefs of Staff, the head of the Central Intelligence Agency, a couple of special advisers, and the council's executive secretary, who managed the council's administration. From the outset the council's staff has always been limited in numbers with much of the information gathering performed by cabinet departments and other agencies.

In the more than 50 years of its existence, the structure, functions, influence, and relationship to the president and various departments have varied greatly depending on the predilections, styles, and policies of the presidents, the personalities and powers of secretaries of state and other departments, and the personal and professional strengths and methods of the council's chief.

During the Korean conflict the NSC became particularly active and met regularly with President Truman, and was involved in considerable strategizing and coordination. One of its recommendations in late 1947 was authorization of a stepup in covert operations involving secret intervention in the affairs of other countries. Truman also set a pattern repeated by several future presidents, by relying on informal contacts and advisers outside any official structure such as the NSC.

President Dwight D. Eisenhower reorganized the council soon after taking office in 1953, creating a more formal structure for receiving policy suggestions and backup data from various departments, evaluating them and developing consensus recommendations for the president. This restructuring was based on a report by Robert Cutler, who successfully recommended that the executive secretary be designated as a special assistant to the president (a pattern followed in several advisory boards situated in the executive offices of the president). Cutler served for five years as the special assistant for national security affairs, but it was principally an administrative post. Cutler was careful not to run afoul of the strong-willed secretary of state John Foster Dulles, who was adamant that the council was limited to reviewing rather initiating foreign policies. Eisenhower felt the policy papers were

useful to him and all agencies related to foreign affairs; he personally held 329 meetings of the council.

President John F. Kennedy, upon taking office in 1961, responded to congressional criticism that the NSC was too bureaucratic by making a change that would have great significance in the long run: The special assistant to the president was given the title of National Security Advisor (a presidential appointee not subject to Senate confirmation) with authority to make proactive reports and recommendations to the council and the president. One function of the Advisor was to chair a semisecret committee to review covert actions proposed or actually undertaken by the Central Intelligence Agency. McGeorge Bundy, who became National Security Advisor on inauguration day in 1961, became an advocate of increased U.S. involvement in Vietnam, coincidentally resigning at the time of the 1966 Tet offensive, in which Viet Cong guerrillas inflicted substantial losses on American troops.

Bundy's role in the administrations of Kennedy and then President Lyndon B. Johnson was mainly individual, since Kennedy usually developed foreign policy through ad hoc groups to meet crises (such as the Cuban Missile Crisis), and small groups of selected advisers (including Bundy) and an informal committee known as the "Standing Group." Stung by the CIA's ineptitude in recommending the ill-fated Bay of Pigs Cuban invasion by anti-Castro insurgents, Kennedy set up a small committee on covert actions chaired by Bundy, but separate from his role as head of the National Security Council. Thus, the National Security Council diminished in importance, while the National Security Advisor became an influential member of the administration—essentially as the position remains today.

President Johnson treated the council's staff as personal to him, ignoring the council itself, while relying on Bundy and his assistant and successor, Walter Rostow, for advice and support of

Johnson's preconceived policies particularly in regard to foreign interventions. At the time of a rapid increase in troops sent to Vietnam in early 1965, Johnson called several meetings of the council in the guise of consultation, but actually to give the appearance of its support, and generally ignored it thereafter. Administration policy was discussed instead by a handful of advisers at Tuesday luncheons. Rostow, even more than Bundy, became a public cheerleader for LBJ's policies even while public opposition to them was growing.

However, it was President Richard Nixon's appointment as National Security Advisor of colorful academic Henry Kissinger, long an adviser on foreign affairs to various political figures, that firmly established the holder of the position as a dominant participant in foreign policy conception and implementation. Any tug-of-war with the State Department (and the secretary of state) over control was quickly awarded to Kissinger. Dr. Kissinger became the point man with foreign leaders and personally chaired interagency committees covering crises, intelligence, and arms control negotiations. He also revived the National Security Council by setting up a working system of committees to prepare research and position papers on a variety of topics that would be reviewed and assist him, the president, and other officials. The council staff was increased and became one of the first governmental agencies to use computers.

Nixon came to rely on Kissinger almost without question and enjoyed his company. It was Kissinger who prepared the way for Nixon's summit meetings, and took the role usually filled by the secretary of state in various international questions. Thus, when Kissinger proposed quiet negotiations to open the door to mainland (Communist) China, Nixon—who had made his political reputation as an indefatigable foe of communism—agreed, in what proved to be an international triumph. Kissinger eventually negotiated a conclusion to the war in Vietnam over a prolonged period, for which he was awarded the Nobel Peace Prize.

In the waning days of the Nixon presidency, Kissinger was appointed secretary of state as well, but it proved to be an untenable confusion of roles, and after a year in office President Gerald Ford named Lieutenant General Brent Scowcroft as National Security Advisor, while leaving Kissinger at state. As a result, the State Department again filled its normal role as the lead in foreign affairs, while Scowcroft refashioned the council to its intended position of analysis and review for the president.

In 1977 President Jimmy Carter downgraded the operation of the National Security Council, cutting staff, limiting the number of meetings, and relying primarily on meetings with Vice President Walter Mondale, the secretaries of state and defense, and a handful of advisers without taking notes or setting fixed agendas. Thus, the president got little benefit from the council's activities and developed no clear foreign policy in the area of national security. On the other hand, Carter steadily gave National Security Advisor Zbigniew Brezinski more functions (including arms control negotiations), and thus increased clout, and listened to him for much foreign policy advice, which annoyed Secretary of State Cyrus Vance. At the time of the taking of 58 American embassy officials by militants in Iran, the National Security Advisor and the secretary of state were completely at odds, and when Brezinski urged a military attempt to rescue the hostages, which turned into a disaster, Vance resigned.

In order to rein in any free-wheeling by the National Security Advisor, President Ronald Reagan attempted a substantial restructuring of the council, in which the Advisor no longer reported to the president, and set up committees on national security topics in which the council's role was only supportive. Pressed by the new secretary of state, Alexander Haig, foreign policy was primarily within the purview of the State Department. But the president had no independent source of advice to assist him in making final international decisions.

A year into his administration Reagan replaced the National Security Advisor with a friend, William P. Clark, whom he trusted. Clark regained the power to directly advise the president, and became a spokesman at times for the president's foreign policies and also carried on negotiations in the Middle East and elsewhere.

Clark was succeeded by Robert McFarlane, who had a unique view of the role of the National Security Advisor: that he could become directly involved in actually implementing policy (with his own view as to what policy was actually that of the president and/or the government). Thus, McFarlane along with Admiral John Poindexter and Lieutenant Colonel Oliver North cooked up a scheme in which arms were secretly sold to Iran in return for freeing hostages held by extremists (contrary to announced Reagan policy) and in turn funneled the money to the contras, who were fighting the leftward government of Nicaragua (contrary to American law). When revealed, the scandal disgraced the office of National Security Advisor, and led to appointment of a special counsel and an investigation by a board made up of Senator John Tower, former Senator and Secretary of State Edmund Muskie, and Scowcroft, which recommended several changes, including reduction of staff and dissolving the activist crisis pre-planning group. McFarlane attempted suicide, Colonel North was convicted of violations of law (overturned on appeal), and the president appointed Frank Carlucci as National Security Advisor to implement the reforms, including getting the NSC out of the operational business.

Within a year Carlucci was appointed secretary of defense, and in his place Reagan named as National Security Advisor the chief deputy on the council, General Colin Powell. Without public fanfare Powell continued the reform toward giving even-handed advice to the president, improving the policy review system, and laid the groundwork for the successful Reagan-Gorbachev summit meeting in 1988.

Under President George H. W. Bush Brent Scowcroft returned as National Security Advisor, who carried out some changes in structure desired by the president, and maintained a both professional and personal relationship with the State Department.

President Bill Clinton took considerable interest in the council, enlarging it by adding the secretary of the treasury (sometimes a member in prior administrations), the ambassador to the United Nations, the assistant to the president for economic policy, and the president's chief of staff. The president required that international economic concerns be added to the mandate of the council. Appointed National Security Advisor was Anthony Lake, a career foreign service officer who had been Kissinger's assistant under Nixon and with Department of State under Carter. He was particularly successful in maintaining effective relations with the secretary of state and other officials. Numerous topics were added to the issues reviewed, evaluated, and recommendations solicited, including drug trafficking, global environment, peacekeeping, and various hot spots around the world. When Lake left, his successor, Samuel "Sandy" Berger—Clinton's personal foreign policy adviser—expanded the council's menu of interest to include Middle East peace negotiations, NATO, and the Chemical Weapons Treaty. Both Lake and Berger worked in tandem with Madeleine Albright, who was U.S. ambassador to the United Nations and then secretary of state.

Dr. Condoleezza Rice had been George W. Bush's leading foreign affairs consultant prior to and during Bush's campaign leading up to his election as president in 2000. Appointed National

Security Advisor, she has been a member of his inner circle of advisers, talking to him almost every day. Despite some media reports of policy differences among members of the president's administration on the direction of foreign policy, Rice and Secretary of State Powell have managed to speak in one voice in support of presidential positions. Their relative roles were tacitly delineated; Rice gives advice to the president, to whom she has ready access, and often serves as a public spokesperson for administration foreign policy. Thus, although technically a special assistant to the president on any table of organization and with a minimal operational staff, in reality she has cabinet-equivalent status. Powell also gives advice and public utterances, and is personally active in direct relations with the heads of state and top foreign affairs officials—to a great degree because of his prestige around the world. President Bush also has sent officials such as Vice President Cheney and Secretary of Defense Rumsfeld overseas to "sell" other world leaders on American international initiatives, particularly since the September 11, 2001, terrorist attack.

Obviously, events have demonstrated that as of 9/11/01 the National Security Council had not resolved the problem of inadequate coordination and communication among government agencies directly responsible for national security by detecting and preventing terrorism.

CONTACT Address: National Security Council, Old Executive Office Building, Washington, DC 20506; Phone: (202) 456-1414; Fax: (202) 456-2461; Website: www.whitehouse.gov/nsc.

COUNCIL OF ECONOMIC ADVISERS

Founded as an element of the Employment Act of 1946, the council is actually only a three-person group appointed by the president and approved by the Senate. By statute the appointees must be exceptionally qualified and experienced economists. The president names one of these three as chairman, as such one of the most influential people in the nation, who is in the words of former chairman Martin Feldman (1982–84) "legally responsible for establishing the positions taken by the Council" per an executive order by President Dwight D. Eisenhower.

The role of the council and its chair is unique to the United States since the president is the ultimate official responsible for economic policy, unlike most nations that have an economics minister at cabinet level. Thus the Council of Economic Advisers is the president's initial source of professional economic advice and information in formulation of fiscal policy. How often the president meets with the council has varied depending on the desires, interests, and styles of the several presidents. The council also acts to provide coordination of economic policy among government agencies with major impact on the nation's economics, such as the TREASURY DEPARTMENT, the OFFICE OF MANAGEMENT AND BUDGET, and the DEPARTMENTS OF COMMERCE, AGRICULTURE, and HOUSING AND URBAN DEVELOPMENT.

The chair of the council is the prime economic adviser to the president and is the public voice of the council. The singular importance of the chairman is buttressed by the fact that the members of the council do not take votes, but work with the chairman in an attempt to reach a consensus. However, if there are differences, the chairman's views control. He or she reports directly and personally to the president and may also deal directly with top-level administration officials such as the secretary of the treasury. Several of the chairs have been heavily relied upon by the incumbent president, and include such luminaries as Leon Keyserling for Truman, Arthur Burns for Eisenhower, Walter Heller for Kennedy, Alan Greenspan for Nixon and Ford, Charles Schultze for Carter, Martin

Feldman for Reagan, Michael Boskin for the senior Bush, and Laura Tyson for Clinton. The chairman appointed by President George W. Bush is R. Glenn Hubbard, and the other members are Mark B. McClellan and Randall S. Kroszner.

Each council member also directs economic research in particular fields and participates in interagency discussions of economic policy, both receiving information and explaining the administration's position on fiscal policy. The staff of the council consists of about a dozen top-level academicians (often on leave from universities), assisted by staff economists and statisticians. Administratively, a career incumbent fills the position of director for macroeconomic forecasting, and a chief of staff and four assistants are appointed by the chair. While the emphasis of the council is on professionalism in the economic field, the recommended policies often reflect the philosophy of the administration, including variations in reliance on governmental use of fiscal policies to affect the economy.

FUNCTIONS

In addition to the direct advice to the president and top executive officialdom on economic policy, the responsibilities of the council include:

Preparing the annual *Economic Report of the President,* which is a substantial volume supported by statistical tables in spreadsheet form. This report, including coverage of several past years, is available from the Government Printing Office in print form, as well as searched through the Internet at http://w.3.access.gpo.gov/eop/index.html. This major document requires substantial staff input.

Gathering current economic information covering trends, developments, and predictions to prepare studies of these activities in order to keep the president on the alert for changing conditions and their effect on administration economic policies. This data is also made available to various administrative agencies as needed.

Preparing and recommending national economic policies that will employ governmental authority to stabilize and stimulate the economy, including input in regard to the proposed budget. Regularly, this includes preparation of legislation to be submitted to Congress by the president. The council and its staff also prepare studies and recommendations upon the request of the president or other executive officials.

Often overlooked is the ongoing "watch dog" function of the council in evaluating programs and activities of the federal agencies in order to determine if these programs are making a positive contribution to the furtherance of the administration's economic policies. To the extent that such programs and actions fall short, the council may make recommendations of changes for the president to consider.

CONTACT Address: The council and its staff operate from offices in the Old Executive Office Building, Washington, DC 20502; Phone: (202) 395-5084; Website: www.whitehouse.gov/cea.

COUNCIL ON ENVIRONMENTAL QUALITY

The council was established by Congress in the National Environmental Policy Act of 1969 (NEPA), to provide an adviser to the president on environmental policy. It consists of three members appointed by the president subject to Senate confirmation, one of whom the president designates as chair. The chair directly advises the president and is the public spokesperson for the council.

With a small administrative staff and associate directors for international affairs, sustainable development, toxics and environmental protection, and outreach, the council is responsible as the chief environmental adviser to the president, prepares an annual report on the environment, and provides oversight as to whether federal agencies are meeting the environmental standards set by NEPA. Often the council strives to strike a policy balance between environmental protections and the competing needs of business and the economy. Also competing for the president's attention is the Environmental Protection Agency, industries affecting the environment, and organizations advocating maximum environmental protection.

CONTACT Address: 722 Jackson Place NW, Washington, DC 20503 and Old Office Building, Room 360, Washington, DC 20501; Phone: (202) 456-6224; Website: www.whitehouse.gov/ceq.

PRESIDENT'S FOREIGN INTELLIGENCE ADVISORY BOARD

Composed of 11 leading private citizens, the mission of this board is to advise the president on the quality of governmental intelligence gathering and analysis, counterintelligence, and the legality of the intelligence (spying) activities of other governments. Principally an "oversight" group, the board is intended to provide independent insight into the effectiveness of the nation's intelligence operation.

Originally formed under President Dwight D. Eisenhower in 1956 as the President's Board of Consultants on Foreign Intelligence Activities, it was continued under President John F. Kennedy, who changed the name to the President's Foreign Intelligence Advisory Board. The board was not appointed by President Jimmy Carter, but was revived by President Ronald Reagan in 1972. Chairs of the board have included several prominent retired military men, such as General Maxwell Taylor, and former congressional leaders, such as Thomas Foley, Les Aspin, and Warren Rudman. In light of the September 11 terrorist attacks and other such threats and the creation of the Homeland Security Council, its future role is unclear.

CONTACT Address: President's Foreign Intelligence Advisory Board, Room 340, Eisenhower Executive Office Building, Washington, DC 20502; Phone: (202) 456-2352; Website: www. whitehouse.gov/pfiab.

WHITE HOUSE OFFICE OF NATIONAL DRUG CONTROL POLICY

Created by the Anti-Drug Abuse Act of 1988, the ONDCP sets policy, priorities, and objectives of the federal drug control program. The program consistently has targeted illicit drug use, manufacturing, trafficking, and the resultant criminal activity and health problems. The goal is a national drug control strategy that establishes not only an action program and budget, but also guidelines for the cooperation of federal, state, and local agencies in fighting the war on drugs. By 2000 an additional goal was to educate young people about the health dangers of tobacco and alcohol use as well as the use of illegal substances.

FUNCTIONS

The recommended antidrug (and anti-tobacco and alcohol abuse by youths) methodologies include public relations, advertising, research, encouraging treatment of those addicted, zero tolerance of drug use in schools, involvement of educational, community, and religious groups in fighting drug use, providing assistance to law enforcement in disrupting drug traffic (especially at the borders), and international cooperation to reduce illegal drug (cocaine, heroin, marijuana) production in countries of origin, as well as smuggling and distribution.

Another prime function of the office is to monitor antidrug efforts by federal agencies, state and local governments, and other nations. Based on this oversight and research the director of the council is mandated to advise the president on recommended changes in direction, policies, programs, and personnel in relation to any anti–illicit drug operations.

ADMINISTRATION

The office is headed by a director appointed by the president subject to Senate confirmation. The media has given the director the popular name *drug czar*. There are also four deputy directors who are presidential appointees confirmed by the Senate. One is the number two official of the office and three are deputy directors for (drug) demand reduction, state and local affairs, and (drug) supply reduction. There are a substantial number of career professionals and assistants providing support.

CONTACT Address: White House Office of National Drug Control Policy, Executive Office of the President, P.O. Box 6000, Rockville, MD 20849-6000; Phone: (800) 666-3332; Fax: (301) 519-5212; E-mail: ondcp@ncjrs.org; Website: www.whitehousedrugpolicy.gov; a useful agency website is www.whitehousedrugpolicy.gov/state-andlocal, which provides a means to click into the state and local drug control offices, publications, related offices in various line agencies and courts dealing with drug-related crime.

UNITED STATES TRADE REPRESENTATIVE

The Office of the United States Trade Representative is headed by and serves to assist the U.S. trade representative, who is appointed by the president with confirmation by the Senate as are the five chief deputies. Created by the Trade Expansion Act of 1962, the office came into being January 15, 1963, as the Office of Special Trade Representative, and was given its present name in 1980, when President Jimmy Carter authorized that the trade representative establish and run overall trade policy and conduct international trade negotiations on behalf of the government. The person holding the title of U.S. trade representative holds the rank equivalent to a cabinet member (regularly sitting in at cabinet sessions) and is also an ambassador in order to negotiate on even diplomatic terms with foreign diplomats.

The office proposes governmental trade policy, resolves differences among various agencies concerned with trade, and presents the results to the president to set administration trade policy. The trade representative is automatically vice chair of the Overseas Private Investment Corporation and serves ex officio on the board of the Export-Import Bank, and serves on the national advisory committee on International Monetary and Financial Policies.

In addition to formulation of trade policy the office is responsible for U.S. participation in the World Trade Organization, expanded American international market access, overseeing trade involving international institutions, negotiating international trade agreements (both bilateral and multilateral) including GATT and NAFTA, import policies, and protection of intellectual property (such as pirating of copyrighted works). The office also monitors compliance with trade agreements. Staff members are primarily career incumbents and experts on various topics.

The office solicits advice from several sources, including from the president's Advisory Committee on Trade Policy and Negotiations, a 45-person body appointed by the president, six policy advisory committees on specific subjects such as defense and the environment. Industry and labor advisory committees deal with such matters as customs valuations and unfair labor practices. Congress is regularly consulted through a statutory committee made up of five representatives and five senators.

An office of the trade representative is maintained in Geneva, Switzerland, to deal with the World Trade Organization and the Textile Surveillance Body. The Geneva-based deputy serves as the American ambassador to the WTO.

CONTACT Address: United States Trade Representative, 600 17th Street NW, Washington DC 20508; Phone: (888) 473-8787; E-mail: contactustr@ustr.gov (general), webmaster@ustr.gov (technical); Website: www.ustr.gov.

OFFICE OF SCIENCE AND TECHNOLOGY POLICY

This small office provides the president expert advice on the impact on executive policies of the latest in science and technology.

CONTACT Address: Old Executive Office Building, Washington, DC 20500; Phone: (202) 395-7347.

PRESIDENT'S COUNCIL OF ADVISERS ON SCIENCE AND TECHNOLOGY: To provide advice to the president on technology, scientific research, mathematics, and science education, the first President George Bush established the council by executive order in 1990. Serving on the council are 18 experts chosen by the president from industrial, academic, and research entities. Cochairs are one of the members and the assistant to the president for science and technology appointed by the president. Prior to the formation of this council there had been various panels of scientific experts advising presidents beginning with President Harry S. Truman in the 1940s.

CONTACT Address: Eisenhower Executive Office Building, Room 431, 1650 Pennsylvania Avenue, Washington, DC 20502; Phone: (202) 395-7347; Fax: (202) 456-6026; E-mail ostpinfo@ostp.eop.gov; Website: www.ostp.gov/pcast.

OFFICE OF THE FIRST LADY

Laura Bush, the librarian/teacher/mother of twin girls, wife of President George W. Bush, has an official office in the East Wing of the White House. Her predecessor, Hilary Rodham Clinton, also had an office, but in the West Wing, somewhat closer to the Oval Office of the president.

This formal recognition of the role of the wife of the president is a far cry from the position of Martha Washington, the wife of George Washington. A wealthy young widow when she married the young Virginia aristocrat, she knew her place as a wife and hostess: Entertain guests, manage the household with the help of servants, provide your husband with a place of shelter from the winds of world and national conflict, and then stay out of the political way. She was noted for being gracious to her husband's critics.

For almost a century and a half, with few exceptions, the first ladies followed Mrs. Washington's example. The sobriquet "first lady" was not used by the press to describe the president's wife until Lucy Hayes in the 1870s. Since that time, the title of first lady has become institutionalized (and sometimes applied to governors' wives as well). To the extent that first ladies exerted influence, it was subtle, and with due respect to the official views of their husbands.

Abigail Adams, the privately outspoken wife of John Adams (whose thoughts are found in the extensive exchange of letters with her husband, who was often away on diplomatic missions in Europe prior to being elected vice president), during an early session of the Continental Congress in 1774, at the risk of being thought "saucy," admonished him "in the new Code of Laws which I suppose it will be necessary for you to make I desire you would Remember the Ladies, and more generous and favourable to them than your ancestors." Specifically, she wanted the women to have the vote. When Adams was president, Abigail's advice was usually personal, but she deeply resented critics of her husband, and urged his signing of the infamous Alien and Sedition Acts, including the unpopular and unconstitutional provision that made public criticism of the president a crime.

Dorothea "Dolley" Madison was an extroverted young widow who cured James Madison of his painful shyness, and was Washington, D.C.'s, most accomplished hostess. She came to the White House with several years of experience gained from the period when Madison had been secretary of state responsible for entertaining foreign diplomats. Rather than concern herself with politics (which she said was "the business of men"), she concentrated on being charming, a leader of the adolescent nation's fashion, planning events and becoming the most popular woman in the United States. Her special mark on history occurred in August 1814, during the War of 1812, while her husband was away inspecting troops. The British army swarmed across Maryland, headed for the capital. While most of official Washington fled, Dolley—with help from servants and a woman friend—loaded a wagon with official documents, silverware, and artworks. With cannons booming in the distance, she would not leave until she had ordered servants to carry out Gilbert Stuart's portrait of George Washington and put it into the wagon. The next day the British soldiers set fire to the president's house, and it was gutted.

The elegant Lucy Monroe was in ill health during her husband's administration, but every two weeks, she held formal receptions with the assistance of her daughters. John Quincy Adams's wife, London-born Luisa, found the White House an unhappy place, primarily due to the mountain of calumny directed toward her husband, multiple miscarriages, and a period of tension between the two of them while he was president. So this talented lady retreated into writing, drawing, and taking various "cures."

Letitia Tyler, John Tyler's first wife, suffered a stroke more than two years before he became president, and only left her bedroom in the White House a couple of times before dying less than 18 months into his administration. In his final year in office he remarried, to vivacious 24-year-old Julia Gardiner, 30 years his junior. Julia renovated the White House, threw a gigantic New Year's party, openly urged annexation of Texas at social events, and in the final month hosted a party celebrating annexation (she wore on a chain the gold presidential pen with which Tyler signed the legislation). Even in her short tenure she was the first overtly political presidential wife.

She was followed by austere Sarah Polk, the most complete political wife in the 19th century. Not only was Sarah the confidante of her workaholic husband, James K. Polk, she culled items from the newspapers, kept track of current political events, and was his number one adviser. Deeply religious, she frowned at dancing at White House events, banned alcoholic beverages in the White House, and barred any business or entertainment of guests on Sundays.

Margaret Taylor was another invalid presidential wife, who seldom left the sitting room where she would chat with friends. White House banquets and dances were managed by daughter Mary Elizabeth "Betty" Taylor, who was in her 20s.

When President Zachary Taylor died suddenly after laying the cornerstone to the Washington Monument, Millard Fillmore became president. His wife, Abigail, had been a schoolteacher who had met her husband when he came to her class to make up for lack of learning so he could study law. She discussed public matters privately with him, but her political influence was negligible—he signed the Fugitive Slave Law despite her advice. Her health was precarious when he suddenly became president, and her comely 18-year-old daughter, Mary, assisted her in entertaining at the White House. On a couple of occasions Mrs. Fillmore attended public functions without her husband, including a concert by Jenny Lind, which was considered forward if not downright scandalous. She caught a cold at the inauguration of Franklin Pierce, which turned into pneumonia, and she died three weeks later.

The story of Jane Pierce is one of tragedy. She was shy and retiring, hated Washington and politics, and was fragile both in physical and mental health. After terms in the House and Senate, Franklin Pierce had declined an appointment as attorney general, and promised his wife he would stay in New Hampshire and abandon politics. However, seeing the possibility of a deadlocked 1852 Democratic convention, without telling Jane, he informed his political allies that he was available as a compromise candidate. It all fell into place, and to Jane's consternation he was elected. But worst of all, their only surviving young son, 11-year-old Benjamin, was killed in a railroad accident virtually before their eyes, just three months before inauguration day. For a time she retreated into an upstairs room in the White House, writing notes to her lost son, and praying. A woman manager was hired to arrange public events. After a time Jane appeared at dinners and receptions, but was quiet and unhappy—nicknamed "the shadow in the White House."

Mary Todd Lincoln was intelligent, a good conversationalist and fashion-conscious, as well as being impulsive and neurotic. More than any president's wife up to her time, she had been politically ambitious for her husband, including having an eye on the presidency even when he was a semiobscure ex-congressman from Illinois—then a frontier state. Lincoln's election was the triumph of her life, and a vindication of her choice of him as a husband, her Whig background, and sacrifices on her husband's behalf.

However, her years in the White House were soured by the constant attacks upon her as a sus-

pected Confederate sympathizer since she had so many Southern relatives and friends from her home state of Kentucky, some of whom visited her at the White House. It is apocryphal that Lincoln appeared before a closed congressional committee hearing to attest to her loyalty to the Union, but the story reflects the degree to which the campaign upon Mary was well known. She was criticized for extravagance in dress both in expense and plunging necklines and as a cheapskate for cutting back on state dinners. The attacks were so vicious that as early as August 1861 the *Chicago Tribune* called for a halt in an editorial captioned "HOLD ENOUGH." The real reason for the attacks was Mary's outspoken belief in emancipation. The death of the Lincolns' 11-year-old Willy from typhoid in 1862 caused a nervous breakdown that kept her deeply depressed for more than a year.

Eliza Johnson, who as a young wife had helped her husband learn to read, was ill with tuberculosis throughout Andrew Johnson's tumultuous term. She had no impact upon his policies other than moral support during his impeachment trial. Surrounded by family members on the second floor of the White House, Eliza only twice descended to the reception rooms on the first floor: to greet the queen of Hawaii and for a children's ball.

Julia Grant was a lively lady, proud of her husband, who loved the ceremonial White House as well as high fashion. By contrast to taciturn Ulysses S. Grant, she liked to talk, and gladly expressed her opinions on public policy and personnel. For his part, President Grant listened and sometimes took her advice, but often fended it off with a jest. She held open receptions that anyone could attend, and put on a lavish wedding for their daughter, Ellen.

History has misunderstood Lucy Hayes, wife of President Rutherford B. Hayes. She is forever known as "Lemonade Lucy" because the Hayes White House refused to serve any alcoholic beverages. Although Lucy was a teetotaler and devout Methodist, the ban on liquor was the president's decision for political advantage with the growing number of prohibitionist voters. Nor was she responsible for her husband's support for legislation that allowed women to practice law before the Supreme Court. Efforts of the women's rights organizations and the Woman's Christian Temperance Union to make her the poster girl for the "new women's" movement were turned away. She did not attempt to influence her husband and followed his lead on all political matters, and despite her advocacy of better pay for women when she was in college, she accepted President Hayes's opposition to the vote for women.

However, Lucy is notable as the first presidential wife to have earned a college degree, graduating from Ohio Wesleyan Female College. She was also the first to be called "first lady," a term employed by reporter Mary Clemmer Ames in a Protestant weekly, the *Independent,* shortly after the inauguration.

The differing personality of shy Lucretia "Crete" Garfield and her gregarious husband, James Garfield, created tensions during much of their marriage, but their shared religion (Disciples of Christ), the raising of five surviving children, and joy in his election had brought them close by the time of his inauguration in 1881. However, she was ill with malaria most of the time before he was shot by a disappointed office seeker only four months into his term. He was carried to the White House, where inept physicians unsuccessfully probed for the bullet, but eventually gave him blood poisoning. Lucretia nursed him, praying for his recovery. On September 6 she accompanied him to the New Jersey shore for the salubrious pleasant weather, but he slipped away, dying on September 19 after singing "Nearer My God to Thee." One recorded shared political sentiment was that they both considered women's suffrage as "atheistic."

Succeeding Vice President Chester Alan Arthur's handsome wife, Ellen, had died a year before he was elected as Garfield's running mate. When Grover Cleveland was inaugurated in 1885, he was a bachelor, a week short of 48 years old. Frances Folsom was just 21, in her final semester before graduation from Wells College. Her father had been killed in a buggy accident when she was 11, so his lawyer friend Cleveland had become administrator of his estate and guardian of the young girl's share of her inheritance. Often she is referred to as his "ward," as if he had some predatory advantage, but it is a legal term for the person whose estate is being managed under court supervision. Although he was 27 years older, they corresponded while she was at college, and shortly after her graduation they became secretly engaged. When the president escorted mother and daughter, the gossip columns predicted his marriage to the widowed Mrs. Folsom, and so when his impending marriage to the daughter was announced, the press was titillated.

On June 2, 1886, they were married at the White House (the only time a president was married there) in a simple ceremony—simple except for the Marine Band, a 21-one gun salute, and a mob of reporters outside, who followed them on their honeymoon, like a 19th-century version of paparazzi the president called "ghouls."

Frances was beautiful, charming, bright, and lively. But she concentrated on being an attentive wife and manager of the White House, and never expressed a word about politics either publicly or privately. She hosted informal Saturday receptions for all women in Washington of whatever social or economic station. The public loved her and appreciated the vitality she brought to the White House and her serious husband. When she gave birth in 1891 to the first of five Cleveland children, a daughter named Ruth, the Baby Ruth candy bar was named in the girl's honor.

After Cleveland lost to Benjamin Harrison in the electoral college in 1888 (although winning the popular vote), Frances urged a White House attendant to take good care of the furniture and chinaware for the Clevelands' return in four years—and that happened. When Cleveland ran and won in 1892 many of his posters featured a picture of Frances between her husband and the vice presidential candidate, Adlai Stevenson.

During most of the four years between the two Cleveland administrations, the first lady was Caroline Harrison. A talented watercolorist and pianist, she directed the refurbishment and modernization of the aging White House (with a budget of only $35,000), including a heating system, several modern bathrooms, electric lights, resurfaced floors, new china, and decorative plants in profusion. She was a popular hostess, particularly in contrast to the stiff-necked Benjamin Harrison. Caroline painted, gave art lessons, and personally decorated the first White House Christmas tree.

One of the organizers of the Daughters of the American Revolution, she became its first president-general in 1890. Her health had not been robust, and in 1891 she contracted tuberculosis and by the new year was bedridden. Harrison declined to campaign for reelection during the summer, and Cleveland, again the Democratic candidate, also stopped campaigning out of respect. Caroline died in the White House on October 25, 1892, two weeks before President Harrison was defeated for reelection. Frances Cleveland would find the White House in better condition than she had left it.

Ida McKinley was epileptic, subject to frequent seizures that rendered her briefly unconscious. Nevertheless, she insisted on entertaining and accompanying the president to most ceremonial functions. The media never mentioned her malady, and to the degree her health was ever mentioned, she was referred to as "delicate." Too frail to handle the work of entertaining and, more important, to disguise the nature of her affliction, the McKinleys' had a system of physical help and assistance for Ida in quietly leaving a gathering or making light of a brief seizure. The solicitous president, noting the onset of an attack, would let her lean on him and place a lace handkerchief over her face. A maid, a niece, and friends (in particular Jennie Hobart, wife of Vice President Garret Hobart) were all enlisted as her ladies in waiting. At times her health was so precarious she could barely walk; she sat at all receptions and held flowers to avoid the burden of shaking hands. When McKinley died from an assassin's bullet and a physician's ineptitude, Ida wrote in her diary: "I pray the Good Lord will take me with my dearest love."

Not since Sarah Polk had a first lady been so involved in the work of a president/husband as was Edith Carrow Roosevelt. The overly energetic, type-A personality of Theodore Roosevelt needed the kind of assistance she was able to give him. She sorted his mail, read newspapers and noted articles of interest, and rechecked documents prepared for his signature. These activities helped keep her in a position to control the boisterous household of a half dozen children, various pet animals, and a husband who needed to be reminded to quit working and prevented from making impolitic remarks in moments of anger or dispute.

Edith was the first president's wife to retain a social secretary. She also met regularly with the cabinet wives. Roosevelt often solicited her advice on political matters, which she was willing to impart. His respect for her mature judgment and his enjoyment of her company were palpable. Somewhat austere, with a touch of the aristocrat in her manner, Edith was also capable of many kindnesses, and was equally gracious to heads of state and average citizens. But it was in her understanding of her husband that she excelled.

Helen "Nellie" Taft had been a schoolteacher known for her keen intellect and blotterlike absorption of knowledge, which along with her good looks attracted William Howard Taft. Before she became first lady, her principal task was to keep her husband from taking an appointment to the Supreme Court, which would frustrate her ambition that he become president. Taft, whose father had been President Grant's attorney general and secretary of war, was appointed a superior court judge at 29, U.S. solicitor general, and then a federal judge by President Harrison. Taft left the bench when McKinley appointed him commissioner of the Philippines, and at her urging twice turned down Teddy Roosevelt's offers to name him to the Supreme Court. Taft said no the second time only after Nellie met with Roosevelt to be sure he would support her husband for the presidential nomination by the Republicans in 1908.

Having achieved her goal, she established her role as first lady on inauguration day by becoming the first presidential wife to ride back to the White House with her husband after the swearing-in, which was held in the Senate due to a blizzard. She took charge of the White House, restaffing it with a female housekeeper and black "footmen" in livery instead of ushers, and converting a couple of public rooms for use of the Taft family. Musicales and Shakespearean productions were performed at the White House, and she pushed through a plan to turn Potomac Drive into a promenade. She planned a cherry blossom festival, and when there were found to be few cherry trees in Washington, the mayor of Tokyo donated 3,000 of them. She immediately began managing the president's schedule and was often present when Taft conferred with various officials.

Her fast-paced style was brought to a crawl only a couple of months into Taft's term, when Nellie suffered a stroke that paralyzed one side and rendered her able to speak only haltingly. Her convalescence took a year, in which the president attended to her, which was the reverse of

the way she had planned it. In the following two years she renewed her role as first lady at a less demanding pace, concentrating on planning events, such as their gala 50th wedding anniversary and quietly making her thoughts known to her husband. After the Tafts left the White House in 1913, she wrote her memoirs, which were serialized in *Delineator Magazine* between May and November 1914. Incidentally, Taft did achieve his goal; he was appointed Chief Justice of the Supreme Court by President Warren Harding in 1921 and served nine years.

When Woodrow Wilson entered the White House in 1913, at his side was his wife of 30 years, Ellen. She had not only raised their three daughters, she managed the household and to a degree the professorial Wilson himself. A graduate of Female Seminary, located in Rome, Georgia, Ellen had helped edit and prep him for speeches and performed research. She took to her role as first lady with enthusiasm and soon became involved in charities, pressed for women's restrooms in government buildings, and lobbied for legislation for assistance to Washington, D.C., slum dwellers (known as "Mrs. Wilson's bill"). She turned one sunlit room into a studio where she could paint. Only a year into the Wilson administration, Ellen fell in her bedroom in March 1914, and an examination revealed she was suffering from Bright's disease (chronic inflammation of the kidneys) and tuberculosis, which had settled in her kidneys. With Wilson often at her bedside, she steadily declined and died on August 6, after whispering to the White House physician, Cary Grayson, "promise me you will take good care of Woodrow."

Wilson recovered from a subsequent depression when seven months later he met Edith Galt, a pretty 43-year-old widow, who was running the family's jewelry business. Well-read but with little formal education, she was pursued by the president for months until they were married at her home in December 1915. Edith handled the social functions, directed the White House staff, traveled with him in the 1916 reelection campaign, but concentrated on making life run smoothly for the president. While the president was on an arduous train tour drumming up public support for U.S. entry into the League of Nations against Senate opposition, on September 26, 1919, he collapsed from the first of two strokes, which left him paralyzed on one side and for a period unable to speak clearly.

Edith and Dr. Grayson decided to keep the presidency operating, but to do so they entered into a cabal in which the public and most officials were kept in the dark about the severity of the president's illness. She made sure Vice President Thomas Marshall did not visit. When senators, foreign diplomats, cabinet members, and agency chiefs had official or personal business with the president, they would meet with Mrs. Wilson, who would meet with the bedridden president and then return to explain the president's response, including his refusal to consider the limitations the Senate leadership demanded if they were to vote for United States entry into the League. Thus, for the last 18 months of Wilson's presidency, the first lady controlled what decisions were made in the name of the president—what her detractors called "petticoat government," or referred to Edith as "the first man." In her memoirs she denied making any decisions that were contrary to the president's wishes. On occasion she was of considerable influence, such as the time of the forced resignation in 1920 of Secretary of State Robert Lansing in reaction to Lansing's calling a cabinet meeting.

Florence Harding was the first president's wife who was a divorcee,[1] having ended a youthful marriage to an alcoholic husband. She went to work for Warren Harding, publisher of the local

Marion, Ohio, newspaper, and soon married Harding, five years her junior. Hard-driving and blunt-spoken, she was a balance to her affable husband in the success of the Marion *Daily Star.*

As first lady, Florence (called "Duchess" by her husband) worked at opening up the White House to the public and nagging the president to be more refined (making him stop chewing tobacco), but for some of the arbiters of Washington society she was considered too hard, too small-town, and without the elegant manners of her recent predecessors. She also suffered from her knowledge of his dalliances with other women, and her kidney ailment. On a western tour, including major speeches in Vancouver, British Columbia, and Seattle, Washington, Harding had a heart attack, and when he reached San Francisco he died suddenly of a stroke while Florence was reading a magazine article praising him; "read some more" were his final words. A sensation-seeking book suggesting the first lady had poisoned Harding to spare him the humiliation of the criminal corruption of members of his administration had no basis in fact or good sense.

The aptly named Grace Coolidge was a popular breath of fresh air in the White House. Lovely, stylish, good-humored, and full of natural kindness for people, she not only was a popular first lady but also sharply contrasted to her tight-lipped and tight-fisted husband, who was called "Silent Cal" for good reason. After graduation from the University of Vermont, Grace left Vermont to teach at an institute for the deaf in Northampton, Massachusetts, where she met and married Coolidge, an attorney and local Republican leader. They lived simply in a duplex throughout his Massachusetts political career, mayor, legislator, lieutenant governor, and governor. Even when he was vice president, the Coolidges stayed in a Washington hotel.

As first lady, she treated the White House naturally as their home, and made a name for herself as a happy hostess, easy to talk to, and most

---

[1] President Andrew Jackson's wife, Rachel, was a divorcee, but she died on December 22, 1828, between the date of his election in 1828 and the inauguration on March 4, 1829.

important as sharp-tongued Alice Roosevelt Longworth (daughter of Teddy) observed, Grace Coolidge was "unimpressed by it all." Grace commented that she was two people, and one was being wife of the president, and that persona took precedence. She provided charm and gaiety, and exchanged bits of "Yankee" humor with her husband. The president's one extravagance was his wife's fashionable clothing, simple but striking. She and Calvin mourned with quiet dignity when their younger son died of blood poisoning from a heel infection in 1924, and the people mourned with them.

The National Institute of the Social Sciences presented Grace with a gold medal for her "fine personal influence exerted as first lady."

The story at Stanford University is that Lou Henry had a higher grade point average than her fellow geology student, Herbert Hoover. Whether or not that is only legend, after they both had graduated and then married in 1899, Lou commented that she "majored in Herbert Hoover." With his wife as an informal assistant (mapmaking, for example), Hoover exercised his knack for making money from mining in a dozen countries, and they were soon multimillionaires. In 1912 Lou translated a 16th century classic on mining and mineralogy from Latin to English.

When Hoover was appointed food administrator by President Wilson and then secretary of commerce for Harding and Coolidge, she entertained modestly and plunged into activities with the Girl Scouts, Campfire Girls, League of Women Voters, and General Federation of Women's Clubs.

As first lady, she earned a surprising reputation as an imperious task mistress for the staff (the president scarcely noticed them at all), demanded efficiency, and spent the Hoovers' own funds on new and refurbished furniture. As the Great Depression deepened, she gave generously to various charities, but she was aggrieved at public blame for her husband's failure to stem the rise of unemployment and financial collapse. While graciously showing her successor, Eleanor Roosevelt, around the White House, Lou said she could not explain the kitchen since she had never been there.

When her husband was elected president, for a time Anna Eleanor Roosevelt feared that her individual personality would be subsumed in the presidency and there would be no clear role for her. Nothing could be further from what actually occurred, for Eleanor Roosevelt became the first lady against whom all others are compared, and her impact on the nation and the world came to be the most extensive of any president's wife.

While raising four exuberant boys and a daughter, Eleanor had to endure dealing with a mother-in-law who tried to dominate the young couple, the trauma of learning of his affair with her former social secretary, and then her husband's crippling attack of polio in 1921. She determined to keep Franklin's political career alive by working with him to gain at least the ability to stand, maintain correspondence throughout the country, and by becoming a leader in the women's division of the Democratic Party. She forced herself to give speeches and discovered she was an able organizer with an empathetic understanding of the poor, the unrepresented, and the downtrodden, from factory girls to black sharecroppers. Her efforts helped him win a tight race for governor of New York in 1928.

As first lady, Eleanor Roosevelt quickly established a number of "firsts." She was the first to hold a press conference—actually a day before the president's initial press conference. With her husband's encouragement she started writing a daily syndicated column, "My Day," which concentrated on daily life, but on occasion discussed issues, which proved very popular. She gave lectures and spoke on radio broadcasts. Since FDR could not travel spontaneously due to the fact his legs had never gained strength, Eleanor became his "eyes and ears," and throughout the 12 years of his presidency she traveled around the country, attended meetings, and during the war went on morale-building and fact-finding tours of American military units—some not too far from the front.

When there were emerging issues in which the president felt he had to be cautious, Eleanor would step out in front, particularly on moving toward equality for blacks, which raised the hackles of southern Democratic politicians. When the outstanding black contralto Marian Anderson was refused the use of an auditorium run by the Daughters of the American Revolution, Mrs. Roosevelt arranged for her to sing at the Lincoln Memorial. Better housing, cooperative communities, farm laborers, and mine safety were issues in which she nudged the president, sometimes coming close to nagging as well as reporting. She became both fearless and politically astute.

A year after her husband's death in 1945, she was named a delegate to the United Nations, and began a new career of working for world health and education.

Elizabeth "Bess" Truman was a complete change of pace as first lady. On the sudden death of President Roosevelt, her first instinct as the new mistress of the White House was to preserve the privacy of her family (Harry, Bess, and daughter, Margaret) to the extent humanly possible. She refused to hold press conferences, although hosting "off the record" teas with the female reporters, would not make speeches, turned down interviews, and eschewed statements on political causes. She continued to entertain her friends, including the ladies of the Independence Tuesday Bridge Club, hand-addressed her Christmas cards, and drove her own car on shopping trips.

Her influence on Harry Truman was generally employed in private when he had been a county official, senator, and vice president, which he readily acknowledged publicly as "always good advice." During his first year as president,

when he got too busy to consult her, Bess threw a fit, and thereafter Harry made sure she was treated as what he called "the boss" or his "partner." She was not a nagger, but did what she could to curb the president's temper and tone down his acerbic language. When he staged his come-from-behind reelection campaign in 1948, she took the national train tour with him, allowing herself to be introduced, then smiled, waved, shook thousands of hands, and said little or nothing. At the same time she sat with the campaign strategists every night.

Bess Truman called the White House the "Great White Jail," but oversaw its budgeting and cleaning, checked daily menus, and one of her first acts was to get rid of an imperious dictator of the White House kitchen. After the presidency she and Harry returned to their home in Independence, where she lived to be 97, the longest-living first lady, whom the *New York Times* obituary called the "President's full partner."

After having been an army officer's wife for more than 30 years, Mamie Eisenhower was used to living in government housing for temporary periods, having a staff of obedient servants, and dedicating her life to a commanding husband. Thus, being mistress of the White House was not an unfamiliar lifestyle for her. With her trademark bangs, feminine clothes (she favored pink), and ability to be charming without expressing strong political opinions, like Bess Truman she cherished privacy and homelife. She managed the White House, sometimes micromanaged it, with a touch of a military officer's sense of order, except for timing since she was often late.

In 1952 and 1956 she campaigned with husband "Ike", fulfilling much the same function as Mrs. Truman, smiling, waving, and shaking hands, without the political strategizing. As the helpmate of the popular general/president she reflected in his triumphs and winning smile.

Mamie said she had "only one career, and his name is Ike."[2]

Like Bess and Mamie, Jacqueline Bouvier Kennedy valued her privacy, but there the comparison stopped, for there was no way "Jackie" would not attract public attention. The dramatic beauty, the background of wealth and social position, the clothes designed by Oleg Cassini, the poised, diffident manner, the knowledge of art, music, and design, and the one-on-one charm quickly captured the nation's interest if not love.

She could write (winning an essay contest when a student at George Washington University), was used to moving among the prominent and powerful, and could romp with her two small children with the wind blowing her auburn hair—a natural photo opportunity (and a target of paparazzi). No first lady was featured on more magazine covers than Jackie Kennedy. As the consort of America's youngest elected president, she was a symbol of a new generation. She set styles without seeming to try, and even challenged the stodginess of her beloved Catholic Church by attending mass bare-headed in a sleeveless dress.

As first lady, she decided to carve out particular specialties to pursue: culture in the White House with concerts by leading musicians, and restoration of White House rooms and furniture by digging out stored artworks and antiques dating back as far as the Monroe administration. She conducted a television tour of the White House, which gave the public an intimate look at their home, for which she was awarded an Emmy. When she and JFK visited France, she was so popular there (demonstrating her easy competence in speaking French) that the president introduced himself as "the man who accompanied Jackie to France."

---

[2] As quoted by Paul F. Boller, Jr., *Presidential Wives*, p. 344.

In the hours after Kennedy was shot by a sniper with Jackie by his side in an open car, the nation grieved with her. With her clothes splattered with her husband's blood, she stood while Lyndon Johnson was sworn in on Air Force One. Her dignity as widow and mother, holding the hand of their little son, John John, while he saluted as the caisson bearing his father's coffin passed by, became an image for the ages.

Claudia (Lady Bird) Johnson had spent almost 30 years married to the hard-driving Lyndon Johnson, representative, senator, Senate leader, and vice president, when she became first lady in the chaotic, tragic aftermath of the killing of President Kennedy in her home state of Texas.

A graduate of the University of Texas, with an extra year studying journalism, she was the most educated president's wife up to that time. Overcoming youthful shyness, Lady Bird (a nickname given her by a childhood servant), knew what it meant to be a hostess in Washington, and how to chat with world leaders, for she had traveled to 33 countries when Lyndon was vice president.

Married in 1934 to congressional aide Lyndon with a $2.50 ring from Sears, three years later she talked her father into lending her husband $10,000 to launch his first campaign for Congress. With an inheritance from her mother in 1943 she bought an Austin radio station. Helped by Lyndon's clout with the Federal Communications Commission, she managed and expanded the communications business that became the basis of their later wealth.

As first lady, she concentrated her influence on the Highway Beautification Act ("Lady Bird Act") and tree-planting programs, and organized a White House Conference on Natural Beauty and her First Lady's Committee for a More Beautiful Capital. She toured Great Society antipoverty programs and took a particular interest in Head Start, the preschool network for disadvantaged children. LBJ listened closely and valued her advice as free of any hidden agenda on her part.

Lady Bird also hosted "Women Doers" at the White House, and planned dozens of dinners and luncheons in Washington and at the Johnsons' ranch in Texas. Her office was the busiest of any first lady so far, and was directed by heady newswoman Liz Carpenter.

In the 1964 presidential reelection campaign she was the first president's wife to make a series of campaign speeches, concentrating on southern states, where her soft drawl was comforting and her feminine charm took the edge off southern white politicos angered over Johnson's support for civil rights legislation. She was bitter about growing opposition to the increasing involvement in the Vietnam War, and was relieved when he announced in January 1968 that he would not seek reelection.

History depicts Pat Nixon as a tragic figure, standing numb, her face a mask of despair as her disgraced husband resigned as president in August 1974 and flew off in the Nixons' final helicopter ride. But it was not always so. She was not born Pat or Patricia, but Thelma Ryan, and not on St. Patrick's Day as her husband would say when it suited his purpose. Born the day before St. Patrick's, her father called her Pat the morning after her birth. Orphaned before she was 18, by holding part-time jobs, she worked her way through the University of Southern California, graduating cum laude. Becoming a high school teacher in Whittier, a Los Angeles suburb, she met Richard Nixon. When her husband ran for Congress, she pitched in at headquarters, but she never cared for politics.

Nixon's election to the vice presidency brought rewards: world travel, meeting interesting people, entertaining, and the opportunity to aid children and charities. When Nixon lost to Kennedy in 1960 in a close election, and then was defeated for governor of California, she was bitter, but was relieved that there was no more politics.

Dick's position as a "rainmaker" for a New York law firm delighted Pat; it was like a new life. But after four years her husband was on the political comeback trail—another grueling campaign—ending with his election in 1968. Being first lady made the burden of endless politics seem worthwhile. Her theme was encouraging volunteer service. Pat held nondenominational church services in the East Room, and invited American musical icons—country, folk, operatic—to perform. She followed Jackie's example by garnering antiques and paintings for the White House.

Besides accompanying Nixon on his historic trip to China, for the first time she acted independently, touring Africa and South America to cheering crowds. With her husband's landslide reelection, only good times seemed ahead for Pat. But soon Nixon was engulfed in the Watergate scandal, which grew worse with each week's revelations of wrongdoing in the Oval Office. Heartbroken, Mrs. Nixon became reclusive, spending most hours in her sitting room writing letters, reading, and nipping bourbon. At such required appearances as the Senate wives' luncheon, Pat would appear briefly, shake a few hands, and then leave. Most evenings in the final year she and Dick ate alone, not speaking to each other. All that was left was her loyalty to her husband and the ride in the helicopter to California.

Elizabeth (Betty) Ford was the most surprising of first ladies. Born Elizabeth Bloomer, she was a natural beauty who learned modern dance first at Bennington College and then as a member of the Martha Graham dance troupe in New York, where she was also a Powers model. Returning to her hometown of Grand Rapids, Michigan, Betty worked as a department store fashion coordinator while teaching dance to handicapped children. After a brief unfortunate marriage and divorce, like Pat Nixon she married a "political animal," Gerald Ford, a young lawyer running for Congress in 1948. The comparison stops there.

While Ford made the slow climb up the Republican leadership ladder in the House of

Representatives, she raised four children, ran the household, and became active in congressional wives' activities. When he became Republican leader in the House, he was regularly called upon to travel in support of candidates throughout the country as well as fulfilling the time-consuming duties while Congress was in session. Finally, in 1972 she expressed her loneliness to her husband and the possibility that with a Democratic majority his hope of becoming Speaker of the House was fading. He was understanding and apologetic, showing his affection for her by agreeing not to seek reelection in 1974.

When he was appointed vice president in late 1973, Betty let him out of his promise and said she welcomed the "challenge" since it meant there were functions for her that she could enjoy, such as entertaining international figures, in which her talents and natural warmth could be on display. When Nixon resigned and Ford became president on August 9, 1974, one of her husband's first comments after taking the oath was: "I am indebted to no man and only one woman—my dear wife."

When they moved into the White House, she cheerily greeted the guards, who did not respond since under Nixon they had been ordered not to speak to the first family. She quickly changed that rule, saying: "This house has been a grave. I want it to sing."

Betty soon displayed an independence and openness that enthralled a nation, particularly in contrast to the previous administration. She urged appointment of more women to high office (which the President did), spent time with retarded children at a Washington hospital, and made a series of pronouncements in speeches and appearances (including a free-form interview on *Sixty Minutes*), which were anathema to some conservative Republicans. On an inside tour of the White House she happily showed the media the bed she and Jerry shared, commenting that, of course, they slept together. She campaigned for adoption of the Equal Rights Amendment, called *Roe v. Wade,* in which the Supreme Court decriminalized abortions, "a great, great decision," said she would not be surprised if her daughter had a premarital affair, and discussed in detail her mastectomy in order to encourage women not to be afraid.

Despite President Ford's half-jocular comment that her remarks would cost him 10 million votes, in reality her public opinion ratings rose rapidly. In the 1976 reelection campaign buttons proclaimed "Keep Betty in the White House." When Ford lost a nail-biter election to Jimmy Carter, they were both upset, but there were no charges of fraud. Betty had more surprises in store.

In 1978 she announced that she had become addicted to painkillers (originally to ease the pain of arthritis) and increasingly to alcohol, and that she was going through rehabilitation in a medical facility. The public admission was a release for her personally and a big step in her complete recovery, and freed her to urge people with addictions to seek help. This became her crusade, which culminated in her founding and raising money for the Betty Ford Center for Drug and Alcohol Rehabilitation, which opened its doors in 1981. She authored *Betty: A Glad Awakening,* and was the subject of a television movie, *The Betty Ford Story.* When asked why there was a film about Betty and not him, the ex-president responded: "My wife is much more interesting."

Rosalynn Carter was a serious small-town (Plains, Georgia) girl who married the boy from up the street when he graduated from Annapolis and she was 19. Although she had only a community college education, the Carters shared and discussed all phases of life, including their "born again" Christian faith. She loved the travel that went with navy life, and when her husband quit the service to take over the family's wholesale peanut business back in Plains, she became downright depressed. But soon she was handling much of the business end of the Carter enterprise.

Besides rearing four children, when Jimmy ran for the state senate then lost, and later won races for governor of Georgia, Rosalynn performed headquarters tasks, chatted, charmed, and played the hostess. She also researched issues for her husband and reviewed his speeches. The Carters were always seeking self-improvement. With Jimmy in the governor's mansion as the new type of southern governor who favored desegregation, Rosalynn conquered her fear of public speaking and became highly proficient in giving detailed talks based on a few notes, speaking in a soft southern drawl. At least one reporter called her a "steel magnolia." By the time he ran for president— starting as a little-known long-shot—they were used to working and thinking together.

Symbolic of their partnership, Rosalynn held the Bible when Carter took the oath of office. Mrs. Carter was the first president's wife to use an office in the East Wing, which was necessary because he asked her to assume an increasing number of quasi-official tasks. She urged her husband to appoint a commission on mental health, and when he did so, she became honorary chairperson. She acted as the president's personal emissary to several Latin American nations, averaged a press conference every two weeks, conducted a telephone campaign with state legislators in favor of ratifying the Equal Rights Amendment, attended cabinet meetings, and planned and hosted numerous White House events, including musical programs. Rosalynn and Jimmy talked to each other about policy, and he listened to her, although not always agreeing. It was Rosalynn's suggestion that led to the famous meeting of Israeli and Egyptian leaders at Camp David—for which Begin and Sadat received the Nobel Peace Prize.

In short, she worked full time at the job of being first lady and the president's alter ego. Not since the administration of James K. Polk had a

presidential couple worked so closely together. Afterward she said she "enjoyed every minute of it." The Carters postpresidential humanitarian and mediation services are matters of international acclaim.

Nancy Reagan (born Anne Frances, but her mother called her Nancy), graduated from Smith College, and became a professional actress who appeared in 11 movies. Mrs. Reagan, who had given up acting in 1957, was concerned about playing the role of first lady and the image she projected. She started out on the wrong foot with the Washington press corps, who were put off by her expensive designer "going to the ball" clothes and jewelry, particularly in comparison with the simplicity of the Carters. She promptly redecorated the residential rooms of the White House, furnished with antiques and china bought with a fund of contributions from friends and supporters of her husband.

Nancy supervised the details of banquets and receptions, but for the first term publicly she shied away from political issues, except that unlike Betty Ford and Rosalynn Carter she stated her opposition to the Equal Rights Amendment. However, her personal influence upon Ronald Reagan began long before he entered politics. She and her stepfather encouraged his transition from a liberal Democrat to conservative Republican. Nancy was intensely antiabortion and backed her husband's decision to support a constitutional amendment to recriminalize it, which became a tenet of the Republican Party platform in 1980 and thereafter.

Her White House office was a converted bedroom in the residential area of the West Wing. She saw her role as giving as much help to her husband as possible, which included giving him comfort and support while he recuperated from his near-fatal wounds after an assassination attempt shortly after he took office.

Mrs. Reagan improved her public image by championing the Foster Grandparents Program and launching a "Just Say No" campaign against drug use, especially by teenagers. She also displayed more humor, including a surprise appearance at a Gridiron Club dinner in tattered clothes and singing a parody of "Second Hand Rose." Eventually, she received high marks in the Gallup Poll.

Early in President Reagan's second term Nancy became increasingly concerned about her husband's health, following two cancer operations and an apparent decline in his energies and attentiveness—at 78 he was America's oldest president. Ever since President Reagan began showing symptoms of Alzheimer's disease after leaving office, Nancy has continued to be lovingly protective and supportive of his personal needs and his reputation.

Few first ladies were to the "manor born" as much as Barbara Pierce Bush. Her father was president of the McCall Publishing Company, and she grew up with live-in servants, debuted in New York City, attended a finishing school for young ladies, lived in posh suburban Rye, New York, and moved in social registry society.[3] It is little wonder that she and another member of the circle, George Herbert Walker Bush, son of a United States senator and an heiress mother, a navy pilot headed for Yale, would meet, be mutually attracted, and marry at the close of World War II.

Barbara Bush was her husband's helpmate when he went into the oil business in Texas and when he tried to raise the Republican banner in that state at a time it was still heavily Democratic. She shared two losing races for the Senate sandwiched around a single term in the House of Representatives. When beleaguered President

Nixon was looking for a simon pure man for Republican chairman, he tapped Bush, who accepted despite Barbara's doubts about his being tainted by the Watergate aftermath. Politics, like Texas oil, was a bit of rough-and-tumble to which she adapted. There followed key posts for George: first American representative to mainland China, then director of the Central Intelligence Agency, followed by his 1980 try for the presidential nomination, which led to the vice presidency under President Reagan. All these experiences prepared her for being wife of a president.

With her prematurely white hair, fine features, and ready smile, Barbara radiated a motherliness as first lady. In reality she was a mother with three sons, a surviving daughter, and daughter Robin, who died of leukemia when only four. Politically, Barbara was in sync with her husband, with a notable exception—when George chose to find reasons to oppose the Equal Rights Amendment, Barbara Bush let it be known she supported it. She also wrote a little book about their dog, Millie, which became a bestseller.

In the White House, she projected a tight-knit family, with all the benefits of wealth and position, beyond the power of the presidency. In that milieu Barbara Bush fit well. She entertained in style, and the Bushes obviously enjoyed life at the top. Barbara became the first first lady since Abigail Adams to be both the wife of a president and mother of a president.

Hillary Rodham Clinton was like no other first lady, if only because she had ambitions not only for her presidential husband, but also for herself. As student government president at Wellesley she insisted on speaking at graduation. She was the most highly educated first lady, with a law degree from Yale. Although she could be circumspect, Hillary's position on political issues was almost always up front—moderately liberal.

At law school she met another ambitious student, Bill Clinton, and there was a chemistry

---

[3] However, she was not a descendant of President Franklin Pierce as usually authoritative writer Bill Minutaglio asserts in *First Son George W. Bush and the Bush Family Dynasty,* Times Books, Random House, 1999, p. 23; President Pierce had no children who lived past 11 years of age.

between them. She told friends she was marrying a future president. From her home city of Chicago, she willingly followed Clinton to Arkansas, where he felt his future lay. She was deeply involved in all his campaigns: state attorney general and multiterms as governor. She was the principal source of income through practicing with a leading Little Rock firm. She insisted on using her maiden name, could swear like a stevedore when angry, raised a bright daughter, and along with her husband developed a list of friends—loyal, influential, informative—for future use.

In the midst of the rigors of Clinton's campaign, Hillary had to face the television cameras and show her support of Bill against a woman who claimed she had been his mistress for years.

President Clinton gave his wife the important official task of developing a promised national health program. It proved a political mistake. As first lady, she and the plan that emerged became a target for those who were not only opposed to the plan, but also to the president himself. The plan died, and Hillary went into a quiet phase. This political disaster may explain the reason that other active first ladies, such as Eleanor Roosevelt and Rosalynn Carter, never took official positions, but only filled honorary posts or acted outside any official role.

Hillary's interest in education led her to write a popular book: *It Takes A Village* [to raise a child]. Her advice was given directly to the president, but she was often on the stump, speaking on political issues.

Mrs. Clinton's toughness was tested again when it became public knowledge—spread across headlines and late-night talk shows—that Bill had sexual encounters with a young female intern. This information came out during questioning of the president under oath in a lawsuit brought by a former Arkansas employee that she had been sexually harassed by Clinton when he was governor. An impeachment charge in the

House of Representatives stated that he had committed perjury in that case. A Senate trial and acquittal followed. Although the result was almost never in serious doubt, Hillary suffered this humiliation with quiet reserve.

As the Clintons were preparing to complete the president's second term, Hillary established residence in New York and announced her candidacy for the United States Senate from that state. And she won. Martha Washington and all the first ladies that followed her would not have believed it.

Laura Welch Bush, as the daughter-in-law of the first President Bush, was very familiar with the White House when she and George W. Bush arrived there in January 2001. A native of Texas—her father was a Midland contractor and real estate man—she graduated from Southern Methodist University in education and taught elementary school for a time before attending the University of Texas to earn a master's in library science, becoming a school librarian in Austin.

While visiting Midland, she met George W. Bush, and in his words they were a perfect match, telling his family that Laura was "one of the great listeners. And since I'm one of the big talkers, it was a great fit."[4] After only three months they were married in 1977, just as George W. Bush began a campaign for Congress, which he eventually lost. He promised his new bride she would not have to make any speeches. While her husband ventured into Texas oil and baseball businesses, she remained the quiet listener. However, it was Laura who brought him into her Methodist church, and when he turned 40 convinced him to stop drinking—which had become a problem—completely and permanently. She also delivered twin girls.

His involvement in politics was revived when he took an active role in his father's 1988 race

[4] Minutaglio, page 184.

for president. When "W" decided to challenge incumbent Ann Richards for the Texas governorship, Laura was at his side. When he was governor, she served as hostess at the governor's mansion and at the ranch they owned. She showed a keen interest in education and literacy, which has continued in the White House. During the presidential campaign, she was present for major events, a vision of calm in the eye of the storm.

Her arrival in the White House was a seamless transition in which she readily assumed the duties as hostess. She set up her office in the East Wing, away from the nerve center in the West Wing, where Hillary Clinton had operated. In a surprising development, Laura Bush was sent on a tour of European nations—important as allies of the United States—where she gave polished speeches outlining the aims of her husband's policies.

Over the course of White House history, the wives of Presidents Thomas Jefferson, Andrew Jackson, Martin Van Buren, and Chester Alan Arthur had died prior to their husband's becoming president. James Buchanan never married. In each case a female relative served as a substitute hostess of the president's household.

The First Ladies
(With Years Served)

Martha Dandridge Custis Washington	(1789–97)
Abigail Smith Adams	(1797–1801)
Dolley Payne Todd Madison	(1809–17)
Elizabeth Kortright Monroe	(1817–25)
Louisa Catherine Johnson Adams	(1825–29)
Anna Tuthill Symmes Harrison	(1841)
Letitia Christian Tyler	(1841–42)
Julia Gardiner Tyler	(1844–45)
Sarah Childress Polk	(1845–49)
Margaret Mackall Smith Taylor	(1849–50)
Abigail Powers Fillmore	(1850–53)
Jane Means Appleton Pierce	(1853–57)
Mary Todd Lincoln	(1861–65)
Eliza McCardle Johnson	(1865–69)
Julia Dent Grant	(1869–77)
Lucy Ware Webb Hayes	(1877–81)
Lucretia Rudolph Garfield	(1881)
Frances Folsom Cleveland	(1886–89, 1893–97)
Caroline Lavinia Scott Harrison	(1889–92)
Ida Saxton McKinley	(1897–1901)
Edith Kermit Carrow Roosevelt	(1901–09)
Helen Harron Taft	(1909–13)
Ellen Louise Axson Wilson	(1913–14)
Edith Bolling Galt Wilson	(1915–21)
Florence Kling Harding	(1921–23)
Grace Anna Goodhue Coolidge	(1923–29)
Lou Henry Hoover	(1929–33)
Anna Eleanor Roosevelt Roosevelt	(1933–45)
Elizabeth Virginia Wallace (Bess) Truman	(1945–53)
Mamie Geneva Doud Eisenhower	(1953–61)
Jacqueline Lee Bouvier Kennedy	(1961–63)
Claudia Taylor (Lady Bird) Johnson	(1963–69)
Thelma Ryan (Pat) Nixon	(1969–74)
Elizabeth Bloomer (Betty) Ford	(1974–77)
Rosalynn Smith Carter	(1977–81)
Anne Frances Davis (Nancy) Reagan	(1981–89)
Barbara Pierce Bush	(1989–93)
Hillary Rodham Clinton	(1993–2001)
Laura Welch Bush	(2001–)

~ THE CABINET ~

The Constitution of the United States does not mention the term *cabinet,* nor does it specifically provide for appointment by the president of members of the cabinet or department secretaries. The power of appointment is couched in the language in Article II, Section 2, that among the powers of the president "He shall nominate, and by and with the advice and consent of the Senate. . . . all other officers of the United States, whose appointments are not herein otherwise provided for. . . ." In the same section the Constitution provides that "The President. . . . may require the opinion, in writing, of the principal officer in each of the executive departments, upon any subject relating to the duties of their respective offices. . . ."

In organizing not only the first presidential administration but also the executive branch of government itself, President George Washington on July 27, 1790, (less than three months after taking office) signed the act passed by Congress creating the Department of Foreign Affairs, which was changed to the DEPARTMENT OF STATE on September 15. He signed into law an act creating the Department of War on August 7, and signed an act establishing the DEPARTMENT OF TREASURY on September 2. Alexander Hamilton was promptly appointed treasury secretary and was sworn in on September 11, becoming the first member of the cabinet. Henry Knox (a bookstore owner and artillery general in the Revolution) was sworn in as secretary of war the following day. On September 26 Washington appointed Thomas Jefferson secretary of state and Edmund Randolph attorney general, who became a cabinet member, but without a Department of Justice. Neither Jefferson nor Randolph took office until 1790.

Washington held the first actual meeting of the entire group on November 26, 1791, at his residence in the temporary capital of Philadelphia, but it was not referred to as a "cabinet"

at that time, but shortly that term came into popular use. The president had the problem that Secretaries Hamilton and Jefferson increasingly represented differing views, and were organizing two competing political parties, the Federalists and the Democratic-Republicans, respectively. Washington's efforts to work out a rapprochement between the two cabinet members was unavailing. Both factions were sponsoring newspapers that were making sharp and sometimes scurrilous attacks on the other.

On May 3, 1798, President John Adams signed an act that created the Navy Department, necessary in the face of threats by British and sometimes French warships to interfere with American shipping. There was no further change in the cabinet positions until the first day of Andrew Jackson's administration, when Congress elevated the postmaster general to cabinet level, although the federal Post Office had existed as a government agency within the Treasury Department since 1790.

During Jackson's administration, the president met often in the warm kitchen of the White House with several advisers, most of whom were not members of the cabinet, and were called in the popular press the "kitchen cabinet." Several presidents thereafter chose to rely for policy on such informal advice from cronies or government officials below cabinet level rather than the official department heads. Theodore Roosevelt had his "tennis cabinet" and Herbert Hoover his "medicine ball" cabinet, who played or exercised together, respectively, as an excuse (or cover) for getting together.

On February 28, 1844, during a demonstration for government leaders of a new cannon called the Peacemaker on the warship *Princeton,* the cannon exploded, killing Secretary of State Abel Upshur and Secretary of Navy Thomas Gilmer, as well as the father of the fiancée of President John Tyler and five others.

President James K. Polk, on his last full day in office, signed into law an act creating the DEPART-

MENT OF INTERIOR (initially called the Home Department) on March 3, 1849, leaving the appointment to incoming President Zachary Taylor. This seemed necessary due to the great increase in western lands acquired in the Mexican War and substantial population of Native Americans there. Included within Interior's jurisdiction were the Bureau of the Census (since removed to Commerce), Indian Affairs, and the General Land Office.

During a continuing dispute between President Andrew Johnson and Congress, on March 2, 1867, both houses passed over the president's veto the Tenure of Office Act, which declared that the president could not remove government officials such as department heads without consent of the Senate. It was patently unconstitutional, and declared so in a 1926 Supreme Court case. Nevertheless, when Johnson asked for the resignation of Secretary of War Edwin Stanton, the secretary not only refused to resign, but declined to physically leave the office. Then the president appointed General Ulysses S. Grant as "acting" secretary. This eventually led to impeachment charges against Johnson in February 1868, a trial before the Senate, and acquittal of President Johnson by a single vote on May 26, 1868.

Although the attorney general had been a member of the cabinet since Washington's time, he had served as an individual, so on June 22, 1870, President Grant signed an act establishing a cabinet-level JUSTICE DEPARTMENT. The DEPARTMENT OF AGRICULTURE, which had been an agency since 1862, was elevated to cabinet status by statute enacted February 9, 1889.

Proactive President Theodore Roosevelt in his first two State of the Union messages asked for a DEPARTMENT OF COMMERCE, but instead Congress passed a bill creating a Department of Commerce and Labor, which he signed on February 14, 1903. In the final hours of his administration President William Howard Taft approved a measure that divided the department into the Department of Commerce and the DEPARTMENT OF LABOR. On his first day in office President Franklin D. Roosevelt appointed the first woman to the cabinet, Secretary of Labor Frances Perkins, who served even beyond FDR's death in 1945.

The most extensive change in the cabinet structure was effected in 1949, with amendments to the National Security Act, which at the urging of President Harry S. Truman had been enacted by Congress on September 18, 1947. The 1947 act had created the Department of the Air Force, the Joint Chiefs of Staff of the various military branches, and an umbrella organization, the Defense Establishment. Also authorized was the independent Central Intelligence Agency. Creating the DEPARTMENT OF DEFENSE formalized the amalgamation of the Department of the Army (originally the War Department), the Department of the Navy, and the Department of the Air Force, which each partially maintained its separate organizational status under the secretary of defense and the Defense Department staff, which directly supervises military operations.

Several agencies were cobbled together as the Department of Health, Education and Welfare, created on April 1, 1953. President Dwight D. Eisenhower appointed as its secretary the second woman cabinet member, Oveta Culp Hobby, who had been head of the WACs, the World War II women's army corps. What had been the Housing and Home Finance Agency (HHFA) was upgraded on January 18, 1966, to the DEPARTMENT OF HOUSING AND URBAN DEVELOPMENT (HUD) in legislation pushed by President Lyndon B. Johnson. He named HHFA chief Robert C. Weaver, the cabinet's first African American, as secretary.

The DEPARTMENT OF TRANSPORTATION came into being on October 15, 1966, and within a short time brought together several transportation-oriented agencies, including the federal administrations of aviation, highways, railroads, transit, maritime, and the Coast Guard (in peacetime). This was followed by the creation of the DEPARTMENT OF ENERGY on October 1, 1977, following several crises in oil shortages and apparent lack of coordination of energy policies.

The DEPARTMENT OF EDUCATION was spun off from Health, Education and Welfare pursuant to the Department of Education Organization Act, signed October 17, 1979. At the same time the remaining functions of HEW were continued under the newly named DEPARTMENT OF HEALTH AND HUMAN SERVICES.

With the millions of military veterans from four wars requiring services including pensions, medical and education benefits, hospitals, and other programs, the Veterans Administration (formed in 1930) was elevated by Congress in 1988 to the DEPARTMENT OF VETERANS AFFAIRS led by a secretary in the cabinet.

The only official cabinet post ever eliminated was that of postmaster general, which had been given cabinet status in 1829 under President Andrew Jackson, who wanted political control of the thousands of post office jobs. Pursuant to the Postal Reorganization Act enacted by Congress and signed by President Richard M. Nixon on August 12, 1970, the United States Postal Service replaced the Post Office Department and became an independent government corporation. The then current postmaster general's position in the cabinet was terminated as of June 30, 1971. Coincidentally, earlier in 1970, on March 18, nearly 200,000 postal workers went on strike and ignored a court injunction against the walkout. President Nixon declared that this largest federal strike in history was a national emergency and directed the U.S. Army to deliver the mail if necessary. By March 25 the postal workers were back on the job.

In the latter half of the 20th century the practice of giving other federal officials cabinet status was adopted by several presidents. Although over the years various nondepartment heads have sat in at cabinet meetings, this was either by courtesy or the desire to have a specialist or political ally of the president involved in discussions. The first official recognition of conferring cabinet status was that given to Adlai Stevenson when he was appointed United States representative to the United Nations and head of the United States Mission by President John F. Kennedy in 1961. Former Illinois governor Stevenson, two-time Democratic nominee for president in 1952 and 1956, wished to be appointed secretary of state, but when Kennedy offered him the noncabinet U.N. post instead, Stevenson let it be known he would take the appointment on condition he was given cabinet status and could participate in cabinet meetings. Faced with the great popularity of Stevenson with Democrats, Kennedy agreed. This status also gave the United Nations ambassador greater prestige in dealing with representatives of other nations.

Henry Kissinger, National Security Advisor under President Richard Nixon, was given similar cabinet status, and was Nixon's de facto foreign policy adviser to a greater extent than the secretary of state. Eventually Kissinger was appointed secretary of state and for a time held both positions, but it did not work well since there was a built-in conflict of interest between the Department of State and the NATIONAL SECURITY COUNCIL, so Kissinger gave up the lesser post.

President Bill Clinton was particularly liberal in giving cabinet status to various officials, such as the director of the OFFICE OF MANAGEMENT AND BUDGET, the U.S. trade representative, the ambassador to the United Nations, the chair of the COUNCIL OF ECONOMIC ADVISERS, the director of the Drug Control Office, the administrator of the Environmental Protection Agency, and the president's chief of staff. However, during Clinton's eight years in office only 18 meetings of the cabinet as a group were held.

The same inclusion was followed to a great extent by President George W. Bush, who granted the director of Homeland Security, former governor Tom Ridge, cabinet status (with little staff), before proposing that Homeland Security become a new cabinet department, which Congress created in the spring of 2003.

The role of the vice president as an ex officio member of the cabinet—sitting in at meetings—is a relatively modern development. Partly this is because with few exceptions the vice president has not been particularly close to the president and was primarily in a "stand by" position. President Warren G. Harding (1921–23) invited Vice President Calvin Coolidge to attend cabinet meetings, but Coolidge said he did not think that was "proper." Franklin D. Roosevelt urged his first vice president, John Nance Garner (1933–41), to come to cabinet sessions. Garner did so for a while and then stopped, as he found he was not in agreement with some of the more innovative New Deal programs and that he had little input on policy. Vice Presidents Walter Mondale, George H.W. Bush, Al Gore, and Dick Cheney all sat with the cabinet.

Soon after President Woodrow Wilson suffered a debilitating stroke in 1919, Secretary of State Robert Lansing called a cabinet meeting to discuss means to continue coordination of the government. This action so infuriated the president's wife, Edith, who regarded it as a traitorous usurpation of power and an admission that the president was too ill to function, that she convinced the ailing Wilson to fire Lansing. Vice President Thomas R. Marshall refused to call the cabinet together. During three illnesses of President Dwight D. Eisenhower, Vice President Nixon held cabinet meetings with the understanding that no decisions would be made that were not approved by the president. Vice President George H. W. Bush handled the situation equally delicately after President Ronald Reagan was severely wounded by a would-be assassin in the early months of his administration.

For the most part, the cabinet meeting together is generally not so much a decision-making body. Thus, actual full sessions tend to be only ceremonial events for public consumption. President John F. Kennedy commented that a secretary of agriculture was not in position to provide input on foreign policy. Legend has it that President Abraham Lincoln would poll his cabinet on a proposed action or policy, and after the majority voted "nay" he would announce that he voted "aye" and the "ayes have it."

Service as a cabinet member has not proved a smooth road to the presidency. Early secretaries of state James Madison and James Monroe were considered designated successors to the voting public, during a time when communication in the United States was slow and erratic. Jefferson and Van Buren served in that position at one point in their careers, but it was the vice presidency that put them in line for the executive office. Thus, only William Howard Taft, who was appointed secretary of war by Theodore Roosevelt in order to give the ponderous Taft a stepping-stone, and Secretary of Commerce Herbert Hoover, who had made his reputation as a relief and food administrator during and after World War I, moved up to the White House.

DEPARTMENT OF AGRICULTURE

The Department of Agriculture is a cabinet-level department of the executive branch, which was originally created as a commission by Act of Congress on May 15, 1862, during the Lincoln administration. It was upgraded to cabinet status by Congress on February 8, 1889. In 1933 it became a proactive department as a key element of President Franklin D. Roosevelt's New Deal, to provide assistance to beleaguered farmers, including subsidies, loans, and marketing programs to maintain profitable prices for agricultural products, under the leadership of Secretary of Agriculture Henry A. Wallace (1933–40).

The department administers many programs involving research, nutrition, consumer services, inspection of agricultural products for public safety, farm price supports, loan and grant programs for rural utilities, housing and disaster relief, antihunger efforts including food stamps, school lunches and breakfasts, conservation assistance and education, and international food aid. Also within its authority is the United States Forest Service, the National Arboretum, and the National Agricultural Library.

ADMINISTRATION

The department is headed by the secretary of agriculture, appointed by the president with confirmation by the Senate. Except for the highest levels, almost all positions are held by career civil servants, most of whom are specialists in their fields of responsibility. Presidential appointees are the secretary; deputy secretary; under secretaries for natural resources and environment, for farm and foreign agricultural service, for rural development, for food, nutrition and consumer service, for food safety, for research, education and economics, and for marketing and regulatory programs; and assistant secretaries for congressional relations and for administration. The other presidential appointees include the chief financial officer, general counsel, and inspector general.

The Department of Agriculture's headquarters at 1400 Independence Avenue, SW, Washington DC 20250, is a four-building complex that stretches along Independence Avenue between 12th and 14th Streets, including the South Building (built between 1930 and 1936), the Sidney R. Yates Federal Building (portions of which date back to 1880), the Jamie Whitten Building (completed in 1930), and the Cotton Annex (dedicated in 1937 and remodeled in 1970).

CONTACT Address: Department of Agriculture, 1400 Independence Avenue SW, Washington, DC 20250; Phone: (202) 720-8732; Fax: (202) 720-5043; Website: www.usda.gov. Regional offices can be reached online via www.offices.usda.gov/scripts/ndISAPI.dll.oip_public/USA_map.

The Department operates the 6,500-acre Beltsville Agriculture Research Center in Belts-ville, Maryland, which includes four research institutes for animal and natural resources, human nutrition, and plant sciences. Also in the center is the George Washington Carver Center, a 45-acre complex of four interconnecting buildings dedicated in 1999, and the 14-story National Agriculture Library at 10301 Baltimore Avenue. The center can be reached from Washington, D.C., by driving on the Beltway or via the Metro to the Greenbelt Metro Station, where there is a free shuttle into the center.

CONTACT Address: Department of Agriculture, Room 1-2250, 5601 Sunnyside Avenue, Beltsville, MD 20705-5128; Phone: (301) 504-1638; Fax: (301) 504-1648; Website: www.nal.usda.gov.

The Center for Nutrition Policy and Promotion was established in 1994, and is located at 1120 29th Street SW, Washington, DC 20036. The offices of the various nutrition agencies are located at 3101 Park Center Drive, Room 1034, Alexandria, VA 22302-1594.

There are also Department of Agriculture service offices throughout the country. The National Agriculture Library (NAL) offers agricultural information to researchers and the public. Information includes domestic and international resources through the Food and Agriculture Organization of the United Nations.

ACTIVITIES, PROGRAMS, AND SERVICES

The activities, programs, and services of the Department of Agriculture are organized into the following categories.

FARM SERVICE AGENCY (FSA) processes loans to farmers, crop, and natural disaster assistance, and a conservation reserve program. Annually more than $4 billion is available for loans and programs, with more than 30,000 loans in force each year for operating costs, farm ownership, emergencies, seeds, boll weevil infestation, apple growing, as well as guarantees of loans through a network of state and county

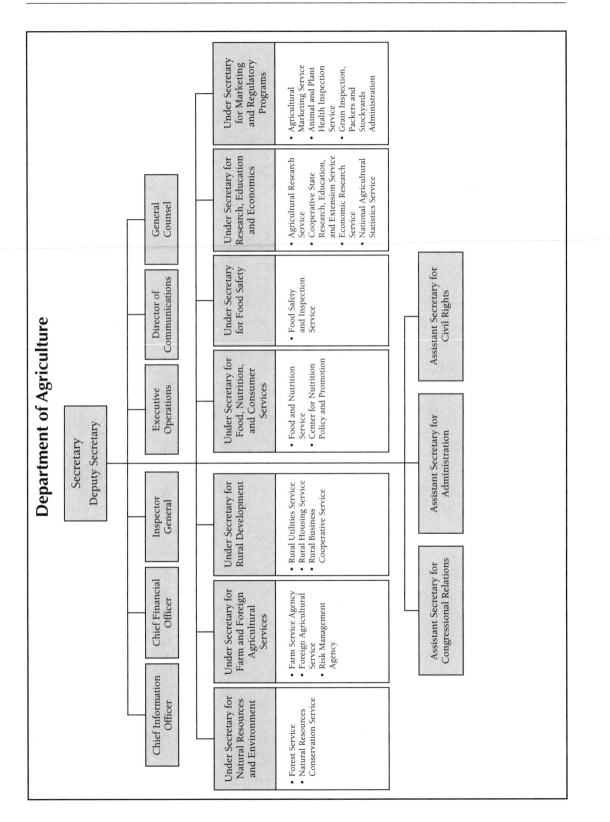

Department of Agriculture

Secretary
Deputy Secretary

- Chief Information Officer
- Chief Financial Officer
- Inspector General
- Executive Operations
- Director of Communications
- General Counsel

Under Secretary for Natural Resources and Environment
- Forest Service
- Natural Resources Conservation Service

Under Secretary for Farm and Foreign Agricultural Services
- Farm Service Agency
- Foreign Agricultural Service
- Risk Management Agency

Under Secretary for Rural Development
- Rural Utilities Service
- Rural Housing Service
- Rural Business Cooperative Service

Under Secretary for Food, Nutrition, and Consumer Services
- Food and Nutrition Service
- Center for Nutrition Policy and Promotion

Under Secretary for Food Safety
- Food Safety and Inspection Service

Under Secretary for Research, Education and Economics
- Agricultural Research Service
- Cooperative State Research, Education, and Extension Service
- Economic Research Service
- National Agricultural Statistics Service

Under Secretary for Marketing and Regulatory Programs
- Agricultural Marketing Service
- Animal and Plant Health Inspection Service
- Grain Inspection, Packers and Stockyards Administration

Assistant Secretary for Congressional Relations
Assistant Secretary for Administration
Assistant Secretary for Civil Rights

offices. The programs are particularly directed toward beginning farmers and "socially disadvantaged applicants" such as women and ethnic minorities.

CONTACT Address: 1400 Independence Avenue SW, Washington, DC 20250; Phone: (202) 720-3467; Fax: (202) 720-9105; Website: www.fsa.usda.gov.

PRICE SUPPORT DIVISION is part of the Farm Service and coordinates and assists commodity loan and information programs for designated crops, as well as cash assistance for problem farm loans, and a bundle of benefits generally known as Farm Subsidies, which amount to over $15 billion annually. Originally intended to save small farmers during the Great Depression, subsidies are now a vital and continuing element of the U.S. farm economy. Subsidies include crop specific assistance and payments in return for conservation activities.

CONTACT Address: 1400 Independence Avenue SW, South Agriculture Building, Room 3071, Washington, DC 20250; Phone: (202) 720-3935; Fax: (202) 690-2159; Website: www.fsa.usda.gov/dafp/psd.

The **AGRICULTURAL MARKETING SERVICE** is located in the Price Support Division. Since 1972 the service has provided information, and it conducts programs for quality assurance and standards. Phone: (202) 720-5115 or, for information: (202) 720-8999; Fax: (202) 720-8477; Website: www.fsa.usda.gov/ams.

The **COMMODITY CREDIT CORPORATION** also in that division, assists in maintaining farm price supports by purchasing agricultural goods that are in short supply and using government guarantees to make sure farmers receive "parity" payments for the crops even if the market price goes down, with the corporation risking the loss.

CONTACT Address: 3101 Park Center Drive, Room 1208, Alexandria, VA 22302; Phone: (703) 305-1386; Fax: (703) 305-2842.

FOREIGN AGRICULTURAL SERVICE manages the International Food Aid program and provides assistance for exporters of agricultural products.

CONTACT Address: 1400 Independence Avenue SW, South Agriculture Building, Room 5071, Washington, DC 20250; Phone: (202) 720-5935; Fax: (202) 690-2159; E-mail: fasinfo@fas.usda.gov; Website: www.fas.usda.gov.

The department also maintains the **EXPORT CREDIT GUARANTEE PROGRAM**. Address: 1400 Independence Avenue, Room 4519, Washington, DC, 20250; Phone: (202) 720-3224; Fax: (202) 720-2949.

OFFICE OF INTERNATIONAL COOPERATION AND DEVELOPMENT is at 1400 Independence Avenue SW, Room 3008; Phone: (202) 690-0776; Fax: (202) 720-6100.

RISK MANAGEMENT AGENCY provides financial aid and emergency loans to farmers suffering losses caused by natural disasters, including coverage for crop damage, rehabilitation of farm land, and emergency loans.

CONTACT Address: 1400 Independence Avenue SW, Washington, DC 20250. Phone: (202) 690-2803; Fax: (202) 690-2818; Website: www.act.fcic.usda/gov.

FOOD SAFETY AND INSPECTION SERVICE inspects and grades meat and poultry and can require recalls of products which fail inspection, and conducts consumer education. As mandated by the Meat Inspection Act, the Poultry Products Inspection Act, and the Egg Products Inspection Act, the service is responsible for making sure the nation's commercial supply of meat, poultry, and egg products is safe, wholesome, and properly labeled and packaged.

CONTACT Address: 1400 Independence Avenue SW, Washington, DC 20250. Hotline to report possible problems: 1-800-535-4555; Phone: (202) 720-7025; Fax: (202) 205-0158; Website: www.usda.gov/fsis; Internet hotline: www.fsis.usda.gov/CA/mphotlin.

ANIMAL AND PLANT HEALTH INSPECTION (APHIS) requires animal dealer registration, inspects to guarantee farm animals are healthy, oversees biotechnology in the field of animal husbandry, and provides information (including warnings) to travelers.

CONTACT Address: 1400 Independence Avenue SW, Room 312E, Washington, DC 20250; Phone: (202) 720-3668; Fax: (202) 720-3054; E-mail: comments@www.aphis.usda.gov; Website: www.aphis.usda.gov.

A *Center for Epidemiology and Plant Health Laboratory* is operated at 555 South Howes Street, Fort Collins, Colorado 80521; Phone: (970) 490-8100, 1(800) 545-8732; Fax: (970) 490-8099; E-mail: comments@www.aphis.usda.gov; Website: www.aphis.usda.gov/vs/ceah.

Also the department runs the *National Veterinary Services Laboratory,* located at 1800 Dayton Road, Ames, IA 50010; Phone: (515) 663-7266; Fax: (515) 663-7397, and the *National Animal Health Program,* at 4700 River Road, Riverside, MD 20737; Phone: (301) 734-6954; Fax: (301) 734-7964; Website: www.aphis.usda.gov/na/ah.

GRAIN INSPECTION SERVICE AND PACKERS AND STOCKYARDS PROGRAMS conducts regular inspection and sampling of grain and meat production to protect the public and enforce standards.

CONTACT Address: 1400 Independence Avenue SW, MS 3601; Phone: (202) 720-0219; Fax: (202) 205-9237; Website: www.usda.gov/gipsa.

RURAL DEVELOPMENT OFFICE targets rural communities and towns with less than 10,000 population.

CONTACT Address: 1400 Independence Avenue SW, MS 0107, Washington, DC 20250; Phone: (202) 720-4581; Fax: (202) 720-2080; Website: www.rurdev.usda.gov. It includes the **RURAL BUSINESS—COOPERATIVE SERVICE** for business development assistance, at 1400 Independence Avenue SW, South Agriculture Building, Room 5045, Washington, DC 20250; Phone: (202) 690-4730; Fax: (202) 690-4737; and the **OFFICE OF COMMUNITY DEVELOPMENT**, which gives low cost loans for empowerment

zones and economic action in rural areas, to be reached at the Rural Development Office. The **RURAL HOUSING SERVICE** (previously the Farmers Home Administration) provides loans and other assistance to promote decent rural housing.

CONTACT Address: 1400 Independence Avenue SW, Washington, DC 20250; Phone: (202) 690-1727; Fax: (202) 690-0500; Website: www.rurdev.usda.gov.rhs.

RURAL UTILITIES SERVICE (founded in 1936 as the Rural Electrification Administration) promotes rural electrification and water programs as well as "telemedicine" and telecommunications.

CONTACT Address: 1400 Independence Avenue SW, South Agriculture Building, Washington, DC 20250; Phone: (202) 720-9450; Fax: (202) 720-1725; Website: www.rurdev/usda/gov/rus.

More than $60 billion has been spent on utility programs over the years. The department also encourages small businesses through its **OFFICE OF SMALL AND DISADVANTAGED BUSINESS UTILIZATION (OSBDU),** which assists small businesses (especially women-owned) to contract for supplies and services with the department. The OSBDU office toll free number is 1-877-99O-SBDU; Fax: (202) 720-3001; Website: www.usda.gov/da/smallbus.

AGRICULTURAL RESEARCH SERVICE provides crop profiles to give current information on all agricultural products, including prices, productivity, and other valuable data.

CONTACT Address: 1400 Independence Avenue SW, Jamie Whitten Building, Room 302A, Washington, DC 20250; Phone: (202) 720-3656; Fax: (202) 720-5427; Website: www.ars.usda/gov. This service also maintains the National Agricultural Library. (See next entry.)

National Agricultural Library is one of four national libraries operated by the federal government and dates its beginnings from the 1860s. It is a 14-story facility in the Beltsville Agriculture Research Center at 10301 Baltimore Avenue, Beltsville, MD 20705-2351; Phone: (301)

504-5755; Fax: (301) 504-6927; E-mail: agref@ nal.usda.gov; Website: www.nal.usda.gov/ref.

National Arboretum at New York and R Streets, Washington, D.C., conserves and displays trees, shrubs, and flowers.

COOPERATIVE STATE RESEARCH, EDUCATION AND EXTENSION SERVICE coordinates locally administered programs, such as technical help for small farms, extension grants for agricultural education, and "Ag in the Classroom."

CONTACT Address: 1400 Independence Avenue SW, Jamie Whitten Building, Room 305A; Phone: (202) 720-4423; Fax: (202) 720-8987; E-mail: csrees@reeusda.gov.; Website: www.reeusda.gov.

Another educational service run by the department is The Graduate School, USDA, which provides agricultural courses at more than 100 locations or on-line, with certificates of completion often useful for professional advancement. The program is supported by tuition fees. Website: www.grad.usda.gov/programs_services includes lists of classes, sites, and enrollment information.

NATIONAL AGRICULTURAL STATISTICS SERVICE (NASS) develops a census of agricultural data and reports.

CONTACT Address: 1400 Independence Avenue SW, South Building, Room 4117, Washington, DC 20250; Phone: (800) 727-9540, (202) 720-2707; Fax: (202) 720-9013; E-mail: nass@ nass.usda.gov; Website: www.usda.gov/nass.

ECONOMIC RESEARCH SERVICE provides economic reports for the services operated by the department.

CONTACT Address: 1800 M Street NW, Washington, DC 20036; Phone: (800) 999-6778, (202) 694-5050; Fax: (202) 694-5700; Website: www. econ.ag.gov.

FOOD AND NUTRITION SERVICE is dedicated to improving the nutrition of the public, while also making certain that agricultural producers have a fuller market for their output.

CONTACT Address: 3101 Park Center Drive, Room 906, Alexandria, VA 22302; Phone: (703)

305-2062 and 1 (800) 221-5689; Fax: (703) 305-2908; E-mail: webmaster@fus.usda.gov; Website: www.fas.usda.gov/fns.

Food Stamp Program provides coupons to low-income recipients certified by local welfare agencies for purchase of food and food plants.

CONTACT Address: 3101 Park Center Drive, Alexandria, VA 22302. Food Stamp hotline: 1-800-221-5689; Phone: (703) 305-2022; Fax: (703) 305-2454; Website: www.fas/isda/gpv/fsp.

National School Lunch Program and the **School Breakfast Program** provide such meals free or at reduced cost (at participating public or private schools) for children of families certified to be close to or below the poverty line. **Milk Programs for Children** and **Special Supplement Food Program for Women, Infants and Children (WIC)** funded through state agencies are also administered by the service. Coordination of the programs promoting good nutrition is managed at the Center for Nutrition Policy and Promotion.

CONTACT Address: 3101 Park Center Drive, Alexandria, VA 22302. For these special nutrition programs: Phone: (703) 305-2052; Fax: (703) 305-2782; Website: www.fns.usda.gov. (See next entry.)

The **CENTER FOR NUTRITION POLICY AND PROMOTION** was created in 1994 to coordinate all of the programs of the Food and Nutrition Services and also promotes nutrition. It is located at 1120 29th Street SW, Suite 2000, Washington, DC 20036; Phone: (202) 418-2312; Fax: (202) 208-2321; E-mail: cnpp-web@www.usda.gov; Website: www.usda.gov/fsc/cnpp.

NATURAL RESOURCES CONSERVATION CENTER produces the National Resources Inventory, operates the Wetlands Reserve Programs, and works to encourage what is called "backyard conservation."

CONTACT Address: P.O. Box 2890, Washington, DC 20013; Phone: (202) 720-7246; Fax: (202) 720-7690; Website: www.ncrs.usda/gov/.

National Resources Inventory is an extensive source of information about land throughout the United States, including detailed reports and maps covering urbanization, land use, prime farmland, erosion, and wetlands. The inventory is fully updated every five years, but issues current reports. Maps can be downloaded and printed. Website: www.nhq.ncrs.usda/gov/land/index. (See next entry.)

UNITED STATES FOREST SERVICE (USFS) Created by Congress in 1905, the U.S. Forest Service is a major, somewhat independent agency within the Department of Agriculture. It functions within the Office of the Under Secretary for Natural Resources and Development and is headed by a chief forester, who is a career incumbent.

The service is responsible for management of 155 national forests, 20 national grasslands, and eight land utilization projects, for a total of 191 million acres in 44 states, the Virgin Islands, and Puerto Rico. Of these, almost 35 million acres are designated wilderness and 175,000 acres are primitive areas where timber harvesting is prohibited. Preventing forest fires and erosion and preserving wildlife habits are major areas of Forest Service responsibility. Research in all these areas is performed by the service, which maintains six regional laboratories and a wood-products laboratory at 1 Gifford Pinchot Drive, Madison, Wisconsin 53705.

The Forest Service negotiates contracts for timber rights under specific requirements and restrictions, giving the service a major role in the lumber industry's conduct and practices. There are nine regional Forest Service offices, each headed by a regional forester.

CONTACT Address: 201 14th Street SW, Washington, DC 20250; Phone: (202) 205-1661; Fax: (202) 205-1765; Website: www.fs.fed.us.

WORLD AGRICULTURAL OUTLOOK BOARD maintains a watch and analyzes agricultural conditions, markets, and needs throughout the world.

CONTACT Address: 1400 Independence Avenue SW, Room 5143; Phone: (202) 720-6030; Fax: (202) 690-1805; Website: www.usda.gov/agency/oce/waob.

DEPARTMENT OF COMMERCE

The Department of Commerce is a cabinet-level department of the executive branch that began life as the Department of Commerce and Labor by act of Congress on February 14, 1903, during the administration of President Theodore Roosevelt. Roosevelt had proposed creation of a "Department of Commerce" in his first State of the Union message in 1902 and again urged it in his State of Union message in January 1903, and Congress promptly enacted the necessary legislation. George B. Courtelyou, a top aide to Presidents William McKinley and Roosevelt and former chairman of the Republican National Committee, was immediately appointed the first secretary. A decade later, the department was divided into the Department of Commerce and the Department of Labor on March 4, 1913, the day Woodrow Wilson was inaugurated.

Secretaries of commerce have included several who were notable in other positions, including Franklin D. Roosevelt confidante Harry Hopkins (1938–40), former Vice President Henry A. Wallace (1945–46), Governors W. Averell Harriman (1946–48) and Luther H. Hodges (1961–65), Eliot Richardson (1976)–77), who had been attorney general, secretary of health, education and welfare, and secretary of defense, and economist Juanita M. Kreps (1977–79), who was the first woman to serve in the position. The most famous was Herbert C. Hoover (1921–28) who served under Harding and Coolidge and was elected president in 1928.

Over the years various functions and agencies were transferred to the department, such as the Patent Office (1925) and the Weather Bureau (1940), while several functions that had originally been under the administration of the department were transferred to other agencies and new departments, including radio (1932), mines (1934), fisheries (1939), aeronautics (1958),

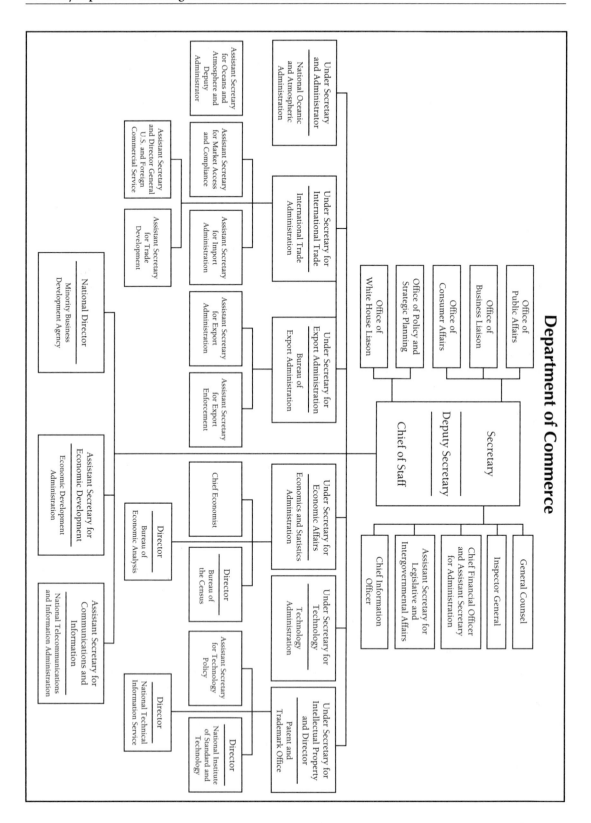

Department of Commerce

transportation (1966), energy (1977), and maritime administration (1981).

The department has numerous goals: stimulate job creation in business, industry, agriculture, and universities, including by strengthening American competitiveness in the global marketplace; community development; assistance for minority businesses; perfecting science and technology; develop the information infrastructure ("information superhighway"); and protect life and property in the case of natural disasters. Commerce also manages, develops, and disseminates a broad spectrum of detailed economic statistics for use by government and private industry. The department was the original creator of national (as well as regional and global) "economic accounts" as well as the Gross Domestic Products (GDP) and Gross Domestic Income (GDI) indices. Also under its aegis are the *Bureau of the Census,* the *Patent and Trademark Office,* the *National Weather Service,* and the *National Maritime Fisheries Service.*

ADMINISTRATION

The department is headed by the secretary of commerce, appointed by the president with confirmation by the Senate. Presidential appointees in addition to the secretary, deputy secretary, and general counsel are several assistant and under secretaries who are responsible for particular administrations, offices, and bureaus. The other presidential appointees include the chief financial officer, general counsel, inspector general, and chief scientist.

The headquarters and principal offices of the Department of Commerce are located in the Herbert Clark Hoover Building, 14th Street and Constitution Avenue NW, (1401 Constitution Avenue) Washington, DC 20230, a three-block-long building bounded by Constitution Avenue and Pennyslvania Avenue, 14th and 15th Streets. It was completed in 1931 and named for President Hoover in 1981. Due to limitations on auto

access in the area and high parking rates, the best means to reach the building is by taxi or the Metro subway, exit at the Federal Triangle stop on the Blue/Orange Line or the Metro Center on the Red Line. The main entrance in the middle of the building on 14th Street can be reached via the tunnel entrance from the food court in the Ronald Reagan International Trade Center across 14th.

The department's National Institute of Standards and Technology also maintains offices and laboratories at 100 Bureau Drive, Gaithersburg, MD 20899, and shares a 208-acre campus in Boulder, Colorado, with the National Oceanic and Atmospheric Administration, and the National Telecommunications and Information Administration. The laboratories are not open to the general public. The National Marine Fisheries Service is headquartered at 1315 East West Highway, Silver Spring, MD 20910.

CONTACT Address: Department of Commerce, 1401 Constitution Avenue NW, Washington, DC 20230. A general telephone number is (202) 482-2000, business liaison at (202) 482-1360, public affairs at (202) 482-5151, press secretary at (202) 482-6001, and information officer at (202) 482-4797. Website: www.doc.gov. Many contacts to the various departments, offices, agencies, and programs are listed with agencies below.

ACTIVITIES, PROGRAMS, AND SERVICES

The activities, programs, and services of the Department of Commerce are organized into several administrations, each directed by an under secretary: *Economic and Statistics, Economic Development, International Trade, National Oceanic and Atmospheric,* and *Technology.* There are also separate agencies: The *Census Bureau,* the *U.S. Patent and Trademark Office,* and within the National Oceanic and Atmospheric Administration, the *National Weather Bureau* and the *National Marine Fisheries Service.*

OFFICE OF POLICY AND STRATEGIC PLANNING

Assists the secretary of commerce in developing policy and strategic planning. New releases and policy documents can be obtained by contacting the department's Office of Public Affairs by telephone at (202) 482-5151; Website: www.doc.gov/opa. To reach the Office of Policy and Strategic Planning directly: Phone: (202) 482-4127; Fax (202) 482-4636; Website: www.osec.doc.gov/opsp.

ECONOMIC AND STATISTICS ADMINISTRATION

The Economic and Statistics Administration includes the Bureau of Economic Analysis, the Census Bureau, and STAT-USA, all of which are administered by the under secretary for economic affairs (who also serves on the Council of Economic Advisers and other governmental interagency economic committees). The administration's principal missions include maintaining and improving a federal statistical system, communicating and publicizing important economic forces that affect American public and private decisions, and providing statistical information and analysis for the executive branch of the federal government. Room 4836; Phone: (202) 482-2235; E-mail: esa.webmaster@mail.doc.gov; Website: www.esa.doc.gov.

BUREAU OF ECONOMIC ANALYSIS, although small in personnel numbers is key to obtaining, analyzing, and promulgating economic statistics relied upon by private and governmental agencies throughout the world. Its greatest informational product is the National Income and Product Accounts (NIPAs). This agency's invention of the Gross Domestic Product (GDP) was a remarkable useful statistical tool in developing economic policies. Economic information includes gross state products, annual state personal income, quarterly state personal income and local area personal income, and industrial accounts that are national, regional, and international. The office is located at 1441 L Street NW, Washington, DC 20230. Phone: (202) 606-9900; Fax: (301) 606-5310; E-mail: webmaster@bea.gov; Website: www.bea.doc.gov.

BUREAU OF THE CENSUS: The U.S. Constitution mandated in Article I, Section 2 that Congress shall provide for an "enumeration" of residents in every state every 10 years, for the purpose of determining the number of members of the House of Representatives and how "direct taxes" shall be allocated to each state. This census is conducted by the Bureau of the Census, also commonly known as the Census Bureau, which is headed by a director appointed by the president with confirmation by the Senate. As early as 1810 the bureau began gathering much more statistical information besides mere counting of people. Additions have been made to the scope of information gathering over the years. For example, home plumbing (e.g., running water, flush toilets/outhouses) was added in 1940. Currently the census (as well as interim estimates) provides extensive statistical information on a wide variety of subjects and is the largest single statistical source in the United States. Its current structure was established by Congress on March 6, 1902, and it became a function of the new Department of Commerce and Labor in 1903.

Every 10 years the bureau hires a large number of enumerators who are trained and then gather information on a door-to-door basis. In addition, the bureau sends out mailings of lengthy forms on detailed subjects such as employment, income, housing conditions, and education. In the 2000 census the use of "samplings" in some areas in which the actual numbers of people is difficult to determine because of transience and other factors was a matter of debate.

Special censuses of various industries such as agriculture, mining, distribution trades, construction, and transportation are conducted every five years, as well as special censuses on the request of state and local governments.

The bureau maintains extensive staff for statistical analysis and a dozen regional offices.

CONTACT   Address: Census Bureau, Washington, DC 20233 (actual office is in Federal Office Building 3, Suitland, MD 20233); Phone: (301) 457-4608, (301) 763-4636 (info) or (301) 457-3030; Fax: (301) 457-4714; E-mail: director@census.gov or customer.services@census.gov; Website: www.census.gov.

The Census Bureau is customer friendly and is organized so that members of the public can make direct telephone calls to staff specialists on subjects ranging from means of commuting to poverty levels by area. The information is entirely statistical, and all individual responses are confidential. A list of subjects and contacting telephone numbers is found at www.census.gov/contacts. To order census reports or other materials telephone (888) 249-7295.

The regional offices can be reached on E-mail by www.census.gov/and the name of the city. They are: Atlanta for Alabama, Florida, Georgia, (404) 730-3833; Boston for Connecticut, Massachusetts, Maine, New Hampshire, most of New York, Rhode Island, Vermont, (617) 424-0510; Charlotte for Kentucky, North Carolina, South Carolina, Tennessee, Virginia, (704) 344-6144; Chicago for Illinois, Indiana, Wisconsin, (708) 562-1791; Dallas for Louisiana, Mississippi, Texas, (214) 253-4434; Denver for Arizona, Colorado, Montana, Nebraska, North Dakota, New Mexico, Nevada, South Dakota, Utah, Wyoming, (303) 969-7750; Detroit for Michigan, Ohio, West Virginia, (313) 259-1875; Kansas City for Arkansas, Iowa, Kansas, Minnesota, Missouri, Oklahoma, (913) 551-6711; Los Angeles for southern and central California and Hawaii, (818) 904-6339; New York City for greater NYC, New Jersey, (212) 264-4730; Philadelphia for Delaware, District of Columbia, Maryland, part of New Jersey, Pennsylvania, (215) 656-7578; Seattle for northern California, Alaska, Idaho, Oregon, Washington, (206) 553-5835.

There are committees that advise the Census Bureau, which can be reached as follows: *Census Advisory Committees* at (301) 457-2070, *Decennial Census Advisory Committee* at (301) 457-2095, and *Race and Ethnic Advisory Committees* at (301) 457-4047. The bureau has developed a list of census information centers that are nongovernmental nonprofit organizations, ethical associations, educational and charitable institutions. The list with telephone numbers can be located on the Internet at www.census.gov/contacts.

STAT-USA has an electronic information system to provide government economic, business, statistics, and foreign trade information to the public and expert information technology to other bureaus in the Department of Commerce. Phone: (202) 482-1405. Nongovernmental use of its Internet site (*STAT-USA/Internet*) is by subscription for a fee that supports the program. Subscribers can download and print out trade opportunities, market reports, as well as information from the STATE DEPARTMENT, the Federal Reserve Board, the Census Bureau, and the Bureau of Industry and Security.

Also available by subscription on-line are up-to-the-minute trade statistics prepared jointly by STAT-USA, the Census Bureau, and a private partner.

In addition, this administration is staffed by the under secretary for economic affairs, who is primarily the chief adviser on economic issues to the secretary of commerce, provides oversight to the Census Bureau and the Bureau of Economic Analysis, and serves as Commerce's representative on the President's Council of Economic Advisers. Another key official within this administration is the chief economist, who acts as an economic adviser, conducts analyses with his own staff, and receives reports from the Office of Economic Conditions. The Offices of Economic Conditions, Policy Development, Policy Analysis, and Business and Industrial Analysis provide further input on economic matters.

ECONOMIC DEVELOPMENT ADMINISTRATION

The Economic Development Administration, created in 1965, focuses on urban and rural areas suffering economic distress that strives to generate and maintain jobs, and stimulate industrial and commercial expansion in those communities, including Indian reservations. In partnership with state and local governmental and private organizations, Economic Development encourages local governmental-business strategies for economic health. It also addresses emergency economic woes due to the impact of natural disasters, depletion of natural resources, or closure of federal government and military facilities.

Of a budget of about a half billion dollars, more than half is spent on public works, while area planning, technical assistance, economic adjustment, and research are the other principal functions.

EDA produces the *Economic Development Directory,* which lists individuals, organizations and activities in every state involved in economic development, which can be contacted by e-mail at edirectory@doc.gov. Since the directory was put together by private organizations and state governments, the department distributes it without guaranteeing its accuracy.

INTERNATIONAL TRADE ADMINISTRATION

The International Trade Administration is responsible for the Bureau of Industry and Security and works to encourage international trade and assist American entrepreneurs involved in international commerce.

TRADE INFORMATION CENTER provides information and basic advice for people interested in international trade. From this center one can obtain answers to export questions, tariff and tax information, export program guidance, information by country and industry, and location of trade offices and trade events. This center brings together information from 20 federal agencies that make up the Trade Promotion Coordinating Committee. The basic telephone number is 1(800) USA TRADE; Fax: (202) 482-4473; Website: www.trade.gov/td/tic.

Trade Advocacy Center, created in 1993, in proper circumstances will assist an American company (or a company primarily American owned, operated, or employing Americans) in dealing with foreign governments acting in cooperation with U.S. embassies and consular officials abroad. The center steps in only under certain guidelines, including prohibitions against bribing foreign officials.

Trade Development Office provides information statistics on particular industries; Market Access and Compliance focuses on the ability to enter various foreign markets.

Trade Compliance Center deals with foreign trade barriers and how to overcome them, and the Import Administration protects American industry against foreign "dumping" and "countervailing duties" by other nations' industries.

BUREAU OF INDUSTRY AND SECURITY (BIS)

Created as a separate bureau within the Commerce Department on October 1, 1987, as the Bureau of Export Administration, until the name was changed by the George W. Bush administration in April, 2002, BIS controls exports of materials and commodities that are restricted by federal laws and regulations to prevent their use by countries for purposes adverse to the United States, subject to embargo or otherwise restricted. These include "dual-use" materials that could be used for military purposes as well as civilian use. BIS's key goals are protection of infrastructure and cyber security by enforcement of export control laws. The bureau assists American exporters to comply with international arms agreements and the Chemical Weapons Conventions.

BIS processes exporter license applications, determines whether an exporter is meeting legal limitations on commodities spelled out in the Export Control Act, provides continuing education on export rules, studies the needs of foreign countries, and after analysis makes recommendations on decontrolling products. Regulations covering export of medical supplies to nations such as Cuba or Iraq may include systems that could be used for military purposes. Export licenses are developed and issued or rejected by the bureau depending on statutes and regulations. License applications can be made on-line, but may require sophisticated knowledge of the regulations on the part of the exporter.

After the September 11, 2001, attack on the World Trade Center and the Pentagon, the bureau participates in homeland defense. Adoption of the bureau's new name did not change the functions or thrust of the bureau, but more accurately reflected its new purpose.

The director of the bureau is an undersecretary for export, appointed by the president with Senate confirmation, as are two assistant secretaries, including one responsible for enforcement.

CONTACT Address: Bureau of Industry and Security, 14th Street and Constitution Avenue, Washington, DC 20230; Phone: (202) 482-2721; Website: www.bis.doc.gov. There are 10 regional offices for assistance to exporters.

NATIONAL OCEANIC AND ATMOSPHERIC ADMINISTRATION (NOAA)

The National Oceanic and Atmospheric Administration (NOAA) is a scientific administration that includes ocean, satellite, and fisheries services and the National Weather Service. It was cre-

ated in a reorganization pursuant to the National Oceanic and Atmospheric Administration, proposed by President Richard Nixon when he also proposed creation of the independent Environmental Protection Agency.

NOAA's historic origins go back to February 10, 1807, when President Thomas Jefferson ordered a survey of coasts of the United States, which then meant the Atlantic Ocean and Lake Erie. That work was performed by the combined efforts of the navy, army topographic engineers, and the Revenue Cutter Service (precursor of the Coast Guard) all under the direction of the TREASURY DEPARTMENT.

In 1878 that office became the Coast and Geodetic Survey, reflecting the fact that it took on responsibility for land surveys as well, including a coast-to-coast survey of the United States. Here and there in the mountains old markers (stakes in piles of rocks) can still be located. The Coast and Geodetic Survey found its way into the Commerce Department in 1966 through a reorganization that preceded NOAA. When it was created in 1968, NOAA also acquired the so-called Lakes Survey covering the Great Lakes, which first began in 1841, the Great Lakes Research Center, and several laboratories.

NOAA creates and tracks aeronautical and nautical charts; coastal aerial photography and maps; tide tables; climate, flood, and storm predictions; environmental, oceanographic, solar, and space data; weather observation stations; oil spills; fish statistics and economics; endangered species, marine mammal, and whale protection; seafood inspections; hurricane and ozone hole research; satellite operations; and several studies on different aspects of global warming.

CONTACT Address: NOAA, 14th Street and Constitution Avenue, Room 6013, Washington, DC 20230; Phone: (202) 482-6090; Fax: 482-3154; E-mail: noaal-outreach@noaa.gov; Website: www.noaa.gov.

NATIONAL WEATHER SERVICE provides weather, hydrologic, and climate forecasts and warnings throughout the United States, its territories, and adjacent waters. It produces and maintains a national database that can be accessed by governmental agencies, private business, and the general public both in the United States and foreign countries. The U.S. Navy, Coast Guard, Corps of Engineers, Federal Emergency Management Agency (FEMA), the U.S. Forest Service, the DEPARTMENT OF THE INTERIOR, fire watch entities, U.S. Geological Survey, the Federal Aviation Administration, civil aviation organizations, the World Meteorological Organization, and the American Red Cross are all regular users of these services.

In addition to gathering information and providing updated warnings and other information, the bureau conducts extensive research, planning, and development of improvements in gathering data, predicting, planning, and responding to weather and oceanic conditions.

The Weather Bureau had its origins in private and local weather reporting and statistics gathering that date back to the 17th century. American government weather observations were initiated in 1817 by the Federal Land Office. Starting in 1849 the Smithsonian Institution ran a network of weather observation reporters that was connected by the newly invented telegraph. Congress established in 1869 a national weather warning service operated by the Army Signal Corps in the War Department. In the 1870s regular weather predictions began to be printed in newspapers, and the Smithsonian operation became part of the weather warning service of the Signal Corps.

The Weather Service Organic Act transferred the Weather Bureau to the newly created DEPARTMENT OF AGRICULTURE, effective July 1, 1891. Over the years before World War II the bureau regularly added innovations such as wireless contacts with ships at sea (1902), weekly forecasts (1910), aerological studies for aviators (1914), "flying weather" forecasts (1919), fruit frost reports (1922), use of radiosondes for measurement of

---

On-line weather information:
www.nws.noaa.gov
For local, regional, and national weather map, forecasts, marine weather warnings, and satellite maps, all of which are kept up-to-date hourly.

---

atmospheric pressure, temperature, humidity, and winds (1936), and five-day forecasts (1940). In 1940 President Franklin D. Roosevelt ordered the Weather Bureau transferred to the Commerce Department, in part because weather has a major impact on production and trade.

With the growth of aviation during and after World War II the bureau greatly expanded its services. Various centers were established, including the National Weather Records Center, the National Meteorological Center, and the National Hurricane Research Project.

In the early 1960s the Weather Bureau was one of the first government agencies to understand, value, and employ the use of computers, which has meant an exponential gain in the ability to collect weather-related information and to process rapidly mounds of data, previously impossible to analyze. The computer-enhanced system was operational by 1978. In the early 1990s it was updated to provide a high-speed nationally connected computer network from data collected at 260 locations.

The bureau is headed by the director of the National Weather Service (technically an assistant administrator for weather services of the Department of Commerce). Its functions are organized under the Office of Climate, Water and Weather Services, Office of Science and Technology, Office of Hydrologic Development, and Office of Operational Systems. The bureau also has six regional headquarters (eastern, southern, central, western, Alaska, and Pacific), 13 river forecast centers, and seven regional climate centers.

CONTACT Website: www.nws.noaa.gov; Phone: (301) 713-0689.

WEATHER AND ENVIRONMENTAL SATELLITES

In concert with NASA and the DEPARTMENT OF DEFENSE, in 1965 the Weather Bureau participated in the launching of a weather satellite synchronized with the sun (TIROS-10), which made possible worldwide observation of weather conditions. Until 1980 NOAA had operational responsibility for the perfection of the satellite system, when it was transferred to the National Earth Satellite Service (NESS) headed by an assistant administrator who reported to the secretary of commerce. Under legislation enacted in 1984, the weather satellite was commercialized in 1985. Using the combined benefits of satellites, radar, and computers, the worldwide weather picture is constantly available (see National Weather Service above), and worldwide mapping has provided a remarkable inventory of photomaps of land surface and conditions.

NATIONAL MARINE FISHERIES SERVICE manages the 2 million square miles of what it describes as "federal fishing waters," in the development and protection of American fishery resources in partnership with the fishing industry and the various coastal states.

CONTACT Website: www.nmfs.doc.gov; Phone: (301) 713-2239.

Governmental involvement with edible fish originated with a one-man United States Fish Commission in 1871 during the administration of President Ulysses S. Grant. In 1903 it became the Bureau of Fisheries within the then-new Department of Commerce and Labor. In 1939, the bureau was transferred to the Interior Department and a year later was shuttled to the Department of Agriculture as part of the Fish and Wildlife Service. Under the Fish and Wildlife Act of 1956, the commercial fishing aspect was sent back to Interior as the Bureau of Commercial Fisheries. Finally in 1970, the bureau and most of

its functions came back to the Commerce Department under the National Oceanic and Atmospheric Administration (NOAA).

Responding to falling fish stock, a decline in catches by American commercial fishermen, and increased incursions by foreign fishing boats along U.S. coasts, in 1976 Congress enacted the Magnuson Fishery Conservation and Management Act (named for Senator Warren Magnuson of Washington state), which claimed American jurisdiction over oceans within 200 miles of the coasts. The act established a United States Fishery Conservation Zone and charged NOAA of the Commerce Department with implementation of the system. Regional Fishery Management Councils were set up, which prepared management plans for each fishing area. Enforcement was given jointly to the Commerce Department and the Coast Guard (ready to chase away foreign poachers and fishing in violation of regulations). In 1983 President Ronald Reagan reinforced the claim of U.S. control of much of the neighboring oceans by declaring sovereignty over what he called the "Exclusive Economic Zone" of 200 miles outward from American land territory.

By various means, including regulations and monitoring, the Fisheries Service has reversed the decline in fishing stocks in recent years, and shows considerable progress in "rebuilding." Methods include fishing "closures" during spawning seasons, halting all fishing of over-harvested fish species until rebuilding has occurred and the stock population has stabilized at higher levels, restrictions on mesh size of nets to protect smaller fish such as sardines, preventing incidental deaths of marine mammals, limiting fishing seasons, and working with local fishing industries and state governments to develop workable management programs. Worldwide, the losses in whale population have been halted.

The Magnuson Act also gave authority and means to the National Marine Fisheries Service for research on seafood quality, market conditions in the fishing industry, and to enter into joint efforts with the State Department to remove barriers to exports of U.S. fish, and development of technology in the industry.

Marine Recreational Fisheries Statistics Program, started in 1979, conducts the Marine Recreational Facilities Statistics for the benefit of 17 million recreational fishers, government agencies, and economic research. Management of recreational fishing is handled by the fish and wildlife managers at the Interior Department.

CONTACT Website: www.st.nmfs.gov.

The work of the service is facilitated through five regional offices (Alaska, Northeast, Northwest, Southeast, and Southwest [including Pacific islands]), each with several laboratories, a science center, and field offices. The Pacific Fisheries Environmental Laboratory is located on Monterey Bay at 1352 Lighthouse Avenue, Pacific Grove, CA 93950; Phone: (831) 648-8515.

Protection of certain marine species became an official function of the service under the Marine Mammal Protection Act (1972) aimed at protecting endangered marine mammals such as whales, porpoises, seals, sea turtles, and otters. The Endangered Species Act (1973) was designed to conserve marine species likely to be wiped out by preventing illegal imports and exports of endangered marine mammals and the accidental catches by fisheries. The NOAA administrator is the U.S. representative on the International Whaling Commission.

COASTAL ZONE AND
OCEAN MANAGEMENT

Pursuant to the 1972 Coastal Zone Management Act, NOAA makes grants to states to improve and protect coastal lands to make them safe, well planned, and attractive. Grant goals include assistance to states and communities dealing with the environmental, social, and economic costs of energy development, such as nuclear power plants and offshore oil and gas drilling, and matching funds to states for acquisition, management, and research of estuaries in their natural state. More than 90 percent of American coasts are covered by plans prepared under these programs.

Also adopted in 1972, the Marine Protection, Research and Sanctuaries Act authorized the secretary of commerce, with concurrence of the president, to designate marine "sanctuaries" to be preserved. The hulk of the Civil War ironclad USS *Monitor,* sunk off Cape Hatteras, North Carolina, was the first to be designated, as were the Northern Channel Islands west of Santa Barbara, California, as a crucial habitat for marine birds and mammals. The same act required NOAA to monitor ocean dumping activities and to perform research on the effects of pollution and human-caused changes in ocean ecosystems. The Ocean Pollution Planning Act (1978) authorized further research of such pollution and the preparation and implementation of a five-year plan of investigation and ameliorative action. Investigation, research, regular reports, studies of coastal regions from New York Bight to Puget Sound, and a plan to provide scientific support to the Coast Guard in battling the effects of an oil spill were among the responsive programs. Since 1983 the Fisheries Service and the Army Corps of Engineers, responsible for navigable waters along the coast, joined together to rejuvenate coastal wetlands and other natural habitats.

There are numerous other programs, offices, and databases under the aegis of NOAA. The *National Sea Grant College Program* supports funding of marine research, education, and advisory services at qualified universities and numerous other institutions. Data collections include: *Strategic Assessment Data Atlases, National Coastal Pollutant Discharge Inventory, National Estuarine Inventory, National Shellfish Register, National Coastal Wetlands Data Base,* and *Living Marine Resources.*

There are thousands of nautical and aeronautical maps; the *North American Horizontal Geodetic Reference System* is a constant readjustment of locations on the Earth's surface (map updating) including shifts due to seismic activity.

NATIONAL TELECOMMUNICATIONS AND INFORMATION ADMINISTRATION

Formed in 1978 as part of a government reorganization under President Jimmy Carter's Executive Order 12046, some elements of its authority date back to the Radio Advisory Committee of 1922. It focuses solely on telecommunications and information and serves as the president's prime adviser on those subjects and works with other executive agencies on telecommunications policy development.

In addition to policy development the administration employs its expertise in a staff of engineers, researchers, and analysts to promote the development of a national information infrastructure ("the Information Highway"), manages grants to maintain and extend public broadcasting, and explores the impact of telecommunication innovations and spread on the society.

NTIA makes sure all Americans have affordable phone and cable television service, brings the Internet to rural and underserved urban regions of the United States, and provides hardware to help public radio and television maintain or extend the reach of programming. The administration advocates liberalization and competition in the telecommunications field around the world (consider the federal government's lawsuits against Microsoft Corporation), negotiates for American companies through government-to-government communication, and works with federal, state, and local public safety agencies to help meet future needs.

CONTACT Address: Herbert C. Hoover Building, 1401 Constitution Avenue, Washington, DC 20230; Phone: (202) 482-7002; Website: www.ntia.doc.gov. Telecommunications Sciences, Commerce Laboratory Complex, 325 Broadway, Boulder, CO 80305-3337; Website: www.ntia.doc.gov.

Administered by the NTIA are grant programs such as the *Public Telecommunications Facilities Program,* which gives equipment grants to public telecommunication entities, the *National Endowment for Children's Educational Television,* and the *Technology Opportunities Program (TOP),* which gives matching grants to nonprofit organizations for projects to improve public access to various community-based services.

PATENT AND TRADEMARK OFFICE (PTO)

Patent laws were adopted by the British parliament in 1623 to protect inventors, and applied to the American colonies. The first U.S. patent act was signed into law by President George Washington on April 10, 1790, under the authority in the Constitution, Article I, Section 8, which states that Congress shall have the power "To promote the progress of science and useful arts, by securing for limited times to authors and inventors the exclusive right to their respective writings and discoveries." The first patent was granted in that year to Samuel Hopkins for a method for manufacturing potash. In 1925 the Patent and Trademark Office was placed within the Commerce Department.

The Patent and Trademark Office principally processes applications for patents and trademarks, and maintains a detailed inventory of existing patents and trademarks to determine if such are truly original or infringe in whole or in part on existing patents or trademarks. In regard to patents, the process is sufficiently complex to require the assistance of patent attorneys for preparation of an application, including detailed drawings and technical explanations. Much of the processing is initiated by a computerized system, which can be entered at the office's website, www.uspto.gov.

Among its useful functions the office maintains search collections of patents, patent applications, expired patents, and trademarks, which often provide a ready test of originality for the applicant. It publishes manuals on "Patent Classification," "Examining Procedure," "Trademark Goods and Services," "Trademark Design Code," a roster of "Patent Attorneys and Agents," and maintains a library. Among its publications are Federal Register Notices, public comments, and job announcements.

CONTACT Phone: (703) 305-8600; E-mail: webmaster@uspto.gov; Website: www.uspto.gov.

Important note: The *Copyright Office,* which protects the original works of authors, composers, and artists is located in the Library of Congress. (See p. 457.)

TECHNOLOGY ADMINISTRATION

The Technology Administration, under the direction of the under secretary for technology, comprises the Office of Technology Policy, the National Institute of Standards and Technology, Measurement and Standards Laboratories, and the National Technical Information Service.

The Technology Administration provides information to industry, various agencies, and the general public by a program of publications, speeches, and maintenance of an updated informational website. Its goal is to "maximize technology's contribution to American growth."

CONTACT Phone: (202) 482-1575; E-mail: public_affairs@ta.doc.gov; Website: www.ta.doc.gov.

NATIONAL INSTITUTE OF STANDARDS AND TECHNOLOGY (NIST), founded in 1901, actually predates the formation of the Department of Commerce. It is a nonregulatory agency that promotes standards and technology intended to increase productivity, works to improve quality of products, and enhances trade, particularly through testing and research at two complexes

of laboratories in Maryland and Colorado. Scientists, engineers, and technicians in the fields of physics, chemistry, engineering, industrial production, and weights and measures provide technological benefits for American industry.

CONTACT Phone: (301) 975-2300.

NIST also offers local technical and business assistance to small manufacturers under the Manufacturing Extension Partnership; website: webmaster@mep.nist.gov. To promote excellence the NIST sponsors the Baldrige National Quality Program highlighted by the Malcolm Baldrige National Quality Award founded in 1987. (Phone: (301) 975-2036; Fax:(301) 948-3716; E-mail: nqp@nist.gov). The Advanced Technology Program cofunds innovative research and development programs by private industry. It also maintains the NIST Research Library, and conducts conferences and educational programs for children.

CONTACT Address: NIST, 100 Bureau Drive, Stop 3460, Gaithersburg, MD 20899-34690; Phone: (301) 975-6478; E-mail: inquiries@nist.gov; Website: www.nist.gov. Boulder, Colorado, laboratories located at 325 Broadway, Boulder, CO 80305-3328; Phone: (800) 287-3863; E-mail: smithcn@boulder.nist.gov. Subject matter telephone numbers can be found at www.nist.gov/public_affairs.

OFFICE OF TECHNOLOGY POLICY is in charge of developing national policies that promote the use of emerging technology to improve the strength of the American economy. Among its programs are an *Office of Technological Competitiveness* to stimulate innovation and exchange of information among competitors, the *Office of International Technology* promoting overseas technological partnerships between American and foreign firms, and the National Medal of Technology to be awarded by the president for outstanding technological innovation.

WEBSITE www.ta.doc.gov/OTPolicy.

NATIONAL TECHNICAL INFORMATION SERVICE amasses and distributes technical information produced by the government as well as foreign sources. Located in Springfield, Virginia, the telephone is (703) 605-6000; Website: www.ntis.gov.

Office of Space Commercialization explores the future commercial use of space.

Partnership for a New Generation of Vehicles is a 10-year study of potentials for fuel-efficiency, lower emissions, and improved vehicle safely.

Miscellaneous Commerce Department offices: There are also staff and administrative offices of the Commerce Department of use to entrepreneurs, researchers, and the general public.

OFFICE OF BUSINESS LIAISON

This is a small office that is an initial point of contact for business people desiring to deal with the Commerce Department. As its "outreach" function the office arranges meetings and briefings with department officials and staff, and can be useful in guiding members of the business public through the labyrinth of the federal government. The Office of Business Liaison also informs the secretary and the department of issues raised by the business community, so if there are questions, complaints, or fears, this is a good place for businesses (particularly those without other government contacts) to speak up. The office can be called directly at (202) 482-1360, or faxed at (202) 482-4054. Website: www.osec.doc.gov/obl.

MINORITY BUSINESS DEVELOPMENT AGENCY

It provides information and advice through publications, conferences, and direct counseling to minority business people, including such items as how to prepare a business plan, how to get

financing, and the like. Its director is appointed by the secretary of commerce.

CONTACT Phone: (202) 482-5061; Website: www.mbda.gov (users must register and obtain a password).

Also contact the *Office of Public Affairs* (phone: [202] 482-5151) and the **OFFICE OF SMALL AND DISADVANTAGED BUSINESS UTILIZATION** (phone: [202] 482-3387).

DEPARTMENT OF DEFENSE

Of all government agencies, the Department of Defense is the largest in number of personnel and in annual budget. Its estimated number of civilian employees is about 670,000, of which approximately 570,000 are allocated to the army, navy, air force, and coast guard, and an additional 100,000 work on various programs. There were 1,380,000 in the active uniformed military as of 2002. Additionally, the ready reserves who could be called upon totaled 1,280,000. The requested budget for fiscal year 2002 was approximately $329 billion (including supplements). These figures change radically when the United States is involved in actual military conflicts.

CONSTITUTIONAL AUTHORITY

Under Article II, Section 2 of the Constitution: "The President shall be commander in chief of the Army and Navy of the United States, and of the militia of the several states, when called into the actual service of the United States. . . ." However, the Constitution also gives the power "to declare war" exclusively to Congress in Article I, Section 8. The same section authorizes (or more accurately, importunes) Congress to "provide for the common defense," "make rules for capture on land and water," "raise and support armies," "provide and maintain a navy," and

Department of Defense

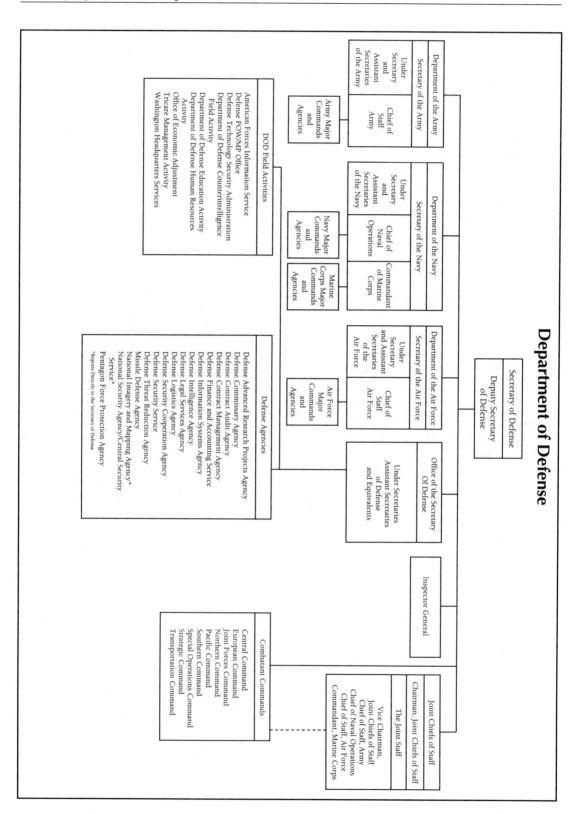

Secretary of Defense

Deputy Secretary of Defense

Department of the Army

Secretary of the Army

Under Secretary and Assistant Secretaries of the Army

Chief of Staff Army

Army Major Commands and Agencies

Department of the Navy

Secretary of the Navy

Under Secretary and Assistant Secretaries of the Navy

Chief of Naval Operations

Commandant of Marine Corps

Navy Major Commands and Agencies

Marine Corps Major Commands and Agencies

Department of the Air Force

Secretary of the Air Force

Under Secretary and Assistant Secretaries of the Air Force

Chief of Staff Air Force

Air Force Major Commands and Agencies

Office of the Secretary Of Defense

Under Secretaries Assistant Secretaries of Defense and Equivalents

Inspector General

Joint Chiefs of Staff

Chairman, Joint Chiefs of Staff

The Joint Staff

Vice Chairman, Joint Chiefs of Staff
Chief of Staff, Army
Chief of Naval Operations
Chief of Staff, Air Force
Commandant, Marine Corps

DOD Field Activities

American Forces Information Service
Defense POW/MP Office
Defense Technology Security Administration
Department of Defense Counterintelligence Field Activity
Department of Defense Education Activity
Department of Defense Human Resources Activity
Office of Economic Adjustment
Tricare Management Activity
Washington Headquarters Services

Defense Agencies

Defense Advanced Research Projects Agency
Defense Commissary Agency
Defense Contract Audit Agency
Defense Contract Management Agency
Defense Finance and Accounting Service
Defense Information Systems Agency
Defense Intelligence Agency
Defense Legal Services Agency
Defense Logistics Agency
Defense Security Cooperation Agency
Defense Security Service
Defense Threat Reduction Agency
Missile Defense Agency
National Imagery and Mapping Agency*
National Security Agency/Central Security Service*
Pentagon Force Protection Agency

*Reports Directly to the Secretary of Defense

Combatant Commands

Central Command
European Command
Joint Forces Command
Northern Command
Pacific Command
Southern Command
Special Operations Command
Strategic Command
Transportation Command

various powers to organize, arm, and maintain any militia called up. These powers are legislative directions, and the actual administration of military preparedness and action ultimately lies with the president and his executive branch, primarily the Defense Department. Constitutionally the U.S. armed forces are under civilian control. Although the president is commander-in-chief of all armed forces, he does not dictate or control the day-to-day operations of military action or preparation.

HISTORY

The creation of the present Department of Defense was a two-step process begun with enactment of the Armed Services Unification Act on July 26, 1947, which created a National Defense Establishment, headed by a secretary of defense. President Harry Truman (who had sent the proposed act to Congress on February 26 of that year) immediately appointed Secretary of the Navy James V. Forrestal as the first secretary of defense, who actually took the new position on September 17. The same act created the Department of the Air Force, which recognized the fact that the former Army Air Corps had been greatly increased and modernized during World War II under the vigorous command of five-star General H. H. "Hap" Arnold.

The three Departments of War (renamed Department of the Army), Navy, and Air Force remained entities, but became subsidiary to the National Defense Establishment as of September 17, 1947. Amendments to the act enacted in 1949 officially made the Defense Establishment a cabinet-level Department of Defense and no longer recognized the secretaries of army, navy and air force as cabinet-level equivalents, but provided that they each report to the Defense Department.

The original War Department had been an executive department since August 7, 1790, and the Navy Department dated back to May 3, 1798. However, the army itself predates the 1776 Declaration of Independence, having been authorized by the Continental Congress on June 14, 1775, shortly after clashes between informal groups of American soldiers ("Minutemen") and British regulars ("Redcoats") in the Massachusetts towns of Lexington and Concord. Two days later, the Congress named George Washington commander of the Continental Army with the rank of general. Washington was a Virginia planter and surveyor, with experience as an officer in the British Army on the western frontier in battles against the French during the French and Indian War in the 1760s.

Historically, the army had been a volunteer organization, with a relatively small number of regulars during peacetime. During the Civil War, President Lincoln asked for and got a draft to meet the increasing needs for men in the Union Army. To provide the soldiers for the American Expeditionary Force in 1917, once again a military draft was inaugurated. With Nazi Germany conquering much of Europe and militant Japan invading China, in 1940 President Roosevelt asked for a new draft law, which passed the previously isolationist Congress by a margin of a single vote. After World War II, while the armed services were drastically reduced, the draft law and the Selective Service System remained on the books, requiring young men to register. Call-ups based on a lottery raised the ranks for the Korean conflict in 1950 and again during the war in Vietnam, with various possible exemptions.

Washington appointed the first naval officer on September 2, 1775, and Congress authorized the arming of fishing boats in October, and on October 13 formed a Naval (later Marine) Committee with a budget of $500,000 to arm and adapt for fighting four merchant ships and to construct 13 frigates. Both Congress and various state governments issued charters as "privateers" to ship owners and captains, which were licenses to attack and rob British merchantmen. The first naval regulations were issued on November 28, 1775. Determined to protect shipments of goods to the American ports and interrupt British supplies to their troops, intrepid captains such as John Paul Jones roamed as far as the coast of England. One problem for the sailors was that the British treated them as pirates if captured, and they ran the risk that they could be hanged as such. The first navy flag, with 13 red and white stripes and the British Union Jack in the upper left-hand corner, was sewn by Margaret Manny of Philadelphia and first flown in December 1775.

After the Treaty of Paris officially ended the War for Independence, the small United States Navy was actually disbanded and its ships were sold. Faced with attacks on American shipping by the revolutionary government of France and the need to respond to the holding of ships for ransom by the semiofficial pirates from Tripoli (hence the refrain "from the shores of Tripoli" in the Marines' Hymn) on the Mediterranean, in 1798 Congress created the Navy Department, and a ship-building program was begun. Over the years the navy grew and contracted in size based on potential threats. In the opening week of the Spanish-American War in 1898, a small American fleet defeated the Spanish in Manila Bay in a single day. President Theodore Roosevelt pushed through a navy rebuilding program, and in 1908 sent the "Great White Fleet" on a trip around the world, putting other nations on notice that the United States was a naval power. Today it is unparalleled in aircraft carriers and nuclear submarines.

From the earliest days of the navy, the Marine Corps was a component, meant to fight to protect ships and carry out coastal forays. By World War I the marines were considered a specialized force of particularly tough units of professional fighters, and during and after World War II the corps was usually in the heart of the fighting.

The United States Air Force traces its roots to the War Department's first purchase of an airplane from Wilbur and Orville Wright in 1909, after flight demonstrations (with President Taft in attendance) on July 27. That day the airplane flew at an average speed of 42 miles per hour, and stayed aloft for more than an hour. The price: $30,000. The aircraft was placed under the purview of the army's Signal Corps, and in 1912 the rating of "Military Aviator" was announced. Two young lieutenants were assigned to experiment with the plane—Thomas Milling and Henry H. Arnold, universally known as "Hap." Between September 1908 and February 1914 there were 11 flying fatalities. On July 18, 1914, President Woodrow Wilson signed legislation creating an "Aviation Section" within the Signal Corps with a goal of 60 pilots and 260 enlisted men. After the United States entered World War I in 1917, there was a quantum leap in funds, planes, and pilots (yet still far less than other major combatants) who began fighting sorties and experimenting with bombing rather than just reconnaissance. Back in Washington, D.C., at the War Department, Arnold (by then a major) was the youthful director of supply and production of the Aviation Section, which had grown from 311 officers and men in 1916 to 195,023 by the end of the war in 1918.

After the war the Aviation Section was sharply reduced to a handful of obsolete aircraft. In 1925 an outspoken advocate of air power, Brigadier General Billy Mitchell, was court-martialed and suspended for his public statements that the army and navy brass were "incompetent" and "criminally negligent" in not developing an air arm. On July 2, 1926, the Aviation Section was reconstituted as the Army Air Corps, but it remained a minor unit in the armed services. Congressional bills to create a separate Department of Aeronautics were routinely shelved. At the time of the start of World War II in September 1939, the United States had only 800 planes, many of which were out of date. With the shocking success of the modern German Luftwaffe, air power appeared to be essential.

Chosen to build a modern air force was Major General "Hap" Arnold. He set up training programs and schools, pressed for plans of bombers of a size not known before (including the future B-29), and pressed converted industries to meet FDR's announced goal of 50,000 planes a year. Four months before the Japanese attack on Pearl Harbor, in a single week Arnold and a handful of air officers produced an air battle plan for potential combat in Europe. Tactical and strategic commands were organized, supply systems established, weapons developed, and the increase in numbers of planes and personnel was staggering (64,000 planes and more than 2,200,000 men and women). During the war, the Army Air Corps was morphed into the United States Air Force with tacit equality of command; Arnold became one of the five five-star generals in American history.[5]

Notable secretaries of war have included future president James Monroe (1814–15) and William Howard Taft (1904–08). Jefferson Davis, who would become the president of the Confederacy in the Civil War, was secretary of war between 1853 and 1857. Abraham Lincoln's son, Robert Todd Lincoln, was secretary of war between 1881 and 1885. Henry L. Stimson, who served as secretary of war (1912–13) appointed by Republican President Taft, was called back to the position by Democrat Franklin D. Roosevelt, a year before American entry into World War II, and served throughout the war. At the same time, Roosevelt chose for secretary of navy Frank Knox, who had been Republican candidate for vice president in 1936. When the United States became involved in the Korean conflict, President Harry S. Truman asked George C. Marshall (former commander of the army during World War II and former secretary of state) to return to service as secretary of defense, which Marshall did for a year. Serving as assistant secretaries of the navy were future presidents Theodore Roosevelt in 1897–98 and Franklin D. Roosevelt between 1913 and 1920.

---

[5] George C. Marshall, Dwight D. Eisenhower, Douglas MacArthur, Arnold, and Omar Bradley.

Secretary of the Navy (1944–47) James V. Forrestal was appointed the first secretary of defense on September 19, 1947, by President Harry S. Truman. A brilliant workaholic, he began to suffer from depression and resigned March 27, 1949. Shortly thereafter, he committed suicide by leaping from a hospital window. The carrier *Forrestal* is named in his honor.

ORGANIZATION

In broad terms this gigantic Defense Department is structured as follows:

The *National Command Authority* consists of the president and the secretary of defense as his chief adviser, in performance of the duties as commander in chief.

The *Office of the Secretary of Defense* with its extensive staff, under secretaries, and technical agencies, is directly below the president. It is directed by the *secretary of defense*, appointed by the president with senatorial confirmation, who is assisted by the deputy secretary of defense, who is also a presidential appointee with Senate confirmation, and an extensive support staff divided into dozens of offices.

Other chief officials appointed by the president are the *under secretaries of defense for acquisition, technology and logistics, for policy, for personnel and readiness, comptroller and chief financial officer,* and *general counsel.* Also in the upper echelon are *assistant secretaries of defense for command, control, communications and intelligence, for public affairs, for legislative affairs,* and *for intelligence oversight.* All of these positions filled by the president must be confirmed by the Senate, as are several internal support officials, such as the *directors of operational test and evaluation* and *administration and management,* and the *inspector general.*

The *Joint Chiefs of Staff* actually plan and coordinate military operations. The Joint Chiefs comprise a chairman appointed by the president from among high-ranking military officers, a vice chairman, the chief of staff of the army, the chief of naval operations, the chief of staff of the air force, and the commandant of the Marine Corps. Thus, the heads of all military services coordinate on policies, strategies, and recommendations in one organization.

Directly responsible to the Joint Chiefs are the nine *United Commands* headed by military officers who actually conduct operations, including military action. These Unified Commands are: *European Command, Pacific Command, Joint Forces Command, Southern Command, Central Command, Space Command, Special Operations Command, Transportation Command,* and *Strategic Command.*

A layer of defense operations more or less parallel to the United Commands are the *Departments of the Army, Navy* (which includes Marines), and *Air Force.* The chiefs of these departments are designated secretary of the army, secretary of the navy, and secretary of the air force, respectively. The role of each of these departments is assistance, backup, training, equipping, and preparation for military action of each service branch, but the office of the secretary of defense is the source of leadership, direct advice to the president, and overall strategy in both preparation and conduct of military operations.

This unusual administrative structure in which these three "departments" and "secretaries" are not cabinet-level but subordinate agencies, is rooted in history: Two existing departments and a long-overdue air force department were brought into the new Department of Defense so the old departments maintained certain functions and prestige while giving top authority over to the secretary of defense. The secretaries of army, navy, and air force are expected to advocate the peculiar needs of each branch of the service, and they do so.

LOCATION The Pentagon, just across the Potomac River from the heart of Washington, D.C., in Langley, Virginia, is the nerve center of the Department of Defense. It is the world's largest building in square footage (3.7 million), with five equal sides, five stories each, with a five-acre open area in the center. The building is 77 feet, 3.5 inches high. Approximately 23,000 people, both civilian and military, work in the Pentagon, look out through 7,754 windows, walk through 17 1/2 miles of corridors (but due to its design all offices are within a short distance of each other), and are served by its own post office, dining facilities, libraries, and 284 rest rooms. The building has a 29-acre footprint surrounded by 200 acres of lawn and 16 parking lots. It is reached by an access highway from Washington as well as a new subway.

Construction began with a groundbreaking ceremony on September 11, 1941, exactly 60 years prior to the day when suicide terrorists crashed a hijacked airliner into the building on September 11, 2001, tearing a gigantic hole in one side, and killing 181 people. At a cost of only $83 million (paid for by sales of obsolete War Department buildings), the Pentagon was completed by January 15, 1943, a span of just 16 months. After the 2001 terrorist attack, the badly damaged side of the Pentagon was completely rebuilt in exactly one year.

Only those with business with the Department of Defense and its employees may visit the Pentagon. Immediately after the 9/11/01 attack, all tours were suspended for the foreseeable future.

By the very nature of its mission the Department of Defense maintains facilities throughout the United States and the world.

DEFENSE DEPARTMENT SERVICE ORGANIZATIONS

Washington Headquarters Services provides support and operational services to the Defense Department, and is headed by the director of administration and management. In-house support includes financial management and accounting, records management, human resource management (both military and civilian), personnel security, office services, facilities management, physical security and law enforcement protection (guards), technology and data systems, and legal services.

Furthermore, Headquarters Services is placed in charge of various mandated programs of the Defense Department, including: Mandatory Declassification Review (what data can be declassified), Federal Voting Assistance (means to give overseas personnel an opportunity to vote), Freedom of Information Act, Privacy, Information Requirements, Directives System, Security Review, Federal Register System, Administrative Space Management for the National Capital Region, Data Collection, and Reports and Forms Management.

Thus, much of the smooth functioning of the tasks that a private corporation would require as well as particular federal mandates are managed and supervised by this service.

CONTACT Website: www.whs.pentagon.mil.

Other so-called *Field Services* are: *American Forces Information Service, Prisoner of War/Missing Personnel Office (POWs/MIAs), Human Resources, Education, TRICARE (medical services),* and *Economic Adjustment.*

AGENCIES WITHIN THE DEFENSE DEPARTMENT

Within the Department of Defense are 16 agencies with specific responsibilities and programs. Some of these are part of the internal management of the department, while several have distinct ongoing programs.

NATIONAL SECURITY AGENCY

This is the American government's cryptologic organization with a dual responsibility: 1) obtaining and deciphering coded messages by foreign powers and their agents and foreign organizations, 2) protecting information systems of the United States government, including the military services and defense contractors. It was created on November 4, 1952, during the Truman administration, based on a secret memorandum dated October 24, 1952, of the NATIONAL SECURITY COUNCIL entitled National Security Council Intelligence Directive Number 9.

For a period of time the NSA was kept a secret from the general public, and it became an internal joke that NSA stood for "No Such Agency." By 1972 its operation was clearly no longer secret, but much of its operation remains classified, including the NSA budget and number of employees. However, an investigative reporter estimates that approximately 50,000 people work for NSA.[6] The agency reports that these employees are equally divided between civilians and those assigned from the various military services. The agency is the second-largest user of electrical power in the state of Maryland, where it is headquartered. The budget figures are known to the OFFICE OF MANAGEMENT AND BUDGET, the Senate Select Committee on Intelligence, the House Permanent Select Committee on Intelligence, and the Appropriations Committees of both houses of Congress.

A presidential directive in 1972 by President Nixon created the *Central Security Service* to coordinate with NSA the cryptology (code-breaking) efforts of the Army, Navy, Air Force, and Marine Corps intelligence divisions. This has become a joint operation of NSA, technically known as NSA/CSS, with the director of the NSA also serving as chief of the CSS.

The objectives, requirements, and priorities of the NSA/CSS are established by the Central Intelligence Agency with input from the National Foreign Intelligence Board and the National Security Council. In particular, these objectives are to design cipher systems to protect American

---

[6] James Bamford, *Body of Secrets*, Anchor Books.

information transmission and "production" of foreign signals information (intercepting and decoding foreign transmissions, often picked up by satellite) as well as ferreting out weaknesses in the code systems of actual and potential adversaries. By directives of the department and executive orders, the NSA cannot spy on American citizens, commit sabotage or such "dark" operations as assassination of foreign leaders or operatives, or gather information by illegal or unethical means (including such methods used by foreign governments even if they are friendly allies). These prohibitions are governed by Executive Order 12333. Nevertheless, sources of intelligence and exact methodology are classified and may not be revealed publicly.

Government oversight is provided by the president's Intelligence Oversight Board, the National Security Council, the Department of Defense, the DEPARTMENT OF JUSTICE, and the oversight committees of both houses of Congress. Regulations governing the operations of the agency require the approval of the secretary of defense and the attorney general.

Clients of the agency include the WHITE HOUSE, the Central Intelligence Agency, the State Department, the Joint Chiefs of Staff, all military services at command levels, NATO forces, and selected allies. The agency also provides assistance and training to defense contractors and other private businesses that have a need to protect national security secrets from compromise, theft, or invasion. These secret protection services are provided through a program entitled *Information Systems Security (INFOSEC)*, which can be reached by telephone at (800) 688-6115.

ORGANIZATION

By regulation, the director of the NSA is always at least of the rank of lieutenant general (three stars) of a military service. The same directive provides that the deputy director, and the deputy directors for operations, technology, and infor-

mation systems security, are all civilians. Pursuant to Section 210 of Title 10 of the United States Code, the director is appointed by the president upon recommendation of the secretary of defense, and requires Senate confirmation. It is probable that NSA/CSS employs more mathematicians than any other entity in the world. Other staffers include linguists, analysts, computer experts, engineers, physicists, researchers, and administrators.

The first federal agency to use computers, the NSA has contributed to many advances in the field of cybernetics. Its *National Cryptologic School* provides training for its employees and other elements within the Defense Department. NSA also finances training for its employees at leading universities and colleges, as well as the war colleges of the several military services.

NSA opened the *National Cryptologic Museum* in December 1993, displaying a history of cryptology (codes, code-breaking) and how they have served, been developed, and have an impact on American lives. The museum is open to the public Monday-Friday, except federal holidays, 9:00 A.M. to 4:00 P.M., reached by turning into Fort Meade from Maryland Route 32 northeast on Colony 7 Road to the parking lot. Within the museum area is the *National Vigilance Park,* honoring aerial reconnaissance crews and cryptologists killed in the line of duty.

LOCATION   NSA headquarters and most of its activities are located in approximately 50 acres and several buildings at Fort George G. Meade in Maryland, reached on Route 295 (Baltimore-Washington Parkway) northeast from Washington, D.C., and southwest from Baltimore to the intersection of Maryland Route 32 and turn south.

CONTACT   Address: National Security Agency/ Central Security Service, 9800 Savage Road, Fort George G. Meade, MD 20755-6000; NSA Public Affairs: Phone: (301) 688-6524; tours of National Cryptologic Museum: Phone: (301) 688-5849; Website: www.nsa.gov.

DEFENSE INTELLIGENCE AGENCY

This is the Defense Department's agency for collection of foreign military intelligence, with 7,000 military and civilian employees worldwide. Directed by a lieutenant general, it provides advice to the Department of Defense, the chairman of the Joint Chief of Staffs, and to appropriate federal agencies. While seemingly somewhat redundant to other intelligence operations within and without the Department of Defense, the DIA specializes in advice directed toward military planning and weapon systems acquisition. Staff specialists include experts in military history, physics, political science, and computers.

The director is also chair of the *Military Intelligence Board,* which coordinates the activities of various segments of defense intelligence operations (sometimes referred to as "the intelligence community"), including intelligence officers from each of the military services. The board meets regularly and considers means of gathering intelligence, including surveillance and reconnaissance, as well as analysis of information so gathered.

In addition to its principal office at the Pentagon, the agency conducts activities at the *Defense Intelligence Analysis Center,* elsewhere in Washington, the *Armed Forces Medical Intelligence Center,* in Frederick, Maryland, and the *Missile and Space Intelligence Center,* in Huntsville, Alabama. Also within its purview is the *Joint Military Intelligence College* to provide advanced training for intelligence professionals. The college is authorized to grant a B.S. in intelligence and an M.S. in strategic intelligence. For staff of the agency and other federal employees for whom military intelligence is important, the agency also conducts the *Joint Military Intelligence Training Center,* which in 2001 created an innovative online virtual university on the Internet for students wherever they may be stationed.

CONTACT Address: Defense Intelligence Agency, the Pentagon, Langley, VA; Phone: (703) 695-0071; Fax (703) 614-3692; E-mail: Afdiapa@dia.osis.gov; Website: www.dia.mil.

IMAGERY AND MAPPING AGENCY

Known as NIMA for short, this agency acquires, prepares, and analyzes geospatial intelligence in various forms to produce magnificent maps, spatial pictures of Earth, a substantial database, and analysis. These include forecasts of future environments through a system called Inno Vision. These are used for various defense operations, including intelligence and combat support, as well as governmental planning by other departments. Many of the maps are also available to the public.

CONTACT Public Affairs Office: 4600 Sangamore Road, Mail Stop D-54, Bethesda, MD 20816-50031; Phone: (301) 227-2057, or Directorate of Public Affairs for comments or questions: (301) 227-7385; Website: www.nima.

For purchase of NIMA aeronautical charts: FAA Distribution Division, AVN-530, National Aeronautical Charting Office, Riverdale, MD 20737-1199; Phone: (301) 436-8301, (800) 638-8972; Fax: (301) 436-6829.

For purchase of NIMA nautical publications contact the United States Government Printing Office, Superintendent of Documents, P.O. Box 371954, Pittsburgh, PA 15250-1954; Phone: (202) 512-1800 (bookstore); Fax: (202) 521-2250.

For purchase of NIMA topographic maps and aerial photographs, the responsible agency is the U.S. Geological Survey (USGS), which also sells NIMA gazetteers and other publications. To order contact: USGS Information Services, Box 25286 DFC, Denver, CO 80225-0286; Phone: (303) 202-4700, (888) 275-8747; Fax: (303) 202-4693; Website: mapping.usgs.gov/mac/nimamaps/index.

MISSILE DEFENSE AGENCY

Since the end of World War II in 1945, there has been interest in defending the United States from intercontinental ballistic missiles (ICBMs). The initial studies of such possible defense were undertaken by the air force and the army. This concern was particularly stimulated by the missile progress by the then Soviet Union during the cold war (1946–88). The Cuban missile crisis in 1962, in which the Soviets began construction of missile sites in Cuba, was resolved by a combination of diplomacy and a tough-minded response by President John F. Kennedy and United Nations Ambassador Adlai Stevenson. Nevertheless, the potential threat remained. Missile defense has often taken a political turn such as the claimed "missile gap" in 1960–61, and the antimissile umbrella advocated in the early 1980s nicknamed by critics as "Star Wars," criticized as too expensive and unworkable. With the dissolution of the Soviet Union in 1989, antiballistic treaties in place, and some mutual reduction of nuclear arsenals by Russia and the United States in 2001, such a massive defense may or may not be practical or necessary.

The Missile Defense Agency is charged with developing defenses against ballistic missiles. In recent years, with the umbrella concept on hold, it has concentrated on interception of missiles. The development of sensors, tracking methods, interceptor missiles, unmanned aircraft, and other advances have been key to this work. On June 13, 2002, after several failures, in cooperation with the navy, a Sea-Based Midcourse intercepting missile hit a programmed target over the Pacific. Hailed as a significant breakthrough by the agency, it has its doubters who are not sure it would be effective in actual attacks by an enemy trying to elude the intercepting missile. The agency successfully tested a modified 747 as a "directed-energy" combat plane on July 18, 2002, in a flight at McConnell Air Force Base lasting an hour and 22 minutes, before landing without incident. The hope is that such an unmanned aircraft can be directed to intercept and shoot down ICBMs.

Administration is headed by a director, with a substantial staff, including research, engineering, and testing elements.

CONTACT Phone: (703) 697-8472; E-mail: external.affairs@bmdo.osd.mil; Website: www.acq.osd.mil.

DEFENSE THREAT REDUCTION AGENCY

This relatively small agency serves as the government's primary implementing organization for arms control inspection and monitoring compliance by signatory governments to several international arms control treaties and other agreements (including those never officially adopted by the United States, but followed as a matter of practice). On-site inspections and verifications in participating nations are standard activities.

By the same token, when foreign officials make on-site inspections of American facilities, they are accompanied by representatives of the Defense Threat Reduction Agency. The agency also provides assistance and personnel to the United Nations Monitoring, Verification and Inspection Commission.

As manager of the *Defense Treaty Inspection Readiness Program,* the agency prepares the Department of Defense and defense contractors for inspections within the United States in order to fulfill treaty obligations and at the same time protect national security and guarantee that the sanctity of sensitive data will not be jeopardized.

ORGANIZATION

The director of the Defense Threat Reduction Agency is an assistant secretary of defense appointed by the president with Senate confirmation. Included in the table of organization are a deputy director, an executive director, a chief of staff, and numerous special offices.

LOCATION The agency is headquartered at Fort Belvoir, Virginia.

CONTACT Website: www.acq.osd.mil.

DEFENSE SECURITY COOPERATION AGENCY

This agency processes the government's programs for providing military equipment and weaponry and military service to its allies both by the federal government and sales by private businesses. The principal programs are: 1) Foreign Military Sales, and 2) International Military Education and Training. The operation of the agency originated with the United States Foreign Assistance Act of 1961 (although providing arms and other military assistance to allies dates back to the eve of American entry into World War II). It was also enhanced by the Arms Export Control Act and related legislation.

International Military and Education is provided on a "grant" basis—essentially a free program to assist designated nations with "similar values and interests" to meet "common defense goals." The decision of making such grants is a policy matter determined by the secretary of state with the Defense Department responsible for implementation.

Governmental sales to foreign governments of military supplies, including arms, and services under Foreign Military Sales require defined procedural steps managed by this agency. The procedures include letters of request made by the hopeful foreign government delivered to the U.S. diplomatic mission in the requesting government, which is first examined by a security assistance organization in the U.S. embassy. Subject to comments by the local security assistance office, it is then sent to Department of State, the

relevant military service (army, navy, air force, marines) or defense office, and the Defense Security Cooperation Agency. Depending on the size and nature of the request, the response to the applicant, if tentatively approved by these three entities, will be either a form detailing price and availability or a letter containing an actual offer that can be accepted. There is a federal charge of a 3 percent fee to pay the cost of administering the program.

Private sales of weaponry are generally subject only to export controls, which can include prohibitions or limitations based on embargoes on recipients or banned weapons.

The United States is the world's largest arms dealer from both government and private sources, supplying almost half of the military arms by cost each year. Arms sales to foreign governments from United States sources amounted to $12.1 billion of the $26.4 billion in international arms sales worldwide in 2001.[7]

ORGANIZATION

The Defense Security Cooperation Agency is headed by a deputy director of the Department of Defense, who is a career officer with divisions covering different areas of the world, information and technology, humanitarian assistance, weapons, programs, and policy.

CONTACT Phone: (703) 601-3710; Website: www.dsca.osd.mil.

DEFENSE LOGISTICS AGENCY

The agency operates a complex network of acquisition, storage, distribution, movement of supplies, and inventory control to meet the supply needs of the various armed services at home

---

[7] Congressional Research Service report, August, 2002.

and abroad. It maintains supply, service, and distribution centers, procures and manages millions of items for the services and other federal agencies as well as American allies. Excess equipment is available to law enforcement agencies. The agency establishes and administers rules for purchases, suppliers, and standards of materiel. Given the danger of fraud, prior scandals over gouging by defense contractors, inflated prices for routine items, and other disturbing events, the Defense Logistics Agency can serve to save the American public millions of dollars.

ORGANIZATION

Logistics lies within the responsibility of the under secretary of defense for acquisition, technology, and is directly administered by the deputy under secretary. There are a dozen centers specializing in supplies, distribution, energy support, stockpiling of strategic materials, reutilization and marketing, printing and duplicating, and foreign distribution. The DLA maintains data on procurement regulations, supplier assessment and capability, pricing, law enforcement support (for sale of excess items), and an Internet library and directory.

CONTACT E-mail: dlapublicaffairs@hq.dla.mil for most questions and contacts; Phone: (877) 352-2255; for technical support (804) 279-HELP, (866) 335-4357, or E-mail dscrithelp@dscr.dla.mil; www.dla.mil.

The agency relies on the Defense Contract Audit Agency for auditing, which saves millions of dollars in contract evaluation. The auditors are located at Fort Belvoir, VA, Phone: (703) 767-3265.

Those agencies performing ministerial duties as part of the Defense Department's internal management apparatus are the following: *Defense Commissary, Defense Finance and Accounting Service, Defense Legal Services, Defense Technical Information Center, Defense Contract Audit Agency, and Defense Logistics.*

U.S. COURT OF APPEALS FOR THE ARMED FORCES

The U.S. Court of Appeals for the Armed Forces is an impartial civilian court established for the ultimate appeals above the structure of the military justice system. It is intended to ensure fair and unbiased protections of due process to members of the armed forces accused of crimes and tried by military courts. The court reinforces the fact that the military is ultimately under civilian control and that service men and women are entitled to the same guarantees of legal rights as civilians.

The Court is specifically *not* "subject to the authority, direction, or control of the Secretary of Defense." Uniquely, it is the one federal court subject to oversight by the Armed Forces Committees of the House and Senate. A Code Committee composed of the judge advocate generals of the army, navy, air force, and marines, the chief counsel of the Coast Guard, and nonservice attorneys appointed by the secretary of defense meets regularly (at least annually by statute). The committee reviews the implementation of the Uniform Code of Military Justice, prepares a report to Congress on the court's conduct and cases, and recommends legislation on such matters as proposed amendments to the Code of Military Justice and standards of uniform sentencing.

Originally established by Congress in 1950 as the Court of Military Appeals, in 1968 Congress redesignated the court as the United States Court of Military Appeals, to make clear it was a federal court and not an agency. Further name changes were made on October 5, 1994, as the United States Court of Appeals for the Armed Forces in the National Defense Authorization Act for 1995. The court is composed of five civilian judges appointed by the president for 15-year terms with Senate confirmation.

LOCATION Judiciary Square at 5th and E Streets NW, Washington, D.C. 20442-0001. The courthouse, originally housing the United States Court of Appeals for the District of Columbia

Circuit, dates from 1910, and is included in the National Register of Historic Places.

CONTACT Address: United States Court of Appeals for the Armed Forces, Clerk of the Court, 450 E Street NW, Washington, DC 20442-0001; Phone: (202) 761-1448; Fax: (202) 761-4672.

JOINT SERVICE SCHOOLS

DEFENSE ACQUISITION UNIVERSITY

The Defense Acquisition University (DAU), created by the Defense Acquisition Workforce Improvement Act of 1990, is the DOD center for acquisition training, education, research, and publishing located across five regional campuses. It performs these functions for the army, navy, air force, and other DOD schools to provide learning products and services to help these agencies make good business decisions and purchase appropriate products.

CONTACT Address: Director for University Operations, Defense Acquisition University, Fort Belvoir, VA 22060-5565; Phone: (800) 845-7606; Website: www.dau.mil.

JOINT MILITARY INTELLIGENCE COLLEGE

Previously called the Defense Intelligence College, the Joint Military Intelligence College was established in 1962 and works under the director of the Defense Intelligence Agency. It teaches military and civilian intelligence professionals and conducts and disseminates intelligence research, granting a bachelor of science in intelligence (BSI) and a master of science of strategic intelligence (MSSI) degrees, as well as conducting undergraduate and postgraduate diploma programs in intelligence.

CONTACT Address: Joint Military Intelligence College, Defense Intelligence Analysis Center, Washington, DC 20340-5100; Phone: (202) 231-5642; Website: www.dia.mil/jmic.html.

NATIONAL DEFENSE UNIVERSITY

Established in 1976, the National Defense University educates military and civilian leaders through teaching, research, and outreach in national security, military, national resource strategy, joint and multinational operations, information strategies, resource management, acquisition, and hemispheric defense studies.

National Defense University operates the National War College, Industrial College of the Armed Forces, Joint Forces Staff College, the Information Resources Management College, and the Uniformed Services University of Health Sciences.

CONTACT Address: National Defense University, Building 62, 300 Fifth Avenue, Fort McNair, Washington, DC 20319-5066; Phone: (202) 685-2169; Website: www.ndu.edu.

The National War College is the only senior service college whose primary mission is to offer an emphasis on national security policy formulation and the planning and implementation of national strategy. In its 10-month program, it provides education in national security policy to selected military officers and federal career civil service employees.

CONTACT Address: Department of Administration, The National War College, Building 61, Room G20, 300 D Street, Fort McNair, Washington, DC 20319-5078; Phone: (202) 685-3674; Website: www.ndu.edu/ndu/nwc/nwchp.html.

Industrial College of the Armed Forces provides study of resources of national power and its integration into national security strategy to prepare selected military and civilian personnel for senior leadership positions. It gives postgraduate executive-level courses and research on materiel acquisition and joint logistics, and their integration into a national security strategy for war and peace.

CONTACT Address: Director of Administration, Industrial College of the Armed Forces, Building 59, 408 Fourth Avenue, Fort McNair,

Washington, DC 20319-5062; Phone: (202) 685-4333; Website: www.ndu.edu/ndu/icaf.

Joint Forces Staff College educates staff officers and other leaders in joint operational-level planning and warfare, with the goal of a commitment to joint, multinational, and interagency teamwork, attitudes, and perspectives. JFSC runs its Joint and Combined Warfighting School, the Joint and Combined Staff Officer School, and the Joint Command, Control, and Information Warfare School.

CONTACT Address: Joint Forces Staff College, 7800 Hampton Blvd., Norfolk, VA 23511-1702; Phone: (757) 443-6185; Fax: (757) 443-6034; Website: www.jfsc.ndu.edu.

Information Resources Management College provides graduate-level courses to military and civilian leaders in information resources management (IRM) as it relates to national power by leveraging information and information technology for strategic advantage.

CONTACT Address: Information Resources Management College, Building 62, 200 Fifth Avenue, Fort McNair, Washington, DC 20319-5066; Phone: (202) 685-6300; Website: www.ndu.edu/irmc.

UNIFORMED SERVICES UNIVERSITY OF THE HEALTH SCIENCES was established on September 21, 1972, to educate career-oriented medical officers for military departments and the Public Health Service. It includes the F. Edward Hebert School of Medicine and the Graduate School of Nursing. Students are selected by board of regents-recommended procedures prescribed by the secretary of defense. Graduating students are obligated to serve not less than seven years, excluding their graduate medical education. Students in the Graduate School of Nursing must be commissioned officers of the army, navy, air force, or public health Service prior to application, serving a post-graduate commitment that varies according to the respective service.

CONTACT Address: Uniformed Services University of Health Sciences, 4301 Jones Bridge Road, Bethesda, MD 20814-4799; Phone: (301) 295-3030; Website: www.usuhs.mil.

DISTRIBUTION OF UNIFORMED MILITARY

Of the uniformed military services slightly over 1 million are stationed within the United States and its territories, and another 100,000 are "afloat." Those nations with major contingents of the more than a quarter of a million overseas American military are Germany 71,000, Japan 39,000, South Korea 38,000, Italy 11,000, United Kingdom 11,000, Serbia (Kosovo) 5,000, Saudi Arabia 4,800, Kuwait 4,300, Bosnia and Herzegovina 3,100, Turkey 2,170, Spain 1,778, Iceland 1,713, Belgium 1,554, and Bahrain 1,280. In addition, as of December 2003, there were 130,000 in Iraq and Afghanistan on combat and/or occupation duty. The number of American uniformed service men and women assigned to NATO countries is approximately 100,000. (Figures as of December 2001).

The total number of active duty service men and women was reduced from 2,168,000 in 1987 to 1,320,000 in 2002.

The ready reserves approximate 1,350,000, made up of Army National Guard (state militias) 367,000, Air National Guard 108,000, Army Reserve 430,000, Navy Reserve 206,000, Marine Corps Reserve 99,000, Air Force Reserve 128,000, and Coast Guard reserve 12,000.

ARMY NATIONAL GUARD: The basis of the National Guard is Article 2, Section 2 of the U.S. Constitution, which provides in part:

> The President shall be commander in chief of the Army and Navy of the United States, *and of the militia of the states, when called into actual service of the United States.*

Each state's National Guard is also available as the National Guard of the United States subject to national mobilization at time of war and for assistance during an emergency such as floods, riots, or enforcement of federal laws.

AIR NATIONAL GUARD: Each of 54 states and territories has a militia unit that maintains, flies, and practices with modern warplanes, called the Air National Guard. It is unique in that it is administered by the *Air National Guard Bureau,* a joint bureau of the Department of the Air Force and the Department of the Army. When mobilized, these units are assigned to air force commands, particularly airlifts and rescues, but may see actual combat.

CONTACT Address: Air National Guard Bureau, 2500 Army Pentagon, Washington, DC 20310-2500; Phone: (703) 607-2613.

SERVICE ACADEMIES

The Defense Department operates five major academies to train future officers of the various services. These are: *Military (Army) Academy* at West Point, New York (often just called West Point or just "The Point"), *Naval Academy* in Annapolis, Maryland, *Air Force Academy* in Colorado Springs, Colorado, *Coast Guard Academy* in New London, Connecticut, *Merchant Marine Academy* in Kings Point, New York. While the Coast Guard and the Merchant Marine have fighting responsibilities only during wartime and are currently managed by the Department of Homeland Security, the training of their officers is overseen by Defense.

UNITED STATES MILITARY ACADEMY (WEST POINT)

The original fort at West Point overlooking the Hudson River from a bluff on the west bank was ordered built in 1778 by General George Washington and designed by Thaddeus Kościuszko, a Polish officer fighting for the Americans, and completed in 1779. The oldest army facility was briskly defended by American troops fighting off attempts at capture by the British. American general Benedict Arnold became a traitor by offering to turn over West Point to the British troops, but the plot was uncovered and thwarted.

In 1802 Congress passed and President Thomas Jefferson signed legislation making West Point the official institution for training army officers, particularly in the field of engineering. Jefferson was especially desirous that the selection of cadets would be based on potential talent and from all states as compared to the officer corps of Great Britain and European powers, which were primarily sons of nobles, royalty, and the wealthy, on the dubious assumption that such upper-class elite were natural leaders. An early superintendent, Colonel Sylvanus Thayer (1817–33) set high academic standards, demanded strict discipline, and placed a premium on honorable conduct. Under Colonel Thayer civil engineering became the premier course of study, which provided two generations of engineers for American roads, bridges, railroad lines, and harbors for the expanding young nation. Between the date of its founding and the end of the Civil War, the academy was administered by the Corps of Engineers.

In the Civil War academy graduates were military leaders for both sides: Ulysses S. Grant and William Tecumseh Sherman for the Union and Robert E. Lee and "Stonewall" Jackson for the Confederacy. After that war the curriculum was broadened to a full academic program. After World War I Superintendent Brigadier General Douglas MacArthur further diversified the course of study and insisted that physical fitness of the future officers had to be an important element of the Point's activities, not only for the intercollegiate teams but intramural sports, under the slogan "Every cadet an athlete."

During World War II West Pointers Dwight D. Eisenhower, Douglas MacArthur, H. H. "Hap" Arnold, and Omar Bradley were four of America's only five five-star generals. The exception was Chief of Staff George C. Marshall, who had graduated from the Virginia Military Institute.

Over the years each member of Congress was entitled to a minimum of two appointments to the academy each year, but any single man or woman between the ages of 17 and 22 can apply, provided the application is approved by a member of Congress, the Department of the Army, or some other agency. Cadets are chosen from those nominees, followed by competitive examinations, meeting physical standards, and evaluation of leadership potential. After President Harry S. Truman ordered desegregation of the military services, the number of minority cadets began increasing, particularly in the last third of the 20th century. By the 1970s women cadets broke the gender barrier and now constitute approximately 15 percent of the cadet corps. In 1964 Congress legislated an increase in the number of cadets from 2,529 to more than 4,417, but since leveled at 4,000, with a graduation rate of over 90 percent. Some 1,200 cadets enter each July.

West Point's curriculum has been expanded to include humanities, cutting-edge sciences, and general education covering 31 fields of study. Much of the military training is conducted during stints at various military facilities after the first year. Graduates are awarded a bachelor of science, commissioned a second lieutenant, and are committed to five years of service in the military.

LOCATION About 50 miles north of New York City on the west bank of the Hudson River sited in a 16,000-acre reservation in Orange County; 600 Thayer Road, West Point, NY 10996-1788.

CONTACT Phone: (845) 938-2006; Fax: (845) 446-5820; Website: www.usma.edu.

UNITED STATES NAVAL ACADEMY (ANNAPOLIS)

Founded in 1845 as the Naval School, the United States Naval Academy trains future professional officers of the United States Navy and the Marine Corps. Like the United States Military Academy, over the years the Naval Academy has developed a full-range curriculum for its current 4,000 students (known as midshipmen), such as eight majors in engineering, six in science, mathematics, and computer science, and four in the humanities and social studies.

The principal campus is 338 acres situated on the south bank of the Severn River where it empties into Chesapeake Bay and borders on Annapolis, Maryland, the state capital. Some of its buildings are over 90 years old, and qualify the academy as a National Historic site. Much more modern are the Nimitz Library (named for World War II admiral Chester Nimitz), the Rickover Hall engineering complex (in honor of nuclear submarine developer Admiral Hyman Rickover), and Hendrix Oceanography Laboratory, in which the waters of Chesapeake Bay flow through the lab.

An early graduate in 1859 was Alfred Thayer Mahan, the leading advocate of the importance of naval power and noted geopolitical expert who contended that control of the central Pacific and northern Atlantic Oceans was crucial to American security. A prolific writer and president of the Navy War College, which provided advanced training to naval officers, he influenced future president Theodore Roosevelt, who was assistant secretary of the navy at the outbreak of the Spanish-American War. In most cases the leading American admirals in the victorious two-ocean battle against Japan and Germany during World War II were Annapolis alumni, including Chief of the Fleet/Chief of Naval Operations Ernest J. King, Pacific Commander Chester Nimitz, South Pacific Commander William F. "Bull" Halsey, and Raymond Spruance, hero of the Battle of Midway. President Jimmy Carter was a postwar graduate, specializing in physics.

For navigation, seamanship, tactics, weaponry, shipboard discipline, and leadership afloat, the midshipmen spend each summer training at naval bases and ships of the fleet. In addition to academics and practical naval experience, all students are expected to maintain a high level of physical fitness and participate in sports ranging from intramural club activity to varsity football.

Admission to Annapolis follows a four-step process, including appointments from the home district member of the House of Representatives, the Navy Department, or other entities. College students in Naval ROTC are encouraged to apply for transfer to Annapolis. A preliminary application for admission is available on the website of the U.S. Naval Academy, which is a simple means to start the process. Applicants must be single, be between the ages of 17 and 22, be prepared for tough competition examinations, be in good health, and show leadership qualities. Like other academies women have become eligible for entry and now make up 15 percent of the academy student body. Recent statute changes permit women to serve in combat roles when in the military services. In the last third of the 20th century minorities increasingly were admitted to the academies (as well as military service in general), and have become high-ranking naval officers.

Naval Academy graduates are awarded a bachelor of sciences with specific major course of study designated on his/her diploma, and then become either a navy ensign or a 2nd lieutenant in the U.S. Marines (a branch within the navy). All are committed to five years of service either in the Naval Reserve or the Marine Reserve, with a strong possibility of making a career as a regular naval officer.

LOCATION   121 Blake Road, Annapolis, MD 21402-5000; 1.6 miles from downtown Annapolis, via Rowe Boulevard to College Avenue, left on College, right on King George Street, after two blocks enter Gate 1, visitor's parking on right.

CONTACT   Phone: (410) 293-1000; Website: www.usna.edu.

UNITED STATES AIR FORCE ACADEMY

The Air Force Academy was authorized on April 1, 1954, by President Dwight D. Eisenhower. In several ways it is patterned upon the format of West Point and the Naval Academy. There are 4,000 cadets, with an entering class of approximately 1,200 each year. Like the other service academies, most of the students receive appointments from their home district members of the House of Representative as well as other sources. They must be single and between 17 and 22, and are subject to rigorous tests, physicals, and a determination of leadership skills. Of the cadet corps 12 percent are women (first admitted in June 1976) and 16 percent are minorities.

The academy is located 7,000 feet above sea level, on the outskirts of Colorado Springs, Colorado, 50 miles south of Denver. This site was recommended by a commission named in 1948 by the first secretary of the air force, Stuart Symington. From 580 considered sites, the commission culled out three possible locations. Secretary of the Air Force Harold Talbott picked the Colorado Springs location. Between July 1955 and August 1958 the academy occupied temporary quarters at Lowry Air Force Base while the new facilities were under construction for an initial cost of $142 million.

The academy's curriculum covers 31 different academic majors from astronautical engineering to foreign area studies. About 60 percent of the cadets major in science or engineering. A core course includes military training and leadership. Physical education and participation in sports, intramural, club, and/or intercollegiate, is a four-year requirement. Cadets are required to take a course in basic aviation, but optional are various studies related to actual flying, such as navigation, parachuting, soaring, and basic flying. Actual flight training awaits graduation for those selected for the flying and navigation programs. The modern laboratories include wind tunnels and rocket engines.

Upon graduation a cadet is awarded a bachelor of science degree, is given a reserve commission as a 2nd lieutenant in the air force, and may be entered in flight programs leading to actual piloting and navigating.

LOCATION   USAF Academy, CO 80840-5025.

CONTACT   Phone: (719) 333-2520, (800) 443-9266; Website: www.af.mil; Mail: United States Air Force Academy, Public Affairs Office, 2304 Cadet Drive, Suite 329, USAF Academy, CO

80840-5016; Admission information mail address: HQ USAFA/RRS, 2304 Cadet Drive, Suite 200, USAF Academy, CO 80840-5025.

DEPARTMENT OF THE ARMY

The principal responsibilities of the Department of the Army are recruiting, organizing, supplying, equipping, and training army personnel. Actual combat operations are planned and supervised by the hierarchy of the Department of Defense and the president in coordination with the army command staff. Obviously, the role of the Department of the Army is intertwined with the entire Defense apparatus.

Heading this department is the *secretary of the army,* who is appointed by the president subject to Senate confirmation. The secretary is assisted by an *under secretary of the army,* also appointed by the president with Senate confirmation required, who also has specific areas of responsibility such as the District of Columbia National Guard, operations research, and international affairs. In the upper echelon of the department are the *assistant secretary for acquisition, logistics and technology, assistant secretary for civil works, assistant secretary for financial management, assistant secretary for installations and environment, assistant secretary for environment,* and *assistant secretary for manpower and reserves* (meaning the ready reserves, who can be called up for active service). All are presidential appointees confirmed by the Senate.

Within the department are offices of the *army's surgeon general* (at Walter Reed Army Medical Center in Washington, D.C.), the *judge advocate general* (in Arlington, Virginia), the **ARMY MATERIEL COMMAND** (Alexandria, Virginia), Army *headquarters in Europe* (Brussels, Belgium), **ARMY SPACE AND MISSILE DEFENSE COMMAND** (Huntsville, Alabama, and Arlington, Virginia), and the *National Committee for Employer Support of the Guard and Reserve* (Arlington, Virginia).

There are also *deputy under secretaries for international affairs* and *for operations research,* who are career staffers. Also within the offices of the secretary are the *Office of Legislative Liaison* and the *Office of the Chief of Public Affairs.*

Managed by the Defense Department are training centers, the Army Reserves, and coordination of the National Guard (organized as state militias).

United States Army: The U.S. Army has (as of April 30, 2002) in uniform on active duty 481,266 men and women (76,067 officers, 401,138 enlisted, and 4,061 cadets) both in the United States or at various bases and assignments throughout the world. Within the Department of Defense are 230,130 civilian employees working for the army.

Direction of the U.S. Army is broken down into a dozen *major commands: Army Forces, Materiel, Training and Doctrine, Medical, Pacific Command, Space and Missile Defense, Special Operations, Intelligence and Security, Military Traffic Management, Criminal Investigation,* and *the Army Corps of Engineers.*

ARMY CORPS OF ENGINEERS: In June 1775 the Continental Congress directed the chief engineer of the Continental army (even before George Washington had been named general of the army) to build a fortification at Bunker's Hill (actually Breed's Hill) outside of Boston, where a troop of American patriots was holed up awaiting a British attack that came on June 17. This was the birth of the Corps of Engineers. After the Revolution the Corps of Engineers was based at West Point, and between 1802 and 1866 was in charge of the new Military Academy, in which civil engineering was the most significant course of study.

The corps has three basic missions: 1) planning, designing, building, and directing civil works projects, including flood control, dredging navigable waters, dams, roads, bridges, and other public facilities where civil engineering is a major element; 2) planning and constructing military facilities for the army and the air force, and in combat building pontoon bridges, laying wire for communications, building temporary structures, repairing rail lines and roads, and other purely military activity often under enemy fire; 3) designing and managing the building of facilities for various Defense Department and other federal agencies. In total the Army Corps of Engineers is the world's largest public engineering and construction management entity.

It is commanded by the army's *chief of engineers,* who lays out policy and directs the organization, as well as directly advising the president on engineering and real estate matters. He is also the army's official topographer, responsible for mapmaking.

While the chief of engineers has an office in the Pentagon, the headquarters are located in Washington, D.C. Geographically, its command is operated through eight divisions in the United States as well as about 40 subordinate commands in the United States, Asia, and Europe. Eight research laboratories are also run by the corps, placed in various locations in the United States. Research includes infrastructure design, structural engineering, ice engineering, coastal and hydraulic engineering, environmental quality, terrain analysis, high-performance computers and information delivery, and geotechnical engineering.

HEADQUARTERS

U.S. Army Corps of Engineers, 441 G Street NW, Washington, DC 20314-1000; Phone: (202) 761-0001; Fax: (202) 761-1683.

Corps of Engineers Major Commands:

U.S. Army Engineering and Support Center Huntsville, 4820 University Square, Huntsville, AL 35816; Mail: P.O. Box 1600, Huntsville, AL 35807; Phone: (256) 895-1300. Military and civil works construction.

U.S. Army Engineer Division, North Atlantic, 302 General Lee Avenue, Fort Hamilton Military Community, Brooklyn, NY 11252; Phone: (718) 491-8707. Military and civil works construction.

U.S. Army Engineer Division, Great Lakes and Ohio River, 550 Main Street, Cincinnati, OH 45202; Mail: P.O. Box 1159, Cincinnati, OH 45201; Phone: (513) 684-3010. Military and civil works construction.

U.S. Army Engineer Division, South Atlantic, Room 9M15, 60 Forsyth Street SW, Atlanta, GA 30303; Phone: (404) 562-5005. Military and civil works construction and real estate.

U.S. Army Engineer Division, Mississippi Valley, 1400 Walnut Street, Vicksburg, MS 39181; Mail: P.O. Box 80, Vicksburg, MS 39181; Phone: (601) 634-5750. Civil works construction and real estate.

U.S. Army Engineer Division, Northwestern, 220 NE 8th Avenue, Portland, OR 97209; Mail: P.O. Box 2870, Portland, OR 97208; Phone: (503) 808-3700. Military and civil works construction and real estate.

U.S. Army Engineer Division, Pacific Ocean, Building 230, Fort Shafter, HI 96858: Phone: (808) 438-1500. Military and civil works construction and real estate.

DISTRICTS

The Corps of Engineers also maintains district offices in Buffalo, New York; Memphis, Tennessee; New Orleans, Louisiana; Chicago, Illinois; Rock Island, Illinois; St. Louis, Missouri; Detroit, Michigan; St. Paul, Minnesota; Vicksburg, Mississippi; Baltimore, Maryland; New York City, New York; Norfolk, Virginia; Philadelphia, Pennsylvania; Concord, Massachusetts; Kansas City, Missouri; Omaha, Nebraska; Portland, Oregon; Seattle, Washington; Walla Walla, Washington; Anchorage, Alaska; Wiesbaden, Germany; Seoul, Korea; and Kanagawa-Ken, Japan.

U.S. ARMY FACILITIES
WITHIN THE UNITED STATES

The army maintains several types of facilities such as forts, camps, arsenals, army airfields, combat training centers, laboratories, depots, medical centers, and proving grounds.

Forts: McClellan, Rucker (Alabama); Greely, Richardson, Wainwright (Alaska); Huachuca (Arizona); Chafee (Arkansas); Irwin, Hunter Liggett (California); Carson (Colorado); McNair (D.C.); Benning (infantry training school), McPherson, Stewart (Georgia); Shafter (Hawaii); Leavenworth, Riley (Kansas); Campbell, Knox (Kentucky); Polk (Louisiana); Detrick, Meade (Maryland); Devens (Massachusetts); Leonard Wood (Missouri); William Henry Harrison (Montana); Monmouth, Dix (New Jersey); Drum, Hamilton (New York); Bragg (North Carolina); Sill (Oklahoma); Indiantown Gap (Pennsylvania); Jackson (South Carolina); Bliss, Hood, Sam Houston (Texas); A. P. Hill, Belvoir, Eustis, Lee, Monroe, Myer, Story, Pickett (Virginia); Lewis (Washington); McCoy (Wisconsin).

Proving Grounds: Yuma Proving Ground (Arizona); Aberdeen Proving Ground (Maryland); White Sands Missile Range (New Mexico); Dugway Proving Ground (Utah)

Training Sites: Joint Forces Training Base, Parks Reserve Forces Training Area (California); Bethany Beach Training Site (Delaware); Pohakuloa Training Area (Hawaii); Regional Training Institute (Nevada); New Jersey National Guard Training Center (New Jersey); Tucumcari Training Site, Carlsbad Training Site, Debremond Training Site, Roswell Local Training Area (New Mexico); Clark Hill Training Site, South Carolina Training Center (South Carolina); Catoosa Training Center (Tennessee); National Guard Readiness Center (Virginia).

Camps: There are 39 army camps spread over the United States, primarily for National Guard and Reserve units.

Defense Language Institute A premier foreign language immersion course center used by the army, but also by other government agencies. Located in Presidio of Monterey, downtown Monterey, California.

DEPARTMENT OF THE AIR FORCE

The Department of the Air Force is responsible for recruiting and training air force personnel, and organizing, supplying, and equipping the personnel and the numerous air bases both within the United States and overseas. The U.S. Air Force has (as of April 30, 2002) in uniform on active duty 362,000 men and women (69,466 officers, 288,720 enlisted) deployed in bases and airfields throughout the United States and in foreign countries. Air force civilian employees number 151,664. The number of aircraft is about 2,000, including approximately 150 heavy bombers.

Heading this department is the *secretary of the air force,* who is appointed by the president subject to Senate confirmation. Second in command is the *under secretary of the air force,* also appointed by the president with Senate confirmation. On the next echelon are the *assistant secretary for financial management,* who is also the comptroller, *assistant secretary for acquisition, assistant secretary for space,* and *assistant secretary for manpower, reserve affairs, installations and environment.* All are appointed by the president as is the *general counsel.*

Career professionals are the *judge advocate general,* and the directors and managers of the ***Air Force Material Command,*** *Aeronautical Systems Center,* and *Air Force Research Center,* each of which is located at a different air force base.

AIR FORCE FACILITIES
WITHIN THE UNITED STATES

Altus Air Force Base, Altus, Oklahoma 73523; Phone: (405) 482-8100; 6,623 acres,

Andersen Air Force Base, APO AP 96543; Phone: 0111-671-366-1110; 20,604 acres two miles north of Yigo, Guam. (Named for General James Roy Andersen)

Andrews Air Force Base, Maryland 20331; Phone: (301) 981-1110; 7,550 acres 11 miles southeast of Washington, D.C. (Named for Lt. General Frank M. Andrews)

Arnold Air Force Base, Tennessee 37389; Phone: (931) 454-3000; 40,118 acres seven miles southeast of Manchester, Tennessee. (Named for first Air Force chief, five-star general H. H. "Hap" Arnold)

Barksdale Air Force Base, Louisiana 71110; Phone: (318) 456-2252; 22,000 acres at Bossier City, Louisiana. (Named for World War I airman Lt. Eugene H. Barksdale)

Beale Air Force Base, California 95903; Phone: (916) 634-3000; 22,944 acres 12 miles east of Marysville, California. (Named for pre–Civil War brig. general E. F. Beale)

Bolling Air Force Base, District of Columbia 20332; Phone: (202) 767-6700; 604 acres 3 miles south of Capitol Building. (Named for highest-ranking flying officer killed in World War II, Lt. Colonel Raynal C. Bolling)

Brooks Air Force Base, Texas 78235; Phone: (210) 536-1110; 1,310 acres at San Antonio, Texas. (Named for Sidney J. Brooks Jr., a cadet killed in 1917)

Cannon Air Force Base, New Mexico 88103; Phone: (505) 784-3311; 25,663 acres seven miles west of Clovis, New Mexico. (Named for World War II general John K. Cannon)

Charleston Air Force Base, South Carolina 29404; Phone: 963-6000; 6,235 acres at North Charleston.

Columbus Air Force Base, Mississippi 39710; Phone: (601) 434-7322; 6,025 acres 10 miles north northwest of Columbus, Mississippi.

Davis-Monthan Air Force Base, Arizona 85707; Phone: (602) 750-3900; 11,000 acres at Tucson, Arizona. (Named for Lt. Samuel H. Davis and 2nd Lt. Oscar Monthan, both killed in crashes in the 1920s)

Dover Air Force Base, Delaware 19902; Phone: (302) 677-3000; 3,908 acres three miles southeast of Dover, Delaware.

Dyess Air Force Base, Texas 79607; Phone: (915) 696-0212; 6,405 acres at Abilene, Texas. (Named for World War II fighter pilot Lt. Colonel William E. Dyess, killed in crash, December 1943)

Edwards Air Force Base, California 93524; Phone: (805) 277-1110; 301,000 acres 20 miles east of Rosamond, California; serves as alternative landing field for space shuttle. (Named for Captain Glen W. Edwards, killed in crash of experimental "Flying Wing", June 5, 1948)

Elgin Air Force Base, Florida 32542; Phone: (904) 882-1110; 463,452 acres seven miles northeast of Fort Walton Beach, Florida. (Named for Lt. Colonel Frederick I. Eglin, World War I pilot, killed in aircraft accident January 1, 1937)

Eielson Air Force Base, Alaska 99702; Phone: (907) 377-1110; 23,500 acres 26 miles southeast of Fairbanks, Alaska. (Named for arctic aviation pioneer Carl Ben Eielson)

Ellsworth Air Force Base, South Dakota 57706; Phone: (605) 385-1000; 10,632 acres 12 miles east-northeast of Rapid City, South Dakota. (Named for Brig. General Richard E. Ellsworth, killed in 1953)

Elmendorf Air Force Base, Alaska 99506; Phone: (907) 552-1110; 13,103 acres at Anchorage, Alaska. (Named for test pilot Captain Hugh Elmendorf, killed in 1933 crash during a flight test)

Fairchild Air Force Base, Washington 99011; Phone: (509) 247-1212; 4,551 acres 12 miles west-southwest of Spokane, Washington. (Named for one-time air force vice chief of staff General Muir S. Fairchild)

Falcon Air Force Base, Colorado 80912; Phone: (719) 550-4113; 3,840 acres 10 miles east of Colorado Springs, Colorado.

Fort Worth NAS JRB, Texas 76127; Phone: (817) 782-5000; located seven miles west-northwest of downtown Fort Worth.

Francis E. Warren Air force Base, Wyoming 82005; Phone: (307) 775-1110; 5,866 acres in Cheyenne, Wyoming. (Named for Francis Emory Warren, first governor of the state of Wyoming)

Goodfellow Air Force Base, Texas 76908; Phone: (915) 654-3217; 1,137 acres two miles southeast of San Angelo, Texas. (Named for World War I pilot Lt. John J. Goodfellow Jr., killed in combat, 1918)

Grand Forks Air Force Base, North Dakota 58205; Phone: (701) 747-3000; 5,422 acres 16 miles west of Grand Forks, North Dakota.

Hanscom Air Force Base, Massachusetts 01731; Phone: (617) 377-4441; 846 acres 17 miles northwest of Boston, Massachusetts. (Named for aviation pioneer Laurence G. Hanscom, killed in crash in 1941)

Hickam Air Force Base, Hawaii 96853; Phone: (808) 471-7110; 2,855 acres nine miles west of Honolulu, Hawaii. Hickam Field was a primary target of Japanese air attack on December 7, 1941. (Named for air pioneer Lt. Colonel Horace M. Hickam, killed in crash, 1934)

Hill Air Force Base, Utah 84056; Phone; (801) 777-7221; 6,698 acres eight miles south of Ogden, Utah. (Named for test pilot Major Ployer P. Hill, killed while testing first B-17 bomber, the "Flying Fortress," in 1935)

Holloman Air Force Base, New Mexico 88330; Phone: (505) 475-8511; 57,000 acres eight miles southwest of Alamogordo, New Mexico. (Named for Colonel George Holloman, killed in B-17 crash, 1946)

Hurlburt Field, Florida 32544; Phone: (904) 884-1000; located five miles west of Fort Walton Beach, Florida. (Named for Lt. Donald W. Hurlburt, World War II pilot killed in crash at nearby Eglin air base in 1943)

Keesler Air Force Base, Mississippi 39534; Phone: (228) 377-1110; 3,546 acres. (Named for World War I aerial observer 2nd Lt. Samuel R. Keesler Jr., killed in action in 1918)

Kelly Air Force Base, Texas 78241; Phone: (210) 925-1110; 4,660 acres five miles southwest of downtown San Antonio, Texas. (Named for Lt. George Kelly, the first Army airman killed in a crash, May 10, 1911)

Kirtland Air Force Base, New Mexico 87117; Phone: (505) 846-0011; 52,678 acres southeast of Albuquerque, New Mexico. (Named for Colonel Roy C. Kirtland, commandant of Langley Field in the 1930s)

Lackland Air Force Base, Texas 78235; Phone: (210) 671-1110; 6,725 acres eight miles southwest of downtown San Antonio, Texas. (Named for Brig. General Frank D. Lackland, pre–World War II commandant of Kelly Field flying school)

Langley Air Force Base, Virginia 23665; Phone: (804) 764-9990; 3,216 acres three miles north of Hampton, Virginia. (Named for Samuel Pierpont Langley, aviation pioneer and inventor, who built an unmanned plane that was briefly airborne before crashing even before Wright brothers' successful flight)

Laughlin Air Force Base, Texas 78843; Phone: (830) 989-3511; 5,228 acres six miles east of Del Rio, Texas. (Named for Del Rio native 1st Lt. Jack Thomas Laughlin, B-17 pilot killed over Java, January 29, 1942)

Little Rock Air Force Base, Arkansas 72099; Phone: (501) 988-3131; 11,373 acres 17 miles northeast of Little Rock, Arkansas.

Los Angeles Air Force Base, California 90245; Phone: (310) 363-1110; 192 acres three miles south of Los Angeles International Airport, Los Angeles, California.

Luke Air Force Base, Arizona 85309; Phone: (602) 856-7411; 4,197 acres 20 miles west-northwest of Phoenix, Arizona, as well as 2.7 million acres at Gila Bend, Arizona. (Named for 2nd Lt. Frank Luke Jr., first U.S. Army aviator to be awarded the Congressional Medal of Honor; Luke was killed September 29, 1918, when his plane was forced down after shooting down two enemy planes, three balloons, and dropping two bombs; on the ground, armed with a .45 pistol he was shot in a fire fight with German soldiers.)

MacDill Air Force Base, Florida 33608; Phone: (813) 830-1110; 5,631 acres adjacent to Tampa, Florida. (Named for Colonel Leslie MacDill, who died in aircraft accident in 1938)

Malmstrom Air Force Base, Montana 59402; Phone: (406) 731-1110; 3,573 acres 1.5 miles east of Great Falls, Montana. (Named for World War II fighter commander Colonel Einar A. Malmstrom, killed in air accident in 1954)

Maxwell Air Force Base, Alabama 36112; Phone: (334) 416-1110; 2,524 acres one mile west-northwest of Montgomery, Alabama. (Named for 2nd Lt. William C. Maxwell, killed in air accident in 1920)

Maxwell Air Force Base Gunter Annex, Alabama 36114; Phone: (334) 416-1110; 368 acres four miles northeast of Montgomery, Alabama. (Named for one-time Montgomery mayor William A. Gunter)

McChord Air Force Base, Washington 98438; Phone: (253) 984-1910; 4,616 acres eight miles south of Tacoma, Washington. (Named for early army pilot Colonel William C. McChord, killed in air crash in 1937)

McClellan Air Force Base, California 95652; Phone: (916) 643-2111; 3,755 acres nine miles northeast of Sacramento, California. To a great extent McClellan has been shut down. (Named for Major Hezekiah McClellan, pioneer in Arctic flying, who died in crash in 1936)

McConnell Air Force Base, Kansas 67221; Phone: (316) 652-6100; 3,113 acres five miles southeast of Wichita, Kansas. (Named for the McConnell brothers, who were both World War II B-24 bomber pilots; 2nd Lt. Thomas L. McConnell was killed in combat in 1943, and Captain Fred J. McConnell was killed in a private plane accident in 1945.)

McGuire Air Force Base, New Jersey 08641; Phone: (609) 724-1100; 3,597 acres 18 miles southeast of Trenton, New Jersey. (Named for World War II P-38 fighter pilot Major Thomas B. McGuire Jr., who was awarded Congressional Medal of Honor after killed in action in 1945)

Minot Air Force Base, North Dakota 58705; Phone: (701) 723-1110; 5,085 acres 13 miles north of Minot, North Dakota.

Mountain Home Air Force Base, Idaho 83648; Phone: (208) 828-2111; 9,112 acres 10 miles southwest of Mountain Home, Idaho.

Offutt Air Force Base, Nebraska 68113; Phone: (402) 294-1110; 4,044 acres six miles south of Omaha, Nebraska. (Named for World War I pilot 1st Lt. Jarvis J. Offutt, who died 1918)

Patrick Air Force Base, Florida 32925; Phone: (407) 494-1110; 2,341 acres two miles south of Cocoa Beach, Florida. (Named for Major General Mason M. Patrick, chief of American Expeditionary Air Service in World War I and chief of Air Service/Air Corps, 1921–27)

Peterson Air Force Base, Colorado 80914; Phone: (719) 554-7321; 1,277 acres east of Colorado Springs (home of Air Academy). (Named for 1st Lt. Edward J. Peterson, who died in air crash at the base in 1942)

Pope Air Force Base, North Carolina 28302; Phone: (910) 394-0001; 1,750 acres 12 miles north-northwest of Fayetteville, North Carolina, near Fort Bragg. (Named for 1st Lt. Harley H. Pope, who died in crash of a "Jenny" into the nearby Cape Fear River, 1917)

Randolph Air Force Base, Texas 78150; Phone: (210) 652-1110; 5,044 acres near San Antonio, Texas. (Named for Captain William M. Randolph, killed in crash on takeoff, 1929)

Robins Air Force Base, Georgia 31098; Phone: (912) 928-1110; 8,700 acres 15 miles southeast of Macon, Georgia. (Named for Brig. General Augustine Warner Robins, pre–World War II chief of Air Corps materiel division)

Scott Air Force Base, Illinois 62225; Phone: (618) 256-1110; 3,000 acres six miles east-northeast of Belleville, Illinois. (Named for Corporal Frank S. Scott, pioneer airman and first enlisted man to die in airplane accident, September 28, 1912)

Seymour Johnson Air Force Base, North Carolina 27531; Phone: (919) 736-5400; 3,233 acres in Goldsboro, North Carolina. (Named for navy Lt. Seymour A. Johnson, a Goldsboro native, killed in air crash, 1941)

Shaw Air Force Base, South Carolina 29152; Phone: (803) 668-8110; 3,363 acres 10 miles west-northwest of Sumter, South Carolina.

(Named for 2nd Lt. Ervin D. Shaw, killed in action in World War I, 1918)

Sheppard Air Force Base, Texas 76311; Phone: (940) 676-2511; 6,158 acres four miles north of Wichita Falls, Texas. (Named for U.S. senator Morris E. Sheppard from Texas, 1913–41)

Tinker Air Force Base, Oklahoma 73145; Phone: (405) 739-7321; 5,000 acres eight miles southeast of Oklahoma City, Oklahoma. (Named for Major General Clarence L. Tinker, who went down at sea during World War II, 1942)

Travis Air Force Base, California 94535; Phone: (707) 424-5000; 7,580 acres next to Fairfield, California. (Named for Brig. General Robert Travis, who died in B-29 accident in 1950)

Tyndall Air Force Base, Florida 32403; Phone: (904) 283-1113; 29,115 acres 12 miles east of Panama City, Florida. (Named for 1st Lt. Frank B. Tyndall, a World War I pilot who was later killed in the crash of P-1 biplane in 1930)

Vance Air Force Base, Oklahoma 73705; Phone: (580) 213-2121; 4,394 acres near Enid, Oklahoma. (Named for Congressional Medal of Honor recipient Lt. Colonel Leon R. Vance Jr., who died when the plane evacuating him to a stateside hospital disappeared over the Atlantic in 1944)

Vandenberg Air Force Base, California 93437; Phone: (805) 734-8232; 98,400 acres on California coast eight miles north-northwest of Lompoc, California. Famed as launching site for missile launch tests down range over the Pacific Ocean. (Named for General Hoyt S. Vandenberg, second chief of staff of United States Air Force)

Whiteman Air Force Base, Missouri 65305; Phone: (816) 687-1110; 4,627 acres two miles south of Knob Harbor, Missouri. (Named for 2nd Lt. George A. Whiteman, first American pilot to die in World War II, in the air defending Pearl Harbor on December 7, 1941)

Wright-Patterson Air Force Base, Ohio 45433; Phone: (513) 257-1110; 8,145 acres 10 miles east-northeast of Dayton, Ohio, the city where the Wright brothers had their shop and trained the first pilots. (Named for Orville and Wilbur Wright, the fathers of heavier-than-air flight achieved in 1903, and 1st Lt. Frank S. Patterson, early airman killed in crash in 1918).

AMERICAN AIR FORCE BASES ON FOREIGN SOIL

Aviano Air Base, Italy, APO AE 09601; Phone: 011-39-434-667-111; 1,140 acres next to Aviano, 50 miles north of Venice, Italy.

Howard Air Force Base, Panama APO AA 34001; Phone: 011-507-84-9805. (Named for Major Charles Harold Howard)

Incirlik Air Base, Turkey APO AE 09824; Phone: 011-90-71-221774; 3,400 acres 10 miles east of Adana, Turkey. (*Incirlik* means "fig orchard" in Turkish)

Kadena Air Base, Japan APO AP 96368; Phone: 011-81-098-938-1111; 12,547 acres 12 miles north of Naha, Japan.

Kunsan Air Base, South Korea APO AP 96264; Phone: 011-82-654-470-1110; 2,174 acres eight miles southwest of Kunsan City.

Lajes Field, Azores, Portugal APO AE 09720; Phone: 011-351-95-540-100; 1,148 acres on Terceira Island 900 miles west of Portugal's mainland.

Misawa Air Base, Japan APO AP 96319; Phone: 011-81-3117-66-1111; 3,865 acres in Misawa, Japan.

Osan Air Base, South Korea APO AP 96278; Phone: 011-82-333-661-1110; 1,674 acres near city of Osan 38 miles south of Seoul, South Korea.

Ramstein Air Base, Germany APO AE 09094; Phone; 011-49-631-536-1110; 5,292 acres next to town of Ramstein.

Royal Air Force Lakenheath, England APO AE 09464; Phone: 011-44-638-52-3000; 2,290 acres near village of Lakenheath 25 miles from Cambridge, England.

Royal Air Force Mildenhall, England APO AE 09459; Phone: 011-44-638-51-1110; 1,121 acres near village of Mildenhall, 30 miles northeast of Cambridge.

Spangahlem Air Base, Germany APO AE 09126; Phone: 011-49-6565-61-1110; 1,282 acres near town of Spangahlem six miles east of Bitburg, Germany.

Yokota Air Base, Japan APO AP 96328; Phone: 011-81-3117-55-1110; 1,750 acres 28 miles west of Tokyo, Japan.

DEPARTMENT OF THE NAVY

The responsibilities of the Department of the Navy are recruiting, organizing, supplying, equipping, and training navy personnel. In addition to numerous naval bases both on the shores of the United States and in strategic overseas locations, the navy operates three fleets: Pacific, Atlantic, and European (although somewhat interchangeable). It operates almost 350 ships of various types, including approximately 260 fighting units, and close to 450 aircraft. Semi-autonomous within the navy are the U.S. Marines with an air arm of more than 300 aircraft.

Heading the department is the *secretary of the navy* assisted by the *under secretary of the navy* (specifically in charge of departmental strategic planning), both appointed by the president with

Senate confirmation. Several assistant secretaries have specific areas of responsibility, which are *assistant secretary for manpower and reserve affairs, assistant secretary for installations and environment, assistant for research, development and acquisition* (who has deputy assistant secretaries for such key elements as ships, planning, program and resources, mine and underseas warfare, air programs, and space), and *assistant secretary for financial management (comptroller).* All of these assistant secretaries are appointed by the president subject to Senate confirmation, as is the *general counsel.* The *chief of naval education and training* advises the department and the active navy on training from an office in Pensacola, Florida, site of the naval air school.

Certain career incumbents in the department are assigned to the Marine Corps Headquarters, the Office of Naval Research, and the Chief of Naval Operations, which are elements of the naval operations conducted by navy officers.

The U.S. Navy has (as of April 30, 2002) in uniform on active duty 381,901 men and women (53,972 officers, 323,745 enlisted) in the United States, overseas bases, and afloat on ships (about 100,000), and 4,184 attending the Naval Academy. The civilian employee navy contingent in the Defense Department is approximately 183,000.

UNITED STATES MARINE CORPS

Although administratively within the Navy Department, the Marine Corps as a fighting force is a distinct entity and has (as of April 30, 2002) in uniform on active duty 172,741 (18,393 officers and 154,348 enlisted) within the United States and overseas. Its civilian employees are counted within those attached to the navy.

Washington Navy Yard: Primarily of historic interest, the Washington Navy Yard is approximately 30 blocks in size and encompasses the *Naval Historical Center,* including the Navy Department Library, Navy Museum, Navy Art Gallery, and several "branches" of various phases of naval history. In the yard itself is the U.S.S.

Barry, a decommissioned destroyer, open to visitors naval ordinance, and a "swift boat." The main entrance is located on M Street at 8th Street (901 M Street SE). Picture ID is required.

UNITED STATES NAVY BASES

Naval Air Station Brunswick, 1251 Orion Street, Brunswick, ME 04011; Phone: (207) 921-2000.

Naval Air Station Corpus Christi, 11001 D Street, Suite 143, Corpus Christi, TX 78419; Phone: (361) 961-2811.

Naval Air Station Fallon, Fallon, NV 89406; Phone: (775) 426-8726.

Naval Air Station Jacksonville, Box 102, Naval Air Station, Jacksonville, FL 32212; Phone: (904) 542-2345; home base of the commander, Navy Region Southeast.

Naval Air Station Key West, P.O. Box 9001, 804 Sigbee Road, Building V-4058, Key West, FL 33040; Phone: (305) 293-4408.

Naval Air Station Kingsville, 554 McCain Street, Kingsville, TX 78363; Phone: (361) 516-6333.

Naval Air Station Lemoore, 700 Avenger Avenue, Lemoore, CA 93246; Phone: (559) 998-3300.

Naval Air Station Meridian, 1155 Rosenbaum Avenue, Meridian, MS 39309; Phone: (601) 679-2528.

Naval Air Station North Island, P.O. Box 357033, San Diego, CA 92135; Phone: (619) 545-1011.

Naval Air Station Oceana, Virginia Beach, VA 23460; Phone: (757) 444-0000 (note: same telephone number as Naval Station Norfolk and Commander, Navy Region Mid-Atlantic).

Naval Air Station Patuxent River, Patuxent River, MD 20670; Phone: (301) 342-1419.

Naval Air Station Pensacola, 190 Radford Boulevard, Pensacola, FL 32508; Phone: (850) 452-0111.

Naval Air Station Whidbey Island, 3730 North Charles Porter Avenue, Oak Harbor, WA 98278; Phone: (360) 257-2211.

Naval Air Station Whiting Field, 7550 USS Essex Street, Milton, FL 32570; Phone: (850) 623-7011.

Naval Amphibious Base Coronado, 3420 Guadacanal Road, San Diego, CA 92155; Phone: (619) 545-6071.

Naval Amphibious Base Little Creek, Tarawa Court, Norfolk, VA 23521; Phone: (757) 444-0000 (note: same telephone number as Naval Station Norfolk and Commander, Navy Region Mid-Atlantic).

Naval Base San Diego, 937 North Harbor Drive, San Diego, CA 92132; Phone: (619) 556-1011, ship tours (619) 532-3130; home base of the commander, Navy Region Southwest.

Naval Base San Francisco, 140 Sylvester Road, San Diego, CA 92106; Phone: (619) 553-1011.

Naval Construction Battalion Center, Gulfport, MS 39503; Phone: (228) 871-2555.

Naval Station Everett, 2000 West Marine View, Everett, WA 98207; Phone: (425) 304-3000.

Naval Station Ingleside, 1455 Ticonderoga Road, Ingleside, TX 78362; Phone: (361) 776-5781.

Naval Station Mayport, P.O. Box 280112, Mayport, FL 32228; Phone: (904) 270-5011.

Naval Station Norfolk, 1653 Morris Street, Norfolk, VA 23511; Phone: (757) 444-0000. For the commander, Navy Region Mid-Atlantic, 6506 Hampton Road, Norfolk, VA 23508; Phone: (757) 444-0000. For ships tours information, 9079 Hampton Road, Norfolk, VA 23505; Phone: (757) 444-7637.

Naval Station Pascagoula, Pascagoula, MS 39595; Phone: (228) 761-2164.

Naval Station Washington, 901 M Street SE, Washington, D.C. 20374; Phone: (202) 433-3612; home base of the commander, Naval District Washington.

Naval Submarine Base Bangor, 1100 Hunley Road, Silverdale, WA 98315; Phone: (360) 396-6111; home base of the commander, Navy Region Northwest.

Naval Submarine Base Groton, P.O. Box 100, Groton, CT 06349; Phone: (800) 694-4636; home base of the commander, Navy Region Northeast.

Naval Submarine Base Kings Bay, 1063 USS Tennessee Avenue, Kings Bay, GA 31547; Phone: (912) 673-2000.

Naval Submarine Base San Diego, 140 Sylvester Road, San Diego, CA 92106; Phone: (619) 553-1011

Naval Training Center Great Lakes, 2601 A Paul Jones Street, Great Lakes, IL 60088; Phone: (847) 688-3500.

Pearl Harbor, 517 Russell Avenue, Suite 110, Pearl Harbor, HI 96860; Phone: (808) 449-7110; home base of the commander, Navy Region Hawaii.

United States Naval Academy, 121 Blake Road, Annapolis, MD 21402; Phone: (410) 293-1000.

MARINE COMMANDS

The top officer of the United States Marines is the *commandant,* who holds the rank of general. The marines are unusual in that they have a special rank for a senior member of the marines particularly concerned with the enlisted men, who is the *sergeant major of the Marine Corps,* respected and revered although not a commissioned officer.

MARINE COMMAND HEADQUARTERS

Fleet Marine Force, Atlantic, Camp Lejeune, North Carolina.

Fleet Marine Force, Pacific, Camp H. M. Smith, Hawaii.

Marine Corps Development Command and Marine Corps Systems Command, Quantico, Virginia.

Marine Expeditionary Forces, Camp Pendleton, California, Camp Lejeune, North Carolina, and Camp Butler, Okinawa.

Marine Corps Air-Ground Combat Center, Twenty-nine Palms, California.

Marine Reserve Forces Command, New Orleans, Louisiana.

CIVIL AIR PATROL

This civilian patrol was founded on December 1, 1941, just a week before the attack on Pearl Harbor, to use the talents of civilian pilots and their light aircraft for civil defense. Within the aegis of the U.S. Army Air Force starting in 1943, it became a permanent organization on July 1, 1946. Under the CAP Supply Bill, Public Law 557, enacted in May, 1948, it became an official "auxiliary" of the air force.

The CAP comprises 35,000 adult volunteers, flying 3,700 private airplanes, and 530 aircraft and 950 vehicles belonging to the patrol. These volunteers wear air force uniforms with Civil Air Patrol emblems and insignia.

Nowadays the patrol has three principal functions: emergency services, aerospace education, and cadet training.

Emergency services include search and rescue, disaster relief and (starting in 1985) assisting the U.S. Customs Service, the Drug Enforcement Administration, and the U.S. Forest Service in antidrug smuggling reconnaissance. Emergency services are headquartered at the Air Force Rescue and Coordination Center at Langley Air Force Base, Virginia, and save dozens of lives each year.

Aerospace education involves more than 200 workshops at the college level annually to train 5,000 teachers on aerospace subjects. It hosts the National Congress on Aviation and Space Education convention annually for teachers. It also publishes educational materials in the field of aerospace.

The Cadet Program with about 26,000 enrollment educates and encourages young people 12 to 21 years old to learn about aerospace, flying, and aviation. They receive ranks, awards, possible scholarships, and upon completion of initial training are eligible to enter the air force as airmen first class if they enlist.

All states, the District of Columbia, and Puerto Rico have Civilian Air Patrol "wings" and other groups of varying size, totaling about 1,700 units. Its national headquarters is at Maxwell Air Force Base in Alabama.

CONTACT Address: Air University, Public Affairs Office, Attention: CAP-USAF, 55 LeMay Plaza South, Maxwell AFB, AL 36112; Phone: (334) 953-4241; E-mail: hyla.pearson@ maxwell.af.mil.

DEPARTMENT OF EDUCATION

The Department of Education's primary mission is to assure equal access to education to every individual; supplement and complement the efforts of states and local school systems, the private sector, public and private nonprofit educational research institutions, community-based organizations, parents, and students to improve the quality of education; encourage increased involvement of students, parents, and public in federal education programs; promote improvements in quality and usefulness of education;

Department of Education

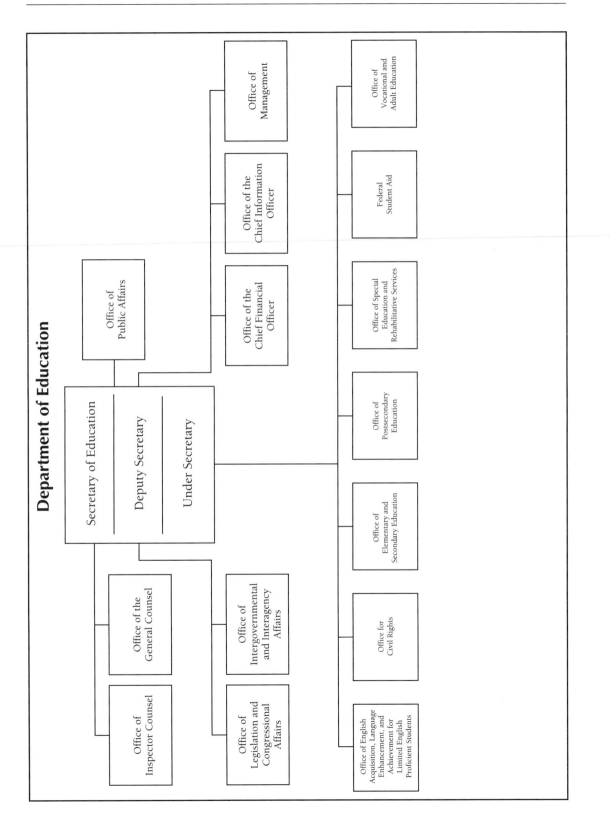

- Secretary of Education
- Deputy Secretary
- Under Secretary

- Office of Public Affairs
- Office of Inspector Counsel
- Office of the General Counsel
- Office of Legislation and Congressional Affairs
- Office of Intergovernmental and Interagency Affairs
- Office of the Chief Financial Officer
- Office of the Chief Information Officer
- Office of Management
- Office of English Acquisition, Language Enhancement, and Achievement for Limited English Proficient Students
- Office for Civil Rights
- Office of Elementary and Secondary Education
- Office of Postsecondary Education
- Office of Special Education and Rehabilitative Services
- Federal Student Aid
- Office of Vocational and Adult Education

improve coordination of federal education programs and activities; and increase the accountability of federal education programs to the public, the Congress, and the president. The department administers programs from preschool education through doctoral research. (See below.)

The federal government sees education as primarily a state and local responsibility, and thus contributes about 10 percent of all education funds, while the states, local communities, and public and private organizations provide 90 percent of the funding.

The original Office of Education was created in 1867 to gather information on schools and teaching to help the states establish better school systems. That function of disseminating information on what works in education to teachers and education staff, school boards, and teachers continues today.

The Second Morrill Act in 1890 made the Office of Education of the period responsible for administering the land-grant colleges and universities. The Smith-Hughes Act of 1917 and the George-Barden Act of 1946 created federal aid to vocational schools for agricultural, industrial, and home economics training for high school students.

The Lanham Act of 1941 and the Impact Aid laws of 1950 gave aid to communities where World War II military and other federal installations created new burdens on communities' educational systems. The "G.I. Bill" of 1944 granted financial aid for college education to 8 million World War II veterans. Thus, the Education Department developed an emergency response system to fill in educational financial gaps in crises.

Responding next to the cold war and then the Soviet Union's *Sputnik* launch, Congress passed the National Defense Education Act (NDEA) in 1958 to upgrade science, mathematics, and foreign language instruction at all educational levels to ensure that the United States could compete with the Soviet Union in scientific and technical fields.

The Department of Education received the role of antipoverty and civil rights enforcer when Congress passed several laws prohibiting discrimination based on race, sex, and disability, including Title VI of the Civil Rights Act of 1964, Title IX of the Education Amendments of 1972, and Section 504 of the Rehabilitation Act of 1973. The Elementary and Secondary Education Act of 1965 created several new Education Department programs, such as the Title I program giving federal aid to disadvantaged (poor) children. Also in 1965, Congress passed the Higher Education Act, partly to help needy college students.

On October 17, 1979, Congress made the Department of Education a cabinet-level agency, with the secretary of education serving in the cabinet.

ORGANIZATION

The secretary of education directs, supervises, and coordinates all activities of the department and serves as principal adviser to the president on federal policies, programs, and activities related to education in the United States. The deputy secretary of education is principal policy adviser to the secretary on all major program and management issues, as well as student financial aid, and is responsible for internal management and daily operations of the department. The undersecretary oversees policy development and administration of the Budget Service and Planning and Evaluation Service. The secretary, undersecretary, and all assistant secretaries in charge of programs are appointed by the president, subject to Senate confirmation.

LOCATION Most of the Department of Education staff works in Washington, D.C. The secretary's office is in Federal Office Building 6 at 400 Maryland Avenue, Washington, D.C. Other offices are located in the Regional Office Building 3 (ROB3), the Mary E. Switzer Building (MES), Capitol Place, 1990 K Street, and at L'Enfant Plaza.

CONTACT Address: U.S. Department of Education, 400 Maryland Avenue SW, Washington, DC 20202; Phone: 1-800-USA-LEARN; TTY: 1-

800-437-0833; Fax: (202) 401-0689; E-mail: customerservice@inet.ed.gov; Website: www.ed.gov.

ACTIVITIES, PROGRAMS, AND SERVICES

FEDERAL STUDENT AID (FSA)

FSA administers Student Financial Assistance Programs of the Department of Education. The largest student aid source in the United States, FSA programs provide over $60 billion a year in grants, loans, and work-study assistance. FSA provides general information about student loans, how to apply, tax credits for education expenses, and other federal, state, and private sources of information and student funds. FSA also offers information on loan deferments and cancellations for teaching in low-income or teacher shortage neighborhoods, direction on consolidating existing loans, and the Stafford Loan Forgiveness Program for teachers. FSA offers student loan applications over the Internet. Website: www.ed.gov/offices/OSFAP/Students/.

OFFICE OF CIVIL RIGHTS (OCR)

OCR enforces federal statutes that prohibit discrimination based on race, color, national origin, sex, age, or disability in education programs that receive federal funds. The federal laws extend to all state, elementary, and secondary school systems and agencies, colleges and universities, vocational schools, private schools, state vocational rehabilitation agencies, libraries, and museums. Areas covered may include admissions, recruitment, financial aid, academic programs, student treatment and services, counseling and guidance, discipline, classroom assignment, grading, vocational education, recreation, physical education, athletics, housing, and employment.

Under Title II of the Americans with Disabilities Act of 1990 (ADA), OCR also has responsibilities to enforce laws against disabilities discrimination by any public entity, whether they receive federal funds or not. Since January 8, 2002, OCR also enforces the Boy Scouts of America Equal Access Act as amended by the No Child Left Behind Act of 2001, which prohibits state or local public or private schools from denying equal access to one youth group listed in Title 36 of the United States Code as a patriotic society if it allows another organization to use school facilities before or after school hours.

CONTACT OCR has 12 enforcement offices throughout the country. Address: OCR National Headquarters: U.S. Department of Education, Office for Civil Rights, Customer Service Team, Mary E. Switzer Building, 330 C Street SW, Washington, DC 20203; Phone: 1-800-421-3481; Fax: (202) 205-9862; TDD: 877-521-2172; E-mail: OCR@ed.gov; Website: Http://bco101.ed.gov/CFAPPS/OCR/.

OFFICE OF ELEMENTARY AND SECONDARY EDUCATION (OESE)

OESE provides financial assistance to state and local education agencies for public and private preschool, elementary, and high school education, promoting and striving for equal educational opportunities and educational excellence for all students, and improving the quality of teaching and learning by providing leadership, technical assistance, and financial support.

OESE directs, coordinates, and recommends policy to assist state and local educational agencies to improve achievement of elementary and secondary school students; ensure equal access to services for all children, particularly those educationally disadvantaged, Native American, children of migrant workers, or homeless; works with state and local educational entities to improve education; and gives financial assistance to local educational agencies whose local revenues are affected by federal activities.

OESE offers information and publications on the No Child Left Behind Act of 2001; early childhood resources; reading resources; teacher and principal resources including Education Department grants at federal, regional, and state levels for local school districts, state agencies of higher education, community organizations and others; pertinent legislation and regulations; and data collection.

CONTACT Address: Office of Elementary and Secondary Education, Department of Education, 400 Maryland Avenue SW, Washington, DC 20202; Phone: (202) 401-0113; Fax: (202) 205-0310; E-mail: oese@ed.gov; Website: www.ed.gov/offices/OESE/.

OFFICE OF ENGLISH LANGUAGE ACQUISITION, LANGUAGE ENHANCEMENT, AND ACADEMIC ACHIEVEMENT FOR LIMITED ENGLISH PROFICIENT STUDENTS (OELA)

Formerly called the Office of Bilingual Education and Minority Language Affairs (OBEMLA), OELA coordinates and promotes high-quality education for English language learners (ELL) to enable students with limited English language proficiency to enhance their English language abilities to meet academic standards and master academic content. OELA works to improve language programs for students of language minorities by emphasizing high academic standards, school accountability, professional development for teachers, family literacy, early reading, and partnerships between parents and communities.

OELA administers grant programs to help every child learn English and content at high lev-els; provides guidance for policy decisions in the best interest of English language learner children; works with other federal, state, and local programs to strengthen and coordinate ELL programs; monitors funded programs; and provides technical assistance.

OELA administers the *Native American and Alaska Native Children in School Program* under No Child Left Behind Act of 2001 to provide grants to entities that support language education projects for limited English proficient children from Native American, Alaska Native, Native Hawaiian, and Native American Pacific Islander backgrounds, while supporting the native language skills of the children of each culture. Website: www.ed.gov/offices/OBEMLA/nativefacts.html

CONTACT Address: Office of English Language Acquisition, U.S. Department of Education, 330 C Street SW, Washington, DC 20202; Phone: (202) 205-5463; Fax: (202) 205-8680; Website: www.ed.gov/offices/OBEMLA. (Note: OBEMLA operates in three regions of the United States. Check the website for regional offices and appropriate staff direct telephone numbers and e-mail address.)

OFFICE OF POSTSECONDARY EDUCATION (OPE)

OPE recommends, coordinates, and directs policies for programs to give financial aid to eligible students; improves postsecondary (college and university) educational facilities and programs; recruits and prepares disadvantaged students for college programs; and promotes U.S. study of foreign languages and international affairs and research, as well as exchange activities. OPE also works to help all Americans reach postsecondary education; improve teaching at all levels; support undergraduate and graduate college and university students; and promote innovation and technology in education. Among its focuses are child care availability; Native Hawaiian higher education; preparation of gifted students from disadvantaged backgrounds to achieve academic potential; and the availability of Robert C. Byrd Honors Scholarship funds to state education agencies to award funds to eligible students, who must use the money for college expenses.

OPE offers concise student aid information on their student website: www.students.gov, including federal student aid programs; tax benefits for higher education and college costs; college and admissions information including links to community colleges, two-year colleges, business, technical, and vocational schools; international educational opportunities; College Board exams and test dates; other financial aid and funding resources; military service; community service; travel and work-study outside United States; diversity; housing; and government.

CONTACT Address: Office of Postsecondary Education, Department of Education, 1990 K Street NW, Room 7063, Washington, DC 20006; Phone: (202) 520-7750; Fax: (202) 502-7677; Website: www.ed.gov/offices/OPE.

OFFICE OF SPECIAL EDUCATION AND REHABILITATIVE SERVICES (OSERS)

OSERS provides support for education of infants, toddlers, children, and adults with disabilities by providing support to parents, school districts, and states in special education, vocational rehabilitation, and research. OSERS seeks to identify what works to best provide assistance, provides guidelines for early identification and intervention in schools, and promotes equal opportunity at work and in communities. OSERS works to maximize the individual's potential, and help foster full inclusion, social integration, employment,

and independent living for people with disabilities. Programs and projects improve results for infants, toddlers, children, and youth with disabilities.

OSERS has three main program emphases: Office of Special Education Programs (OSEP), the National Institute on Disability and Rehabilitation Research (NIDRR), and the Rehabilitation Services Administration (RSA). The office of the assistant secretary for special education and rehabilitative services (OSERS) administers the American Printing House for the Blind, the National Technical Institute for the Deaf, Gallaudet University, and the Helen Keller National Center Program.

CONTACT Address: Office of Special Education and Rehabilitative Services, Department of Education, 330 C Street SW (Mary E. Switzer Building), Washington, DC 20202; Phone: (202) 205-5465; Fax: (202) 205-9252; E-mail: usa.learn @ed.gov; Website: www.ed.gov/offices/OSERS.

OFFICE OF VOCATIONAL AND ADULT EDUCATION (OVAE)

OVAE supports policies, programs, and activities to help high school students gain knowledge and skills needed to succeed in the workforce and in life through high schools, career and technical education, community colleges, and adult education and literacy.

OVAE's "Preparing America's Future" initiative under President George W. Bush aims to help every American youth to graduate from high school and be well prepared for postsecondary education and employment; help community and technical colleges to offer career preparation, workforce development, and economic development; and expand adult learning to achieve higher levels of literacy and English fluency to millions of underserved Americans.

Specific OVAE programs include grants under the Carl D. Perkins Vocational-Technical Education Act Amendments of 1998 to state agencies for vocational-technical education; the Appalachian Regional Commission; Correctional Education for people in prison; Native American Vocational-Technical Education; National Centers for Research and Dissemination in Career and Technical Education; National Hawaiian Vocational Education Program; and Tribally Controlled Postsecondary Vocational Programs. OVAE assists with programs to train career and technical instructors, including the University of Minnesota, the Ohio State University, the University of Illinois, Oregon State University, and the Pennsylvania State University.

CONTACT Address: Office of Vocational and Adult Education, Department of Education, 4090 MES, 400 Maryland Avenue SW, Washington, DC 20202; Phone: (202) 205-5451; Fax: (202) 205-8748; E-mail: ovae@ed.gov; Website: www.ed.gov/offices/OVAE.

FEDERALLY FUNDED EDUCATIONAL CORPORATIONS

American Printing House for the Blind (APH) produces and distributes educational and other materials adapted for sight-impaired people who are enrolled in primary and secondary school programs. Assistance products provided by APH include Braille and large type textbooks, Braille typewriters, microcomputer software and hardware, special tests, and other innovative methods of measuring learning and performance.

CONTACT Address: American Printing House for the Blind, P.O. Box 6085, Louisville, KY 40206; Phone: (502) 895-2405; Website: www.aph.org.

Gallaudet University: Originally created by act of Congress in 1857 as the Columbia Institution for the Instruction of the Deaf and Dumb and the Blind, the institution's name changed in 1865, 1911, 1954, and 1986, finally becoming Gallaudet University. Currently a private, nonprofit educational institution, Gallaudet actually provides education at every level, including elementary, secondary, undergraduate, and continuing education programs for people with hearing impairments. Widely accredited, Gallaudet's curriculum includes basic liberal arts courses and courses in fields related to deafness. The school also conducts basic and applied deafness research. It provides public service programs for the hearing impaired and for people who work with deaf people.

Gallaudet's Laurent Clerc National Deaf Education Center runs two federally funded programs on the campus: the Kendall Demonstration Elementary School and the Model Secondary School for the Deaf, both of which are authorized under the Education of the Deaf Act of 1986.

The Kendall Demonstration Elementary School was created by congressional act as the United States's first demonstration elementary school for the deaf in 1970. The school serves Washington, D.C., area children from the onset of their deafness through age 15 or through the eighth grade.

The Model Secondary School for the Deaf, created by a 1966 congressional act, offers day and boarding facilities for secondary school students in grades 9 through 12 from throughout the United States.

CONTACT Address: Gallaudet University, 800 Florida Avenue NW, Washington, DC 20002; Phone: (202) 651-5505; Website: www.gallaudet.edu.

Howard University: Established in 1867, Howard University offers special interest and traditional education in its 12 schools and colleges, including arts and sciences; dentistry; engineering, architecture, and computer sciences; medicine; pharmacy; nursing; allied health sciences; the school of business, communications; divinity; education; law; and social work.

Howard University also houses centers, research institutes, and specialized programs on disability and socioeconomic policy; African-American resources; sickle cell disease; the human genome project; terrestrial and extraterrestrial atmospheric studies; aerospace science and technology; the W. Montague Cobb Human Skeletons Collection; drug abuse; science, space, and technology; cancer; child development; computational science and engineering; and international affairs.

CONTACT Address: Howard University, 2400 Sixth Street NW, Washington, DC 20059; Phone: (202) 806-0970; Website: www.howard.edu.

National Institute for Literacy works to reach a standard where all Americans can read by making available education in basic reading skills to those in need, through collaboration with schools, workplaces, families, and communities.

CONTACT Address: National Institute for Literacy, Suite 730, 1775 I Street NW, Washington, DC 20006; Phone: (202) 233-2025.

National Institute for the Deaf at the Rochester Institute of Technology (NTID): Created by the National Technical Institute for the Deaf Act of 1965, NTID operates under Department of Education contract with the Rochester Institute of Technology (RIT). DOE has RIT run a residential facility for postsecondary training and education for persons with hearing impairment (deaf) so that NTID students can benefit from education in a general technology university, its facilities, its institutional services, and career options. Deaf students enrolled at NTID receive special support services to prepare themselves for successful careers, including specialized educational media, cooperative work experience, and specialized job placement assistance.

NTID conducts applied research in occupational and employment concerns associated with deafness, communication assessment, NTID target population demographics, and specialized secondary education learning processes for the deaf. It also offers training seminars and workshops for professionals who employ, work with, teach, or serve persons with hearing impairment in other ways.

CONTACT Address: Rochester Institute of Technology, National Technical Institute for the Deaf, Lyndon Baines Johnson Building, 52 Lomb Memorial Drive, Rochester, NY 14623-5604; Phone: (716) 475-6700; Website: www.ntid.edu.

DEPARTMENT OF ENERGY

The late 1970s energy crisis led to a unification of energy planning, development, and coordination under one department umbrella. Signed into law by President Jimmy Carter on October 1, 1977, the Department of Energy Organization Act brought all of the federal government's nuclear programs together into one agency, the Department of Energy.

American nuclear energy activities began with the World War II development of the atomic bomb and continued through nuclear weapons research and production in the 1980s. In the 1990s and early 2000s the department's stated goals focused on environmentally sound clean up of the nuclear weapons complex, nonproliferation and maintenance of the country's nuclear stockpile and its safety, energy conservation and efficiency, and keeping nuclear technology and business competitive and profitable for the nuclear industry.

HISTORY

In 1942 the U.S. Army Corps of Engineers established the Manhattan Engineer District to manage the Manhattan Project to develop the atomic bomb. The Atomic Energy Act of 1946 created the Atomic Energy Commission to keep civilian government control of atomic research and development, giving the control of atomic development, as well as the Manhattan Engineer

Department of Energy

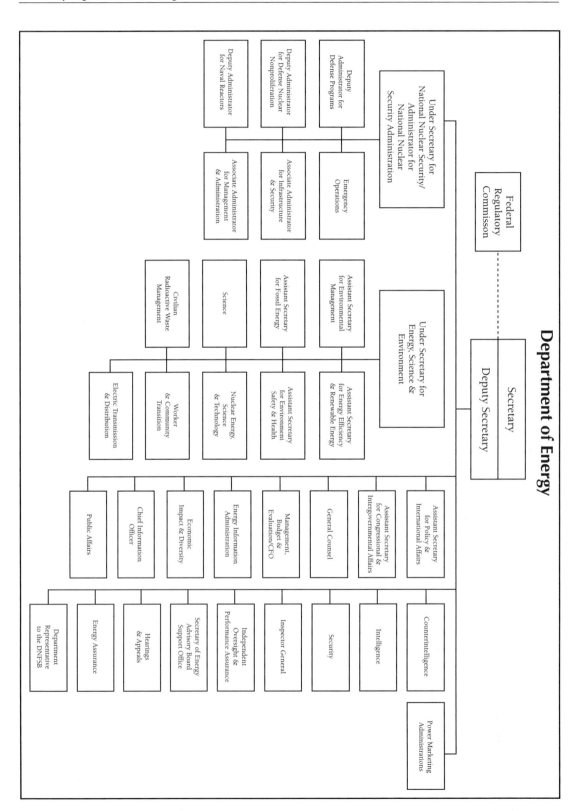

District's huge real estate complex, to the commission.

During the cold war years when the U.S. government feared attack by the Soviet Union, the commission worked to design and produce nuclear weapons and develop nuclear reactors for naval propulsion.

The Atomic Energy Act of 1954 undid the Atomic Energy Commission's sole corner on nuclear development, and instead gave it regulatory control of a new commercial nuclear power industry, ending the government's exclusive use of the atom.

In the 1970s the Atomic Energy Commission was abolished, and the Energy Reorganization Act of 1974 resulted in two new agencies. These were the Nuclear Regulatory Commission to regulate the nuclear power industry and the Energy Research and Development Administration to manage naval reactors, nuclear weapons, and energy development programs.

The Department of Energy became responsible for the Federal Energy Administration, the Energy Research and Development Administration, and the Federal Power Commission, and brought existing programs from other agencies together under the Energy Department roof. The department also oversees long-term, high-risk research and development of energy technology, federal power supplies and marketing, the nuclear weapons program, energy conservation and regulatory programs, and a central energy data center.

In July 2002 the U.S. Senate voted to allow burial of nuclear waste near Yucca Mountain in Nevada, a decision of substantial concern to Nevada residents. Following attacks on the World Trade Center in New York on September 11, 2001, the Department of Energy's role in protecting the country's energy supply has taken on new meaning. From 2000 to 2002 the Department of Energy also had a strong role in the western states energy crisis after run-ups in energy prices put California's residents and government in jeopardy. Accounting scandals and overcharging California for energy bankrupted some of the United States's largest commercial energy providers, such as Enron of Texas.

The Department of Energy now operates facilities in 35 states.

ORGANIZATION

The Department of Energy is organized into four business areas: National Security, Energy Resources, Science and Technology, and Environmental Quality. Crisscrossing and sharing those responsibilities are the Headquarters Program Offices; Area, Field, and Operation Offices; National Laboratories and Technology Centers; and Power Marketing Administrations.

CONTACT Address: U.S. Department of Energy, 1000 Independence Avenue SW, Washington, DC 20585; Phone: 1-800-dial-DOE (202) 586-5000; Fax: (202) 586-4403; Website: www.energy.gov.

REGIONAL OFFICES

Atlanta Regional Office, U.S. Department of Energy, Richard B. Russell Federal Building, 75 Spring Street SW, Suite 200, Atlanta, GA 30303; Website: www.eren.doe.gov/aro/.

Boston Regional Office, U.S. Department of Energy, John F. Kennedy Federal Building, Suite 675, Boston, MA 02203; Phone: (617) 565-9700; Fax: (617) 565-9723; Website: www.eren.doe.gov/bro/.

Chicago Regional Office, U.S. Department of Energy, One South Wacker Drive, Suite 2380, Chicago, IL 60606-4616; Phone: (312) 353-6749; Fax: (312) 886-8561; Website: www.eren.doe.gov/cro/.

Denver Regional Office, U.S. Department of Energy, 1617 Cole Boulevard, MS 1521, Golden, CO 80401; Phone: (303) 275-4826; Fax: (303) 275-4826; Website: www.eren.doe.gov/dro.

Philadelphia Regional Office, U.S. Department of Energy, Wanamaker Building, 100 Penn Square East, Suite 890, Philadelphia, PA 19107-3396; Phone: (215) 656-6950; Website: www.eren.doe.gov/pro/.

Seattle Regional Office, U.S. Department of Energy, 800 Fifth Avenue, Suite 3950, Seattle, WA 98104; Phone (206) 553-1004; Fax: (206) 553-2200.

Pacific sites: Address: P.O. Box 50168, Honolulu, HI 96850; Phone: (808) 541-2564; Fax: (808) 541-2562.

FEDERAL ENERGY REGULATORY COMMISSION (FERC)

The Federal Energy Regulatory Commission is an independent regulatory agency within the Department of Energy with the following specific responsibilities: It regulates transmission and sale of natural gas for resale in interstate commerce; regulates transmission of oil by pipeline in interstate commerce; regulates transmission and wholesale sales of electricity between states; licenses and inspects all private, regional, city, and state hydroelectric projects; oversees environmental issues re: natural gas, oil, and electricity and hydroelectric projects; and approves new sites and abandonment of interstate pipeline facilities.

FERC succeeded the old Federal Power Commission (FPC) and assumed most of its duties when the FPC was abolished and FERC was created through the Department of Energy Organization Act on October 1, 1977. FERC's legal authority derives from several federal acts, the Federal Power Act of 1935, the Natural Gas Act of 1938, the Natural Gas Policy Act of 1978, and the Energy Policy Act of 1992.

FERC has five members, all appointed by the president and confirmed by the Senate, and no more than three of whom may belong to the same political party. Members serve five-year terms, and the president names the chair.

CONTACT FERC's headquarters is at 888 First Street NE, Washington, DC. Regional offices include: *Dam Safety Program:* Division of Dam Safety and Inspections, Federal Energy Regulatory Commission, 888 First Street NE, Washington, DC 20426; Phone (202) 502-6734; Fax: (202) 219-2731. *Chicago Regional Office,* 230 South Dearborn Street, Room 3130, Chicago, IL 60604; Phone: (312) 353-6171; Fax: (312) 353-0109. *New York Regional Office,* 19 West 34th Street, Suite 400, New York, NY 10001; Phone (212) 273-5900; Fax: (212) 631-8124. *Portland Regional Office,* 101 S.W. Main Street, Suite 905, Portland, OR 97204; Phone: (503) 944-6700; Fax: (503) 944-6799. *San Francisco Regional Office,* 901 Market Street, Suite 350, San Francisco, CA 94103; Phone: (415) 369-3300; Fax: (415) 369-3322.

OFFICE OF THE SECRETARY

The secretary of energy oversees the Department of Energy and advises the president on all issues related to energy. The secretary is appointed by the president, with Senate confirmation. There are two deputy secretaries. Six assistant secretaries are responsible for economic impact and diversity; energy efficiency and renewable energy; environment, safety and health; fossil energy; international affairs; and congressional and intergovernmental affairs.

NATIONAL NUCLEAR SECURITY ADMINISTRATION (NNSA)

The National Nuclear Security Administration, headed by a deputy secretary, designs and develops nuclear energy and weapons to "enhance security." NNSA also maintains and monitors U.S. nuclear weapons stockpiles and provides the navy with nuclear propulsion plants and nuclear reactors. At the same time, NNSA claims to promote nuclear safety and nuclear nonproliferation and works to reduce global danger from weapons of mass destruction. Website: www.nnsa.doe.gov/.

NNSA sites include the following bases and offices, some of which have restricted addresses: **BECHTEL BETTIS ATOMIC POWER PLANT LABORATORY**, a subsidiary of Bechtel International, researches and designs nuclear propulsion technology, 814 Pittsburgh McKeesport Boulevard, West Mifflen, Pennsylvania 15122-0079; Phone (412) 476-5000; Website: www.bettis.gov/ and Scoville, Idaho 83404; Phone (412) 476-5000; Website: www.bettis.gov/. **BWTX PANTEX PLANT**, run by BWXT Pantex, U.S. Army Corps of Engineers, and Sandia National Laboratory, is America's only nuclear weapons assembly and disassembly facility and takes care of security and reliability of America's nuclear weapons stockpile on the High Plains of the Texas Panhandle, just 17 miles northeast of Amarillo on Highway 60 in Carson County; Website: www.pantex.com. **HONEYWELL FEDERAL MANUFACTURING AND TECHNOLOGIES**, 2000 East 95th Street, P.O. Box 419159, Kansas City, MO 64141-6159; Phone: (816) 997-2000; Fax: (816) 997-3331; Website: www.kcp.com. **KNOLLS ATOMIC POWER LABORATORY**, run by KAPL, Inc., a Lockheed Martin company, produces nuclear power plants for navy submarines and trains sailors to operate the onboard nuclear reactor plants, 2401 River Road, Niskayuna, NY 12309; Phone (518) 395-4000 and at West Milton, NY, both suburbs of Schenectady, P.O. Box 1072, Schenectady, New York 12301-1072; Fax only: (518) 395-4658; Website: www.kapl.gov/. Restricted New York nuclear sites exist at Kesselring and in Schenectady.

LAWRENCE BERKELEY NATIONAL LABORATORY, the oldest national lab, researches particle physics, materials, life sciences, energy efficiency, detectors, and accelerators, 1 Cyclotron Road, B-90, MS; 102, Berkeley, CA 94720; Phone: (510) 486-5111; Website: www.lbl.gov/. **LAWRENCE LIVERMORE NATIONAL LABORATORY**, operated by the University of California for DOE to design nuclear weapons and research energy, biomedicine, and environmental science, 7000 East Avenue, Livermore, CA 94550-9234; Phone: (925) 422-1100; Fax: (925) 422-1370; Website: www.llnl.gov/. **LOS ALAMOS NATIONAL LABORATORY (LANL)**, 1619 Central Avenue, MSA 117, Los Alamos, NM 87545; Phone: (505) 665-4400 or 1-800-508-4400; Fax: (505) 665-4411; Website: www.lanl.gov/; Bradbury Science Museum, 1350 Central Avenue, MS C330, Los Alamos, NM 87545; Phone: (505) 667-4444; Fax: (505) 665-6932; Website: www.lanl.gov/worldview/museum/index.shtml. Area office, 528 35th Street, Los Alamos, NM 87544; Phone: (505) 667-5105. Albuquerque Operations Office, P.O. Box 5400, Albuquerque, NM 87185-5400; Phone: (505) 845-0011; Website: www.dreal.gov/. **OAKLAND OPERATIONS OFFICE**, 1301 Clay Street, Oakland, CA 94612-5208; Phone: (510) 637-1762; Website: www.oak.doe.gov/. **NEVADA OPERATIONS OFFICE**, 232 Energy Way, P.O. Box 98518, Las Vegas, NV 89193-8518; Phone: (702) 295-1212; Website: www.nv.doe.gov/. *Nevada Test Site* (larger than Rhode Island) for open air nuclear weapons testing, hazardous and toxic chemicals spill testing (HAZMAT Spill Center) near Mercury, Nevada, 75 miles northwest of Las Vegas and includes the Big Explosives Experimental Facility (BEEF).

OAK RIDGE Y-12 NATIONAL SECURITY COMPLEX, managed by Bechtel's BWXT Y-12, makes nuclear weapons, maintains its nuclear weapons stockpile through disassembly and inspection, produces stockpile hardware, dismantles retired nuclear weapons, and works on environmental restoration and waste management and making nuclear facilities safe for shutdown, in the Bear Creek Valley of East Tennessee in Oak Ridge, 15 miles from Knoxville; Bethal

Valley Road, P.O. Box 2009, Oak Ridge, TN 37831-8245; Phone: (865) 574-1000; Website: www.y12.doe.gov/. **SANDIA NATIONAL LABORATORIES**, is run by Lockheed Corp. at Kirtland Air Force Base on Gibson Boulevard. While maintaining the U.S. nuclear stockpile, Sandia reduces "proliferation of weapons of mass destruction, the threat of nuclear accidents, and the potential for damage to the environment," and "addresses new threats to national security"; 1515 Eubank Street SE, Albuquerque, NM 87185; Phone: (505) 845-0011; Website: www.sandia.gov/; *Sandia National Laboratories/California* develops nuclear weapons systems, does combustion and renewable energy research, environmental research, responses to chemical and biological threats, biotechnology, and microsystems technologies, 7011 East Avenue, Livermore CA 94551-0969; Phone: (505) 845-0011. **SAVANNAH RIVER OPERATIONS OFFICE** stockpiles nuclear weapons 12 miles south of Aiken, South Carolina, and 25 miles southeast of Augusta, Georgia, manages excess nuclear materials and weapons, and works to safely dispose of radioactive and nonradioactive wastes from its operations, Building 737-A, Drawer E, Aiken, SC 29802; Phone (803) 725-2472; Website: http://sro.srs.gov/. **STANFORD NUCLEAR ACCELERATOR CENTER** focuses on particle physics and high-energy astrophysics using synchrotron radiation to provide accelerators and technologies, 2575 Sand Hill Road, Menlo Park, CA 95025; Phone: (650) 926-2204; Website: www.slac.stanford.edu.

HEADQUARTERS
PROGRAM OFFICES

CHIEF INFORMATION OFFICER The chief information officer advises the secretary of energy and senior managers on acquisition of information technology and manages information to implement department policies and legislation, including the Paperwork Reduction Act and Clinger-Cohen Act. The chief information officer is also responsible for cyber/computer security of DOE's classified and unclassified information and information technology, as well as information system integration.

CONTACT Website: www.cio.doe.gov/mission.htm.

OFFICE OF CIVILIAN RADIOACTIVE WASTE MANAGEMENT (OCRWM)

[Special note: Following the September 11, 2001, attacks on the World Trade Center in New York City and the Pentagon, OCRWM removed technical information and documents from its website. Some documents have again been posted on the website. If the information you seek is not available on the Internet, call the information line at 1-800-228-6972 for information on procuring the documents you want.]

The Nuclear Waste Policy Act of 1982 established the Office of Civilian Radioactive Waste Management to develop and establish a federal system to dispose of all spent nuclear fuel from commercial nuclear reactors, as well as high-level radioactive waste from federal atomic energy activities. The act also sets licensing requirements for nuclear waste management facilities and gives licensing power to the Nuclear Regulatory Commission (NRC).

The Nuclear Waste Policy Amendments Act of 1987 designated Yucca Mountain, Nevada, as the sole potential site to be researched as a potential disposal site for spent nuclear fuel and high-level radioactive waste. DOE Secretary Spencer Abraham submitted a recommendation to President George W. Bush that the president approve Yucca Mountain as the country's first geologic repository for spent nuclear fuel and high-level radioactive waste. President Bush sent the recommendation to Congress on February 15, 2002, and on July 9, 2002, the U.S. Senate agreed with the House of Representatives and passed the legislation, despite protests from environmentalists and Nevada residents. Nevada had little clout to defeat the measure, which no one else wanted in their state either. The Nuclear Regulatory Commission will review 24 years of scientific study and consider the site for a license as a repository for the country's nuclear waste.

Efforts of OCRWM are regulated and reviewed by several organizations. The U.S. Nuclear Regulatory Commission certifies and licenses components on the nuclear waste management system, including the sites where the material is placed as well as the casks in which it is transported.

The Environmental Protection Agency sets standards of public protection from radiation and dangers caused by disposal of high-level radioactive waste and spent nuclear fuel. The Department of Transportation regulates routing and transportation of highly radioactive materials, including spent nuclear fuel. The Nuclear Waste Technical Review Board looks at technical and scientific appropriateness of sites and packaging or transportation of high-level radioactive waste or spent nuclear fuel.

The General Accounting Office audits and prepares special reports on DOE's Yucca Mountain Project activities, and the state of Nevada and local governments oversee activities at the Yucca Mountain site. Nevada agencies involved in scrutinizing DOE's activities at Yucca Mountain include the Nevada Nuclear Waste Project Office; Clark County Nuclear Waste Program; Nye County Nuclear Waste Repository Project Office; Eureka County, Nevada, Nuclear Waste; and Inyo County Yucca Mountain Repository Assessment Office.

OCRWM also works with other countries and international organizations toward information exchange and consensus building on common issues, including technical information sharing re: Yucca Mountain Site Characterization Project, as well as geological disposal of commercial and defense spent nuclear fuel, waste acceptance, storage, and transportation activities.

OCRWM interacts with the International Atomic Energy Agency (IAEA), the Organization for Economic Cooperation and Development's Nuclear Energy Agency (NEA), and the International Association for Environmentally Safe Disposal of Radioactive Materials (EDRAM).

In 1999 DOE held an international nuclear waste disposal conference attended by 20 nations' representatives that have commercial nuclear power programs. Some of the nations agreed to a joint declaration pledging to work together to address safe management of nuclear waste.

CONTACT Website: www.rw.doe.gov/homejava/homejava.htm.

OFFICE OF CONGRESSIONAL AND INTERGOVERNMENTAL AFFAIRS (CI)

The Department of Energy's Office of Congressional and Intergovernmental Affairs, led by an assistant secretary, promotes DOE policies, programs, and initiatives through interaction with Congress, state, tribal, city, and county governments, other federal agencies, stakeholders, and the general public.

CI seeks input from the public to bring a broad range of two-way communication and diverse stakeholder viewpoints into the department's decision-making process.

CONTACT Website: www.ci.doe.gov/.

OFFICE OF THE DEPARTMENTAL REPRESENTATIVE TO THE DEFENSE NUCLEAR FACILITIES SAFETY BOARD

The Department of Energy has a designated member on the Defense Nuclear Facilities Safety Board, an independent organization created in 1989 within the Executive Branch. The board recommends and advises the president and the secretary of energy on public health and safety issues and evaluates safety, health, design, construction, operation, and decommissioning of the DOE's defense nuclear facilities. Board staff work on two- to three-year assignments at Rocky Flats, Pantex, Hanford, Oak Ridge, and Savannah River sites.

The Defense Nuclear Facilities Safety Board also investigates any event or practice at a DOE defense nuclear facility that the board decides has or may adversely affect public health and safety; conducts public hearings; issues subpoenas of witnesses and evidence; requests information and establishes reporting requirements; stations on-site resident inspectors; conducts special studies; seeks input from the public; and gets assistance from the Nuclear Regulatory Commission and the National Research Council of the National Academy of Sciences.

Among the board's goals are to help DOE develop appropriate and meaningful workable safety standards and convey those requirements clearly to DOE management and contractors; raise the technical expertise of the DOE; and identify the nature and consequence of significant potential threats to public health and safety and inform the public of those threats.

DOE and the board work to ensure public and worker health safety, as well as environmental safety at and around defense nuclear facilities. Safety issues being followed by the board include stabilizing excess nuclear material for interim, long-term, and final disposition; development and implementation of a safety management system that allows for work along with public, worker, and environmental protection; development of a process to integrate oversight findings to correct system problems; use of nuclear safety requirements according to the Integrated Safety Management implementation; and coordination of management of vital safety systems.

CONTACT Address: Office of the Departmental Representative to the Defense Nuclear Facilities Safety Board, 1000 Independence Avenue SW, Room 6H-025, Washington, DC 20585; Phone:

(202) 586-3887; Fax: (202) 586-3472; Website: www.deprep.org. Defense Nuclear Facilities Safety Board: 625 Indiana Avenue NW, Washington, DC.

OFFICE OF ECONOMIC IMPACT AND DIVERSITY (ED)

The Office of Economic Impact and Diversity, managed by an assistant secretary, advises the secretary of energy on the impact of energy policies, programs, regulations, and other DOE actions on under-represented communities, minority educational institutions, and small and women-owned businesses.

ED funds support the Minority Economic Impact (MI) Programs to conduct a Socio-Economic Research and Analysis Program to develop and assess energy consumption data and integrate that information with the National Energy Modeling System to look at equity issues; provide Management and Technical Assistance Programs to support minority educational activities; and provide technical training, financial aid, and small business assistance programs to augment economic development abilities to under-represented segments of the population. The Minority Energy Information Clearinghouse collects and disseminates information and designs and maintains the ED websites.

As part of its goals, MI works to integrate minority education institutions into DOE missions and activities; conducts research to determine socioeconomic and environmental effects of national energy programs, policies, and regulations of DOE on minorities; bolster and develop financial business incentives and initiatives to encourage minority-owned financial institutions to link with minority businesses to help in long-term economic development; to work with educators; support programs to encourage youths to study energy-related curricula and technologies; and provide management and technical assistance to minority businesses to help their communities with economic development efforts.

MI also works with historically black colleges to develop programs in mathematics and science and support research and educational infrastructure at high schools, colleges, and universities with financial support for scientific training and research experiences in mathematics, science, and engineering for teachers and students, using federal and private sector laboratories and energy technology industries.

MI looks to soften adverse impacts of energy and environmental programs and regulations on various population segments.

ED offices include *Office of Minority Impact (MI)*, *Office of Small and Disadvantaged Business Utilization (OSDBU)*, *Office of Civil Rights (OCR)*, *Office of Employee Concerns (OEC)*, and *Office of the Ombudsman*.

CONTACT Address: 1000 Independence Avenue, Washington, DC 20585; Phones: (202) 586-8383; Office of Minority Economic Impact (202) 586-8383; Office of Civil Rights (202) 586-2218; Office of Small & Disadvantaged Business Utilization (202) 586-7377; Office of Employee Concerns (202) 586-6530; Office of the Ombudsman (202) 586-2234; Website: www.hr.doe.gov/ed/.

OFFICE OF ENERGY EFFICIENCY AND RENEWABLE ENERGY (EERE)

The Office of Energy Efficiency and Renewable Energy, directed by an assistant secretary, works to strengthen energy security, environmental quality, and economic vitality between public-private partnerships. All of its efforts are to enhance energy efficiency and productivity; bring clean, reliable, and affordable energies to the marketplace; and enhance the public's energy choices, and thereby their quality of life.

EERE's priorities include: Reduce or end dependence on foreign oil and energy; reduce energy prices for the disadvantaged population; improve renewable energy technologies; increase reliability and efficiency of electricity generation, delivery, and use; increase building and appliance energy efficiency; increase efficiency and reduce energy use of industry; create a new domestic bioindustry; lead by example through government actions, i.e. energy conservation in the federal government; and change the way EERE does business.

EERE conducts its programs in conjunction with private, state, and local government, DOE national laboratories, and universities. EERE's 11 energy programs are: Biomass Program; Building Technologies Program; Distributed Energy & Electricity Reliability Program; Federal Energy Management Program; FreedomCAR & Vehicle Technologies Program; Geothermal Technologies Program; Hydrogen, Fuel Cells & Infrastructure Technologies Program; Industrial Technologies Program; Solar Energy Technology Program; Wind & Hydropower Technologies Program; and Weatherization & Intergovernmental Program.

EERE's Golden, Colorado, field office coordinates partnerships between DOE, its laboratories, and the private sector.

EERE also has six regional offices in Atlanta, Georgia; Boston, Massachusetts; Chicago, Illinois; Denver, Colorado; Philadelphia, Pennsylvania; and Seattle, Washington. The regional offices coordinate project management and technology deployment and serve as EERE liaisons with state and local governments, regional industries, and other users to encourage adoption of new technologies.

CONTACT Address: Office of Energy Efficiency and Renewable Energy, Mail Stop EE-1, Department of Energy, Washington, DC 20585; Phone: (202) 586-9220; Website: www.eren.doe.gov/eere/.

Biomass Program: Biomass power is fuel, power, and chemicals produced from plants and plant-derived materials.

Created by the Biomass Research and Development Act of 2000, EERE's Biomass Program works to develop and improve technology for biomass power, make biofuels such as ethanol from biomass residues and grain, and make renewable diesel fuel; and develop ways to make plastics and chemicals from renewable bio (plant)-based materials. The Biomass Program also coordinates the multiagency Biomass Research and Development Initiative to accelerate all federal bio-based products and bioenergy research.

Building Technologies Program: The Office of Building Technology, State and Community Programs has been reorganized into two offices, the Building Technologies Program and the Weatherization and Intergovernmental Program.

The Building Technologies Program works with the building industry and manufacturers on research and development of technologies and practices for energy efficiency; promotes energy and money-saving opportunities to builders and consumers, including their Zero Energy Buildings program; and works with state and local regulatory groups to change building codes and energy standards for appliances.

WEBSITE www.eren.doe.gov/building/html.

Distributed Energy & Electricity Reliability Program (DER): The Distributed Energy & Electricity Reliability Program (formerly the Office of Distributed Energy Resources) was created in October 2000, when the TER Taskforce combined DER-related programs in the Office of Energy Efficiency with the Renewable Energy office. DER runs four primary programs: Distributed Energy; Energy Storage; Superconductivity; and Transmission Reliability.

To meet the nation's increased needs for high-quality, reliable electricity, distributed energy resources offer a less expensive alternative to construction of large, central power plans and high-voltage transmission lines. To this end, DER works with "industry stakeholders" (power companies) to coordinate distribution of energy through the electricity grid. DER works toward the goal of the United States having a secure, efficient, and reliable energy infrastructure.

DER's efforts have intensified and accelerated since the massive August 14, 2003, blackout in the northeastern states and eastern Canada. DER is working to develop a national power grid, identify transmission bottlenecks, and identify ways to remove transmission bottlenecks; develop integrated energy systems to provide heating, cooling, and better indoor air quality; and develop next-generation technology including hydrogen and fusion. To accomplish the latter, DER is developing advanced microturbines, reciprocating engines, and fuel cells.

WEBSITE www.eren.doe.gov/der/.

Energy Storage Systems Program: The Energy Storage Systems Program seeks to ensure that power is available during electricity shortage and supply fluctuations. Working with the power industry, Energy Storage Systems works toward minimizing costs due to power quality and reliability problems; increase technology choices in deregulated competitive electricity markets; and increase the value of resources.

Other goals of the program include finding industry interest in a quantitative study of transmission power quality and reliability; completing research, development, and testing of a 400-kWh Advanced Battery Energy System, a prototype storage system, a 5-MW transmission power quality system; and installing and testing a mega-storage system (up to 10-MWh capacity) in partnership with industry.

The program also performs research and development for storage technologies and systems that incorporate broad technologies including batteries; flywheels; high-energy and high-density capacitors; superconducting energy storage (SMES); power electronics; and control systems.

WEBSITE www.eren.doe.gov/der/energy_storage/html.

Superconductivity for Electric Systems Program: Superconductivity Magnetic Energy Storage (SMES) systems store energy in a magnetic field created by the flow of direct current in a coil of superconducting material that has been cooled cryogenically. Electric currents encounter almost no resistance in cooled superconducting materials. High-temperature superconductivity lends promise of providing more efficient and higher capacity transmission of electricity.

Since the discovery of high-temperature superconductivity (HTS) in 1986, researchers have been racing to develop this form of power's technology. The U.S. Department of Energy launched the Superconductivity for Electric Systems Program in 1988 to develop and commercialize electric power applications of HTS, working with high-tech companies and the DOE's national laboratories.

CONTACT Phone: (202) 586-1165; Website: www.erendoe.gov/superconductivity.

Transmission Reliability Program: Congress reestablished the Transmission Reliability Program in 1999 to conduct research on the reliability of the nation's electricity infrastructure, because according to the program, "competition and market forces are creating an explosion of power transactions that are causing the grid to be used in ways for which it was not designed."

WEBSITE www.eren.doe.gov/der/transmission/.

OFFICE OF ELECTRIC TRANSMISSION & DISTRIBUTION

A program created October 1, 2003, in response to the August 14, 2003, massive power outage throughout the U.S. northeast and the Canadian southeast, the Office of Electric Transmission & Distribution aims to modernize and expand the U.S. electric delivery system to ensure economic and national security.

OETD's goals include reducing regulatory and institutional barriers to efficient transmis-

sion and distribution; acting as facilitator to find energy solutions; providing public-private partnership linking; research and development; modeling and analysis; electricity import/export authorization; and power marketing liaison.

WEBSITE www.electricity.doe.gov/.

FEDERAL ENERGY MANAGEMENT PROGRAM (FEMP)

Chartered in 1973, the Federal Energy Management Program works to reduce energy use, to improve utility management decisions, and to promote water conservation and use of distributed and renewable energy at federal facilities. Since the federal government is the nation's largest single energy consumer, energy management, that is, efficient use of energy, assurance of reliable supplies, and cost reduction must be achieved.

Charged with leading the federal government toward more efficient use of energy resources, FEMP claims to have reduced the government's building-related energy costs by 20 percent per square foot since 1985 to $4 billion annually. Pursuant to the Energy Policy Act of 1992 President Bill Clinton issued directives and executive orders requiring federal agencies to reduce their energy use by 35 percent of the 1985 consumption levels by 2005. In 2002 the compliance date was extended to 2010 by President George W. Bush.

To reduce energy use, FEMP advises federal facility and energy managers on new construction, building retrofits, equipment purchases, operations and maintenance, and utility management with technical assistance and new partnerships with the private sector.

The *Federal Energy Management Advisory Committee* was created by President Bill Clinton to advise the Department of Energy on meeting federal energy management goals. In October

2000, the secretary of energy appointed 11 members of the committee, chaired by the director of FEMP, and including officials from state government agencies, energy service, utility and equipment manufacturing industries, building design and construction industries, and energy companies.

CONTACT Address: FEMP Administration, EE-90, 1000 Independence Avenue SW, Washington, DC 20585-0121; Phone: Help desk: 1-800-363-3732 (DOE-EREC); Main Office: (202) 586-5772; Fax: (202) 586-3000.

FreedomCAR & Vehicle Technologies Program: Much of the former Office of Transportation Technologies is now incorporated into the FreedomCAR & Vehicle Technologies Program, a new government and industry program to develop technologies for hydrogen-powered fuel cell cars and trucks that will require no foreign oil and emit no harmful pollutants or greenhouse gases. The C-A-R in FreedomCAR stands for Cooperative Automotive Research, meaning a cooperative effort by the Department of Energy and the U.S. Council of Automotive Research (USCAR), an organization formed by the Ford Motor Company, General Motors Cooperation, and DaimlerChrysler Corporation during the administration of President George W. Bush.

Among the goals of the program are reduction of the United States' consumption of 10 million barrels of foreign oil every day (2002), with transportation using 67 percent of the petroleum used in the United States. Other goals include reduction of "the annual increase in use of petroleum fuels by highway transportation vehicles to zero or less," to develop mass production hydrogen-powered fuel cell vehicles that will require no foreign oil, emit no harmful pollutants or greenhouse gases, and to contribute to the nation's economic growth.

One of FreedomCAR's aims is to help manufacturers make these new cars by reducing the vehicle weight by 50 percent, which could create some safety issues.

Within the FreedomCAR bureaucracy are the Office of Advanced Automotive Technologies, the Office of Heavy Vehicle Technologies, the Office of Fuels Development, and the Office of Technology Utilization.

WEBSITE www.cartech.doe.gov/freedomcar/.

The Office of Advanced Automotive Technologies (OAAT) works to develop automobiles using electric and hybrid technologies, advanced heat engines, fuel cells, alternative fuels, and advanced propulsion materials.

WEBSITE www.ott.doe.gov/oaat/.

The *Office of Heavy Vehicle Technologies (OHVT)* helps the auto industry develop heavy vehicles and equipment become more energy efficient and capable of running on alternative fuels, while reducing their polluting emissions.

WEBSITE www.ott.doe.gov/ohvt.shtml.

The *Office of Fuels Development (OFD)* works on reducing costs of cleaner, domestic ethanol, a renewable and easy-to-use alternative fuel. Ethanol can be made from biomass feedstocks such as corn fiber, bagasse, and rice straw, all of which contain cellulose. Cellulose can be converted to sugars that can be fermented into ethanol. OFD is also working on making ethanol out of plants, trees, and other feedstocks grown specifically to create energy. OFD is also contributing to the effort to create biodiesel fuels, that is, truck fuel made from plant sources.

The *Office of Technology Utilization* seeks to furnish alternative fuel vehicles (AFV) to federal fleets of vehicles along with the Clean Cities Program, provide information, and help develop state grants and regulatory information.

CONTACT Address: Office of Transportation Technologies, EE-30, 1000 Independence Avenue SW, Washington, DC 20585; Phone: (202) 586-8594.

Geothermal Technologies Program: Formerly sharing quarters in the Office of Energy Efficiency & Renewable Energy, the Geothermal Technologies Program and the Wind & Hydropower Technologies Program run their own operations.

The program's three focus areas are: energy systems research and testing; drilling technologies research; and geoscience and support technologies research.

Geothermal (*geo*=earth, *thermal*=heat) energy is a huge and underutilized clean and reliable heat and power source available on American soil. Geothermal energy sources range from just under shallow ground to hot water and rock several miles below the Earth's surface. At its deepest, geothermal energy comes from extremely hot molten rock called magma. All three sources can be converted to heat and electricity by geothermal heat pumps, direct-use applications, and power plants.

Geothermal heat pumps use shallow (to 10 feet) ground energy to heat and cool buildings with pipes buried in the ground near a building with a heat exchanger, and ductwork into the building. In cooler seasons heat from the warmer ground goes through the heat exchanger into the building and heats it. In hot weather hot air from the house is pulled through the heat exchanger into the relatively cooler ground. Heat removed from a building in hot weather can be used to heat water at no cost. In some locales the hot water is used to melt snow on nearby sidewalks. All of this is based on the premise that the Earth's surface remains between 50–60°F. American geothermal reservoirs are located in the contiguous western states, Alaska, and Hawaii.

Power plants generate electricity by drilling a mile or more into underground reservoirs to tap steam and extremely hot water that drive turbines and electricity generators. The three types of geothermal power plants operating today are dry steam plants, which use geothermal steam to turn turbines; flash steam plants, which bring high-pressure hot water into lower-pressure tanks and use the resulting steam to drive turbines; and binary-cycle plants, which pass hot geothermal water past another fluid that has a much lower boiling point than water. This causes the secondary fluid to turn to steam, which then drives the turbines.

Geothermal energy is available several miles below the surface of the entire Earth in dry rock that is heated by the magma below it. Government-industry partners are developing technology to drill into the rock, inject cold water down one well and circulate it through the hot, fractured rock, and draw the heated water off from another well.

Benefits of geothermal energy: Compared to coal-fired energy plants, it prevents emission of 22 million tons of carbon dioxide, 200,000 tons of sulfur dioxide, 80,000 tons of nitrogen oxides, and 110,000 tons of matter every year; it takes only 400 square meters of land to produce a gigawatt of power over 30 years; currently produces the third-most energy of all renewable sources after hydroelectricity and biomass; for each 1,000 houses using geothermal heat pumps, utility companies can avoid installing 2–5 megawatts of energy capacity. Geothermal power plants produce at most 1/1,000th as much carbon dioxide as fossil-fuel power plants, and geothermal produces no nitrogen oxides and low amounts of sulfur dioxide. Steam and flash plants emit mostly water vapor, and binary power plants run on a closed-loop system, and no gases are emitted from them.

The Geysers power plant in Sonoma and Lake Counties, California, emits a stinky smell from the hydrogen sulfide contained in the geothermal fluid. The sulfur is extracted and recycled to make sulfuric acid. At the Salton Sea plants in Imperial County, California, corrosive salts and heavy metals require extraction from the mineralized geothermal brine and careful disposal. The salts are crystallized, removed, and recycled. Silica is extracted and recycled as concrete filler for use in roads and flood levees. Zinc is extracted and sold. Water from the Salton Sea is sold for various uses by the Imperial Irrigation District. The Salton Sea was created in 1905 to hold water brought by canal from the Colorado River.

Greenhouse plant growers could cut their power costs by up to 80 percent, while homeowners who invest in a heat pump save on their electricity bills.

CONTACT Address: General: Geothermal Technology Development Program, EE-12, 1000 Independence Avenue SW, Washington, DC 20585; Phone: (202) 586-5348.

National laboratories researching and developing geothermal energy include the following.

BROOKHAVEN NATIONAL LABORATORY-GEOTHERMAL MATERIALS DEVELOPMENT PROGRAM: Brookhaven conducts research on the properties and behavior of engineering materials and develops durable materials needed and used in renewable energy extraction and production.

CONTACT Address: Building 526, P.O. Box 5000, Upton, NY 11973-5000; Phone: (631) 344-3060; Fax (631) 344-2539; Website: www.bnl.gov.est/.

IDAHO NATIONAL ENGINEERING AND ENVIRONMENTAL LABORATORY: INEEL has been researching and developing geothermal resource technologies for direct use and to generate electricity since the mid-1970s. INEEL currently works with private energy plant owners and operators in California, Nevada, and Utah to reduce costs of building and running geothermal plants. INEEL also runs the Geothermal Energy Program's geoscience research into geothermal reservoirs and coordinates DOE's international geothermal program.

CONTACT Address: Idaho National Engineering and Environmental Laboratory, 2525 North Fremont, Idaho Falls, ID 83415; Phone: (208) 526-9824; Website: http://geothermal.id.doe.gov/.

LAWRENCE BERKELEY NATIONAL LABORATORY-GEOTHERMAL ENERGY DEVELOPMENT: Since 1974 The Lawrence Berkeley lab has developed geothermal exploration technologies, reservoir characterization, and performance evaluation technologies. Research endeavors include development of computer codes for forward and inverse modeling of reservoir processes, use of noble gas and other isotopic techniques to define and identify reservoirs, and development of seis-mic and electrical geophysics techniques for reservoir characterization. Some of LBNL's work is now used in nuclear waste storage efforts, environmental improvements, and recovery of oil and gas from tight reservoirs.

LBNL has also contributed significantly to understanding and utilization of the Geysers geothermal field in Sonoma and Lake Counties of northern California, including consideration of the new signs of over exploitation of the geothermal field, such as changes in the chemistry of the steam from the Geysers.

CONTACT Address: Lawrence Berkeley National Laboratory, One Cyclotron Road, Berkeley, CA 94720 and 700 East Avenue, Livermore, CA 94550; Phone: (510) 486-6451; Website: www.esd.lbl.gov/ER/geothermal.html.

NATIONAL RENEWABLE ENERGY LABORATORY (NREL)-GEOTHERMAL TECHNOLOGIES PROGRAM: Geothermal Technologies promotes economical production of electricity from low- to moderate-temperature geothermal resources. It encourages such economies via increased plant cycle utilization efficiency, maximizing efficiency and productivity of geothermal plant design, and lowering costs of operations and management.

CONTACT Address: National Renewable Energy Laboratory, 1617 Cole Boulevard, Golden, CO 80401.

SANDIA NATIONAL LABORATORIES-GEOTHERMAL RESEARCH DEPARTMENT: Sandia is a multiprogram laboratory operated by Sandia Corp., a Lockheed Martin Company, for the U.S. Department of Energy. Sandia's Geothermal Research Department's main goal is to develop well construction technologies that reduce costs of drilling geothermal wells, and theoretically costs of geothermal energy. The methods they explore include hard rock drill bit technology, high-temperature instrumentation, lost-circulation (into surrounding rock) control, rig instrumentation, high-speed data telemetry, and slimhole drilling. Sandia also works to develop better downhole reservoir characterization tools and exploration techniques with industry partners for geothermal energy development.

CONTACT Address: Sandia National Laboratories, 1515 Eubank SE, P.O. Box 5800, Albuquerque, NM 87158-1033; Phone: (505) 844-3933; Website: www.sandia.gov/geothermal/.

Hydrogen, Fuel Cells, & Infrastructure Technologies Program: The Hydrogen, Fuel Cells, & Infrastructure Technologies Program is an outgrowth and expansion of the one-time Hydrogen Program/Hydrogen Information Network and now also includes fuel cells and infrastructure research and development and hydrogen system research and development.

Work to develop fuel cells for transportation focuses on polymer electrolyte membrane (PEM) fuel cells. Research and development is going on at three government labs: Los Alamos National Laboratory is conducting research in automotive fuel cell technology under the Hydrogen Program; Argonne National Laboratory's Fuel Cells for Transportation Program focuses on FreedomCAR to develop hydrogen-powered fuel cell cars and light trucks; and the National Renewable Laboratory has the Alternative Fuels Data Center (AFDC), which provides information on fuel cell use in vehicle fleets.

Fuel cell research also focuses on providing electricity to the grid and to consumers in buildings, as well as how to develop the best fuel cell infrastructure and distribution system, including hydrogen production, storage facilities, transportation, and distribution systems.

Hydrogen production technologies under development include: thermochemical production technologies and natural gas steam reforming (making hydrogen from natural gas); a partial oxidation ceramic membrane reactor to separate oxygen from air and to accomplish partial oxidation of methane; plasma reforming could provide hydrogen for industrial, consumer, and refueling of vehicles; biomass gasification and pyrolysis can produce hydrogen via pyrolysis (decomposition by heat) and gasification using agricultural residues and wastes or biomass grown for energy users; electrolytic production technologies; reversible fuel cells and electrolyzers; photolytic production technologies; photobiological technologies in which microbes produce hydrogen during their metabolic activities; photoelectrolysis; hydrogen transport and storage technologies; compressed gas storage tanks including hydrides and gas-on-solid absorption; and hydrogen utilization and its enabling technologies including fuel cells, internal combustion engines, and hydrogen sensors.

WEBSITE www.eren.doe.gov/hydrogen/.

Industrial Technologies Program (ITP): The Industrial Technologies Program works with industrial partners to develop and deliver advanced technologies to increase energy efficiency, improve environmental performance, boost productivity, and increase profits.

Industries of the Future program aids commercial partners financially with research and development in nine energy-intensive industries: agriculture, aluminum, chemicals, forest products, glass, metal casting, mining, petroleum, and steel.

The agriculture program brings together experts from biobased products industries, agriculture, forest products, and chemical industries to create plastics, chemicals, and materials from agricultural crops and residues, trees and forest residues, animal wastes, grasses, and organic solid wastes from municipalities (sewage).

WEBSITE www.oit.doe.gov/agriculture/.

The forest products program goals, known as Agenda 2020 as developed by the American Forest and Paper Association (AF&PA) in 1994, oversees research in sustainable forest management, environmental performance, energy performance, improved capital effectiveness, recycling, and sensors and control.

WEBSITE www.oit.doe.gov/forest/.

BestPractices program furnishes in-plant assessments, tools, training, and other resources to help identify ways to reduce energy use and save money.

WEBSITE www.oit.doe.gov/bestpractices.

Enabling Technologies program offers cost-shared funding for research and development in technologies common to many energy-intensive industries, such as combustion, sensors and controls, and industrial materials for the future.

State Industries of the Future relays federal energy and environmental benefits to states to distribute on a statewide or regional basis.

Financial Assistance: OIT offers financial aid to inventors and small businesses to launch energy-saving ideas. OIT also provides money to promote demonstrations of energy-efficient technologies through state industry partnerships (NICE3).

International Programs: OIT provides funding for American business leaders to work on energy efficiency, sustainable energy development, and economic progress with their equivalents in China, Ghana, India, and South Africa, where the American businesspeople may be doing business or having products made for them.

WEBSITE www.oit.doe.gov/programs.shtml.

Solar Energy Technology Program: The Solar Energy Technology Program works to speed development of solar technologies and educate the public on the value of solar energy as a secure, reliable, and clean energy source. The program's three main emphases include photovoltaic cells, concentrating solar power technologies, and low-temperature solar collectors.

Photovoltaic cells convert sunlight to electricity to provide power for everything from wristwatches to supplying a massive grid. The cells are made of semiconductors such as crystalline silicon or thin-film materials.

Concentrating solar power technologies use reflective materials to gather and concentrate the Sun's heat energy. That energy eventually drives a generator to produce electricity.

Low-temperature solar collectors absorb the Sun's heat energy, and then the heat is used directly to heat water or space in residential, commercial, and industrial buildings.

WEBSITE www.eren.doe/gov/solar.html.

Wind & Hydropower Technologies Programs: The Wind Energy Program and the Hydropower Program have been combined to form the Wind and Hydropower Technologies Program. The National Renewable Energy Laboratory (NREL) in Golden, Colorado, the home of the National Wind Technology Center (NWTC), is the lead wind technology research center and laboratory. Sandia National Laboratories in Albuquerque, New Mexico, takes the lead in applied wind energy research. Researchers study characteristics of the wind, how wind interacts with turbine rotors, physical, and chemical properties of materials used to make turbine blades and other parts, and develop dissemination of the science of wind technology.

The **Wind Energy Program** includes wind energy research, wind turbine research and development, and research and financial support for utilities', industries', and international wind energy projects. The program's goals are to develop wind turbine technologies able to reduce energy costs from wind to 2.5 cents per kilowatt-hour; establish the U.S. wind industry with 25 percent of world markets; and achieve a U.S. capacity of 10,000 megawatts of electricity from wind-powered generators.

Research projects include wind forecasting to help utilities anticipate the next day's wind and wind integration studies on wind generation, transmission, and distribution. Government programs help wind industries by certification testing for new wind turbines, helping U.S. wind power developers agree on international standards for safety, power performance, and blade testing; and technical assistance with wind project planning and implementation.

The National Renewable Energy Laboratory at Golden, Colorado, also advises wind projects in Argentina, Brazil, Chile, China, the Dominican Republic, India, Indonesia, Mexico, the Philippines, Russia, and South Africa.

Utilities utilizing the Wind Energy Program assistance include Cedar Falls Utilities/Iowa

Utilities, Algona, Iowa; Central and South West Services, Inc., Fort Davis, Texas; Green Mountain Power Corporation, Searsburg, Vermont; Kotzebue Electric Association, Kotzebue, Alaska; Nebraska Public Power District/Nebraska Utilities, Springview, Nebraska; TXU Electric/York Research Corporation, Big Spring, Texas; and Wisconsin Public Service Corporation/Wisconsin Utilities, Glenmore, Wisconsin.

WEBSITE www.eren.doe.gov/wind/.

The **Hydropower Program's** mission is to work with industry and other federal agencies to research and develop technical, societal, and environmental benefits that can be derived from hydropower (the force of water falling).

Hydropower is one of the United States's largest renewable local resources. Hydropower emits no pollution and produces energy at low cost, although dam and reservoir systems can interrupt ecological systems such as fish migration and altering of stream flows.

Use of hydropower is one of civilization's oldest forms of power generation. More than 2,000 years ago the Greeks used turning waterwheels to grind wheat into flour. Jumping to the United States, the Grand Rapids Electric Light & Power Co. of Michigan lit 16 lamps at the Wolverine Chair Factory by using a water turbine. The next year the city of Niagara Falls lit streetlamps with hydropower. And by 1886 nearly 45 water-powered electric plants existed in the United States and Canada. In 1887 San Bernardino, California, introduced the first hydroelectric plant in the western states.

Other important steps in hydropower development include the first Federal Water Power Act (1901); establishment of the Bureau of Reclamation (1902); the Federal Power Act gave the Federal Power Commission power to issue licenses for hydropower development on public lands and 25 percent of all U.S. power generation was hydroelectric (1920); Tennessee Valley Authority was established (1933); the first federal dam, Bonneville Dam, opened on the Columbia River and the Bonneville Power Administration was established (1937). By then 40 percent of electrical power generation in the U.S. was hydropower.[8] Currently hydroelectric power supplies only 7 percent of U.S. electricity.

Hydropower plants use water and the kinetic energy created by water falling to generate electricity. Hydropower plants utilize one or a combination of three methods to produce electricity: run-of-river, peaking, or storage.

Run-of-river projects capture the energy of the natural river flow to make power. Peaking projects hoard water and then release it when energy is needed. Storage projects retain more water longer during high-flow periods than peaking systems and then release it during low-flow periods.

Most hydropower plants consist of the following parts: a dam to store water/energy; a penstock that carries the water from the reservoir formed by the dam to the turbine engine in the power plant; a turbine, whose blades are turned by the force of flowing water; a generator, that because it is connected to the turbine, rotates to produce electrical power; a transformer that converts the generator's electricity to voltage; and transmission lines to take electricity from the hydropower plant to consumers.

WEBSITE http://hydropower.id.doe.gov/more.htm.

Weatherization & Intergovernmental Program: The Weatherization & Intergovernmental Program provides information on cost, energy efficiency, and renewable energy projects to consumers, businesses, government entities, Native American tribal governments, and international agencies.

Alternative Fuels Data Center offers information for alternative fuel vehicles (AFVs), including on-line alternative fuel station maps, alternative fuel vehicle fleet buyer's guide, EPAct

---

8 [Source: http://hydropower.id.doe,gov/facts/history.htm]

fleet information and regulations, help to calculate ozone emission reduction credits for Clean Cities AFVs, and information on how to convert public vehicle fleets to alternative fuel vehicles.

WEBSITE www.afdc.doe.gov/fleet.shtml

Clean Cities Program works with local businesses and governments to use alternative fuel vehicles. Clean Cities helps develop new commercial opportunities for AFVs; facilitate production of and conversion to AFVs; expand network of refueling stations; increase use of alternative fuels; develop "clean corridors"; increase public awareness of values and availability of alternative fuels; and give support to regulated AFV fleets.

Municipalities and other government entities may achieve the Clean Cities designation. For more information contact Clean Cities Hotline at 1-800-224-8437 (1-800-CCITIES)

CONTACT Address: Clean Cities Program, EE-34, 1000 Independence Avenue SW, Washington, DC 20585-0121; Website: www.ccities.doe.gov/what_is.html.

Energy Star Program works to increase consumer awareness, interest, and demand for energy efficient products.

The Department of Energy and EPA gives Energy Star® labels to appliances and electronic equipment that do better than minimum national efficiency standards. Energy Star works with more than 4,000 retailers, including national big names, to label qualified refrigerators, dishwashers, washing machines, and room air conditioners. Energy Star works with the window industry to promote sales of energy efficient windows, doors, and skylights, granting some the Energy Star label, and has introduced and encouraged production and use of Compact Fluorescent Light Bulbs (CFLs).

WEBSITE www.eren.doe.gov/buildings/energystar.html.

Fuel Economy Program offers on-line and hardcopy information to help consumers compare gas mileage, greenhouse gas emissions, air pollution ratings, and safety information for new and used cars and trucks. The program also provides updated gasoline prices, gas mileage tips, links to advanced technology resources, information on vehicle safety and fuel economy, possible tax incentives for driving hybrid vehicles and alternative fuel vehicles, and the latest news on hybrid cars and alternative fuel vehicles.

WEBSITE www.fueleconomy.gov/.

International program involvement includes participation with other countries and resources throughout the world. Programs in which the Office of Technology participates on behalf of the Department of Energy and the United States include the following:

Committee on Energy Efficiency Commerce and Trade (COEET), in which the Office of Technology Access (OTA) helps U.S. companies increase their share of the international energy market.

Asia-Pacific Economic Cooperation (APEC): OTA represents the United States in APEC's energy and energy efficiency working groups. APEC is a regional trade organization.

Energy Efficiency and Sustainable Development Centers: OTA has helped start nonprofit centers in six developing market countries to give them access to American technologies for renewable energy and energy efficiency.

International Renewable Energy Program helps United States renewable energy companies expand their businesses abroad.

Hemispheric Energy Initiative involves OTA working with countries of the Organization of American States energy ministers to support their renewable energy programs and sell U.S. energy companies' technologies and systems abroad.

U.S.-China Renewable Energy Cooperation works to enhance business in China for U.S. renewable energy efficiency companies.

Russian programs enable OTA to help multilateral agencies to develop renewable energy products in Russia.

Eastern Europe: OTA works to find ways to use U.S. developed renewable energy and energy efficient technologies in Eastern European countries.

Africa Projects: OTA supports and holds workshops on renewable energy at a Conference of Energy Ministers in Africa.

Tribal Energy Program: OTA gives financial and technical help to tribes for feasibility studies and shares expenses of installing sustainable renewable energy projects on tribal lands.

Inventions and Innovation Program provides financial help up to $40,000 or up to $200,000 to work on early development and establish technical performance of new ideas and inventions in the renewable energy field. Inventors may gain financial support for ideas that have significant energy savings impact and have commercial market potential in industry, power, transportation, or buildings. The program also gives nonmonetary aid to some innovators by helping them find technical partners, commercial sponsors, business plan developers, financial resources, commercialization planning, market potential assessment, and access to regional service providers.

CONTACT OIT Clearinghouse: Phone: 1-800-862-2086; Fax: (360) 586-8303; E-mail: clearinghouse@ee.doe.gov; Website: www.oit.doe.gov/inventions/about.html.

National Industrial Competitiveness Through Energy, Environment, and Economics (NICE3): NICE3 funds the first commercial demonstration of a new manufacturing or industrial process up to $525,000, with matching funds from nonfederal sources. High-energy-using and waste-generating industries of interest to NICE3 funding include agriculture, aluminum, chemicals, forest products, glass, metal casting, mining, petroleum, steel, and at a secondary level, buildings, transportation, and power.

CONTACT OIT Clearinghouse: Phone: 1-800-862-3086; Fax: (360) 586-8303; E-mail: clearinghouse@ee.doe.gov; Website: www.oit.doe.gov/nice3/about.shtml.

Rebuild America is a national forum and network of public-private partnerships that work to make their communities more energy efficient by sharing information on downtown revitalization, building renovation, new construction, renewable technologies, green buildings, city lighting, and alternative fuel vehicles. Civic improvements may include making schools, homes, workplaces, recreation centers, and other public buildings more energy efficient and friendly to renewable energy. Rebuild America also runs the Energy-Smart Schools program that focuses on revolutionizing the way American schools are designed and built and on energy education.

WEBSITE www.rebuild.org/aboutus/.

State Energy Program (SEP) provides funds to states to design and implement energy efficient and renewable energy programs. Created by Congress in 1996 by combining two existing programs—the State Energy Conservation Program (SECP) and the Institutional Conservation Program (ICP), the old SECP provided funding to states for energy efficiency and renewable energy projects. ICP had provided schools and hospitals with technical analysis of their buildings, offering potential savings from proposed energy conservation improvements.

The Energy Policy Act of 1992 (EPAct) expanded states' roles in regulating energy industries, promoting new energy technologies, developing policy, and deploying technology. SEP takes it all further and gives states responsibility for developing clean energy technology through SEP special projects and gives states more flexibility.

Tribal Energy Activities: The Tribal Energy Program gives financial aid to tribes for feasibility studies, installation of sustainable renewable energy installations on tribal lands, tribal energy self-sufficiency, and employment and economic development on tribal lands.

Title XXVI of the Energy Policy Act of 1992 enabled the Department of Energy to help Indian tribes pursue energy self-sufficiency and to promote development of energy industries on tribal lands of Indians or Alaskan Natives.

In 1994 President Bill Clinton met with tribal leaders and signed a presidential memorandum reaffirming the federal government's commitment to operate within a government-to-government relationship with federally recognized American Indian and Alaska Native tribes. In 1996 President Clinton signed an executive order on sacred sites (Executive Order 13007) directing federal agencies to allow access by Indian religious practitioners to, and ceremonial use of, Indian sacred sites. Clinton also signed the Tribal Colleges and Universities Executive Order (Executive Order 13021) to expand federal assistance for Indian institutions of higher education, promote tribal sovereignty and individual achievement, and advance national education goals and federal policy in Indian education. Subsequently, tribal colleges received grants to conduct feasibility studies to show viability of installing renewable energy technologies on tribal college and university sites and introduce renewable energy courses into the curricula.

Under EPAct (1999), DOE funded eight renewable power systems on reservations or other tribally owned lands, using solar and wind resources. Tribes have installed solar electric (photovoltaic), solar hot water heating systems, and wind turbines, with a spin-off benefit of employment, potential energy self-sufficiency, and potential sales to other markets.

Title XXVI Indian Energy Resource Projects in the late 1990s include: *Atka IRA Council* hydropower feasibility study and preliminary facility design; *Blackfeet Tribe* small-scale wind turbine demonstration project; *Cape Fox Corporation* licensed for a hydroelectric power project on the Upper and Lower Mahoney Lakes; *Crow Indian Tribe* feasibility study for coal-fired cogeneration plant; *Fort Peck Tribes* feasibility study for wind energy project at the Fort Peck Tribes Reservation; *Haida Corporation* feasibility study and application for license for proposed water power project, known as the Reynolds Creek Hydroelectric Project; *Hoopa Valley Tribe* energy efficient community swimming pool and energy efficient youth center; *Hualapai Tribe* feasibility study on photovoltaic pumping system and water pipeline; *Jicarilla Apache Tribe* study to create a Jacarilla

Apache Tribe hydroelectric facility at the Heron Dam Site; *Lower Brule Sioux Tribe* feasibility study on renewable energy products; *Manzanita Band of Mission Indians'* Manzanita Wind Energy Office & Education Project; *Mohegan Tribe of Connecticut* energy efficiency and feasibility study; *Nambe Pueblo* feasibility study of a 1 megawatt solar electric generating facility on the Nambe Pueblo; *Native Village of Chignik Lagoon* Village Power Energy Efficiency Study; *Nez Perce Tribe* biodiesel pilot project; *Oneida Housing Authority* energy efficient home improvement program; *Pueblo of Jemez* wind study; *Pueblo of Laguna* feasibility study of photovoltaic module and system production; *Pueblo of Picuris* multipurpose community center "Tol-Pit-Tah," The Sun Center; *Pueblo of Zuni* solar water pumping feasibility study; *Spirit Lake Sioux* wind energy project for the Spirit Lake Sioux tribe on the Fort Totten Reservation; *Standing Rock Sioux Nation* electric energy supply integrated resource plan; *Turtle Mountain Band of Chippewa Indians* wind resource assessment; *Ute Mountain Ute Tribe* solar water pumping demonstration project; and the *White Mountain Apache Tribe* feasibility study on the potential for biomass energy use.

CONTACT Address: Office of Power Technologies, U.S. Department of Energy, Forrestal Building, 5H-021, 1000 Independence Avenue SW, Washington, DC 20585; Phone: (202) 586-0759; Fax: (202) 586-1605; Website: www.eren.doe.gov/power/tech_access/tribalenergy. Golden Field Office: 1617 Cole Boulevard, M/S 1734, Golden, CO 80401; Phone: (303) 275-4727; Fax: (303) 275-4753; Sandia National Laboratory, P.O. Box 5800, M/S 0753, Albuquerque, NM 87185; Phone: (505) 844-5418; Fax: (505) 844-6541.

Weatherization Assistance Program (Wx) advises residents of low-cost housing, including single-family homes, multiunit buildings, and manufactured homes, based on research done at the Oak Ridge National Laboratory (ORNL).

Whole-house weatherization looks at the whole house as an energy-consuming entity, as opposed to looking at individual parts of the home's energy system. Steps taken to improve energy consumption include energy assessment of the home, deciding what to do to improve the system, correcting and installing improvements, and then verification of the improvements. Improvements might include air and moisture leakage control such as applying caulking or weather-stripping; installing blower doors; making sure there is sufficient insulation in the walls; updating heating equipment, ventilating fans, ceiling fans, or whole house fans; adding insulation to water heaters; improving efficiency of lighting and electric appliances; and improving health effects of heating systems.

Intergovernmental Program, known as the Office of Environment, Safety and Health, works primarily to protect the environment and health and safety of workers at DOE, as well as of the public.

Office of Worker Advocacy provides help to former and current employees of DOE contractors with illnesses or physical problems resulting from work for DOE to get benefits through state workers' compensation programs. The office also provides worker advocates to serve as liaison with state workers' compensation officials, benefits administrators, physicians, union representatives, and others.

WEBSITE http://tis.eh.doe.gov/eshorg/eh12.htm.

Office of Price-Anderson Enforcement enforces DOE's mandated nuclear safety program, and investigates potential and alleged violations of safety requirements and some nuclear safety concerns brought to management's awareness by workers. Price-Anderson expects voluntary compliance and self-reporting by contractors to nuclear safety regulations.

WEBSITE http://tis.eh.doe.gov/eshorg/eh11.htm.

Office of Special Projects and Investigations performs special inspections of problems that affect several DOE sites and programs; investigates safety and health allegations; evaluates accidents and disseminates information on what was

learned from the incident; deploys and runs accident response teams; oversees startups and restarts of nuclear facilities; and reviews new environment, safety, and health efforts to improve inspections and standards.

WEBSITE http://tis.eh.doe.gov/eshorg/eh21.htm.

Office of Environment, Safety and Health Programs, headed by an assistant secretary, evaluates environment, safety, and health programs throughout DOE to facilitate improvement. ES&H's studies include construction, operation, deactivation, decontamination, decommissioning, and environmental restoration of facilities.

WEBSITE http://tis.eh.doe.gov/eshorg/eh22.htm.

Office of Authorization Bases Oversight conducts independent technical reviews to ensure protection of the public's and workers' health and safety and that of the environment in the use of nuclear and other hazardous materials at DOE nuclear sites.

WEBSITE http://tis.eh.doe.gov/eshorg/eh23.htm.

OFFICE OF ENVIRONMENT, SAFETY AND HEALTH

The Office of Environment, Safety and Health, directed by an assistant secretary, serves safety and health needs in various departments, particularly regarding nuclear accidents and injuries.

WEBSITE http://tis.eh.doe.gov/portal/strategic_plan/sec2.htm.

OFFICE OF ENVIRONMENTAL MANAGEMENT

The Office of Environmental Management, run by an assistant secretary, cleans up and manages waste from more than 130 nuclear sites in the

United States, including former nuclear weapons production facilities, research labs, uranium milling sites, older manufacturing sites, and other secret sites as ordered by Congress. Nuclear Waste Fund activities are managed by the Office of Civilian Radioactive Waste Management.

WEBSITE www.em.doe.gov/.

FOSSIL ENERGY OFFICE

The Fossil Energy Office consists of about 1,000 scientists, engineers, technicians, and administrators, directed by an assistant secretary, who conduct research and development in fuel sources found in the ground and which develop from fossil decomposition. The organization has field offices in Morgantown, West Virginia; Pittsburgh, Pennsylvania; Tulsa, Oklahoma; New Orleans, Louisiana; and Casper, Wyoming.

WEBSITE www.fe.doe.gov/organization/.

Electric Power Research and Development: Research on electric power falls into the following categories. *Central Power Systems* research focuses on advanced gas turbine systems; innovations for existing plants; low emission boiler systems; fluidized bed coal combustion; gasification technologies; and indirect fired cycles. *Distributed Generation* researches fuel cell technology; distributed generation turbine systems; and fuel cell/turbine hybrid systems. *Greenhouse Gas Control* works on carbon sequestration. *Advanced Research* efforts go into materials research, computational energy sciences, biopressing, coal utilization science, coal research at universities, and research at historically black colleges and universities.

Oil and Natural Gas Research and Development works to discover new technologies to keep existing oil and gas fields pumping, to find new fields with the least environmental disturbance, and to deliver cleaner fuels.

To get the resources out of the ground, this office tries to create or support creation of new drilling techniques, diagnostics and imaging,

reservoir efficiency processes, reservoir life extension, and methane hydrates. They also perform environmental research, try to improve the gas delivery infrastructure and storage, and explore offshore drilling technologies.

WEBSITE http://fossil.energy.gov/programs_oilgas.html.

Clean Fuels Research and Development seeks to develop new fuels resulting in cleaner air and get more miles per gallon. The new generation of liquid and solid fuels the office is exploring include ultra-clean transportation fuels; natural gas-to-liquids; solid fuels and feedstocks; and coal-based liquid fuels.

WEBSITE http://fossil.energy.gov/program_fuels.html.

Petroleum Reserves consist of crude oil stored in salt caverns that a president can release in emergencies, such as cutoffs of oil supplies from abroad. Home heating oil is also stored for emergencies in commercial tank farms in the northeastern United States. The nation also holds the Naval Petroleum Reserves left from the early 1900s, which are now being released to commercial developers and vendors.

WEBSITE http://fossil.energy.gov/program_reserves.html.

Electricity Regulation by the Fossil Energy's Coal & Power Office authorizes export of electricity and issues permits for construction, connection, operation, and maintenance of electricity transmission systems across U.S. borders. Among the office's objectives are economic and energy security, environmental improvements, country-specific studies of electric power systems, and ensuring availability of domestic electric power supply.

WEBSITE http://fossil.energy.gov/coal_power/elec_reg/ele_reg.htm.

Natural Gas Regulation Import Export Office keeps statistics on the North American natural gas and petroleum trade, finds new export business opportunities for U.S. energy companies, and works to make U.S. energy competitive in foreign markets.

CONTACT To fax an application to import or export natural gas, fax it to (202) 586-6050 or (202) 586-4062. Phone: (202) 586-9478; Website: http://fossil.energy.gov/oil_gas/im_ex/gasimex.htm.

OFFICE OF NUCLEAR ENERGY, SCIENCE & TECHNOLOGY

Under the direction of an assistant secretary, this office is responsible for research and development in the field of nuclear energy. Nuclear power provides about 20 percent of U.S. electricity, second only to coal, which produces 55 percent, with nuclear power plants in 32 states. Five states get more than 50 percent of their electricity from nuclear power. Nuclear energy does not produce air emissions, although occasional leakage or terrorist plots make nuclear plants potential major hazards.

The Atomic Energy Commission, formed in 1947, was the DOE's predecessor agency. The AEC was given the charge to develop nuclear energy technology, beginning with designing propulsion systems for navy vessels. The USS *Nautilus,* launched in 1954, represented the first practical use of nuclear power, and the USS *Sea Wolf* was the second.

The Atomic Energy Act was amended in 1954 to allow private ownership and operation of nuclear reactors, and the AEC set up a cooperative program to help the new industry, with the United States's first nuclear power plant built by Pittsburgh, Pennsylvania's, Duquesne Light Company and called Shippingport Station.

As fossil fuel development waned, nuclear science then focused on space reactors, radioisotope production, nuclear medicine, and new power reactors. Recession, energy conservation, and accidents at Three Mile Island and Chernobyl all contributed to the public's reduced interest in nuclear power.

In the early 2000s, the department continues research and development, as well as clean up of nuclear wastes left by nuclear weapons production and nuclear technology research. In 2002, the U.S. Senate voted to dispose of much of the nation's nuclear waste near Yucca Mountain, Nevada.

CONTACT Address: U.S. Department of Energy, Office of Nuclear Energy, Science and Technology, NE-80, 19901 Germantown Road, Germantown, MD 20874-1290 Phone: (202) 586-5000 (through Department of Energy).

AREA, FIELD, AND OPERATIONS OFFICES

Operations Offices

ALBUQUERQUE OPERATIONS OFFICE: Rooted in the Manhattan Project, Albuquerque Operations was established by the Atomic Energy Commission in 1956. It now oversees maintenance of the nation's nuclear weapons stockpile, works to improve the environmental quality of the site's operations, as well as to develop new security and defense devices.

CONTACT Address: Albuquerque Operations Office, P.O. Box 5400, Albuquerque, NM 87185-5400; Phone: (505) 845-0011; Website: www.doeal.gov/.

CHICAGO OPERATIONS OFFICE: Oversees five government-owned and contractor-operated national laboratories, and two government-owned, and-operated labs in New York, New Jersey, Iowa, Illinois, and Idaho.

CONTACT Address: Chicago Operations Office, University of Illinois, Chicago, IL 60637; Phone: (630) 242-2018; Fax: (630) 252-9473; Website: www.ch.doe.gov/.

IDAHO OPERATIONS OFFICE: Established in 1949 as the National Reactor Testing Station, the Idaho Operations Office oversees operations of the Idaho National Engineering and Environmental Laboratory (INEEL), which conducts nuclear, energy, environmental, and technology research, and builds experimental nuclear reactors. One local controversy includes public concern about treatment and removal of spent fuel and old nuclear waste.

CONTACT Address: INEEL Research Center, 2351 N. Boulevard, P.O. Box 1625, Idaho Falls, ID 83415; Phone: (208) 526-7300; Website: www.id.doe.gov/.

NEVADA OPERATIONS OFFICE: Conducts open air nuclear weapons tests and houses spent nuclear fuel and residue from all over the country. Located near Mercury, Nevada, 75 miles northwest of Las Vegas.

CONTACT Address: 232 Energy Way, P.O. Box 98518, Las Vegas, NV 89193-8518; Phone: (702) 295-1212; Website: www.nv.doe.gov/.

OAKLAND OPERATIONS OFFICE: Oversees nuclear and environmental research activities at nearby Lawrence Berkeley Laboratory and Lawrence Livermore Laboratory.

CONTACT Address: 1301 Clay Street, Oakland, CA 94612-5208; Phone: (510) 637-1762; Website: www.oak.doe.gov/.

OAK RIDGE OPERATIONS OFFICE: Oversees Oak Ridge Y-12 National Security Complex managed by Bechtel Corporation's BWXT Y-12 to make and stockpile nuclear weapons. Oak Ridge also includes The Oak Ridge Institute for Science and Education, The American Museum of Science and Energy, and The Thomas Jefferson National Accelerator Facility.

CONTACT Address: P.O. Box 2009, Oak Ridge, TN 37831-8245; Phone: (865) 574-1000; Website: www.y12.doe.gov; www.oakridge.doe.gov/.

OHIO FIELD OFFICE: Oversees clean up of 50 years of nuclear weapons production and uranium use and waste, and operates the Oak Ridge National Laboratory on the Oak Ridge Reservation, the Y-12 National Security Complex, the

East Tennessee Technology Park, the Thomas Jefferson National Accelerator Facility, the Newport News, Virginia, nuclear physics research center, and uranium facilities in Paducah, Kentucky, Portsmouth, Ohio, and at the Weldon Spring Site near St. Louis, Missouri.

CONTACT Address: 200 Administrative Road, Oak Ridge, TN 37831; Phone: (865) 576-0885; Fax: (865) 576-1665.

RICHLAND OPERATIONS OFFICE: Works to clean up nuclear weapons testing waste at the Hanford nuclear site in eastern Washington.

CONTACT Address: 2890 Horn Rapids Road, Richland, WA 99352; Phone: (509) 372-3143; Website: www.hanford.gov/.

SAVANNAH RIVER OPERATIONS OFFICE: Stockpiles nuclear weapons 12 miles south of Aiken, South Carolina, and 25 miles southeast of Augusta, Georgia, manages nuclear materials and weapons, and works to dispose of its radioactive wastes safely.

CONTACT Address: Building 737-A, Drawer E, Aiken, SC 29802; Phone: (803) 725-2472; Website: http://sro.srs.gov/.

Field and Project Offices

ALBANY RESEARCH CENTER: Established in 1942 as part of the U.S. Bureau of Mines at then vacant Albany College in Albany, Oregon, the Albany Research Center produced the first zirconium, and eventually titanium. Zirconium was used in the reactor of the *Nautilus,* the United States' first nuclear submarine. The Albany Research Center is now part of the Office of Fossil Energy of DOE.

CONTACT Address: Albany Research Center, 1450 Queen Avenue SW, Albany, OR 97321-2198; Phone: (541) 967-5892; Fax: (541) 967-5936; Website: www.alrc.doe.gov.

CARLSBAD FIELD OFFICE: Carlsbad's Waste Isolation Pilot Plant (WIPP) works to clean up transuranic (uranium) materials and radioactive waste from nuclear weapons production. The repository for these materials is 2,150 feet underground in a 2,000-foot-thick salt formation in the Chihuahuan Desert of southeastern New Mexico.

CONTACT Address: 4021 National Parks Highway, Carlsbad, NM 88221; Phone: (800) 336-9477; Website: www.wipp.carlsbad.nm.us/index.htm.

GOLDEN FIELD OFFICE: Works with commercial partners researching photovoltaics (solar cells), wind energy, biomass, hydrogen, superconductivity, and geothermal energy.

CONTACT Address: 1617 Cole Boulevard, Golden, CO 80401; Phone: (303) 275-4700; Fax: (303) 275-4788; Website: www.golden.doe.gov/.

NATIONAL PETROLEUM TECHNOLOGY OFFICE: Works to increase domestic oil production with oil companies, universities, and national laboratories.

CONTACT Address: One West Third Street, Suite 1400, Tulsa, OK 74103-3519; Phone: (918) 699-2000; Fax: (918) 699-2005; Website: www.npto.doe.gov/. Other offices in Pittsburgh, Pennsylvania, and Morgantown, West Virginia.

RIVER PROTECTION OFFICE: Established in 1998, RPO works to remove, treat, and bury nuclear waste at the Hanford nuclear site near Richland, Washington, and clean up past and current damage to the Columbia River. Hanford stores 60 percent of the United States's radioactive waste in deteriorating old tanks.

CONTACT Address: 2440 Stevens Drive, P.O. Box 450, Richland, WA 99352; Phone: (509) 376-7411; Website: www.handford.gov/orp/.

ROCKY FLATS FIELD OFFICE (ROCKY FLATS ENVIRONMENTAL TECHNOLOGY SITE): Oversees clean up of nuclear and chemical contamination from the former nuclear weapons production facility 16 miles northwest of Denver, Colorado. More information at Front Range Community College, Westminster, CO 80031.

CONTACT Phone: (303) 966-7000; Website: www.rfets.gov/ and www.rf.doe.gov/.

STRATEGIC PETROLEUM RESERVE OFFICE: Oversees crude oil storage in 50 huge salt caverns holding up to 30 million barrels of oil, to be released by the president if necessary. These salt deposits underlie most of Texas's and Louisiana's coastline. Strategic Petroleum Reserves are located at Bryan Mound and Big Hill, Texas, and at West Hackberry and Bayou Choctaw, Louisiana. From these sites, strategic reserve oil can be distributed through pipelines, barges, and ships to refineries throughout the country.

CONTACT Address: Office of Fossil Energy, 1000 Independence Avenue SW, Washington, DC 20585; Website: www.spr.doe.gov/.

YUCCA MOUNTAIN SITE OFFICE: Over objections of Nevada residents, this site was approved by Congress in 2002 as the best place to store spent nuclear fuel and highly radioactive waste, the result of nuclear power generation and national defense nuclear weapon development. The materials remain highly radioactive for thousands of years and will be buried deep underground.

CONTACT Address: P.O. Box 364629, North Las Vegas, NV 89036-8629; Phone: (800) 225-6972; Fax: (702) 295-5222; Website: www.ymp.gov/.

National Laboratories & Technology Centers

ALBANY RESEARCH CENTER (See above, page 114.)

AMES NATIONAL LABORATORY: Founded in 1942 to produce purified uranium for the Manhattan Project, Ames partners with companies such as Du Pont, Ford, General Motors, Maytag, and American Superconductor at Iowa State University in Ames. Ames conducts research in chemical, materials, mathematical, engineering, environmental sciences, and physics. Its Materials Preparation Center creates and provides advanced materials to industry, university, and government research centers.

CONTACT Address: Ames Laboratory, Iowa State University, Ames, IA, 50011; Phone: (515) 294-2770; Website: www.external.ameslab.gov/.

ARGONNE NATIONAL LABORATORY (EAST, WEST): With roots in the Manhattan Project and the University of Chicago's Metallurgical Laboratory, where Enrico Fermi and friends created the first nuclear chain reaction on a squash court at the University of Chicago (Dec. 2, 1942), Argonne switched to developing nuclear reactors for peaceful purposes. Its scientists' research now ranges from the atomic nucleus and hazardous waste analysis, to global climate change, working with and for industry, universities, and other national labs. Argonne houses the Intense Pulsed Neutron Source and the Argonne Tandem Linear Accelerator System.

CONTACT Address: Argonne National Laboratory, East, University of Chicago, Chicago, IL and Idaho Falls, ID; Website: www.anl.gov/.

BROOKHAVEN NATIONAL LABORATORY: (See above, p. 104.)

ENVIRONMENTAL MEASUREMENTS LABORATORY (EML): Established in 1947 and formerly known as the Health and Safety Laboratory (HASL), EML is a government-operated lab based in the Manhattan Project. It measures radiation and radioactivity for environmental restoration, global nuclear nonproliferation, and national security.

CONTACT Address: 201 Varick Street, New York, NY 10014-4811; Website: www.eml.doe.gov/.

FERMI NATIONAL ACCELERATOR LABORATORY (FERMILAB): Originally called National Accelerator Laboratory when founded in 1967, the lab was renamed for 1938 Nobel Prize winner Enrico Fermi in 1974. Two major components of the Standard Model of Fundamental Particles and Forces were discovered here, and it is home to the four-mile-across Tevatron, the world's highest-energy particle accelerator, 45 miles west of Chicago.

CONTACT Address: Pine Street, Batavia, IL; Phone: (630) 840-3351; Fax: (630) 840-8780; Website: www.fnal.gov/.

IDAHO NATIONAL ENGINEERING LABORATORY (INEEL): Run by Bechtel BWXT Idaho, LLC, INEEL engages in environmental nuclear and hazardous waste clean up of its one-time world's largest concentration of nuclear reactors. INEEL is the leading nuclear and radiological research lab and researches fossil energy, energy efficiency, and building technologies.

CONTACT Address: 2525 North Fremont, Idaho Falls, ID 83415; Phone: (208) 526-0075; Website: www.inel.gov/.

LAWRENCE BERKELEY LABORATORY: (See above, pp. 95, 104.)

LAWRENCE LIVERMORE LABORATORY: (See above, p. 95.)

LOS ALAMOS NATIONAL LABORATORY: (See above, p. 95.)

NATIONAL ENERGY TECHNOLOGY LABORATORY (NETL): Having absorbed the National Petroleum Technology Office, federally run NETL develops advanced technologies to enhance exploration of fossil energy resources including coal, natural gas, and domestic oil while partnering with industry, academia, and other governmental agencies. NETL also develops environmental technologies important to the clean up of DOE's weapons complex.

CONTACT Address: 626 Cochrans Mill Road, P.O. Box 10940; Phone: (800) 553-7681 or (412) 386-6000; Fax: (412) 386-4604; and 3610 Collins Ferry Road, P.O. Box 880, Morgantown, WV 26507-0880; Phone: (800) 553-7681 or (304) 285-4764; Fax: (304) 285-4403; Website: www.netl.doe.gov/. National Petroleum Technology Office, One West Third Street, Suite 1400, Tulsa, OK 74103-3519; Phone: (918) 699-2000; Fax: (918) 699-2005; Website: www.npto.doe.gov/.

NATIONAL RENEWABLE ENERGY LABORATORY (NREL):
Established by the Solar Energy Research Development and Demonstration Act of 1974, and originally called the Solar Energy Research Institute, NREL develops new renewable energy technologies. NREL is managed by the Midwest Research Institute, Battelle Memorial Institute, and Bechtel National, Inc. Areas of endeavor include research and development of solar energy, photovoltaics, energy efficiency for buildings, alternative fuels, and wind sources.

CONTACT Address: 15013 Denver West Parkway, Golden, CO 80401-3393; Phone: (303) 384-6565; Fax: (303) 384-6568; Website: www.nrel.gov/.

NEW BRUNSWICK LABORATORY:
Functions as the U.S. government's Nuclear Materials Measurements and Reference Materials Laboratory and the National Certifying Authority of nuclear reference materials. It measures quantities and suggests safeguard measures for nuclear materials at federal labs. The New Brunswick Lab is not in New Brunswick. It is located in the Argonne National Laboratory enclave 25 miles southwest of Chicago, Illinois.

CONTACT Address: 9800 S. Cass Avenue, Argonne, IL 60439-4802; Phone: (630) 252-9473; Website: www.ch.doe.gov/.

OAK RIDGE NATIONAL LABORATORY (ORNL):
Within the Oak Ridge complex are ORNL, the Y-12 National Security Complex, the East Tennessee Technology Park, and the Graphite Reactor Museum. The American Museum of Science and Energy (an affiliate of the Smithsonian), 300 South Tulane Avenue, in downtown Oak Ridge, holds the history and memorabilia of the World War II Manhattan Project. Visitors are cautioned about "several radiological areas."

CONTACT Address: One Bethal Valley Road, P.O. Box 2008, Oak Ridge, TN 37831; Phone: (865) 574-7199; Website: www.ornl.gov/.

PACIFIC NORTHWEST NATIONAL LABORATORY:
Works to eliminate environmental hazards, prevent pollution, and minimize waste produced by the Hanford (nuclear) Site north of the city of Richland, Washington. In 1964 Gordon Battelle received a contract from the Atomic Energy Commission to run Hanford Laboratories for the Hanford Site, as well as permission to research beyond Hanford's nuclear-related needs. Pacific Northwest developed vitrification, that is, turning hazardous waste and glass-forming materials into glass, as well as acoustic holography to view human internal organs, the first portable blood irradiator, and techniques for cleaning groundwater and soils, and is home to the William R. Wiley Environmental Molecular Sciences Laboratory.

CONTACT Address: 902 Battelle Boulevard or 790 6th Street, Richland, WA 99352; Phone: (509) 375-2927; Website: www.pnl.gov/.

PRINCETON PLASMA PHYSICS LABORATORY (PPPL):
Managed by Princeton University, PPPL focuses on fusion energy and plasma physics research. Begun at Princeton in 1951 under the code name of Project Matterhorn, PPPL has worked on controlled fusion, magnetic fusion research, and magnetic confinement experiments using the tokamak approach, resulting in the Tokamak Fusion Test Reactor (TFTR).

CONTACT Address: P.O. Box 451, Princeton, NJ 08543-0451; Phone: (609) 243-2750; Fax: (609) 243-2751; Website: www.pppl.gov/.

RADIOLOGICAL AND ENVIRONMENTAL SCIENCES LABORATORY (RESL):
Research focuses on analytical chemistry, radiation protection, and as a reference laboratory for many other programs.

CONTACT Address: Idaho Operations Office, MS 4149, 850 Energy Drive, Idaho Falls, ID

83401-1562; Phone: (208) 526-2765 or (208) 526-2143; Fax: (208) 526-2548; Website: www.inel.gov/resl/.

SANDIA NATIONAL LABORATORIES: Operated by Lockheed Martin for the DOE's National Nuclear Security Administration, Sandia works to ensure safety of the U.S. nuclear weapons stockpile and to assure that it can "support the United States' deterrence policy"; reduce proliferation of weapons of mass destruction, nuclear accidents, and potential environmental damage; protect energy and other critical infrastructures, and "address new threats to national security."

CONTACT Address: 1515 Eubank Street SE, Albuquerque, NM 87185; Phone: (505) 845-0011 and 7011 East Avenue, Livermore, CA 94551-0969; Phone: (505) 845-0011; Website: www.sandia.gov/.

SAVANNAH RIVER ECOLOGY LABORATORY (SREL): Founded in 1951 by Dr. Eugene P. Odum of the University of Georgia, the lab evaluates ecological effects of the Savannah River (nuclear) Site.

CONTACT Address: Savannah River Ecology Laboratory, Savannah River Site, Building 737-A, Drawer E, Aiken, SC 29802; Phone: (803) 725-2472; Fax: (803) 725-3309; Website: www. uga.edu/~srel/SREL_info.htm.

THOMAS JEFFERSON NATIONAL ACCELERATOR LAB (JLAB): Managed by a 59-university consortium called the Southeastern Universities Research Association (SURA), JLab probes the nucleus of the atom to learn more about the quark structure of the matter with the world's most powerful microscope. Its accelerator tunnel is 25 feet below the Earth's surface on an old seabed called the Yorktown Formation and uses 2,200 magnets.

CONTACT Address: 12000 Jefferson Avenue, Newport News, VA 23606; Phone: (757) 269-7100; Fax: (757) 269-7363; Website: www.jlab.org/.

POWER MARKETING ADMINISTRATIONS

BONNEVILLE POWER ADMINISTRATION: A power wholesaler that sells power generated by 31 federally owned dams and one nuclear power plant in the Pacific Northwest of the United States, including Washington, Oregon, Idaho, and Montana west of the Continental Divide. BPA works with Native tribes, other federal agencies, and states on fish and wildlife programs, as well as salmon recovery efforts in the Columbia River Basin.

CONTACT Address: Executive Office-A, Bonneville Power Administration, P.O. Box 3621, Portland, OR 97208-3621; Website: www.bpa.gov/.

SOUTHEASTERN POWER ADMINISTRATION: Created in 1950 to carry out duties in the Flood Control Act of 1944, Southeastern markets electric power and energy generated at reservoirs operated by the U.S. Army Corps of Engineers in Alabama, Florida, Georgia, Kentucky, Mississippi, North Carolina, South Carolina, Tennessee, Virginia, West Virginia, and southern Illinois.

CONTACT Address: 1166 Athens Tech Road, Elberton, GA 30635-4578; Phone: (706) 213-3800; Fax: (706) 213-3884; Website: www.sepa.fed.us/.

SOUTHWESTERN POWER ADMINISTRATION: Established by the Flood Control Act of 1944, Southwestern markets hydroelectric power produced at 23 U.S Army Corps of Engineers multipurpose dams.

CONTACT Address: One West 3rd Street, Tulsa, OK 74103; Phone: (918) 595-6600; Fax: (918) 595-6656; Website: www.swpa.gov/.

WESTERN AREA POWER ADMINISTRATION: Markets and transmits wholesale hydroelectric power from 56 power plants operated by the Bureau of Reclamation, U.S. Army Corps of Engineers, and the International Boundary and Water Commission. Western also markets 24.3

percent of the power produced by the coal-fired Navajo Generating Station that the United States allowed to access. Customers include energy consumers in Arizona, California, Colorado, Iowa, Kansas, Minnesota, Montana, Nebraska, Nevada, New Mexico, North Dakota, South Dakota, Texas, Utah, and Wyoming.

CONTACT Address: P.O. Box 281213, Lakewood, CO 80228; Phone: (720) 962-7050; Fax: (720) 962-7059; Website: www.wapa.gov/.

SECRETARY OF ENERGY ADVISORY BOARD (SEAB): In 1990 the SEAB replaced the Energy Research Advisory Board (ERAB), which had existed since 1978 as the main advisory board to the Department of Energy. The board advises and provides information and recommendations to the secretary of energy on DOE's applied research activities, economic and national security policy, educational issues, and laboratories.

Members of SEAB serve pro bono for two-year terms and usually have expertise in the energy field, particularly related to research and development, energy, and national defense. Members have included two Nobel laureates, a Pulitzer Prize winner, and experts from universities, business, public and environmental groups, labor, and federal and state governmental agencies.

CONTACT Address: Office of the Secretary of Energy Advisory Board, U.S. Department of Energy, AB-1, 1000 Independence Avenue SW, Washington, DC; Phone: (202) 586-7092; Fax: (202) 586-6279.

DEPARTMENT OF HEALTH AND HUMAN SERVICES

GENERAL

The Department of Health and Human Services (HHS) works to protect the health of all Americans and provides essential human services, particularly to Americans who are least able to help themselves or pay for medical care. To achieve this goal, HHS offers more than 300 programs, including medical and social science research, prevention of infectious diseases, immunization services, efforts toward food and drug safety, health insurance for elderly, disabled, and low-income Americans, better maternal and infant health, the Head Start program for disadvantaged children, the fight against child abuse and domestic violence, treatment and prevention of substance abuse, the financing of home-delivered meals for seniors, and health services for Native Americans.

HHS's offices are headquartered in the Hubert H. Humphrey Building (1977), the first federal building dedicated to a living person. Hubert Humphrey (1911–78) was a Democrat who served as U.S. senator from Minnesota and as vice president of the United States. Many Public Health Service offices are located in the Parklawn Building in Rockville, Maryland. The National Institutes of Health does biomedical research in its 40-building campus in Bethesda, Maryland. The Centers for Disease Control is located in Atlanta, Georgia.

HISTORY

Varied steps taken throughout the early United States and its burgeoning government came together to constitute what is now the Department of Health and Human Services.

The first marine hospital, a forerunner of the Public Health Services, was established in 1798 by statute signed by President John Adams to take care of seafaring Americans. President Abraham Lincoln appointed chemist Charles M. Wetherill to serve in the then new Department of Agriculture. Wetherill's appointment led to the Bureau of Chemistry, a forerunner of the Food and Drug Administration, which Congress actually established with the Food and Drug Act of

1906, authorizing the government to monitor food purity and medicine safety.

Other significant dates in HHS's evolution include President Theodore Roosevelt's White House Conference urging creation of a Children's Bureau to fight exploitation of children. Congress passed the Social Security Act in 1935, and in 1939 federal functions in the fields of health, education, human services, and social insurance came together under the new Federal Security Agency. Forerunner of the Centers for Disease Control and Prevention, the Communicable Disease Center was established in 1946.

The Department of Health, Education and Welfare (HEW) was created on August 11, 1953, as a cabinet-level entity under President Dwight D. Eisenhower's administration, and the Department of Education Organization Act was signed into law by President Jimmy Carter in 1979, shifting the educational function to the new Department of Education as of October 17, 1979. Then on May 4, 1980, under President Carter, HEW became the Department of Health and Human Services (HHS).

MILESTONES

1955:   Salk polio vaccine licensed

1961:   First White House Conference on Aging under President John F. Kennedy

1962:   Migrant Health Act passed to provide support for clinics serving migrant agricultural workers, signed by President John F. Kennedy

1964:   First Surgeon General's Report on Smoking and Health released under President Lyndon B. Johnson

1965:   Medicare and Medicaid programs created; Older Americans Act enables HHS's Administration on Aging to create nutritional and social programs for seniors; Head Start Program created by President Lyndon B. Johnson

1966:   Under President Lyndon B. Johnson, U.S. Public Health Service leads International Smallpox Eradication program, with worldwide success accomplished in 1977. Establishment of Community Health Center and Migrant Health Center programs

1970:   The National Health Service Corps created

1971:   President Richard M. Nixon signs National Cancer Act into law

1975:   Under President Gerald R. Ford, Child Support Enforcement program established

1977:   During President Jimmy Carter's administration, the Health Care Financing Administration created to manage Medicare and Medicaid separately from the Social Security Administration

1980:   For the first time, states received federal funding for foster care and adoption assistance

1981:   In President Ronald Reagan's administration, AIDS (Acquired Immune Deficiency Syndrome) was identified in 1981

1984:   U.S. Public Health Service and French scientists identified the HIV virus; National Organ Transplantation Act was signed into law

1985:   A blood test to detect HIV was licensed

1988:   JOBS program created and federal money for child care support began; President Ronald Reagan signs McKinney Act into law to provide health care to the homeless (Reagan

Department of Health and Human Services

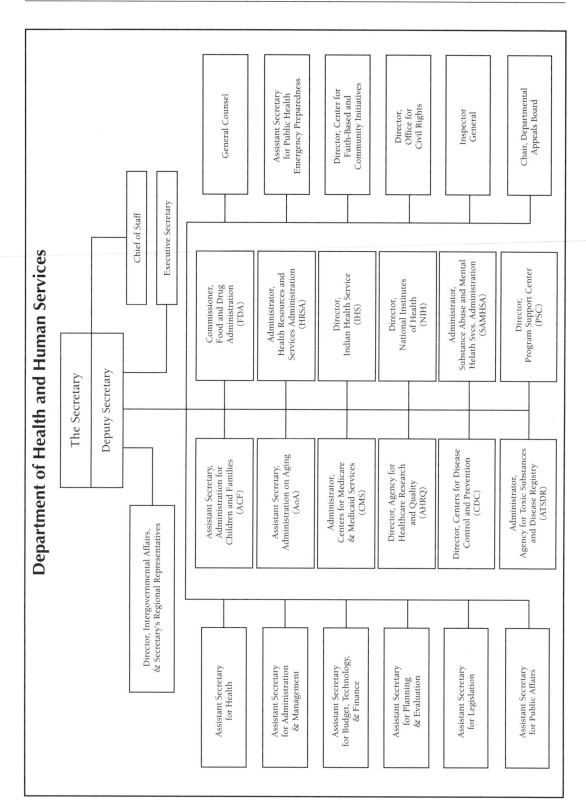

The Secretary

Deputy Secretary

Chief of Staff

Executive Secretary

General Counsel

Assistant Secretary for Public Health Emergency Preparedness

Director, Center for Faith-Based and Community Initiatives

Director, Office for Civil Rights

Inspector General

Chair, Departmental Appeals Board

Director, Intergovernmental Affairs, & Secretary's Regional Representatives

Commissioner, Food and Drug Administration (FDA)

Administrator, Health Resources and Services Administration (HRSA)

Director, Indian Health Service (IHS)

Director, National Institutes of Health (NIH)

Administrator, Substance Abuse and Mental Helath Svcs. Administration (SAMHSA)

Director, Program Support Center (PSC)

Assistant Secretary, Administration for Children and Families (ACF)

Assistant Secretary, Administration on Aging (AoA)

Administrator, Centers for Medicare & Medicaid Services (CMS)

Director, Agency for Healthcare Research and Quality (AHRQ)

Director, Centers for Disease Control and Prevention (CDC)

Administrator, Agency for Toxic Substances and Disease Registry (ATSDR)

Assistant Secretary for Health

Assistant Secretary for Administration & Management

Assistant Secretary for Budget, Technology, & Finance

Assistant Secretary for Planning & Evaluation

Assistant Secretary for Legislation

Assistant Secretary for Public Affairs

closed many halfway houses in California while governor)

1989:   Agency for Health Care Policy and Research created, now called Agency for Healthcare Research and Quality

1990:   President George H. W. Bush signed Nutrition Labeling and Education Act into law, the Human Genome Project was established, and the Ryan White Comprehensive AIDS Resource Emergency (CARE) Act began to provide financial support to communities for aid to AIDS patients

1993:   In President Bill Clinton's administration, Vaccines for Children Program was established, giving free immunizations to all children of low-income families

1994:   National Institutes of Health (NIH)–paid scientists discover genes inclined toward hereditary colon cancer and breast cancer, and some kidney cancer

1995:   Social Security Administration became an independent agency

1996:   President Bill Clinton signed welfare reform law, the Personal Responsibility and Work Opportunity Reconciliation Act

1998:   Clinton administration established the State Children's Health Insurance Program, and launched the Initiative to Eliminate Racial and Ethnic Disparities in Health

1999:   President Clinton signed the Ticket to Work and Work Incentives Improvement Act of 1999, allowing millions of Americans with disabilities to work without fear of losing their Medicare and Medicaid coverage, while modernizing the employment services

system for people with disabilities, and launched the Initiative on Combating Terrorism

2000:   First publication of human genome sequencing

2001:   Centers for Medicare and Medicaid Services established under President George W. Bush, replacing the Health Care Financing Administration; HHS responded to U.S.'s first bioterrorism attack via anthrax deliveries through the U.S. Mail

ORGANIZATION

The Department of Health and Human Services consists of 10 operating divisions and 12 major agencies, some of which duplicate divisions or agencies with the same name. Those entities include Office of the Secretary, Administration for Children and Families, Administration on Aging, Agency for Healthcare Research and Quality, Agency for Toxic Substances and Disease Registry, Centers for Disease Control and Prevention, Centers for Medicare and Medicaid Services, Food and Drug Administration, Health Resources and Services Administration, National Institutes of Health, Substance Abuse and Mental Health Services Administration, Indian Health Service, U.S. Public Health Service Corps, and a Program Support Center. Now an independent agency, the Social Security Administration was part of HHS until March 31, 1995.

The Library of Medicine offers medical information and bibliographic research through MEDLINE and TOXLINE

CONTACT Phone: (301) 496-6308; Website: www.nlm.nih.gov.

CENTRAL AND REGIONAL OFFICES

U.S. Department of Health and Human Services:
  Address: Hubert H. Humphrey Building, 200

Independence Avenue SW, Washington, DC 20201; Phone: (202) 619-0257; toll-free: 1-877-696-6775; Fax: (202) 690-7203; Website: www.hhs.gov/.

Region I (Connecticut, Maine, Massachusetts, New Hampshire, Rhode Island, Vermont): Address: John F. Kennedy Federal Building Government Center, Room 2100, Boston, MA 02203; Phone: (617) 565-1500; Fax: (617) 565-1491; Website: www.hhs.gov/.

Region II (New Jersey, New York, Puerto Rico, Virgin Islands): Address: Jacob K. Javits Federal Building, 26 Federal Plaza, Room 3835, New York, NY 10278; Phone: (212) 264-4600; Fax: (212) 264-3620; Website: www.hhs.gov/.

Region III (Delaware, District of Columbia, Maryland, Pennsylvania, Virginia, West Virginia): Address: Public Ledger Building, 150 South Independence Mall West, Suite 436, Philadelphia, PA 19106-3499; Phone: (215) 861-4633; Fax: (215) 861-4625; Website: www.hhs.gov/.

Region IV (Alabama, Florida, Georgia, Kentucky, Mississippi, North Carolina, South Carolina, Tennessee): Address: Atlanta Federal Center, 61 Forsyth Street, Room 5B95, Atlanta, GA 30303-8909; Phone: (404) 562-7888; Fax: (404) 562-7899; Website: www.hhs.gov/.

Region V (Illinois, Indiana, Michigan, Minnesota, Ohio, Wisconsin): Address: 233 North Michigan Avenue, Suite 1300, Chicago, IL 60601; Phone: (312) 353-5160; Fax: (312) 353-4144; Website: www.hhs.gov/.

Region VI (Arkansas, Louisiana, New Mexico, Oklahoma, Texas): Address: 1301 Young Street, Suite 1124, Dallas, TX 75202; Phone: (214) 767-3301; Fax: (214) 767-3617; Website: www.hhs.gov/.

Region VII (Iowa, Kansas, Missouri, Nebraska): Address: 601 East 12th Street, Room 210, Kansas City, MO 64106; Phone: (816) 426-2821; Fax: (816) 426-2178; Website: www.hhs.gov/.

Region VIII (Colorado, Montana, North Dakota, South Dakota, Utah, Wyoming): Address: 1961 Stout Street, Room 1076, Denver, CO 80294; Phone: (303) 844-3372; Fax: (303) 844-4545; Website: www.hhs.gov/.

Region IX (Arizona, California, Hawaii, Nevada, Guam, Pacific Islands of Commonwealth of the Northern Mariana Islands, Federated States of Micronesia, Guam, Marshall Islands, Republic of Palau, American Samoa): Address: Federal Office Building, Room 431, 50 United Nations Plaza, San Francisco, CA 94102; Phone: (415) 437-8500; Fax: (415) 437-8505; Website: www.hhs.gov/.

Region X (Alaska, Idaho, Oregon, Washington): Address: 2201 6th Avenue, Room 911F, Mail Stop RX-O, Seattle, WA 98121; Phone: (206) 615-2010; Fax: (206) 615-2087; Website: www.hhs.gov/.

OFFICE OF THE SECRETARY

The Office of the Secretary of Health and Human Services oversees and guides the entire department, but has specific administrative responsibility for the Office of Public Health and Science. The secretary is appointed by the president and approved by the Senate, as are a deputy secretary, several assistant secretaries, administrators, the Food and Drug Commissioner, and the surgeon general.

CONTACT Address: Office of Secretary of Health and Human Services, 200 Independence Avenue SW, Washington, DC 20201; Phone: (202) 690-7000; Website: www.hhs.gov/.

OFFICE OF PUBLIC HEALTH AND SCIENCE: The Office of Public Health and Science oversees the offices of Disease Prevention & Health Promotion; Emergency Preparedness; Global Health Affairs; HIV/AIDS Policy; Human Research Protections; Minority Health; Population Affairs; Research Integrity; Surgeon General; Women's Health; President's Council on Physical Fitness and Sports; and Regional Health Administrators.

CONTACT Address: 200 Independence Avenue SW, Room 716-G, Washington, DC 20201; Phone: (202) 690-7694; Website: www.osophs.dhhs. gov/ophs.

Office of Disease Prevention & Health Promotion (ODPHP): Works to improve disease prevention and communications within HHS and to the public. It offers several websites, links, and publications. On-line publications include *Healthy People 2010, Nutrition and Your Health: Dietary Guidelines for Americans,* and listings of health information centers and clearinghouses. ODPHP websites include healthfinder®, Healthy-People2010, National Health Information Center, www.health.gov, www.surgeongeneral. gov, and a gateway to U.S. state and local government health information.

CONTACT Address: Office of Disease Prevention and Health Promotion, Office of Public Health and Science, 200 Independence Avenue SW, Room 738G, Washington, DC 20201; Phone: (202) 401-295; Fax: (202) 205-9478; Website: http://odphp.osophs.dhhs.gov.

As the health part of the Federal Response Plan, and working with the Federal Emergency Management Agency (FEMA), the *Office of Emergency Preparedness* manages and coordinates federal health, medical, and health-related services and recovery in emergencies and federally declared disasters including natural disasters, technological disasters, major transportation accidents, and terrorism involving weapons of mass destruction, such as biological and nuclear weapons.

CONTACT Address: Office of Emergency Preparedness, 200 Independence Avenue SW, Room 716-G, Washington, DC 20201; Phone: (202) 690-7694; Website: www.ndms.dhhs.gov/. Regional

Offices: Region I: John F. Kennedy Federal Building, Government Center, Room 2126, Boston, MA 02203; Phone: (617) 565-1693; Region II: Jacob Javits Federal Building, 26 Federal Plaza, Room 3835, New York, NY 10278; Phone: (212) 264-2802; Region III: 150 South Independence Mall West, Suite 436, Public Ledger Building, Philadelphia, PA 19106-3199; Phone: (212) 861-4635; Website: hhs.gov/region3; Region IV: Sam Nunn Atlanta Federal Center, 61 Forsyth Street SW, Room 5398, Atlanta, GA 30303-8909; Phone: (404) 562-7911; Website: www.hhs.gov /region4; Region V: 233 N. Michigan Avenue, Room 1300, Chicago, IL 60601; Phone: (312) 353-4515; Website: www.hhs.gov/region5; Region VI: 1301 Yount Street, Suite 1124, Dallas, TX 75202; Phone: (214) 767-3843; Website: www.hhs.gov/region6; Region VII: 601 East 12th Street, Room 210, Kansas City, MO 64106; Phone: (816) 426-2829; Website: www.hhs.gov/ region7; Region VIII: 1961 Stout Street, Room 498; Denver, CO 80294-3538; Phone: (303) 235-4800; Website: www.hhs.gov/region8; Region IX: 50 United Nations Plaza, Room 329, San Francisco, CA 94102; Phone: (415) 437-8071, 8516, and 8386; Website: www.hhs.gov/region9; Region X: 2201 Sixth Avenue, Mail Stop RX-29, Seattle, WA 98121-1831; Phone: (206) 762-0889; Website: www.hhs.gov/region10.

Office of Global Health Affairs: Deals with health risks moved around the world to the United States in international commerce such as contaminated food, biological and chemical terrorism threats, and toxic substances. Focusing primarily on Americans' health, the Office of Global Affairs looks at world health problems in terms of how they might affect Americans and American business, and sees that "healthy populations and healthy economies are vital for a healthy world economy and strong markets." Global Health also says that smallpox eradication and tobacco control are two examples of their work, while the United States worries about smallpox terrorism and the U.S. government subsidizes tobacco farmers.

CONTACT Address: Office of Global Health Affairs, 5600 Fishers Lane, Rockville, MD 20857; Director, Phone: (301) 443-1774; Fax: (301) 443-6288; Multilateral Affairs, Phone: (301) 443-1774; Fax: (301) 443-6288; African Affairs, Phone: (301) 443-9942; Fax: (301) 443-8382; The Americas, Phone: (301) 443-4010; Fax: (301) 443-4549; Middle East Affairs, Phone: (301) 443-4010; Fax: (301) 443-4549; Asia and the Pacific, Phone: (301) 443-1410; Fax: (301) 443-1397; Europe and New Independent States, Phone: (301) 443-9624; Fax: (301) 443-0742; Refugee Health Affairs, Phone: (301) 443-1774; Fax: (301) 443-6288; Website: www.global-health.gov.

Office of HIV/AIDS Policy: Works to prevent further spread of HIV/AIDS through education, HIV testing, prevention through promotion of responsible sexual behavior, and quality health care. The office promotes coordination and collaboration among HHS health agencies on HIV/AIDS activities to develop efficiency and progress, surveillance and prevention, and care and treatment.

CONTACT Address: Office of HIV/AIDS Policy, 200 Independence Avenue, Room 736E, Washington, DC 20201; Phone: (202) 690-5560; Fax: (202) 690-7560; Website: www.osophs.ddha.gov/ophs/hivaids.htm.

Office of Human Research Protections: Provides access to all regulations covering protections of infant to elderly humans used in research for any purpose and aspires to enforce compliance with those regulations.

CONTACT Address: Office of Health Research Protection, 1101 Wootton Parkway, Suite 200, Rockville, MD 20852; Phone: (301) 496-7006; Fax: (301) 402-0527; Website: www.ohrp.osophs.dhhs.gov.

Office of Minority Health: Works within HHS and with other federal, state, and local agencies on public health issues affecting American Indians, Alaska Natives, Asian Americans, Native Hawaiians and other Pacific Islanders, African American/Blacks, and Hispanics/Latinos. Its main goal is to eliminate disparities in health care and results for racial and ethnic minorities. OMH operates the Minority Community Health Coalition Demonstration Program and other programs on HIV/AIDS under 18 cooperative agreements. Services offered include referrals, publications, reference information, resource persons' network, the *Closing the Gap* print and online newsletter covering health topics, and federal, state, and community efforts and resources.

CONTACT Address: OMH Resource Center, P.O. Box 37337, Washington, DC 20013-7337; Phones: 1-800-444-6472, TDD for hearing impaired: (301) 230-7199; Fax: (301) 230-7198; Website: www.omhrc.gov/OMH/. Regional Minority Health Consultants available at: Region 1: Government Center, John F. Kennedy Federal Building, Room 2126, Boston, MA 02203; Phone: (617) 565-1064; Fax: (617) 565-4365; Website: www.hhs.gov/region1. Region II: Jacob Javits Federal Building, 26 Federal Plaza, Room 3835, New York, NY 10278; Phone: (212) 264-2127; Fax: (212) 264-1324; Website: www.hhs.gov/region2. Region III: 150 S. Independence Mall West, Suite 436, P.O. Box 13716, Mail Stop 14, Philadelphia, PA 19106-3499; Phone: (215) 861-4618; Fax: (215) 861-4623; Website: www.hhs.gov/region3. Region IV: Sam Nunn Atlanta Federal Center, 61 Forsyth Street SW, Suite 5B-95, Atlanta, GA 30303-8909; Phone: (404) 562-7905; Fax: (404) 562-7899; Website: www.hhs.gov/region4. Region V: 233 North Michigan Avenue, Suite 1300, Chicago, IL 60601-5519; Phone: (312) 353-1386; Fax: (312) 353-7800/1710; Website: www.hhs.gov/region5. Region VI: 1301 Young Street, Suite 1124, Dallas, TX 75202; Phone: (214) 767-8433; Fax: (214) 767-3209; Website: www.hhs.gov/region6. Region VII: 601 East 12th Street, Room 210, Kansas City, MO 64106; Phone: (816) 426-3291; Fax: (816) 426-2178; Website: www.hhs.gov/region7. Region VIII: 1961 Sout Street, Room 498, Denver, CO 80294-3538; Phone: (303) 844-7858; Fax: (303)

844-2019; Website: www.hhs.gov/region8. Region IX: 50 United Nations Plaza, Room 329, San Francisco, CA 94102; Phone: (415) 437-8124; Fax: (415) 437-8069; Website: www.hhs.gov/region9. Region X: 2201 Sixth Avenue, Mail Stop RX-20, Seattle, WA 98121-1831; Phone: (206) 615-2475; Fax: (206) 615-2481; Website: www.hhs.gov/region10.

Office of Population Affairs (OPA): Includes the Title X Family Planning Program and the Title XX Adolescent Family Life Program, both authorized by the Public Health Service Act (1970). The Family Planning Program is within the Office of Family Planning.

The Title X Family Planning Program is the only federal program devoted solely to family planning and reproductive health care, although what it does varies according to the beliefs of a president. The program is supposed to provide access to contraceptives and information on contraceptives and their use to anyone who wants it, with special focus on low-income persons. It also offers other family planning alternatives on a voluntary and confidential basis through 4,600 clinics nationwide.

Patient education and counseling, breast and pelvic examinations, cervical cancer, STD and HIV screenings, and pregnancy diagnosis and counseling are also supposed to be available at these clinics. Title X clinics provide the only health care, health education, and reproductive and pregnancy education available to some people.

Title X family planning services are provided through 85 public and private organizations and a network of community and independent clinics including state and local health departments, hospitals (some Catholic hospitals do not participate), university health centers, Planned Parenthood, and public and nonprofit agencies. At the time of President George W. Bush's inauguration in 2001, nearly 75 percent of U.S. counties offered at least one provider of contraceptive services funded by Title X. For millions of uninsured, under-insured, and low-income women,

Title X clinics provide no-cost or reduced-cost contraceptive services, devices, drugs, and education, especially racial and ethnic minorities, and may be their entry point into the health care system. Title X services help couples plan and space pregnancies and births with the goal of healthy births, healthy starts for infants, and healthy mothers, as well as help people avoid sexually transmitted diseases including HIV.

Office of Adolescent Pregnancy Programs (OAPP) within the Office of Population Affairs was created in 1981 as Title XX of the Public Health Service Act. OAPP's Adolescent Family Life (AFL) Demonstration and Research Program now works to promote abstinence from or postponement of sexual activity among adolescents and provides comprehensive health care, education, and social services to pregnant and parenting adolescents. AFL also develops and promotes interventions with pregnant and parenting teens, their infants, male partners, and family members. AFL funds grants for research on the causes and consequences of adolescent premarital sexual relations, adolescent pregnancy, and parenting. AFL supports about 100 demonstration projects across the country, including 55 abstinence education programs and 45 care programs.

CONTACT Address: Office of Population Affairs, 4350 East West Highway, Suite 200 West, Bethesda, MD 20814; Phone: (301) 594-4000; Fax: (301) 594-5980; Office of Family Planning: Phone: (301) 594-4008; Office of Adolescent Pregnancy Programs: Phone: (301) 594-4004; Website: http://opa.osophs.dhhs.gov/.

Office of Research Integrity: Monitors integrity in biomedical and behavioral research at about 4,000 institutions worldwide. It develops ways to detect, investigate, and prevent research misconduct and promotes responsible research; relays misconduct findings to the assistant secretary of health; and administers programs to maintain institutional assurances, respond to allegations of retaliation against whistleblowers, and respond to requests under the Freedom of Information Act and Privacy Acts.

CONTACT Address: Office of Research Integrity, 5515 Security Lane, Suite 7000, Rockville, MD 20852; Phone: (301) 443-3400; Fax:(301) 594-0039; Website: www.ori.hhs.gov/.

Office of the Surgeon General: Derives from an 1798 act of Congress when it created the U.S. Marine Hospital Service, the predecessor of the U.S. Public Health Service, now Health and Human Services. Dr. John Woodworth became the first supervising surgeon of the Marine Hospital System in 1871, and Congress created the Commissioned Corps on January 4, 1889, to establish a mobile medical corps to meet military medical needs. Until 1968 the surgeon general directed PHS, and the surgeon general reported to the secretary of health, education, and welfare. In 1977 the positions of assistant secretary of health and surgeon general were combined, and then separated again in 1981. In 1987, when the Office of Surgeon General was reestablished, the surgeon general again became responsible for the Commissioned Corps, which Surgeon General C. Everett Koop worked hard to revitalize. Koop sought out women and minorities, and now more than 6,000 officers are on active duty assigned to Public Health Service agencies, the Bureau of Prisons, U.S. Coast Guard, Environmental Protection Agency, Health Care Financing Administration, and the Commission on Mental Health of the District of Columbia.

The surgeon general is appointed by the president for a four-year term and holds the rank of vice admiral in the U.S. Public Health Service Commissioned Corps, a uniformed service parallel to the air force, army, marines, navy, Coast Guard, and NOAA Corps, which can be called upon in the event of a national health emergency. Responsibilities of the office include educating the public on health matters, advocating effective disease prevention, representing scientific health policy analysis to the president and the secretary of HHS, promoting departmental health initiatives such as tobacco hazards and HIV prevention efforts at home and abroad, and raising the level of public health practice.

CONTACT Address: Office of the Surgeon General, 5600 Fishers Lane, Room 18-66, Rockville, MD 20857; Phone: (301) 443-4000; Fax: (301) 443-3574; Website: www.surgeongeneral.gov.

Office of Women's Health (OWH): Works with government agencies, nonprofits, consumer groups, and health care professionals' organizations to improve women's health by directing, developing, stimulating, and coordinating research on women's health, health care services, and public and health professional education and training within HHS and with other government agencies. Established in 1991 to advance a comprehensive women's health agenda, OWH addresses health care prevention and service, research, public and health care professional education, and career advancement for women in health and scientific professions, with new emphasis on the millions of underserved American women, particularly those at special risk.

OWH addresses health needs of women of different ages, cultures, and races and ethnicities by bringing comprehensive and culturally appropriate prevention, diagnostic, and treatment services to women according to regional needs in high-priority health areas. OWH strives to develop and implement effective women's health policies at the highest levels of national, state, and local governments.

OWH programs include Girl and Adolescent Health, Minority Women's Health, breast cancer, gastrointestinal health, environmental health, HIV/AIDs in Women, violence against women, reproductive health, older women's health, National Town Hall on Menopause, A Breath of Fresh Air to create independence from smoking, and Powerful Girls Have Powerful Bones.

CONTACT Address: Office on Women's Health, 200 Independence Avenue SW, Room 730B,

Washington, DC 20201; Phone: (202) 690-7650; Fax: (202) 205-2631; Website: www.4woman.gov/.

Regional offices: Region I: John F. Kennedy Federal Building, Room 2126, Boston, MA 02203; Phone: (617) 565-1071; Fax: (617) 565-4265; Website: www.4women.gov/owh/reg/1. Region II: 26 Federal Plaza, Room 3835, New York, NY 10278; Phone: (212) 264-4628; Fax: (212) 264-1324; Website: www.4women.gov/owh/reg/2. Region III: 150 South Independence Mall West, Suite 436, Philadelphia, PA 19106-3499; Phone: (215) 861-4637; Fax: (215) 861-4623; Website: www.4women.gov/owh/reg/3. Region IV: Sam Nunn Atlanta Federal Center, 61 Forsyth Street SW, 5 B95, Atlanta, GA 30303-8909; Phone: (404) 562-7904; Fax: (404) 562-7899; Website: www.4women.gov/owh/reg/4. Region V: 233 North Michigan Avenue, Suite 1300, Chicago, IL 60601; Phone: (312) 353-8122; Fax: (312) 353-7800; Website: www.4women.gov/owh/reg/5. Region VI: 1301 Young Street, Suite 1124, Dallas, TX 75202; Phone: (214) 767-3482; Fax: (214) 767-3209; Website: www.4women.gov/owh/reg/6. Region VII: 601 East 12th Street, Room 218, Kansas City, MO 64106; Phone: (816) 426-2926; Fax: (816) 426-2178; Website: www.4women.gov/owh/reg/5. Region VIII: 1961 Stout Street, Room 498, Denver, CO 80294-3538; Phone: (303) 844-7854; Fax: (303) 844-2019; Website: www.4women.gov/owh/reg/8. Region IX: 50 United Nations Plaza, Room 327, San Francisco, CA 94102; Phone: (415) 437-8119; Fax: (415) 437-8004; Website: www.4women.gov /owh/reg/9. Region X: 2201 Sixth Avenue, M/S RX-29, Seattle, WA 98121; Phone: (206) 615-2024; Fax: (206) 615-2481; Website: www. 4women.gov/owh/reg/10.

President's Council on Physical Fitness and Sports (PCPFS): Established by President Dwight D. Eisenhower by executive order in 1956, with 20 members appointed by the president. The goal of the Council on Physical Fitness and Sports is to get more Americans physically active and works with individuals, civic groups, private enterprise, and volunteer organizations.

It encourages research in sports medicine, physical activity and fitness, and sports performance; physical education programs and recreation programs; and education of the public on the link between physical activity and health, character, discipline, confidence, self-esteem, and a sense of well-being.

CONTACT Address: President's Council on Physical Fitness and Sports, Dept. W., 200 Independence Avenue SW, Room 738-H, Washington, DC 20201-004; Phone: (202) 690-9000; Fax: (202) 690-5211; Website: www. fitness.gov/.

ADMINISTRATION FOR CHILDREN AND FAMILIES (ACF)

The Administration for Children and Families partners with state, local, and tribal governmental agencies to oversee and finance services and assistance to and promote economic and social well-being of children, youths, families, persons with developmental disabilities, refugees, migrants, Native Americans, legalized aliens, and others. AFC's ultimate goal is to empower families and children to increase their own economic independence and productivity.

CONTACT Address: 370 L'Enfant Promenade SW, Washington, DC 20477; Phone: (202) 401-9200 or (202) 401-9215 for general information; Website: www.acf.gov.

WELFARE PROGRAMS

Temporary Assistance for Needy Families (TANF): TANF replaces former Aid for Dependent Children (AFDC) and JOBS programs. Under TANF (1996), states and territories operate welfare programs, and tribes have the option to operate their own, administering block grants from the federal government. The block grant covers benefits, administrative expenses, and services. States, territories, and tribes determine clients' eligibility and benefits and what services should be provided to needy families.

Goals of TANF include providing help to needy families to assure children may be cared for in their own homes or in the homes of relatives; ending dependence of needy families on government benefits by job training, work, and marriage; preventing and reducing out of wedlock pregnancies; and encouraging two-parent families.

States, territories, and tribes make initial assessment of the clients' skills, and recipients must work after two years on assistance. To qualify for assistance, recipients must work a certain number of hours, either for unsubsidized or subsidized employment, on-the-job training, work experience, community service, 12 months of vocational training, or by providing child care to people who are participating in community service. Families who have received assistance for five cumulative years (or less according to individual states) are ineligible for cash aid.

In order to receive benefits, unmarried minor parents are required to live with a responsible adult or in an adult-supervised setting and take part in education and training activities. According to law, women on welfare get continued health coverage for their families, including at least one year of Medicaid, when they move from welfare to work.

The tribal programs enable Tribal TANF grantees to independently design, administer, and operate their own programs. Tribes are supposed to have flexibility to decide who is eligible, what benefits and services they should have, and to develop strategies for reaching program goals.

CONTACT Address: 370 L'Enfant Promenade SW, Washington, DC 20447; Phone: (202) 401-5139; Fax: (202) 205-5887; Website: www.acf.dhhs.gov/programs/ofa/. Tribal Programs: Address: Division of Tribal Services, 370 L'Enfant Promenade SW, Washington, DC 20447; Phone: (202) 401-2418; Fax: (202) 401-4745; Website: www.adf.dhhs.gov/programs/dts/.

Welfare to Work: Welfare to Work Jobs Challenge gives a tax credit to employers who hire long-term welfare recipients, in an effort to move long-term welfare recipients into lasting, private, unsubsidized jobs.

Refugee Assistance: The 1980 Immigration and Nationality Act created refugee assistance to help new arrivals from Cuba and Haiti to gain employment, become economically self-sufficient, and assimilate into American society. The federal government gives funds to states and some nonprofit organizations to help offset resettlement through cash and medical assistance, social services, preventive health services, and a volunteer agency matching grant program.

CONTACT Address: Office of Refugee Assistance, 370 L'Enfant Promenade SW, 6th Floor, Washington, DC 20447; Phone: (202) 401-9246; Fax: (202) 401-5487; Website: www.acf.dhhs.gov/programs/orr/.

Repatriation: The Repatriation Program helps U.S. citizens and dependents return to the United States with approval of the STATE DEPARTMENT. Causes of repatriation from a foreign country may include illness, no money, or necessity to return to the United States due to a threatening situation in a foreign country. Repatriation assistance must be repaid to the U.S. government. In cooperation with federal and state agencies and volunteer organizations, HHS also has an Emergency Repatriation Program to return large numbers of Americans home in a national security emergency.

CONTACT Address: Office of Refugee Resettlement, 370 L'Enfant Promenade SW, 6th Floor, Washington, DC 20447; Phone: (202) 401-9246; Fax: (202) 401-5487; Website: www.acf.dhhs.gov/programs/orr/.

CHILDREN AND YOUTH

Foster Care, Adoption Assistance, and Independent Living: Foster Care and Adoption Assistance programs offer help to children who cannot remain safely in their family homes. Foster Care seeks to offer a stable environment that assures a child's safety and well-being while the parents or adults in the household work out their problems, or when the family cannot be reunited. Foster Care also provides a home environment until the child can be adopted.

Foster Care and Adoption Assistance also provide help for children determined to have "special needs," which may include older children, members of minority or sibling groups, or are physically, mentally, or emotionally disabled. Title IV-E adoption assistance is available to families who adopt special needs children.

Due to the Foster Care Independence Act of 1999, Independent Living assistance is available to current or former foster care youth age 16 and older to help them transition to adulthood and independent living, help in getting high school diploma or receive vocational training, employment assistance, training in daily living skills, leads to housing, and individual and group counseling. Payments to families, individuals, and institutions vary by state.

CONTACT Address: Children's Bureau, Administration on Children, Youth and Families, 330 C Street SW, Room 2422, Washington, DC 20201; Phone: (202) 205-8618; Fax: (202) 205-8221; Website: www.acf.dhhs.gov/programs/cb/.

Promoting Safe and Stable Families: PSSF works to improve the quality of care and services to children and their families, to prevent unnecessary separation of children from their families, and to give permanency and stability to children by reuniting them with their parents, by adoption, or by finding another permanent living arrangement.

The program gives funds directly to state child welfare agencies and eligible Indian tribes to establish and operate family support services for families at risk or in crisis. PSSF's motivations include the welfare and safety of children and family members, and making needed services flexible and easily accessible (even delivered in the home or in community settings), with respect for cultural and community pride and differences.

Child Abuse and Neglect Prevention and Treatment: Maltreatment (formerly known as abuse) of children categories include neglect, medical neglect, physical abuse, sexual abuse, and psychological "maltreatment." Child deaths are the worst result of "maltreatment," and recent increases in child fatalities compared to recent years due to abuse and neglect are now attributed to better reporting. Children younger than one year account for 44 percent of child fatalities, and 85 percent of child fatalities due to maltreatment were younger than six years of age.

The Child Abuse Prevention and Neglect Program provides grants to states to improve and increase prevention and treatment activities. The Office of Child Abuse and Neglect of the Children's Bureau at ACF coordinates federal activities and allocates child abuse and neglect funds from Congress.

CONTACT Address: Office of Child Abuse and Neglect Prevention, Children's Bureau, Administration on Children, Youth and Families, 330 C Street SW, Room 2422, Washington, DC 20201; Phone: (202) 205-8618; Fax: (202) 205-8221; Website: www.acf.dhhs.gov/programs/cb.

Child Welfare Services: Child Welfare Services helps state and tribal child welfare agencies keep families together by serving children and their families regardless of their income. Services provided by states include preventive intervention to keep children within the family home; development of alternative placements such as foster care or adoption; and reunification services to help children return home if possible.

CONTACT Address: Office of Child Welfare Services, Children's Bureau, Administration on Children, Youth and Families, 330 C Street SW, Room 2422, Washington, DC 20201; Phone: (202) 205-8618; Fax: (202) 205-8221; Website: www.acf.dhhs.gov/programs/cb/.

The *Adoption Opportunities* program helps eliminate barriers to adoption and helps find permanent homes for children, especially special needs children. The *Abandoned Infants Assistance* program gives grants to find ways to prevent abandonment of children in hospitals and to identify and address needs of infants and young children, particularly those with AIDS and pre-natal drug or alcohol exposure. The *Infant Adoption Awareness Training* program funds development of curricula and training programs to train staff in eligible health centers to provide information and referrals to pregnant women.

CONTACT Address: Children's Bureau, Administration on Children, Youth and Families, 330 C Street SW, Room 2422, Washington, DC 20201; Phone: (202) 205-8618; Fax: (202) 205-8221; Website: www.acf.dhhs.gov/programs/cb/.

Head Start: Head Start provides comprehensive developmental services of low-income pre-school children aged three to five and social services for their families. Grants made to local public or private nonprofit agencies must include at least 10 percent of their enrollment opportunities to children with disabilities.

Head Start is the most popular and long-lasting program initiated by Lyndon B. Johnson's Great Society in 1964. Its school soon opened in cities throughout the country with a corps of teachers quickly trained in pre-school techniques. These pre-schools are targeted toward children below or near the poverty line and also provide social services and health care referrals.

President Bill Clinton signed the Head Start Act Amendments in 1994 to establish the Early Head Start program to extend early childhood development benefits to low-income families with children under three and pregnant women. Early Head Start services include quality early education in and out of the home (sometimes in the family's native language); home visits; parent education including parent-child activities; health services, including services to women before, during, and after pregnancy; nutrition; and case management and peer support groups for parents. Other specialized programs include American Indian Head Start and Migrant Head Start. In 2003 President George W. Bush proposed steps to move Head Start from Health and Human Services to the DEPARTMENT OF EDUCATION, a change that would eliminate the social and food programs of Head Start.

CONTACT Address: Head Start Bureau, 330 C Street SW, Room 2018, Washington, DC 20201; Phone: (202) 205-8572; Fax: (202) 205-9336; Website: www2.acf.dhhs.gov/programs/hsb/.

Child Care and Development Fund (CCDF): Authorized by the Personal Responsibility and Work Opportunity Reconciliation Act of 1996, CCDF helps low-income families who receive temporary public assistance and those moving off public assistance to get child care services so the parents can work or attend training or education. All child care funding is now under one umbrella, the Child Care and Development Block Grant (CCDBG) Act. Block grants go to states and tribes, which then fund the programs. Services include those to parents, such as counseling on what resources are available and referrals, how to select the right child care provider for a child's needs, quality care for infants and toddlers, and improved school-age child care.

CONTACT Address: Child Care Bureau, Administration on Children, Youth and Families, 330 C Street SW, Room 2046, Washington, DC 20201; Phone: (202) 690-6782; Fax: (202) 690-5600; Website: www.acf.dhhs.gov/programs/ccb/.

Child Support Enforcement Program (CSE): CSE is a federal/state partnership working to make sure child support payments are made regularly and on time by locating parents, establishing paternity, establishing and enforcing support orders, and even collecting payments. Signed by President Bill Clinton (1996), CSE legislation strives to make sure children get the support due them, and makes tough penalties for not paying child support, including revoking drivers' licenses and seizure of assets. CSE also works to assure children access to their noncustodial parent.

Families receiving assistance under Temporary Assistance for Needy Families (TANF) as well as families not receiving TANF funds are eligible to use CSE services.

CONTACT Address: Office of Child Support Enforcement, 370 L'Enfant Promenade SW,

Washington, DC 20447; Phone: (202) 401-9370; Website: www.acf.dhhs.gov/programs/cse/.

Youth Programs

The *Runaway and Homeless Youth Act* (1974) and its amendments are designed to help runaways who cross state lines and become exposed to exploitation. Estimates of runaway and homeless youths range from 500,000 to 3 million a year. Grants to public and private agencies provide short-term shelter, crisis intervention, family reunification services, shelter, food, clothing, counseling, and other support services.

The Runaway and Homeless Youth Program includes the Traditional Living Program for Homeless Youth, which helps homeless youths aged 16–21 make the transition to independent, sheltered living through Basic Center and Transitional Living programs.

CONTACT Address: Family and Youth Services Bureau, 330 C Street SW, Washington, DC 20201; Phone: (202) 205-8102; Fax: (202) 260-9333; Website: www.acf.dhhs.gov/programs/fysb/.

Critical and Emergency Phone Numbers:

Child Abuse: 1-800-422-4453 (Childhelp's National Abuse Hotline)

Child Care: 1-800-424-3346 (Child Care Aware)

Domestic Violence: 1-800-799-7233 (National Domestic Violence Hotline)

Missing and Exploited Children: 1-800-843-5678 (National Center for Missing and Exploited Children

Runaway Youth: 1-800-621-4000 (National Runaway Switchboard)

COMMUNITY PROGRAMS

Social Services Block Grant (SSBG): SSBG awards block grants to states based on population, and allows the states to decide what services they provide, how they distribute the services, and who is eligible. Most frequently offered services include child day care; home-based services to help individuals or families with household and personal care; protective services to prevent or stop abuse, neglect, or exploitation of children or adults; special needs services for people with physical, mental, or emotional disabilities, and social support; transportation; and family planning. Other goals include avoidance or reduction of inappropriate institutionalization, referral for institutional care when appropriate, and social support.

CONTACT Address: Office of Community Services, Division of State Assistance, 370 L'Enfant Promenade SW, Washington, DC 20447; Phone: (202) 401-5281; Fax: (202) 401-5718; Website: www.adf.dhhs.gov/programs/ocs/ssbg/.

Low Income Home Energy Assistance Program (LIHEAP): LIHEAP provides federal funds to states, territories, tribes, Alaskan Natives, and tribal organizations to help low-income households pay for home heating and cooling by making payments either directly to the households or to the energy suppliers. Funds may also be given to low-income households to meet energy-related crises or to pay for repairs to make recipients' homes more energy efficient.

CONTACT Address: Division of Energy Assistance, 370 L'Enfant Promenade SW, Washington, DC 20447; Phone: (202) 401-9351; Fax: (202) 401-5661; Website: www.acf.dhhs.gov/programs/liheap/liheap.htm. Or Address: Office of Community Services, Demonstration and Special Projects Division, 370 L'Enfant Promenade SW, Washington, DC 20447; Phone: (202) 401-5318; Fax: (202) 401-5538; Website: www.acf.dhhs.gov/programs/ocs/demo/.

Community Service Programs: Community Services funds, including Community Services Block Grants (CSBG), provide help with employment, education, housing, income management, energy, health, and other emergency needs of the poor. Most funds filter from the federal government to states, territories, tribes, tribal organizations, universities, and other nonprofits such as community action agencies to assist low-income people in local communities.

CONTACT Address: Office of Community Services, Division of State Assistance, 370 L'Enfant Promenade SW, Washington, DC 20447; Phone: (202) 401-9343; Fax: (202) 401-5718; Website: www.acf.dhhs.gov/programs/ocs/csbg/.

Developmental Disabilities: Developmental Disabilities programs serve nearly 4 million Americans who suffer severe, chronic disabilities due to mental or physical impairment, or a combination of both, and which are manifested before the person reaches the age of 22. Potential recipients' needs must be likely to continue indefinitely, resulting in substantial limitations to life activities.

Goals of developmental disabilities grants fund programs are to protect the rights and promote self-sufficiency of Americans with developmental disabilities and their families. Funds help governments, local communities, and the private sector integrate recipients socially and economically into society. Part of the grants go for advocacy of recipients' human and legal rights, technical assistance, information dissemination, and interdisciplinary training for service givers.

CONTACT Address: Administration on Developmental Disabilities, 200 Independence Avenue SW, Room 300-F, Washington, DC 20201; Phone: (202) 690-6590; Fax: (202) 690-6904; Website: www.acf.dhhs.gov/programs/add/.

Native Americans: Under the Native American Programs Act of 1974, the Administration for Native Americans (ANA) works toward social, governmental, and economic self-sufficiency of Native Americans, including American Indians, Alaska Natives, Native Hawaiians, and other Native American Pacific Islanders, including American Samoans.

ANA's goals include improving local decision making among community and tribal governments, developing and attracting enterprises that increase jobs that lead to increased economic self-sufficiency and self-supporting communities, and promoting local control and access to services to safeguard the health and well-being of Native Americans.

CONTACT Address: Administration for Native Americans, 370 L'Enfant Promenade SW, Mail Stop 8th floor Aerospace, Washington, DC 20447; Help Desk Phones: (202) 690-7776 or (877) 922-9ANA; Fax: (202) 690-8145 or (202) 690-7441; Website: www.acf.dhhs.gov/programs/ana/.

President's Committee on Mental Retardation (PCMR): Created in 1966 to advise the president and secretary of health and human services (then health, education and welfare) on programs and services for people with mental retardation, the President's Committee on Mental Retardation coordinates federal activities in mental retardation, conducts studies of existing programs, points out changes needed, and promotes research in the field.

PCMR consists of 21 citizen members appointed by the president and six appointees who are professionals in the mental retardation field, developmental disabilities, and related areas of study.

ADMINISTRATION ON AGING (AOA)

The Administration on Aging provides services to senior citizens through its network, with the goal of helping seniors remain independent. AOA finances 240 million meals fed to seniors every year, with some help to their meals on wheels program (not part of Meals on Wheels), helps provide transportation and at-home services, supports ombudsman services for the elderly, and provides some policy advocacy on issues affecting the aging, including costs of health care and medications and housing.

By 2030 the U.S. population will include 85 million people 60 or more years old, double the figure for the year 2000. The minority senior population will increase by 265 percent, Hispanic

Americans by 530 percent, and white seniors by 97 percent. Reasons for the greater increase in minority seniors may include better health care and nutrition than in the past.

The Older Americans Act of 1965 as amended provides services and opportunities for older Americans, with special emphasis on helping seniors live independently. Those at most risk of losing their independence may include millions of Americans over 85, those living alone without a caregiver, members of minority groups, older persons with physical or mental impairments, low-income seniors, and those who are abused, neglected, or exploited by others, including their families.

The Administration on Aging works with federal government agencies, national organizations, businesses, states, area agencies, and 27,000 provider agencies throughout the country. Through Title III of the Older Americans Act it supports nutrition, transportation, senior centers, health promotion, and homemaker services. Title IV finances research projects about subgroups of the elderly to assess needs and plan services and opportunities. Titles III and VII give funds to 57 states' Agencies on Aging (also called state Units on Aging). Title VI gives funds to 220 tribes and native organizations to meet needs of older American Indians, Aleuts, Eskimos, and Hawaiians to provide services with sensitivity to Native Americans' cultural heritage.

Each state receives funds according to its senior population, for a total of 650 Area Agencies on Aging (AAA). The AAAs contract with the private or public groups to actually provide services, or provide services themselves where no subcontractors are available.

The Nutrition Program for the Elderly provides communal and home-delivered meals to seniors. The Eldercare Volunteer Corps enlists senior volunteers to work with the elderly to enhance independence of both the volunteer and the person in need of help.

Toll-free hotline: 1-800-677-1116.

National Family Caregiver Support Program (NFCSP): Created by the Older American Act Amendments of 2000, NFCSP gives money to states to partner with area agencies on aging and local community service providers to provide information to caregivers about help available to them; help to caregivers in getting supportive services; individual counseling, organization of support groups, and caregiver training; respite care of senior family member to give caregivers a break; and other care services for caregivers. Priority services go to people with the greatest economic and social needs, especially low-income and minority individuals; and seniors who provide care and support to people with mental retardation and other developmental disabilities.

The amendments of 2000 also established a Native American Caregiver Support Program, particularly serving Native Americans with chronic illnesses or disabilities, with sensitivity to the recipients' cultural and varied needs.

CONTACT For local offices on aging, look in city or county government sections of the telephone directory under Aging or Social Services. State units or agencies are available via www. aoa/pages/state.html; 330 Independence Avenue SW, Washington, DC 20201; Phones: (202) 401-4634; Eldercare Locator: (800) 677-1116 to find senior services in a senior's locale; public use: (202) 619-0724; assistant secretary of HHS: (202) 401-4634; E-mail: aoainfo@aoa.gov.

AGENCY FOR HEALTHCARE RESEARCH AND QUALITY (AHRQ)

The AHRQ gives support and money for research into how to improve the quality of health care; reduce health care costs and medical mistakes; and provide information to help patients make better health care decisions.

Created in December 1989 as the Agency for Health Care Policy and Research (AHCPR), it was a public health service agency in HHS. As of December 6, 1999, it became the Agency for Healthcare Research and Quality and reports directly to the secretary of health and human services. Almost 80 percent of AHRQ's budget goes out as grants and contracts to researchers at universities and other research centers throughout the United States. AHRQ's stated ultimate goal is to improve quality, availability, and value of health care services. Federal, state, and local policymakers have access to AHRQ-sponsored research to set public policy on health care.

AHRQ works to study the disparities in health care services to wealthy and poor U.S. residents, and to serve needs of low-income groups, minorities, women, children, the elderly, and special health care needs patients.

AHRQ's Translating Research Into Practice (TRIP) initiative (1999) aims to close the gap between research and practice and focuses on improving patient care through studies on smoking cessation; chlamydia screening among adolescents; diabetes care in underserved populations; and treatment of respiratory distress syndrome in preterm or premature infants.

AHRQ's work on diabetes treatment has resulted in what seems like an automatic collaboration among the Health Care Financing Administration, National Committee for Quality Assurance, American Academy of Family Physicians, American Diabetes Association, and the Foundation for Accountability toward the Diabetes Quality Improvement Project (DQIP).

AHRQ research shows that minorities receive less acute care than Caucasians. For example, blacks are about one-third less likely to have bypass surgery than whites, and 13 percent less likely to have coronary angioplasty, which is not to suggest they do not need it; 7 percent of blacks and 2 percent of Hispanic preschool children hospitalized for asthma are prescribed drug treatment to prevent future hospitalizations,

compared to 21 percent of white preschool asthma patients. AHRQ research also shows that three times as many Hispanics as whites and twice as many blacks as whites have no regular health care provider.

AHRQ researchers investigate drug, medicine, and procedural errors in hospitals.

AHRQ projects to improve patient safety aim at identifying causes of mistakes and when and how errors occur; developing a national strategy to improve patient safety; and working with public and private partners to use research to improve patient safety. Research also includes the safety, well-being, and productivity of health care workers.

Centers for Education and Research on Therapeutics (CERTs): Works to reduce adverse drug events and promote safe use of pharmaceuticals through research on uses and risks of new drugs, combination of drugs, biological products, and medical devices in people's systems.

Consumer Assessment of Health Plans (CAHPS®): Offers tools for individuals or groups make their best choice among health plans.

CONQUEST (Computerized Needs-oriented Quality Measurement Evaluation System): A computer software tool of two linked databases that can help identify, understand, compare, and choose ways to assess and improve performance in acute, ambulatory, long-term, and home health care settings.

Healthcare Cost and Utilization Project (HCUP): A nationwide partnership to develop a multi-state health care data system.

Medical Expenditure Panel Survey (MEPS): An ongoing national survey of health care use, costs, sources of payment, insurance coverage, and nursing homes and their residents. MEPS data provide the healthcare expenditure part of the Gross Domestic Product (GDP).

National Guideline Clearinghouse™ (NGC): A Web-based resource of information on clinical practice guidelines developed in partnership with the American Medical Association and the

American Association of Health Plans. On NGS's website, www.guideline.gov, healthcare professionals and health system leaders select appropriate treatments for patients and compare recommendations.

Evidence-based Practice Centers (EPCs): Twelve centers that analyze and synthesize scientific literature and develop reports on clinical topics on topics such as sleep apnea, traumatic brain injury, alcohol dependence, cervical cytology, urinary tract infection, depression, dysphagia, sinusitis, stable angina, testosterone suppression, and attention deficit and hyperactivity disorders.

U.S. Preventive Services Task Force (USP-STF): An independent panel of preventive care experts who evaluate a range of clinical preventive services and make age-specific and risk factor-specific recommendations for these services.

Quality Interagency Coordination (QuIC) Task Force: Works to make sure all federal agencies that purchase, provide, research, or regulate health care services are working together toward a common goal of improving health care quality.

CONTACT Address: Office of Health Care Information, Executive Office Center, 2101 Jefferson Street, Suite 501, Rockville, MD 20852; Phone: (301) 594-1364; E-mail: info@ahrq.gov; Website: www.ahrq.gov/.

AGENCY FOR TOXIC SUBSTANCES AND DISEASE REGISTRY (ATSDR)

This extremely important agency works with states, tribal organizations, and other federal agencies to prevent and control public exposure to hazardous substances and materials from and at waste sites and spills, meaning nuclear and biological weapons materials being dumped. ATSDR evaluates human health risks and studies the relationship between exposure to toxic substances and disease. Toward these goals, ATSDR makes public health assessments, health studies, surveillance activities, and health education training in communities around waste sites listed on the Environmental Protection Agency's National Priorities List. In this role ATSDR also decides how much information to give the public, which may be more or less information than the people actually need for the best decisions about residency, workplace, and health care.

ATSDR was created by Congress in 1980 to implement laws to protect the public from hazardous waste and environmental spills of hazardous substances, as part of the Comprehensive Environmental Response, Compensation, and Liability Act of 1980 (CERCLA). This so-called Superfund act makes ATSDR the Public Health Service leader to clean up abandoned and inactive hazardous waste sites and provide federal assistance in toxic substance emergencies. ATSDR also helps the EPA decide which hazardous substances should be regulated and at what concentration levels substances pose a threat to human health.

The Superfund Amendments and Reauthorization Act of 1986 (SARA) gave ATSDR new responsibilities including assessments and identification of communities where people might be exposed to hazardous substances, determination of the level of public health hazards, actions needed to protect people's health, and establishment and maintenance of toxicologic databases, information dissemination, and medical education. ATSDR also plans emergency responses, applied research, and education of doctors, other health care professionals, and community members on health effects of exposure to hazardous substances, and how to protect people and lessen their exposure to hazardous waste. The agency also keeps registries of victims of toxic exposures, visits communities to discuss exposure, draw blood, collect urine to test for exposure, and occasionally provide ongoing medical monitoring of exposed or potentially exposed communities.

ATSDR must help all sites on or proposed to be on the National Priorities List (NPL). Individuals may petition ATSDR to conduct a public health assessment of a site or community, but most requests acted on come from the EPA and state and local agencies.

CONTACT Address: Agency for Toxic Substances and Disease Registry, 1600 Clifton Road, Atlanta, GA 30333; Phone: (404) 498-0004, public: (404) 498-0110, toll free: 1-888-422-8737; Fax: (404) 498-0081.

REGIONAL OFFICES:

Region I (Connecticut, Maine, Massachusetts, New Hampshire, Rhode Island, Vermont): 1 Congress Street, Suite 1100 (HBT), Boston, MA 02114-2023; Phone: (617) 918-1495.

Region II (New Jersey, New York, Puerto Rico, U.S. Virgin Islands): 290 Broadway North, 18th Floor, New York, NY 10007; Phone: (212) 637-4305; 2890 Woodbridge Avenue, Building 209, Edison, NJ 08837; Phone: (732) 906-6931.

Region III (Delaware, District of Columbia, Maryland, Pennsylvania, Virginia, West Virginia): 1650 Arch Street, Philadelphia, PA 19103-2029; Phone: (215) 814-3140.

Region IV (Alabama, Florida, Georgia, Kentucky, Mississippi, North Carolina, South Carolina, Tennessee): Atlanta Federal Center, 61 Forsyth Street SW, 10th Floor, Atlanta, GA 30303; Phone: (404) 562-1788.

Region V (Illinois, Indiana, Michigan, Minnesota, Ohio, Wisconsin): 77 West Jackson Boulevard, Room 413, M/S 4J, Chicago, IL 60604; Phone: (312) 886-0840.

Region VI (Arkansas, Louisiana, New Mexico, Oklahoma, Texas): 1445 Ross Avenue, Dallas, TX 75202; Phone: (214) 665-6615.

Region VII (Iowa, Kansas, Missouri, Nebraska): Robert J. Dole Federal Courthouse, 500 State Avenue, Suite 182, Kansas City, KS 66101; Phone: (913) 551-1313.

Region VII (Colorado, Montana, North Dakota, South Dakota, Utah, Wyoming): 999 18th Street, Suite 500, Denver, CO 80202-2466; Phone: (303) 312-7012.

Region IX (American Samoa, Arizona, California, Guam, Hawaii, Nevada, Trust Territories of the Pacific Islands, Marshall Islands, Palau, Ponape, the Navajo Nation): 75 Hawthorne Street, Room 100, Mail Code HHS-1, San Francisco, CA 94105; Phone: (415) 744-1771.

Region X (Alaska, Idaho, Oregon, Washington): 1200 6th Avenue, Suite 1930, Seattle, WA 98101; Phone: (206) 553-1049.

CENTERS FOR DISEASE CONTROL AND PREVENTION (CDC)

The CDC works with other health and community organizations and public and private partners throughout the world to promote health and quality of life by controlling and preventing disease, injury, and disability. It monitors health, detects and investigates health problems, conducts research to help disease prevention, develops and advocates sound public health policies, implements prevention strategies, promotes healthy behaviors and environments, and provides leadership and training in disease control and prevention.

CDC also works to limit and prevent international disease transmission, keeps national health statistics, provides immunization services, and supports research into prevention of disease and injury. It aims to prevent the spread of infectious diseases, such as HIV/AIDS, tuberculosis, and new diseases, some of which are capable of transferring or killing quickly. CDC uses "fingerprinting" technology to identify food-borne illnesses, to evaluate a family violence prevention program in a particular urban community, to educate partners on HIV, and to protect children by giving immunizations against preventable diseases.

CDC has special in-depth programs to prevent violence and unintentional injury, to help meet health and safety needs of changing workforces, to use new technologies to produce new ways to deliver health information, to protect people from new infectious diseases (including bioterrorism), to eliminate ethnic and racial disparities in health education and availability of health services, to foster safe and healthy living and work environments, and to work with partners to improve global health.

CDC is headquartered in Atlanta, Georgia, and has employees working in 47 states and 45 other countries. Other locations of CDC offices include Anchorage, Alaska; Cincinnati, Ohio; Fort Collins, Colorado; Morgantown, West Virginia; Pittsburgh, Pennsylvania; Research Triangle Park, North Carolina; San Juan, Puerto Rico; Spokane, Washington; and Washington, D.C. area. It comprises 12 centers, institutes, and offices.

CONTACT Address: Centers for Disease Control and Prevention, 1600 Clifton Road, Atlanta, GA 30333; Phone: (404) 639-3311; Website: www.cdc.gov/.

ORGANIZATION

Following are the major organizations within the CDC, all of which operate on their own and work together on certain common health issues and specific health threats.

NATIONAL CENTER ON BIRTH DEFECTS AND DEVELOPMENTAL DISABILITIES (NCBDDD): Works to make possible optimal fetal, infant, and child development; to prevent birth defects and children's developmental disabilities; and to better the quality of life and prevent secondary conditions in children, adolescents, and adults who are living with disabilities.

Birth Defects

Within NCBDDD, the *Centers for Birth Defects Research and Prevention* research causes of birth defects in the National Birth Defects Prevention Study (NBDPS). Material gained from the study will identify causes and risk factors of birth defects and lead to new approaches to prevention of major birth defects.

The *National Birth Defects Prevention Network (NBDPN)*, an independent organization that was formed and is financed by the NCBDDD, collects birth defect statistics, coordinates a state-based birth defects surveillance system, and helps use the data to develop prevention and intervention programs. Topics worked on include spina bifida, anencephaly, and the impact of folic acid education and fortification on the incidence of the two problems.

Developmental Disabilities

The *Autism Program* funds state Centers of Excellence on Autism Epidemiology programs to determine the prevalence and causes of autism and related disabilities. In Atlanta the Autism Program is engaged in a study to discover a possible connection between MMR vaccination and autism by comparing vaccination histories of children with and without autism, including school systems, age, and gender. The issue was still open by the close of 2003.

In the five-county metropolitan Atlanta area, CDC studies the prevalence of mental retardation, autism, cerebral palsy, hearing deficits, and vision deficits to determine children's functional status, how to study their social participation, and independence.

Fetal Alcohol Syndrome (FAS) program: Through CDC, FAS funds FASSNet, a five-state program to improve studies of FAS and Project CHOICES, a clinical trial on intervention for women who drink and are at high risk of having an alcohol exposed fetus. New funding helps fetal alcohol syndrome awareness and education and helps develop and test new interventions for children with FAS.

Disability and Health: The Behavioral Risk Factor Surveillance Survey (BRFSS), used in all 50 states, aims to assess and understand the health status of Americans with disabilities, and compare that status to that of Americans who do not have disabilities. CDC funds 14 states with Disability and Health State Programs to help people with disabilities, such as better surveillance activities, better health promotion interventions, better monitoring policies for people with disabilities, and improving research partnerships between states and agencies.

The 11 Disability and Health Research Programs study the secondary conditions of specific disability populations; figure out risks and possible protections to avoid or prevent occurrence of secondary conditions; conduct and measure effectiveness of health promotion efforts to prevent secondary conditions; and understand the effectiveness of health promotion efforts and cost-effectiveness of these interventions.

This program also supports the National Limb Loss Information Center, the Christopher and Dana Reeve Paralysis Resource Center, and National Center on Physical Activity and Disability.

Legacy for Children® studies involve families gathered at the University of California at Los Angeles and at the University of Miami, with the goal of better understanding how to help the families of children with disabilities. Mothers who participated thought their parenting skills improved through the study experience.

Early Hearing Detection and Intervention (EHDI): Through grants from CDC, Early Hearing Detection and Intervention funds 30 states to see that every baby receives hearing screening shortly after birth, and that infants with hearing loss and their families receive appropriate and timely follow-up services. Research projects include study of causes of hearing loss disabilities; study of costs and effectiveness of newborn hearing screening, evaluation, and intervention programs; study of psychosocial issues for children who are deaf or hard of hearing as well as for their families; and study of the risk factors associated with progressive and late-onset hearing loss.

CONTACT Phone: (770) 488-7150; Website: www.cdc.gov.ncbddd/.

NATIONAL CENTER FOR CHRONIC DISEASE PREVENTION AND HEALTH PROMOTION (NCCDHP): Works toward prevention of premature death and disability from chronic diseases and promotes healthy personal behaviors to control and prevent diseases, such as heart disease, cancer, and diabetes, the leading causes of death and disability in the United States. These three diseases are involved in 70 percent of American deaths and might be prevented or controlled by healthy eating habits, exercise, and avoidance of tobacco use.

The National Center for Chronic Disease Prevention and Health Promotion studies causes of these diseases, monitors the nation's health, and partners with local, state, private, and volunteer agencies to create a more healthy American people.

CONTACT 4770 Buford Highway N.J., Mail Stop K 40, Atlanta, GA 30341; Phone: (770) 489-5131; Fax: (770) 488-5962.

NATIONAL CENTER FOR ENVIRONMENTAL HEALTH (NCEH): Works to prevent illness, disability, and death due to environmental factors around the world, particularly in children, the elderly, and people with disabilities.

Established by the CDC in 1980 as the Center for Environmental Health (CEH), it took on responsibility for nonoccupational injury control programs and evolved into the Center for Environmental Health and Injury Control (CEHIC). By 1992 the two centers grew so much that they split into two: the National Center for Environmental Health (NCEH) and the National Center for Injury Prevention and Control (NCIP).

NCEH does research in laboratories and in the field on the effects of the environment and man-made hazards on human health; follows and evaluates environment-related health problems; and prepares international and domestic organizations and agencies to respond to natural, technologic, humanitarian, and terrorism related emergencies. Other goals include preventing birth defects and developmental disabilities; promoting optimal fetal, infant, and child development; and preventing secondary conditions of people of all ages with disabilities.

NCEH has a global health office to deal with epidemiology and diseases that know no borders, protecting health of the public visiting U.S. national parks and people on cruise ships that dock at U.S. ports, who may bring disease into the United States or catch disease while visiting the United States. NCEH also conducts studies about how genetics knowledge might be used for effective and ethical public health development.

Among NCEH's accomplishments are disseminating information on childhood lead poisoning, guidelines for preventing spina bifida, and developing ways of measuring toxins in humans.

NCEH's emergency services focus on helping local, state, federal, and international agencies plan responses to emergency problems such as technologic disasters and radiation, chemical, or biological releases; guidance for dealing with natural disasters such as earthquakes, floods, hurricanes, windstorms, volcanic eruptions, civil strife, and famine. NCEH also has responsibility for the National Pharmaceutical Stockpile to be used in terrorism attacks or releases of biological weapons to ensure rapid deployment of potentially life-saving pharmaceuticals.

NCEH's environmental health services also work to protect the public and workers during disposal of chemical weapons; and during exposure to air pollution, nuclear radiation, lead, and other toxicants, as well as from natural and technologic disasters. Links studied include air pollution and respiratory health; asthma; cancer clusters; radiation; and prevention of lead poisoning in young children.

NCEH also works toward demilitarization of chemical weapons by other nations, disaster epidemiology research, emergency response coordination, environmental health services, international emergency and refugee health, and sanitary inspection of international cruise ships.

CONTACT Emergencies: (770) 488-7100; other health information: 1-888-232-6789.

NATIONAL CENTER FOR HEALTH STATISTICS (NCHS): Compiles health statistics to guide government and private actions and policies to improve health of the American people. NCHS uses the statistics to record the health status of the American people and certain subgroups; to identify disparities in health status, health care, and use of health care according to race, ethnicity, region, and other factors; to relate information gathered to health care system participants; to track trends in health status, health trends, and health care delivery; to identify national trends and health problems; to support biomedical and health services research; to provide information and suggestions to public policy makers for changing and improving policies and programs; and to evaluate the effects of existing health programs and policies.

NCHS gets its information from birth and death records, medical records, survey interviews, physical examinations, and laboratory testing. Much of NCHS information is available to the public and health care practitioners on their website.

CONTACT Address: National Center for Health Statistics, Division of Data Services, Hyattsville, MD 20782-2003; Phone: (301) 458-4636; Website: www.cdc.gov/nchs/.

NATIONAL CENTER FOR HIV, STD, AND TB PREVENTION (NCHSTP): Works with government and private partners at public health surveillance, prevention research, and programs to control and prevent HIV (human immunodeficiency virus) and AIDS (acquired immunodeficiency syndrome), STDs (sexually transmitted diseases), and TB (tuberculosis).

The Division of HIV/AIDS Prevention—Surveillance and Epidemiology (DHAP-SE) does epidemiologic and behavioral research to monitor trends in risk behaviors in developing countries as well as in the United States. The Intervention Research and Support Division (DHAP-IRS) seeks to educate and change people's risky behaviors, and gives financial and technical help to state, local, and territorial health agencies, as well as national minority organizations, community groups, business, labor, religious, and training organizations for HIV prevention programs. The Division of STD Prevention (DSTDP) researches epidemiologic and behavioral trends in sexually transmitted diseases such as syphillis, gonorrhea, chlamydia, human papillomavirus, genital herpes, and hepatitis B. It also helps states and communities communicate with people vulnerable to STDs due to risky behavior, and works to prevent infertility and pelvic inflammatory disease that can lead to ectopic pregnancy, cancer, and fetal or infant death. The Division of TB Elimination (DTBE) conducts research and helps state and local agencies deal with preventing and controlling tuberculosis by education; observing therapy to make sure patients complete their treatments; following patients with TB, people exposed to TB, and people suspected of having TB; and increasing TB screening among high risk people.

CONTACT Address: Centers for Disease Control and Prevention, 1108 Corporate Square, Atlanta, GA 30329; Phone: (404) 639-8040; Website: www.cdc.gov/nchstp/od/.

NATIONAL CENTER FOR INFECTIOUS DISEASES (NCID): Works to prevent illness, disability, and death caused by infectious diseases in the United States and around the world. Worldwide, infectious diseases are the leading cause of death, and they ranked third in the United States in 1992. Emergence of new diseases and resurgence of old diseases caution researchers and medical practitioners that the world cannot assume that infectious diseases have been eliminated due to antibiotics, universal immunizations of children in the United States, and eradication of polio. In fact, infectious diseases are again on the rise and may be introduced as biological terrorism.

NCID does specialized research in the Arctic; bacterial and mycotic diseases; bioterrorism preparedness and response; global migration and quarantine; health care quality promotion; para-sitic diseases; vector-borne diseases (such as West Nile Virus); viral hepatitis; and viral and rickettsial diseases.

CONTACT Address: Office of Health Communication, National Center for Infectious Diseases, Centers for Disease Control and Prevention, Mailstop C-14, 1600 Clifton Road, Atlanta, GA 30333; Website: www.cdc.gov/ncidod/.

NATIONAL CENTER FOR INJURY PREVENTION AND CONTROL (NCIPC): Works to prevent disability and death from nonoccupational injuries, unintentional injuries, and violence-related injuries.

NCIPC researches and develops solutions for injuries that including acute care injury, disability and rehabilitation, and traumatic brain injury; violent injuries due to intimate and sexual violence, suicide, homicide, or youth violence; unintentional injuries such as those incurred riding bicycles, and those incurred at home or at recreation and in motor vehicles; and injuries incurred in fires, crossing streets, drowning, sports, and day-care centers.

CONTACT Address: National Center for Injury Prevention and Control, Mailstop K65, 4770 Buford Highway NE, Atlanta, GA 30341-3724; Phone: (770) 488-1506; Fax: (770) 488-1667; Website: www.cdc.gov/ncipc/ncipchm.htm.

NATIONAL IMMUNIZATION PROGRAM (NIP): Gives consultation, training, and epidemiological and technical services to help local and state health departments immunize children in their constituencies. NIP helps health departments identify children who need vaccinations; helps parents get their children immunized at the right age; assesses state and local vaccination levels; and keeps track of vaccine safety and availability by knowing disease outbreak patterns. It also researches prevention and control of vaccine-preventable diseases.

CONTACT Address: NIP Public Inquiries, Mailstop E-05, 1600 Clifton Road, NE, Atlanta, GA 30333; Immunization hotlines: English- (800) 232-2522, Spanish- (800) 232-0233, TTY- (800) 243-7889; Fax: 1-888-232-3299; International Travel Information: 1-877-394-8747 or www.cdc.gov/travel; Website: www.cdc.gov/nip/.

NATIONAL INSTITUTE FOR OCCUPATIONAL SAFETY AND HEALTH (NIOSH): Works to prevent work-related injury and disease, ranging from coal miners' lung disease to computer users' carpal tunnel syndrome. To this end, NIOSH researches potentially hazardous work conditions when investigation is requested by either employers or employees; makes recommendations and puts out information on how to prevent workplace injury, disease, and disability; and provides training to health care and occupational safety professionals.

NIOSH and the Occupational Safety and Health Administration (OSHA) were created by the Occupational Safety Health Act of 1970, although they are separate agencies with different responsibilities. OSHA creates and enforces workplace safety and health regulations, while NIOSH mainly does research.

NIOSH also works with states to improve the health and safety of workers by evaluating workplace hazards and recommending solutions when asked by workers, employers, state, or federal agencies; gives grants and cooperative agreements to improve worker safety in states; and funds occupational safety and health research and occupational safety and health training programs.

CONTACT Address: National Institute for Occupational Safety and Health, 200 Independence Avenue SW, Room 715 H, Washington, DC 20201 or 24 Executive Park Drive, Mailstop E-20, Atlanta, GA 30329; Phone: 1-800-356-4674, outside U.S. (513) 533-8328; Fax: (513) 533-8573 or toll free 1-888-232-3299; Website: www.cdc.gov/niosh/.

EPIDEMIOLOGY PROGRAM OFFICE (EPO): Coordinates public health surveillance at CDC and provides domestic and international scientific communications, statistical and epidemiologic consultation, and training of experts in those fields as well as applied public health and prevention. EPO's Division of Prevention Research and Analytic Methods works on preven-

tion effectiveness; statistics and epidemiology; evaluation and behavioral science methods; and works with a network of health care partnerships. The Division of Applied Public Health includes the Epidemic Intelligence Service; a Preventive Medicine Residency; Public Health Prevention Service; Epidemiology Elective for Senior Medical and Veterinary Students; state branches; and Training Development and Management. The Division of International Health offers program development assistance; data for decision making; and effective use of data and policy. The Division of Public Health Surveillance and Informatics engages in software development activity, surveillance and collection of statistics in areas such as medical examiner and coroner information, offers information technology information, and information on applied sciences in the field of epidemic diseases.

CONTACT Address: Epidemiology Program Office, Centers for Disease Control and Prevention, 1600 Clifton Road, Atlanta, GA 30333; Fax: (404) 639-4198; Website: www.cdc.gov/epo/.

PUBLIC HEALTH PRACTICE PROGRAM OFFICE (PHPPO): Works to strengthen community public health practices by developing the best health care workforce possible, developing public health information channels and networks, conducting research, and keeping laboratory accuracy and quality as high as possible.

CONTACT Address: Public Health Practice Program Office, 1600 Clifton Road, Atlanta, GA 30333; Phones: (404) 639-3534 or (800) 311-3435; Website: www.phppo.cdc.gov/.

CENTERS FOR MEDICARE AND MEDICAID SERVICES (CMS)

The Health Care Financing Administration (HCFA) became the Centers for Medicare and Medicaid Services on July 1, 2002. Both created in 1965 by the Social Security Act, Medicare was run by the Social Security Administration, while Social and Rehabilitation Service oversaw federal assistance to state Medicaid programs. Both were agencies of the Department of Health, Education and Welfare (HEW). The Health Care Financing Administration was created in 1977 under HEW to coordinate the functions of Medicare and Medicaid. Then in 1980 HEW was divided into the Department of Education and the Department of Health and Human Services (HHS).

President Harry S. Truman first proposed a prepaid health insurance plan for all people through Social Security on November 19, 1945, called "National Health Insurance" covering doctors, hospitals, nursing, laboratory, and dental care. Truman's total plan was never adopted, but a program for Social Security recipients' health care did pass eventually, advocated by President John F. Kennedy, and actually enacted and signed by President Lyndon B. Johnson as H.R. 6675, the Social Security Act of 1965.

President Johnson signed the Medicare and Medicaid Bill (Title XVIII and Title XIX of the Social Security Act) in the presence of former president Harry S. Truman in Independence, Missouri, where Truman lived. During the ceremony President Truman received the first Medicare card in front of his wife, Bess, and first lady Lady Bird Johnson. Medicare made health coverage available to most Americans 65 or older, and Medicaid gave health care services for some low-income people and added to the existing federal-state welfare structure to assist the poor.

The 1972 Social Security Amendments extended Medicare to disabled individuals who receive cash benefits for 24 months under Social Security, and to people suffering from end-stage renal disease.

Currently CMS runs two national health care programs and with the Health Resources and Services Administration, runs the State Children's Health Insurance Program (SCHIP). CMS regulates all laboratory testing on humans in the United States through 158,000 laboratory set-tings, and establishes how much health care providers are paid by its programs.

During the administration of President George W. Bush, HHS secretary Tommy Thompson reorganized the department and developed three new bureaucracies. The Center for Medicare Management developed payment and management policies for Medicare's fee-for-service contractors, meaning private doctors and labs. The Center for Beneficiary Choices provides recipients and potential recipients with information on Medicare, Medicare Select, Medicare+Choice, and Medigap options, and oversees Medicare+Choice plans, consumer research, and grievance and appeals. The Center for Medicaid and State Operations is meant to focus on state-run programs, including Medicaid, State Children's Health Insurance Program (SCHIP), insurance regulation, certification, and the Clinical Laboratory Improvements Act (CLIA).

PROGRAMS

Medicare

Medicare provides health insurance to people aged 65 or older, some people under 65 with certain disabilities, and individuals with kidney failure requiring dialysis or a transplant. Medicare's coverage includes Part A, hospital insurance, and Part B, medical insurance. Part A helps pay for hospital stays and services, skilled nursing facility services, home health care, and hospice care. Part B helps pay for doctor fees, outpatient hospital services, medical equipment and supplies, and some other health services. In some states Medicare managed care plans and private fee-for-service plans might be offered. Check www.medicare.gov for local options. Website: http://cms.hhs.gov/about/mission.asp.

Medicaid

Medicaid provides health insurance for some low-income individuals and is administered through state-federal partnerships. States establish their own standards of eligibility, decide what benefits and services they will offer, and set rates of what fees they will pay to health care providers. All states must provide inpatient and outpatient hospital services, laboratory and X-ray services, skilled nursing and home health services, doctors' services, family planning, and periodic health checkups, diagnosis, and treatment for children.

Those eligible include people who receive federal-assisted income payments such as low-income families with children; low-income people who are old, blind, or disabled; low-income pregnant women; low-income children; and people with exceedingly high medical needs and bills. Website: http://dms.hhs.gov/medicaid/.

Administration for Children and Families

State Children's Health Insurance Program (SCHIP): Administers coverage for some poor children through approved state plans.

WEBSITE http://cms.hhs.gov/schip/.

Health Insurance Portability and Accountability Act of 1996 (HIPAA): HIPAA is supposed to protect workers' and their families' health insurance coverage when the workers change or lose their jobs, establish national standards for electronic health care transactions, and work on security and privacy of personal health care information while encouraging widespread interchange of electronic data in health care.

WEBSITE http://cms.hhs.gov/hipaa/.

Clinical Laboratory Improvement Amendments (CLIA): CLIA is the agency actually responsible for ensuring quality laboratory testing and for overseeing all laboratory testing (except research) performed on human beings at approximately 175,000 labs in the United States.

WEBSITE http://cms.hhs.gov/clia/.

CONTACT Address: Centers for Medicare and Medicaid General Offices: 7500 Security Boulevard, Baltimore, MD 21244-1850; Phones: local-(410) 786-3000, toll free-(877) 267-2323; TTY local-(410) 786-0727, TTY toll free-(866)

226-1819; Website: http://cms.hhs/gov/. Regional offices: Atlanta Regional Office, Office of the Consortium/Regional Administrator, Atlanta Federal Center, 4th Floor, 61 Forsyth Street SW, Suite 4T20, Atlanta, GA; Phone: (404) 562-7150. Boston Regional Office, JFK Federal Building, Room 2325, Boston, MA; Phone: (617) 565-1188. Chicago Regional Office, 233 North Michigan, Suite 600, Chicago, IL 60601; Phone: (312) 886-6432. Dallas Regional Office, 1301 Young Street, Room 714, Dallas, TX 75202; Phone: (214) 767-6427. Denver Regional Office, 1600 Broadway, Suite 700, Denver, CO 80202; Phone: (303) 844-2111. Kansas City Regional Office, 601 East 12th Street, Room 235, Kansas City, MO 64106; Phone: (816) 426-5233. New York Regional Office, 26 Federal Plaza, Room 3811, New York, NY 10278; Phone: (212) 264-4488. Philadelphia Regional Office, 150 South Independence Mall West, Philadelphia, PA 19106; Phone: (215) 861-4140. San Francisco Regional Office, 75 Hawthorne Street, 4th Floor, San Francisco, CA 94105; Phone: (415) 744-3501. Seattle Regional Office, 2201 6th Avenue, RX 40. Seattle, WA 98121; Phone: (206) 615-2306.

FOOD AND DRUG ADMINISTRATION (FDA)

The Food and Drug Administration has legal jurisdiction over pertinent consumer products marketed and shipped in interstate commerce, and usually not products that are manufactured, shipped, and marketed within one state. It works to promote and protect the public health by reviewing clinical research and allowing or disallowing marketing of regulated products. It seeks to ensure that foods (except for meat and poultry) are safe, wholesome, sanitary, and properly labeled; that prescription and nonprescription human and veterinary drugs are safe and effective; that medical assistance devices are safe and effective; that cosmetics are safe and properly labeled; and that the public is protected from electronic products' radiation.

The FDA also communicates with other countries to reduce regulation and make regulatory requirements more equal, although pharmaceutical companies resist Americans' purchase of drugs abroad at lower prices.

Among other functions FDA protects the public from food-borne illnesses through safer food handling, and provides more effective detection, tracking, and prevention of these diseases; works toward a safer blood supply by improving donor screening, blood testing, and blood banking; provides better detection and prevention of disease-causing organisms and chemicals in food products; and provides increasing testing and surveillance of new medicines, medical devices, vaccines, blood products, gene therapy, toothbrushes and thermometers, pacemakers, dialysis machines and transplant tissues and organs, tanning salons, and infant formula. FDA oversees regulation of radiation exposure from electronic devices such as microwave ovens, cell phones, X-ray and mammogram machines, lasers, MRI machines and medical ultrasound equipment and regulates animal medicines, cosmetics and their ingredients, and truth in food and product ingredients and labeling.

Signed June 30, 1906, by President Theodore Roosevelt, the Food and Drugs Act created the first consumer protection law and made it illegal to distribute mislabeled and adulterated foods, drinks, and drugs across state lines, having grown out of the Division of Chemistry which, in July, 1901, became the Bureau of Chemistry. Before 1906 testing had amounted to checking the safety of food additives by feeding them to federal employees, known affectionately as the "Poison Squad." In 1927 the Bureau of Chemistry morphed into the Food, Drug, and Insecticide Administration, with the name shortened to the Food and Drug Administration in July 1930.

Until 1937 law did not require testing of products' safety before making them available to the public, a point made disastrously public by the deaths of 107 people who were given elixir of sulfanilamide, marketed for children, and including a chemical used to make antifreeze. Congress responded to this crisis by passing the federal Food, Drug and Cosmetic Act in 1938, which required companies to prove new drugs' safety before selling them, and regulated cosmetics and therapeutic devices. Now drugs and medical devices must be proven safe as well as effective before they go on the market. In 1940 the agency moved from the DEPARTMENT OF AGRICULTURE to the new Federal Security Agency, and then in 1953 the FDA was placed in the Department of Health, Education, and Welfare (HEW). The FDA became part of the Public Health Service within HEW in 1968, and in May 1980 HEW was divided into the DEPARTMENT OF EDUCATION and the DEPARTMENT OF HEALTH AND HUMAN SERVICES, where the FDA now resides.

After products are on the market, the FDA inspects manufacturers and their products in the United States and abroad, checks shipments of imported products, and collects and tests samples for contamination. The FDA watches for adverse reactions to drugs and devices on the market, and processes more than 400,000 complaints each year. If problems are detected, the FDA follows steps and works with the manufacturer to voluntarily correct the problem, takes legal steps if that fails including possibly asking the manufacturer to recall the product, having federal marshals seize products if the manufacturer refuses to recall the product, withdrawing approval of a drug or product, requiring label changes and corrections, and sending warnings to health practitioners. The FDA may also detain imports at their port of entry into the United States, and even may ask the courts for injunctions or to prosecute deliberate law violators.

In the veterinary field the FDA oversees veterinary devices and drugs, pet foods, and livestock feeds, which eventually find their way into the human food supply.

The FDA offers numerous consumer publications on new products and other topics, and much of this information is also available and updated regularly on the FDA website. One of the public's most frequent complaints is the slowness of the FDA's drug and device approval process in the United States, although the FDA claims that new breakthrough products are now reviewed in six months or less, with a 40 percent increase in new drugs approved in each year, all enabled by increased funding and staff from the Prescription Drug User Fee Act of 1992. Until that act was passed, the time for drug approvals averaged 30 months.

CONTACT Address: 5600 Fishers Lane, Rockville, MD 20857; Phone: (888) 463-6332; Website: www.fda.gov/. Hotlines: Food information: (888) 723-3366; Vaccine Adverse Event Reporting System: (800) 822-7967; Mammography Information Service: (800) 838-7715; AIDS Clinical Trials Information Service (ACTIS): (800) TRIALS-A.

FDA Centers and Offices: All FDA centers and offices have extensive advisory committees of professionals in each field of expertise.

CENTER FOR BIOLOGICS EVALUATION AND RESEARCH (CBER): Regulates biological products including blood, vaccines, tissue, allergenics, and biological therapeutics. In contrast to chemically made drugs, biologics derive from living sources such as humans, animals, or microorganisms, as complex mixtures occasionally made using biotechnology.

CBER takes responsibility for making sure the nation's blood supply and products made from it are safe; approval and production of safe and effective childhood and AIDS vaccines; oversight of human tissues to be used in transplantation; making sure the nation has a sufficient safe supply of allergenic materials and antitoxins; and development and approval of safe and effective biological therapeutics, including new biotechnology-derived products used against AIDS and cancer.

CBER evaluates new and already approved biological products by requiring evaluation of the scientific and clinical data submitted by manufacturers. After a close look, CBER weighs the risks and benefits of the new drug, considering its intended use and the population it is supposed to serve. In this case "safe" does not mean a drug or device is void of risk. All medical products afford some risk. CBER balances "safe" and "risk," protecting itself legally within the following definition: "A safe biological product is one that has reasonable risks, given the patient's condition, the magnitude of the benefit expected, and the alternatives available. The choice to use a biological product involves balancing the benefits to be gained with the potential risks."

CONTACT Address: Center for Biologics Evaluation and Research (CBER), Food and Drug Administration, 1401 Rockville Pike, Rockville, MD 20852-1448; Phones: (301) 827-1800, (800) 835-4709; blood and plasma information: (301) 827-4604, (888) CBER-BPI; consumer product questions E-mail: OCTMA@CBER.FDA.GOV; Website: www.fda.gov/cber.

CENTER FOR DEVICES AND RADIOLOGICAL HEALTH (CDRH): CDRH is responsible for a variety of in vitro diagnostic tests; review, monitoring, evaluation, and surveillance of the medical device industry; clearance of devices for clinical trials and marketing including investigative and humanitarian device exemption; follow-up after medical devices are approved for marketing, including analyzing reports of adverse events during or after use, recalls, and other corrective actions; guidance for design and labeling of medical devices to reduce hazards that may result from use; disclosure requirements for devices made in the United States or in foreign countries intended for commercial distribution in the United States.

CDRH also makes available guidance, regulations, and laws applicable to the manufacture and use of radiation emitting products and devices. It disseminates information for mammogram consumers, facility personnel, and inspectors; regulates products that emit electromagnetic radiation; works toward prevention of unnecessary radiation exposure from such products; provides information on CT (whole body computed tomography) scanning; and makes recommendations on measuring and recording information from and about patients using electromagnetic signals in wireless medical telemetry. The technical electronic product radiation safety standards committee advises the FDA on current and proposed performance standards for electronic products.

CONTACT For accidental radiation occurrence, Address: Office of Compliance (HFZ-300), 2094 Gaither Road, Rockville, MD 20850. For radiation defect or failure to comply with standards, Address: Notice of Defect/Noncompliance, Office of Compliance (HFZ-300), 2098 Gaither Road, Rockville, MD 20850, and Electronic Product Reports, Office of Compliance (HFZ-307), 2098 Gaither Road, Rockville, MD 20850; Website: www.fda.gov/cdrhy/radhlth/.

CENTER FOR DRUG EVALUATION AND RESEARCH (CDER): CDER focuses on new drug development and review, generic drug review, over-the-counter drug review, and post-drug approval. CDER's goal is to make sure safe and effective medicines and drugs are available to Americans.

New drug applicants need to have the following reviews completed to place their products on the market: medical, chemical, pharmacological, and statistical reviews; safety reviews, a judgment of whether the drug is acceptable for the approval study to proceed; and further reviews and notification of the applicant of either acceptability or deficiency of the application.

In its role of checking the safety and effectiveness of drugs already available for use in the United States, CDER monitors post-marketing product qualities; prescription drug advertising and promotional labeling; medication errors; drug shortages; pharmaceutical industry surveillance; and therapeutic inequivalence reporting.

Post-Marketing Surveillance (PMS) monitors safety of drugs on the market by reassessing drug risks based on new data, and recommending ways of managing that risk through the Division of Pharmacovigilance and Epidemiology. PMS tracks drug experiences and epidemiologic sources, monitors Adverse Drug Reaction Reports, and offers drug safety data on a national level.

To monitor prescription drug advertising and promotional labeling, CDER's Division of Drug Marketing, Advertising and Communications (DDMAC) provides guidelines to drug firms, advertising and labeling definitions to the industry and to the public, and engages in patient education.

CDER estimates that medication errors cause at least one death daily and injure 1.3 million Americans each year. Medication mistakes happen most frequently at the following stages of the medical system: prescribing, repackaging, dispensing, administering, job stress, and monitoring, often due to poor communication, confusion in product names, directions for use, and hand writing or abbreviations, poor procedures or techniques including haste, and patient mistake due to misunderstanding directions for use of the product.

To reduce medication errors, CDER works to prevent errors prior to a drug's approval; monitors, evaluates, and takes action on medication errors after the drug is approved; gives feedback and improves education to health professionals; and shares information with organizations outside the U.S. government that are involved in preventing medication errors.

WEBSITE www.fda.gov/cder/handbook/mederror.htm.

In 1992 a Medication Errors Subcommittee began to evaluate and code MedWatch reports of medication errors. Health care professionals and consumers can report medication errors to the FDA and get medical products safety information through MedWatch.

CONTACT (800) FDA-1088; Website: www.fda.gov/medwatch/.

Medical drug shortages should be reported by consumers through the Drug Shortage System, maintained by CDER's Drug Quality Reporting System (DQRS). Drug shortages result from changes in marketing and production; voluntary or FDA recalls; shortages of raw materials; unpredicted or unanticipated disease outbreaks, even due to terrorism; shortages caused when one producer controls and supplies the entire quantity available; actual shortages of drugs; a lack of a medically necessary product when there is no substitute that has been approved; and insufficient production or stockpile of particular medicines or vaccines.

When a shortage is reported and deemed valid, the FDA decides whether the cause of the shortage is production or distribution. The FDA has uncovered these problems and helped correct them in cases involving tuberculosis drugs, antibiotics, antihypertensives, and insulin products.

WEBSITE www.fda.gov/cder/handbook/shortage.htm.

Pharmaceutical Industry Surveillance breaks down into preapproval and postapproval categories. FDA works to make sure pharmaceutical firms adhere to the terms and conditions approved in their application for drug approval, and that the drug is actually produced in a required consistent and controlled manner.

The FDA makes unannounced inspections of factories, vehicles, equipment, records, process, and controls required by their regulations. Those regulations, entitled the Current Good Manufacturing Practice for Finished Pharmaceuticals, are included in Part 211 of Title 21 of the U.S. Code of Federal Regulations. They include requirements for organization and personnel, buildings and facilities, equipment, components, containers, closures, production and process control, packaging and labeling, distribution, laboratories, and reports and records.

The regulations apply to everything from dosages of drugs to topical ointments, creams, sterile injectables, and ophthalmics. They also require testing of every batch before release to the market for conformance to specific master formulae and processes, validation of manufacturing and control processes, investigation of complaints and failures, testing of a product for stability during its shelf life as specified by the label's expiration date, and testing of ingredients and components.

Created in 1988, the FDA established the Therapeutic Inequivalence Action Coordinating Committee (TIACC) to find and evaluate reports of drug products that fail to work for patients, either because the drug has no effect or has a toxic effect. Sometimes these are the results of substituting one drug for another, when the two drugs are not actually the same. TIACC may conduct a full-scale investigation.

Once the inequivalence of the product is proven, TIACC might remove the inequivalent product from the market; evaluate and change the therapeutic equivalence rating; recommend that an existing product manufacturer file a new application for approval of the drug; test and evaluate the inconsistencies of the inequivalent drug; recommend changes to make the drug identical to the one it replaces; and evaluate the toxicity profile of injectables and require appropriate controls to create equivalency.

WEBSITE www.fda.gov/cder/handbook/tiacc.htm.

CDER's Office of Generic Drugs works to assure that generic drugs offered are safe and effective. A generic drug is the identical or bioequivalent to a brand name drug in composition, safety, strength, route of administration, quality, performance, and use. Generic drugs are usually sold at a much lower cost than their brand name counterparts.

Drug manufacturers have to submit an abbreviated new drug application (ANDA) for official approval to market a generic product, due to the Drug Price Competition and Patent Term Restoration Act of 1984, also known as the Hatch-Waxman Act. Drug manufacturers get patents for new drug formulae to keep others from duplicating their product, giving them the sole right to sell the drug while the patent is in effect. When the patent or other forms of exclusive rights expire, other manufacturers can apply to the FDA to sell generic versions of the drug. ANDA speeds the generic approval process by not requiring the new, current, or former manufacturer to repeat expensive animal and clinical research on ingredients or dosage that have been approved since 1962.

To be approved, a generic drug must contain the same active ingredients as the original drug; be identical in strength, dosage form, and route of administration; have the same use directions and indications; be the bioequivalent; meet the same batch requirements for identity, strength, purity, and quality; and be manufactured according to the same FDA standards required of new product manufacturers. For generic drug approvals, generic drug labeling updates, therapeutic equivalence of generic drugs, generic drug development, and new drug applications, contact: www.fda.gov/cder/ogd/.

Over-the-counter drugs (OTC), drugs that are available without a prescription, account for six out of ten medicinal drug purchases by Americans, and are reviewed by CDER's Division of Over-the-Counter Drug Products. OTC products range from acne products to weight control drug products and aspirin.

CDER makes sure OTCs are properly and accurately labeled and that their benefits outweigh their risks to consumers through the OTC Drug Review Program. This program establishes OTC monographs (recipes) for acceptable ingredients, doses, formulations, and labeling. Monographs are updated continually, adding ingredients and labeling. Products that conform to a monograph may be marketed without new approval, while those that do not have to go through the New Drug Approval System. New OTC products that were previously available only by prescription first have to go through the New Drug System and then switch to OTC status if the New Drug System approves.

WEBSITE www.fda.gov/cder/handbook/otcintro.htm.

Other CDER functions in assuring safe and effective drugs include keeping a drug registration and listing system, doing environmental assessments, focusing on women's health issues, and creating pediatric initiatives.

CONTACT Phones: (800) 741-8138, (301) 443-0572; Fax-on-demand: (800) 342-2722; drug information branch: (301) 827-4573; Website: www.fda.gov/cder/. FDA Office of Consumer Affairs: Phone: (800) 532-4440, (301) 827-4420.

CENTER FOR FOOD SAFETY & APPLIED NUTRITION (CFSAN): Promotes and protects U.S. public health by working to ensure that the nation's food supply is safe, sanitary, wholesome, and truthfully labeled, and by working to make cosmetic products safe and appropriately labeled. To that end, CFSAN regulates the products' port of entry to the United States or processing until they go to market, including 50,000 food establishments (including more than 30,000 domestic food manufacturers and processors and more than 20,000 food warehouses) and 3,500 cosmetic firms. This does not include nearly 1 million restaurants, institutional food establishments, supermarkets, grocery stores, convenience stores, and other food outlets. The FDA works with state and local authorities toward uniform food establishment and retailer standards.

In the food area FDA is responsible for all domestic and imported food except for meat, poultry, and frozen, dried, and liquid eggs, which fall under U.S. Department of Agriculture's (USDA) Food Safety and Inspection Service control. FDA is not responsible for labeling of alcoholic beverages (those above 7 percent alcohol), which are the responsibility of the U.S. DEPARTMENT OF THE TREASURY's Bureau of Alcohol, Tobacco, and Firearms (ATF). The U.S. Environmental Protection Agency (EPA) establishes "tolerance levels" for pesticide residues in foods and works to ensure safe drinking water.

FDA oversees food products sold in interstate commerce. Foods grown or produced and sold entirely within a state are regulated by that state.

CFSAN programs address acidified and low-acid canned foods; biotechnology; color additives; cosmetics; dietary supplements; food ingredients and packaging; food-borne illnesses; food labeling and nutrition; imports and exports; inspections, compliance, enforcements and recalls; pesticides and chemical contaminants including diets; a seafood and regulatory fish encyclopedia; food allergens; produce and imports; eggs, fruit juice, sprouts, listeria, milk and shellfish. Its seafood Hazard Analysis and Critical Control Point (HACCP) regulations attempt to make sure seafood that makes it to market is safe for human consumption.

CFSAN also pays special attention to young children, teens, and educators; seniors; and women's health, with a large consumer advice section.

A particular CFSAN focus is contamination that may enter the food product while it is growing or during the food's processing, packaging, transportation, and preparation. Areas of concern include biological pathogens such as bacteria, viruses, and parasites; naturally occurring toxins such as mycotoxins, ciguatera toxin, and paralytic (to the consumer) shellfish poison; dietary supplements such as ephedra; pesticide residues; toxic metals such as lead and mercury; decomposition and contaminants such as insect fragments; food allergens such as eggs, peanuts, wheat, and milk; nutrient concerns such as Vitamin D overdoses and iron toxicity in children; dietary components such as fat and cholesterol; radionuclides; TSE-type diseases such as chronic wasting disease found in elk; and product tampering.

To monitor food safety, CFSAN inspects food establishments; collects and analyzes samples; monitors imported foods; conducts premarket reviews of food and color additives; conducts notification programs of food contact substances and infant formula; publishes regulations and agreements with producers; conducts consumer studies and focus groups; and performs laboratory research in many fields.

CFSAN works on joint projects such as the Joint Institute for Food Safety and Applied Nutrition (JIFSAN) with the University of Maryland, and the National Center for Food Safety and Technology (NCFST) with the Illinois Institute of Technology, in a government, academia, and industry effort.

CONTACT Address: 5100 Paint Branch Parkway, College Park, MD 20740-3835; Phone: (301) 935-6074; Website: www.cfsan.fda.gov or www.FoodSafety.gov.

CENTER FOR VETERINARY MEDICINE (CVM): Regulates production and distribution of food additives and drugs to be given to animals, including to animals that end up as human food, as well as food additives, feed, and drugs for domestic animals. CVM also regulates drugs, devices, and food additives used on or given to companion animals, poultry, cattle, swine, and minor animal species, the latter of which may include animals other than cattle, swine, chickens, turkeys, horses, dogs, and cats. Among CVM's goals is to increase availability of safe and effective products to relieve animal pain and suffering, and extend their health, with sensitivity to owners' cultural diversity. Another is to make sure animal drugs do not result in unsafe residue levels in human foods.

To bring producers into compliance, CVM educates consumers and producers; evaluates data on proposed veterinary products before they go to market; initiates legal action if necessary to bring violators into compliance with law; and conducts research.

CVM approves New Animal Drug Applications (NADAs) and Abbreviated New Animal Drug Applications (ANADAs) and withdraws new animal drug approvals when hearings have been waived.

CONTACT Address: 7519 Standish Place, HFV-12, Rockville, MD 20855; Phone: (301) 827-3800; Website: www.fda.gov/cvm/.

NATIONAL CENTER FOR TOXICOLOGICAL RESEARCH (NCTR): Researches what causes toxicity of products regulated by the FDA to assess human exposure, susceptibility, and risk at their laboratory complex near Little Rock, Pine Bluff, and Benton, Arkansas. The 35 buildings house general purpose and high-containment laboratories, specific pathogen-free "barrier" laboratory animal breeding and holding rooms, conventional laboratory animal holding rooms, primate research facilities, diet preparation facilities, pathology laboratories, hazardous waste disposal, and an extensive scientific and technical library.

CONTACT Address: 3900 NCTR Road, Jefferson, AR 72079; Phone: (870) 543-7000; Website: www.fda.gov/nctr/.

OFFICE OF REGULATORY AFFAIRS: Produces publications on FDA regulations, import programs for brokers, wholesalers, retailers, and consumers that have been detained; manuals containing procedures and guidance for conducting or submitting to inspections; promotes uniform policies on food and drug-related matters between the federal government and state governments; offers access to FDA consumer health information such as the FDA Bulletin Board, History, and Public Affairs offices; offers local contacts for industry assistance and information; and publicizes recalls.

CONTACTS *Headquarters:* Regional offices: *Northeast Region* and New York District, 158-15 Liberty Avenue, Jamaica, NY 11433; Phone: (718) 340-7000; Fax: 622-5434. New England Office, One Montvale Avenue, Stoneham, MA 02180; Phone: (781) 279-1675. Winchester Engineering & Analytical Center (WEAC), 109 Holton Street, Winchester, MA 01890; Phone: (781) 729-5700. Buffalo Office, 300 Pearl Street, Suite 100, Buffalo, NY 14202; Phone: (716) 551-4461, Ext., 3103; Fax: (716) 551-4470. *Central Region* and Philadelphia District Office, 900 U.S. Customhouse, 2nd & Chestnut Streets, Philadelphia, PA 19106. Baltimore Region, 900 Madison Avenue, Baltimore, MD 21201; Phone: (410) 779-5102. Chicago Field Office, 20 North Michigan Avenue, Room 510, Chicago, IL 60602. Forensic Chemistry Center (FCC) and Cincinnati District Office, 6751 Steger Drive, Cincinnati, OH 45237; Phone: (513) 679-2700; Fax: (513) 679-2761. Baltimore District, 6000 Metro Drive, Baltimore, MD 21215; Phone: (410) 779-5424; Fax: (410) 779-5707. Chicago

District: 300 South Riverside Plaza, 5th Floor, Suite 550 South, Chicago, IL 60606; Phone: (312) 353-7379; Fax: (312) 886-3280. Detroit District, 1560 East Jefferson Avenue, Detroit, MI 48207-3179; Phone: (313) 226-6260; Fax: (313) 226-3076. Minneapolis District, 240 Hennepin Avenue, Minneapolis, MN 55401; Phone: (612) 334-4100; Fax: (612) 334-4134. New Jersey District, Waterview Corp. Center, 10 Waterview Boulevard, 3rd Floor, Parsippany, NJ 07054; Phone: (973) 526-6000; Fax: (973) 526-6069. *Southeast Region,* 60 Eighth Street NE, Atlanta, GA 30309; Phone: (404) 253-1171; Fax: (404) 253-1207. Florida Office, 555 Winderley Place, Suite 200, Maitland, FL 32751. New Orleans District Office, 6600 Plaza Drive, Suite 400, New Orleans, LA 70127; Phone: (504) 253-4500; Fax: (504) 253-4504. San Juan Region, 466 Fernandez Juncos Avenue, San Juan, Puerto Rico 00901-3223; Phone: (787) 729-6842; Fax: (787) 729-6851. *Southwest Region,* 7920 Elmbrook Road, Suite 102, Dallas, TX 75247-4982; Phone: (214) 655-8100; Fax: (214) 253-5318. Denver Office, 6th & Kipling Street, P.O. Box 25087, Denver, CO 80225-0087; Phone: (303) 236-3016; Fax: (913) 752-2111. *Pacific Region,* 1301 Clay Street, Suite 1180-N, Oakland, CA 94512-5217. Pacific Regional Lab Northwest and Seattle District Office, 22201 23rd Street WE, Bothell, WA 98021-4421; Phone: (425) 483-4901. Pacific Lab Southwest, 1521 West Pico Boulevard, Los Angeles, CA 90015-2486; Phone: (213) 252-7592; Fax: (213) 251-7142. Los Angeles District Office, 19900 MacArthur Boulevard, Suite 300, Irvine, CA 92612-2445; San Francisco District, 1431 Harbor Bay Parkway, Alameda, CA 94502-7070; Phone: (510) 337-6700.

FDA-AFFILIATED ORGANIZATIONS

Joint Institute for Food Safety and Applied Nutrition (JIFSAN): A public and private partnership between the U.S. Food and Drug Administration and the University of Maryland created in 1996, JIFSAN is a multidisciplinary research and education program that includes the Centers for Food Safety and Applied Nutrition (CFSAN), Veterinary Medicine (CVM), and the University of Maryland. JIFSAN researches food supply safety and wholesomeness, human nutrition, and animal health, including human exposure to microbial pathogens, natural toxins, and other chemical compounds such as pesticides and animal drug residues in the food supply.

JIFSAN's Hazard Analysis Critical Control Point (HACCP) works to reduce Americans' exposure to microbial hazards in the food supply, along with researching emerging pathogens, virulence factors, and better detection of pathogenic organisms and microbial toxins.

JIFSAN studies food composition and how it affects safety and applied nutrition, including trace elements, special dietary needs (especially among more susceptible populations), beneficial nonnutritive components, dietary supplements, potential human health hazards in the food supply, help in compliance with Nutrition Labeling and Education Act, and the results in humans of some food processing techniques that may first appear as new foods or dietary supplements in the diet.

Research in animal health sciences and food safety contributes data to establish and support public health policies in animal drugs, food additives in animal feeds, and veterinary medical devices, with the assumption that these ingredients, additives, and processes make their way into the human food supply. JIFSAN also investigates human resistance to antibiotics that results from antibiotics given to food animals.

CONTACT Address: University of Maryland, JIFSAN, 0220 Symons Hall, College Park, MD 20742; Phone: (301) 405-8382; Website: www.jifsan.umd.edu/.

The *National Center for Food Safety and Technology (NCFST)* emphasizes research and outreach by encouraging exchange of scientific and technical information among academics, government, and food science and industry members. Funded through the Center for Food

Safety and Applied Nutrition, the U.S. FDA, and the Illinois Institute of Technology, NCFST also conducts research into regulating food safety, and research into promoting the importance of the U.S. food supply's safety and quality. NCFST's Oversight Advisory Committee establishes operating policy for research, and the Technical Advisory Committee reviews research proposals and establishes research project priorities. Researchers working on these projects include food scientists, and experts in technology, food process engineering, biotechnology, chemistry, chemical engineering, packaging, microbiology, and nutrition. The center includes research laboratories, pilot plants, and a huge scientific library.

CONTACT Address: National Center for Food Safety and Technology, Illinois Institute of Technology, Moffett Campus, 6502 South Archer Avenue, Summit-Argo, IL 60501; Phone: (202) 205-4064; Website: www.iit.edu/~ndfs/.

HEALTH RESOURCES AND SERVICES ADMINISTRATION (HRSA)

The Health Resources and Services Administration works to make quality health care accessible and available to everyone, particularly low-income, uninsured, isolated, vulnerable, and special needs people and those with unique health care needs. It aims to provide 100 percent health care access with no disparities in levels of health care available to all Americans, through improving public health care and American general health care systems.

HRSA supports a network of 643 community and migrant health centers nationwide, and 144 primary care programs for homeless adults and children and for public housing residents. HRSA also runs the National Health Service Corps, oversees and coordinates the organ transplantation system throughout the country, works to improve infant health and decrease infant mortality among HRSA's service population, and provides AIDS services through the Ryan White CARE Act programs.

HIV/AIDS BUREAU: The largest source of federal HIV/AIDS care funding for low-income, uninsured, and underinsured individuals and the homeless outside of Medicaid and Medicare, thanks to the Ryan White CARE Act. The HIV/AIDS Bureau began in 1997 to consolidate programs covered by the Ryan White Comprehensive AIDS Resources Emergency (CARE) Act, which was signed into law August 15, 1990, by President George H.W. Bush. Reorganized and amended in November 2000, it was named for Ryan White, an inspired and inspiring hemophiliac teenager from Indiana who contracted HIV/AIDS from blood transfusions and died of AIDS in 2000 after appearing on worldwide television shows to educate the public on the disease.

The Ryan White CARE Act includes emergency funding relief to metropolitan areas with a disproportionate number of the population affected by HIV/AIDS; helps states and territories improve availability, quality, and delivery of health care support services to patients and families of HIV/AIDS patients; provides access to pharmaceuticals through the AIDS Drug Assistance Program (ADAP); works to provide early intervention and primary care to people with HIV/AIDS; works to improve access to care for children, youth, women, and their families who are at risk for HIV/AIDS; encourages and supports innovation in care development models; supports training for health care workers and providers to counsel, diagnose, and treat HIV patients, and to work toward preventing high risk behaviors that cause HIV/AIDS infection; gives financial support to dental schools, postdoctoral dental education programs, and dental hygiene programs to care for persons with HIV disease when other sources (insurance companies) would not pay for the care. Website: http://hab.hrsa.gov

HRSA's HIV/AIDS Bureau takes special initiatives, including HIV and AIDS role in border health, services to people in correctional facilities, injection drug users, integrating health care networks, people with multiple diagnoses, Native Americans including American Indians and Alaskan Natives, outreach programs, end-of-life (palliative) care, HIV/AIDS prevention, quality of care, substance abuse, unmet care needs, and unavailability of pharmaceuticals.

Along the U.S.-Mexico border efforts focus on community-based health care and identification of HIV for people who live and/or work on the U.S. side of the border, especially those who are at high risk for HIV or have HIV/AIDS. Programs include the Centro de Evaluacion, San Ysidro Health Center, El Rio Health Center, Camino de Vida, Centro de Salud Familiar La Fe, and Valley AIDS Council. Website: http://hrsa.gov/special/border_overview.htm

With the support of CDC and HRSA, the HIV/AIDS Bureau works toward HIV prevention, intervention, and care in prisons and other correctional facilities. This special initiative aims to improve access to health care for both incarcerated and at-risk African Americans and other racial minorities. Goals include increasing access to HIV/AIDS prevention and health care services; improving transitional health care services for HIV/AIDS infected prisoners moving from correctional institutions to outside communities; forming more effective links and coordinating health care and social services; improving networks and health services for HIV/AIDS, STD, TB, hepatitis, and substance abuse prevention and treatment and how it relates to HIV/AIDS during and after incarceration; and developing prevention, primary care, and psychosocial support and referral systems.

Services to People with HIV in Correctional Settings has given grants to develop these projects at the following sites: Baltimore City Office of Homeless Services, Baltimore, Maryland; Emory University, Atlanta, Georgia; Fortune Society, Inc., New York, New York; Health Care for the Homeless, Inc., Baltimore, Maryland; Housing Authority of Santa Cruz County,

Capitola, California; Miriam Hospital, Proficence, Rhode Island; Montefiore Medical Center, Bronx, New York; Trustees of Columbia University, New York, New York; University of Miami School of Medicine, Miami, Florida; University of Washington, Seattle, Washington; Volunteers of America, Alexandria, Virginia. Website: http://hab/hrsa.gov/special/spnspopulations.htm.

Another special initiative, the bureau focuses on HIV-seropositive injection drug users (IDUs) researching and working to prevent HIV transmission through drug injection and high-risk sexual practices. It also works to increase access to and actual use of primary health care and HIV treatments, including prophylaxis for drug injectors, some aimed at preventing side infections.

The HIV/AIDS Bureau also targets individuals with "multiple diagnoses," such as people suffering from HIV/AIDS, mental illness, chronic substance abuse, tuberculosis, hepatitis, and/or are homeless. One goal is to coordinate housing, support, counseling, and health care services. Website: http://hav.hrsa.gov/special/facts.

The American Indian/Alaskan Native (AI/AN) Initiative focuses on American Indians and Alaskan Natives who have higher rates of "comorbidities" than other populations, meaning these groups are more likely to suffer HIV/AIDS in conjunction with substance abuse and/or chemical dependency, including alcoholism, sexually transmitted infections, and mental illnesses such as depression.

Grants for these projects have gone to the Alaska Native Tribal Health Consortium, Anchorage, Alaska; Na'Nizhoozi Center, Inc., Gallup, New Mexico; Robeson Health Care corporation, Fairmount, North Carolina; South Puget Intertribal Planning Agency, Shelton, Washington; Urban Indian Health Board Inc., Oakland, California; Yukon-Kuskokwim Health Corporation, Bethel, Alaska; and the University of Oklahoma, Norman, Oklahoma. Website: http://hab.hrsa.gov/special/na_an.htm.

Through the HIV/AIDS Bureau, an effort is being made via HIV Outreach and Intervention Models to reach underserved HIV positive people who are especially vulnerable and marginalized. Some people suffering from the disease are not being treated at all for a variety of reasons, which may include cultural and linguistic biases, racial and gender discrimination, and lack of health insurance. Some sufferers who are African American, Latino, or are intravenous drug users have not been diagnosed for these reasons, or may be diagnosed and treated later than average. Ways of reaching potential patients in rural areas, or who are racial and ethnic minorities living in ghettos, or those just released from correctional institutions, include street outreach and mobile vans.

Grants for researching needs include to the Access Community Health Network, Chicago, Illinois; AIDS Service Center, Anniston, Alabama; Blacks Assisting Blacks Against AIDS, St. Louis, Missouri; Charles Drew University, Los Angeles, California; Community AIDS Resources, Inc., Coral Gables, Florida; Fenway Community Health Center, Boston, Massachusetts; Harm Reduction Services, Sacramento, California; Miriam Hospital, Providence, Rhode Island; Montefiore Medical Center, Bronx, New York; Multnomah County, Oregon, Portland, Oregon; UCLA Schools of Medicine & Public Health, Los Angeles, California; University of Miami School of Medicine, Miami, Florida; University of Texas Health Science Center, San Antonio, Texas; University of Washington Dept. of Psychiatry, Seattle, Washington; Wayne State University, Detroit, Michigan; Well Being Institute, Detroit, Michigan; and Whitman Walker Clinic, Washington, D.C.

The *End-of-Life/Palliative Care Initiative* under the HIV/AIDS Bureau aims at providing end-of-life care for HIV/AIDS patients and evaluate five demonstration projects in rural, urban, and suburban settings that are testing end-of-life care with medically underserved and hard to reach populations who are dying of HIV/AIDS and cannot be saved. Care services range from full palliative care to hospice care. All of this research is overseen by the Columbia University Mailman School of Public Health and covers quality of care, quality of life, symptoms, psychological function, physical function, client service, client demographics, client medical status, and client medical treatment history.

Grants for palliative/end-of-life study and care have gone to the AIDS Services Center, Inc., Aniston, Alabama; Catholic Community Services, Jersey City, New Jersey; Montefiore Medical Center-Palliative, Bronx New York; Montefiore Medical Center-Prisons, Bronx, New York; University of Maryland, Baltimore, Maryland; and Volunteers of America, New Orleans, Louisiana.

CONTACT Address: General Offices: 5600 Fishers Lane, Rockville, MD 20857; Phone: (301) 443-3376; Website: www.hrsa.gov. Regional offices: Northeast: 150 S. Independence Mall West, Suite 1172, Philadelphia, PA 19106-3496; Phone: (215) 861-4396; Fax: (215) 861-4385. Southeast: 61 Forsyth Street, South West, Suite 3M60, Atlanta, GA 30303; Phone: (404) 562-4195; Fax: (404) 562-7974. Pacific West: 50 United Nations Plaza, Room 349 A, San Francisco, CA 94102; Phone: (415) 437-7691; Fax: (415) 437-7664. Midwest: 233 North Michigan Avenue, Suite 200, Chicago, IL 60601-5519; Phone: (312) 886-1631; Fax: (312) 886-3770. West Central: 1301 Young Street, 10th Floor, Dallas, TX 75202; Phone: (214) 767-3872; Fax: (214) 767-8049.

BUREAU OF PRIMARY HEALTH CARE (BPHC): Started the Movement Toward 100% Access and 0% Health Disparities in 1998, also known as the 100%/0 Movement. The movement's goal is to get community leaders and business groups to set and achieve clear goals of everyone having equal access to primary health care in their communities, free of disparities based on race, ethnicity, gender, age, sexual preference, or income, and utilizing and re-organizing existing community health assets. The stress is on reforming health care from the bottom up, maintaining and expanding databases of community resources and teams, and providing electronic, print, and other materials to help community organizations achieve their goals.

CONTACT Address: Center for Communities in Action, Bureau of Primary Health Care, East West Towers, 4350 East West Highway, Bethesda, MD 20814; Phone: (301) 594-3801; Fax: (301) 594-4987.

Healthy Aging Initiative aims to improve access to comprehensive health care for underserved Americans 50 years of age and older by giving both Medicare and Medicaid coverage, outreach to bring care to older people, quality appropriate health care, and information on how to use these methods in other constituencies. Healthy Aging coordinates communication and management of all activities concerning adult health care, emphasizing care for women and older persons. Among Healthy Aging health center users, patients frequently suffered from hypertension, heart disease, diabetes, mental health problems, asthma, and bronchial emphysema. Mental health and substance abuse needs frequently include depression, anxiety, alcohol dependency, and drug dependency. In 2000 persons aged 65 and over in the United States represented 13 percent of the population, with that number and percentage expected to rise as baby boomers age, to 70 million or 20 percent of the population by 2030, at which time 25 percent of the older population will be of racial and/or ethnic minorities. Website: http://bphc.hrsa.gov/Aging.

Black Lung Clinics Program: Originally funded under the Black Lung Benefits Reform Act of 1977 and amended in 1985, reinstating a part of the Federal Mine and Safety Act so the secretary of health and human services can support clinics specifically to evaluate and treat coal miners with respiratory problems resulting from their occupation. The program's goal is to provide health services to coal miners and others with occupation-related respiratory disease through publicly funded clinics that provide diagnosis, treatment, and rehabilitation of active and retired coal miners with respiratory and lung impairments, counsel them and their families on benefits programs, and reduce care and funeral costs for black lung disease sufferers. The 17 grantee organizations also provide educational programs for respiratory disease patients and their families to help them cope with the disease, improve their breathing and endurance, and improve the quality of their lives through 49 clinics.

The Black Lung Program also works to reach out to current and former miners to inform them of services available and to improve cooperation, education, and communication between coal mining companies and mining communities on risks and methods of prevention of black lung disease.

CONTACT Address: Program Director, Black Lung Clinics Program, Division of Programs for Special Populations, Bureau of Primary Health Care, 4350 East-West Highway, 9th Floor, Bethesda, MD 20814; Phone: (301) 594-4100; Fax: (301) 594-2470; Website: http://bphc.hrsa.gov/programs/BLProgramInfo.htm.

HRSA Border Health Initiative: Refers to the U.S.-Mexico border. Under President Bill Clinton, the U.S.-Mexico Border Health Task Force was established when the administrator of HRSA named U.S.-Mexico border health one of HRSA's eight top priority programs, focusing on the Mexican border with Arizona, California, New Mexico, and Texas. Various problems are unique to U.S.-Mexico border residents, particularly in communities with people moving frequently between the two countries. Some of those health problems may include high rates of hepatitis, intestinal infections due to lack of clean water and proper sewage disposal, high rates of communicable diseases such as tuberculosis and vaccine-preventable diseases, poverty, unemployment, and lack of health insurance.

The Border Health Program's (BHP) goals include: partnerships with state health departments and public health advisers in Arizona and California and medical epidemiologists in New Mexico and Texas; funding for hew health centers and satellite clinics; support for the Border

Vision Fronteriza project to train 800 lay health workers (*promotoras*); enrolling 15,000 children in CHIP and Medicaid in Arizona, California, New Mexico, and Texas; grants of $12 million over five years to five organizations to provide health care to HIV/AIDS patients; working with Environmental Protection Agency (EPA) to train health center clinicians and *promotoras* on pesticide exposures, asthma surveillance, and safe water; and support of Ten Against TB, a U.S.-Mexico initiative to reduce tuberculosis cases by direct observed therapy (DOT) intervention.

Other developing programs include better and more primary health care clinics; maternal and child health care; HIV/AIDS detection and treatment; better and more available health care to this uniquely mobile population; and pursuit of environmental and workplace exposure to chemicals and other workplace health concerns.

CONTACT Address: Border Health Program, Division of Community and Migrant Health, Bureau of Primary Health Care, 4350 East West Highway, 7th Floor, Bethesda, MD 20814; Phone: (301) 594-4897; Fax: (301) 594-4997; Website: http://bphc.hrsa.gov/programs/BorderProgram. For field office, epidemiologist activities under the HRSA/New Mexico State Health Department of Understanding information,

CONTACT Address: Border Health Coordinator, Region VI, 1200 Main Tower Building, Room 1800, Dallas, TX 75202; Phone: (214) 767-3872 or (214) 767-3922; Fax: (214) 767-0404; E-mail: fcantu@hrsa.gov. For field office, public health adviser, and epidemiologist activities information,

CONTACT Address: Border Health Coordinator, Region IX, Federal Office Building, 50 United Nations Plaza, San Francisco, CA 94102; Phone: (415) 437-8090; Fax: (415) 437-8003; E-mail: gsoares@hrsa.gov. For questions re: contracts and other issues when the director is not available,

CONTACT Address: Program Management Officer, BPHC/DPSP/Border Health Program Priority, 4350 East-West Highway, Bethesda, MD

20814; Phone: (301) 394-4891; Fax: (301) 594-4997; E-mail: ampuente@hrsa.gov.

Center for Communities in Action (CCA): Targets poor, underserved, and vulnerable populations in an effort to make primary health care available to everyone in America. Created between 1998 and 2000 under the administration of President Bill Clinton, CCA works to find and help needy communities build networks and links to pool health care resources, including federal and state funding. CCA looks for alternative funding; involves local leaders to develop and inform the public of new policy; finds and supports community-based organizations to deliver 100 percent access with zero health care delivery disparities; provides technical assistance to help communities collaborate to develop strategies for local health care for needy persons; and supports a "faith partnership initiative" (inserted under President George W. Bush) to forge cooperation between faith-based and health care providers to coordinate services.

CONTACT Address: Center for Communities in Action, Bureau of Primary Health Care, 4350 East-West Highway, 3rd Floor, Bethesda, MD 20814; Phone: (301) 443-0536; Fax: (301) 443-0248; Website: http://bphc.hrsa.gov/programs/CCA/.

Community Access Program (CAP): Helps health care providers coordinate all the safety net services for Americans who have too little or no health insurance. Some communities have reorganized to better coordinate delivery of health care services to the underinsured and uninsured, including efforts to create networks so that health providers share delivery of uncompensated health care; use of up-to-date data systems to coordinate information, hospital, and clinic services; and use of local tax increases to fund managed care networks for the indigent. CAP grants help improve needed access to health care by making delivery of services more coordinated; improve efficiency among and between health care providers; and encourage private sector involvement. Some CAP projects bring mental health and substance abuse care into primary care, and involve faith communities, social, *promotores,* and human services organizations.

CAP supports 136 community projects and works to redirect patients to appropriate treatment when emergency rooms are inappropriately used or overused. Partners in these projects include local health departments, private nonprofit and public hospitals, community health centers, universities, and state governments. CAP funds are used to create and improve collaboration in integrated information systems, intake and enrollment, referral networks, and coordination of services.

CONTACT Address: Community Access Program Office, Health Resources and Services Administration, 4350 East-West Highway, 3rd Floor, Bethesda, MD 20814; Phone: (301) 443-0536; Fax: (301) 443-0248; Website: http://bphc.hrsa.gov/cap/.

Community Health Center (CHC) Program: Gives grants under Section 330 of the Public Health Service Act of 1996 to provide preventive and primary health care to medically underserved communities throughout the United States and its territories. First funded during President Lyndon B. Johnson's War on Poverty in the mid-1960s, in 1969 the Public Health Service began funding neighborhood health centers. By the early 1970s the Office of Economic Opportunity (OEO) opened about 100 neighborhood health centers, which went under Public Health Service control when OEO was phased out.

CHC provides family health and preventive care services for people in medically underserved communities either in rural or urban settings, particularly where a large percentage of the population lacks access to primary health and dental care due to economic, geographic, or cultural barriers. These populations may include African Americans, Hispanics/Latinos, poor people of any race, and other immigrant and migrant populations.

CHC also provides laboratory tests, X rays, environmental health, pharmacy, transportation to care, and prenatal care services for populations in need. It also offers connections to services including welfare, Medicaid, mental health, substance abuse treatment, and other services. CHC also strives to collaborate with private and public partners to assure funding and resources to provide health care to America's medically underserved people.

CONTACT Address: Division of Community and Migrant Health, Bureau of Primary Health Care, 4350 East-West Highway, 7th Floor, Bethesda, MD 20814; Phone: (301) 594-4300; Fax: (301) 594-4497.

Office of Data Evaluation, Analysis and Research (ODEAR): Collects and makes available data analysis and research findings to health care providers to best assure health care access and better health, and to eliminate disparities in health care delivery between well-served and underserved and vulnerable segments of the U.S. population. ODEAR involves collaborative efforts with experts, organizations, federal agencies, state agencies, primary care giver organizations, constituency advocacy organizations, and the general public.

CONTACT Address: Office of Data Evaluation, Analysis and Research, 4350 East-West Highway, 7th Floor, Bethesda, MD 20814; Phone: (301) 594-4280; Fax: (301) 594-4986; Website: http://bphc.hrsa.gov/ODEAR/.

Faith Partnership Initiative: Is intended to develop partnerships between federally funded community health centers and faith-based organizations to improve health and social well-being through a new environment of hope and healing. It also aims to help faith-based institutions engage in dialogue with public and private sector stakeholders. The Faith Partnership Initiative, created under President George W. Bush, works to develop relationships with the faith community throughout the United States.

To this end the Faith Partnership Initiative has developed a brochure to let potential partners understand the mission; and developed a network of people and organizations with expertise in working with faith-based organizations such as the Congress of National Black Churches, Interfaith Health Partnership at the Emory University School of Public Health, and the National Black Church Family Council. Specifically, Faith Partnership works with the Congress of National Black Churches to disseminate diabetes information and education. Other Faith Partners include Bridge Over Troubled Waters, Peninsula Baptist Pastors Council, Howard University School of Divinity, and the Northside Ministerial Alliance.

CONTACT Faith Partnership Initiative, Center for Communities in Action, Bureau of Primary Health Care, 4350 East-West Highway, 3rd Floor, Bethesda, MD 20814; Phone (301) 594-4494; Fax: (301) 594-4987; Website: http://bphc.hrsa.gov/programs/Faith/or www.hhs.gov/faith/.

To apply for health center grants, including expanding medical, mental health, and substance abuse capacities, contact the HRSA Grants Application Center, Attn.: Grants Management Officer, 901 Russell Avenue, Suite 450, Gaithersburg, MD 20879; Phone (877) HRSA-123; Fax: (877) HRSA-345; E-mail: hrsagac@hrsa.gov. Website: http://bphc.hrsa.gov/DPSnewcenters/. Letters of intent should be mailed to: Bureau of Primary Health Care, 4350 East-West Highway, 7th Floor, Bethesda, MD 20814.

National Hansen's Disease Programs (NHDP): Runs in- and out-patient care and treatment of leprosy, formally known as Hansen's disease. With its center in Baton Rouge, Louisiana, NHDP conducts clinical programs and out-patient care for Hansen's disease patients, education programs for international health care workers, and provides information on Hansen's disease care throughout the United States. NHDP operates laboratory research programs to improve detection, diagnosis, prevention, and treatment of Hansen's disease. The Ambulatory Hansen's Disease Program maintains a physician referral list of 900 private physicians who will treat Hansen's disease patients who do not require hospitalization throughout the United States.

CONTACT Address: National Hansen's Disease Programs, 1770 Physicians Park Drive, Baton

Rouge, LA 70816; Phone: (800) 642-2477. In Hawaii call (808) 733-9831. Website: http://bphc.hrsa.gov/nhdp/.

Health Care for the Homeless Program (HCH): Works with community health providers and social service agencies to combine aggressive street outreach, varied approaches to primary care, mental health and substance abuse services, case management, and client advocacy to best deliver health care to homeless adults and children.

First authorized under the Stewart B. McKinney Homeless Assistance Act of 1987, HCH tries to provide primary care and substance abuse services convenient to homeless people's gathering places; provides some 24-hour emergency health services; refers homeless people to hospitals; refers homeless persons to mental health services when HCH facilities cannot provide appropriate treatment; works in the streets, shelters, and transitional housing to inform homeless people of services available to them; and educates and helps homeless people seeking assistance to establish their eligibility for housing and other service under entitlement programs.

HCH gives 135 grants to community-based organizations, migrant health centers, local health departments, hospitals, and community coalitions, serving nearly 500,000 patients nationwide.

CONTACT Address: Health Care for the Homeless Program, Division of Programs for Special Populations, Bureau of Primary Health Care, 4350 East-West Highway, 9th Floor, Bethesda, MD; Phone: (301) 594-4430; Fax: (301) 594-2470; Website: http://bphc.hrsa/gov/programs/homeless/.

LEAP Program (Lower Extremity Amputation Prevention Program): Works to reduce the need for amputation of lower extremities (legs and feet) due to diabetes mellitus, Hansen's disease, or any condition that results in loss of one's self-protective sensations in the feet. The LEAP Program includes annual foot screenings, patient education, instruction in daily self-inspection of the feet, management of simple foot problems, and footwear selection advice.

CONTACT Address: Lower Extremity Amputation Prevention Program (LEAP), Bureau of Primary Health Care, Division of Programs for Special Populations, 4350 East-West Highway, 9th Floor, Bethesda, MD 20814; Phone: (888) ASK-HRSA or (888) 275-4772; Website: http://bphc.hrsa.gov/leap/.

Mental Health in Primary Care Program: Seeks to include mental health in the U.S. health care system in the spirit of the World Health Organization's 1946 definition of health as "the complete state of physical, mental, and social well-being and not merely the absence of disease." Mental Health focuses on primary mental health conditions such as depression, alcohol use, anxiety, sleep problems, chronic fatigue, and unexplained somatic symptoms and the mind-body relationship that leads to early death in persons with mental health and substance abuse disorders.

The Mental Health Program works with certain premises: People with mental and substance abuse problems are twice as likely to smoke and bring on risk for heart disease, lung disease, and cancer; some patients who have experienced heart attacks, diabetes, cancer, and HIV/AIDS have some depression or adjustment disorders; and some depressed people have higher incidence of cancers or heart disease. The Mental Health Program focuses on integrating mental health treatment with primary care centers to integrate treatment of the whole person. Website: http://bphc.hrsa.gov/bphc/mental/.

Migrant Health Program (MHP): Originated in 1962 as part of the Public Health Service Act, funds local nonprofit organizations to hire bilingual and culturally sensitive primary medical and other support services for migrant and seasonal farmworkers and their families (MSFW), whose incomes average $7,500 annually. MHP funds migrant health services such as primary and preventive health care, transportation, outreach, dental, pharmaceutical, occupational health and safety, and environmental health through 125 public and private nonprofit organizations with 400 clinic sites in 42 states and Puerto Rico.

Obstacles to providing care to migrant farmworkers include occasional fear of authorities and the transient nature of their work and lives. MHP also provides infant immunizations, well baby care, developmental screenings, and other prevention-oriented and pediatric services.

MHP works to improve Migrant Health Centers delivery of mental health and substance abuse treatment services, as well as oral and dental health services. MHP cooperates with federal services such as Migrant Labor, Migrant Head Start, Migrant Education, and with the Migrant Supplemental Food Program for Women, Infants and Children and the State Child Health Insurance Program (SCHIP). MHP also works with state, regional, and local agencies and health departments and helps migrant and seasonal workers access Medicaid and SCHIP benefits. The goal is to expand health care availability to migrant and seasonal workers in 1,200 communities by the end of fiscal year 2006.

CONTACT Address: Division of Community and Migrant Health, Bureau of Primary Health Care, 4350 East-West Highway, 7th Floor, Bethesda, MD 20814; Phone: (301) 594-4303; Fax: (301) 594-4997; Website: http://bphc.hrsa.gov /programs/MHCProgramInfo.htm.

Office of Minority and Women's Health (OMWH): Established in 1994 to improve health care services to women, minorities, and other at-risk special populations served by BPGC programs and serves as a think tank and respository of information on health issues specifically concerning women and ethnic and racial populations. It also serves as administrator of the Health and Human Services Academy at Eastern Senior High School, which is working to develop a model to help public high school students explore interests in health and human-service-related fields.

OMWH seeks to rid the country of disparities in the health of women and certain racial and ethnic populations and to create collaborative partnerships for health care that are sensitive to cultural and linguistic needs of its clients. OMWH publishes information and research articles and is developing special projects on women's health, older persons' needs, rural health, breast cancer, migrant health, cultural competence, and violence prevention and reduction. Other projects include a holistic program to integrate care for the physical, mental, and spiritual needs of women and ethnic and racial communities, and translating useful documents into several languages.

To these ends, OMWH works with several governmental and special needs interest organizations, from federal agencies to the American Association of Retired Persons, Congress of National Black Churches, Health and Human Services Academy, and the Inter-American College of Physicians and Surgeons.

CONTACT Address: Office of Minority and Women's Health, Bureau of Primary Health Care, 4350 East-West Highway, 3rd Floor, Bethesda, MD 20814; Phone: (301) 594-4490; Fax: (301) 594-0089; Website: http://bphc.hrsa.gov/programs/ OMWHProgramInfo.htm.

Models That Work Campaign (MTW): Identifies and encourages replication of innovative community primary health care models of service to underserved and various vulnerable segments of the population. Models That Work Campaign gives support to groups and organizations that want to increase access to primary health care and eliminate disparities in health services available to needy citizens.

CONTACT Phone: (800) 859-2386; E-mail: models@hrsa.gov; Website: http://bphc.hrsa.gov/ mtw/.

Office of Pharmacy Affairs (OPA): Formerly the Office of Drug Pricing, runs the drug discount program that makes available low-cost prescription drugs to people receiving federal assistance.

CONTACT Address: 4350 East-West Highway, 10th Floor, Bethesda, MD 20814; E-mail: opastaff@ hrsa.gov; Website: http://bphc.hrsa.gov/opa/.

Public Housing Primary Care Program (PHPC): Created under the Disadvantaged Minority Health Improvement Act of 1990, was reauthorized under the Health Centers Consolidation

Act in 1996. PHPC defines its public housing community as residents of public housing; low-income people who live near public housing; and low-income people who get public rent subsidies.

PHPC funds and coordinates health delivery services to provide primary health care services including direct medical care, health screening, health education, dental, prenatal and perinatal care, preventive health care, and case management to residents of public housing. It also conducts outreach services to inform residents of health services available to them; helps residents establish eligibility for assistance for health, mental health, and social services; and trains and employs public housing residents to do health screenings and give health education services.

Among the challenges PHPC faces are rapid changes in public housing environments to mixed income populations, moving populations, immigrant populations, cultural traditions, and language.

CONTACT Address: Public Housing Primary Care Program, Division of Programs for Special Populations, Bureau of Primary Health Care, 4350 East-West Highway, 9th Floor, Bethesda, MD 20814; Phone: (301) 594-4420; Fax: (301) 594-2470; Website: http://bphc.hrsa.gov/phpc/.

Radiation Exposure Screening and Education Program (RESEP): Helps people who have been exposed to radiation through mining, processing, and transport of uranium, and testing of nuclear weapons as part of the U.S. nuclear weapons arsenal. RESEP makes grants to develop education programs on radiogenic diseases, early detection of cancer, screening of appropriate people for cancer and other diseases due to their exposure; offers referrals for medical treatment; and helps with processing documents for Radiation Exposure Compensation Act (RECA) claims.

CONTACT Address: Radiation Exposure Screening and Education Program, Division of Programs for Special Populations, Bureau of Primary Health Care, 4350 East-West Highway, 9th Floor, Bethesda, MD 20814; Phone: (301)

594-5105; Fax: (301) 594-2470; Website: http://bphc.hrsc.gov/resep/.

Center for School-Based Health Care: Provides funding for 512 school-based health center programs (SBHCs) through the Consolidated Health Centers Program. The center coordinates expansion of the program by offering policy leadership, technical assistance, training, successful standards, and models of programs that work.

To accomplish these goals, the Center for School-Based Health Care identifies issues, policy options, guidelines, and ways to effectively organize and manage school health programs. It also coordinates child and adolescent health services for medically underserved communities; gives guidance and leadership to the Healthy Schools, Healthy Communities Program; coordinates funds, grants, contracts, and other assistance for child and adolescent health services; serves as liaison with other federal, state, and local agencies and governments, consumer groups, and organizations involved with health care for at-risk childen and youth; directs Health and Human Services Academics Program; coordinates Health Status and Performance Improvement Collaborative; and leads and coordinates the Clinical Network.

CONTACT Address: Director, Center for School-Based Health, Division of Programs for Special Populations, Bureau of Primary Health Care, 4350 East-West Highway, 9th Floor, Bethesda, MD 20814; Phone: (301) 594-4470; Fax: (301) 594-2470; Website: www.bphc.hrsa.gov/programs/csbh.

Healthy Schools, Healthy Communities Program (HSHC): Works with Center for School-Based Health to focus on school-based health centers to give health care to high-risk children. Created in 1994 under President Bill Clinton, HSHC works to establish comprehensive health centers in schools to treat vulnerable children and adolescents, and provide counseling, mental, and dental health services, nutrition guidance, and health education. Other projects include violence prevention and fitness programs, home visits, wellness promotion, establishing and conducting parenting groups, and activities to establish and enhance self-esteem.

HSHC funds 76 organizations that created new school-based health centers including community health centers, local health departments, private nonprofit health centers, university medical centers, and hospitals.

CONTACT Address: Director, Center for School-Based Health, Division of Programs for Special Populations, Bureau of Primary Health Care, 4350 East-West Highway, 9th Floor, Bethesda, MD 20814; Phone: (301) 594-4470; Fax: (301) 594-2470; Website: http://bphc.hrsa.gov/programs/HSHCProgramInfo.htm.

Office of State and National Partnerships (OSNP): Focuses on underserved and vulnerable populations and works with and coordinates federal-state primary care partnerships; coordinates state interests in health care programs with BPHC and the HRSA; gathers policy and priority information from states; and works with private, nonprofit groups of community-based primary health care providers to identify and solve states' health care needs and improve primary health care delivery to underserved and vulnerable people.

CONTACT Address: Office of State and National Partnerships, Bureau of Primary Health Care, 4350 East-West Highway, 3rd Floor, Bethesda, MD 20814; Phone: (301) 594-4488; Fax: (301) 480-7833; Website: http://bphc.hrsa.gov/programs/OSNPOfficeInfo.htm.

Center for Risk Management: Makes available information and instructors from the ProNational Insurance Company on "Minimizing Your Health Center's Malpractice Risk." The office also offers a risk management hotline.

CONTACT Address: Center for Risk Management, 150 South Independence Mall West, Suite 1172, Philadelphia, PA 19106-3499; Phone: (215) 861-4373; Fax: (215) 861-4391; Risk Management training: (202) 659-8008; Risk Management hotline toll free: (888) 800-3772; Website: http://pbhc.hrsa.gov/risk/.

Native Hawaiian Health Care Program: Created in 1988 to provide health promotion, disease prevention, and primary care services for Native Hawaiians and persons of Hawaiian origin. By the Native Hawaiian Health Care Program's definition, "Native Hawaiians are defined as those peoples with historical continuity to the original inhabitants of the Hawaiian archipelago whose society was organized as a Nation prior to the arrival of the first non-indigenous people in 1778." The program was organized by Papa Ola Lokahi, the local coordinating agency, and grants were given to five Native Hawaiian organizations to deliver services to nine Hawaiian Islands in 1992.

Some Hawaiians are affected more acutely than other Americans by the same diseases, possibly due to cultural behaviors. According to the Bureau of Primary Health Care, Native Hawaiian women have the highest breast cancer mortality rates in the United States, Hawaiians have the highest rate of "years of productive life lost", as well as the shortest life expectancy rate. Among problems suffered by full or part Native Hawaiians are highest rates of chronic obstructive lung disease, highest infant mortality rate, highest accident rate, highest suicide rate, highest blood pressure, most new cases of HIV, and highest inclination toward obesity.

The Native Hawaiian Health Care Act funds Papa Ola Lokahi, the coordinating agency that works with five Native Hawaiian Health Care Systems to certify them, plans, gives training and technical assistance, helps with research, serves as a clearinghouse for information and data, helps develop special projects, and with the Native Hawaiian Scholarship Program gives scholarships to Native Hawaiian students interested in health care professions.

It also funds localized and culturally appropriate health care systems on the islands, including eligibility and emergency assistance, health and risk screenings, support groups and counseling, transportation, referrals, and health and nutrition education to people from seven islands.

CONTACT Address: Native Hawaiian Health Care Program, Division of Programs for Special Populations, Bureau of Primary Health Care, 4350 East-West Highway, 9th Floor, Bethesda, MD 20814; Phone: (301) 594-4476; Fax: (301) 594-2470; Website: http://bphc.hrsa.gov/programs/HawaiianProgramInfo.htm.

Health Disparity Collaboratives: Work to eliminate disparities in health care, such as in detection and treatment of diabetes, asthma, or depression and to help families and patients participate in their own care. The collaboratives coordinate with over 240 health centers, their efforts based on a model developed by Dr. Ed Wagner at the MacColl Institute for Healthcare Innovation. Among their goals are developing collaboratives for care and prevention of cancer, discounted pharmaceuticals, making more lab equipment available, and creating and disseminating health and nutrition education materials.

CONTACT Address: Chief, Clinical Branch, 4350 East-West Highway, Bethesda, MD 20814; Phone: (301) 594-4292; Fax: (301) 443-4983; or Director, Health Disparity Collaborative, 1961 Stout Street, Room 360, Denver, CO 80294; Phone: (303) 844-7890; Fax: (303) 844-2019; Website: http://bphc.hrsa.gov/programs/HDCProgramInfo.htm.

Integrative Medicine and Alternative Health Practices Initiative (IMAHP): Aims to integrate acupuncture, massage, chiropractic, homeopathic medicine, Native American medicine, and other indigenous healing practices with conventional U.S. allopathic medicine. IMAHP works to provide greater access to complementary and alternative medicine (CAM), a glossary of CAM terms, and training, technical assistance, and consultation to health care providers and patients.

CONTACT Address: Bureau of Primary Health Care, Integrative Medicine and Alternative Health Practices Initiative, 4350 East-West Highway, 8th Floor, Bethesda, MD 20814; Phone: (301) 594-4241; Fax: (301) 594-4987; Website: http://bphc.hrsa.gov/programs/IMAHProgramInfo.htm.

Division of Immigration Health Services: Aims to support delivery of primary health care to undocumented immigrants; hopes to be the preeminent provider for the Immigration and Naturalization Service by 2005.

CONTACT Address: Division of Immigration Health Services, 1220 L Street NW, Washington, DC 20005.

Asian American and Pacific Islander Initiative (AAPI Initiative): Made a reality by President Bill Clinton's executive order in 1997, seeks to improve Asian Americans' and Pacific Islanders' (in the United States and its territories) access to health and human services, better data collection and research on AAPI health, training of AAPI health professionals, and extending care in a culturally and linguistically appropriate manner to medically underserved Asian and Pacific Islander patients.

CONTACT Website: www.healthfinder.gov/justforyou.

Together for Tots Immunization Initiative: Pulls together resources of various federal health agencies, clinical networks, local community, and migrant health centers in a community-based initiative to increase immunizations of infants and children aged two and under who receive health care at Community and Migrant Health Centers (C/MHC's) in the states participating in the program. TOTS and an adult/adolescent immunization project are scheduled to join together in the Preventive Services Collaborative.

CONTACT Address: Together for Tots Immunization Initiative, Division of Community and Migrant Health, Bureau of Primary Care, 4350 East-West Highway, 7th Floor, Bethesda, MD 20814; Phone: (301) 594-4397; Fax: (301) 594-4983; Website: http://bphc.hrsa.gov/programs/TotsProgramInfo.htm.

Maternal and Child Health Bureau (MCHB): Works to create equal access for all to quality health care that is culturally appropriate and supportive in family and community situations. Building on the establishment of the Children's Bureau in 1912, Congress enacted Title V of the

Social Security Act in 1935, creating the Maternal and Child Health Services programs to assure health for American mothers, adolescents, children with special health care needs, and other children and infants. In 1981 the Omnibus Budget Reconciliation Act converted the program to block grants to the states.

MCHB's general goals include: reduction of infant mortality and handicaps among children; increase of immunizations among children; increase of the number of health assessments and follow-up diagnostic and treatment services for children in low-income households; prenatal (before pregnancy) health care for women; preventive and child care services; comprehensive long-term care for children with special needs; rehabilitation services for children under 16 who are blind and/or disabled and are eligible for Supplemental Security Income; and family-centered, community-based health care for children with special needs.

MCHB offers programs and health guidelines for families with children from birth to age 21; Healthy Start program to reduce infant mortality and increase health of infants in high-risk communities; prenatal care, healthy pregnancy tips, and sources for low-cost care for unborn children and pregnant mothers; and a Sudden Infant Death Resource Center.

MCHB also works to reduce illness, injury, and death among children and youths by encouraging healthy behaviors and provides comprehensive community-based health care through the Children's Safety Network, emergency medical services for children, the Get the Right Care Where It Counts program for information for parents on how to respond to emergencies and prevent injuries, and the National Resource Center for Health and Safety in Child Care.

For children with special health care needs, MCHB works to coordinate health care resources for children at risk for chronic behavioral, emotional, developmental, or physical conditions who may also need care beyond what most children require. The Family Voices clearinghouse provides education and information on health care for special needs children; contacts with state directors of special needs services; and information on cross-cultural needs and issues.

MCHB offers information for adolescents at its National Adolescent Health Information Center; education on abstinence from sexual relations; and guides to improving adolescent nutrition. In the genetics field MCHB supports screening of newborns for genetic diseases through the National Newborn Screening and Genetic Resource Center, at gene tests-gene clinics; offers newborn hearing screening for all, and a Genetics in Primary Care initiative. Additionally, MCHB conducts and supports research into better maternal and child health services, with emphasis on preventive care and early intervention.

MCHB offers training, faculty, continuing education, and technical assistance to train caregivers for children and mothers, emphasizing interdisciplinary, family-centered, and culturally appropriate care through training and education for health care professionals; provides the Bright Futures Health Supervision Guidelines for parents and professional caregivers; and the Healthy Tomorrows Partnership to foster health promotion and disease prevention in communities.

MCHB's Division of State and Community Health administers the whole program and coordinates relations with the 10 HRSA field offices, runs a national data and information reporting system, and oversees state grant applications.

CONTACT Address: Maternal and Child Health Bureau, Parklawn Building, Room 18-05, 5600 Fishers Lane, Rockville, MD 20857; Phone: (301) 443-2170; Fax: (301) 443-1797; Website: http://mchb.hrsa.gov/.

BUREAU OF HEALTH PROFESSIONALS (BHPr): Provides assistance and education to health care professionals throughout the United States and promotes cultural and ethnic diversity in the health care service, with the goal of increased health care delivery to needy communities. To increase the number of health care workers caring for underserved people, BHPr seeks to attract diverse people as health professions students and to expose health care trainees to the experience of caring for underserved communities.

CONTACT Address: Bureau of Health Professionals, Health Resources and Services Administration, Parklawn Building, 5600 Fishers Lane, Rockville, MD 20857; Phone: (301) 433-3376.

The *Office of Special Programs's Division of Facilities Compliance* runs the Health Care and Other Facilities grant program for construction funds for health care facilities, and manages the Hill-Burton program to make sure health care facilities offer free or reduced-cost medical services to uninsured and underinsured people. The Division of Facilities and Loans manages the Health and Human Services's existing direct and guaranteed loans and helps the DEPARTMENT OF HOUSING AND URBAN DEVELOPMENT run hospital mortgage insurance programs.

The *Division of Transplantation* manages the Organ Procurement and Transplantation Network (OPTN), the Scientific Registry of Transplant Recipients (SRTR), and the National Marrow Donor Program (NMDP), and coordinates the organ and tissue donations. The State Planning Grants Program gives one-year grants to the states to develop plans to provide affordable health insurance coverage to all citizens, with attention to programs similar to the Federal Employees Health Benefit Plan, Medicaid, coverage for state employees, or other standards. The National Childhood Vaccine Injury Compensation Program (VICP), begun in 1988, compensates individuals, families of individuals, and people negatively affected by childhood vaccines. Website: http://www.hrsa.gov/osp/.

Division of Facilities Compliance and Recovery (DFCR): Runs the program that gives grants to build health facilities. DFCR also manages the Hill-Burton program to ensure health facilities provide free or reduced-cost medical services to uninsured and underinsured people. Such obligated facilities that receive Hill-Burton money must maintain public or nonprofit status for 20 years. Website: www/jrsa/gpv/osp/dfcr/.

Known as the Hill-Burton Act (1946), the Hospital Survey and Construction Act, sponsored by Senators Lister Hill and Harold Burton, is the primary program to fund health facility construction in the United States under Title VI of the Public Health Service Act. The original intent of Hill-Burton was to give federal grants to bring obsolete hospitals up to date, particularly those that had been neglected from 1929 to 1945, during the Great Depression and World War II. Eventually $4.6 billion has been granted and $1.5 billion loaned to 6,800 health facilities. In return for the federal money, the health facilities have to give free or reduced-cost medical services to people who cannot pay for them.

Congress amended Hill-Burton in 1975 with Title XVI of the Public Health Service Act, and established federal grants, loan guarantees, and interest subsidies for health facilities. Recipients of these funds under Title XVI must provide health services to the uninsured and underinsured as long as they receive federal funds, and responsibility for keeping track of compliance was transferred from the states to the federal government. Title XVI also allowed the federal government to take back grant funds when a facility is sold, transferred to an entity that does not qualify, or stops being used for an appropriate purpose during the 20-year obligation period.

CONTACT Phone: Hill-Burton Hotline 24 hours (800) 638-0742, Maryland residents: (800) 492-0359; Website: www.hrsa.gov/dfcr/.

OFFICE OF RURAL HEALTH POLICY (ORHP): Created by President Jimmy Carter in August 1987, as part of the Health Resources and Services Administration, and then authorized by Congress in December to coordinate rural health care activities and hospitals, and maintain a national clearinghouse of information and data on rural health needs and care.

Additionally, ORHP contributes to rural health policy; works with state offices of rural health; promotes and sponsors rural health research; funds innovative rural health programs; supports National Advisory Committee on Rural Health; advocates for rural hospitals, clinics, and other rural health care providers; serves as liaison with national, state, and local rural health organizations; works with minorities in rural areas; and runs an Office of Rural Health Policy Grants that gives out money to states.

ORHP gives grants to improve quality of essential health care and access to it at low cost to rural areas through its Rural Health Outreach Program; Network Development Grant Program; Mississippi Delta Rural Development Initiative; Rural Access to Emergency Devices (RAED) Grant Program for rural purchase of automated external defibrillators; and Small Rural Hospital Improvement Grant Program.

State programs funded by ORHP include state offices of Rural Health Grant Program and the Rural Hospital Flexibility Grant Program.

CONTACT Address: Office of Rural Health Policy, Health Resources and Services Administration, 5600 Fishers Lane, 9A-55, Rockville, MD 20857; Phone: (301) 443-0835; Fax: (301) 443-2903; Website: http://ruralhealth.hrsa.gov/.

HRSA launched a new *Bioterrorism Hospital Preparedness Program* (grants) in 2002 for American states, territories, and the large cities of New York, Chicago, and Los Angeles. Programs include the Hospital Preparedness Program to provide equipment and training to respond to bioterrorism and mass casualties; the Trauma/Emergency Medical Services to states to improve the country's trauma and EMS systems; Emergency Medical Services for Children for grants to states or to accredited medical schools for demonstration projects to expand and improve emergency medical services for children needing trauma or critical care; and Poison Control Centers program for special grants to increase availability and access to poison control centers.

HRSA also gave $10 million in emergency grants to New York and New Jersey community health centers to support services required following September 11, 2001, terrorist attacks on the World Trade Center in New York City. HRSA granted $35 million in emergency awards for health care on November 19, 2001, to 131 public and nonprofit entities in New York, New Jersey, Connecticut, Virginia, Pennsylvania, and Washington, D.C. for health care costs incurred by organizations affected by the World Trade Center attacks. In 2002 $140 million more was granted by Congress.

CONTACT Address: Health Resources and Services Administration, U.S. Department of Health and Human Services, Parklawn Building, 5600 Fishers Lane, Rockville, MD 20857; Website: www.hrsa.gov/bioterrorism.htm for a broad range of information on biological terrorism, infection control, epidemiology, Federal Emergency Management Agency (FEMA) (www.fema.gov), poison control centers (www.aapcc.org/), and the National Institutes of Health (NIH) (www.nih.gov).

INDIAN HEALTH SERVICE (IHS)

HISTORY

American Indians first received U.S. government health services in the 19th century when army physicians tried to curb smallpox and other contagious diseases introduced by the white man ("Europeans") to Indians living around federal military posts. Since the Indian custom was to gather around those who were ill, instead of isolating the victim or patient, diseases spread rapidly and disastrously among the tribes. Prior to the Europeans' arrival, at least 10 million Indians lived in good health in what is now the United States.

In 1849 the Bureau of Indian Affairs (BIA) was transferred from the War Department to the

DEPARTMENT OF THE INTERIOR, and health care services grew to include civilian physicians working among the Indians. In the 1890s nurses joined the 83 doctors in Indian Medical Services, with 25 nurses serving by 1900, primarily in government-run Indian boarding schools, which many Indian children were forced to attend, leaving their families. In 1891 field matrons worked with Indians, providing practical instruction in sanitation and hygiene, emergency nursing services, and prescribing medicine for some illnesses, all of which duties eventually fell to Public Health Service nurses.

The first hospital built by the federal government to treat American Indians appeared in the 1880s in Oklahoma, the beginning of an effort to establish hospitals or infirmaries on every Indian reservation and at every Indian boarding school. The position of chief medical supervisor of Indian health activities was appointed in 1908, and Congress first appropriated funds for American Indian and Alaska Native health care in 1911, although the legislation did not include continuing appropriations. Disease-specific programs, such as for tuberculosis, and health education began in the early 1900s, with dental services first offered in 1913.

In 1921 Congress passed the Snyder Act, which authorized continuing and accelerating appropriations for "the relief of distress and conservation of health" of American Indians and Alaska Natives, and led to creation of the Bureau of Indian Affairs Health Division and appointment of district medical directors to minister specifically to the health of the two groups. Medical officers of the Public Health Service were assigned to work for the Indian Health Program by 1926. The precursor to the Indian Health Service remained part of the Bureau of Indian Affairs from 1924 to 1955.

Public Health Law 83-568 (known as the Transfer Act), passed by Congress in 1954, transferred responsibility for American Indian and Alaska Native health care from the Department of Interior's Bureau of Indian Affairs to the Department of Health, Education and Welfare's Public Health Service. HEW is now the Department of Health and Human Services. Initial goals of the then-new Division of Health included attracting competent staff to care for American Indians and Alaska Natives; establish facilities to deliver services; provide treatment for seriously ill patients; and develop and start a preventive program to reduce high rates of illness and early deaths from preventable diseases and conditions.

In the early 1900s the government began health surveys of American Indians and Alaska Natives such as the Trachoma Survey (1909) to study unusually high incidence of blindness among American Indians. The Miriam Report of 1928 showed early mortality and disease rates far in excess of those of the general U.S. population, that one in 10 Indians had active or inactive tuberculosis, that 29 percent of all American Indian and Alaska Native deaths were from tuberculosis, and that 37 percent of all American Indian deaths were children under the age of three. Other surveys included the Public Health Service Survey and the Hoover Commission Report.

American Indians and Alaska Natives are citizens of both their tribes and bands and of the United States. Their relationship with the U.S. government is based on more than 350 treaties signed between the federal government and Indian tribes, from the first treaty signed with the Delaware Nation in 1784 to the last treaty signed with the Nez Perce tribe of what is now Idaho in the late 1800s. The federal government–tribal relationship is based on Article 1, Section 8 of the U.S. Constitution.

According to "treaty rights" specified in the treaties, the U.S. government has a "trust responsibility" entitling Indians to participation in federal financial programs and services, including health care and education. The IHS has a trust responsibility to provide health care to American Indians and Alaska Natives who are members of federally recognized tribes. Not all tribes are recognized by the federal government because they do not have signed treaties with the United States, so those tribes are not recognized by Congress, and therefore are not eligible to benefit from federal programs, including health care from the Indian Health Service.

Many Indian Health Service clients live in what is now the state of Alaska. "Alaska Natives" include those of Athabascan, Tsimpsian, Tlingit, Haida, Eskimo, and Aleut descent.

Many American Indians belong to one of about 560 recognized Indian tribes, bands, pueblos, and villages, which have tribal governments organized or recognized under the Indian Reorganization Act, the Oklahoma Indian Welfare Act, and the Alaska Native Act. Some tribes have written constitutions approved by the U.S. secretary of interior, and many operate their own traditional governments based on tribal customs instead of written constitutions.

The Indian Self-Determination and Education Act (Public Law 93-638) of 1975, amended, gives tribes the right to choose whether to run IHS programs on their reservations or in their communities with federal funds, have IHS administer the health programs, or employ a combination of both methods. More and more tribes are opting for operating hospitals, outpatient facilities, and other health care programs.

Poor nutrition, unsafe water, inadequate waste disposal systems, and an increasingly mobile Indian population contribute to the difficulty in improving health for many American Indians and to the status of health unequal with that of the general U.S. population.

Major health concerns for American Indians and Alaska Natives include maternal and child health, HIV/AIDS, otitis media, aging problems, heart disease, alcoholism, mental health, diabetes, accidents, and suicide. Environmental planning (sanitation and contamination), clean water treatment systems, educational outreach, life support for trauma victims, and plague control are examples of developing programs.

The Indian Health Service works to (1) help Indian tribes develop health programs through health management training, technical assistance, and human resource development, e.g. training of health care professionals; (2) help Indian tribes coordinate health planning, get health care funds from federal, state, and local programs to operate health care programs and services; (3) provide health care services such as hospital and ambulatory care, preventive and rehabilitative services, and develop sanitation facilities; and (4) serve as advocate in health care field for Indians to make sure American Indians and Alaska Natives get the health care to which they are entitled.

GENERAL INFORMATION

In addition to services mentioned above, IHS offers special initiatives in traditional medicine, elder care, women's, children's, and adolescent's health, injury prevention, domestic violence and child abuse, health care financing, state health care, sanitation, and oral health. While most health services are delivered on reservations and in other Indian and Native communities, some health care services are available to Indians who live in urban environments.

While many American Indians and Alaska Natives receive health services through tribally contracted and operated health systems, health services also include health care purchased from more than 9,000 private providers. The Indian Health Service system itself includes 43 hospitals, 63 health centers, 44 health stations, five residential treatment centers, and 34 urban Indian health centers. American Indian tribes and Alaska Native corporations run 13 hospitals, 158 health centers, 28 residential treatment centers, 76 health stations, and 170 Alaska village clinics.

IHS has provided funding for water and sewer facilities and solid waste disposal systems to 230,000 Indian homes since 1960, decreasing the death rate among American Indians and Alaska Natives by more than 91 percent since 1955.

About 93 percent of client populations have received sanitation facilities.

According to the IHS, 100 percent of its senior executive staff are of American Indian or Alaska Native descent. The Indian Health Care Improvement Act provides scholarship programs to train recipient populations to be health professionals to meet the program's needs, as well as a Loan Repayment Program to help attract health professionals to service IHS needs. The Indian Health Professions Program gives scholarships, loans, and summer jobs in return for commitments to serve in IHS, tribal, or urban Indian programs. The public Health Service's National Health Service Corps program offers scholarships and stipends to medical students who agree to specialize in primary care needs of native populations and to a minimum of a two-year commitment working in Public Health Service programs, including IHS tribal programs.

The 35 states that have American Indian reservations or Alaska Native communities where IHS delivers services are: Alabama, Alaska, Arizona, California, Colorado, Connecticut, Florida, Idaho, Indiana, Iowa, Kansas, Louisiana, Maine, Massachussetts, Michigan, Minnesota, Mississippi, Montana, Nebraska, Nevada, New Mexico, New York, North Carolina, North Dakota, Oklahoma, Oregon, Pennsylvania, Rhode Island, South Carolina, South Dakota, Texas, Utah, Washington, Wisconsin, and Wyoming.

IHS has 12 administrative area offices, which oversee 127 local service units at hospitals and clinics and are defined by the Indian reservations or tribes they serve. A service unit may have several smaller satellite facilities and field health stations. Health care at these sites may be delivered directly by IHS, by facilities operated by tribes, or by health care services on private contract with the federal government and/or the tribes.

IHS runs medical centers in Phoenix, Arizona; Gallup, New Mexico; and Anchorage, Alaska. In other places, IHS contracts with local hospitals, local and state health agencies, tribal health institutions, and individual health care providers. Clinical staff include physicians, dentists, nurses, pharmacists, therapists, dietitians, laboratory and radiology technicians, medical and dental assistants, community health medics, nurse practitioners, and nurse-midwives.

HEALTH CARE PROGRAMS

IHS's health care programs include the following:

Preventive Health Services works to improve American Indian and Alaska Native health and prevent or reduce the need for acute medical care, primarily in the fields of prenatal, postnatal, and well-baby care, family planning, dental health, nutrition, immunizations, environmental health activities, and health education. *Emergency Medical Services* strives to make available and train "first responders" (police officer or community health person) personnel to react to a health crisis within 15 minutes and communicate by radio to get advice on next-step health care, particularly in remote locations on Alaska Native and American Indian reservations where ambulances are rare.

Environmental Health and Engineering Services provides preventive programs to improve workplace, community, and home environmental conditions through environmental planning, food protection, occupational health and safety education, injury prevention, pollution control, control of insects and other carriers of pathogens to limit communicable disease outbreaks and environmental health on reservations. These efforts also include coordination with the Environmental Protection Agency (EPA); working with tribes to develop sanitary ordinances and codes; and finding alternatives to crowded, substandard housing, water supplies, and inadequate waste disposal facilities.

Pharmacy Services offers medications compatible with traditional remedies, as well as primary care to some outpatients. *Contract Health Services* (CHS) links up with private physicians or hospitals and funds care for American Indians and Alaska Natives, based on prioritizing medical care needs, when no government facility can provide the services.

IHS's *Health Education Program* promotes health-promoting lifestyles; teaches how to select and use health care resources, products, and services to best advantage; influences policy, health care, and environmental health planning; and guides Alaska Native and American Indian communities to better understanding of disease and how lifestyle and changes in behavior can reduce disease, reduce accidents and injuries, and lead to general health. *Community-based Programs* combine public health care and traditional medicine with local tradition to create community-oriented primary care (COPC).

The *Alcoholism and Substance Abuse Program* addresses the most urgent health problems for American Indian and Alaska Native populations by offering more than 200 treatment and prevention educational services. Four of the top 10 causes of death among Indians are alcohol related, including accidents, cirrhosis of the liver, suicide, and homicide. The Indian Alcohol and Substance Abuse Prevention and Treatment Act of 1986 authorizes one regional youth treatment center within each IHS area (see areas below). *School-Based Programs* involve teachers, teachers' aides, students, parents, and counselors in Alcohol and Other Drug Abuse (AODA) programs, through school-based student and parent groups such as Students Against Drunk Driving, Chemical People, Mothers Against Drunk Driving, and some peer counseling groups. These programs combine cultural support with traditional counseling, recreational and therapeutic activities, family support, Alcoholics Anonymous, and Narcotics Anonymous groups and strategies.

IHS's *Diabetes Program* approaches one of the major causes of death among adult American Indian patients at IHS facilities by teaching nutrition's role in diabetes, and training caregivers to recognize, treat, and help patients make lifestyle changes, including nutrition and exercise. The *Nutrition Program* works to educate American Indians and Alaska Natives on nutrition as a leading cause of death through heart disease, cancer, cirrhosis of the liver, diabetes, obesity, hypertension, and dental infections. The program attempts through education to teach the importance of proper nutrition in the case of infants, preschool children, adolescents, pregnant and nursing women, and the chronically ill. Food-assistance programs attempt to meet cultural needs of clients.

The *Mental Health Program* attempts to help American Indians and Alaska Natives deal with constantly increasing differences between their traditional cultures and modern American society. Due to problems experienced in trying to deal with contrasting cultures, American Indians and Alaska Natives have more mental health problems and emotional struggles, leading occasionally to alcoholism and suicide. According to IHS, Indian communities' feelings of frustration, hopelessness, depression, and low self-esteem lead to high rates of alcoholism, violence, homicide, and family problems, including abuse. By trying to understand Indians' and Natives' way of life, ideas, and language, the program works to change self-destructive behaviors and encourage mentally healthy environments.

The *Community Health Representative Program* (CHR), begun in 1968, uses CHRs, who are American Indians and Alaska Natives trained to work as paraprofessional health care providers for and among their tribes and communities. Conversant with the dialects and social and cultural facets of their people's lives, and trained by IHS, CHRs are in a unique position to promote health and prevent disease within their communities through early intervention. CHRs' health care training by IHS includes basic health skills, health and disease, home nursing, emergency medical services, nutrition, environmental health, how to teach others about health, communication, group organization, and planning. Through CHRs, many tribes are managing their own health care for the first time ever.

CONTACT Address: General offices: Indian Health Service Headquarters, 801 Thompson Avenue, Suite 120, Rockville, MD 20852; Phone: (301) 443-4242. Administrative area offices: Aberdeen Area IHS, Federal Office Building, 115 Fourth Avenue SE, Aberdeen SD, 57401; Phone: (605) 226-7581. Alaska Area Native Health Service, 4141 Ambassador Drive, Anchorage, AK 99508-5928; Phone: (907) 729-3686. Albuquerque Area IHS, 5300 Homestead Road NE, Albuquerque, NM 87110; Phone: (505) 284-4500. Bemidji Area IHS, 522 Minnesota Avenue NW, Bemidji, MN 56601; Phone: (216) 759-3412. Billings Area IHS, 2900 4th Avenue, North, Billings, MT 59101 or P.O. Box 2143, Billings, MT 59103; Phone: (406) 247-7107. California Area IHS, 6500 Capitol Mall, Suite 7100, Sacramento, CA 95814; Phone: (916) 930-3937. Nashville Area IHS, 711 Stewarts Ferry Pike, Nashville, TN 37214-2634; Phone: (615) 736-2400. Navajo Area IHS, P.O. Box 9020, Window Rock, AZ 86515-9020 or Highway 264-St. Michaels, Window Rock, AZ 86515; Phone: (520) 871-5811. Oklahoma City Area IHS, Five Corporate Plaza, 3825 NW 56th Street, Oklahoma City, OK 73112; Phone: (405) 951-3768. Phoenix Area IHS, Two Renaissance Square, 40 N. Central Avenue, Suite 600, Phoenix, AZ 85004-4424; Phone: (602) 364-5039. Portland Area IHS, 1220 SW Third Avenue, Room 476, Portland OR, 97204-2892; Phone: (503) 326-4998. Tucson Area IHS, 7900 SJ Stock Road, Tucson, AZ 85746-7012; Phone: (520) 295-2406. Environmental Health Offices include the Santa Fe Service Unit, 1700 Cerrillos Road, Santa Fe, NM 87501; Phone: (505) 946-9462. ACL Hospital, P.O. Box 130, San Fidel, NM 87049; Phone: (505) 552-6641. Escondido District Office, 1249 Simpson Way, Escondido, CA 92029-1406; Phone: (760) 735-6884.

The *Dental Program* works to provide preventive and corrective dental care to prevent disease and reduce losses of teeth among the American Indian and Alaska Native populations, who have more dental disease than the rest of the U.S. population. Originally a service provided by itinerant dentists dealing with emergencies, the Dental Program now functions in 250 locations in IHS and tribal hospitals, health centers, and other facilities, along with nearly 200 field locations and 26 mobile dental sites. Fluoridation is encouraged.

IHS's *Accident and Injury Reduction Program* includes community alcoholism programs, which address accidents as the second leading cause of injury and death among American Indians and Alaska Natives. Death due to accidents among these communities ia about 2.5 times that for all other U.S. races. The *Laboratory Program* operates accredited hospital and clinic laboratories that perform about 15 million lab tests annually from screening tests to detection and monitoring of diseases such as diabetes, heart disease, and cancer.

Among IHS's nonmedical programs, *Environmental Health and Engineering* works on construction and engineering of facilities, engineering, real property management, sanitation construction, and program development with the goal of delivering safe water, wastewater, and solid waste systems to American Indian and Alaska Native communities.

CONTACT Address: Director, Office of Environmental Health and Engineering, Indian Health Service, Twinbrook Metro Plaza Building, 12300 Twinbrook Parkway, Suite 600A, Rockville, MD 20852; Phone: (301) 443-1247; Fax: (301) 443-5697.

IHS's *Environmental Health Support Center* sponsors training courses for American Indians and Alaska Natives to help them understand, improve, and work in the Indian Health Service's Office of Environmental Health and Engineering.

CONTACT Address: 5300 Homestead Road NE, Albuquerque, NM 87110; Phone: (505) 248-4258.

The Indian Health Service *Head Start Program* provides health training and technical assistance for Head Start's Bureau–American Indian/Alaska Native-run Head Start programs. IHS Head Start develops preventive health service and intervention programs and health education for Head Start families and children and helps develop health care mobilization programs by providing medical, dental, mental health, nutrition, and environmental health technical assistance and training. More than 150 American Indian/Alaska Native Head Starts in 27 states receive this help through grants. Target problems include prevention and treatment of dental caries, environmental health, childhood obesity and diabetes prevention (including nutrition), and playground safety.

CONTACT Address: Indian Health Service-Head Start Program, Suite 450, Twinbrook Metro Plaza, 12300 Twinbrook Parkway, Rockville, MD 20852; Phone: (301) 443-0046; Fax: (301) 443-1522.

The *Health Education Program*'s goals include educating American Indians/Alaska Natives to participate actively in their own health care and maintenance, and preventive strategies, based on how to make the best behavior and lifestyle choices. The program gives support, information, and resources to health care providers in the field. The *Indian Health Service Research Program* coordinates community research into American Indian/Alaska Native health problems, the communities' health status, and their health care systems.

CONTACT Address: Office of Public Health, Office of Program Support, 12300 Twinbrook Parkway, Suite 450, Rockville, MD 20852; Phone: (301) 443-6258; Fax: (301) 594-6213.

Project *TRANSAM* is a Civilian-Military Cooperative Action Program linking the Indian Health Service and the DEPARTMENT OF DEFENSE to distribute medical equipment and supplies obtained from closures of military bases and military installations. TRANSAM results from the National Defense Authorization Act of 1995, Section 8032 of Public Law 103-335, led by U.S. Senators Daniel Inouye of Hawaii and Ted Stevens of Alaska.

Tribal Health Programs include the *California Rural Indian Health Board* (CRIHB), created in 1969 as a consortium of nine California Indian Tribes to advocate return of federal health care services to California's American Indians; the *Center for Native American Health* (CNAH), a joint effort of the University of Arizona and southwest tribes to create the Center for Native American Health; the *Intertribal Council of Arizona*, which provides lobbying and organizational efforts to member tribes' sovereignty and to strengthen tribal governments; the *Northwest Portland Area Indian Health Board*; and the *National Indian Health Board*.

The *National Indian Health Board* (NIHB), a nonprofit organization, advocates on behalf of all federally recognized American Indians and Alaska Natives and all tribal governments to obtain and provide quality health care and communicates between the federal government and tribes in both directions. NIHB represents those tribal governments that choose to operate their own health care delivery systems either on-site or by contract, as well as those that receive health care services directly from the Indian Health Service. To these ends NIHB monitors federal legislation; analyzes policy; conducts research, program assessment, and development; plans national and regional meetings; and provides training and technical assistance programs, as well as project management. It provides such services to tribes and tribal organizations, Area Health Boards, federal agencies, and private foundations.

NIHB consists of representatives from each of the 12 IHS areas, and includes an elected representative and alternate from each area health board or tribal government in places where there is no area health board. Area health boards communicate between NIHB and tribes, advise on health policy development, plan, design programs, gather information, and review public opinion and proposals.

CONTACT Address: NIHB, 101 Constitution Avenue NW, Suite B-809, Washington, DC

20001; Phone: (202) 742-4262; Fax: (202) 742-4615; or 1385 S. Colorado Boulevard, Suite A-707, Denver, CO 80222; Phone: (303) 759-3075; Fax: (303) 759-3674.

Area Health Boards: Aberdeen Area Tribal Chairman's Health Board, Berkshire Plaza, Suite 205, 405 8th Avenue NW, Aberdeen, SD 57401; Phone: (605) 229-3846. Alaska Native Health Board, 4201 Tudor Center, Suite 105, Anchorage, AK 99508; Phone: (907) 562-6006; Fax: (907) 563-2001. Albuquerque Area Indian Health Board, 2301 Renard Place, SE Suite 101, Albuquerque, NM 87106; Phone: (505) 764-0036; Fax: (505) 764-0466. Montana-Wyoming Area Indian Health Board, 2900 4th Avenue NW, Billings, MT 59103; Phone: (406) 252-2550; Fax: (406) 254-6355. Bemidji Area Representative, Oneida Tribe of Wisconsin, P.O. Box 365, Oneida, WI 54155; Phone: (920) 869-2711; Fax: (920) 869-1780. California Rural Indian Health Board, 1451 River Park Drive, Suite 220, Sacramento, CA 95815; Phone: (916) 929-9761; Fax: (916) 929-7246. United South & Eastern Tribes, 711 Stewarts Ferry Pike, Nashville, TN 37214; Phone: (615) 872-7900; Fax: (615) 872-741. Navajo Area Health Board, P.O. Box 1390, Window Rock, AZ 86515; Phone: (928) 871-6350; Fax: (928) 871-6255. Oklahoma City Area Inter-Tribal Health Board, Chickasaw Nation, P.O. Box 425, Tishomingo, OK 73460; Phone: (580) 924-8280; Fax: (580) 920-3126. Inter-Tribal Council of Arizona, Inc., 4205 N. 7th Avenue, Suite 200, Phoenix, AZ 86013; Phone: (602) 248-0071; Fax: (602) 248-0080. Northwest Portland Area Indian Health Board, 527 SW Hall Street, Suite 300, Portland, OR 97201; Phone: (503) 228-4185; Fax: (503) 228-8182. Tucson Area Representative, Department of Health and Human Services, Tohono O'oodham Nation, P.O. Box 815, Sells, AZ 85634; Phone: (520) 383-6000.

NIHB informs its clients and advocates on their behalf on the status and changes in health financing via Medicare and Medicaid; performs case studies in managed care among Indian populations and state Medicaid programs; and researches how Arizona, California, Michigan, Minnesota, New York, New Mexico, Oklahoma, Oregon, Washington, and Wisconsin are addressing American Indian needs in Medicaid managed care programs.

In the field of self-determination, the NIHB works to better serve tribal governments' health policy needs, including a national study on self-determination contracts and self-determination, as well as a new system to use the Internet for health policy information. The board is also developing a "Strengthening Tribal Management Capabilities in Health and Human Service Delivery" program funded by the Administration for Native Americans to develop health care curricula and distance-based learning on-line and through video conferencing. The project will also involve tribal views in redefining the NIHB and improve national and intertribal meetings and health care programs. NIHB also holds an Annual Consumer Conference to help tribal leaders and health care providers communicate and improve health care to families, and provide training, technical assistance, and policy discussions. NIHB also conducts studies to assess tribal views of how tribes taking over their health care systems works and affects lives. A Henry J. Kaiser Family Foundation study of nine tribes in four IHS areas looked at how tribes make decisions whether and how to take over management of their own health care systems. Results included four factors: the political process of tribal decision making; underlying tribal cultural values; perceptions of likely outcomes; and unmet needs for information, technical assistance, and training in planning and negotiating.

As some administrations divest federal management to states through block grants, NIHB monitors how states taking over management of Indian programs fare as tribes may see state governments as working against their interests.

NIHB is working on a National Native American Breast Cancer Survivor's Network involving data on 500 American Indian breast cancer survivors. The Native C.I.R.C.L.E. provides cancer-related information and materials to health care professionals and other providers of health information education to develop and disseminate culturally appropriate cancer information for American Indian and Alaska Native health care workers and leaders, students, and educators. Through the American Indian/Alaska Native Leadership Initiative on Cancer, NIHB works with universities, cancer centers, cancer research facilities, and particularly the Mayo Clinic on cancer research among its peoples.

NIHB works to expand diabetes programs, working with the National Diabetes Prevention Center to research and expand treatment services to American Indians and Alaska Natives.

NIHB and the National Congress of American Indians (NCAI) cosponsored a Tribal Leader Summit on Alcohol and Substance Abuse with the Healing Our Spirit Worldwide Conference in Albuquerque, New Mexico, in 2002 to deal with the intensifying problem of alcoholism among American Indians and Alaska Natives, resulting in a Tribal Leader Proclamation on alcohol and substance abuse, requesting permanent funding for education and treatment.

In the mental health field, NIHB works toward improving the disproportionate mental health problems among the American Indian/Alaska Native populations. All minorities suffer more mental and emotional disorders because they have less access to mental health services, often receive inferior mental health care when they do get it, and are underrepresented in mental health research.

With the Environmental Protection Agency, NIHB works with tribes to study the health impact of hazardous substances such as lead and its poisons, including removing causes and reducing exposure, and improving community education on substances containing lead.

Traditional healing is not funded by the Indian Health Service, although some programs claim to integrate traditional healing with "modern" medicine. In a quest for holistic approaches

to health care, future budgets might include a culturally appropriate approach that takes advantage of successful traditional care.

NATIONAL INSTITUTES OF HEALTH

The National Institutes of Health (NIH) is made up of 27 separate institutes and is the largest medical research organization in the world. NIH involves government, university, and private researchers who work to detect, diagnose, treat, and eradicate a multitude of diseases, from the common cold to cancer, diabetes, Alzheimer's, heart ailments, AIDS, genetic disorders, spinal cord injuries, schizophrenia, depression, respiratory distress syndrome, and arthritis. To accomplish these goals, NIH helps train research investigators and helps to foster communication of medical information throughout the world.

NIH occupies 75 buildings on its 300-acre campus in Bethesda, Maryland, alone. Its first "budget" was about $300 in 1887, and rose to $23.4 billion in 2002. Its grants and contracts support more than 2,000 research institutions throughout the United States and in other countries. Currently it funds 46,700 grants at universities, medical schools, and other research and research training institutions worldwide.

HISTORY

The National Institutes of Health began in 1887 as a one-room laboratory in the Marine Hospital Service (MHS), which was the earliest version of the Public Health Service (PHS). The Marine Health Service originated in 1798 to provide health care for merchant seamen, paid for by a single clerk collecting 20 cents a month from each seaman's wages. In the 1880s Congress expanded MHS's duties to examine passengers on arriving ships for signs of infectious diseases, particularly cholera and yellow fever.

In 1887 the MHS authorized young Dr. Joseph J. Kinyoun to set up a one-room lab at the Marine Hospital at Stapleton, Staten Island, New York. Kinyoun called the lab a "laboratory of hygiene" to imitate German labs and to suggest that its purpose was to serve the public's health. Eventually called the Hygienic Laboratory, it moved to Washington, D.C., in 1891, where Kinyoun served as the lab's only staff member for 10 years. Dr. Kinyoun started a training program in bacteriology for MHS officers and conducted innovative tests of water purity and air pollution in D.C.

In 1901 Congress authorized $35,000 to build a new building at 25th and E Streets NW for the lab to research "infectious and contagious diseases and matters pertaining to the public health." In 1902 the Marine Hospital Service became the Public Health and Marine Hospital Service (PH-MHS), setting the groundwork for it to become the nation's federal research center and public health agency. The same congressional act began the formal research programs by designating the Division of Pathology and Bacteriology, the Division of Chemistry, the Division of Pharmacology, and the Division of Zoology, and allowed PH-MHS to start hiring Ph.D. specialists to head them, instead of just M.D.s.

The Biologics Control Act (also of 1902) designated the laboratory to regulate production of vaccines and antitoxins, making PH-MHS the new regulatory agency four years before the 1906 Pure Food and Drugs Act was passed. Following contamination of vaccines that eventually killed 13 children in 1901, regulations and standards were established between 1903 and 1907 to license pharmaceutical firms to make smallpox and rabies vaccines, diphtheria and tetanus antitoxins, other antibacterial antisera, thyroidectomized goat serum, and horse serum. Research involved in setting these standards led to the new field of immunology.

Another congressional act reorganized PH-MHS into the Public Health Service (PHS) in 1912, and authorized the lab to conduct research on noncontagious diseases and pollution of streams and lakes in the United States. During World War I (1917–18), the Public Health Service focused primarily on sanitation issues around military bases in the United States, tracing the cause of anthrax outbreaks among soldiers to contaminated shaving brushes. They also discovered that bunion pads used to cover smallpox vaccinations could harbor tetanus spores. In 1916 lab director Dr. George McCoy hired the laboratory's first female bacteriologist, Dr. Ida Bengtson.

The Ransdell Act (1930) changed the Hygienic Laboratory's name to the National Institute of Health (NIH) and authorized its first fellowships for research into biological and medical problems. Use of outside investigators originated in 1918, when chemists who had worked with the Chemical Warfare Service in World War I tried to establish a private sector institute to apply chemistry to medical problems. When the chemists failed to find a private benefactor, they worked with Louisiana senator Joseph E. Ransdell to get federal government support.

Every U.S. senator voted for the act creating the National Cancer Institute (NCI) in 1937, foreshadowing the disease-specific institute structure that developed within NIH. The National Cancer Institute's legislation allowed it to award grants to nonfederal scientists for research on cancer and to fund fellowships for young researchers. Building 6 on the NIH campus in Bethesda, Maryland, housed the National Cancer Institute, where it remained from 1938 to 1941. In 1944 Public Health Service legislation, NCI became part of the National Institutes of Health.

NIH focused primarily on war-related problems during World War II, starting with a Division of Public Health Methods working with the Selective Service to figure out why 43 percent of potential inductees were unfit for military service. Results showed that the most common reason for rejection was bad teeth, and, incidentally, many of those rejects also had syphilis. The Division of Industrial Hygiene worked with the

Divisions of Pathology and Pharmacology to research hazardous substances and conditions to protect workers in war industries. Also related to the war was research on vaccines and therapies against tropical disease, including research at NIH's Rocky Mountain Laboratory in Hamilton, Montana, on yellow fever and typhus vaccines. At the Bethesda, Maryland, facility and through grants to university researchers, a synthetic substitute for quinine was sought to treat malaria. The Division of Biologics looked into the fever-producing properties of bacteria that might appear as contaminants of plasma, serum albumin, or whole blood, and developed sampling techniques to avoid contamination. The Division of Chemotherapy discovered that a lack of sodium in the system was the critical element that could lead to death after burns or traumatic shock, which led to the use of oral saline therapy as a first-aid measure on wartime battlefields.

As World War II ended, Congress passed the 1944 Public Health Service Act, which defined public health and medical research for the future. The new act expanded the grants program to outside and university researchers throughout NIH. New institutes proliferated from 1946 to 1949. Congress created institutes to conduct research on mental health, dental disease, and heart disease.

As part of the National Heart Act in 1948, the name of the National Institute of Health was changed to the plural: National Institutes of Health, with reorganization of the two original divisions into two new institutes: the National Microbiological Institute (NMI) and the Experimental Biology and Medicine Institute (EMBI). Researchers and public health leaders realized that institutes named for specific diseases passed Congress faster than academic-medical named programs, so in 1950 EMBI was absorbed by the National Institute of Arthritis and Metabolic Diseases. In 1955 the National Microbiological Institute became part of the National Institute of Allergy and Infectious Diseases. By 1960 there

were 10 institutes, and in 2003 there were 27 institutes and centers, and several specialized research offices, such as the Office of AIDS Research.

Back in 1944 the Public Health Service Act also authorized NIH to conduct clinical research, beginning with the Warren Grant Magnuson Clinical Center on the NIH campus in Bethesda, Maryland. The clinical center opened in 1953 with 540 beds, designed to bring research labs close to hospital wards to promote collaboration between lab scientists and clinicians. In the '50s there was a real fear of "socialized medicine," particularly on the part of physicians, and great efforts were taken to assure them and the public that this government clinical center existed only for research purposes. Because of inhuman Nazi medical experiments during World War II, the clinical center's board set standards to make sure humans were not harmed in the name of research. Toward this goal, the resultant NIH Office for Protection from Research Risks now monitors 450 major institutions and more than 5,000 smaller institutions, community hospitals, and clinics where research is conducted. In 1963 NIH issued a guide for care and use of laboratory animals. Now institutional animal care committees review animal research practices at institutions that receive NIH funds.

CONTACT Address: Warren Grant Magnuson Clinical Center, 6100 Executive Boulevard, Suite 3C01, MSC7511, Bethesda, MD 20892-7511; Phone: (301) 496-2563; Fax: (301) 402-2984.

Congress meted out "health-funding" more moderately in the 1960s, partly due to inflation and partly due to new programs such as Medicare and Medicaid. Congress funded disease specific research in the 1970s. The National Cancer Act of 1971 created 15 new research, training, and demonstration cancer centers. In 1972 the National Heart, Blood Vessel, Lung, and Blood Act mandated and expanded programs to fight all aspects of heart disease, including high blood pressure, elevated cholesterol levels, stroke, and specific blood diseases, such as sickle-cell anemia. The AIDS crisis of the 1980s and 1990s also resulted in disease-specific research funding.

Also in the 1980s, NIH and the DEPARTMENT OF ENERGY launched the Human Genome Project to map and sequence the entire range of human genes.

NIH also works internationally through the Pan American Sanitary Bureau, now called the Pan American Health Organization. The first NIH grants funding researchers in foreign universities were awarded in 1947. Creation of the John E. Fogarty International Center in 1968 formalized coordination of international exchanges at NIH, and the Fogarty Center maintains liaisons with the World Health Organization and European medical research organizations even today, in efforts to reduce disparities in global health, give international research grants, fellowships, and training, and lead internationally in science policy and global research strategies. Fields of interest include tuberculosis, malaria, maternal and child health, genetics, infectious diseases, environmental and occupational health, medical informatics, minority training, brain disorders in the developing world, HIV/AIDS, biodiversity groups, health and economic development, and tobacco and health research. The Fogarty Center also offers and connects to research opportunities in many centers throughout the world.

CONTACT Address: Fogarty International Center, Building 31, Room B2C29, 31 Center Drive MSC 2220, Bethesda, MD 20892-2220; Phone: (301) 496-2075; Fax: (301) 594-1211; Website: www.fic.nih.gov.

The 1986 Technology Transfer Act established and codified partnerships between NIH research and private-sector development of therapeutic products.

The *National Library of Medicine (NLM)* is the world's largest medical library, holding more than 5.1 million items, including books, journals, technical reports, manuscripts, microfilms, photographs, and images. Originating in 1836 as the library of the surgeon general of the army, the National Library of Medicine became part of NIH in 1968. Most of the NLM's current medical literature is available on the Web as MEDLINE, which includes AIDSLINE, which contains AIDS research information. CATLINE is an on-line catalog of books and manuscripts in the library. NLM also publishes Index Medicus®, a monthly guide to articles in 3,400 journals. The Lister Hill Center houses the Lister Hill National Center for Biomedical Communications (explores use of computers, communication, and audiovisual technologies) and the National Center for Biotechnology Information (stores and makes available data on the human genome) (www.ncbi.nih.gov), as part of the National Library of Medicine.

CONTACT Address: 8600 Rockville Pike, Bethesda, MD 20894; Phone: (888) 346-3656; Tours: (301) 496-6308; Website: www.nlm.nih.gov.

NLM holds materials in all areas of biomedicine and health care, as well as works on biomedical technology, the humanities, and the physical, life, and social sciences.

Construction began in 1997 on the Mark O. Hatfield Clinical Research Center, expected to open in 2004. Intended to adjoin the Magnuson Clinical Center, the Hatfield Center will have 250 beds for inpatient and outpatient care, outpatient care facilities, and research laboratories.

NIH also holds Consensus Development Conferences of investigators, researchers, and physicians from around the world who meet and sit on panels to examine new methods of therapy or to evaluate existing therapies about which there may be questions or doubts.

NIH-supported investigators have won more than 80 Nobel Prizes.

INSTITUTES AND CENTERS

NIH is headed by the Office of the Director and comprises various offices or departments and 27 institutes and centers.

OFFICE OF THE DIRECTOR (OD): The Office of the Director is NIH's central office and sets NIH scientific and administrative policy, and plans, manages, and coordinates programs and activities of all NIH components. While each NIH institute and center formulates its own mission, the OD helps shape each agency's research agenda, and participates in coordinating efforts that involve more than one institute. The director identifies areas of research emphasis that show potential for future benefits, while each institute develops initiatives within the area of research. Office of the Director Program Offices stimulate and occasionally initiate specific areas of research, which currently include minority health, women's health, AIDS research, disease prevention, and behavioral and social sciences research.

Within the OD are the following offices:

Office of Extramural Research (OER): Guides and supports institutes in research and training programs through grants, contracts, or cooperative agreements. Some of its projects include bioinformatics and bioengineering.

Office of Intramural Research (OIR): Coordinates research conducted by in-house NIH personnel. Areas of exploration include animal care, human subjects research, technology transfer, graduate partnerships, education, and loan repayment for students. OIR has facilities in Bethesda, Baltimore, and Frederick, Maryland; Research Triangle Park, North Carolina; Hamilton, Montana; and Phoenix, Arizona.

Office of Administration (OA): Advises NIH director and staff on administration, management, policy, and oversees information resources management, management assessment, grant administration, and contract management, procurement, and logistics.

Office of AIDS Research (OAR): Formulates scientific policy and recommends allocation of research resources for AIDS research.

Office of Behavioral and Social Sciences Research (OBSSR): Advises NIH director on research on the role of human behavior in the development of health, prevention of disease, and therapeutic intervention.

Office of Communications and Public Liaison (OCPL): Communicates information about NIH policies, programs, and research results to the general public.

Office of Community Liaison (OCL): Plans, directs, and oversees activities promoting collaboration between NIH and research community.

Office of Disease Prevention (ODP): Coordinates actual application of NIH research to disease prevention, nutrition programs, and medical practice, including dietary supplements and rare diseases.

Office of Education (OE): Provides a guide to postdoctoral training opportunities available at NIH.

Office of Equal Opportunity (OEO): Advises the director and staff on equal opportunity policies and programs.

Office of Financial Management (OFM): Works on budgets and allocation of funds.

Office of Human Resource Management (OHRM): Oversees all matters of human resource management (personnel) and leadership.

Office of Research on Women's Health (ORWH): Coordinates women's health research at NIH and promotes, stimulates, and supports efforts to improve women's health through biomedical and behavioral research. ORWH also works to make sure women's health research is an important part of research throughout the scientific community.

Office of Research Services (ORS): Manages and provides technical and administrative services throughout NIH, including engineering, safety, space and facility management, support services, and security.

Office of Science Policy (OSP): Helps develop new policy and program initiatives, monitors and coordinates planning and evaluation, plans and runs a science education program, and develops and implements NIH policy and procedures for safe conduct of DNA activities.

Office of Legislative Policy and Analysis (OLPA): Develops legislative policy and proposals and provides liaison (lobbying) with Congress, and with the rest of the Department of Health and Human Services and other federal agencies.

Office of Technology Transfer (OTT): Serves as the lead public health coordinator of technology transfer activities for the Public Health Service, NIH, Centers for Disease Control (CDC), and the Food and Drug Administration (FDA).

NATIONAL INSTITUTE ON AGING (NIA): Conducts and financially supports biomedical, social, and behavioral research to increase knowledge and improve life through the aging process. It also studies the physical, psychological, and social factors of aging. Congress authorized funding for NIA in 1974, and it now looks into the aging process, age-related diseases, and the special problems and needs of the aged. It also trains and develops research scientists, state-of-the-art resources, and disseminates information to the public on its findings.

NIA's research programs include Extramural Programs of Biology of Aging, Behavioral and Social Research, Neuroscience and Neuropsychology of Aging, and the Geriatrics and Clinical Gerontology Program. Intramural programs include primarily laboratory and clinical research done at the Gerontology Research Center in Bethesda, Maryland.

CONTACT Address: National Institute on Aging, Building 31, Room 5C27, 31 Center Drive, MSC 2292, Bethesda, MD 20892; Phone: (301) 496-1752; Website: www.nia.nih.gov/.

NATIONAL INSTITUTE ON ALCOHOL ABUSE AND ALCOHOLISM (NIAAA): Supports financially and conducts biomedical and behavioral research on the causes, consequences, treatment, and prevention of alcoholism and alcohol-related problems. NIAAA also looks for how alcohol damages body organs; medication; rehabilitation; risks of alcohol-related problems among population groups; works with local and international program coordinators; and disseminates research findings to health care providers, researchers, policy makers, and the public.

CONTACT Address: National Institute on Alcohol Abuse and Alcoholism, Willco Building, 6000 Executive Boulevard, Bethesda, MD 20893-7003; Phone: (301) 443-3885 or 433-3860; Website: www.niaaa.nih.gov/.

NATIONAL INSTITUTE OF ALLERGY AND INFECTIOUS DISEASES (NIAID): Supports and conducts research and clinical evaluations on the causes, treatment, and prevention of infectious, allergic, and immunologic diseases, including autoimmune diseases, AIDS, transplantation, microbiology and infectious diseases, and vaccines at the Dale and Betty Bumpers Vaccine Research Center (VRC).

With its origins in the 1887 Hygienic Laboratory, Congress gave the current name in 1955 to include its predecessors, the Rocky Mountain Laboratory, the Biologics Control Laboratory, NIH Division of Infectious Diseases, and the Division of Tropical Diseases. NIAID operates in Bethesda, Maryland; Rockville, Maryland; and at the Rocky Mountain Laboratories in Hamilton, Montana. Intramural research includes virology, biochemistry, parasitology, epidemiology, mycology, molecular biology, immunology, immunopathology, and immunogenetics.

Extramural research includes AIDS; asthma and allergic diseases, including the National Cooperative Inner-City Asthma Study to reduce occurrences and severity of asthma episodes and deaths among African-American and Hispanic children; biodefense to research pathogens to be used as agents of bioterrorism, including treatments, diagnostics, and vaccines; new diseases and reemerging old diseases, as well as Lyme disease, and multidrug-resistant tuberculosis; enteric diseases that cause severe diarrhea such as cholera and rotavirus infection; genetic regulation of immune system responses through immunosuppressive therapies; diseases experienced due to malfunctions of the immune system; research into malaria, filariasis, typanosomiasis, and leprosy, including tropical medicine research in Brazil, China, Mali, and Thailand; sexually transmitted diseases (STD) such as gonorrhea, syphilis, Chlamydia, genital herpes, and human papillomavirus; and work to develop new vaccines for many diseases, which have included rabies, meningitis, whooping cough, hepatitis A and B, chickenpox, and pneumococcal pneumonia. NIAID also researches fungal diseases, hospital-associated infections, respiratory diseases, and antiviral and antimicrobial drug development.

CONTACT Address: NIAID, Building 31, Room 7A-50, 31 Center Drive, MSC 2520, Bethesda, MD 20892-2520; Phone: (301) 496-2263, 496-5717; Website: www.niaid.nih.gov/.

NATIONAL INSTITUTE OF ARTHRITIS AND MUSCULOSKELETAL AND SKIN DISEASE (NIAMS): Works to find causes, treatment, and prevention of arthritis and musculoskeletal and skin diseases, such as atopic dermatitis, bunions, bursitis, carpal tunnel syndrome, fibromyalgia, gout, heel pain, hip replacement, juvenile rheumatoid arthritis, lupus, muscular dystrophy, osteoporosis, psoriasis, psoriatic arthritis, Raynaud's phenomenon, rosacea, scoliosis, sports injuries, and sweating disorders.

CONTACT Address: NIH Osteoporosis and Related Bone Diseases-National Resource Center: 1232 22nd Street NW, Washington, DC 20037-1292; Phone: (202) 223-0344 or (800) 624-BONE, TTY: (202) 466-4315; Fax: (202) 293-2356; Website: www.osteo.org. NIAMS Information Clearinghouse, National Institutes of Health, 1 AMS Circle, Bethesda, MD 20892-3675; Phone: (301) 495-4484, 496-4353, or (877) 226-4267, TTY: (301) 565-2066; Fax: (301) 718-6366; Website: www.niams.nih.gov/.

NATIONAL INSTITUTE OF BIOMEDICAL IMAGING AND BIOENGINEERING (NIBIB): Created by legislation signed December 29, 2000, by President Bill Clinton, NIBIB works to improve health through coordinating use of technology with biomedical imaging, bioengineering, physics, chemistry, mathematics, materials science, and computer sciences and transferring and applying such technologies to medial applications.

CONTACT Address: NIBIB, 31 Center Drive, Room 1B37, Bethesda, MD 20892-2077; Phone: (301) 451-6768; Website: www.nibib.nih.gov/.

NATIONAL CANCER INSTITUTE (NCI): Works toward complete control and elimination of cancers through interdisciplinary collaboration to develop interventions and new technology and delivery of new interventions through clinical and public health programs. Cancer death rates have decreased from 1993 to 1999. NCI also encourages reduction of tobacco use, weight gain, and sun exposure, while increasing physical activity. Cancers still increasing include non-Hodgkin's lymphoma, melanoma, cancers of the liver and esophagus, and breast and lung cancer in women.

NCI has developed an extensive research program, which includes investigator-initiated research including novel approaches to solutions and progress review groups; NCI-supported centers, networks, and consortia; a National Clinical Trials Program in Treatment and Prevention to move new interventions into practical health care delivery; bioinformatics for cancer research to coordinate the huge quantity of relevant scientific information and translating it to medicine to reach the public; studies of genes and the environment to understand the relationship between inherited susceptibility to cancer and environmental risk factors in collaborations with such groups as the Cohort Consortium; studies of signatures of the cancer cell, its microenvironment, and its co-conspirators; molecular targets of prevention and treatment looking at low toxicity, high efficacy against molecular features that cause tumor growth to try to make them become normal, stop replicating themselves, or self-destruct; cancer imaging and molecular sensing to detect, diagnose, and treat cancer; and improved cancer information availability to help patients and their families make informed cancer-related decisions.

NCI also works to improve the quality of cancer care, reduce cancer-related health disparities, increase cancer survivorship and quality of life, and do more research on tobacco and tobacco-related cancers and the role of tobacco exposure on the incidence of cancer.

CONTACT Address: NCI, Suite 3036A, 6116 Executive Boulevard, MSC8 322, Bethesda, MD 20892-8322; Phone: (301) 435-3848 or (800) 422-6237; Website: www.nci.nih.gov/.

NATIONAL INSTITUTE OF CHILD HEALTH & HUMAN DEVELOPMENT (NICHD): NICHD's goal is to ensure that every person is born healthy and wanted, that women suffer no harmful effects from any part of the reproductive process, and that all children have the chance to live a healthy and productive life, free of disease or disability.

Created by Congress in 1962, NICHD supports and conducts research on topics related to the health of children, adults, families, and populations, with the goals of reducing infant deaths; improving the health of women and men; understanding reproductive health; learning about growth and development; examining birth defects and mental retardation; the effects of events that happen throughout pregnancy or during childhood; human growth and development; reproductive health of men and women; and developing medical rehabilitation interventions to help people with disabilities.

Among the topics studied are infant deaths through Sudden Infant Death Syndrome and other infant breathing problems; managed care for premature infants; mental retardation; infertility; contraceptive methods; transmission of HIV from infected mothers to their babies; and social, physical, and behavioral treatments to remove barriers and increase mobility for people with mental, developmental, and physical disabilities.

NICHD maintains three centers and two divisions to conduct research on specific health topics and areas: Center for Research for Mothers and Children (CRMC); Center for Population Research (CPR); National Center for Medical Rehabilitation Research (NCMRR); Division of Epidemiology, Statistics and Prevention Research (DESPR); and Division of Intramural Research.

CONTACT Address: NICHD Information Resource Center, P.O. Box 3006, Rockville, MD 20847; Phone: (800) 370-2943; Fax: (301) 984-1473; Website: www.nichd.nih.gov/publications/health.cfm. Public Information and Communications, NICHD, 31 Center Drive, Building 31, Room 2A32, Bethesda, MD 20892-2425; Phone: (301) 496-5133; Fax: (301) 496-7101; Website: www.nichd.nih.gov.

NATIONAL CENTER FOR COMPLEMENTARY AND ALTERNATIVE MEDICINE (NCCAM): Supports clinical and basic science research through grants for studying complementary and alternative medicines and integration of alternative and conventional medicine. NCCAM also works to educate and train complementary and alternative medicine researchers and disseminates information to the public and to professionals.

CONTACT Address: NCCAM, National Institutes of Health, Bethesda, MD 20892; Website: http://nccam.nih.gov/. NCCAM Clearinghouse, P.O. Box 7923, Gaithersburg, MD 20898-7923; Phone: (888) 644-6226, (301) 519-3153, TTY: (866) 464-3615; Fax: (866) 464-3616.

NATIONAL INSTITUTE ON DEAFNESS AND OTHER COMMUNICATION DISORDERS (NIDCD): Supports and conducts 600 biomedical and behavioral research projects and research training to analyze and improve disorders of hearing, balance, smell, taste, voice, speech, and language. NIDCD also researches ear infections, creates hearing aids, investigates noise-induced hearing loss, Ménière's disease, auditory processing disorder in children, dysphagia, and traumatic brain injury. NIDCD's extramural research includes development of a vaccine against otitis media, identification and characterization of genes responsible for hereditary hearing impairment, genes associated with neoplasms that affect human communications, and treatment of voice disorders.

CONTACT   Address: NIDCD, 31 Center Drive, MSC 2320, Bethesda, MD 20892-2320; Phone: (301) 496-7243, TTY: (301) 402-0252; Website: www.nidcd.nih.gov.

NATIONAL INSTITUTE OF DENTAL AND CRANIOFACIAL RESEARCH (NIDCR): Works to promote people's general health by improving their oral, dental, and craniofacial health through support and conduct of research to promote health, prevent diseases and conditions, and develop new diagnostics and therapeutics.

CONTACT   Address: NIDCR, National Institutes of Health, Bethesda, MD 20892-2190; Phone: (301) 496-4261; Website: www.nidcr.nih.gov.

NATIONAL INSTITUTE OF DIABETES AND DIGESTIVE AND KIDNEY DISEASES (NIDDK): Supports and conducts research on metabolic diseases such as diabetes, inborn metabolism errors, endocrine disorders, mineral metabolism, digestive diseases, nutrition, urology and renal disease, and hematology. Basic research studies include biochemistry, nutrition, pathology, histochemistry, chemistry, physical, chemical and molecular biology, pharmacology, and toxicology.

NIDDK's Division of Intramural Research conducts research at its 10 branches and 10 laboratories. Eight branches in Bethesda, Maryland, conduct basic and clinical research on diabetes, bone metabolism, endocrinology, obesity, hematology, digestive diseases, kidney diseases, and genetics. The Phoenix branch in Arizona develops and applies epidemiologic and genetic methods to the study of diabetes and obesity. The 10th branch looks at mathematical modeling of biological problems. The laboratories do fundamental research in molecular biology, structural biology, chemistry, cell biology, pharmacology, chemical physics, biochemistry, neuroscience, and developmental biology. The Laboratory

Animal Science section provides research animal collaboration and support for institute research programs.

CONTACT   Address: General inquiries: NIDDK, Building 31, Room 9A04, Center Drive, MSC 2560, Bethesda, MD 20892-2560; Phone: (301) 496-3583; Website: www.niddk.nih.gov.

NATIONAL INSTITUTE OF DRUG ABUSE (NIDA): Claims to support more than 85 percent of the world's research on the health aspects of drug abuse and addiction. Established in 1974, NIDA became part of NIH in October 1992. NIDA studies how drugs of abuse change the brain and behavior, and works to quickly communicate scientific data to policy makers, drug abuse and health care practitioners, and the general public. NIDA also works on the dual and sometimes parallel epidemics of drug use and HIV/AIDS. Research is sometimes conducted through block grant programs to the states.

CONTACT   Address: NIDA, National Institutes of Health, 6001 Executive Boulevard, Room 5213, Bethesda, MD 20892-9561; Phone: (301) 443-1124; Website: www.drugabuse.gov/.

NATIONAL INSTITUTE OF ENVIRONMENTAL HEALTH SCIENCES (NIEHS): Based on the belief that human health and disease result from the interaction of environmental factors, individual susceptibility, and age, NIEHS works to reduce human illness and dysfunction from environmental causes by researching and understanding each of these factors and how they interrelate through multidisciplinary biomedical research programs. Working in a rare setting of 509 acres of North Carolina rolling hills covered with rhododendrons, oak, and pine trees, NIEHS has discovered the deadly effects of asbestos exposure, the developmental impairment of children exposed to lead (in paint), the health effects of urban pollution, and contributed to the identification of the first breast cancer gene, BRCA1. In 1995 NIEHS scientists identified a gene that suppresses prostate cancer. NIEHS staff have also developed genetically altered mice to use in screening potential toxins and to help develop aspirinlike anti-inflammatory drugs with fewer side effects than aspirin.

NIEHS funds centers for environmental health studies at Harvard, Oregon State, Vanderbilt, University of California at Berkeley, and MIT, among others.

Specific current projects are environmental influences on health including health disparities research; studies of birth and developmental defects, sterility, and breast and testicular cancers; women's health; Alzheimer's and other neurologic disorders; lead poisoning; hazards to the poor and minorities; agricultural pollution; signal error in which environmental chemicals mimic hormonal growth factors and activate receptor proteins that stimulate cell growth and division; reduction in number of animals used in research (while developing genetically altered mice for testing); practical application of research on impacts of waste sites, pesticides used in farms and homes, Lyme disease–carrying ticks, water and air pollution, power lines, and electric and magnetic fields; and studying biomarkers to measure the body's exposure to and uptake of toxins.

CONTACT Address: NIEHS, P.O. Box 12233, 111 Alexander Drive, Research Triangle Park, NC 27709; Phone: (919) 541-3345; Website: www. niehs.nih.gov/.

NATIONAL EYE INSTITUTE (NEI): Established by Congress in 1968 to protect and prolong the vision of the American people, NEI works to develop sight-saving treatments, reduce visual impairment and blindness, and thereby improve the quality of life for everyone. NEI awards about 1,600 research grants and training awards to scientists at more than 250 medical centers, hospitals, universities, and other institutions throughout the world, and conducts research at its own facility in Bethesda, Maryland.

Eye diseases and problems addressed by NEI include diabetic retinopathy; amblyopia; age-related macular degeneration (AMD); glaucoma;

retinopathy of prematurity; corneal stromal keratitis; cytomegalovirus retinitis; uveitis; retinitis pigmentosa; Leber's congenital amaurosis; and laser treatment for AMD, glaucoma, and myopia. Currently NEI is working on developing techniques to transplant healthy cells into diseased retinas; gene-based treatments to slow some kinds of retinal degeneration; and "neuroprotection" techniques to prevent or slow glaucoma cell damage and promote survival of retinal cells damaged by glaucoma.

NEI has established the National Eye Health Education Program (NEHEP) among 65 professional, civic, and volunteer organizations and government agencies to develop public and professional education programs to prevent blindness, reduce visual impairment, and communicate possible remedies available to people with vision problems.

CONTACT Address: NEI, National Institutes of Health, Building 31, Room 6A32, 31 Center Drive, MSC 2510, Bethesda, MD 20892-2510 or National Eye Institute, 2020 Vision Place, Bethesda, MD 20892-3655; Phone: (301) 496-5248; Website: www.nei.nih.gov.

NATIONAL INSTITUTE OF GENERAL MEDICAL SCIENCES (NIGMS): Supports basic biomedical research that is not aimed at specific diseases or disorders, and looks at mechanisms involved in certain diseases. Established in 1962, NIGMS's 2002 budget was $1.73 billion. Currently, its major initiatives include stem cell research, structural genomics, pharmacogenetics, complex biological systems, and collaborative research initiatives.

The *Division of Cell Biology and Biophysics* researches analytical and separation techniques; biomedical instrumentation; cell organization, motility, and division; lipid biochemistry; membrane structure and function; molecular biophysics; spectroscopic techniques; structural biology; and structural genomics. The *Division of Genetics and Developmental Biology* works on cell growth and differentiation; chromosome organization and mechanics; complex biological systems; control of gene expression; control of the cell cycle; developmental genetics and cell biology; extrachromosomal inheritance; mechanisms of mutagenesis; neurogenetics and the genetics of behavior; population genetics, evolution and the genetics of complex traits; and replication, recombination, and repair of genes.

The *Division of Pharmacology, Physiology, and Biological Chemistry* researches anesthesiology; biochemistry; bioenergetics; bio-organic and bioinorganic chemistry; biotechnology; glycoconjugates and glycobiology; medicinal chemistry; molecular immunobiology; pharmacogenetics; pharmacology and clinical pharmacology; physiology; synthetic chemistry; trauma and burn injury; and wound healing.

The *Division of Minority Opportunities in Research* includes the Minority Access to Research Careers Branch that supports research training at the undergraduate, graduate, and faculty levels. The Minority Biomedical Research support branch finances research projects at educational institutions whose enrollments substantially consist of minorities.

The *Center for Bioinformatics and Computational Biology* conducts and supports research on the interlinking of biology and computer sciences, engineering, mathematics, and physics. The center also manages NIH's *Biomedical Information Science and Technology Initiative.*

CONTACT Address: National Institute of General Medical Sciences, 45 Center Drive, MSC 6200, Bethesda, MD 20892-6200; Phone: (301) 496-7301; Website: www.nigms.nih.gov.

NATIONAL HEART, LUNG, AND BLOOD INSTITUTE (NHLBI): Leads research nationally on the causes, diagnosis, and treatment of diseases of the heart, blood vessels, lung, blood, sleep disorders, and stroke, and administers the Woman's Health Initiative. Among NHLBI's fields of focus are prevention, education, and control of the above problems; science and technology; minority health; epidemiology and clinical applica-

tions, including the Framingham Heart Study and the Jackson Heart Study; hematology; animal medicine and surgery; biochemical genetics; biophysical chemistry, cardiac energetics; cell biology; cell signaling; developmental biology; kidney and electrolyte metabolism; lymphocyte biology; molecular cardiology; molecular immunology; and pathology science. It also runs the National Center on Sleep Disorders.

CONTACT Address: NHLBI Health Information Center, P.O. Box 30105, Bethesda, MD 20824-0105; Phone: (301) 496-4236; or NHLBI, Building 31, Room 5A52, 31 Center Drive, MSC 2486, Bethesda, MD 20892; Phone: (301) 496-2411; Website: www.nhlbi.nih.gov.

NATIONAL HUMAN GENOME RESEARCH INSTITUTE (HGP): Works to understand genomes of various organisms used in biomedical research, such as model organisms mice, fruit flies, and roundworms to figure out how the human organism behaves. The Human Genome Project is an international research program trying to complete mapping, sequencing, and understanding all genes of human beings, which are collectively known as the human genome. NIH created the institute in 1989, and it works with the DEPARTMENT OF ENERGY (DOE), and universities and research facilities throughout the United States, United Kingdom, France, Germany, Japan, and China.

HGP has discovered that there are between 30,000 and 40,000 human genes.

CONTACT Address: National Human Genome Research Institute, NIH, Building 31, Room 4B09, 31 Center Drive, MSC 2152, 9000 Rockville Pike, Bethesda, MD 20892-2152; Phone: (301) 402-0911 or 496-0844; Website: www.genome.gov.

NATIONAL INSTITUTE OF MENTAL HEALTH (NIMH): Works to reduce the burden of mental illness and behavioral disorders through research on the mind, brain, and behavior. Current goals of NIMH include to find vulnerability genes and diagnostic biomarkers for major mental disorders; find and produce information to help reduce suicide; improve behavioral interventions to reduce HIV/AIDS transmission; and develop new strategies to prevent mental disorders. NIMH researches and offers information on depression and bipolar disorder; schizophrenia; anxiety disorders; eating disorders; suicide related to mental disorders; and childhood disorders such as autism, attention deficit hyperactivity disorder, conduct disorder, and other behavioral conditions that can affect a child's development.

NIMH's clinical division includes study of behavioral endocrinology, biological psychiatry, child psychiatry, brain disorders, neuroendocrinology, neurogenetics, neuroscience, experimental therapeutics, geriatric psychiatry, labs of brain and cognition and clinical science, and mood and anxiety disorders.

The National Advisory Mental Health Council, made up of scientists and public representatives, advises the institute on how to exploit existing scientific opportunities to best cope with urgent public health needs. The council has helped develop the Strategic Plan for Mood Disorders Research and holds community forums to discuss research needs and priorities with people in local communities.

CONTACT Address: NIMH, 6001 Executive Boulevard, Room 8184, MSC 9663, Bethesda, MD 20892-9663; Phone: (301) 443-4513; Fax: (301) 443-4279, TTY: (301) 443-8431; Website: www.nimh.nih.gov.

NATIONAL INSTITUTE OF NEUROLOGICAL DISORDERS AND STROKE (NINDS): Conducts and supports research on brain and nervous system disorders to reduce frequency and burden of neurological disease. Created by Congress in 1950, NINDS now knows of and works on 600 disorders that afflict the nervous system, including stroke, epilepsy, Parkinson's disease, AIDS, Alzheimer's disease, brain tumors, developmental disorders, motor neuron diseases, muscular dystrophies, multiple sclerosis, neurogenetic disorders, pain, spinal cord injuries, sleep disorders, traumatic brain injury, and autism. Other problems it researches include narcolepsy, Jakob disease, Lou Gehrig's disease, St. Vitus' dance, postpolio syndrome, and lupus.

Currently NINDS research areas include biology of the cells of the nervous system; brain and nervous system development; genetics of the brain; cognition and behavior; neurodegeneration; brain plasticity and repair; neural signaling; learning and memory; motor control and integration; sensory function; and neural channels, synapses, and circuits.

CONTACT Address: BRAIN or NIH Neurological Institute, P.O. Box 5801, Bethesda, MD 20824; Phone: for health or medical questions and general information: (800) 352-9424 or (301) 496-5751, TTY: (301) 468-5981; Website: www.ninds.nih.gov. For extramural programs: NINDS, Division of Extramural Research, 6001 Executive Boulevard, Suite 3309, Bethesda, MD 20892-9531.

NATIONAL INSTITUTE OF NURSING RESEARCH (NINR): Focuses on clinical care in community and home, as well as in traditional health care situations. It deals with problems encountered by patients, families, and caregivers, with emphasis on special needs of at-risk and under-served populations. NINR supports grants to universities and other research organizations and conducts research at its labs in Bethesda, Maryland, pertaining to long-term care for the elderly, special needs of women throughout their lives, bioethical issues regarding genetic testing, biobehavioral aspects of managing and treating infectious diseases, end-of-life (palliative) care, and environmental influences on risk factors and chronic illnesses.

NINR looks for, supports, and researches chronic illness experiences; cultural and ethnic considerations; health promotion and disease prevention; implications of genetic advances; quality of life and quality of care; symptom management; telehealth interventions and monitoring; chronic illness and long-term care; health promotion and risk behaviors; cardiopulmonary health and critical care; neurofunction and sensory conditions; immune responses and oncology; reproductive and infant health; low birth weight in minority populations; diabetes self-management; and health disparities among minority populations.

CONTACT General information: Address: NINR, 31 Center Drive, Room 5B-10, Bethesda, MD 20892-2178; Phone: (301) 496-0207. For extramural programs, grants and contracts, and Office of Review: 6701 Democracy Boulevard, Room 710, One Democracy Plaza, Bethesda, MD 20892-4870; Website: www.nih.gov/ninr/.

CENTER FOR INFORMATION TECHNOLOGY (CIT): Coordinates and manages information technology and works to advance computational science, while working to collaborate in discovering and developing biomedical knowledge.

CONTACT Address: CIT, 10401 Fernwood Drive, Bethesda, MD 20892-5651; Phone: (301) 496-6203; Fax: (301) 402-4437; Website: www.cit.nih.gov.

NATIONAL CENTER ON MINORITY HEALTH AND HEALTH DISPARITIES (NCMHD): Promotes minority health and leads, coordinates, supports, and assesses NIH's effort to study and eliminate disparities in health care for minorities in relationship to majority Americans. Established in 1990, NCMHD supports and conducts clinical, social, and behavioral research, promotes training of minority researchers, and reaches out to and disseminates information to minority and other health disparity communities. NCMHD's overall goal is that all U.S. populations have equal opportunity to enjoy long, healthy, and productive lives.

CONTACT Address: NCMHD, 6707 Democracy Boulevard, Suite 800, MSC 5465, Bethesda, MD 20892-5465; Phone: (301) 402-1366; Fax: (301) 480-4049; Website: http://ncmhd.nih.gov.

NATIONAL CENTER FOR RESEARCH RESOURCES (NCRR): Creates and provides research technologies and shared resources in biomedical research by providing cost-effective, multidisciplinary resources to investigators, particularly to institutions that have not participated in NIH research programs previously. It supports patient-oriented research on human diseases, using animals that model human reactions.

CONTACT Address: National Center for Research Resources, 6705 Rockledge Drive, Suite 5140, Bethesda, MD 20892-7965; Phone: (301) 435-0888; Fax: (301) 480-3558; Website: www.ncrr.nih.gov.

CENTER FOR SCIENTIFIC REVIEW (CSR): Interacts with extramural research community and provides information on how to apply for grants, requirements for scientific review by scientific peers, and employment opportunities.

CONTACT Address: Center for Scientific Review, 6701 Rockledge Drive, MSC 7768, Bethesda, MD 20892-7768; Phone: (301) 435-1115 or 435-1111; Website: www.csr.nih.gov.

PROGRAM SUPPORT CENTER

Health and Human Services' Program Support Center works to provide measurable, qualitative, and cost-effective administrative and logistical services to HHS, other executive departments, and independent federal agencies. It processes grant payments, automated personnel and payroll services, training, personnel support for the Public Health Service Commissioned Corps, management and award acquisitions, and distribution and management of more than 5,000 pharmaceutical items and health supplies to government agencies, ships at sea, and embassies throughout the world. PSC also provides accounting and financial management services, information technology and telecommunications services, and occupational health services. PSC has offices in Atlanta, Georgia; Boston, Massachusetts; Chicago, Illinois; Dallas, Texas; Denver, Colorado; Kansas City, Missouri; New York, New York; Philadelphia, Pennsylvania; San Francisco, California; and Seattle, Washington.

CONTACT Address: Program Support Center, 5600 Fishers Lane, Room 13-12, Rockville, MD

20857; Phone: (301) 443-1494; Fax: (301) 443-2909; E-mail: ocr@psc.gov; Website: www.psc.gov.

SUBSTANCE ABUSE AND MENTAL HEALTH SERVICES ADMINISTRATION (SAMHSA)

The Substance Abuse and Mental Health Services Administration (SAMHSA) works to improve the quality and availability of substance abuse prevention, treatment of addictions, and mental health services. SAMHSA was established by Congress October 1, 1992, to provide prevention, diagnosis, and treatment services for people suffering substance abuse and mental illnesses. SAMHSA also works with communities, states, American Indian tribes, and private organizations, and considers community risk factors involved in substance abuse and mental illness, and coordinates the functions of the Center for Mental Health Services, the Center for Substance Abuse Prevention, and the Center for Substance Abuse Treatment. Federal block grants help states with substance abuse and mental health services programs, and Targeted Capacity Expansion grants help fund community programs to identify and address substance abuse and mental health service needs as early as possible.

CENTER FOR MENTAL HEALTH SERVICES (CMHS): Creates and coordinates community-based nationwide mental health services to improve availability and accessibility of high-quality care for at-risk people or people with mental illness and their families, which includes 44 million Americans. Through Community Mental Health Services block grants, CMHS supports community-based practices to reach highest-risk people, such as adults with serious mental illnesses, such as schizophrenia, bipolar disorder, and severe depression, and children with serious emotional disturbances. CMHS also works on stigma issues, and collects and disseminates national mental health services data,

addresses disaster mental health services, school violence, mental illness and drug addiction suffered by the homeless, and influences of drug abuse and mental illness on HIV/AIDS. It assists patients with treatment, employment, housing, transportation, and community involvement, and focuses on rural mental health, faith-based mental health initiatives (instigated by President George W. Bush), and refugee mental health.

CMHS's Comprehensive Community Mental Health Services for Children Program offers "system of care" teams featuring the families of children with serious emotional disturbances to help them improve their lives and not lapse into juvenile justice systems.

CONTACT Address: SAMHSA, 5600 Fishers Lane, Rockville, MD 20857; Phone: (800) 789-2647; Website: www.mentalhealth.org or www.samhsa.gov.

CMHS's American Indian/Alaska Native Circles of Care program helps federally recognized tribes and urban Indian communities to design culturally appropriate mental health services for their children with serious emotional disturbances and their families. Circles of Care is a three-year grant collaborative program including financial and technical assistance from the Indian Health Service, Department of Health and Human Services, and the Department of Justice's Office of Juvenile Justice Delinquency Prevention. Technical assistance comes from the National Center on American Indian and Alaska Native Research, and the National Indian Child Welfare Association.

CONTACT Address: National Center for American Indian and Alaska Native Mental Health Research, University of Colorado Health Sciences Center, Campus Box AO11-13, 4455 East 12th Avenue, Denver, CO 80220; Phone: (303) 315-9232; Fax: (303) 315-9579; Website: www.uchsc.edu/ai/ncaianmhr/ or National Indian Child Welfare Association, 5100 SW Macadam Avenue, Suite 300, Portland, OR 97201; Phone: (503) 222-4044; Fax: (503) 222-4007; Website: www.nicwa.org or Website: http://mentalhealth.

samhsa.gov/cmhs/childrenscampaign/nativeamerican.asp.

CENTER FOR SUBSTANCE ABUSE PREVENTION (CSAP): Runs federal programs to make substance abuse prevention services better and more accessible for problems such as illicit drug use, misuse of legal medications, use of tobacco, or excessive or illegal use of alcohol. CSAP also aims to inform all Americans of how to avoid substance abuse by strengthening families and communities, and what prevention methods work best for populations at risk of substance abuse, for preschool-age children, youth, and even older Americans. CSAP also supports the National Clearinghouse for Alcohol and Drug Information on substance abuse research, treatment, and prevention

CONTACT Phone: 800-662-HELP; Website: www.health.org.

CSAP Comprehensive Prevention System focuses collecting and disseminating information on children of substance abusing parents; a family-strengthening program; a federal drug-free workplace program; high-risk youth; parenting adolescents and welfare reform; and two special programs: Project Youth Connect and Starting Early, Starting Smart.

CONTACT Phone: (301) 443-8956 or (301) 443-0365; Website: http://prevention.samhsa.gov.

CSAP also maintains a prevention decision support system (www.preventiondss.org), model programs and training support (www.samhsa.gov/centers/csap/modelprograms/contact.cfm), a Fetal Alcohol Syndrome Center for Excellence (http://fascenter.samhsa.gov), and several other on-line training programs.

CENTER FOR SUBSTANCE ABUSE TREATMENT (CSAT): Works to improve lives of people and families affected by alcohol and drug abuse. CSAT aims to ensure access to clinically sound, cost-effective addiction treatment to reduce health and social costs of addictions.

CSAT's Office of Managed Care keeps track of changes in behavioral health services throughout the United States; studies alternative services and their effects on access, quality, costs, and clinical outcomes; and helps public officials, consumers, families, and service providers take advantage of health care services. CSAT runs five sites that study adults with chemical dependencies who are involved in publicly funded managed care systems, and six sites that study adolescents with chemical dependencies in managed care. Among CSAT's data collections are the Children's Health Care Reform Tracking Project, the Employer Mental Health and Substance Abuse Benefits program; Mental Health and Substance Abuse Services in HMOs and PPOs; the Integrated Mental Health, Substance Abuse, and Medicaid Data Project; and the State Managed Care Evaluation Project.

CONTACT Phone: (800) 662-HELP, (301) 443-2817, (800) 789-2647; Website: www.samhsa.gov, www.mentalhealth.org, or www.health.org.

CSAT's Office of Pharmacologic and Alternative Therapies (OPAT) educates the professional treatment community and the public about use of medications such as methadone and Levo-Alpha-Acetyl-Methadol (LAAM) for detoxification or maintenance treatments of opioid addictions and develops and recommends federal policy on use of pharmacologic and alternative therapies for substance abuse. OPAT works with the Food and Drug Administration, National Institute on Drug Abuse, and the Drug Enforcement Administration to coordinate their efforts.

CONTACT Address: Center for Substance Abuse Treatment, 5600 Fishers Lane, Rockwall II, 6th Floor, Rockville, MD 20857; Phone: national helpline: (800) 662-HELP or (800) 662-4357, (301) 443-5052; Fax: (301) 443-7801; Website: www.samhsa.gov/csat/csat.htm.

OTHER CONTACT Address: SAMHSA's National Clearinghouse for Alcohol and Drug Information (NCADI), P.O. Box 2345, Rockville, MD 20847-2345; Phone: (800) 729-6686 or (301) 468-6433; Fax: (301) 468-6433; E-mail: info@health.org; Website: www.health.org.

President George W. Bush announced the creation of the President's New Freedom Commission on Mental Health on April 29, 2002, to address the stigma that surrounds mental illness, saying: ". . . Mental disability is not a scandal; it is an illness. And like physical illness, it is treatable, especially when the treatment comes early." Bush stated he created the new commission to close the cracks of the fragmented mental health service delivery system.

DEPARTMENT OF HOMELAND SECURITY

The Department of Homeland Security came into being on November 25, 2002, at least on paper, when President George W. Bush signed the Homeland Security Act, which was an element of an overall Homeland Security Reorganization Plan. This reorganization was the most extensive restructuring of the federal government since 1947, when the DEPARTMENT OF DEFENSE and the CENTRAL INTELLIGENCE AGENCY were created. The new department replaced the old presidential adviser status on January 24, 2003, and opened for business on March 1, 2003.

The original impetus for this 2002 reorganization were the problems raised in response to the threat of terrorist attacks after September 11, 2001. On that date organized foreign nationals hijacked four airliners and crashed suicidally into the World Trade Center and the Pentagon, and were prevented from attacking a third national icon (presumably the White House or the Capitol) when heroic passengers started a fight with the hijackers who caused it to crash.

The basic concept of the new department was to provide a center for intelligence analysis and dissemination of intelligence gathered by "the intelligence community," meaning the FEDERAL BUREAU OF INVESTIGATION, the Central Intelligence Agency, the NATIONAL SECURITY AGENCY, the

Department of Defense, and other collectors of intelligence. However, those agencies remain in the same administrative locations where they were before creation of Homeland Security. It also disseminates to the general public, as well as government agencies, the results of this analysis, including the well-known *Advisory System of Current Threat Levels,* which is illustrated by a color code of levels ranging from green (low danger) through shades of yellow and orange (moderate danger) to red (high risk).

HISTORY

The legislation creating this cabinet-level department survived a circuitous route to the president's desk. Shortly after the 9/11 attack, the president by executive order on October 8, 2001, created an Office of Homeland Security and named Pennsylvania governor Tom Ridge as assistant to the president for homeland security within the Executive Office of the President. Ridge's job was primarily as a coordinator of existing efforts by various agencies scattered throughout the government. This office had no operating budget and no separate headquarters.

During congressional hearings in the first half of 2002, various witnesses who were past or present employees of governmental intelligence agencies testified about breakdowns in communications between intelligence-gathering agencies such as the FBI and the CIA, and intelligence mishaps that occurred particularly during the months prior to 9/11. Members of the Senate Government Affairs Committee , which was conducting those hearings, concluded that a mere advisory office was not sufficient to provide the level of coordination necessary to improve a homeland security network.

The original suggestion for a cabinet-level department to unite those government agencies and functions relevant to protection from actual or potential future foreign terrorists was embodied in a bill proposed by Democratic senator

Joseph Lieberman, chairman of the Government Affairs Committee in May 2002. At first, President Bush opposed the idea, but shortly embraced it, and on June 18, 2002, submitted similar legislation. During the 2002 congressional campaign, President Bush made support for his version a cornerstone of his campaign for Republican candidates.

However, there was a new wrinkle: The president's bill gave the president the right to hire and fire the federal employees of the new department who would not fall within the civil service system and its employee protections. Most Senate Democrats opposed the bill with the new language, and the president and some Republican congressional candidates equated the reluctance to take away civil service rights with lack of patriotism or charged the opposition with being lackeys to labor unions. After the November 2002 election, in which the Republicans gained a one-vote majority in the Senate, the bill was enacted with several amendments: (a) a mediation board to arbitrate labor disputes, but without civil service protections and with the power of the secretary to overrule board decisions; and (b) compliance with the protections of the 1989 Whistleblowers Act, which prohibited discriminatory penalties as retribution for detection of lapses in security.

Last-minute amendments gave pharmaceutical companies limited immunity from lawsuits due to allegedly defective vaccines or other products supplied as part of homeland security programs.

On March 1, 2003, the new department was in business with 177,000 federal employees nationwide moved to Homeland Security, but almost all of them physically worked out of the same quarters as before the changeover. Approximately 1,000 people moved into the temporary headquarters in buildings provided by the United States Navy. Another 16,000 are employed in the Washington, D.C., area, while the remainder are spread around the nation. Estimates are that the eventual number of employees would reach 190,000, the third-largest department.

The first-year budget was $33 billion, somewhat greater than the sum of the budgets of the agencies conjoined in the department. The second annual budget was $36 billion. Newspapers reported that the amount was considered inadequate for local homeland security needs by cities and counties that were under mandate for improvements and equipment (such as respirators) that had not been funded. A study by the Coast Guard stated that an immediate $1 billion was necessary to begin upgrading port security, and only $318 million had been actually paid after 9/11/01. The department's website offers advice on what to do during biological, chemical, or radiation disasters, explosions, and nuclear blasts.

AGENCIES BROUGHT INTO THE NEW DEPARTMENT

Moved to the new department were all or part of 22 different governmental agencies. The functions are organized into four *directorates* with related responsibilities in order to improve coordination and communication in planning and response to crisis. These are: Border and Transportation Security, Emergency Preparedness and Response, Science and Technology, and Information Analysis and Infrastructure Protection. A few absorbed units will be situated outside these directorates and will report directly to the secretary, and one reports to a deputy secretary. Thus, the elements (and their current designations) placed in each directorate and their agencies of origin are as follows:

BORDER AND TRANSPORTATION SECURITY DIRECTORATE: Responsible for border security and transportation operations and encompasses:

U.S. Customs Service from Treasury, where it was previously for historical reasons since it originally was concerned with collection of import

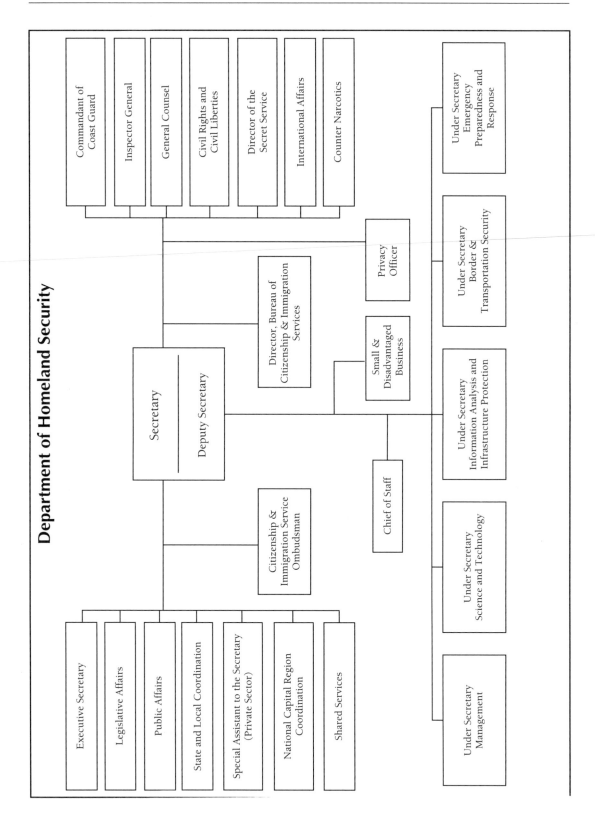

Department of Homeland Security

duties and not primarily security and smuggling at entry points, including airports, seaports, and border crossings. The *Commissioner of Customs* has headed the Customs Service in the TREASURY DEPARTMENT and is an appointee of the president with senatorial confirmation. The number of employees is about 22,000;

CONTACT Address: 1300 Pennsylvania Avenue NW, Washington, DC 20229; Phone: (202) 354-1000; Website: www.customs.gov/.

Immigration and Naturalization Service, which previously had about 40,000 employees, is split between its border control functions such as the *Border Patrol* agents and investigators, which are placed in this bureau and the oversight of citizenship, visas, and services for immigrants placed in the newly formed *Bureau of Citizenship and Immigration* discussed below. The old INS had been subject to adverse comments since it was overwhelmed by its dual responsibilities of border security and processing documentation of would-be citizens and visitors who often disappeared into the general population. Moving the INS to the Department of Homeland Security and dividing its functions was a major change to achieve efficiency and effectiveness;

Federal Protective Service from the General Services Administration, to give greater emphasis to protection of government buildings, with fewer than 1,500 in its workforce;

Transportation Security Administration from the DEPARTMENT OF TRANSPORTATION, the TSA deals with the problems of airport, airliner, and ship security, including all those inspectors who operate the metal detectors, request removal of shoes, and question those people either randomly or those they feel may be up to no good. Prior to transition to the new department, numerous new personnel were hired as federal employees to replace many contract workers and people who were not American citizens. The number of employees exceeds 41,000;

Federal Law Enforcement Training Center, which had resided in Treasury as its training base for its own enforcement officers;

Animal and Plant Health Inspection Service was excised from Agriculture to meld it with other border-crossing protections with the new department. The staff approximates 4,000;

Office for Domestic Preparedness was one of many Justice Department Programs, where it was called the Office for State and Local Domestic Preparedness. Statistics for staff and budget are lumped into that of the FEDERAL EMERGENCY MANAGEMENT ADMINISTRATION;

Added to the functions of this directorate is the *Counternarcotics Officer/Interdict Coordinator* as the department's role in the effort to prevent smuggling of illegal drugs into the United States.

EMERGENCY PREPAREDNESS AND RESPONSE DIRECTORATE: Brings together and oversees government disaster response offices with disaster training and includes:

Federal Emergency Management Administration (FEMA): A formerly independent agency now under the Homeland Security umbrella, as of March 2003. Established by President Jimmy Carter's executive order on March 31, 1979, FEMA is the primary federal agency for emergency planning, preparedness, mitigation, response, and recovery to disasters. FEMA works closely with state and local governments and disperses federal staff and resources following a catastrophic disaster.

President Carter's order brought together historically evolved disaster agencies including the Reconstruction Finance Corporation of the 1930s (had authority to make disaster loans for repair and reconstruction following earthquakes and other types of disasters), the Flood Control Act, the Federal Disaster Assistance Administration within Housing and Urban Development, the National Flood Insurance Act of 1968, and the 1974 Relief Act. FEMA absorbed the Federal Insurance Administration, the National Fire Prevention and Control Administration, the National Weather Service Community Preparedness Program, the Federal Disaster Preparedness Agency of the General Services Administration, and the Federal Disaster Assistance Administration from the DEFENSE DEPARTMENT's Defense Civil Preparedness Agency.

The end of the cold war led to redirection of resources from civil defense to disaster relief, recovery, and mitigation programs. In 2001 President George W. Bush again refocused FEMA's effort to national preparedness and homeland security following September 11, 2001. FEMA then joined 22 other agencies, programs, and offices in becoming part of the new DEPARTMENT OF HOMELAND SECURITY, and FEMA is one of four branches of Homeland Security.

ORGANIZATION

FEMA is headed by a director appointed by the president with senate confirmation, assisted by the deputy director, also a presidential appointee. Functions are divided among several directorates: Preparedness, Training and Exercises; Mitigation, Response and Recovery, Operations and Support; and Information Technology Services. There are also the Federal Insurance Administration and United States Fire Administration. Their administrators are appointed by the president and confirmed by the Senate, as the associate directors in charge of Preparedness and Mitigation.

FEMA runs the *U.S. Fire Administration* and its *National Fire Academy,* with all fire and emergency medical service programs and training activities. Its Federal Insurance and *Mitigation Administration* works on protection, prevention, and partnerships with federal, state, local, and individual entities to educe the impact of disasters on families, homes, communities, and the economy. The *National Flood Insurance Program* works to mitigate damages from national disasters. FEMA's *Emergency Management Institute* gives professional courses for emergency managers. Its *Office of National Preparedness* works to prepare the United States for potential acts of terrorism, works to improve efforts and effectiveness of first responders (police, firefighters, and Emergency Medical Service workers), coor-

dinates programs and resources to respond to terrorist acts, and coordinates state and local Citizen Corps volunteer programs. FEMA also works with state and local governments to prepare for accidental or terrorist releases of nuclear power plant contents and the army's chemical stockpiles.

CONTACT Address: FEMA, 500 C Street SW, Washington, DC 20472; Phone: (202) 566-1600; Website: www.fema.gov. Regional offices: 3003 Chamblee-Tucker Road, Atlanta, GA 30341; Phone: (770) 220-5200. Room 442, J.W. McCormack Post Office and Courthouse Building, Boston, MA, 02109-4595; Phone: (617) 223-9540. 130 228th Street SW, Bothell, WA 98021-9796; Phone: (206) 487-4765. 4th Floor, 175 West Jackson Boulevard, Chicago, IL 60604-2698; Phone: (312) 408-5504. 800 N. Loop 288, Denton, TX 76201; Phone: (817) 898-5104. Box 25267 Building 710, Denver Federal Center, Denver, CO 80225-0267; Phone: (303) 235-4812. Suite 900, 2323 Grand Boulevard, Kansas City, MO 64108-2670; Phone: (816) 283-7061. Room 1337, 26 Federal Plaza, New York, NY 10278-0002; Phone: (212) 225-7209. 2nd Floor, 105 South 7th Street, Philadelphia, PA 19106-3316. Building 105, Presidio of San Francisco, San Francisco, CA 94129-1250; Phone (415) 923-7105.

FEMA's staffing exceeds 5,000 and recent budgets exceed $6 billion.

Strategic National Stockpile and the National Disaster Medical System, a portion of which was handled by the DEPARTMENT OF HEALTH AND HUMAN SERVICES as chemical, biological, radiological, and nuclear response units; there are 150 workers and a $2 billion budget, which calculates out as $1.2 million per person.

Nuclear Incident Response Team is comprises experts on nuclear energy, science, and technology as well as security in the DEPARTMENT OF ENERGY, including its National Security Administration. In essence the department is concerned about a nuclear disaster whether caused by terrorists or from some internal failure. Its most recent budget was $91 million and the number of employees is classified.

Domestic Emergency Support Teams have been taken from the DEPARTMENT OF JUSTICE specialists in legal reactions to emergencies and draw from various agencies at times of emergency.

National Domestic Preparedness Office is staffed by 15 former Federal Bureau of Investigation personnel expert in investigating domestic crimes and national security threats and has a budget of $2 million.

Science and Technology Directorate sponsors and manages scientific and technological information useful in guarding the nation from potential attack. These include

Civilian Biodefense Research Countermeasures Programs bring the technical experience of 150 people from the Department of Energy on countering certain threats with a budget of almost $2 billion.

Environmental Measurements Laboratory also is transferred from Energy.

National Biological Warfare Defense Analysis Center was new and given an initial budget of $420 million.

Plum Island Animal Disease Center is moved from the DEPARTMENT OF AGRICULTURE to help protect the American public from disease-ridden animals, either by negligence or intentional threat. It has a staff of 124 and only $25 million in its annual budget.

In addition the Homeland Security Act provided for creation of the *Science and Technology Advisory Committee*, which has 20 members. The department also coordinates research with the Technology Administration of the DEPARTMENT OF COMMERCE.

Information Analysis and Infrastructure Protection Directorate: Brings together protective agencies to prevent harm to America's infrastructure (buildings, bridges, highways, energy production) computers, the Internet, and databases. These conjoined agencies are

Critical Infrastructure Assurance Office is an office with fewer than 70 employees and a budget

of approximately $27 million formerly in the COMMERCE DEPARTMENT, which provides expertise to assist in analysis related to infrastructure protection.

Federal Computer Incident Response Center was a small office previously in the GENERAL SERVICES ADMINISTRATION, with about 23 employees and $11 million to spend annually.

National Communications System was sliced off from the communications and intelligence arm of the DEPARTMENT OF DEFENSE. It has a staff of about 90 and budget of $155 million.

National Infrastructure Protection Center is composed of a number of former agents of the FBI; it has about 800 workers and a budget of $151 million.

Energy Security and Assurance Program came from the ENERGY DEPARTMENT's office for Environment, Safety and Health and has 65 employees and a budget of $27 million.

The *Bureau of Immigration and Citizenship,* which had been a segment of the Immigration and Natural Service (INS) of the JUSTICE DEPARTMENT, is new as a separate entity. Dividing the INS between the *Border and Transportation Security Directorate,* discussed above, and the newly created *Bureau of Immigration and Citizenship* was intended to focus the work of the previously overburdened (and often criticized) INS. The Bureau of Immigration and Citizenship can now concentrate on processing applications for citizenship, granting of and enforcing the terms of visas for visitors, issuance of work permits (often specialized or temporary), and tracking entrants into the United States, many of whom violate visas or are "lost" among the population.

Independent Agencies: Independent agencies were incorporated into the Department of Homeland Security and positioned outside the directorate structure. The *Secret Service* was transferred intact from the TREASURY DEPARTMENT, where it had served since 1865. The *United States Coast Guard,* which had been under the aegis of the Treasury Department, except during wartime when it had served as an element of the Defense

Department, also moved into the new department as an entire unit.

From the DEPARTMENT OF TRANSPORTATION came the *Transportation Security Administration,* which had been set up in November 2001 by the Aviation and Transportation Act to federalize (and make more professional) screening of passengers and baggage at commercial airports.

CONTACT   The temporary headquarters of the Department of Homeland Security Station, a four-story building within the Naval District of Washington facility at Nebraska and Massachusetts Streets NW (across from American University), Washington, DC; Address: Department of Homeland Security, Washington, DC 20528; Phone: (202) 282-8000; Website: www.dhs.gov or www.ready.gov.

UNITED STATES
SECRET SERVICE

Transferred intact from the DEPARTMENT OF THE TREASURY to the Department of Homeland Security in March 2003, the U.S. Secret Service has two particular lines of responsibility. Best known is protection of the president, vice president, leading candidates during campaigns, and members of the president's family. The image of the Secret Service to the public is that of athletic men, with trim haircuts and business suits, accompanying the president, omnipresent but unobtrusive, with identifying pins in their lapels. During parades or events in which a president or other high official could be vulnerable, Secret Service officers are on rooftops with sniper rifles, trotting beside a limousine, or diplomatically clearing the way. Their professionalism is famous, and their scope of authority is much broader.

The service investigates violations of laws dealing with financial crimes including counterfeiting, financial institution fraud, identity theft, computer fraud, and the computer attacks and invasion of American financial, bank, and telecommunications systems. In recent years other protective services have been added to its curriculum such as mandated by the Safe School Initiative and responsibility for preparing and carrying out plans to protect major occurrences, known as National Special Security Events.

There are slightly more than 6,000 employees of the Secret Service. Its recent annual budget has been $1.25 Billion.

HISTORY

Although the Secret Service Division of the Treasury Department was inaugurated on July 5, 1865, less than three months after the assassination of President Abraham Lincoln, its initial purpose was not to guard the president, but was intended to suppress the counterfeiting of currency because the government had begun issuing paper money. In 1867 the office's responsibilities were expanded to include the detection of people perpetuating frauds against the government, which included smugglers, illegal liquor distillers, mail robbers, and other violators of federal laws (there was no Federal Bureau of Investigation). Within a decade this authorization empowered the office to investigate the terrorist Ku Klux Klan.

In 1883 the service was upgraded from just an office in the Treasury Department to a distinct agency. Despite the fatal shooting of President James A. Garfield as he walked through Union Railroad Station in Washington, D.C., no government agency was designated to protect the president. Informal part-time protection of the president by the Secret Service began for President Grover Cleveland in 1894. This occasional guarding proved inadequate when President William McKinley was shot and killed while shaking hands at an exposition in Buffalo, New York, in 1901. Congress immediately requested the Secret Service to protect the new president, Theodore Roosevelt. The following year full-time protection was provided with two agents assigned full-time at the WHITE HOUSE, and in 1906 the federal budget contained a specific item for presidential protection called the Executive Protection Service.

A massive fraud in the acquisition of western open space for settlers was investigated in 1906 and 1907 by the Secret Service, and millions of acres were recovered by the government. One of the service's operatives, Joseph A. Walker, was murdered during this investigation.

In 1908 the executive protection was expanded to include the president-elect. Also that year President Theodore Roosevelt by executive order transferred eight Secret Service agents to the DEPARTMENT OF JUSTICE, forming the nucleus of the future Federal Bureau of Investigation. In 1913 Congress passed legislation permanently authorizing the Secret Service to protect the president. When war broke out in Europe, President Woodrow Wilson ordered the Secret Service in 1915 to investigate possible espionage.

Protecting the members of the president's immediate family was added to its duties in 1917, and Congress made credible physical "threats" against the president a federal crime. The White House Police Force (created in 1922) was incorporated into the Secret Service in 1930.

On November 1, 1950, a group of Puerto Rican nationalists opened fire on the House of Representatives and attempted to invade Blair House, where President Truman was residing during renovations to the White House, to assassinate the president. Secret Service agents fought off the attackers in a firefight in which Officer Leslie Coffelt was killed. The threat resulted in mandatory protection of the president-elect and the president's family, and the vice president if he or she wished it.

Congress expanded the coverage for protection by the Secret Service several times: former presidents for a reasonable period of time (1961), the vice president-elect, next in line if the vice presidency is vacant (1962), Jacqueline Kennedy and her children for two years after President Kennedy was assassinated (1963), former presidents and their spouses for their lifetimes and their children until age 16 (1965), major presidential and vice presidential candidates, party nominees, widows of presidents until death or remarriage (1968, following the fatal shooting of Senator Robert F. Kennedy, who was campaigning for the Democratic presidential nomination), diplomatic missions in the Washington, D.C., area (1970), and foreign diplomatic missions throughout the United States and territories (1975). In 1997 protection for future ex-presidents would be reduced to 10 years after leaving office.

In 1977 the Executive Protective Service was renamed the Secret Service Uniformed Division.

Starting in 1984, new legislation to combat various types of modern fraud was enacted, and the Secret Service was given the task of investigating such fraud. Credit card, debit card, computer fraud, and fraudulent identification documents were all addressed. The Secret Service was given concurrent jurisdiction with the Justice Department in 1990 to investigate federally insured financial institutions. The 1994 Crime Bill included a "long arm" provision, which permitted prosecution within the United States of any person counterfeiting American currency or trafficking in counterfeit bills overseas.

Telemarketing fraud and identity theft were made specific crimes in 2000, and the Secret Service was assigned the task of investigating in order for prosecution or exposing these illegal schemes.

The so-called Patriot Act enacted within a few days after the 9/11 terrorist attacks, among other provisions, authorized the director of the Secret Service to set up electronic task forces to investigate computer-based crime, and suppress transnational financial crimes—in part to halt transfer of funds to terrorist organizations in the guise of charitable or personal transactions.

Following creation of the Department of Homeland Security, on March 1, 2003, the Secret Service moved from Treasury to the new department.

ORGANIZATION

The Secret Service is headed by a professional nonpolitical director. Its structure is based on functions, task forces, and specializations. Basic functional areas are: *Protection, Investigations* (particularly involving financial crimes and fraud), a partnership with the DEPARTMENT OF EDUCATION implementing the *Safe School Initiative* to develop means to protect schools from external and internal violence, and since 1998 developing and implementing plans for *National Special Security Events.*

CONTACT Address: 950 H Street NW, Washington, DC 20233. There are also about 134 *Field Offices* situated in all 50 states, District of Columbia, Puerto Rico, and 15 foreign countries. Phone: (202) 406-5708 (Public Affairs), (202) 406-5800 (Personnel).

UNITED STATES COAST GUARD

The Coast Guard is a military-style agency with a substantial fleet of ships, boats, and aircraft with responsibility for search and rescue in the oceans along the coasts of the United States as a result of storms or accidents, intercepts, illegal smuggling operations; inspection of marine vessels (including off-shore drilling platforms) in order to enforce maritime laws and safety regulations (including safety training); operation of ice-breaker ships; and management of the federal Lighthouse Service. During wartime the Coast Guard has become a fully active fighting force, usually under the Navy Department.

HEADQUARTERS, LOCATION, AND CONTACT Address: Commandant, U.S. Coast Guard, 2100 Second Street SW, Washington, DC 20593; Phone: (202) 267-2229. Public Affairs: Phone: (202) 267-1587. Boating Safety: Phone: (800) 368-5647 (8 A.M.–4 P.M., eastern time).

There are approximately 37,000 Coast Guard personnel, men and women, (6,931 officers,

29,138 enlisted, and 845 at the Coast Guard Academy in 2002). Some 5,700 civilians are assigned to the Coast Guard. The most recent annual budget is $7.27 billion. The Coast Guard operates a fleet of cutters, ranging in size between 65 and 378 feet, larger icebreakers, approximately 1,400 boats (primarily motor lifeboats), and more than 200 aircraft, including airplanes flying from air stations and helicopters operating from both air stations and aircraft carriers.

HISTORY

The first element of what would eventually become the United States Coast Guard was the establishment of the Lighthouse Service on August 7, 1789. That service was placed under the authority of the TREASURY DEPARTMENT, which was inaugurated a month later. A year later, Secretary of Treasury Alexander Hamilton authorized formation of the Revenue Service to enforce customs laws by suppressing smuggling. Concern about the safety of passengers in steamboats caused Congress to pass legislation authorizing the attorney general to inspect steamboats. In August 1852, Congress passed the Steamboat Inspection Service, which operated in the Treasury Department until 1903, when it was transferred to the Bureau of Navigation in the new Department of Commerce and Labor.

Formal creation of the Coast Guard came on January 20, 1915, when President Woodrow Wilson signed an act combining the Life-Saving Service and the Revenue Cutter Service to form the Coast Guard. During World War I it was controlled by the navy, but afterward returned to the Treasury Department.

On July 1, 1939, the Lighthouse Service, an independent agency, was brought into the Coast Guard. Once again the Coast Guard came under navy control during World War II. In July 1946 the Bureau of Marine Inspection in the DEPARTMENT OF COMMERCE was abolished, and its function returned to the Coast Guard, where it had been until 1903.

The Coast Guard was transferred from the Treasury Department to the new DEPARTMENT OF TRANSPORTATION on April 1, 1973, and from there to the Department of Homeland Security on March 1, 2003.

ORGANIZATION

With a headquarters in Washington, D.C., the operational sea arm of the Coast Guard is divided into two parts: Atlantic Area and Pacific Area, each of which is divided into districts. These are:

Atlantic Area: Headquarters: Portsmouth, Virginia;
Districts: Boston, Massachusetts; Portsmouth, Virginia; Miami, Florida; New Orleans, Louisiana; and Cleveland, Ohio.

Pacific Area: Headquarters: Alameda, California;
Districts: Seattle, Washington; Honolulu, Hawaii; and Juneau, Alaska.

U.S. Coast Guard Academy: As a facility for training potential Coast Guard officers the academy, which was founded in 1876, is located at New London, Connecticut.

CONTACT Address: U.S. Coast Guard Academy, 15 Mohegan Avenue, New London, CT 06320; Phone: (860) 444-8500; for information on admissions, Phone: (800) 883-USCG; E-mail: admissions@cga.uscg.mil.

DEPARTMENT OF HOUSING AND URBAN DEVELOPMENT (HUD)

The Department of Housing and Urban Development, commonly referred to as HUD, traces its program beginnings to the innovative New Deal housing programs enacted in the 1930s. Its mission has matured beyond stimulating the housing industry and providing housing for people of both low-income and modest means, so that it finances public facilities and has created a format for community planning and development. HUD's arsenal of methods to achieve these goals includes loans, guarantees of loans, grants, matching grants, and technical assistance to states, local agencies, individuals, developers, sponsors of projects, Indian tribes, and both urban and rural communities.

HISTORY

The New Deal housing programs were originally separately administered, and included the Federal Housing Administration (FHA), which guaranteed home loans so financial institutions would more readily lend to home buyers and thus stimulate the housing market as well as provide the social benefit of housing for first-time buyers, which stemmed from legislation to prevent foreclosure of home mortgages on thousands of families caught in the throes of the Great Depression.

Subsidies for construction and maintenance of low-cost public housing administered by the Public Housing Administration (PHA) were inaugurated by the Housing Act of 1937. There followed urban renewal funding and loans by the Urban Renewal Administration, and the Community Facilities Administration provided loans for college housing, hospitals, and public facilities. Established in 1938, the Federal National Mortgage Association (FNMA—generally referred to as Fannie Mae), is a corporation that originally only purchased FHA-guaranteed loans to provide a cash flow for home financing.

In 1947 under the Truman administration these agencies were brought together under the newly created Housing and Home Financing Agency (HHFA). While HHFA was the administrative center of federal housing action, the amount of funding was increased, and various specialized programs, such as housing for the elderly and moderate-priced housing projects sponsored by local organizations, were inaugurated. Since many of its programs provided economic stimulus as well as a social good, much of the housing legislation had some bipartisan support.

With the encouragement of President Lyndon B. Johnson, Congress passed the Department of Housing and Urban Development Act, which upgraded HHFA as the Department of Housing and Urban Development, which came into being on November 9, 1965. This provided the opportunity for President Johnson to appoint HHFA administrator and noted housing expert Robert C. Weaver as secretary of HUD, the first African-American member of the cabinet in U.S. history.

The Fair Housing Act (Civil Rights Act of 1968) outlawed housing discrimination because of race and gave HUD the responsibility for federal enforcement. The same year the Housing Act of 1968 created the Government National Mortgage Association (Ginnie Mae), providing government guaranteed mortgages that were backed by Ginnie Mae securities, particularly aimed at moderate-income families, as a spin-off from the Federal National Mortgage Association (Fannie Mae) and constituted as a private corporation under a strict congressional charter. Also established that year was a third entity to provide funding for acquisition of home loans and thus increase the flow of funds into the housing market, entitled Federal Mortgage Securities Association, commonly called Freddie Mac.

The Housing and Urban Development Act of 1970 introduced a federal Experimental Housing Allowance Program and the Community Development Corporation. However, President Richard Nixon suspended housing and community development assistance in 1973. A year later, the Housing and Community Development Act consolidated various programs into the Community Development Block Grant program and inaugurated rental supplements for low-income families, commonly referred to as Section 8. Rental supplements were in the form of certificates (vouchers) to assist families to pay rent and thus not be limited to public housing projects. Using block grants decentralized administration of community programs.

Urban Development Action Grants for distressed communities for residential and nonresidential use were inaugurated in 1977. In 1983 Housing Development Grants and Rental (unit) Rehabilitation were instituted under the Housing and Urban-Rural Recovery Act.

A major new responsibility was added to HUD through the 1988 Indian Housing Act, which provided for assistance in meeting the housing needs of Native Americans and Alaskan Indians. That same year the sale of public housing to resident management corporations was authorized by a new Housing and Community Act. It became easier for victims of housing discrimination to sue under the Fair Housing Amendments Act, enacted in 1988.

The savings and loans crisis, in which savings institutions that had originally been legally limited to loans for housing and home rehabilitation, came to a head in the late 1980s when dozens of such institutions went bankrupt. These savings and loans had gone into the quasi-banking business and made risky loans for various purposes including land developments without sufficient security, financed projects of their own officers, and employed either dishonest or negligent practices. This resulted in default of billions of dollars of loans guaranteed by federal programs, and the loss of the savings of thousands of innocent depositors. Underlying this crisis was the so-called deregulation of savings and loans by the Depository Institutions' Deregulation and Monetary Control Act of 1980. One of the supposed benefits of deregulation was to stimulate home loans with less regulation. Actually the act was "a license to steal" for many savings and loans associations that operated recklessly through ignorance and/or venality.

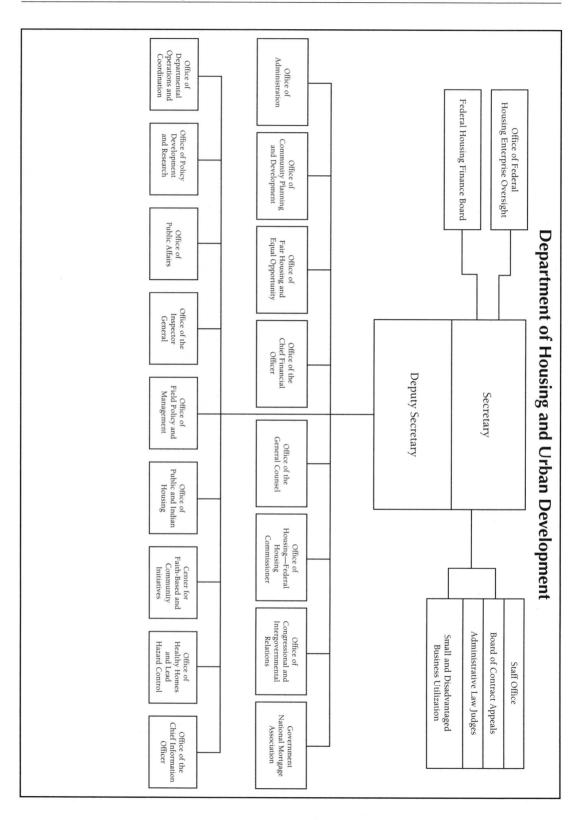

Department of Housing and Urban Development

To bail out many such institutions, primarily to soften the burden on depositors, in 1989 Congress enacted the Financial Institutions' Reform, Recovery and Enforcement Act. The reputations of several otherwise respected United States senators were tarnished by their assistance to constituent savings and loans under federal investigation, who had been major campaign contributors to the senators or their political parties. The friendship of future president Bill Clinton with a savings and loan official convicted of misuse of funds would be a source of problems for Clinton for several years, although Clinton was cleared after lengthy investigation.

A package of housing assistance programs was initiated by the Cranston-Gonzalez National Affordable Housing Act (named for Senator Alan Cranston and Representative Henry Gonzalez) in 1990, including homeowner and tenant-based assistance and the HOME housing block grant program, which directed funds to state agencies that made the final decision on allocation. Also adopted at the same time was the Low-Income Preservation and Residential Homeownership Act of 1990, which increased support for families in apartments, town houses, condominiums, and cooperatives.

In the wake of the savings and loan scandals, in 1992 Congress passed the Federal Housing Enterprises' Financial Safety and Soundness Act, which set up the HUD Office of Federal Housing Enterprise Oversight, charged with public oversight over the two giants making secondary purchases of mortgages, Fannie Mae (Federal National Mortgage Association) and Freddie Mac (Federal Home Loan Mortgage Corporation).

Under the Omnibus Budget Reconciliation of 1993, Congress established the Empowerment Zone and Enterprise Community Program (championed by former HUD secretary Jack Kemp), which provided funding and advice to urban communities (including racial ghettos) to stimulate community identity, improvements, and businesses.

Discrimination in housing was the target of two 1998 developments. An Enforcement Center was opened by HUD to take direct action against federally assisted multiunit property owners (apartment building landlords) and any other people who have any form of federal financing. The center receives complaints of discrimination and takes direct action if violations of law or regulations seem likely. Public housing reforms were adopted by Congress with the goal to reduce segregation based on race or income in public housing projects, encourage and reward those working to lift themselves above the low-income level, permit more working families to occupy public housing (lifting limits on income to encourage working out of poverty), and increase the subsidized housing for the poorest families.

Following Robert Weaver as secretary were Robert C. Wood (interim appointment, December 18, 1968–January 22, 1969), former Michigan governor George W. Romney (January 22, 1969–January 20, 1973), James T. Lynn (February 2, 1973–February 5, 1975), Carla Hills (March 10, 1975–January 20, 1977), Patricia Harris, first African-American woman in the cabinet (January 23, 1977–September 10, 1979), Moon Landrieu (September 24, 1979–January 20, 1981), Samuel R. Pierce Jr. (January 23, 1981–January 20, 1989), Jack F. Kemp, former NFL quarterback, congressman, and 1996 Republican vice presidential candidate (February 13, 1989–January 19, 1993), Henry G. Cisneros, a former mayor (January 22, 1993–January 19, 1997), Andrew M. Cuomo (January 29, 1997–January 20, 2001), Mel Martinez (January 24, 2001–December 10, 2003), and Alphonso Jackson (Acting; January 28, 2004 –).

The administration of Secretary Pierce, who served 1981 to 1989, was scandal ridden, involving bribery for favorable approval of loans and grants, and resulted in criminal convictions of some HUD officials. Similar problems of illegal and/or unethical practices, such as purchase of favors, overlooking violations, and maladministration by local housing authorities have plagued HUD over the years.

HEADQUARTERS

HUD headquarters and most of its administrative offices are located in the Robert C. Weaver Federal Building, at 451 Seventh Street SW, Washington, DC 20410. It was built between November 1966 and November 9, 1968, when it opened after dedication ceremonies led by Secretary Weaver. Ten stories high, it was designed by architect Marcel Breuer, a leader in the modern design movement, Herbert Beckhard, and Nolen Swinburne Associates. On July 11, 2000, the building was named for Weaver.

CONTACT The general telephone number is (202) 708-1112.

ORGANIZATION

The *secretary of housing and urban development* is given almost total control of administration over the department, which authority flows to the under secretary, eight assistant secretaries, and program directors. Any delegation of authority is subject to statutory restrictions. The power of the secretary to reorganize the administrative field structure requires a cost-benefit analysis published in the Federal Register for 90 days.

The secretary's office is located in Room 1000; and the telephone number is (202) 708-0417. Providing administrative support for the secretary's office are chief of staff (Phone: (202) 708-2713), press secretary (Phone: (202) 708-2236), and chief executive officer (Phone: (202) 708-3750).

The *under secretary* assists the secretary and has concurrent powers, except to sue or be sued, so that he/she can serve in various functions of the secretary, and could serve as interim secretary during any temporary vacancy. (Phone: (202) 708-0123).

The eight assistant secretaries, all appointed by the president with Senate confirmation, are assigned specific responsibilities as follows:

Assistant secretary for administration is responsible for executive scheduling, managing the secretariat, oversight of the Office of Management and Planning, the Office of Budget and Administrative Support, the HUD Training Academy, human resources, and the Office of Field Operations with service centers in New York, Atlanta, and Denver. The assistant secretary is aided by *deputy assistant secretaries for resource management and for operations.*

Assistant secretary for public and indian housing is responsible for funding, maintaining, and planning the program of public housing for low-income families actually managed by local Public Housing Authorities, and for public housing for Native American communities. The assistant secretary operates through a substantial field operations staff, an Office of Policy Program and Legislative Initiatives, Grants Management Center, Section 8 (rental supplements for low-income families) Financial Management Center, and offices for Troubled Agency Recovery run by two deputy assistant secretaries. There are also deputy secretaries for Native American Programs, Public and Assisted Housing, and for Public Housing Investments.

Assistant secretary for community planning and development is charged with programs for community assistance, including technical assistance, various services, an Office of Community Visibility, with deputy assistant secretaries for Community Empowerment, Economic Development, Grant Programs (both block grants and affordable housing programs), and for special needs such HIV/AIDS and the homeless.

Assistant secretary for fair housing and equal opportunity (established by Title VIII of the Civil Rights Act of 1966) is primarily responsible for directing programs aimed at prevention of discrimination in housing due to race, gender, or age, and requiring compliance. It is broken down into offices of Programs, Enforcement, Information, Management and Planning, and one for Economic Opportunity, Monitoring and Compliance, each directed by a deputy assistant secretary.

Assistant secretary for housing (who is also designated the *federal housing commissioner*) directs the most extensive and time-honored federal housing programs (other than public housing), including the Office Of Housing/FHA (Federal Housing Administration), administered by four deputy assistant secretaries, including for Finance and Budget, which has oversight on FHA, which guarantees home loans, making them available for a larger segment of the population.

The other deputy assistant secretaries direct the *Office of Multifamily Housing, Office of Single Family Housing,* and *Office of Management and Business Development.*

Assistant secretary for congressional and intergovernmental relations follows legislation, and works with members of Congress and other government agencies explaining and providing information on HUD activities, programs, and positions in regard to legislation, regulations, and interaction with other agencies. The assistant secretary is supported by deputy assistant secretaries for Congressional Relations, Intergovernmental Relations, Legislation, and Strategic Planning.

Assistant secretary for policy development and research directs studies on economic affairs, develops policy positions for HUD consideration, and runs an Office of University Partnerships for studies, research, and policy development. The assistant secretary is responsible for overseeing evaluation and monitoring of HUD programs. The assistant secretary is supported by deputy assistant secretaries for Economic Affairs, Policy Development, and Research, Evaluation, and Monitoring.

Assistant secretary for public affairs is responsible for media relations, HUD publications, and speechwriting.

The secretary, the deputy secretary and the assistant secretaries (except for Public Affairs) are all appointed by the president, subject to Senate confirmation.

Other Officials Established by Statute

Director of the Office of Federal Housing Enterprise Oversight (created by 1992 HUD Act), is a presidential appointee with Senate confirmation, for a five-year term. The responsibility of the office is to ensure that the Federal National Mortgage Association (Fannie Mae) and the Federal Home Loan Mortgage Corporation (Freddie Mac) are adequately and safely funded. The director may issue regulations and investigate, and file enforcement actions independent of the secretary.

President of the Government National Mortgage Association (Ginnie Mae), which is described below.

Director of Office of Lead-Based Paint Abatement and Poisoning Prevention is a career senior executive of this office created by the 1992 HUD Appropriations Act, and directs these activities within the department.

Special assistant for Indian and Alaska Native Programs.

Director of Urban Program Coordination (filled by assistant secretary for community planning and research).

Director of Small and Disadvantaged Business Utilization tracks and reports to the secretary information concerning opportunities for small and disadvantaged businesses that may be assisted by any HUD program, including technical assistance.

Chief procurement officer directs the contract administration of purchasing including for projects around the nation. Regional offices of the office are located in New York City, Chicago, and Fort Worth for operations, and in Philadelphia, Atlanta, and Denver for contracting.

General counsel provides legal advice to HUD, analyzes proposed legislation, and oversees legal actions involving HUD. The *inspector general* conducts and supervises investigations of the operation of the department and by statute reports only to the secretary or the deputy secretary, the attorney general, and Congress. The *Chief Financial Officer* reports directly to the secretary in regard to the department's financial management. *Chief information officer* and *Federal Housing Administration comptroller* perform professional services in their fields.

Statutory officials appointed by the president with Senate confirmation are the chief financial officer, the director of Federal Housing Enterprise Oversight, inspector general, director of the Office of Multifamily Housing Assistance Restructuring, and the president of the Federal National Mortgage Association ("Fannie Mae").

Specialized Offices

Office of Departmental Grants Management and Oversight was created to provide department-wide perspective on grant applications, approval, and management. This office prepares and publishes notices of available grant funds, lists of people and organizations that have been awarded grants, an inventory of descriptions of every HUD program, and links to government-wide lists of federal grant and BusinessLaw.gov relative to small businesses. It strives to improve management efficiencies, streamline grant procedures, create better internal controls, and implement policies and procedures in relation to grants. Integrity is enhanced by making certain that those establishing programs are separated from those selecting grantees.

Office of Multifamily Housing Assistance Restructuring was established by the Multifamily Assisted Housing Reform and Affordability Act of 1997 to deal with the expiration of housing subsidy contracts on thousands of privately owned multifamily properties (apartment buildings) with federally insured mortgages. Since with rental subsidies the rental level can be higher than market, the rental levels need to be adjusted, and existing loan debts need to be restructured to be supportable by the new rent levels. This is a sensitive matter (entitled "Market-to-Market") affecting both owners and tenants, scheduled to

"sunset" September 30, 2006. Given the size of the challenge and the need for expert diplomacy, the director of the office is appointed by the president and requires Senate confirmation.

CONTACT Website: www.hud.gov:80/offices/ombar.

Office of Healthy Homes and Lead Hazard Control is responsible for removal of lead-paint hazards and unhealthy conditions in homes.

Office of Departmental Operations and Coordination is a catchall office responsible for developing the website, migrants in the southwest border region, and farmworker initiatives (migrant labor housing).

Secretary's Responsibilities and ex officio Positions

The secretary of HUD has numerous responsibilities as ex officio to his office. Thus, the secretary has the following positions outside of the direct administration of the department:

Director, *Federal Housing Finance Board;* and chairman, board of directors, *National Homeownership Trust.*

The secretary is also a member of the following: Thrift Depositor Protection Oversight Board, Advisory Council on Historic Preservation, Martin Luther King, Jr. Federal Holiday Commission, Coordinating Council on Juvenile Justice and Delinquency Prevention, board of directors of Neighborhood Reinvestment Corporation, National Commission on Manufactured Housing, National Interagency Task Force on Multifamily Housing, National Drug Policy Board, President's Committee on Mental Retardation, and Community Empowerment Board.

In addition, the secretary or his/her designee from the HUD staff (which is usually the case) serves as a member of the following: Community Enterprise Assessment Credit Board, Appraisal Subcommittee of the Federal Financial Institutions Examination Council, Architectural Transportation Barriers Compliance Board, Economic Adjustment Committee, Task Force on Environmental Health Risks and Safety Risks to Children, American Heritage Rivers Interagency Committee, President's Council on the Future of Princeville, North Carolina, Interagency Task Force on the Economic Development of the Southwest Border, and Interagency Task Force on the Economic Development of the Central San Joaquin Valley [California].

All of these organizations have some relation to housing, community development, and programs directed by HUD. For example, such topics as drug policy and mental retardation are related because there are problems of drug use in public housing projects or special programs for persons with disabilities serve some people who have drug addiction problems (or are distributors of drugs) and others who are mentally retarded. Many of the subjects of the varied agencies are involved in efforts for community development, empowerment zones, and other concerns within the HUD umbrella of activities. The assignment of designees to meet with some technical entities provides a level of expert involvement by HUD without requiring the attendance of the secretary.

Appointments by Secretary Mandated by Law or Executive Order

The secretary of HUD is required by statute or executive order to make appointments to various governmental agencies such as:

Nine members to the *Federal Housing Advisory Board,* individuals with expertise in housing and home finance;

24 members to the *National Manufactured Home Advisory Council,* divided eight each from consumer and community groups, from the industry and government agencies;

one member of the HUD staff to the Federal Coordinating Council on Science, Engineering and Technology;

Secretary's Task Force to Establish Reasonable Criteria for Federally Assisted Housing, composed of representatives of owners, managers, tenants, tenant advocacy organizations, persons with disabilities, organizations assisting the homeless, and nonprofit providers of social service, mental health and other services, the number to be at the discretion of the secretary;

12 members of the *Community Outreach National Advisory Council* from state and local governments, higher education, community advisory committees, and organizations with expertise in urban matters;

HUD staff representatives designated by the secretary to the following: Task Force on Lead-Based Paint Hazard Reduction and Financing (which also has representatives from the Veterans Administration, FNMA, Environmental Protection Agency, and other entities), the Consumer Affairs Council, the Commission on Alternative Utilization of Military Facilities, the President's Council on Management Improvement (a senior HUD management official), the Interagency Council on Administrative Management (a senior HUD management official), and the American Indian and Alaska Native Education Task Force.

Administrative Law Judges: There are five administrative law judges, including a chief administrative law judge, who determine various disputes arising from actions of HUD offices. The administrative law courts are located at

CONTACT Address: Washington Office Center, 409 Third Street SW, Suite 320, Washington, DC 20024. Phone: (202) 708-5004.

HUD BOARD OF CONTRACT APPEALS: Disputes in regard to procurement contracts to which HUD is a party are heard by this board, composed of three administrative judges, including a chairperson and vice chairperson. The board was established pursuant to the Contract Disputes Act of 1978.

CONTACT Address: HUD Office Building, 1707 H Street NW, 11th Floor, Washington, DC 20004; Room 2131, HUD Building, 451 7th Street SW, Washington, DC 20410.

PROGRAMS

Approximately 70 programs are managed by HUD, including various loan guarantees; public housing for low-income persons and families; community development; grants for technical assistance; special programs for Native Americans, the elderly, and people with disabilities; certain educational institutions; disaster and emergency assistance; fair housing protections; and various special programs for public safety and protection.

FEDERAL HOUSING ADMINISTRATION (FHA) HOUSING PROGRAMS

These housing programs are mainly mortgage insurance (or guarantee) provided under statutorily established methods to assist both low- and moderate-income families to become homeowners by lowering the cost of their home loans and thus the monthly mortgage payments. By insuring payment of the loans made by conventional lenders such as banks, mortgage companies, and savings and loan institutions, such lenders can require downpayments that are a much smaller percentage of the purchase price (for example only 3 percent rather than 10 percent or 20 percent of purchase price) and thereby open up the market to many people who do not have the funds for the larger down payment. So-called closing costs are limited, but the cost of the FHA insurance is folded into the monthly installments. FHA mortgage insurance is only available to people who will be the homeowners and not for nonres-

ident speculators. Since these loans are intended for persons and families of modest means, the amount of the mortgage is limited and is therefore available only for medium-priced housing.

The FHA has a list of approved institutions. A prospective homeowner desiring an FHA-guaranteed loan will apply directly to the lending institution, which can make a "direct endorsement" of the application if the applicant qualifies under the FHA established requirements as to amount of downpayment available (second mortgages not allowed), credit status, and ability to make monthly mortgage payments. If the lender tentatively approves, it will request FHA approval of the loan insurance through processing by the local HUD field office.

As a practical matter the initial application and supporting documents are often supplied by a developer of a housing subdivision or the builder or sponsor of a multifamily project or other developer, who assists the buyer in preparing the documentation and then submits them to the lending institution. Some mortgage companies specialize in FHA loans. These guaranteed loans are routinely sold to "secondary" mortgage entities such as Federal National Mortgage Association (FNMA, Fannie Mae.). These purchases maintain a steady flow of money into the home mortgage market.

FHA loan guarantees are available for many different types of housing and developments, which are commonly identified in the housing industry by the nature of the housing and the National Housing Act Code Section, which authorized the insurance. The borrower must qualify for the specific program, and in the case of multifamily housing it must qualify as a project. The various types of housing covered by the mortgage insurance must meet rather strict standards as to construction, configuration, space, and amenities that have been established (and updated) by FHA housing specialists. Builders, developers, sponsors, and designers who deal with larger projects are generally aware of these standards.

Particular *FHA Loan Insurance Programs* include the following:

a. One- to four-family homes, Section 203(b);

b. Single family disaster victims, Section 203(h);

c. Single family in outlying areas, Section 203(i);

d. For rehabilitation loans, Section 203(k);

e. Single family condominium unit, Section 234(c);

f. Single family cooperative unit purchase, Section 203(n);

g. Adjustable rate mortgage loans, Section 251;

h. Graduated payment mortgage loans, Section 245(a);

i. Growing equity mortgage loans, Section 245(a);

j. Certain low/moderate buyers, Section 221(d)(2);

k. For members of the armed forces, Section 222;

l. For housing in older, declining areas, Section 223(e).

The FHA also operates loan guarantee programs that are supportive of other housing programs for the elderly, persons with disabilities, and for assisted-living conversions, often administered by the Office of Multifamily Housing. These include:

a. Construction or rehabilitation of condominium projects, Section 234(d);

b. Rental housing for the elderly, Section 231, administered by the Multifamily Office described below;

c. Nursing homes, board and care, assisted-living projects, Section 232;

d. Manufactured homes, Title I;

e. Construction or rehabilitation of condominium projects, Section 234(d);

f. Hospitals and group practice facilities, Sections 242 and Title IX, respectively;

g. Manufactured lot and combination loan;

h. Property improvements, Title I;

i. For energy efficiency improvements;

j. Rental housing and manufactured home parks, Section 207;

k. Rental housing projects in urban renewal and concentrated development areas, Section 220;

l. Rental and cooperative housing, and single-room occupancy, Section 221(d)(3) and (4);

m. Two-year operating loss loans, Section 223(d);

n. Entities risk-sharing programs, Section 542(b) and (c).

By far the most extensive program is the single-family home loan guarantees under Section 203(b), which met the needs of post–World War II housing construction and purchase needs, particularly for new families of returning servicemen. Section 203(b) became the framework for much of the nation's home finance system, including non-FHA loans. Section 203 loan insurance is available for detached or semidetached homes, row houses, or a multifamily building. The 203(n) loan guarantees for cooperative housing are applied in the same fashion, although a cooperative unit purchaser technically owns a share in the cooperative entity, which entitles the purchaser to live in the unit as well as share in the use of nonresidential areas, rather than specific real estate.

Currently there are more than 7 million FHA loans in effect covering almost $400 billion in outstanding mortgages. The premiums for the loan insurance are placed in the *FHA's Mutual Mortgage Insurance Fund,* which sustains the program without cost to the federal government.

The Federal Housing Administration (FHA) is administered by HUD's Office of Housing directed by assistant secretary of housing (who also holds the title of federal housing commissioner). Within that office are sub-offices of *Single-Family Housing Programs* and *Multi-Family Housing Programs,* which are discussed in detail below under those separate categories.

Information is available on the FHA Mortgage Hotline: 1(800) CALLFHA, FHA: 1 (800) 697-4287 or the Housing Counseling Hotline: 1 (800) 569-4287.

PUBLIC HOUSING ADMINISTRATION

PUBLIC HOUSING DEVELOPMENT

Dating back to the Public Housing Act of 1937, this program issues federal grants to local public housing authorities, which are established by cities and counties, to develop and manage "decent, safe and affordable" housing for low-income families unable to afford private housing, provided the local government approves the specific project. There are three means by which public housing is developed by the local housing authority: (1) contracts to construct a project on property owned by the housing authority; (2) selects a developer to build a project on land owned by the developer, and then buys the completed project from the developer; (3) purchases existing units such as a refurbished apartment building or finances rehabilitation by a developer prior to purchase of the renovated project by the PHA.

In addition to providing 100 percent of the funding for development of the project, HUD furnishes technical assistance in planning, development, and management of public housing projects. Debt service on loans to the local authority can be covered by the PHA. When a development has mixed-income (and mixed-value) projects, the Public Housing Administration may provide assistance to the local authority.

The units in the projects are rented for rates well below the market, and can be adjusted based on income and other factors. Eligible tenants are low-income families who are citizens or some eligible immigrants; "families" may be with or without children living at home, elderly or "near elderly" families, the disabled, the "displaced" (including when moved due to urban renewal of blighted substandard housing), the survivor of an eligible family, and single persons. The local public housing authority can set up priority lists of potential eligibles depending upon the number of available units. Often this means long waits. When a low-income family raises its income to moderate income level, often they are permitted to continue in the project, but will have their rents increased, though still on the low side of the market rate.

Public housing has a reputation as having dull, institutionalized designs, which sacrifice attractiveness for inexpensive cost. Television and movie dramas and celebrities often refer to the depressed nature of life when growing up "in the projects." Since the hands-on management is often directed by an ill-prepared, poorly funded local housing authority, many projects suffer from ill-repair, graffiti splattered walls, broken public lighting, drug dealing, prostitution, gang activity, and violence. HUD officials in cooperation with local governments have been working to alleviate these conditions, and encourage attractive design, repairs, professional management, and particularly positive tenant activities to develop community leadership and control.

Some public housing projects feature playgrounds, lawns, plantings, and safe conditions. Outstanding designs are possible, as witnessed by the award-winning buildings in Marin City,

California. Mixing private housing or moderate-priced sponsored projects with public housing units and/or siting public housing in a redeveloped area (with separate community funding) are means some cities and counties have employed to make public housing attractive and an integral part of the community.

The *Public Housing Operating Fund* is a major fund (more than $3 billion annually) to meet operating expenses of local public housing authorities. The amount of the subsidy to each housing authority is the shortfall between the total annual expenses of its operations and the amount of rentals it receives. This is especially necessary for maintenance of public housing because the amount of rental of public housing is limited to 30 percent of the tenant's adjusted income.

These operating subsidies are calculated for every housing authority by HUD based upon an established regulatory formula called the *Performance Funding System*, with audits of some expenses. Statutorily, this funding has been in place since the enactment of Section 9 of the United States Housing Act of 1937, as amended by the Public Housing Reform Act.

Public housing authorities, tenant organizations, or nonprofit corporations supported by residents can obtain services to the projects through application to HUD for inclusion in the *Resident Opportunity and Self-Sufficiency Program (ROSS)* to assist residents to become economically and/or physically self-sufficient, including assistance to the elderly and persons with disabilities. Funds granted under this program can cover: (1) training in management of the project and HUD program possibilities; (2) hiring experts and trainers with housing project expertise; (3) limited expenses for such experts and training such as child care and transportation; (4) legal expenses of creating a tax-exempt nonprofit corporation; and (5) some costs of renovation or conversion. The funds available are limited, and applications should be prepared with the aid of the local field office of HUD.

Capital Fund Program (Public Housing) provides annual subsidies from HUD to local public housing authorities for capital improvements, management and/or development, and other activities of a one-time nature, rather than the initial funding, and the regular support payments to the authorities. The fund may finance modernization, redesign, reconstruction, reconfiguration including accesses, vacancy reduction, deferred maintenance, meeting modern building codes, demolition and replacement, relocation, assistance in promotion of economic self-sufficiency of tenants, encouragement of tenant participation in management, improvement of security and safety within the projects, and promotion of homeownership. This is essential to many of the older public housing projects that date back as far as the late 1930s.

Applications by local public housing authorities should be submitted to local HUD field offices, usually followed by a 75-day review, including consultation to perfect any inadequacies and obtain advice. Proposed programs should be capable of completion within two years. Annual funds appropriated are in the neighborhood of $2.9 billion. Approval of applications is made by HUD's Office of Public and Indian Housing based on various factors. There are limitations on amounts approved for operations, and the authorities cannot use the funds for lobbying.

HOPE VI Revitalization and Demolition provides funds to local public housing authorities faced with obsolete or otherwise distressed projects (some dating back to the late 1930s) to revitalize demolish, rehabilitate, reconfigure, and/or replace all or a portion of obsolete public housing projects. Funds may be made available to public housing authorities providing the local authority is making an effort to revitalize its program and is capable of making progress in improvement. The application by such authorities is complex, including a narrative of proposed activities, each demonstrating its "appropriateness," a budget of projected costs, and a series of federal forms and certifications (see www.

hudsclips.org). Applications to the Office of Public and Indian Housing are due prior to May 18, except for funds specifically for demolition, which may be submitted before June 14. Recent availability of funds has been $513 million for revitalization (including technical support, monitoring, and resident studies), and in addition $50 million primarily for demolition.

Housing Choice Voucher Program (Section 8 rental supplements) is a program to assist in adequately housing low-income persons and families who cannot afford the entire rent for public housing or rent in the private sector. Commonly called Section 8, eligible applicants are public housing authorities and nonprofit disability organizations sponsoring housing projects. Particularly benefited are the elderly, people with disabilities, and those for whom inadequate housing or inability to afford decent housing is a prime factor in separation of families, under the Family Unification Program. The result is that low-income families and individuals can rent decent private housing in lieu of using public housing or waiting for years for public housing, or where none is available. For the disabled, vouchers can also be used to meet public housing rentals, or housing sponsored by nonprofit organizations.

Individual applicants who believe they may qualify should apply at the local public housing authority. In turn, the housing authorities submit applications to the Grants Management Center, HUD, 501 School Street SW, Suite 800, Washington, DC 20024. Administered by the HUD Office of Public and Indian Housing, the available funding is as high as $613 million. Approval is discretionary, but is based on various factors, including the need to maintain families intact, persons with disabilities, and availability of housing outside of the public housing projects.

Single-Room Occupancy Program Under Section 8 provides rental assistance to homeless persons in connection with the moderate rehabilitation of single-room occupancy dwellings.

HUD enters into contracts with local public housing authorities for administration and dealing both with tenants and landlords to whom the rental assistance is paid on behalf of the tenants. The rental assistance covers the difference between 30 percent of the tenant's income and the fair market for the unit, which may include sanitary and/or food preparation facilities. Rental assistance is allowable for a period of no more than 10 years. The program was authorized by Section 441 of the McKinney-Vento Homeless Assistance Act, which also provides for payment of $3,000 or more for the limited rehabilitation to make the unit decent and livable. This program is particularly appropriate for bringing up to standard a rundown hotel, an old school, or a large abandoned home to house previously homeless people.

Indian Community Development Block Grant is similar to redevelopment programs, and directly benefits Indian tribal organizations, bands, and Alaska native villages that qualify under 31 USC 1221, with development of those communities with funding for decent housing, "suitable" living environment, and increased economic opportunities. Of the expected $67 million annual amount available, the HUD secretary may designate 5 percent for special grants to deal with threats to public health or safety.

Under the HUD Office of Public and Indian Housing, it is directly administered by six area Offices of Native American Programs (ONAP) under policies determined by the National Program Office of ONAP. These area offices are located at: Eastern Woodlands ONAP, 77 West Jackson Boulevard, Chicago, IL 60604-3507; Southern Plains ONAP, 500 West Main Street, Suite 400, Oklahoma City, OK 73102-3202; Northern Plains ONAP, 633 17th Street, Denver, CO 80202-3607; Southwest ONAP, 400 North 5th Street, Suite 1650, Phoenix, AZ 85004-2361; Northwest ONAP, 909 First Avenue, Suite 200, Seattle, WA 98104-1000; and Alaska ONAP, 949 East 36th, Suite 401, Anchorage, AK 99508-4309.

Applications must be submitted by May 24 of the year and require an authorizing resolution by the governing body of the applicant. Application kits can be obtained at www.codetalk.fed.us/ Community_Developl. (Note that "codetalk" honors the heroic Navaho codetalkers during World War II.)

Indian Housing Block Grants is similar to grants for public housing, but is directed toward providing housing for low-income Native American families in Indian tribes as defined in the Native American Housing Assistance and Self-Determination Act of 1996. A recipient Indian tribe becomes eligible to administer the program locally by designating an Indian housing authority or equivalent entity. Such an Indian authority has the latitude to determine the tribal housing needs, providing they are principally for low-income families. The funding can be used for either rental or privately owned housing. The local authority must submit an annual detailed plan before July 1 of each year.

HUD's Office of Public and Indian Housing administers the program and allocates the funds based upon an annual formula, which it develops. A typical total annual fund for all such block grants is over $600 million.

Gun Buyback Program is intended to reduce crime and gun violence by providing funds (approximately $10 million per year recently) to purchase weapons. The program is facilitated through local public housing authorities and Indian tribal housing entities working with local law enforcement. HUD's Office of Public and Indian Housing provides technical assistance, training, and assessment as well as allotment of funds for this program.

Public Housing Technical Assistance for Safety and Security provides expert advice to local public housing authorities on means to prevent both personal and property crime in the projects. This can include design of security including gates, fences, and other facilities, prevention of areas that are difficult to observe or police, as well as organizing tenants for leadership and cooperation to prevent criminal activity.

COMMUNITY PLANNING AND DEVELOPMENT

Urban Renewal (Redevelopment) is assisted by the federal government through HUD's *Community Development Block Grant Program,* pursuant to the Housing and Community Development Act of 1974, as amended. The CDBG program assists local redevelopment agencies of cities and urban counties, nonentitlement communities (nonurban) assisted by the state, or nonentitlement communities eligible under the HUD-administered *Small Cities Community Development Block Grant Program.*

In charge of the Community Development Block Grant Program is HUD's *Office of Community Planning and Development.* Essentially the three methods of federal assistance (with controls) are grants, loan guarantees, and technical assistance.

The objectives of urban renewal must be to redevelop large-scale urban communities by funding acquisition of assembled land, rehabilitating property, building or improving public facilities, providing economic development (land and facilities for businesses), and paying related expenses to create a suitable living environment primarily for people of low and moderate income. Over the years since the current program's predecessor was inaugurated in the late 1940s, almost all major cities and hundreds of smaller communities have cleared or substantially renewed blighted areas (based on definitions of blight in federal regulations) pursuant to redevelopment plans.

Replacing the previous slums are various new or rehabilitated buildings, in various mixes of public housing, moderate-priced affordable housing, elderly or cooperative housing sponsored by nonprofit organizations, elegant condominiums, businesses of all sizes from community grocery stores to gigantic hotels, improved traffic patterns, parks, schools, and even land provided for churches. Local planning and administration is the responsibility of redevelopment agencies appointed and supervised by the city or urban area with jurisdiction. Applications and guarantees must be approved by the governing body as well as by the redevelopment agency.

In order to assemble the necessary real property each local redevelopment agency has the power of eminent domain to acquire private property since urban renewal has been ruled by federal courts to be a "public use" required by the Fifth Amendment to the Constitution. "Just compensation" based on professional appraisals is determined either by negotiation or litigation, but acquisition can precede such judicial determination.

An abiding problem is the question of relocation and/or rehousing for people displaced by removal of substandard housing. Funding must be provided for moving, and decent housing must be provided either within the project area or nearby. Relocation programs must be included in the redevelopment plans. The adequacy of such programs has been a source of considerable litigation. Statistics demonstrate that some of those whose dwellings have been removed move elsewhere or "filter" down to substandard housing with low rents.

Section 108 is the loan guarantee portion of the Community Development Block Grant Program. The program's goal is the development of viable urban communities with decent housing, a suitable living environment, and increased economic opportunities primarily for persons of low and moderate income. These objectives are to be achieved by providing a source of financing for land acquisition, economic development of local business, property rehabilitation, and public facilities, all as part of large-scale development. Thus, it is a loan guarantee segment of urban renewal (redevelopment).

Authorized by the Housing and Community Development Act of 1974 as amended, it is administered by the Office of Community Planning and Development. Available guarantees in a single year are in the neighborhood of $1.25 billion.

To obtain the guarantee of the loan for these purposes a detailed application and a submitted plan meeting standards set by HUD are required. A plan for repayment of the funds must be included. Security for the loan must be pledged by the local entity. The application must be developed with the assistance and advice of a HUD field office and the headquarters of the Financial Management Division of the Office of Planning and Development, which is located at 451 7th Street SW, Washington, DC 20410.

Disaster Recovery Initiative is a community development block grant program to help communities recover from presidentially declared natural disasters such as floods, tidal waves, earthquakes, or massive fires. The direct financial assistance is made upon application by state governments, local governments (but not to local agencies such as housing authorities), Indian tribes, and insular areas in those geographic locations designated as disaster areas. Grants are restricted for the purposes spelled out in Section 105(a) of the Housing and Community Development Act of 1974, must be related to the specific disaster, and must be concentrated (at least 50 percent) on activities benefiting low and moderate-income people. Annual funding has varied broadly ($20 million to $500 million in one four-year period) since it is based on supplemental appropriations depending on the severity of disasters.

Grantees are required to report quarterly on progress resulting from use of the emergency grants to the Web-based Disaster Recovery Grant Reporting system.

HOME Disaster Grants are funds specifically appropriated by Congress to specific state and local governments for housing damaged by a natural disaster such as a hurricane or flood. Usually the grant funds are distributed to low-income families for essential tenant assistance, housing rehabilitation, home reconstruction, or new homes. Grants are administered by the Office of Community Planning and Development, which notifies the states of the availability of congressional authorized funding. In most cases technical red tape is waived to hasten delivery of needed funds to the disaster area. Available funding varies annually based on the extent and location of disasters, ranging from $60 million to $170 million in a period of four years, for example.

HOME Investment Partnerships Program is an affordable housing development program designed to finance plans consolidated among states, cities, counties, local jurisdictions, private businesses, and nonprofit organizations. The submitted consolidated plans must be directed toward strategies that provide decent and affordable housing for people of very low and low income. While the emphasis is on rental housing, home ownership may be possible. Both financial and technical assistance is funded under the partnership program. Approved strategies may include acquisition and rehabilitation of housing, rental and home ownership assistance (such as rental supplements), new construction, site acquisition and improvement, demolition if necessary, and relocation. The basic concept is to design a partnership plan that meets local needs and priorities, as long as the goal of an increase of affordable housing units is achieved. Administrative costs are limited to 10 percent of costs of a plan.

For participation in an investment partnership program applications in the form of a proposed "Consolidated Plan" and accompanying report must be submitted between November 15 and the following August 16 of the fiscal year. Available funding in recent years has exceeded $1.5 billion. The program is managed by the Office of Community Planning and Development. Submissions should be made to the local HUD field office.

HOME Technical Assistance is available from HUD's Office of Community Planning and Development to assist local authorities in developing and managing HOME programs.

Church Arson Loan Guarantee Recovery Fund was created by the Church Arson Recovery Act of 1996 in response to several arson attacks on churches with African-American congregations. The program gives financial assistance and guarantees of loans to victimized churches in rebuilding places of worship damaged or destroyed by arson or terrorism. HUD also set in motion the National Rebuilding Initiative, which is a public and private partnership of HUD, the National Council of Churches, and the Congress of National Black Churches. Any church congregation may apply for direct assistance providing it can demonstrate that the damage was caused by arson or terrorism and proof that it is a nonprofit organization as defined in IRS Code Section 501(c)(3). Lenders to such eligible churches can apply for the loan guarantee, making them easier to grant to congregations with limited resources. Applications can be made at any time for the limited amount of funds. Applicants should contact the local HUD field office or the HUD Office of Community Planning and Development at 1(800) 998-9999.

Emergency Shelter Grants is a program intended to provide some shelter for the homeless. Eligible applicants are states, local governmental agencies, Indian tribal governments, and nonprofit organizations participating in rehabilitation or conversion of a shelter, as well as maintenance and supportive services, and homeless prevention. These funds are given on a 50-50 matching basis, requiring states, local agencies, or nonprofits to equal the federal contribution, with some exemptions in certain circumstances. Grants for emergency or transitional shelter for the homeless are limited to the following activities: (1) renovation, rehabilitation, or conversion of buildings for shelters, (2) essential services for the homeless not to exceed 30 percent of grant, (3) operations not to exceed 10 percent, and (4) homeless prevention not to exceed 30 percent. New construction is not an eligible expense.

Applicants must submit a five-year plan, as well as a first-year plan that must be updated each year. As is true with most such agencies with constituencies of people without influence, the grantees may not participate in lobbying.

A consolidated plan which is, in effect, an application for funding, must be submitted to the local or state HUD office 45 days before the local program's year. Most recently the available funding was $150 million. Grants have ranged between $75,000 and $7.8 million. All funds distributed to a state agency must be transmitted to the local government or nonprofit organization actually managing the homeless program.

The Emergency Shelter Grant program is managed by the Office of Community Planning and Development. Application forms are also available from state or local HUD offices, which is the practical method of beginning the processing of a submission.

Homeless people are defined as those who regularly sleep in places not meant for human habitation, such as sidewalks, parks, cars, and abandoned buildings, or sleep in emergency shelters as a primary nighttime residence. They also include those who recently come from the streets or emergency shelters to transitional housing, or those recently evicted or discharged from an institution who have neither a residence nor funds to obtain housing.

Rural Housing and Economic Development is a program intended to stimulate and support innovative housing and economic development activities in rural areas. Of the approximately $25 million a year available, about 75 percent goes for innovation, and the remainder is allocated to organizations to improve their ability to sponsor housing and economic development ("capacity building") and for new organizations in the field ("seed support"). Eligible applicants are local rural nonprofit organizations, community development corporations, and Indian tribes. State housing finance agencies, and state community or economic development agencies are limited to grants for innovation only. To obtain an application kit, call the Office of Rural Housing and Economic Development at (202) 708-2290. Applications are due by April 7.

Empowerment Zone/Enterprise Community Initiative is directed toward "underserved" areas in order to create self-sustaining, long-term economic development. These "underserved" communities or neighborhoods (called "empowerment zones" in this context) are economically depressed, often containing substandard housing and deteriorating business locations, inadequate public facilities, and high unemployment particularly among minorities. The methodology involves the use of innovative and comprehensive strategies developed and implemented by partnerships of private, public, and nonprofit entities in the particular community.

Zones for consideration must be nominated by the state and/or a local government, and the application rated by the Office of Community Planning and Development, which manages the initiative, based on the scope of the plan, the amount of community involvement, and the ability of the community to commit local resources. Essential inclusions are (1) nomination forms, (2) a strategic plan, (3) census tract maps delineating the zone, and (4) an environmental impact statement. Typical funding is $55 million for a "round" of applications.

This "empowerment zone" program was first authorized by the Taxpayer Relief Act of 1997, and was originally promoted by HUD secretary Jack Kemp as early as the late 1980s.

The Office of Community Development and Planning manages programs to assist local community development, including *Community Development Work Study* and *Community Development Block Grant Technical Assistance.*

State Administered Community Development Block Grant is a program in which cities of fewer than 50,000 people and counties of fewer than 200,000 people can receive block grant funds administered by the participating states (all but Hawaii, which chose not to apply), provided the state fulfills certain responsibilities. These are: (a) formulating community development objectives, (b) determining how to distribute the funds, and (c) ensuring that recipient local governments comply with applicable state and federal law and requirements. State-administered block grants were inaugurated by a 1981 amendment to the Housing and Community Development Act.

This program provides the state the opportunity to apportion among local governments and supervise the use of the development funds, of which 70 percent must be used for activities that benefit low- and moderate-income people and families and meet urgent community development needs that have suddenly arisen within 18 months. The community development activities can include the usual redevelopment purposes, such as property acquisition, demolition, rehabilitation, planning, and assistance to nonprofits for development and to private small businesses to promote economic development.

These are matching funds that must be equaled dollar-for-dollar by each state's contribution. There are limitations on the amount that may be used for administration and technical assistance. Apportionment among the states is based on a statutory formula factoring in population, poverty, amount of overcrowded housing, and age of housing. In recent years the annual amount available is $1.267 billion.

Community Development Block Grants to Entitlement Communities are similar to State Administered Development Block Grants, except they are granted directly to more populous (entitlement) cities and counties. The cities must exceed 50,000 in population, and the counties, excluding entitlement cities, must have populations in excess of 200,000. The eligible amount of a grant is determined by a statutory formula taking into consideration poverty, population, housing overcrowding, and age of population. Another factor, unlike the state managed block grant, is the "population growth lag" in comparison to other metropolitan areas.

For funding, the city or county must submit a consolidated plan that includes some or all of various available programs, of which at least 70 percent will benefit low- and moderate-income persons. Just as in the state administered block grants, the basic redevelopment activities to eliminate blight will be acquisition, demolition, relocation, rehabilitation, construction of public facilities and improvements, limited public services, achieving energy conservation and renewable energy methods, economic development, and job creation of local businesses. Prohibited are: (a) acquisition, construction or reconstruction of government buildings, (b) political activity, (c) certain income payments, and (d) construction of housing by general local government (but permitted by public housing authorities).

After review, HUD will approve a grant if the submission is complete, its goals are consistent with the National Affordable Housing Act, and the plan appears effective to achieve them. However, the secretary may determine that the municipality or county lacks a continuing capacity to complete the proposed activities in a timely manner, or has previously failed to carry out assisted activities in accordance with the Housing and Community Development Act or other laws.

Local citizens interested in urging their community to apply for block grant funds should contact the local HUD field office.

Housing Opportunities for Persons with AIDS (HOPWA) are two types of programs to respond to the special needs of those persons with the disease HIV/AIDS. The "formula" program funds "consolidated plans" developed by local jurisdictions, which receive 90 percent of the approximately $200 million per year appropriated for these housing opportunities. The second type is entitled the "competitive" program, which provides grants in two categories: 1) Special Projects of National Significance with innovative features available to states, units of local government, and nonprofit organizations, and 2) long-term grants to states and local government agencies that do not qualify for the formula grants. Although not able to obtain grants under this category, nonprofit organizations can become sponsors of housing projects if approved by the local government or the state.

About 100 jurisdictions have received the formula grants, which must be reviewed and renewed each year. The consolidated program brings to bear all available programs on the special problems of those with AIDS to achieve not only decent, safe, and affordable housing, but also all the services that will maintain a full life. Under HUD's jurisdiction are funds from Community Block Grants, HOME Investment Partnerships, and Emergency Shelter Grants.

HOPWA funding may be used for a broad range of housing and services. In the housing arena jurisdictions receiving grants can acquire, rehabilitate, or build community residences, operate and maintain community residences, and provide rental assistance and emergency payments to prevent homelessness. To round out the assistance within a consolidated program, HOPWA funding can be spent on health care and mental health services, drug- and alcohol-abuse treatment and counseling, intensive care, nutrition, case management, daily living assistance, and placement assistance.

Consolidated plans must be submitted to HUD's Office of Community Planning and Development 45 days prior to the end of the applicant jurisdiction's fiscal year.

As well as this direct assistance to provide housing, health care, and supportive services, HOPWA officials authorize funds to states to develop long-term strategies that may be of help in conquering the AIDS epidemic.

The remaining 10 percent funding available by competition must be applied for by May 23 by the state or local governmental bodies. Acceptable uses of the funding are similar to those of the formula funds, except there need not be a consoli-

dated plan, the number of grantees is much fewer (about 20 percent), and has greater latitude in eligible grantees. It also requires applications that compete with other applications for the funds. The application kit for the competitive funding can be acquired from SuperNOFA Center at 1(800) HUD-8929 or through the Internet at www.hud.gov/fundsavl or www.hud.gov/cpd/hopwahom.

Community Development for Historically Black Colleges and Universities is a program managed by the Office of Community Planning and Development to provide neighborhood revitalization, housing, and economic assistance in the locality of one of the historically black colleges (which are now integrated, but with predominately African-American students). It is administered by the Office of Community Planning and Development under the Housing and Community Act of 1974. Funding is only $10 million. The annual application deadline is May 10 at HUD headquarters, 451 7th Street SW, Washington, DC 20410; application kits may be obtained at HUD's on-line address: Website: www.hud.gov.

Self-Help Homeownership Opportunities Program (SHOP) provides up to $10,000 per unit for land acquisition and infrastructure improvements as assistance to people willing and able to provide "sweat equity" (personal labor by the prospective owner and volunteers) into the construction or rehabilitation of a dwelling. The concept is that this grant, plus the sweat equity, reduces the cost of the dwelling so that the remainder may be financed within the means of families with modest financial means. SHOP was originally set aside for Habitat for Humanity International, but all such nonprofit organizations, including Habitat for Humanity, compete for these funds, which are available only for self-help projects of 30 or more units.

Applications must be submitted to the Office of Community Planning and Development before May 29 each year. There is approximately

$20 million available. Applications should be in narrative form covering five aspects of the proposed program: 1) capacity of the organizational application, including its staffing and a copy of the most recent audit; 2) extent of the need; 3) the approach developed by the organization, emphasizing the soundness of it; 4) the ability to leverage (find other financing to complete construction); and 5) means of coordination and the comprehensive nature of the project. The project applicant must also provide the formal Application for Federal Assistance (Standard Form 424), proof of nonprofit status, and related forms such as budget information.

Colonias (State Block Grant Set Aside) are communities along the southern border of the United States (within 150 miles of Mexico) that fall below a decent standard of community facilities (since they are often originated by squatters). The Colonias often lack potable water, an adequate sewage system, and/or safe and sanitary housing. Under Section 916 of the National Affordable Housing Act of 1990, Congress urged the states of Texas, New Mexico, Arizona, and California to set aside some of their Community Development Block Grants for assistance to these Colonias, which became mandatory in 1996 and permanent in 1997. The amounts required are 2 percent for California and 10 percent by the other three states. The bulk of the funds have been expended on water, sewer, and housing projects.

Assistance through the *Rural Housing and Economic Development Program,* previously described, is also available to the Colonias. Phone: (202) 708-2290.

For the people in these communities to discuss necessary benefits, they should contact the HUD field offices in the border area, and/or the HUD state office in each of the four states.

Youthbuild is a grant program that assists disadvantaged (minorities, low-income, and needing educational opportunity) youths to complete high school education and learn construction and related skills gained on worksites for construction of housing for low-income families and for the homeless. Eligible grantees are public and private nonprofit agencies, state and local housing authorities, or other governmental bodies. Administered by the Office of Community Planning and Development, the opportunities are encompassed within housing creation and rehabilitation programs for low and very low income people. The annual amount available has been about $27 million. For application information call 1 (800) HUD-8929 and ask for "Youthbuild" information and kit.

The *Office of Economic Development* is maintained by the Office of Community Planning and Development to monitor HUD-approved and -assisted economic development projects. It also provides technical assistance to recipients to ensure that the investment of funds is successful and achieves the intended goals. It is particularly intent that federal investments stimulate an involvement and increase in private opportunity in the communities served.

Fair Housing Compliance

Fair Housing Initiative Program grants funds to organizations to foster compliance with the Fair Housing Act as well as state and local fair housing laws, all of which attempt to prevent any form of discrimination in housing, including that allegedly based on race, gender, and/or age. Eligible for the grants are fair housing organizations, state and local governments, and Fair Housing Assistance Program agencies. There are four types of initiatives: (1) administrative enforcement of fair housing laws, (2) education and outreach on fair housing, (3) private enforcement by those receiving federal housing assistance, and (4) so-called organization capacity building, which attempts to maximize the ability of organizations to promote fair housing. The funding (as much as $24 million in some years) is divided approximately two-thirds for competitive applicants and one-third to specific named organizations. Applications should be made to the Office of Fair Housing and Equal Opportunity by May 16 each year. Information on a detailed application can be obtained from the SuperNOFA Clearinghouse.

The legislative grounding for these programs are the laws promoting nondiscrimination in federally assisted housing (Sections 504, Title VI, and Section 109), and the Age Discrimination Act. In addition, Section 3 deals with employment and economic opportunity for low-income persons.

Fair Housing Assistance Program is intended to assist state and local fair housing agencies in their efforts to enforce legislation that prohibits discrimination in housing. Among the funded activities are complaint processing, administration, special enforcement efforts (investigations, administrative hearings, and trials), and training. Goals include creation and maintenance of data and information systems.

Directed by the Office of Fair Housing and Equal Opportunity, the annual funding in recent years has been $20 million. Contributions of funds to participating agencies are made pursuant to a complex set of restrictions and regulations and reporting requirements, indicating concern by lawmakers that local and state fair housing agencies must confine their activities in regard to the politically sensitive issues of preventing discrimination by landlords, real estate agents, and local governments. The participating agencies are prohibited from lobbying for legislation, by 31 U.S.C. 1352, adopted in 1990.

The program is managed by the Office of Fair Housing Equal Opportunity.

Housing Discrimination Hotline: 1 (800) 669-9777.

Healthy Homes and Lead Paint Hazard Control

Lead Hazard Control Program provides funding by grants to assist states, local governments, and Indian tribes to identify and control the hazards of lead-based paint on existing homes. Administered by the HUD Office of Healthy Homes and Lead Hazard Control, available funding is approximately $59 million. As delineated in the Housing and Community Development Act of 1992 (42 USC 4851 et seq.) participation in the program by local governmental bodies requires a plan including: (1) maximize the number of children protected; (2) strive for cost-effective approaches; (3) employ renovation, remodeling, and maintenance of housing to reduce the dangers; and (4) guarantee that the program furthers fair housing, advanced technology, and environmental "justice."

Eligible applicants must submit a series of documents explaining the proposed project, detailed estimated budget with costs justifications, any research program, résumés of key personnel, and HUD forms such as 2880, certifications, and assurances. The application kit can be found at www.hud.gov/lea/. Numerous states, cities, and counties have joined the program, and individuals desiring assistance, reporting problems, or seeking information would be advised to contact the state or local government if it is participating.

State governments that have applied and received grants are: California, Delaware; Georgia, Illinois, Maryland, Massachusetts, Maine, New Hampshire, New Jersey, Michigan, Nebraska, Pennsylvania, Rhode Island, Vermont, and Wisconsin. Some of the major cities with lead-based control projects are: Birmingham, Alabama; Phoenix, Arizona; Los Angeles, California, Denver, Colorado; New Haven, Connecticut, Boston, Massachusetts; Baltimore, Maryland; Portland, Maine; Detroit, Michigan, Minneapolis, Minnesota; Charlotte, North Carolina, Omaha, Nebraska; New York, New York; Cleveland, Ohio, Portland, Oregon; Charleston, South Carolina; Memphis, Tennessee; Fort Worth, Texas; Richmond, Virginia; Milwaukee, Wisconsin. For counties and other cities that have received grants check the website: www.hud.gov/offices/lead. The

Lead Paint Safety Field Guide booklet is available in English and Spanish by calling the National Lead Information Center at 1(800) 424-LEAD. The Lead-Safe Housing Website: www.hud.gov/offices/lead.

The *Healthy Homes Initiative* is directed at removing housing hazards to health, such as asbestos, radon, fire, structural, and electrical dangers. This is accomplished by developing, demonstrating, and promoting preventive measures to correct hazards in the home that result in illness or injury. Eligibility is open to a broad class of organizations, profit and nonprofit, state and local governmental agencies, and Indian tribes. Grants ranging between $250,000 to $2,500,000 may be available from an annual availability of about $6.5 million. Selection of grantees is based on evaluation of programs factors, such as reducing health threats to the maximum number balanced against cost effectiveness. To order an application kit, go to www.hud/gov/lea/healthy-homes. Healthy Homes performs research on home health and safety and has prepared detailed lists of tips, many of which are found in pamphlets and brochures that can be obtained from The Office of Applied Economics 100 Bureau Drive Stop 8603 Gaithersburg, MD 20899-8603; Fax: (301) 975-5337.

Multifamily Housing

Almost all of the multifamily housing programs, including FHA loan insurance, are eligible for Multifamily Accelerated Processing (MAP) for review, approval, and HUD commitment of proposals and applications.

Assisted-Living Conversion Program is a concomitant to various elderly housing programs to provide a grant to the nonprofit owners with grants to convert dwelling units into facilities in which frail elderly with some disabilities can live independently if provided with special facilities and protections for daily living such as eating, bathing, grooming, dressing, and home management. It is authorized under Section 202b of the Housing Act of 1959 and is intended to encourage independent living of the elderly.

These grants are given only to operators of elderly housing under Sections 202, Section 8, housing services under 515, Section 221(d)3 (a moderate-priced multiunit housing program), and Section 236. The existing projects must have a central kitchen or dining facility, lounges, and recreation areas available to the residents. Also they must have met all local and state licensing requirements.

The funds are allocated by HUD's Multifamily Office, and there can be competition for a limited amount available. Those entities desiring funding should check the Notice of Fund Availability published in the Federal Register each year.

Support Housing for the Elderly (Section 202) is a capital advance program for development of below-market rental housing for very low income people 62 years or older. The capital advance carries no interest and is not repayable so long as the project remains available for occupancy by such low-income elderly for at least 40 years. Thus, for current purposes this is a direct grant, in which the only profit would be the limited profit margin permitted under the program. The development may be a new construction, rehabilitation, or purchase of a building that had been acquired by the FEDERAL DEPOSIT INSURANCE CORPORATION from a defaulting financial institution such as one of the failed savings and loans. Each project may not exceed 200 living units.

The only entities authorized to apply for the Section 202 program are private nonprofit organizations or nonprofit consumer cooperatives (such as housing cooperatives), but not PHAs or government bodies. An application kit and related materials may be acquired by calling HUD's SuperNOFA Information Center at 1(800) HUD-8929, or from a Multifamily Hub or Multifamily Program Center. Applications are due on or before May 18 of each year. Recent annual funds available have been around $426 million.

Coupled with the development advances are contracts for the *Rental Assistance Program (Section 8)* to provide sufficient funds to keep the rent paid by the elderly low enough for them to subsist, and for certain supportive services peculiar to housing for the elderly, including the frail.

Supportive Housing for Persons With Disabilities (Section 811) is a capital advance program for development of below-market rental housing for very low income people with disabilities. The capital advance carries no interest and is not repayable so long as the project remains available for occupancy by such low-income disabled for at least 40 years. Thus, for current purposes this is a direct grant, in which the only profit would be the limited profit margin permitted under the program. The development may be independent living projects, condominiums, or small group homes with supportive services available. Every project must provide a supportive services plan, which may vary depending on the needs of the particular population in the project. A test of eligibility of tenants is that at least one member of the family (which can be a single person) is at or below 50 percent of the median income, and one member is 18 years or older.

Coupled with the assistance to developers of housing for the disabled, HUD also provides rental assistance for tenants under the Section 8 Housing Assistance Payments Program. Section 811 refers to that section entitled Supportive Housing for Persons With Disabilities in the authorizing legislation, the National Affordable Housing Act.

The only entities authorized to apply for the Section 811 capital advances are private nonprofit organizations with an IRS Section 501(c)(3) exemption and the proven ability to make a small capital investment. An application kit and related materials may be acquired by calling HUD's SuperNOFA Information Center at 1(800) HUD-8929. Applications must be submitted to HUD's local field office. The supportive services portion of the project must be certified to be well designed for these special tenants and their needs.

Mortgage Insurance for Rental and Cooperative Housing (Sections 221(d)(3) and 221(d)(4) is a long-standing program of mortgage guarantees to assist and stimulate multifamily housing for moderate-income families, the elderly, the handicapped, and even single-room occupancy. Section 221(d)(3) insures nonprofit sponsors of projects, while Section 221(d)(4) is available to for-profit developers and/or project owners. The great attraction of these programs is their scope and flexibility. It is limited to tenants or co-op owners of moderate income, the elderly, the handicapped, or families displaced by urban renewal. A unique facet is that the mortgages are financed by Government National Mortgage (Ginnie Mae) mortgage-backed securities.

Projects eligible for mortgage insurance may be new construction or rehabilitation, detached, semidetached, row, walkup, or elevator-served construction of five units or more. It is not unusual that the units are pure rental or cooperative shares (in which the tenant family owns a share of the cooperative that has title to the project) and with each shareholder owning the right to occupy the unit and use of the common areas.

Section 221(d)(3) is intended for nonprofit sponsors (such as church organizations, labor unions, service organizations, community groups, or cooperatives) and can guarantee loans up to 100 percent replacement value of the project. For-profit developers and project owners are covered by Section 221(d)(4) and have loan guarantee limits of 90 percent of replacement cost estimates. Mortgages may be up to 40-year terms. The maximum amount of each insured mortgage varies depending on the size of the units, the type of construction, and the location of the project.

Although the aim of these programs is to provide housing at moderate prices for people of moderate income, actually there are no income limits. Designs suitable for elderly or handicapped family members are encouraged.

Applying for loan insurance follows negotiations between the borrowing sponsor and the lending institution in developing the loan package, which is then submitted as an application to the local multifamily hub or program center, which can issue a loan insurance commitment upon approval.

Mortgage Insurance for Single Room Occupancy is available for sponsors of projects under Sections 221(d)(3) or 221(d)(4). Thus, studio apartments of limited space may be included in the projects, under the terms described above. While there is no strict income limitation for a tenant or co-op shareholder, the housing is intended for single low-income persons on the theory that the small size of the apartments will provide low-cost rental within the project. There is no limit to the number of people who may occupy the single-room unit; the occupancy requires adherence to local and state occupancy codes. Occupants of these units may not be beneficiaries of rental assistance or other subsidies.

Mortgage Insurance for Nursing Homes, Intermediate Care, Board and Care, and Assisted-Living Facilities (Sections 232 and 232/223(f) is an FHA mortgage insurance program for construction, rehabilitation, or purchase of existing facilities for people requiring care and medical attention. Like 221(d)(3), the guarantees are made by Ginnie Mae mortgage-backed securities. Covered financing is either 35 years for existing properties or 40 years for new construction, and is fixed rate, based on 85 percent of value for profit-making entities and 90 percent for nonprofits.

Mortgage Insurance for Supplemental Loans for Multifamily Projects (Section 241(a) guarantees loans to repair and improve multifamily rental housing, including those with existing HUD guaranteed loans, to maintain the housing as decent, containing modern equipment and making it economically viable. Borrowers can include nursing homes, hospitals, or assisted-living facilities as well as multifamily (apartment-style buildings). While the loans are FHA insured, the program is administered by the Office of Multifamily Housing Development.

Housing Finance (State) Agency Risk-Sharing (Section 542(c) provides loan insurance to state housing authorities for multifamily projects, by HUD sharing the risk with the state housing agency, if the state agency can meet some fairly strict standards, including a high credit rating. In a typical recent year HUD insured 78 projects with 8,565 units, covering $430 million in loans. The actual borrowers are investors, builders, developers, local public entities, and nonprofit sponsoring corporations or associations. Potential borrowers apply through an approved state housing authority.

Mortgage Insurance for Rental Housing (Section 207) was originally designed to provide mortgage guarantees of multifamily rental housing including new construction. It is now limited to rehabilitation or refinance of all multifamily projects if there is a need. However, as a practical matter, starting in 2001, no loans have been insured under this program. Sections 221(d)(3) and 221(d)(4) are more advantageous to builders, developers, and sponsors of multifamily housing.

Mortgage Insurance for Rental Housing for the Elderly (Section 231) has essentially been replaced by guarantees under Sections 221(d)(3) and 221(d)(4), with only six projects approved in 2001.

Mortgage Insurance for Manufactured Home Parks is also a Section 207 mortgage insurance program for families (including the elderly) who own manufactured homes or wish to lease spaces in a "manufactured park," which is commonly called a mobile home park, although the homes are stationary. In 2001 only five parks were provided insurance for a total of 1,265 units.

Mortgage Insurance for Rental Housing for Urban Renewal and Concentrated Development Areas (Section 220) is a loan insurance program directed to rental housing construction or rehabilitation in areas of urban renewal, strict code enforcement, neighborhood development, or housing having suffered from a natural disaster.

Guaranteed loans may not exceed 90 percent of replacement cost and can be as long as 40 years. Borrowers can be private developers and public bodies that can meet HUD standards. The potential borrower must prepare a detailed application with the potential lender before it is submitted to the local HUD multifamily hub or center for review.

Multifamily Housing Service Coordinators are available to local agencies, projects, and sponsors upon request.

Multifamily Housing Complaint Line: 1 (800) MULTI-7 (685-8470).

Single Family Housing

Manufactured Home Construction Safety Standards is a program mandated by the National Manufactured Housing Construction and Safety Standards Act of 1974. Builders of manufactured homes (off-site construction and sale to move to a lot) are required to comply with HUD design and construction standards. This program responds to customer complaints, investigates, inspects, and reviews for compliance with the so-called HUD codes. The enforcement is handled either directly by the Office of Single Family Housing in HUD or by state agencies in 36 states.

The designs of each model must be approved and certified, which earns a manufacturer's certification label that assures the purchaser that it meets federal standards. Funding is primarily by user fees, which amount to more than $10 million annually.

CONTACT Address: Office of Single Family Housing, Office of Consumer and Regulatory Affairs, Manufactured Housing and Standards Division, HUD, 451 7th Street SW, Washington, DC 20410; Phone: 1(800) 245-2691. Program standards can be found in 24 CFR 3280, and can be acquired on-line at HUDCLIPS or in print through HUD USER, P.O. Box 6091, Rockville, MD 20849; Phone: 1(800) 245-2691. Also contact Manufactured Housing Institute; Phone: (703) 558-0400.

Single Room Occupancy Program (for Homeless) provides grant funds to local public housing authorities for moderate rehabilitation of buildings up to a sufficiently decent standard as to be appropriate to house homeless people with very low incomes. Typical units in which rehabilitation assistance is provided are rundown hotels, abandoned schools, homes, or a charitable organization's older building. The assisted owners will be allowed a minimum of $3,000 per unit to meet housing quality standards. This program is usually coupled with rental assistance payments previously described for a period of 10 years, with the rent level approved by HUD and the portion paid by the tenant limited to 30 percent of income. The program was authorized by the McKinney-Vento Homeless Assistance Act, and is intended to alleviate some of the heartbreak of homelessness by putting into use buildings that could house very low income single persons.

Policy Development and Research

Community Outreach Partnerships Centers Program is a demonstration program to assist universities in using resources to benefit the surrounding communities, authorized by Section 851 of the Housing and Community Development Act of 1992. Grants are available up to $400,000 for two or three years. University resources may include economics and technology as well as local major employers, investors, real estate developers, and other people. Target issues are housing, infrastructure, economic development, neighborhood revitalization, health care, crime, and planning. Suggested methodology includes community cooperation with the university for job training and counseling, developing strategies to spur economic growth, combating crime and housing discrimination, financial and technical assistance for new businesses, and mentoring of young people.

This is a matching grant program in which the local community must provide 75 percent of the cost in cash and/or activity, and the research element is limited to 25 percent of project costs.

Applications and information may be acquired from the *University Partnership Clearinghouse* at 1(800) 245-2691.

The *Office of University Partnerships* within the Office of Policy Development and Research administers the outreach program, which can be reached at (202) 708-1537. That office also administers grants for *Doctoral Dissertation Research* on housing topics (information at (202) 708-3061), and the *Community Development Work Program*, created by Congress, which grants two-year scholarships to economically disadvantaged and minority graduate students in the field of community planning and economic development. The scholarships include work stipends up to $9,000 per year and $5,000 for costs of education. Total funding each year is $2 to $3 million. An application and/or informational brochures can obtained by calling 1(800) 245-2691.

Hispanic Serving Institutions Assisting Communities is designed to provide community development assistance to localities in which there are colleges or universities that serve the needs of Hispanic students. Targets of the assistance are neighborhood revitalization, better housing, and economic development, euphemisms for a desire that Hispanic-origin students can live in a decent, vital neighborhood while attending an institution of higher learning. The program is administered by HUD's Office of Policy Development and Research. The available funds are typically $6.5 million. Phone: 1(800) HUD-8959 (483-8959).

National American Indian Housing Council is eligible for grants to provide technical assistance for Indian housing on an annual basis. The Office of Policy Development and Research administers this grant, which has not exceeded $2.2 million.

Alaskan Native and Hawaiian Institutions is designed to provide community development assistance to localities in which there are colleges or universities that serve the needs of Alaskan or Hawaiian natives, with the institutions of higher learning serving as the applicants. Targets of the assistance are neighborhood revitalization, better housing, and economic development, so that students of these two native groups can live in a decent, vital neighborhood while attending an institution of higher learning. The program is administered by HUD's Office of Policy Development and Research. The available funds are typically $2 million, divided equally at $1 million for each ethnicity. No project can exceed one-third of the available funding. The application deadline is May 10, to be sent to the Processing and Control Branch, Office of Community Planning and Development, HUD, 451 Seventh Street SW, Room 7251, Washington, DC 20410. For information call SuperNOFA Information Center at 1(800) HUD-8929.

HUD Regional and Field Offices

HUD has administratively divided the country into 10 regions, each supervising numerous field offices. The regions and their field offices are:

Region I - New England Regional Office: 10 Causeway Street, Room 301, Boston, MA 02222-1092; Phone: (617) 994-8200; Fax: (617) 565-6558.

Field Offices: Bangor, Maine, 202 Harlow Street, Chase Building, Suite 101, Bangor, ME 04402-1384; Phone: (207) 945-0468. Hartford, Connecticut, One Corporate Center, Hartford, CT 06103-3220; Phone: (860) 240-4850. Manchester, New Hampshire, Norris Cotton Federal Building, 275 Chester Street, Manchester, NH 03103-248; Phone: (603) 666-7682. Providence, Rhode Island, 10 Weybosset Street, 6th Floor, Providence, RI 02903-2808; Phone: (401) 528-5352. Burlington, Vermont, 159 Bank Street, 2nd Floor, Burlington, VT 05401; Phone: (802) 951-6290.

Region II - New York/New Jersey Regional Office: 26 Federal Plaza - 3541, New York, NY 10278-0068; Phone: (212) 264-1161.

Field Offices: Albany, New York, 52 Corporate Circle, Albany, NY 12203-5121; Phone: (518) 464-4200. Buffalo, New York, Lafayette

Court, 5th Floor, 465 Main Street, Buffalo, NY 14203-1780; Phone: (716) 551-5733. Syracuse, New York, 128 Jefferson Street, Syracuse, NY 13202; Phone: (315) 477-0616. Newark, New Jersey, One Newark Center, 13th Floor, Newark, NJ 07102-5260; Phone: (973) 622-7619. Camden, New Jersey, 800 Hudson Square, 2nd Floor, Camden, NJ 08102-1156.

Region III - Mid-Atlantic Regional Office: Philadelphia, Pennsylvania, Wanamaker Building, 100 Penn Square East, Philadelphia, PA 19107-3380; Phone: (215) 656-0600.

Field Offices: Pittsburgh, Pennsylvania, 339 Sixth Avenue - 6th Floor, Pittsburgh, PA 15222-2515; Phone: (412) 644-5945. Wilmington, Delaware, 920 King Street, Suite 404, Wilmington, DE 19801-3016; Phone: (302) 573-6300. Baltimore, Maryland, 10 South Howard Street, 5th Floor; Phone: (410) 962-2520. Richmond, Virginia; Phone: (804) 771-2100. Washington, DC, 820 First Street NE, Suite 300, Washington, DC 20002-4205; Phone: (202) 275-9200. Charleston, West Virginia, 405 Capitol Street, Suite 708, Charleston, WV 25301-1795; Phone: (304) 347-7000.

Region IV - Southeast/Caribbean Regional Office: Atlanta, Georgia, Marietta Street - Five Points Plaza, Atlanta, GA 30303-2806; Phone: (404) 331-4111.

Field Offices: Birmingham, Alabama, 950 22nd Street North, Suite 900, Birmingham, AL 35203-2617; Phone: (205) 731-2630. Louisville, Kentucky, 601 West Broadway, Louisville, KY 40402; Phone: (502) 582-5251. Jacksonville, Florida, 301 West Bay Street, Suite 2200, Jacksonville, FL 32202-5121; Phone: (904) 232-3759. Miami, Florida, 909 SE First Avenue, Miami, FL 33131; Phone: (305) 536-5678. Orlando, Florida, 3751 Maguire Boulevard, Room 270, Orlando, FL 32803-3032; Phone: (407) 648-6441. Tampa, Florida, 500 Zack Street, Suite 402, Tampa, FL 33602; Phone: (813) 228-2026. Greensboro, North Carolina, Koger Building, 2306 West Meadowview Road, Greensboro, NC 27401-3707; Phone: (336) 547-4001. Columbia, South Carolina, 1835 Assembly Street, Columbia, SC 29201-2480; Phone: (803) 765-5592. Jackson, Mississippi, 100 West Capitol Street, Room 910, Jackson, MS 39269-1096; Phone: (601) 965-4700; Nashville, Tennessee, 235 Cumberland Bend, Suite 200, Nashville, TN 37228-1803; Phone: (615) 736-5213. Knoxville, Tennessee, 710 Locust Street SW, Knoxville, TN 37902-2526; Phone: (803) 765-5592; Memphis, Tennessee, 200 Jefferson Avenue, Suite 1200, Memphis, TN 38103-2335; San Juan, Puerto Rico, 171 Carlos East Chardon Avenue, San Juan, PR 00918-0903; Phone: (787) 766-5201.

Region V - Midwest Regional Office: Chicago, Illinois, Ralph Metcalfe Federal Building, 77 West Jackson Boulevard, Chicago, IL 60604-3507; Phone: (312) 353-5680.

Field Offices: Springfield, Illinois, 320 West Washington, 7th Floor, Springfield, IL 62707; Phone: (217) 492-4120. Indianapolis, Indiana, 151 North Delaware Street, Suite 1200, Indianapolis, IN 46204-2526; Phone: (317) 226-6303; Detroit, Michigan, 477 Michigan Avenue, Detroit, MI 48226-2592; Phone: (313) 226-7900. Flint, Michigan, 1101 South Saginaw Street, Flint, MI 48502-1953; Phone: (810) 766-5110. Grand Rapids, Michigan, Trade Center Building, 50 Louis Street NW, Grand Rapids, MI 49503-2633; Phone: (616) 456-2100. Minneapolis, Minnesota, Kinnard Financial Center, 920 Second Avenue South, Minneapolis, MN 55402; Phone: (612) 370-3000. Columbus, Ohio, Phone: (614) 469-7540. Cincinnati, Ohio, 415 East Seventh Street, Cincinnati, OH 45202-2401; Phone: (513) 684-3451; Cleveland, Ohio, 1350 Euclid Avenue, Suite 500, Cleveland, OH 44115-1815; Phone: (216) 522-4058. Milwaukee, Wisconsin, 310 West Wisconsin Avenue, Room 1380, Milwaukee, WI 53203-2289; Phone: (414) 297-3214.

Region VI - Southwest Regional Office: Fort Worth, Texas, 801 Cherry Street, P.O. Box 2905, Fort Worth, TX 76113-2905; Phone: (817) 978-5980.

Field Offices: Dallas, Texas, 525 Griffin Street, Room 86, Dallas, TX 75202-5007; Phone: (214) 767-8300. Houston, Texas, 2211 Norfolk, #200, Houston, TX 77098; Phone: (713) 313-2274. Lubbock, Texas, 1205 Texas Avenue, Room 5111, Lubbock, TX 79401-4093; Phone: (806) 472-7265. San Antonio, Texas, 800 Delorosa, San Antonio, TX 78207-4563; Phone: (210) 475-6806. Little Rock, Arkansas, 425 West Capitol Avenue, 900, Little Rock, AR 72201-3488; Phone: (501) 324-5931. New Orleans, Louisiana, Hale Boggs Building, 501 Magazine Street, 9th Floor, New Orleans, LA 70130-3099; Phone: (504) 589-7201. Shreveport, Louisiana, 401 Edwards Street, Room 1510, Shreveport, LA 71101-3289; Albuquerque, New Mexico, 625 Silver Avenue SW, Suite 100, Albuquerque, NM 87102; Phone: (505) 346-6463. Oklahoma City, Oklahoma, 500 West Main Street, Suite 400; Phone: (405) 553-7500. Tulsa, Oklahoma, 1516 South Boston Avenue, Suite 100, Tulsa, OK 74119; Phone: (918) 581-7496.

Region VII - Great Plains Regional Office: Kansas City, 400 State Avenue, Room 200, Kansas City, KS 66101-2406; Phone: (913) 551-5462.

Field Offices: Des Moines, Iowa, 210 Walnut Street, Room 239, Des Moines, IA 50309-2155; Phone: (515) 284-4573. Omaha, Nebraska, 10909 Mill Valley Road, Suite 100, Omaha, NE 68154-3955; Phone: (402) 492-3103. St. Louis, Missouri, 1222 Spruce Street, #3207, St. Louis, MO 63103-2836; Phone: (314) 539-6384.

Region VIII - Rocky Mountains Regional Office, Denver, Colorado, 633 17th Street, 14th Floor, Denver, CO 80202-3607; Phone: (303) 672-5440.

Field Offices: Helena, Montana, 7 West 6th Avenue, Helena, MT 59601; Phone: (406) 449-5050. Fargo, North Dakota, 657 Second Avenue North, Room 366, Fargo, ND 58108; Phone: (701) 239-5040. Sioux Falls, South Dakota, 2400 West 49th Street, Room I-201, Sioux Falls, SD 57105-6558; Phone: (605) 330-4223. Salt Lake City, Utah, 125 South State Street, Suite 3001, Salt Lake City, UT 84138; Phone: (801) 524-6070. Casper, Wyoming, 100 East 8 Street, Room 1010, Casper, WY 82601-1969; Phone: (307) 261-6251.

Region IX - Pacific/Hawaii Regional Office, San Francisco, California, 450 Golden Gate Avenue, San Francisco, CA 94102-3448; Phone: (415) 436-6560.

Field Offices: Los Angeles, California, 611 West Sixth Street, Suite 800, Los Angeles, CA 90017; Phone: (213) 894-8007. Fresno, California, 2135 Fresno Street, Suite 100, Fresno, CA 93721-1718; Phone: (559) 487-5032; Sacramento, California, 925 L Street, Sacramento, CA 95814; Phone: (916) 498-5220. San Diego, California, Symphony Towers, 750 B Street, Suite 1600, San Diego, CA 92101-8131; Phone (619) 557-5310. Santa Ana, California, 1600 North Broadway, Suite 101, Santa Ana, CA 92706-2927; Phone: (714) 796-TK. Phoenix, Arizona, One Central Avenue, Suite 600, Phoenix, AZ 85004; Phone: (602) 379-7100. Tucson, Arizona, 160 North Stone Avenue, Tucson, AZ 85701-1467; Phone: (520) 670-6000. Honolulu, 500 Ala Moana Boulevard, Suite 3A, Honolulu, HI 96813-4918; Phone: (808) 522-8175. Las Vegas, Nevada, 333 North Rancho Drive, Atrium Building, Suite 700, Las Vegas, NV 898106-3714; Phone: (702) 388-6500. Reno, Nevada, 3702 South Virginia Street, Reno, NV 89502-6581; Phone: (775) 784-5356.

Region X - Northwest/Alaska Regional Office: Seattle, Washington, 909 First Avenue, Suite 200, Seattle, WA 98104-1000; Phone: (206) 220-5101.

Field Offices: Spokane, Washington, U.S. Courthouse Building, 920 West Riverside,

Suite 588, Spokane, WA 99201-1010; Phone: (509) 353-0674. Anchorage, Alaska, 949 East 36th Avenue, Suite 401, Anchorage, AK 99508-4399; Phone: (907) 271-4470. Boise, Idaho, Plaza IV, Suite 220, 800 Park Boulevard, Boise, ID 83712-7743; Phone: (208) 334-1990. Portland, Oregon, 400 SW 6th Avenue #700, Portland, OR 97204-1632; Phone: (503) 326-2561.

Housing Counseling: HUD maintains a housing counseling service to give members of the public advice on home purchase, renting, defaults, mortgage foreclosures, credits, and various types of mortgages, including so-called reverse mortgages. This counseling service can be reached by telephone at 1(888) 466-3487. The caller can ask for a Spanish-speaking adviser. In each state there is a HUD-approved agency for housing counseling, and the list of such local services can be obtained at the above toll-free number.

Secondary Mortgage Market

Background: Prior to the enactment of the National Housing Act in 1934, the average family had a difficult time in financing a home because the usual down payment was not less than 40 percent of the purchase price with a loan secured by a relatively short-term mortgage (in some states like California, called a deed of trust) on the purchased property. Worse yet, as the Great Depression deepened, many homeowners with mortgages defaulted due to unemployment or depressed business conditions. Many banks were in financial jeopardy or bankrupt since they could not collect on the mortgages. The home building industry, including the workers in construction such as carpenters, plumbers, electricians, and both skilled and unskilled tradesmen, were in economic distress.

The FHA loan insurance program inaugurated in 1934 permitted qualified banks to make home loans without fear of default, and in amounts and at rates that the average family could afford, thus stimulating movement of funding into the housing finance market. However, the financial institutions needed a source to replace the funds, which were loaned so that there could be even more money to fund home loans.

FEDERAL NATIONAL MORTGAGE ASSOCIATION (FANNIE MAE)

The solution was the chartering on February 10, 1938, of a government corporation entitled the Federal National Mortgage Association, more commonly known by the friendly name Fannie Mae. This was possible under existing authority included in the 1934 Federal Housing Act, but Fannie Mae was the only corporation chartered under that act. Its purpose was to refinance FHA-insured mortgages, thus in effect buying from banks and other lending institutions existing insured promissory notes secured by these mortgages. Thus was born the government-supported "secondary mortgage market."

Facing the pent-up demand for new housing that had accumulated during World War II, Congress enacted the Serviceman's Readjustment Act of 1944, pursuant to which the Veterans' Administration began guaranteeing the so-called VA loans to ex-servicemen along the lines of the existing FHA loan insurance. Fannie Mae also served as a secondary market for these loans. In 1954 this government corporation was converted to a private-government corporation in which the United States government owned the preferred shares and the common stock was sold to the public.

Under the leadership of Fannie Mae president Raymond Lapin, previously the innovative founder of a major mortgage brokerage, appointed by President Lyndon Johnson, FNMA was divided by Congress into two entities: (1) Fannie Mae, to be transformed into a fully private corporation concentrating on the purchase of government insured mortgages subject to considerable government control through HUD, and (2) a new entity, the Government National Mortgage Association, called Ginnie Mae, which would be a secondary mortgage market for FHA, VA, and certain other government guaranteed loans.

Under its statutory charter, Fannie Mae received the right to purchase loans in excess of FHA limits, but its concentration would be for acquiring loans for low-, moderate- and middle-income home owners or multifamily building tenants. The annual share of the loans that must be made available to low- and moderate-income families is set by the secretary of HUD. The standard maximum limitation for home owners is at or below the estimated "median" family income in the population of the particular community. Because of exceptionally high real estate prices in certain areas, there are exceptions that allow loans well in excess of the median family income. For example, in 2002 there were eight areas in which loans at higher percentages of the median were permitted: California 140 percent, Hawaii 170 percent, New York City 165 percent, Boston 135 percent, Seattle 120 percent, Newark 125 percent, Bergen Passaic, New Jersey 120 percent, and Portland, Oregon 120 percent.

Beginning in 1971, Fannie Mae was authorized by the Emergency Home Finance Act of 1970 to purchase "conventional" loans that were not insured by the government and to introduce its own mortgages secured by securities based on a pool of mortgages. By the 1980s the more flexible Fannie Mae began purchasing second mortgages, which had become increasingly popular in the spiraling increase in home prices. This private source provided an additional flow of funds into the mortgage market.

Like all the government-initiated home loan programs, it is subject to strict fair-housing requirements. It has become proactive by establishing a program of secondary financing of minority and women-owned businesses, or MWOB. For information contact: MWOB Program, 4000 Wisconsin Avenue NW, Mailstop: 2H-4N-05, Washington, DC 20016. Over $200 million in various products and services are sold each year in addition to its secondary mortgage purchases.

Fannie Mae's popularity and effectiveness are demonstrated by the fact that over the years it has indirectly financed more than 40 million homes, and is the nation's largest source of home mortgage financing. It receives no assistance from the government, is traded on the New York Stock Exchange, and has been consistently profitable to its investors. However, in 2003, there were claims of mismanagement which led to executive resignations.

CONTACT Address: Federal National Mortgage Association, 4000 Wisconsin Avenue NW, Washington, DC 20036; Phone: (202) 752-6770; Website: www.fanniemae.com; for direct business www.eFannieMae.com.

GOVERNMENT NATIONAL MORTGAGE ASSOCIATION (GINNIE MAE)

Ginnie Mae is owned by the government and remains an integral part of HUD, and is particularly useful in purchasing FHA-insured loans for low- and moderate-income sponsors. The president of Ginnie Mae is appointed by the president with Senate confirmation, with career incumbents filling the positions of executive vice president and senior adviser to the president of the corporation.

Ginnie Mae also began issuing loans secured by mortgages with the loans funded through the issuance of mortgage-backed securities (MBS). Sale of these securities is attractive as they are backed by a pool of mortgage loans, mortgage backed bonds, so-called pass through securities, and other instruments in which real property is the ultimate underlying security. The success of the Ginnie Mae MBS program is demonstrated by the fact that on average there is more than

$600 billion of these mortgages outstanding at any one time, and the cumulative amount issued has surpassed $1.7 trillion. More than 23 million households have benefited by the purchase of their mortgages by Ginnie Mae.

CONTACT Address: Government National Mortgage Association, HUD headquarters, Room 6100; Phone: (202) 755-5926; Website: www.ginniemae.gov.

FEDERAL HOME LOAN MORTGAGE CORPORATION (FREDDIE MAC)

Freddie Mac is a stockholder-owned corporation chartered by Congress in 1970 at the same time Fannie Mae and Ginnie Mae were divided. It provides an additional mechanism for funding home loans by providing a stream of investment funds for purchase of home mortgages of both individual home owners and for rental housing. Since its founding it has funded more than 26 million families.

The key financing mechanism of Freddie Mac is the participation certificate (Gold PC), each of which represents an undivided interest in a pool of residential mortgages. For investors interested in both safety and liquidity these certificates are a popular investment. The goal of Freddie Mac is to provide funding for affordable housing, both ownership and rental, at an annual required percentage of loans set annually by the secretary of HUD.

CONTACT There are several headquarters offices located in northern Virginia: three buildings 8100, 8200, and 8250 Jones Branch Drive, McLean VA 22102-3110, 1769 and 1771 Business Center Drive, P.O. Box 4180, Reston, VA 20195-1759, with telephone numbers at (703) 903-2000, 918-5000, 714-2500, 450-3199, and 450-3000. Any of these numbers will connect the caller to an information center. Try also www.freddiemac. com, which will provide means to apply for busi-

ness or other information. There are also regional offices: Northeast: 1410 Springhill Road, Suite 600, McLean, VA 22101-8922; Phone: (703) 902-7700. North Central: 333 West Wacker Drive, Suite 2500, Chicago, IL 60606-1287; Phone (312) 407-7400. Southeast: North Tower Suite 200, 2300 Windy Ridge Parkway SE, Atlanta, GA 30339-5671; Phone (770) 857-8800. Southwest: 5000 Plano Parkway, Carrolton, TX 75010; Phone: (972) 395-4000. Western: 21700 Oxnard Street, Suite 1900, Woodland Hills, CA 91367-3821; Phone: (818) 710-3000. There are also offices in New York: 975 Lexington Avenue, Suite 1800, New York, NY 10022-6102; Phone: (212) 418-8900 and Washington, DC: 401 9th Street NW, Suite 600 South, Washington, DC 20004; Phone: (202) 434-8600.

OFFICE OF FEDERAL HOUSING ENTERPRISE OVERSIGHT

Fannie Mae and Freddie Mac, privately owned corporations with publicly traded shares, under congressionally granted charters, are exempt from SECURITIES AND EXCHANGE COMMISSION registration and from state and local taxation. At the same time their combined assets (2000) exceed $2.4 trillion, and their impact on the economy is tremendous. To provide independent oversight of these corporations necessary to guarantee prudent and legal conduct, Congress enacted the Federal Housing Enterprises Financial Safety and Soundness Act of 1992 to create the Office of Federal Housing Oversight.

The director of this office is appointed by the President for a five-year term subject to Senate confirmation.

Primary responsibility of the office is to ensure the financial soundness of the two institutions, much like the comptroller of the currency, the FEDERAL DEPOSIT INSURANCE CORPORATION, or the governors of the Federal Reserve System. It conducts quarterly examinations of both corporations, and by regulation sets minimal capital standards based on a low level of risk and low-stress interest rates. The office also prohibits excessive executive compensation. It also determines whether Fannie Mae and Freddie Mac met the annual share of purchasing loans for low- and moderate-income persons established each year by the secretary of HUD. It may also take legal action to require compliance. It is a self-supporting agency as its costs are paid by fees charged to the two regulated corporations.

WEBSITE www.ofheo.gov.

FEDERAL HOUSING FINANCE BOARD

Established as an independent regulatory agency by the Financial Institutions Reform, Recovery and Enforcement Act of 1989. Although independent, the board is an adjunct to the DEPARTMENT OF HOUSING AND URBAN DEVELOPMENT as a guarantor of the fiscal and management integrity of the home loan functions of the 12 regional Federal Home Loan Banks. To a considerable extent it replaces the former Federal Home Loan Bank Board, which had monitored these banks, which were established by legislation in 1932 as a pre–New Deal effort to provide a flow of funds for home ownership.

ORGANIZATION

The board is composed of five members, four presidential appointees with Senate confirmation for staggered seven-year terms, and the secretary of housing and urban development or his/her designee. It is funded by assessments from the 12 regional banks without any government appropriations. There are currently 7,929 banks, savings and loan associations (generically called "thrifts"), credit unions, and insurance companies that make home loans through various government-guaranteed programs such as

Federal Housing Administration. The staff is primarily technical personnel with knowledge of finance, economics, housing, and banking.

CONTACT Address: 1777 F Street NW, Washington, DC 20006; Phone: (202) 408-2500; Website: www.fhfb.gov.

FUNCTIONS

The board's key activity is constant supervision of the member regional banks and the institutions to which they provide a flow of funds, and to insure that the banks are adequately capitalized, that their lending practices, including levels of interest charged and sufficiency of loan security, are prudent and safe. To fulfill this function the board: (a) prescribes rules and regulations governing these practices, (b) maintains databases and records, (c) oversees implementation of programs such as affordable housing and community investment guaranteed through HUD, (d) requires independent audits of all banks making home loans, (e) makes an annual examination of each of the 12 Home Loan Banks, (e) every two years reviews community support performances of each member bank, (f) appoints a "public interest" member to the board of directors to each of the Federal Home Loan Banks, (g) sets rules for election of other FHMLB bank directors, (h) establishes standards for approval of membership of individual banks in the home loan bank system, and (i) supervises the operation of the Office of Finance, which is the fiscal agent for the Home Loan Banks.

The Housing Finance Board issues the results of a monthly Interest Rate Survey, and maintains a reading room at its headquarters.

The dozen supervised regional Home Loan Banks provide a steady flow of funds to allow member institutions to lend to home buyers. This is a complex and varied process that includes making sure that all loans are adequately collateralized, purchasing mortgages from member banks (so they can make new loans), issuing short-term letters of credit, and providing subsidized funds for affordable rental housing programs for lending banks with a solid financial record. Certain community-based programs for small businesses and family farmers are also financed by these banks.

In the wake of the crisis of failing and poorly managed savings and loans, the Competitive Equality Banking Act of 1987 created the Financing Corporation (FICO) to issue bonds that could be used to fund resolution of thrift underfunding. FICO consists of the managing director of the Office of Finance and two Home Loan Bank presidents, based on regulations set out and monitored by the Federal Housing Finance Board.

DEPARTMENT OF INTERIOR

GENERAL

The Department of Interior's eight bureaus act as the nation's principal conservation agency to protect and provide access to our nation's natural and cultural resources and heritage and honor the trust responsibilities to American Indians and Alaska Natives and commitments to island communities. It also conducts scientific research; manages energy, mineral, land, and water resources; and works to conserve and protect fish and wildlife at 2,400 locations throughout the United States, Puerto Rico, U.S. territories, and "freely associated states." At the same time it leases out federal land for mining and energy production.

The Department of Interior (DOI) manages 507 million acres of surface land, including 262 million acres managed by the Bureau of Land Management, 95 million acres managed by the Fish and Wildlife Service, 84 million acres managed by the National Park Service, 8.6 million acres managed by the Bureau of Reclamation, 56 million acres managed by the

Bureau of Indian Affairs, and 180,000 acres of abandoned coal mines reclaimed by the Office of Surface Mining's Abandoned Mine Land Program.

According to DOI, federally managed lands and offshore acreage supply about 28 percent of the national energy production, including 35 percent of natural gas, 29 percent of oil, 35 percent of coal, 17 percent of hydroelectric power, and 40 percent of geothermal power.

ORGANIZATION

The department is headed by a secretary, who is appointed by the president and confirmed by the Senate and aided by a deputy secretary and five assistant secretaries, each appointed by the president and approved by the Senate. Assistant secretaries are responsible for wildlife and parks, land and mineral management, Indian affairs, and science, respectively, and one serves as the chief financial officer of the department.

HISTORY

Congress passed a bill on March 3, 1849, creating the Home Department to take charge of internal affairs of the United States, thereby consolidating the General Land Office from the DEPARTMENT OF THE TREASURY; the Patent Office from the DEPARTMENT OF STATE; the Indian Affairs Office from the War Department; and military pension offices from the War and Navy Departments. DOI originally had a much wider range of responsibilities than it does now, including construction of the national capital's water system; taking a census; colonization of freed slaves in Haiti; exploration of the western wilderness; oversight and management of the District of Columbia jail; regulation of territorial governments; management of all hospitals and universities; public park management; and management of Indian affairs, public lands, patents, and pensions.

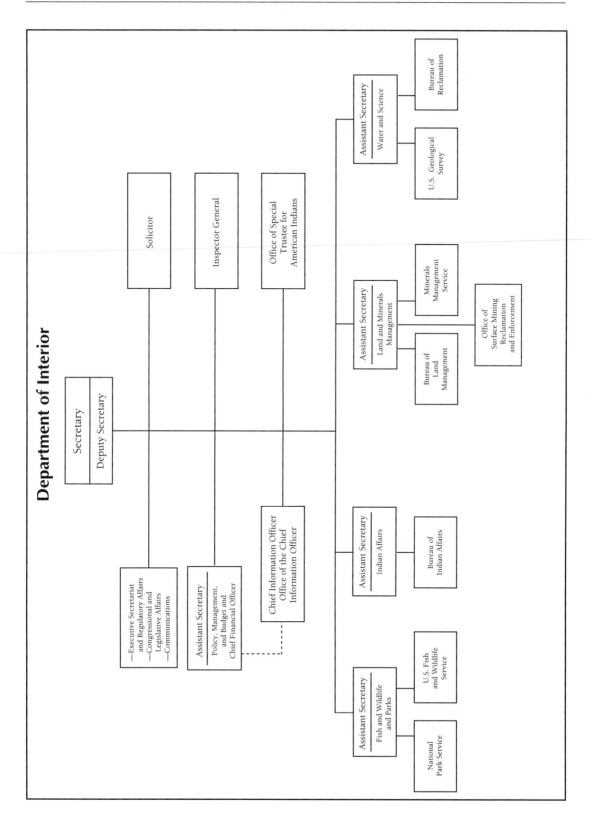

Department of Interior

From 1850 to 1900 Interior's predecessors were busy. Its Mexican Boundary Commission established the border between the United States and Mexico; its Pacific Wagon Road Office improved western emigrant routes and began its geological survey of the western territories with the Hayden expedition, and created the U.S. Geological Survey; the Bureau of Education came under Interior's purview; established Yellowstone as the first national park; established the Bureau of Labor, which became the DEPARTMENT OF LABOR; Congress established Interstate Commerce Commission within the department; and the Dawes Act authorized land allotments to Indians.

The Bureau of Reclamation was created in 1902 to build dams and aqueducts in the West. In 1903 President Theodore Roosevelt established the first National Wildlife Refuge at Pelican Island, Florida (not to be confused with Pelican Bay federal prison in California). The Bureau of Mines was created in 1910 to promote mine safety and minerals technology, and in 1916 President Woodrow Wilson signed legislation creating the National Park Service. The Mineral Leasing Act of 1920 gave the federal government the right to rental payments and royalties on oil, gas, and mineral production. Between 1925 and 1930 the Patent Office was transferred to the Department of Commerce, and the Bureau of Pensions went to the Veterans Administration.

1934 was a busy year at Interior: The Taylor Grazing Act gave the government the right to regulate economic (business) use of public lands; the first Migratory Bird Hunting stamp was issued; the Indian Reorganization Act got rid of the land allotment system dating from 1887, allowed formation of tribal governments, and affirmed the secretary of interior's Indian trust responsibilities. Alaska, Hawaii, Virgin Islands, and Puerto Rico oversight responsibilities were transferred to the Department of Interior.

The Bureau of Reclamation completed Hoover Dam in 1935. In 1940 the Bureau of Fisheries and the Bureau of Biological Survey combined to form the U.S. Fish and Wildlife Service. The General Land office and the Grazing Service merged to create the Bureau of Land Management in 1946. In 1950 and 1951 Interior expanded its jurisdiction to include Guam, American, Samoa, and the Trust Territory of the Pacific Islands.

Following strip mining abuses, the office of Surface Mining Reclamation and Enforcement was established in 1977 to oversee state regulation of strip coal mining and the repair of environmental damage left by mining companies and practices. 1980's Alaska National Interest Lands Conservation Act added 47 million acres to the National Park System and 54 acres to the National Wildlife Refuge System. Two years later, the Minerals Management Service was established to collect mineral revenues and manage the Outer Continental Shelf offshore lands.

In 1993 President Bill Clinton convened the Northwest Forest Plan Summit and released the "Forest Plan for a Sustainable Economy and Sustainable Environment," and in 2002 President George W. Bush introduced the so-called Healthy Forests Initiative. In the mid-90s Interior introduced gray wolves into Yellowstone National Park, and Interior's science and technology's functions were consolidated under the U.S. Geological Survey.

BUREAUS

NATIONAL PARK SERVICE

Created by Congress on August 25, 1916, under President Woodrow Wilson, the National Park Service now includes 8,000 miles of roads, 763 miles of paved trails, 12,250 miles of unpaved trails, 1,804 bridges and tunnels, 680 water and wastewater systems, 8,505 monuments, more than 400 dams, and more than 200 solid waste operations, with properties in every state except Delaware. By executive order, President Franklin D. Roosevelt transferred 63 national monuments and military sites from the Forest Service and from the War Department to the National Park Service in 1933.

The original "National Park Service Organic Act" signed by Wilson stated that "the Service thus established shall promote and regulate the use of Federal areas known as national parks, monuments and reservations . . . by such means and measures as conform to the fundamental purpose of the said parks, monuments and reservations, which purpose is to conserve the scenery and the natural and historic objects and the wild life therein and to provide for the enjoyment of the same in such manner and by such means as will leave them unimpaired for the enjoyment of future generations."

The National Park Service oversees 83.6 million acres in 49 states, the District of Columbia, American Samoa, Guam, Puerto Rico, Saipan, and the Virgin Islands. It holds 54.7 million acres in Alaska, which has the largest park, Wrangell-St. Elias National Park and Preserve with 13.2 million acres (16.3 percent of the National Park System). The largest park in the contiguous states is Death Valley National Park (3.3 million acres), the smallest is Thaddeus Kosciuszko National Memorial in Pennsylvania, and the oldest is Yellowstone (1872). Approximately 3.2 percent of U.S. land is in the National Park System.

Currently, additions to the National Park System and new parks are made by congressional act, although under the Antiquities Act of 1906, the president may proclaim national monuments on lands already under federal jurisdiction.

The National Park System Advisory Board advises the secretary of the interior on policies for management of the parks as well as on potential additions to the system.

The National Park Service also runs the National Register of Historic Places, national historic landmarks, historic and technical preservation services, the historic American buildings survey, the historic American engineering record, interagency archeological services, the national wild and scenic rivers system, and the national trails system.

National Park System designations all have equal legal standing. *National Park* is usually a large natural place with various attributes, including possibly historic. No hunting, mining, or "consumptive activities" are allowed. *National Monument* includes structures or other historic or scientific objects on land owned or controlled by the government. *National Preserve* is similar to a national park, except Congress permits public hunting, trapping, and oil and gas exploration and extraction. Some national preserves where there is no sport hunting, could be switched to national parks. *National Historic Site* usually has one primary historic feature and is designated by acts of Congress, although some are established by the secretary of the interior. *National Historic Park* applies to historic parks that include more than one property or building. *National Memorial* commemorates a historic person or occurrence, and does not have to be located in a site related to it historically. *National Battlefield* may include a national battlefield or national battlefield park, a national battlefield site, or a national military park.

The designation *National Cemetery* includes 14 cemeteries in the National Park System. *National Recreation Area* includes 12 areas on large reservoirs and features water-based recreation, and five are in or near major population centers, the latter providing urban open space with preservation of historic resources and natural areas. *National Seashore* includes 10 seashores on the Atlantic, Gulf, and Pacific coasts, many of which allow hunting. *National Lakeshore* is similar to a designated seashore, but is all on the Great Lakes. *National River* includes national river and recreation area, national scenic river, wild river, and others. *National Parkway* is a roadway or parkland parallel to a roadway, intended for scenic driving along a protected corridor, sometimes connecting historic or cultural sites. *National Trail* may be a national scenic trail or a national historic trail, which are linear parklands and are authorized under the National Trails System Act of 1968. *Affiliated Areas* includes certain locations in the United States and Canada that preserve properties outside the National Park System. *Other Designations* in the National Park Service are unique and include the WHITE HOUSE and Prince William Forest Park.

CONTACT Address: National Park Service, 1849 C Street NW, Washington, DC 20240; Phone: (202) 208-6843. Regional Offices: Alaska Area, 2525 Gambell Street, Room 107, Anchorage, AK 99503; Phone: (907) 257-2687. Midwest Region, 1709 Jackson Street, Omaha, NE 68102; Phone: (402) 221-3471. Intermountain Region, 12795 Alameda Parkway, Denver, CO 80225; Phone: (303) 969-2500. Pacific West Region, One Jackson Center, 1111 Jackson Street, Suite 700, Oakland, CA 94607; Phone: (510) 817-1300. Northeast Region, U.S. Custom House, 200 Chestnut Street, 5th Floor, Philadelphia, PA 19106; Phone: (215) 597-7013. National Capital Region, 1100 Ohio Drive SW, Washington, DC 20242; Phone: (202) 619-7222. Southeast Region, 100 Alabama Street SW, 1924 Building, Atlanta, GA 30303; Phone: (404) 562-3100.

UNITED STATES FISH AND WILDLIFE SERVICE

The Bureau of Fisheries was established in 1871 and was later put under the Department of Commerce. The Department of Agriculture's Bureau of Biological Survey started in 1885, and in 1939 the two offices were moved to the Department of Interior. In 1940 they were consolidated into the Fish and Wildlife Service. The U.S. Fish and Wildlife Service (FWS) works to conserve, protect, and enhance fish, wildlife, and plants and their habitats. It improves habitats for migratory birds, some marine animals, freshwater and anadromous fish, works to protect 1,818 endangered or threatened species, and to prevent and control invasive species.

FWS runs 540 National Wildlife Refuges covering about 95 million acres, 69 National Fish Hatcheries that produce 150 million fish annually, and includes 3,000 miles of dikes, 10,000 miles of fencing, and 23,000 water control structures.

CONTACT Address: 1849 C Street NW, Washington, DC 20240, 4401 N. Fairfax Drive, Arlington, VA 22203; Phone: (202) 208-5634; Website: http://fws.gov.

PROGRAMS

FWS national programs include Bird Habitat Conservation, Coastal Habitat Conservation, contaminants, cultural and archeological resources, duck stamps, ecosystems, environmental quality, fire management, fisheries, medicinal plants, migratory bird management, national surveys of fishing, hunting, and wildlife-associated recreation National Wildlife Refuges, geographic information systems and spatial data, wetlands habitat conservation, shorebirds, sport fishing and boating, and waterfowl.

The Endangered Species Program works with American Indians to conserve natural habitats with sensitivity to tribal culture and tradition; works on habitat conservation planning with landowners to integrate building development plans with conservation of endangered species in the area; works on international agreements to protect migratory species across North America and to regulate trade in endangered species; and makes up the lists of endangered species. As follow-up, ESP also recovers and enhances populations of listed species so that they can be taken off the list. It also makes up the lists of threatened and endangered plants, compiles statistics, and maintains a Kids Corner on its website.

CONTACT Address: General: Endangered Species Program, 4401 N. Fairfax Drive, Room 420, Arlington, VA 22203. Regional offices:

Division of Endangered Species, Eastside Federal Complex, 911 NE 11th Avenue, Portland, OR 97232-4181; Website: http://pacific.fws.gov/es/endsp.htm. Division of Endangered Species, P.O. Box 1306, Albuquerque, NM 87103; Website: http://ifw2es.fws.gov/EndangeredSpecies. Ecological Services Operations, Bishop Henry Federal Building, One Federal Drive, Fort Snelling, MN 55111-4056; Website: http://midwest.fws.gov/endangered. Division of Endangered Species, 1875 Century Boulevard, Suite 200, Atlanta, GA 30345. Division of Endangered Species, 300 Westgate Center Drive, Hadley, MA 01035; Website: http://northeast.fws.gov. Endangered Species Program, U.S. Fish and Wildlife Service, Lakewood, CO 80225; Website: http://mountain-prairie.fws.gov/endspp/. Division of Endangered Species, 1011 E. Tudor Road, Anchorage, AK 99503; Website: http://www.r7.fws.gov/es/te.html.

The National Wildlife Refuge System includes more than 500 national wildlife refuges, and recognizes sport fishing and hunting as acceptable, traditional forms of wildlife-oriented recreation to manage and manipulate wildlife population levels.

WEBSITE http://refuges.fws.gov/.

Its Fire Management Branch in Boise, Idaho, works to manage fire use and fire preparedness and suppression.

The National Wetlands Inventory is a computer center in Florida that keeps track of the characteristics, extent, and status of U.S. wetlands and deepwater habitats, and has mapped 90 percent of the lower 48 states and 34 percent of Alaska. NWI also must produce status and trends reports to Congress every 10 years. NWI also produces manuals, plant and hydric soils lists, field guides, posters, wall-sized maps, atlases, and state reports.

WEBSITE http://wetlands.fws.gov/.

The Division of Migratory Bird Management tracks, manages, and conserves migratory birds and their habitats in sufficient quantities to keep them off the threatened or endangered lists in the United States. It also works to make sure U.S. citizens can enjoy "consumptive and nonconsumptive uses of migratory birds and their habitats." MBM also produces handy bird pamphlets on migratory and backyard birds.

WEBSITE http://migratorybirds.fws.gov/.

FWS's Air Quality Branch works to protect air quality in support of ecosystem management in the National Wildlife Refuge System, particularly in the 21 wilderness areas designated as Class I under the Clean Air Act through air quality monitoring and research, regulatory development, permit reviews, and public awareness.

WEBSITE http://www2.nature.nps.gov/ard/fws/fwsaqb.htm.

The Coastal Habitat Conservation Programs identify coastal resource problems and solutions, and develop public and private partnerships to work the on-the-ground conservation projects in the country's 15 highest-priority coastal areas. This program has protected 1,066,460 acres and restored 100,720 acres of coastal habitats since 1994, reopened 3,330 miles of coastal streams for anadromous fish passage, and restored 825 miles of riparian or streamside habitats. Coastal Wetlands Conservation Grants are awarded yearly on a competition basis to coastal states for acquisition, restoration, or enhancement of coastal wetlands and tidelands.

CONTACT Address: U.S. Fish and Wildlife Service, Branch of Habitat Restoration, 4401 N. Fairfax Drive, Arlington, VA 22203; Phone: (703) 358-2201; Fax: (703) 358-2232; Website: www.fws.gov/cep/coastweb.html.

FWS's Division of Environmental Quality honors former colleague and author Rachel Carson, whose 1962 book *Silent Spring* outlined the widespread harmful effects of pesticides in and on the environment. The public awakening caused by that book contributed to development and enactment of the National Environmental Policy Act, the Clean Water Act, the Clean Air Act, the Federal Insecticide, Fungicide and Rodenticide Act, the Safe Drinking Water Act, the Toxic Substances Control Act, and the "Superfund" toxic waste clean up law.

CONTACT Address: Division of Environmental Quality, 4401 N. Fairfax Drive, Suite 322, Arlington, VA 22203; Phone: (703) 358-2148; Website: http://contaminants.fws.gov/.

Today the Environmental Contaminants Program has contaminants specialists at more than 75 locations throughout the United States who specialize in detecting toxic chemicals; looking at the effects of those chemicals; preventing harm to fish, wildlife, and their habitats; and removing toxic chemicals and restoring a habitat when harm is already done. They also focus on oil and chemical spills, pesticides, water quality, hazardous waste disposal, and general pollution biology.

The Green Medicine Program actually encourages and does research on use of plants for natural medicines, from goldenseal and ginseng, to echinacea, ginkgo, and taxol from the bark of the Pacific yew in the Pacific Northwest.

WEBSITE www.nps.gov/plants/medicinal/.

President George W. Bush proposed a $698.7 million Healthy Forests Initiative to cut forest to prevent fires and manage forests, including continued funding of the hazardous fuels treatment program, fire preparedness including contracts with airplane fire fighters, fire suppression, rehabilitating burned areas, and Rural Fire Assistance. This proposal produced a firestorm of controversy over the amount of logging permitted in this program.

BUREAU OF INDIAN AFFAIRS

Established by the secretary of war on March 11, 1824, the Bureau of Indian Affairs (BIA) works to fulfill its trust responsibilities and promote self-determination on behalf of tribal governments, American Indians, and Alaska Natives. BIA is the principal agent of the U.S. government in rela-

tionships among more than 562 sovereign, federally recognized American Indian tribes and 223 village groups in Alaska, including 275 Indian reservations with their own local governing authority. The Navajo Reservation includes about 16 million acres in Arizona, New Mexico, and Utah, and is the largest reservation. The Department of Interior manages 185 Indian schools.

Once the enforcer of federal policies that subjugated and assimilated American Indians, matters relating to Indians were governed by the Continental Congress, which created the Committee on Indian Affairs in 1775, headed by Benjamin Franklin. Once run by the superintendent of Indian trade in the War Department (1806), BIA's predecessor was established in the War Department in 1824, where it was referred to as the "Indian Office." In 1887 the General Allotment Act opened Indian lands west of the Mississippi River to non-Indian settlers. In 1924 the Indian Citizenship Act gave Indians the right to vote, and the Indian Reorganization Act of 1934, part of President Franklin D. Roosevelt's New Deal, established and allowed modern tribal governments. In 1949 BIA moved to the Department of the Interior. From World War II through the 1950s, Indians were relocated. The 1960s and 1970s saw Indians and their supporters protest and actually invade the Bureau of Indian Affairs' headquarters.

Further progress was made with the Indian Self-Determination and Education Assistance Act of 1975 and with the Tribal Self-Governance Act of 1994.

BIA administers and manages 56 million acres of land held in trust by the United States for American Indians, Indian tribes, and Alaska Natives. Such responsibility fulfilled agreements with American Indians and Alaskan Natives includes developing forest lands, leasing assets on the lands, directing agricultural programs, protecting water and land rights, developing and maintaining infrastructure, providing health and human services (see pp. 170–174), economic development, education, agriculture, roads, housing, employment, training, and judicial and social services.

Since 1824 BIA had 45 commissioners of Indian affairs, six of whom have been American Indian or Alaska Native. Since the position of assistant secretary of the Department of the Interior was created in 1977 under President Jimmy Carter, six men and one woman have served in the position, and all were American Indians. Currently, about 90 percent of BIA employees are either American Indians or Alaska Natives.

BIA serves about 1.5 million American Indians and Alaska Natives who are members of more than 562 federally recognized Indian tribes in 32 contiguous states and in Alaska. BIA works to move away from its original role to subjugate American Indians and Alaska Natives and toward partnerships with and service to them, while tribes view the relationship as one of love/hate.

CONTACT Address: BIA, 1849 C Street NW MS2472MIB, Washington, DC 20240; Phone: (202) 208-3710, (202) 208-3338, tribal leaders directory (202) 208-3711; Website: www.doi.gov/bureau-indian-affairs.html (unavailable due to lawsuits as of 02/07/03).

INDIAN ARTS AND CRAFTS BOARD: A separate agency within the Department of Interior, the Indian Arts and Crafts Board promotes the economic development of American Indians and Alaska Natives by expanding the market for Indian arts and crafts, and implements and enforces the Indian Arts and Crafts Act of 1990. The Arts and Crafts Act is a truth-in-advertising law that enforces criminal and civil penalties for marketing non-Indian-made products as Indian when they are not.

The board gives professional business advice, fund-raising assistance, promotion advice and assistance, and promotes Indian arts and crafts. The board operates three regional museums: the Sioux Indian Museum in Rapid City, South Dakota; the Museum of the Plains Indian in Browning, Montana; and the Southern Plains Indian Museum in Anadarko, Oklahoma. It also produces a consumer directory of 190 Native American owned and operated arts and crafts businesses.

CONTACT Address: 1849 C Street NW, MS4004-MIB, Washington, DC 20240; Phone: (202) 208-3773; Fax: (202) 208-5196; Website: www.doi.gov/iacb/museum/general_museum.html.

BUREAU OF LAND MANAGEMENT

The Bureau of Land Management (BLM) resulted from the 1946 merger of the Grazing Service and the General Land Office. BLM works to maintain and sustain the health, diversity, and productivity of public lands for the use and enjoyment of the public. Most BLM lands are intended for multiple uses, which might include extraction of resources, intensive recreation, and sustained yield and conservation. Some BLM lands are set aside for landscape conservation while allowing traditional uses such as grazing.

BLM manages about 262 million surface acres of federally owned land, more than any other federal agency, and about one-eighth of all U.S. land area, or 40 percent of all lands managed by the federal government. Its acreage exists in 12 western states, with 87 million acres in Alaska alone, comprising about one-quarter of Alaska, and 48 million acres in Nevada, about two-thirds of that state. BLM also manages about 700 million subsurface acres of minerals that produce 35 percent of U.S. coal production, 11 percent of gas production, and 5 percent of domestic oil production. It administers 205,498 miles of fishable streams, 2.2 million acres of lakes and reservoirs, 6,600 mile of floatable rivers, more than 500 boating sites, 69 National Back Country Backways, 300 Watchable Wildlife sites, 4,500 miles of National

Scenic, Historic, and Recreational Trails, and thousands of miles of multiple-use trails for motorcycling, hiking, horseback riding, mountain biking, and off-highway vehicles (OHVs).

Among the wide range of resources, extractions, grazing, and other uses of BLM land are resource material mining; forests and timber; geothermal energy and mineral extraction; wild horse and burro grazing; fish and wildlife habitats; wilderness areas; archaeological, paleontological, and historical sites; endangered plant and animal species; wild and scenic rivers; and some wilderness areas. Public recreational opportunities on BLM lands include hunting, fishing, camping, hiking, boating, hang gliding, off-highway vehicle driving, mountain biking, birding, and visiting natural and cultural historical sites. It also works to enhance vegetation where appropriate and to rid the land of noxious weeds, and works toward clean water.

BLM manages watersheds to protect soil and enhance water quality; develops public recreational opportunities on public lands; and sometimes sells land to individuals, organizations, local governments, and federal agencies, or leases land to state and local government agencies and nonprofit organizations. The bureau also oversees leases of federal land under its jurisdiction for energy and mineral development, and issues rights-of-way, leases, and permits for extraction.

BLM surveys federal lands, establishes and maintains public land records, and keeps track of mining claims records. It also coordinates payments made by counties and other local government entities in lieu of taxes based on the amount of federally owned land in the governmental units' jurisdictions.

BLM's other functions include a database on current and historical cadastral (ownership registration), including information on mineral estate, resource conditions, and permits or leases on federal lands. Details available include land patent records through the General Land Office, land survey information, and public land orders.

In the field of energy and minerals, BLM oversees commercial opportunities on federal lands, including forest products, grazing forage, and pipeline and transmission line rights-of-way. In the field of fluid minerals, BLM leases federal oil, gas, and geothermal minerals and supervises exploration, development, and production operations on federal and Indian lands, and manages helium operations on federal lands. BLM oversees mining law and leasing of sites for extraction of solid minerals such as coal and nonenergy materials including hardrock minerals, locatable minerals, salable minerals, and "solid leasables" such as phosphate, potassium, and sodium.

BLM also engages in public education on environmental balances on federal lands, and maintains the Geospatial Information Systems (GIS), which tracks information on each piece of land and the resources on and under it. Such data might include bird nesting sites or locations of wild horse herds. BLM has a Geospatial Clearinghouse, and an interactive web portal to locate, access, and share current geographic information called Geocommunicator (www.geocommunicator.gov/). The National Information Resources Management Center provides information technology services to BLM, the states, partners, and connected centers to share information.

BLM also maintains extensive Web pages for children, partnerships, and public information on public lands and monuments.

CONTACT Address: U.S. Bureau of Land Management, LS-406, 1849 C Street, Washington, DC 20240; Phone: (202) 452-7732, (202) 452-5125; Fax: (202) 452-5124; Website: www.blm.gov. Regional offices: No. 13, 222 W. 7th Avenue, Anchorage, AK 99513-7599; Phone: (907) 271-5080. 222 N. Central Avenue, Phoenix, AZ 85004-2203; Phone: (602) 417-9500. 2800 Cottage Way, Suite W-1834 Sacramento, CA 95825-0451; Phone: (916) 978-4600. 2850 Youngfield Street, Lakewood, CO 80215-7076;

Phone: (303) 239-3700. States east of Mississippi River: 7450 Boston Boulevard, Springfield, VA 22153; Phone: (703) 440-1700. 1387 S. Vinnell Way, Boise, ID 83709-1657; Phone: (373-4001). P.O. Box 36800, 5001 Southgate Drive, Billings, MT 59107-6800; Phone: (406) 896-5012. P.O. Box 12000, 1340 Financial Boulevard, Reno, NV 89520-0006; Phone: (702) 861-6590. P.O. Box 27115, 1474 Rodeo Road, Santa Fe, NM 87502-0115; Phone: (505) 438-7501. P.O. Box 2965, 333 SW 1st Avenue, Portland, OR 97208; Phone: (503) 808-6024. P.O. Box 45155, 324 S. State Street, Salt Lake City, UT 84145-0155; Phone: (801) 539-4010. P.O. Box 1828, 5353 Yellowstone Road, Cheyenne, WY 82003; Phone: (307) 775-6001.

UNITED STATES GEOLOGICAL SURVEY

Established by the Organic Act of 1879, the United States Geological Survey (USGS) is an independent fact-finding agency that collects and classifies public lands, and examines geological structure, mineral resources, and potential products on federal and nongovernmental lands in the United States. Its goal is to provide reliable scientific information to describe and understand the Earth; minimize loss of life and property from natural disasters; manage water, biological, energy, and mineral resources; and protect and enhance quality of life. USGS serves as the sole science agency for the Department of Interior, and maintains vast data banks of Earth and biological information on biological resources, natural hazards, and ground-water availability. USGS prides itself on providing impartial science, since it has no regulatory or management role, and focuses on four major areas: natural hazards, resources, environment, and information and data management.

USGS' Biological Resource Division (BRD) works to manage and conserve U.S. biological resources, to understand causes of biological and ecological trends, and to predict the ecological consequences of management practices. BRD develops technologies to synthesize, analyze, and disseminate biological and ecological information, working together with private partners and scientific collaborators.

Over 10,000 USGS scientists, technicians, and support staff work in 400 offices in every state and some foreign countries. USGS also works with more than 2,000 agencies of state, local, and tribal governments, as well as with academics, other federal agencies, nongovernmental organizations, and the private sector. USGS produces and distributes more than 100,000 different maps and more than 600 terabytes of cartographic and digital data, archive aerial photographs, and global satellite data.

For USGS purposes, natural hazards include earthquakes, volcanic eruptions, landslides and other forms of ground failure, geomagnetic storms, floods, droughts, coastal storms, wildfires, fish and wildlife diseases, and invasive species. USGS scientists figure out and assess where natural hazards may occur, and what the risks are to the people who live in the area. Environmental scientists also focus on the physical, chemical, and biological processes involved in those natural systems, and how those processes are affected by human activities.

USGS operates the National Earthquake Information Center and the National Landslide Information Center, as well as the National Water Quality Laboratory, the Hydrologic Instrumentation Facility, the EROS Data Center with 30 years of global imaging, and biological research and science centers.

USGS scientists also focus on long-term data collection, monitoring, analysis, and predictive modeling, and have made important contributions to keys to toxic substances and water-borne pathogens in the water supply; understanding the physical processes that control contaminants in the environment and the impact they may have on living resources; assessing the status and trends in water quality; working on an integrated approach to understand ecosystems such as those found in San Francisco Bay, in the Everglades, and in Chesapeake Bay; and collecting geographic data to ensure biological diversity throughout the American landscape.

In real-life terms, USGS scientists developed hydrologic techniques to gauge various discharges in rivers and streams, trained astronauts who landed on the Moon in 1969 in geology, and worked with the private sector to give worldwide access to digital images of neighborhoods and communities. USGS studies in seismology will possibly enable scientists to give advance warnings of earthquakes to save lives.

CONTACT Address: United States Geological Survey, 12201 Sunrise Valley Drive, Reston, VA 20192; Phone: (888) ASK-USGS or (703) 648-4000; Website: www.usgs.gov.

USGS is affiliated with 39 Cooperative Research Units and 54 state Water Resources Research Institutes.

As the primary science agency for water resource information, USGS' Cooperative Water Program (Coop) monitors the quantity and quality of water in American rivers and aquifers, assesses sources and end results of aquatic systems' contaminants, develops tools to improve use of hydrologic information, and makes this information available to potential users. The cooperative program is a partnership between USGS and 1,400 water resource agencies of state, local, and tribal governments, including Puerto Rico and several former U.S. territories.

USGS' Cooperative Water Program includes the National Water Quality Laboratory, the National Water Information System, the National Research Program, instrumentation testing facilities, and a national system of quality assurance. The Coop Program does or funds about 750 hydrologic studies annually, with recent emphasis on water quality issues, such as aquifer contamination, land application and injection of reclaimed water, river quality, storm runoff water

quality, and the effects of acid rain, urban development, mining, and agricultural chemicals and practices on water resources.

A unique project of the Cooperative Water Program is that it brings together information on water-related topics from throughout the United States and makes trends and the large picture available to the public. Topics studied nationally in the National Synthesis project include: recharge to groundwater systems; fluvial (river) sediment; changes in flood frequencies, sometimes due to land use changes; and synthesis of water quality information.

CONTACT Address: 409 USGS National Center, 12201 Sunrise Valley Drive, Reston, VA 20192; Phone: (703) 648-6843; Website: http://water.usgs.gov/coop. Regional contacts: Address: Eastern: USGS, Spalding Woods Office Park, Suite 160, 3850 Holcomb Bridge Road, Norcross, GA 30092; Phone: (770) 409-7700; Fax: (770) 409-7725. Central: USGS, Denver Federal Building 53, P.O. Box 25046, Mail Stop 406, Denver, CO 82335; Phone: (303) 236-5950; Fax: (303) 236-5919. Western: USGS, MS470, 345 Middlefield Road, Menlo Park, CA 94025-3591; Phone: (650) 329-4087.

BUREAU OF RECLAMATION

Founded in 1902 as part of the Reclamation Act, the Bureau of Reclamation (BOR) is the largest wholesaler and manager of water in the United States. Best known for the 600 dams, power plants, canals, and reservoirs it built in 17 western states, the Bureau of Reclamation's mission is to manage, develop, and protect water and related resources in an environmentally and economically sound way for the public welfare of western Americans and American Indian tribes. Reclamation works to meet increasing water demand while attempting to protect the environment and the public investment in the dams and other structures. Among the bureau's best-known dams are Hoover Dam on the Colorado River and Grand Coulee Dam on the Columbia River. The bureau also works to deliver water on demand, and encourage water conservation, water recycling, and water reuse by encouraging partnerships between itself and customers, states, and Indian tribes.

As western settlers required irrigation for agriculture, they diverted water from streams that usually dried up in summer months and could not meet the demand. Settlers realized it might help to trap the runoff of rainwaters and melting snow and save it for summer use. Many such efforts did not work, either for lack of engineering expertise or lack of funds, or both.

Westerners urged Congress to invest in water as part of America's infrastructure (although the word did not exist), since they had already spent money on roads, river navigation, harbors, canals, and railroads. In 1900 the platforms of both the Republican and Democratic parties included planks on funding irrigation. After an ill-fated filibuster by eastern and midwestern representatives, Congress passed the Reclamation Act on June 17, 1902, requiring that water consumers repay the government for the construction costs of dams and irrigation projects. Irrigation was then known as "reclamation" in the sense that irrigation would allow people to "reclaim" arid lands for human use, implying prior entitlement. "Homemaking" became a key sales point for reclamation, because supporters believed and campaigned on the claim that reclamation would encourage western settlement of family homes on family farms, a concept that had great appeal to the public as well as to President Theodore Roosevelt.

Secretary of Interior Ethan Allen Hitchcock established the United States Reclamation Service within the U.S. Geological Survey (USGS) in July 1902. First, the Reclamation Service studied potential water development projects in each western state with federal lands, utilizing funds from sales of federal lands to fund the program. Congress had to pass a special act in 1906 to include Texas, as it had no federal lands.

In 1907 the secretary of the interior took the Reclamation Service out of USGS and created an independent bureau within the Department of Interior. In 1923 the agency was renamed the Bureau of Reclamation, and in 1928 Congress authorized building of the Boulder Canyon Project, now called Hoover Dam. Reclamation's grand era of building occurred during the Great Depression and in the 35 years following World War II, with the last major funding authorization for construction in the 1960s. Environmental concerns slowed development of projects, along with the 1976 failure of Teton Dam when it was filled for the first time.

The Bureau of Reclamation is the second-largest producer of hydroelectric power in the western United States, utilizing 456 dams, 348 reservoirs, and 58 power plants to produce more than 42 billion kilowatt hours annually to serve 31 million people in 6 million homes and thousands of businesses. BOR also provides one-fifth (140,000) of western farmers with irrigation water for 10 million acres of farms, which produce 60 percent of the nation's vegetables and 25 percent of American nuts and fruits.

BOR operates approximately 180 projects on about 8.6 million acres in 17 western states, providing 5 percent of western land with irrigation. The bureau now helps to develop and support or enhance recreational uses at Reclamation projects; conducts research and encourages technology transfer; works to make its lands and waters free of hazardous and toxic wastes; operates and maintains its facilities; and provides technical and engineering support to federal and state agencies, to American Indian tribes, and to other nations.

Since 1994 Reclamation has focused on operation and maintenance of existing facilities instead of on its previous goal of building them, on the contention that "the arid West essentially has been reclaimed. . . ."

The Bureau of Reclamation's new mission is to "manage, develop, and protect water and related resources in an environmentally and economically sound manner in the interest of the American public."

CONTACT Address: Bureau of Reclamation, 1849 C Street NW, Washington, DC 20240-0001; Phone: (202) 513-0501; Fax: (202) 513-0314; Website: www.usbr.gov. Regional offices: Reclamation Service Center, Building 67, Box 25007, Denver, CO 80225; Phone: (303) 445-2692. Great Plains Region: Box 36900, 316 N. 26th Street, Billings, MT 59107; Phone: (406) 247-7614. Lower Colorado Region: Box 61470, Nevada Highway and Park Street, Boulder City, NV 89005; Phone: (702) 293-8000. Upper Colorado Region: 125 S. State Street, Room 6107, Salt Lake City, UT 84147; Phone: (801) 524-3793. Mid-Pacific Region: 2800 Cottage Way, Sacramento, CA 95825; Phone: (916) 978-5100. Pacific Northwest Region, 1150 N. Curtis Road, Boise, ID 83706; Phone: (208) 378-5012.

OFFICE OF SURFACE MINING

Congress passed the Surface Mining Control and Reclamation Act of 1977 to establish the Office of Surface Mining Reclamation and Enforcement (OSM) in the Department of Interior. The office's purpose is to help states protect the environment and citizens from the adverse effects during coal mining, restore the mined land to beneficial use after mining is completed, and mitigate the effects of past mining by cleaning up and restoring abandoned mine lands. So far more than 180,000 acres of abandoned coal mine sites have been reclaimed under this program.

The Surface Mining Law gives primary responsibility for regulating surface coal mine reclamation to the states. Twenty-four coal mining states are regulating surface mining and coal mine reclamation. In states that have not set up their own regulatory and reclamation programs (Tennessee and Washington), and on federal lands and Navajo, Hopi, and Crow Indian reservations, OSM issues coal mine permits directly, conducts inspections, and enforces regulations.

Related to coal mining, OSM oversees regulation of environmental protections, environmental restoration, technology development and transfer, regulatory grants, abandoned mine land grants, and federal reclamation.

OSM's goals and results include: Coal mine operators now often reclaim land as they mine; mined lands should not be abandoned without proper reclamation; 13,000 acres of abandoned mine waste piles have been restored to productive use; 2.4 million linear feet of dangerous cliff-like high walls have been eliminated; and 23,000 dangerous abandoned portals and vertical openings to mines have been sealed.

OSM also collects, disburses, and accounts for abandoned mine land reclamation fees; administers civil penalties programs for violators of surface mining laws; sets technical standards and regulatory policy for reclamation and enforcement efforts; and coordinates the Appalachian clean streams initiative to clean up streams and rivers polluted by acid mine drainage.

The states where OSM oversees coal mining activities include: Alabama, Alaska, Arkansas, Colorado, Illinois, Indiana, Iowa, Kansas, Kentucky, Louisiana, Maryland, Mississippi, Missouri, Montana, New Mexico, North Dakota, Ohio, Oklahoma, Pennsylvania, Texas, Utah, Virginia, West Virginia, and Wyoming.

CONTACT Address: OSM, 1951 Constitution Avenue NW, Washington, DC 20240; Phone: (202) 208-2719; Website: www.osmre.gov.

MINERALS MANAGEMENT SERVICE

Created by the secretary of the interior on January 19, 1982, the Minerals Management Service (MMS) manages mineral resources on the Outer Continental Shelf (OCS) in an environmentally sound and safe way to collect, verify, and distribute mineral revenues generated from extraction from federal waters and on federal and Indian lands. The Outer Continental Shelf begins three miles off coastal shorelines and extends 200 miles out to sea, including about 1.76 billion acres under a few to thousands of feet of water. MMS's primary programs are Minerals Revenue Management and Offshore Minerals Management, which function in three regions: Alaska, Gulf of Mexico, and the Pacific Ocean.

More than 25 percent of U.S. domestic natural gas and 28 percent of domestic oil production occurs on the OCS, referred to as "off shore." MMS collects and distributes $5 to $10 billion in revenues annually that it collects from federal offshore mineral leases and onshore mineral leases on federal and Indian lands. About 57 percent of that money goes to the U.S. Treasury, 26 percent to "special purpose funds" such as the Land & Water Conservation Fund and to the National Historic Preservation Fund, 13 percent to the states, and 4 percent to American Indians.

Offshore Minerals Management evaluates resources available, projects for environmental review, leasing activities, lease management, and inspection and enforcement programs.

OMM works with state officials before issuing leases, and grants five-year oil and gas leases. Once the leases are granted, inspectors review offshore operations, and conduct offshore environmental studies in an effort to protect marine environments from pollutants.

The Minerals Revenue Management office collects and distributes royalty payments, rentals, bonus payments, fines, penalties, assessments, and other monies owed to the federal government or to Indian lessors as royalties-in-kind for the permit to extract mineral resources onshore as well as from leases and extraction of mineral resources offshore.

In the Alaska region, MMS manages mineral resources on 600 million acres along 6,000 miles of Alaska coastline, encompassing wide-ranging ecosystems of the Arctic Ocean, the Bering Sea, and the Northern Pacific Ocean. MMS's goal in Alaska is to find a way to provide exploration for oil while preserving the environment and lifestyle of local residents.

CONTACT Address: MMS, Alaska OCS Region, 949 East 36th Avenue, Anchorage, AK; Website: www.mms.gov/alaska/.

The Gulf of Mexico OCS Region (GOMR) has produced more than 97 percent of the 10.9 billion barrels of domestic oil and 133 trillion cubic feet of gas from offshore sources. More than 55,000 petroleum-related workers are employed in the Gulf of Mexico offshore oil industry, only 542 of whom work for GOMR as petroleum engineers, geologists, geophysicists, inspectors, physical scientists, technicians, environmental scientists, and administrators. GOMR has offices in Houma (504-868-4033), Lafayette (335-262-6632), Lake Charles (337-480-4600), and New Orleans (504-736-2504), Louisiana, as well as in Lake Jackson, Texas (979-265-7147).

CONTACT Address: Minerals Management Service, Public Information Office, 1201 Elmwood Park Boulevard, New Orleans, LA 70123-2394; Phone: (504) 736-0557 or (800) 200-GULF; Fax: (504) 736-2620; Website: www.gomr.mms.gov/.

The Pacific OCS Region manages 79 federal oil and gas leases off Southern California's coast (much off Santa Barbara County), producing more than 1 billion barrels of oil and 1.22 trillion cubic feet of gas since 1970. OCS estimates that there are about 400 million barrels of oil left offshore within the existing 43 producing leases, and possibly 1 billion more barrels available in locales of undeveloped leases. In 2002 California governor Gray Davis asked President George W. Bush to cancel some undeveloped offshore oil leases as Republican Bush had for his brother, Florida governor Jeb Bush, but the Bush administration denied the request of Democratic governor Davis.

CONTACT Address: Pacific OCS Region, 770 Paseo Camarillo, Camarillo, CA 93010; Website: www.mms.gov/omm/pacific/.

OTHER PROGRAMS

The *U.S.-Mexico Border Field Coordinating Committee (FCC)* works to promote, facilitate, and enhance binational communication and coordination on U.S.-Mexico border environmental issues pertaining to natural and cultural resources such as national parks, wildlife refuges, forests, conservation areas, wilderness areas, waterways, natural resources, and special areas for protection on the Outer Continental Shelf. FCC also protects water resources, endangered and threatened species, migratory birds, and some marine mammals along the border, as well as on American Indian reservations along the border.

Pilot projects include some for water in the Western Sonoran Desert, the Chihuahuan Desert–Big Bend Region, and the Lower Rio Grande Basin, known as the Rio Bravo del Norte in Mexico.

CONTACT Address: International Affairs, Department of the Interior, 1849 C Street NW, Washington, DC; Phone: (202) 208-5160; Fax: (202) 208-4867; Website: www.cerc.usgs.gov/fcc/.

The *National Park Service Archeology and Ethnography Program* strives to preserve the American heritage of places, objects, and traditions, including archeology and ethnography of archeological sites on and off public land, and artifacts, including those of ancient civilizations of the lower Mississippi Delta and American Indians.

The *Western Water Policy Review Advisory Commission* is a commission created under the Western Water Policy Review Act of 1992 to review allocation and use of water resources in 19 western states.

CONTACT Address: P.O. Box 25007, D-5010, Denver, CO 80225-0007; Phone: (303) 445-2100; Fax: (303) 445-6693; Website: www.den.doi.gov/wwprac/.

DEPARTMENT OF JUSTICE

A cabinet-level department headed by the attorney general, who is appointed by the president with Senate confirmation, the Department of Justice provides legal representation for the United States government in civil legal disputes, prosecution of those charged with violation of federal penal statutes, and enforcement of many federal statutes. Actual criminal prosecutions are conducted by United States attorneys in districts throughout the United States and territories.

The attorney general is chief of the department, with a deputy attorney general, and the solicitor general, who is the chief trial counsel of the department and who conducts cases before the UNITED STATES SUPREME COURT.

In the realm of federal criminal law the Department of Justice has jurisdiction over investigation and imprisonment, directly through the Federal Bureau of Investigation and the Federal Bureau of Prisons, and other offices in the department.

Historically, the department is unique in that the position of attorney general preceded the creation of the Department of Justice by 80 years. President George Washington appointed Edmund Randolph (former aide de camp to Washington and governor of Virginia) the first attorney general as a member of the original cabinet on September 26, 1789, the same day Washington named Thomas Jefferson the first secretary of state. Randolph casually started to work in early 1790. While a member of the cabinet, unlike other members, the attorney general served as an individual with a small staff, and no department, until June 22, 1870, when President Ulysses S. Grant signed legislation creating the

Department of Justice. The largest law office in the United States, it has more than 80,000 employees (after losing the Immigration and Naturalization Service to the new Department of Homeland Security).

While there have been many distinguished lawyers serving as attorney general, as well as an occasional politician, it has been a stepping-stone to the Supreme Court, but seldom to political office. Roger Taney (1831–33), Harlan F. Stone (1923–25), Frank Murphy (1939–1940), Robert H. Jackson (1940–41), and Tom C. Clark (1945–49) all moved on to the high court. John Breckinridge (1805–06), William Wirt (1817–23), Benjamin Butler (1833–38), John J. Crittenden (1841, 1850–53), Caleb Cushing (1853–57), Edwin M. Stanton (1860–61), Richard Olney (1893–95), Philander C. Knox (1901–04), Homer S. Cummings (1933–39), and William P. Rogers (1956–61) were influential political figures of their time. Elliot L. Richardson (1973), who also served in two other cabinet posts, is a hero in the history of the department for his refusing to discharge special counsel Archibald Cox, who was closing in on evidence of President Richard Nixon's involvement in the White House cover-up of the Watergate scandal. Nixon fired Richardson as part of what became known as the "Saturday Night Massacre." Of less distinguished reputation are attorneys general A. Mitchell Palmer (1919–21), who conducted constitutionally dubious raids and imprisonment on people he claimed were "Bolsheviks" in a blatant publicity stunt that he hoped would propel him into the Democratic presidential nomination, Harry Daugherty (1921–24), who was the leader of the "Ohio Gang" that ripped off the government in the corrupt administration of Warren G. Harding, and John M. Mitchell (1969–72), who was convicted and went to federal prison for his part in the Watergate scandal, when he authorized the break-in of Democratic offices and then lied to Congress about it. Robert F. Kennedy (1961–64) was appointed attorney general by his brother, President John F. Kennedy. The first woman to hold the office was Janet Reno, 1993–2001.

LOCATION The headquarters of the Department of the Justice and most of its functions is located at 950 Pennsylvania Avenue NW, Washington, DC 20530, and is officially named the Robert F. Kennedy Justice Building. The Federal Bureau of Investigation, a key component of the department, is located in the J. Edgar Hoover Building, 935 Pennsylvania Avenue NW, Washington, DC 20535, across the avenue from the Department of Justice building. The Bureau of Prisons is at 320 First Street NW, Washington, DC 20534; the Drug Enforcement Administration at 600–700 Army Navy Drive, Arlington, VA 22202, the U.S. Parole Commission in Chevy Chase, MD 20815, and the Office of Justice Programs at 810 Seventh Street NW, Washington, DC 20531. There are also regional offices.

CONTACT The central telephone number for the department is (202) 514-2000, and the Internet address is www.usdoj.gov. Various divisions, offices, and departments have direct telephone numbers and Internet addresses.

ORGANIZATION

In the administrative office of the attorney general are a deputy attorney general, an associate attorney general, and several associate deputy attorneys general, as well as a chief of staff and his/her deputy. Operating from a separate office is the solicitor general, ranking number three in the department's hierarchy, responsible for litigation before the Supreme Court. Directly responsible for major areas of enforcement of federal laws and litigation in which such statutes are a factor are the Criminal Division, the Civil Division, the Antitrust Division, the Tax Division, the Civil Rights Division, the Environment and Natural Resources Division, and the Justice Management Division. Except for the Criminal Division, which works closely with the Federal

Department of Justice

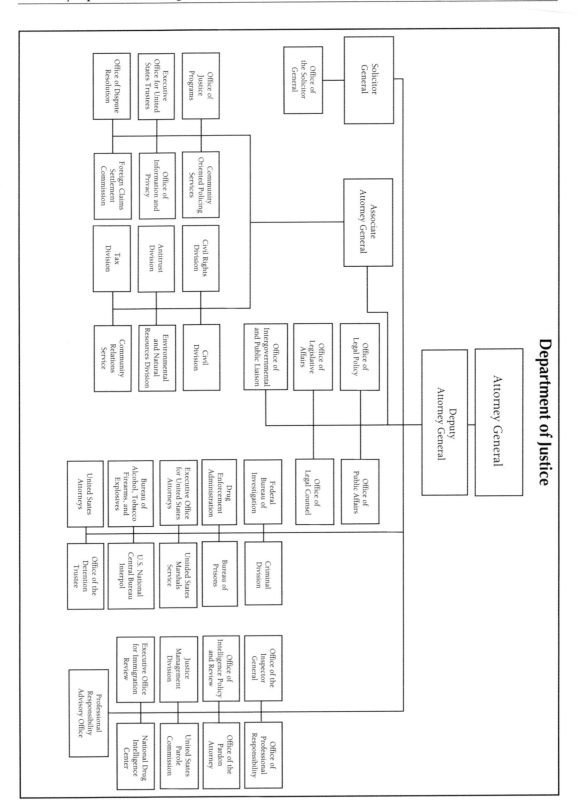

Attorney General

Solicitor General

Office of the Solicitor General

Associate Attorney General

Office of Justice Programs

Executive Office for United States Trustees

Office of Dispute Resolution

Foreign Claims Settlement Commission

Office of Information and Privacy

Community Oriented Policing Services

Civil Rights Division

Antitrust Division

Tax Division

Community Relations Service

Environmental and Natural Resources Division

Civil Division

Office of Intergovernmental and Public Liaison

Office of Legislative Affairs

Office of Legal Policy

Deputy Attorney General

Office of Legal Counsel

Office of Public Affairs

Federal Bureau of Investigation

Drug Enforcement Administration

Executive Office for United States Attorneys

Bureau of Alcohol, Tobacco Firearms, and Explosives

United States Attorneys

Office of the Detention Trustee

U.S. National Central Bureau Interpol

Unided States Marshals Service

Bureau of Prisons

Criminal Division

Office of the Inspector General

Office of Intelligence Policy and Review

Justice Management Division

Executive Office for Immigration Review

Professional Responsibility Advisory Office

National Drug Intelligence Center

United States Parole Commission

Office of the Pardon Attorney

Office of Professional Responsibility

Bureau of Investigation and the Justice Management Division, which is somewhat independent, the other divisions are each directed by an assistant attorney general and overseen by the associate attorney general.

More than a dozen offices and services manage various functions within the department. Major semi-autonomous bureaus within the department are the *Federal Bureau of Investigation, Bureau of Prisons, Bureau of Alcohol, Tobacco and Firearms (ATF), Drug Enforcement Administration,* and the *United States Parole Commission.* Under the terms of the legislation adopted by Congress in November 2002, which created the Department of Homeland Security, the Immigration and Naturalization Service and its nearly 40,000 employees were transferred to the new department.

Deputy attorney general is the chief assistant to the attorney general in all phases of the administration of the department, and is directly responsible for the Office of Legal Policy, Office of Public Affairs, Office of Legislative Affairs, Office of Legal Counsel, and Office of Inter-Governmental Affairs.

CONTACT Address: 950 Pennsylvania Avenue NW, Washington, DC 20530; Phone: (202) 514-2000 (main number of Department of Justice).

Solicitor general argues cases before the United States Supreme Court on behalf of the government. The solicitor general's office determines which cases the government should ask the Supreme Court to review and prepares the briefs for argument. It also decides which cases that the government has lost at the APPEALS COURT level should be appealed to the Supreme Court.

CONTACT Address: Room 5734, 950 Pennsylvania Avenue NW, Washington, DC 20530.

Associate attorney general, the number four position in the table of organization of the department, has a dual role: (1) giving advice and assistance to the attorney general in developing policy (although it is clear that the attorney general calls the shots); and (2) has supervisorial oversight over the divisions (Civil, Criminal, Antitrust, Civil Rights, Tax, Environment and Natural Resources), Offices of Justice Programs, Community Oriented Policing, Community Relations, Dispute Resolution, Violence Against Women, Information and Privacy, U.S. Bankruptcy Trustees, and the Foreign Claims Settlement Commission.

CONTACT Website: www.usdoj.gov/aag.

Pardon attorney and his/her staff investigate and review all requests for presidential pardons, commutations of sentence, or other forms of clemency. The pardon attorney recommends to the president disposition of such requests. However, on a few occasions a president has bypassed the pardon attorney and granted a pardon or commutation without consultation. The pardon power given to the president under Article II, Section 2 of the Constitution is absolute and is thus final and cannot be appealed or reviewed.

CONTACT Address: Office of the Pardon Attorney, Department of Justice, Suite 400, 500 First Street NW, Washington, DC 20530; Phone: (202) 616-6070.

Administratively, the Department of Justice is organized under six major divisions, the Civil Division, the Criminal Division, the Tax Division, the Antitrust Division, the Civil Rights Division and the Environment and Natural Resources Division. For specialized functions there are more than 20 separate offices, as well as bureaus and programs.

CIVIL DIVISION

The Civil Division, directed by an assistant attorney general, is the largest division in the Justice Department with a staff of more than 700 attorneys. They represent over 100 different federal agencies, members of Congress, and the federal judiciary. The subject matter of litigation, negotiations, and other matters runs the legal gamut.

They defend the federal government in lawsuits that challenge the constitutionality or legality of federal laws, government programs, and executive actions. Also, the civil division responds to lawsuits against individual government officials arising out of their official activities, lawsuits alleging either civil negligence (torts) by government employees and agencies, or bringing suits for damages against the government under the Federal Tort Claims Act (permitting persons injured by alleged negligence by government employees and entities) ranging from truck accidents to spread of toxic substances such as oil tanker spills and air crashes. More than a billion dollars in clean-up costs and fines was recovered for the government in a case involving the wreck and million-gallon oil spill of the tanker *Exxon Valdez*. Some 170 lawyers are involved in the torts branch of the civil division.

Also on the proactive front, the Civil Division enforces consumer protection statutes, pursues claims of alleged fraud by firms contracting with the government and welfare claimants, pursues bankruptcy and patent claims, fights fraud in banking, insurance, welfare, and Medicare, and advises federal officials throughout the government. It is also involved in representing the government in its various commercial and international operations. In total, billions of dollars in either recovery or defense are involved in the thousands of cases handled by the Civil Division each year.

In complex and specialized cases (such as environmental torts) the torts office in Washington often handles the cases directly, as it has the expertise, experienced staff, and the resources necessary to adequately represent the government, rather than refer the cases to the U.S. attorney in charge of the jurisdiction in which the problem or case arose. This is particularly necessary when the government has been sued by a "class" of plaintiffs representing large numbers of people, and often scattered over the nation. An example of this is the "Agent Orange" cases in which numerous service veterans brought lawsuits claiming that their health had been seriously affected by the use of the defoliant agent orange during the Vietnam War.

CONTACT FOR CIVIL DIVISION Phone: (202) 514-3301.

The Civil Division's activities are divided among several "branches" that are specialized teams of attorneys.

Commercial Litigation Branch: The largest branch with a staff of more than 280 attorneys, which both bring legal actions and defend the federal government and its agencies. The work is broken down into several legal areas: civil frauds (as distinguished from criminal fraud), contract disputes, customs and international trade, corporate and financial litigation, intellectual property, and foreign cases.

Recovery of claims by the government in cases in which it is alleged that contractors with the federal government, fraudulent receipt of funds through Medicare and health insurance phony or inflated claims, improperly acquired or overpayment of federal subsidies, grants, and loans. Many of the claims by the Department of Justice are based on revelations by whistle-blowers, people who were employees of the contracting organizations. A major example is the investigation of the nation's largest for-profit hospital chain, Columbia/HCA, which raised issues of inflated fees for outpatient laboratory work, home health, community education and management, and "up-coding" (charging for a procedure with a higher established fee code than the procedure actually performed); Columbia/HCA settled with a payment of $745 million.

Torts Branch: Employs about 130 lawyers, who are divided into four sections: Federal Tort Claims Act cases, Aviation and Admiralty, Environmental Torts, and Constitutional and Specialized Torts. Incidentally, the word *tort* means a civil wrong that causes damage, often through negligence, which may not necessarily be criminal, but causes accidents through carelessness, violations of rules, or by means under the control of federal employees. The torts branch may defend the government and its agencies from claims of damages allegedly caused by the government, or bring legal actions for damages to federal property and employees due to the misfeasance or negligence of private parties.

The cases handled by this branch are usually more complex, extensive, and expensive (such as class actions) or possibly precedent-setting. More run-of-the-mill tort cases are handled by the United States attorney in the jurisdiction where the case arose.

The *Federal Tort Claims Act* provides a system under which people claiming injury due to governmental negligence can file their claims, and also sorts out alleged demands that are clearly not based on the elements necessary to at least make a prima facie case. The litigation includes personal injuries from reckless driving by federal employees, animal attacks in national parks, and professional malpractice by federally employed physicians or blood banks. In this context torts are not based on questioning government policy, but on errors in conduct. A typical defense would be contesting claims that a Forest Service control burn got out of hand and destroyed property.

The *Aviation and Admiralty Section* is responsible for government legal involvement in air traffic control, regulation of commercial airlines, weather services, aeronautical chartering, all forms of aircraft activity, oil spills, cargo damage claims, and ship collisions and groundings. Following the 1989 1 million-gallon oil spill by the tanker *Exxon Valdez,* for which the government through several agencies recovered over a billion dollars, Congress enacted the Oil Pollution Act of 1990, which increased the involvement of the Civil Division in recovering clean-up costs from pollution.

Primarily defending the government is the *Environmental Torts Section,* which resists claims of contamination as a result of government activity. These include defeating an attempt by the manufacturers of "Agent Orange" to receive reimbursement for claims by ex-servicemen and women, and claims from nuclear radiation.

The legal staff of the *Constitutional and Specialized Torts Litigation Section* represents federal employees, particularly in law enforcement, from allegations of breaches of constitutional and other legal protections.

Appellate Staff: All of the appeals resulting from cases handled by the Civil Division are the responsibility of a staff of approximately 60 lawyers. Many of the appeals are challenges to the rulings of administrative agencies before federal appeals courts. It is a basic rule of administrative law that parties must "exhaust their administrative remedies," but having done so the next step is filing an action or directly appealing to a federal appeals court having jurisdiction. This specialized staff has been operative for 50 years, and was originally created by then assistant attorney general Warren Burger, who was later appointed to the U.S. Supreme Court.

The appeals attorneys prepare and argue cases before the courts of appeals. They also draft briefs and petitions (including for certiorari asking the Supreme Court to hear a case) involving cases before the Supreme Court, although the arguments are made by the Office of the Solicitor General.

Office of Consumer Litigation: The branch responsible for both civil and criminal litigation involving laws intended to protect public health and safety. The client agencies of this office include the Food and Drug Administration, the FEDERAL TRADE COMMISSION, the CONSUMER PRODUCT SAFETY COMMISSION, and the National Highway Traffic Safety Administration. Its staff of about 25 lawyers files actions to enforce statutes prohibiting unfair and deceptive trade practices. On occasion they may defend federal actions promoting consumer protection.

Some topics that have been the subject of litigation are prosecuting drug manufacturers who falsified test data, car dealers who falsified mileage use by "rolling back" odometers, and a manufacturer of children's cribs known to have openings that could trap a baby's head and strangle the child.

Office of Immigration Litigation: Has attorneys who review alien petitions that dispute orders of deportation, denials of political asylum, and requests such as claims that an alien immigrant might be entitled to certain constitutional rights, including a hearing on detention, or protest by an employer charged with hiring an illegal alien. The lawyers may act directly on individual cases or assist U.S. attorneys or counsel for the Immigration and Naturalization Service. In general, the courts have limited the rights of illegal aliens, refusing to reverse denials of asylum without overwhelming evidence of the need for asylum, and that the Fourth Amendment (including the exclusion of illegally obtained evidence) does not apply in deportation proceedings.

Federal Programs Branch: Employs about 100 attorneys to represent approximately 100 federal agencies, the president, cabinet officers, and other officials. Subject matter includes national security, foreign relations, law enforcement, interstate and foreign commerce, employment litigation, constitutional challenges to government operations, validity of executive orders, freedom of information and privacy, regulatory enforcement, banking, disability, international terrorism, pornography on the Internet, negotiations relative to negotiating recovery for Holocaust families, and dealing with foreign assets. In addition to cabinet offices, government clients include the U.S. POSTAL SERVICE, the SOCIAL SECURITY ADMINISTRATION, and the Federal Bureau of Investigation.

CIVIL RIGHTS DIVISION

The Civil Rights Division was established in 1957 at the time of the enactment of the Civil Rights Act of 1957, to enforce that act's prohibitions against discrimination. Since that time further legislation has greatly expanded the purview of the Civil Rights Division. These were the Civil Rights Acts of 1957, 1960, 1964, and 1968, as well as the Voting Rights Act of 1985, plus its amendments and extensions through 1992. In addition, there are several acts intended to facilitate voter registration and voting, including the National Voter Registration Act (1993), the Uniformed and Overseas Citizens Absentee Voting Act (1986), and the Voting Accessibility for the Elderly and Handicapped Act (1984).

Other major legislation now enforced by the Civil Rights Division include the Equal Credit Opportunity Act (1999), the Americans with Disability Act (1986), the Civil Rights of Institutionalized Persons Act (1997), the Freedom of Access to Clinic Entrances Act (1984), the Police Misconduct Provision of the Violent Crime Control and Law Enforcement Act (1994), and Section 102 of the Immigration Reform and Control Act. In addition, there are Education Amendments of 1972 to the Civil Rights Act 1964, and Section 504 of the Rehabilitation Act of 1973, the Equal Pay Acts (1963 and 1970), the Church Arson Prevention Act (1996) and antidiscrimination provisions contained in other laws.

Under the direction of an assistant attorney general, assisted by deputy assistant attorneys general, the Civil Rights Division enforces both by criminal prosecution and civil actions the statutory protections of Americans from violation of their civil rights. It is divided into 10 sections plus a special office. The sections are: criminal, employment litigation, housing and civil enforcement, disability rights, educational opportunities, voting, administrative management, special litigation, coordination and review, and appellate. In addition, there exists the Office of Special Counsel for Immigration Related Unfair Employment Practices.

CONTACT FOR CIVIL RIGHTS DIVISION Phone: (202) 514-2151; Fax: (202) 514-0293; Website:

www.usdoj.gov/crt. Appellate Section: Phone: (292) 514-2195; Fax: (202) 514-8490.

Coordination and Review Section: This section aims at consistent enforcement of the various civil rights acts prohibiting discrimination based on race, color, national origin, gender, or religion in 30 or more federally assisted programs and almost 100 federal agencies. It reviews regulations, policies, standards, procedures, and plans of federally funded agencies to prevent violations of civil rights. Elements of its activities are investigations, training programs, interagency meetings, and determination of noncompliance. Many of these activities have been mandated by a series of executive orders.

The section publishes *Title VI Legal Manual, Title IX Legal Manual, Investigative Procedures Manual,* and *Civil Rights Forum,* a quarterly newsletter. It also issues numerous guidance documents, including such items as useful assistance to persons with limited English proficiency.

Attorneys in the section review complaints of discrimination by state and local law enforcement agencies, courts, correctional systems, and federally funded nongovernmental entities. They attempt mediation leading to compliance, but if unsuccessful, refer the matter to other sections such as the Criminal Section.

CONTACT Phone: (202) 307-2222, (888) 848-5306; Fax: (202) 307-0595.

Appellate Section: The team of lawyers in the Appellate Section represents the government in appeals from federal district court judgments arising from cases tried by the trial attorneys in the Civil Rights Division, and also assists the office of the solicitor general in such cases appealed to the Supreme Court. Further, the section monitors private cases in which civil rights is a significant issue, and will state the government's position by filing an *amicus curiae* (friend of the court) brief, which can have significant impact on the judges of the appeals courts.

CONTACT Phone: (202) 514-2195; Fax: (202) 514-8490.

Criminal Section: Of the 12,000 annual civil rights complaints received by the Department of Justice, the Federal Bureau of Investigation, United States attorneys, and other agencies, the Criminal Section prosecutes civil rights cases of national significance and public concern. These high-profile cases usually involve violence based on race, ethnicity, or religion, abuse of authority by law enforcement and local officials at all levels, violence to prevent access to reproductive health services, virtual slavery of illegal sweat shop and immigrant workers, or conspiracies to suppress voting, housing, educational, and employment rights. About 100 cases a year are actually prosecuted by the section.

The majority of the prosecutions brought by the section are the abuse of authority by public officials, including both federal and state law enforcement, state judges, and prison officials. These include use of their police powers to carry out sexual assaults, beatings, illegal searches and arrests, and theft. Some are the result of refusal or delay by state officials to take action upon evidence of obvious civil rights violations. Most of these follow an investigation by the FBI upon referral by the section.

Most cases are referred to the United States attorney where the alleged infraction occurred or to state authorities.

CONTACT Phone: (202) 514-3204; Fax: (202) 514-8336.

Disability Rights Section: Its area of responsibility is enforcement of the three titles (I, II, and III) of the Americans With Disabilities Act, which bans discrimination against persons with disabilities in public accommodations, of state and local government activities, employment practices of state and local governments employing more than 15 persons, and establishing accessibility standards for new nonresidential construction. The effect of the act has led to creation of ramps for wheelchair use on sidewalks and building entrances, installation of elevators to upper stories of public buildings, wheelchair lifts on municipal buses, and special seating in auditoriums, theaters, and stadiums. In educational and entertainment venues special facilities to equalize the opportunities of the blind and the deaf are being installed throughout the country.

Specifically, the attorneys for the section handle enforcement litigation under the three titles of the act, certification of state and local government building codes that access equivalency under act standards, information and outreach to educate business, governments, people with disabilities, and the general public in regard to the requirements of the Americans With Disabilities Act and the means for enforcement, coordinating enforcement of the act by various federal agencies.

Legal action against public employers for discrimination in employment are usually upon referral from the Equal Employment Opportunity Committee as well as the Justice Department's own authority. At the same time many of the section's successes have been by agreements with local governmental jurisdictions, industries, and individual businesses to establish "comparable" access (such as wheelchair locations in theaters) and facilities assisting those with hearing, visual, and other disabilities.

CONTACT Phone: (202) 307-0663, ADA Hotline: (800) 514-0301; Fax: (202) 307-1198; Website: www.usdoj.jov/crt/ada.

Educational Opportunities Section: Assigned the task of enforcement of portions of the Civil Rights Act of 1964, the Educational Opportunities Act of 1974, the Rehabilitation Act of 1973, and the Americans With Disabilities Act. Its highest priority is to monitor more than 400 school districts under court orders for desegregation. This includes monitoring and responding to issues of student and teacher assignment, transportation (busing), and equitable use of resources.

Many of the cases handled by this section are on behalf of the DEPARTMENT OF EDUCATION. Some of the most significant cases included a 25-year-long struggle to properly desegregate the state of Mississippi's colleges ($500 million settlement), covering such matters as equalizing financial support for historically black colleges, and allowing Jackson State University to use Mississipi Veterans Memorial Stadium for its home football games. Other equalization of opportunity and facilities cases have been settled in Illinois and New York among other states.

CONTACT Phone: (202) 514-4092; Fax: (202) 514-8337.

Employment Litigation Section: Enforces against state and local governments federal laws banning discrimination in employment based on race, sex, religion, or national origin. These include the Civil Rights Act of 1964 and the Pregnancy Discrimination Act of 1978.

The section's lawyers are proactive in initiating lawsuits when investigation demonstrates there is an apparent pattern or practice of discrimination in employment recruiting, hiring, job assignments, and promotions, which limit employment and promotional opportunities to a class of individuals (meaning those of a particular race, gender, or other identifiable group). In most cases the result is a settlement and stipulated "consent" decree of the court.

Also prosecuted are individual cases of employment discrimination including harassment, failure to promote, retaliatory assignments, unlawful discharges, discrimination against pregnant women, and various forms of discrimination. Most of these cases are on referral from the EQUAL EMPLOYMENT OPPORTUNITY COMMISSION. While individually less sweeping than the class-action decrees, they put the power of the government, including expertise, against discriminatory activities on behalf of people unable to afford the legal cost of pursuing the legal route by themselves.

The section defends claims against the DEPARTMENTS OF LABOR and TRANSPORTATION and other agencies sued for alleged overly aggressive enforcement of antidiscrimination or suits involving affirmative action requirements of those contracting with the government.

CONTACT   Phone: (202) 514-3831; Fax: (202) 514-1105.

Housing and Civil Enforcement Section: Enforces civil rights statutes that prohibit discrimination in housing transactions (the Fair Housing Act), lending (the Equal Credit Opportunity Act), and public accommodations including hotels, restaurants, and places of entertainment (Civil Rights Act of 1964), and opportunity to exercise religion (Religious Land Use and Institutionalized Persons Act).

The lengthy and disgraceful history of discrimination in housing that established ghettoes, attempted to preserve all-white neighborhoods, refused to show or sell housing to minorities, and encouraged various dodges by builders, developers, real estate agents, and local governments was the target of the federal Fair Housing Act. This measure had particular teeth since so much of housing is funded directly by federal programs or by government guaranteed loans, and secondary mortgage funding (as by the Federal National Mortgage Association) give the government the power to halt these practices.

The Fair Housing Act authorizes the department to file lawsuits to enforce bans on discriminatory housing practices (both by sale or rental) based on race, color, religion, sex, national origin, handicap, or familial status. The cases are initiated by the Department of Justice through this section or from referrals by the HOUSING AND URBAN DEVELOPMENT DEPARTMENT (HUD). Often the results include civil penalties that provide monetary damages to the people who were objects of discrimination. Defendants have included local governments, banks, insurance companies (funding developments), real estate professionals, and landlords.

One technique employed by the section is fair housing "testing" by sending both a white and minority person to attempt to buy or rent the same unit and compare the treatment by the landlord or real estate office. They have also successfully sued landlords who sexually harassed female tenants by demanding sexual favors or face retaliatory eviction.

Lending institutions are the target of the section pursuant to the Equal Credit Opportunity Act, for such practices as refusing to make or offer loans to nonwhites, failure to make loans to qualified minorities, and offering loans to minorities only at higher interests rates or other more onerous terms than to white applicants.

CONTACT   Phone: (202) 514-4713; Housing Discrimination Hotline (800) 896-7743; Fax: (202) 514-1116.

Voting Section: Enforces key provisions of the Voting Rights Act of 1965 (particularly targeting the Jim Crow laws and practices in southern states to prevent African Americans from registering, voting, and participating in the political process), the National Voter Registration Act of 1993 (providing for registration at Departments of Motor Vehicles), the Voting Accessibility for the Elderly and Handicapped Act, and the Uniformed and Overseas Citizens Absentee Voting Act.

Pursuant to Section 8 of the Voting Rights Act, the section is empowered to assign federal observers to election day activities. In 2002 observers were assigned to eight cities in Mississippi, as well as Los Angeles, St. Louis, and New York City, but oddly enough not to Dade and Broward Counties in Florida, which had been the subject of many complaints of intimidation of minority voters, irregularities, and vote suppression in the 2000 election.

Under Section 203 of the Voting Rights Act, in areas with 5 percent of the population or 10,000 persons with limited English, voting officials are required to provide bilingual voting materials (ballots and sample ballots) for those with significant numbers speaking another language. The section enforces this provision and can seek court orders requiring the provision of such materials.

Other areas of responsibility include determining whether local redistricting plans meet the constitutional requirements of one-person-one-vote or result in discriminatory dilution of minority votes preventing any possible election of a minority person, badly gerrymandered districts (drawn in peculiar shapes for one-party advantage), and adequate provisions for absentee voting by the elderly or men and women in the service. The section has had considerable success, including achieving a redrawing of a state senate plan in Georgia, and in preventing the splitting of Native American voters in Montana.

CONTACT Phone: (202) 307-2767, (800) 253-3931; Fax: (202) 307-3961.

Special Litigation Section: This special section has been assigned enforcement of four major areas of civil rights protection enforcement as a sort of legal "strike force": conditions in prisons and other institutions, misconduct by law enforcement, protection from interference with access to reproductive clinics (providing abortions and/or family planning information) and places of worship, and the guarantees of prisoners' religious rights (particularly of Muslims).

Investigations of over 350 facilities and actual or threatened legal action to correct the conditions in those institutions has corrected dangerous, often inhuman, conditions, and lack of services and adequate medical treatment. They have also attacked the problems of inadequate educational opportunity for juvenile offenders, lack of mental health treatment, the problem of sexual victimization of female prisoners, and inadequate protections for pretrial detainees. In other types of institutions the section has investigated abuse and neglect in facilities for people with developmental disabilities, and conditions in nursing homes for the elderly. They have also acted to make provision for worship by Muslim prisoners who have daily prayers and dietary requirements.

Often through negotiation, settlement, consent decrees, and informal agreements, police departments have set up programs to avoid discrimination both in employment and treatment of suspects, and even entire states have adopted reforms of their institutional programs.

Attorneys in the Special Litigation Section provide assistance to relevant divisions within the Department of Justice (such as the Health Care Fraud Working Group and the Task Force on Violence Against Reproductive Health Providers) and other federal agencies operating on the four major concerns of the section. These include the Office of Juvenile Justice and Delinquency Protection, the National Institute of Corrections, the Bureau of Prisons, and the Departments of Education and Health and Human Services.

CONTACT Phone: (202) 514-6273; Fax:(202) 514-6273 or (202) 514-0212.

Administrative Management Section: Provides technical support for the entire Civil Rights Division, including software, an Internet site, recruitment and personnel management, demographic and geographic information, and case management of legal actions. It also ensures that the division complies with the Freedom of Information and Privacy Acts.

CONTACT Phone: (202) 514-4224; Fax: (202) 514-1783.

Office of Special Counsel for Immigration Related Unfair Employment Practices: This office was established to protect the rights of American citizens and legal immigrants with work permits from employment discrimination. One of the most common discriminatory actions rejects American citizens for regular employment in favor of temporary foreign workers who are willing to work for less money or without payroll deductions. Another type of case involves discrimination against citizens or legal immigrants eligible for employment on the employer's claim that they "looked" or "sounded" like foreigners, who might have forged documentation.

CONTACT Phone: (202) 616-5594; Fax: (202) 616-5509.

Office of Redress Administration: During World War II, pursuant to presidential order, starting in April 1942, many thousands of American citizens of Japanese ancestry as well as Japanese aliens resident in the United States were abruptly interned and relocated in internment camps for the duration of the war. This removal program (particularly sweeping the West Coast) was criticized for possible unconstitutionality and resulted in massive economic harm to the interned families who had to sell or give up farms, businesses, and possessions at distress prices. They also suffered abuse of their dignity without cause—no cases of sabotage or espionage were attributed to any persons of Japanese background, and those young men who were allowed to enlist in the U.S. Army served with distinction, primarily in the campaign to take Italy.

Eventually, legislation was enacted to provide some financial redress for those survivors of the internment camps. This office processes the claims for such redress.

CONTACT Phone: (202) 219-6900.

CRIMINAL DIVISION

This division is responsible for prosecuting violations of federal criminal laws, other than those types of criminal activity specifically assigned to other divisions. Its responsibilities include developing and supervising the application of criminal laws, setting enforcement policies, and conducting investigations in preparation of prosecutions.

In addition, the division monitors the Witness Security Program (to protect witnesses from harm in retaliation), and use of electronic surveillance (which must meet certain constitutional standards). It also advises the attorney general, Congress, the Office of the President, and the OFFICE OF MANAGEMENT AND BUDGET on criminal law, and gives legal advice and assistance to federal, state, and local prosecutors and investigating agencies.

The areas handled by the Criminal Division include:

a. Money laundering and forfeiture of assets seized in certain types of cases;

b. Child exploitation and obscenity, including child pornography creation and distribution, international abduction of children by parents, and child support;

c. Computer crime and theft of intellectual property, including illegal hacking and viruses and other computer crimes;

d. Supervising use of informants and electronic surveillance, the return of prisoners to countries of origin for completion of sentences, and approving or denying requests for immunity in return for testimony;

e. Fraud and white collar crime, including illegal activities on the Internet, telemarketing, insurance, bankruptcy, health care, securities, commodities, and housing;

f. National security and export of military and strategic materials and technology;

g. Enforcement of federal statutes on drugs and controlled substances, and developing strategies to combat the organized illegal drug trade, often in concert with state and local agencies;

h. Terrorism, including immigration enforcement efforts relative to alien terrorists;

i. Firearms and explosives violations;

j. Public corruption by government officials and contractors at all levels where prohibited by federal law;

k. Foreign assistance and training to criminal justice systems of other nations;

l. Investigations of ex-Nazis who entered the country under fraudulent pretenses, and investigation into assets looted from victims of Nazi persecutions;

m. Policy and legislative advice on pending legislation and recommendations on sentencing issues.

CONTACT FOR CRIMINAL DIVISION Phone: (202) 514-2601.

ANTITRUST DIVISION

The Antitrust Division is responsible for using its powers to maintain and promote competitive markets and prevent business activities that tend to monopolize, restrict, or control interstate commerce in a particular field. The legislative basis dates back to 1890 (Sherman Anti-Trust Act), and subsequent additions in the area of preventing monopolies and anticompetition, and oppressive and unfair trade practices based on market control, such as the Clayton Act.

Targets of Antitrust Division actions include vertical and monopolistic control of an industry to the extent that smaller businesses cannot compete or the monopoly is able to fix prices and demand special treatment from suppliers and distributors. In addition to bringing federal criminal charges for willful violation of antitrust statutes, the division often opposes mergers or other reorganizations that tend toward limits on interstate commerce, monopolies, and noncompetition, which may result in substantial fines and jail terms for individuals responsible. It also uses the threat of prosecution to negotiate voluntary judgments or agreements.

During the past century the prevention of monopolistic practices and entities has greatly benefited consumers as well as smaller businesses.

CONTACT FOR ANTI-TRUST DIVISION 325 Seventh Street NW, Washington, DC 20530; Phone: (202) 514-2692.

TAX DIVISION

The primary objective of the Tax Division is the collection of federal taxes through enforcement of the federal tax laws. By volume, most efforts involve settling disputes as to the amount of tax owed by taxpayers when the issue could not be settled by Internal Revenue Service actions, audits, and negotiations, which have reached the level of claims before the U.S. tax courts. This civil litigation (mainly based on taxpayer claims of incorrect or improper tax assessment) generally results in a settlement between the government and taxpayer, but can also result in a civil trial before the tax court.

More serious and less routine are the following types of litigation handled by the Tax Division:

a. Lawsuits by the federal government to collect unpaid taxes, to foreclose federal tax liens, to obtain judgments against delinquent taxpayers, and to establish claims in various legal proceedings;

b. Defending the government in actions by individuals to foreclose on property on which there is a federal tax lien;

c. Lawsuits to enjoin misuse of claimed tax shelters and schemes to understate tax liabilities;

d. Defendant suits against the Internal Revenue Service and its employees, and the secretary of treasury in the performance of their duties;

e. Various legal actions in furtherance of the other responsibilities of this division, including collection of delinquent tax judgments.

CONTACT FOR TAX DIVISION Phone: (202) 514-2901; Website: www.usdoj.gov/tax.

ENVIRONMENT AND NATURAL RESOURCES DIVISION

This division has the duty of acting as the government's attorney in cases enforcing or implementing federal environmental statutes.

The specific types of litigation included within its responsibilities are as follows:

a. Protection, use, and development of natural resources and public lands, wildlife protection, and Indian rights and claims;

b. Prosecuting individuals and corporations charged with violating laws for environmental protection;

c. Litigating on behalf of the ENVIRONMENTAL PROTECTION AGENCY (EPA., DEPARTMENTS OF AGRICULTURE, COMMERCE and INTERIOR for damages to natural resources caused by contamination of public land, and for the costs of cleaning up oil spills on behalf of the U.S. Coast Guard;

d. Prosecution of smugglers and black-market dealers in protected wildlife areas;

e. Litigation to protect federal public lands and natural resources from damaging improper and/or illegal use;

f. Legal action to protect Indian resources such as establishing tribal water, hunting, and fishing rights, establishment of Indian reservation boundaries and rights, and seeking damages for trespass on Indian lands;

g. Bringing legal actions or negotiating acquisition of land for federal public use by the constitutional right of eminent domain at the proven value of the property.

CONTACT FOR ENVIRONMENT AND NATURAL RESOURCES DIVISION Phone: (202) 514-2701.

BUREAUS

The Department of Justice maintains several semi-independent bureaus, which are directly responsible to the attorney general. The best-known is the venerable Federal Bureau of Investigation (FBI), but also there are the Bureau of Prisons, and the National Central Bureau of INTERPOL.

FEDERAL BUREAU OF INVESTIGATION

Prior to May 1908, if the Justice Department needed to investigate corruption and/or federal crimes, it hired detectives by contract, used its own "examiners" to review commercial transactions, and borrowed experts from other departments, especially Secret Service agents. When the department used Secret Service agents, they still reported to the chief of the Secret Service.

The seeds of the FBI were planted on May 27, 1908, when Congress enacted legislation prohibiting the department from using Secret Service operatives, and in response President Theodore Roosevelt authorized Attorney General Charles Bonaparte to create a self-contained corps of special agents. Within a month Attorney General Bonaparte named a force of special agents, including 10 ex–Secret Service employees and several Department of Justice investigators trained in accounting, to be responsible to the department's chief examiner, Stanley W. Finch.

Less than two weeks into the administration of President William Howard Taft, the new attorney general, George Wickersham, named the group the Bureau of Investigation (then with 34 agents) on March 16, 1909, and entitled the chief examiner as chief of the Bureau of Investigation.

During its first decade the bureau concentrated on a limited number of federal crimes involving violations of banking, bankruptcy, naturalization, antitrust, peonage (de facto slavery), and land fraud. It had no training program and generally hired people with prior law-enforcement experience. Its jurisdiction was expanded in 1910 with the enactment of the Mann Act, which made it a federal crime to transport a female across state lines for immoral purposes (an attempt to crack down on "white slave" prostitution rings, which often operated by intimidation, use of drugs, and outright kidnapping of women). When the United States entered World War I in 1917, the bureau became responsible for investigating alleged espionage, sabotage, avoidance of the selective service (draft), and enemy aliens—a duty that terminated when the war ended.

By that time there were 300 agents and a support staff of another 300, with field offices in the larger American cities. When William J. Flynn, a former head of the Secret Service, took over as chief of the bureau in 1919, he was given the title of director of the bureau. The October 1919 passage of the National Motor Vehicle Theft Act gave the bureau responsibility for tracking criminals who crossed state lines after committing state crimes.

Former owner of the Burns Detective Agency, William J. Burns, was the next director, with a young lawyer, J. Edgar Hoover, as his assistant director. Following the scandals of President Warren Harding's administration, in which the attorney general was a key corrupt figure, Harlan Fiske Stone (later chief justice of the Supreme Court) was appointed attorney general, and he appointed young Hoover as director of the bureau on May 10, 1924. Hoover set about modernizing the bureau, dismissing those agents he felt were incompetent, abolishing the seniority system, bringing the inefficient fingerprint identification system (first created in the department in 1907) into the bureau's office, and establishing divisional headquarters in nine cities and expanded field offices to 30.

Hoover also inaugurated training programs, emphasized lawyers and accountants in new hires, set 35 as the maximum age of new agents, created a technical laboratory, and started reporting crime statistics. He also began a personal public relations effort for the bureau. Although the advent of Prohibition gave rise to organized crime in the distribution of illegal alcohol, murders, and big-time gang wars, the control of Prohibition-related crime was not within their purview. On occasion its agents made arrests of gang leaders by using other crimes such as Mann Act violations and income tax evasion.

In response to the kidnapping and murder of the baby of air hero Charles Lindbergh, Congress adopted the federal statute making kidnapping a federal crime, and thus within the authority of the bureau. Supported by President Franklin D. Roosevelt and Attorney General Homer Cummings, there followed other statutes covering crimes that appeared to cross state lines such as bank robberies, and the authority for agents to carry guns and make arrests. The name Federal Bureau of Investigation was adopted in 1935. Many major gangsters were either imprisoned (Al Capone) or killed (John Dillinger) through FBI efforts, including those of intrepid agent Melvin Purvis.

With World War II already under way in Europe and Asia, beginning in 1939 the FBI was directed to investigate threats to national security. Ironically, at the time of the Japanese surprise bombing of Pearl Harbor, the FBI had a definitive list of those relatively few people of Japanese nationality or descent who were suspected of potential pro-Japanese activity, which would have made unnecessary the removal and detention of hundreds of thousands of American citizens of Japanese ancestry in 1942.

After the war the bureau was given the responsibility of investigating the background of all federal employees (even those in such low-level jobs as highway surveyors), which became a major occupation of FBI agents. Hoover directed agents to infiltrate organizations he suspected of communist influence, on the basis that all American communists were being directed by the Soviet Union. He also wrote a book entitled *Masters of Deceit* and numerous articles on the communist menace. The bureau investigated violations of the Smith Act (a law that made membership in the small American Communist Party a crime), which resulted in several convictions, but the Supreme Court ruled the statute was unconstitutional. It was a time (1940s and 1950s) when the House un-American Activities Committee and Senator Joseph McCarthy were using unsupported claims of communists in government and influential occupations as a political weapon to stifle public debate. As HUAC and McCarthy were discredited, there were many who felt that the FBI was less politically motivated, while other critics complained that Hoover was misdirecting the bureau's efforts against left-wing politics to the neglect of major criminals.

In 1950 the list of wanted fugitives became the FBI Most Wanted List, which gave publicity to criminals on the loose, and favorable attention to the bureau. The technical skills of the bureau made it a valuable resource in assisting local and state law enforcement. Congress enacted new federal laws expanding FBI jurisdiction, including the Civil Rights Acts of 1960 and 1964, the Crimes Aboard Aircraft Act (1961), and the Sports Bribery Act (1964). Each of these was in response to revelations of crimes that were interstate in nature.

The assassination of President John F. Kennedy on November 22, 1963, revealed that federal law was hazy on jurisdiction when a president was murdered, but soon the FBI was given that authority. Nevertheless, President Lyndon Johnson ordered the FBI to investigate, and Congress soon legislated such authority. A similar lack become evident after a series of murders of civil rights leaders and activists in 1964 during the efforts in Mississippi and other southern states to register African Americans to vote, desegregate public facilities and schools, and achieve equality in civil rights. After the Supreme Court ruled in 1966 that federal prosecution of civil rights violations were appropriate, the FBI could act directly in investigating such crimes, including the murder of Medgar Evers (which took 30 years to gain a conviction), and tracked down James Earl Ray, the killer of Reverend Martin Luther King Jr. (ironically personally disliked by Director Hoover).

Organized crime through Mafia "families" and other gangs that operated illegal gambling, extortion, drug traffic (increasingly a major crime problem), smuggling, prostitution, loan sharking, labor union corruption, money laundering, and related violence and murders, were increasingly uncovered by FBI agents, who often felt hamstrung by lack of full power to investigate. Congress attempted to provide fuller authority by enacting the Omnibus Crime Control Act of 1968 and the 1970 Racketeer Influenced and Corrupt Organizations (RICO) Act. In the next 30 years a significant dent was put in these criminal cartels, with numerous convictions of organized crime figures.

During Director Clarence M. Kelley's administration the FBI set three top priorities: foreign counterintelligence, organized crime, and white collar crime. The size of the bureau continued to grow, reaching almost 8,000 agents, a support force of 11,000 in 59 field offices, and 13 legal attaché offices. Director Kelley took steps to increase the number of women and ethnic minorities as agents.

When Kelley resigned in 1978 he was succeeded by William H. Webster, a judge of the

UNITED STATES COURT OF APPEALS, appointed by President Jimmy Carter.

Webster made counterterrorism a fourth national priority in 1982, following several terrorist attacks around the world, and created the National Center for the Analysis of Violent Crime. In 1985 the FBI uncovered two spy rings of government employees who were selling secret information to foreign governments. In response to the growing illegal narcotics trade, in 1982 the then attorney general gave the FBI concurrent jurisdiction with the Drug Enforcement Administration over narcotics violations, in particular the heroin trade.

At the same time the bureau discovered several cases of public corruption, especially in so-called ABSCAM, involving members of Congress, as well as involvement of judges, state legislators in two states, and defense procurement contracts. It also conducted extensive investigations involving fraudulent operation of savings and loans (which had been deregulated), which had resulted in almost 300 bank failures. The FBI's ability to investigate was enhanced by the 1987 Financial Institution Reform, Recovery and Enhancement Act.

Before Judge Webster left the FBI to become director of the Central Intelligence Agency in May 1987, 282 bank failures were under investigation by the FBI, the most extensive fraud investigation in national history.

After several terrorist attacks on American personnel overseas, in 1986 for the first time the FBI was given authority to investigate terrorist activities outside U.S. borders, and added authorization to make arrests in foreign countries. Acting Director John E. Otto, who served for five months in 1987, made investigations of illegal drug traffic a fifth national priority.

The next director was another former federal judge, William Steele Sessions. Sessions launched an outreach program, in part in response to revelations of unfavorable conduct of the late Director Hoover, ranging from personal idiosyncrasies, favoritism, obsession with liberal-left activists, and use of personal dossiers as a threat to guarantee his support from political leaders.

After the September 11, 2001, attacks by terrorists, the FBI performed significant investigations, but came under sharp criticism, including from some of its most experienced agents, for its failure to process information from agents and informants such as the evidence against one of the terrorists, the substantial suspicions due to the enrollment of potential terrorists in flying schools around the country, and the bureau's failure to coordinate with the CIA and other intelligence agencies.

Former United States attorney Robert S. Mueller III was appointed as the new director of the FBI, taking office a few days before the 9/11 disaster.

CONTACT   Address: J. Edgar Hoover Building, 935 Pennsylvania Avenue, Washington, DC 20535; Phone: (202) 324-3000; Website: www.fbi.gov; further information: Phone: (202) 317-2727.

BUREAU OF ALCOHOL, TOBACCO, FIREARMS AND EXPLOSIVES (ATF)

The Bureau of Alcohol, Tobacco, Firearms and Explosives (ATF) collects taxes and enforces regulations of the Department of Treasury as its law-enforcement arm. ATF has a colorful if complicated history, which began in 1789, when Congress imposed a tax on imported spirits under the new Constitution to pay off the debt for the Revolutionary War. Treasury Secretary Alexander Hamilton had the responsibility to collect the taxes he had suggested. Taxpayers grumbled and rumbled at the new tax, resulting in the Whisky Rebellion of 1794. Congress created the office of Internal Revenue within the Treasury Department in 1862, partly to collect taxes on distilled spirits and tobacco products, eventually hiring "three detectives to aid in the prevention, detection and punishment of tax evaders," bringing tax collection and enforcement under one roof.

In 1875 federal investigators broke up the "Whisky Ring" of grain dealers, politicians, and revenue agents who defrauded the government of millions of dollars in taxes from distilled spirits imports and sales. In 1886 one lone employee of the DEPARTMENT OF AGRICULTURE moved to the Bureau of Internal Revenue to establish the Revenue Laboratory to enforce the Oleomargarine Act, designed to test adulteration of butter with oleomargarine. In the 21st century, ATF labs now employ chemists, document analysts, latent print specialists, and firearms and toolmark examiners in Rockville, Maryland, Atlanta, Georgia, and Walnut Creek, California.

In 1919 the Eighteenth Amendment to the Constitution was ratified, prohibiting the manufacture, sale, or transportation of liquor. The Internal Revenue's investigators and enforcers became known as "revenoors" and became the Prohibition Unit, which gained bureau status on April Fool's Day, 1927. In 1930 Congress moved Treasury's Bureau of Prohibition to the Department of Justice, while the tax collection part stayed at Treasury. Eliot Ness, known as the "T-man" from Treasury, gained respect and fear as the new Bureau of Industrial Alcohol's most illustrious enforcer, having got Chicago's organized crime king Al Capone on tax-evasion charges.

After the Twenty-first Amendment to the Constitution was ratified by the states with unexpected speed in 1933, President Franklin Roosevelt established the Federal Alcohol Control Administration (FACA) by executive order under the National Industrial Recovery Act. FACA worked with the Departments of Agriculture and Treasury to point wineries and distilleries toward brewers' voluntary codes of fair competition. FACA disappeared quickly when President Roosevelt signed the Federal Alcohol Administration (FAA) Act in August 1935.

The Alcohol Tax Unit moved back from Justice to Treasury in 1934 to collect data, establish license and permit requirements, and define regulations to ensure an open and fair marketplace to benefit both the consumer and the alcohol industry. In 1940 the Federal Alcohol Administration merged with the Alcohol Tax Unit (ATU).

Use of weapons by organized crime during Prohibition led to the National Firearms Act in 1934, and that was replaced by the Federal Firearms Act of 1938, with the goal of regulating and taxing guns. Tax monies were collected by the Bureau of Internal Revenue's ancient Miscellaneous Tax Unit, which was then dismantled in 1952, with the Bureau of Internal Revenue officially becoming the Internal Revenue Service (IRS). IRS then renamed ATU the Alcohol and Tobacco Tax Division.

With passage of the Gun Control Act of 1968, after the assassinations of President John F. Kennedy, his brother Senator Robert Kennedy, and Reverend Martin Luther King Jr., the division got responsibility for explosives in addition to guns, and became the Alcohol, Tobacco, and Firearms Division (ATF) and, subsequently, Bureau, removing it from IRS.

ATF now has several state-of-the-art systems, including the Integrated Ballistic Identification System to match weapons and fired ammunition, dogs that detect explosives weapons, and the Gang Resistance Education and Training (GREAT) program to give children the hope of resisting the pressure to join gangs.

ATF's overall goals are to reduce and prevent crime and violence through enforcement and community outreach; to ensure fair and proper revenue collection; to support and help federal, state, local, and international law-enforcement agencies; and to provide innovative training programs. ATF enforces federal laws and regulations concerning alcohol, tobacco, firearms, explosives, and arson.

Firearms: To regulate and enforce controls of firearms, investigators focus on armed violent offenders, career criminals, narcotics traffickers, narco-terrorists, violent gangs, and domestic and international arms traffickers. ATF works with state and local agencies to increase awareness of federal prosecution possibilities under Sections 924© and (e) of Title 18 of the United States Code.

ATF issues firearms licenses and conducts compliance inspections to determine licensee qualifications and traces guns used in crimes, particularly targeting licensees who might divert firearms from legitimate trade to criminal use and dealers with bad compliance histories.

Achilles and Violent Offenders: The Achilles Program works with task forces to target neighborhoods with the highest rates of gang-related violence, drug trafficking, homicides, and other violent crimes. The Achilles Program was created by the Armed Career Criminal and Comprehensive Crime Control Acts of 1984, and has had success due to the mandatory minimum sentence requirements for recidivist criminals and armed narcotics traffickers.

The *Violent Offender Program* complements the Achilles Program and identifies up to 1,000 career criminals at a time who are most likely to be dangerous to society. Offenders who qualify by their crime records are entered into the National Crime Information Center file for ATF violent felons. When it is working right, the system's computer alerts an arresting law-enforcement officer to dangerous situations. If the person the officer is apprehending has a firearm, the officer must notify ATF immediately. If convicted, such criminals often receive mandatory sentencing of 15 years to life in prison without possibility of parole or probation.

CEASEFIRE: CEASEFIRE uses state-of-the-art technology in violent crimes involving shooting with a ballistic comparison system called Integrated Ballistic Identification System (IBIS). This system digitizes and automatically sorts bullet and shell casing identification markings, enabling local police to link projectiles and shell casings in seemingly unrelated shooting incidents. CEASEFIRE has systems in the District of

Columbia; Atlanta, Georgia; New Orleans, Louisiana; Oakland, California; and Boston, Massachusetts.

G.R.E.A.T.: The Gang Resistance Education and Training Program (G.R.E.A.T.) began in 1992 in Phoenix, Arizona. It is a school-based program conducted in places where gang activity exists or is emerging. Uniformed police officers teach seventh and eighth graders to resist gang membership and the violent crimes and drugs that may be part of some of them.

Arson and Explosives: ATF's Explosives Program gives information to local communities to investigate explosives incidents and arson-for-profit schemes through National Response Teams, International Response Teams, and Arson Task Forces that include special agents, auditors, technicians, laboratory personnel, and dogs.

ATF takes the lead in investigating arson and bombing incidents at abortion clinics, and works with other countries on postblast investigations to determine cause and origin of bombing attacks.

National and International Response Teams: The National Response Team (NRT) helps federal, state, and local investigators in on-site fire and explosives investigations, such as suspicious commercial fires, bombings, and accidental explosions at explosives, ammunition, and pyrotechnics manufacturing plants. Each team includes special agents with postblast and fire origin and cause expertise, forensic chemists, fire protection engineers, dog handlers with dogs capable of detecting explosives, and explosives technology experts. Every team of federal, state, and local officials reconstruct the scene, identify the site of the blast or fire's origin, conduct interviews, and sift through debris to gather all evidence related to the fire or bombing.

The International Response Team (IRT) extends the NRT to work with the DEPARTMENT OF STATE and the Diplomatic Security Service. IRT's team includes supervisory special agents, fire origin-and-cause specialists, explosives enforcement officers, and special agent certified explosives specialists with postblast expertise, working with fire protection engineers and forensic chemists.

Alcohol and Tobacco Programs: ATF regulates qualification and operation of distilleries, wineries, breweries, and importers and wholesalers of alcoholic beverages. ATF's National Laboratory Center tests new products and tests to determine if current products pose a health risk to consumers. ATF also examines all label applications for approval to make sure alcoholic beverage labels do not contain misleading information.

The Alcohol Program's goals are to collect alcohol beverage excise taxes; provide deposit and accurate accounting for these taxes; to try to prevent criminals or persons whose business experience or associations suggest a risk of tax fraud from entering into the industry; and to suppress label fraud, commercial bribery, diversion and smuggling, and other unlawful practices.

The Tobacco Program's goals include ensuring collection of tobacco excise taxes qualifying applicants for permits to manufacture tobacco products or to operate tobacco export warehouses. Tobacco inspectors check and verify an applicant's qualifications, check the warehouse's security, and ensure tax compliance. ATF special agents investigate trafficking of contraband tobacco products that violate federal law and some sections of the Internal Revenue Code.

CONTACT Address: Bureau of Alcohol, Tobacco, and Firearms, 650 Massachusetts Avenue NW, Washington, DC 20226; Phone: (202) 927-8500; Fax: (202) 927-8868; Website: www.atf.treas.gov. Field Operations Offices—Offices of Enforcement: 2600 Century Parkway, Suite 300, Atlanta, GA 30345-3104; Phone: (404) 417-2600. 32 Hopkins Plaza, 5th Floor, Baltimore, MD 21201; Phone: (410) 779-1700. 10 Causeway Street, Room 253, Boston, MA 02222-1047; Phone: (617) 557-1200. 5300 Maryland Way, Suite 200, Brentwood, TN 37107; Phone: (615) 565-1400.

6701 Carmel Road, Suite 200, Charlotte, NC 28209; Phone: (704) 716-1800. 300 So. Riverside Plaza, Suite 350, Chicago, IL 60606; Phone: (312) 353-6935. 37 West Broad Street, Columbus, OH 43215; Phone: (614) 469-5303. 1114 Commerce Street, Suite 303, Dallas, TX 75242; Phone: (469) 227-4300. 15355 Vantage Parkway, Suite 210, Houston, TX 77032; Phone: (281) 372-2900. 1155 Brewery Park Boulevard, Suite 300, Detroit, MI 48207-2602; Phone: (313) 259-0700. 2600 Grand Avenue, Suite 200, Kansas City, MO 64108; Phone: (816) 559-0700. 350 So. Figueroa Street, Suite 800, Los Angeles, CA 90071; Phone: (213) 534-2450. 600 Dr. Martin Luther King, Jr. Place, Suite 322, Louisville, KY 40202; Phone: (502) 753-3400; 111 Veterans Boulevard, Suite 1008, Metairie, LA 70005; Phone: (504) 841-7000. 5225 NW 87th Avenue, Suite 300, Miami, FL 33178; Phone: (305) 597-4800. 300 Coffey Street, New York, NY 11231; Phone: (718) 254-7883. 2nd and Chestnut Streets, Room 607, Philadelphia, PA 19106; Phone: (215) 717-4700. 3003 N. Central Avenue, Suite 1010, Phoenix, AZ 85012; Phone: (602) 776-5400. 221 Main Street, San Francisco, CA 94105. 915 2nd Avenue, Room 790, Seattle, WA 98174; Phone: (206) 220-6440. 1870 World Trade Center, 30 E. 7th Street, St. Paul, MN 55101; Phone: (651) 290-3092. 501 E. Polk Street, Room 700, Tampa FL 33602; Phone: (813) 228-2021; 607 14th Street NW, Suite 620, Washington, DC 20005; Phone: (202) 927-8810.

BUREAU OF PRISONS

Responsible for the safe incarceration of those prisoners convicted of federal crimes, the Bureau of Prisons attempts to make the facilities humane, efficient, and safe while providing self-improvement opportunities and work for offenders. Under its jurisdiction the bureau maintains prisoners not only in federal prisons, but also in community-based programs (halfway houses in some cases), detention centers, local jails, and even privately operated prisons. The central office of the bureau is located in Washington, DC.

CONTACT Address: 320 First Street NW, Washington, DC 20534; Phone: (202) 307-3198; Website: www.bop.gov.

To perform its mandated functions the bureau has divided its administration into three divisions and the National Institute of Corrections. The divisions and their missions are:

a. Community Corrections and Detention Division has contracts and other relationships with the various non-bureau entities such as community-based programs, detention centers, state prisons, local jails, and privately operated prisons. It also promotes and coordinates programs of citizen and inmate volunteers to improve facilities and activities;

b. Correctional Programs Division develops programs to prevent inmate idleness and to encourage rehabilitation such as psychological services, religious services, substance abuse treatment, discipline, computing sentence, inmate receipt and discharge formalities, transfers of foreign prisoners, and protecting inmates in the *Federal Witness Protection Program* operated by the United States Marshal Service;

c. Industries, Education and Vocational Training Division oversees these programs as well as the operation of Federal Prison Industries, a government-owned corporation that provides employment for federal inmates. The aim is to provide not only employment but also training for life after prison.

The *National Institute of Corrections* gives technical assistance, training, and information on prisons and correctional activities to state and local agencies that operate prison facilities.

Training services to local correctional employees are held at the institute.

CONTACT Address: 320 First Street NW, Washington, DC 20534; Phone: (202) 307-3198.

UNITED STATES NATIONAL CENTRAL BUREAU—INTERPOL

The International Criminal Police Organization, known commonly as INTERPOL, is an organization of 178 nations to gather information and promote mutual assistance among law-enforcement authorities to combat international crime. Essentially an information-gathering, storing, and disseminating operation, INTERPOL also conducts symposia on various topics related to criminal activity and the means to fight it.

The United States National Central Bureau represents the American government in INTERPOL. Pursuant to the bureau's State and Local Law Enforcement Program leads from American law enforcement agencies can be directed into INTERPOL upon investigation requests. In return, INTERPOL disburses information on international crime activity to local and state law-enforcement authorities throughout the United States. All 50 states and the District of Columbia are involved in the program, as well as sub-bureaus in Puerto Rico, American Samoa, and the Virgin Islands.

CONTACT Address: Interpol, Washington, DC 20530; Phone: (202) 616-9000.

UNITED STATES MARSHALS SERVICE

The United States Marshals Service, which dates back to the founding of the federal court system in 1789, is responsible for protecting and assisting the federal courts, the judges and justices, and their staffs. Famed in history and fiction for serving as law enforcement in the western territories before they became states, today the marshals protect 800 federal court facilities, 2,000 judges and magistrates, and perform various services for the justice system, including:

a. apprehension of most federal fugitives;

b. running the *Federal Witness Protection Program* to guarantee the safety of witnesses against retribution or elimination by criminal defendants, including providing new identities and secret locations for the witnesses;

c. transporting thousands of federal prisoners;

d. making arrests and seizing evidence under warrants and court orders;

e. holding and selling property seized for use in crimes (particularly vehicles used to transport illegal drugs);

f. running the United States Marshals Service Training Academy;

g. providing law-enforcement services during riots, mob violence, and other emergencies; one of the most famous was providing backup in the attack on the Waco Branch Davidians ordered by the Justice Department under Attorney General Janet Reno, which turned out disastrously when the buildings of this religious sect caught fire and numerous followers died, including many children.

The most famous case of judicial protection by a U.S. marshal involved Supreme Court Justice Stephen Field, who had been threatened by David Terry, a former chief justice of the California Supreme Court. When Terry pulled a knife on Field in a railroad dining room, he was shot dead by the marshal, who had been assigned to protect Field. When the authority to empower the marshal to use deathly force was challenged, the Supreme Court ruled in the landmark case, *In re Neagle* (1890), that there was "inherent" power in the president to take such reasonable steps without specific statutory authority.

A U.S. marshal's office headed by the local marshal is located in the federal courthouse in every federal court district throughout the nation.

CONTACT   Phone: (202) 307-9065.

DRUG ENFORCEMENT ADMINISTRATION

Established in July 1973, the Drug Enforcement Administration is the chief federal agency for enforcement of laws against manufacture, cultivation, trafficking, smuggling, sale, and use of illegal narcotics. Authorized to act worldwide, its activities include arresting members of organizations involved in the drug trade both within and without the United States, presenting cases for prosecution before courts with jurisdiction, and assisting law-enforcement antidrug programs.

The DEA is headed by an administrator, popularly known as the Drug Czar. With liaison to the United Nations, INTERPOL, and other organizations, the DEA maintains offices throughout the United States and in more than 55 countries.

Its responsibilities include:

a. investigating major traffickers of illegal narcotics both domestically and internationally;

b. seizing assets involved in narcotics trafficking;

c. managing a narcotics intelligence system;

d. coordinating American law-enforcement efforts against illegal narcotics at every level and abroad;

e. training, conducting scientific research, and facilitating the exchange of information on anti-illegal drug efforts;

f. supervising registration under the Controlled Substances Act.

CONTACT Address: 600-700 Army Navy Drive, Arlington, VA 22202; Phone: (202) 307-1000. Public Affairs Section, DEA, Department of Justice, Washington, DC 20537; Phone: (202) 307-7977; Registration Section, DEA, P.O. Box 28083, Central Station, Washington, DC 20038; Phone: (202) 307-7255.

OFFICE OF JUSTICE PROGRAMS

The Department of Justice conducts several programs directed to crime control and related activities, all of which are coordinated by the Office of Justice Programs. This office was established under the 1984 Justice Assistance Act and renewed in 1994. Under this umbrella are the following bureaus and offices:

BUREAU OF JUSTICE ASSISTANCE: Gives local and state law-enforcement funding, training, and technical assistance in combating violent and drug-related crime, and improvement of the criminal justice systems.

BUREAU OF JUSTICE STATISTICS: Collects, analyzes, and makes available data on crime, convicted criminals, victims of crime, and justice systems throughout the country.

NATIONAL INSTITUTE OF JUSTICE: Sponsors research, develops programs, conducts demonstration of new methodology, and develops new technologies, all directed toward the improvement of criminal justice.

OFFICE OF JUVENILE JUSTICE AND DELINQUENCY PREVENTION: Processes and issues financial grants and contracts to the states for the improvement of their juvenile justice systems. It also sponsors programs of research, demonstrations, evaluation, statistical collection and dissemination, training, and technical assistance intended to promote understanding of and assist states in responding to juvenile criminality, violence, and delinquency.

OFFICE FOR VICTIMS OF CRIME: Administers the actual compensation program for victims of crimes, and assists local organizations serving the victims of crime and local criminal justice offices with funding, training, and technical help aimed at improving the response to the needs of crime victims.

VIOLENCE AGAINST WOMEN OFFICE: Administers grants to local and state organizations that strive to prevent domestic violence, sexual assault, and stalking against women, all of which are crimes. The office also develops legislation and initiatives to assist law enforcement in relation to violence against women.

DRUG COURTS PROGRAM OFFICE: Provides training, technical assistance, and grants to local, state, and tribal governmental bodies and courts to support the development and improvement of so-called drug courts.

CORRECTIONS PROGRAM OFFICE: Provides assistance to state and local governments to help in prison construction and drug treatment programs in prisons and jails.

EXECUTIVE OFFICE FOR "WEED AND SEED": Provides assistance to local communities to develop "weed and seed" programs of neighborhood involvement in multidisciplinary programs to combat crime. These are types of neighborhood watch efforts and conflict resolution.

Office for State and Local Preparedness: Part of the government's response to the 9/11 terrorist attacks, and is intended to provide advice to local jurisdictions on response to potential terrorism by chemical, biological, or radiological "weapons of mass destruction." This is possibly redundant to other antiterrorism efforts by other elements of the United States government.

Office of the Police Corps and Law Enforcement Education: Administers a program of scholarships and other financial aid to college students who have committed to careers in law enforcement and to dependents of law-enforcement officers who were killed in the line of duty.

CONTACT Address: Office of Justice Programs, 810 Seventh Street NW, Washington, DC 20531; Phone: (202) 307-0703; or contact the Department of Justice Response Center by telephone at (800) 421-6770; E-mail: askojp@ojp.usdoj.gov; Website: www.ojp.usdoj.gov.

UNITED STATES PAROLE COMMISSION

For federal prisoners serving more than one year, the U.S. Parole Commission has the exclusive authority to grant, modify, or revoke paroles. The commission follows up to supervise parolees, determine amount of allowances for good behavior in prison, and set conditions of parole, which are supervised by probation officers. It also calculates release dates for American citizens returned to the United States to complete foreign criminal sentences.

Based on specific statutory requirements the commission determines whether former prisoners convicted of crimes involving organized labor can become officials of labor unions or their employment benefit plans.

CONTACT Address: Chairperson, United States Parole Commission, Department of Justice, 5550 Friendship Boulevard, Chevy Chase, MD 20815; Phone: (301) 492-5990; Website: www.usdoj.gov/uspc/parole.

FEDERAL LAW ENFORCEMENT TRAINING CENTER (FLETC)

The Federal Law Enforcement Training Center (FLETC) works to provide world-class law-enforcement training for more than 70 federal law-enforcement agencies. Skills taught range from basic law enforcement to state and local police and investigative personnel, to antiterrorism techniques, microcomputers in investigations, advanced law-enforcement photography, continuing legal education, marine law enforcement, and courses to train law-enforcement instructors.

Other areas of education made available by FLETC include fraud and financial investigations, small-town and rural law enforcement, advanced medical fraud training, international banking and money laundering, and training in protection of archeological resources.

FLETC operates its instructional institutions in Glynco, Georgia, between Savannah and Jacksonville, Florida; Artesia, New Mexico; Charleston, South Carolina; and a new location at Cheltenham, Maryland, all of which are designed for training programs in which learners stay at the facilities, much like law-enforcement training camps. The new Cheltenham program will focus on in-service and requalification training for officers and agents in the Washington, D.C., area. More than 20 partner organizations have training offices at FLETC to coordinate training.

CONTACT Address: FLETC, Glynco, Georgia 31524; Phone: (912) 267-2224. Washington, DC; Phone: (202) 927-8940. Artesia, New Mexico; Phone: (505) 748-8000; Website: www.fletc.gov or www.ustreas.gov/fletc.

OFFICE OF COMMUNITY ORIENTED POLICING SERVICES (COPS)

Based on the program initiated by the Clinton administration to put 100,000 more police officers into communities, COPS' principal function is to award competitive discretionary grants to local law-enforcement agencies. The office follows up to determine progress and compliance with the terms of the grants.

COPS also:

a. develops and designs new programs for officer recruiting and resources for community policing;

b. reviews grant applications and assists grantees in carrying out the grant programs;

c. checks compliance with conditions of grants;

d. gives on-site technical assistance;

e. collects and disseminates the results of successful policing strategies.

All of these functions are intended to coordinate training and technical advances in order to promote and sustain better policing in thousands of American communities. However, as of 2004 the COPS program was underfunded.

CONTACT Address: Office of Community Oriented Policing Services, Department of Justice, 100 Vermont Avenue NW, Washington, DC 20530; Phone: (202) 514-2058; Website: www.usdoj.gov/cops.

FOREIGN CLAIMS SETTLEMENT COMMISSION OF THE UNITED STATES

Over the years since World War II many American citizens and businesses have made claims against foreign governments for alleged loss of property, appropriation and nationalization of commercial enterprises, injuries, treatment of prisoners in violation of international law, as the result of international claims settlement agreements, or authorized by the War Claims Act of 1948. Congress has given jurisdiction to adjudicate such claims to the Foreign Claims Settlement Commission of the United States. In some cases the U.S. government has

foreign assets impounded, which can be used to satisfy such claims.

The commission's decisions are final and are not reviewable by any American or international court. It also maintains records of individual claims by the U.S. government that have been made against the governments of Vietnam, Iran, both German republics, Yugoslavia, Cuba, China, Albania, the former Soviet Union, and a dozen other nations.

CONTACT Address: Foreign Claims Settlement Commission of the United States, Department of Justice, Suite 6002, 600 E Street NW, Washington, DC 20579; Phone: (202) 616-6975; Fax: (202) 616-6993.

COMMUNITY RELATIONS SERVICE

In order to resolve disputes related to race, color, or national origin without employing the enforcement powers of the Division of Civil Rights or other compelling actions, the department operates the Community Relations Service. This service employs mediation, voluntary agreements, and stimulation of community measures to alleviate tensions.

CONTACT Address: Community Relations Service, Department of Justice, Suite 2000, 600 E Street NW, Washington, DC 20530; Phone: (202) 305-2935.

There are also 10 regional offices of the service: 308 Atlantic Avenue, Suite 222, Boston, MA 02201; Phone: (617) 424-5715. 28 Federal Plaza, New York City, NY 10278; Phone: (212) 264-0700. Second and Chestnut Streets, Philadelphia, PA 19206; Phone: (215) 597-2344. 75 Piedmont Avenue, Atlanta, GA 30303; Phone: (404) 331-6883. 55 West Monroe Street, Chicago, IL 60603; Phone: (312) 353-4391. 323 West Eighth Street, Kansas City, MO 64105; Phone: (816) 426-7434. 1420 West Mockingbird Lane, Dallas, TX 75247;

Phone: (214) 655-8175. 1244 Speer Boulevard, Denver, CO 80204; Phone: (303) 844-2973. 888 South Figueroa Street, Los Angeles, CA 90017; Phone: (213) 894-2941. 915 Second Avenue, Seattle, WA 98101; Phone: (206) 220-6700.

UNITED STATES TRUSTEE PROGRAM

In response to problems of the conduct of bankruptcy trustees representing either bankrupt persons or businesses or the creditors, the United States Trustee Program was created by the Bankruptcy Reform Act of 1978 (11 USC 101, et seq.) to oversee the conduct of the trustees. The trustees manage billions of dollars of assets, including those corporations still in business while seeking to reorganize and refinance under Chapter 11.

The Trustee Program sets policies for the trustees, gives legal direction, and investigates claims or suspicions of fraud with so-called U.S. trustees in place in almost every state. They require that trustees file reports and in turn advise federal bankruptcy judges when necessary.

CONTACT Address: Executive Office for U.S. Trustees, Department of Justice, Suite 700, 901 E Street NW, Washington, DC 20530; Phone: (202) 307-1391; Website: www.usdoj.gov/ust.

EMPLOYMENT AT JUSTICE DEPARTMENT

Those interested in applying for jobs at the Department of Justice may contact the website of the Office of Attorney Recruitment and Management at www.usdoj.gov/arm or telephone the job line: (202) 514-3397.

Attorneys applying for employment contact: Director, Office of Attorney Personnel Management, Department of Justice, Room 6150, Tenth Street and Constitution Avenue NW, Washington, DC 20530; Phone: (202) 514-1432. Applications to be assistant United States attorneys (located in each federal court district) should apply to the United States attorney in your area.

For applications to the Federal Bureau of Investigation, write the central office or check with the local field office. For the Bureau of Prisons, U.S. Marshals, Office of Justice Programs, U.S. Trustee Program, or the Foreign Claims Settlement Commission contact those agencies directly at the address and/or telephone number listed with the description of the agency.

DEPARTMENT OF LABOR

The Department of Labor (DOL) works to promote and preserve the welfare of workers, job seekers, wage earners, and retirees by improving work conditions, improving employment opportunities, protecting retirement and health care benefits, linking employers to workers, strengthening free collective bargaining, and tracking changes in employment, prices, and other national economic measurements. DOL also administers federal labor laws such as those that guarantee workers' rights to safe and healthful working conditions; minimum hourly wages and overtime pay; freedom from discrimination in employment; unemployment insurance; and income support. DOL provides some job training and gives special attention to helping older workers, youths, minority group members, women, and handicapped individuals.

The department formulates, gathers, researches, reports, and publishes economic statistics including the Consumer Price Index, the unemployment rate, payroll employment, average hourly earnings, Producer Price Index, the Employment Cost Index, Productivity, U.S. Import Price Index, unemployment initial claims, and the current federal minimum wage.

HISTORY

The first American Bureau of Labor was created by Congress in 1884 as part of the INTERIOR DEPARTMENT, subsequently achieving independence as the Department of Labor, but without cabinet rank. In 1903 Labor returned to bureau status as part of the Department of Commerce and Labor.

After a lengthy campaign by the progressive movement, Congress passed a bill creating the separate Department of Labor, which defeated Republican President Howard Taft grudgingly signed into law just hours before he was succeeded by Democrat Woodrow Wilson. The new department included a new U.S. Conciliation Service (USCS) to mediate labor disputes; the Bureau of Labor Statistics (BLS); the Bureau of Immigration; the Bureau of Naturalization; and the Children's Bureau. President Wilson appointed as first secretary of labor congressman William B. Wilson, a founder and former secretary-treasurer of the United Mine Workers of America.

Secretary Wilson reiterated that the department was created "in the interest of the wage earners," which most secretaries of labor have believed since. During World War I working conditions and labor peace became more important than ever, and DOL took the forefront to implement war labor policies, which included the right to bargain collectively, establishment of methods to adjust grievances, and an eight-hour workday.

Following World War I, labor-management conflicts brought about a strike wave that threatened the postwar economy rebound. At the same time there arose a national "red scare" and fear of "communists," referred to by Attorney General A. Mitchell Palmer as "Bolsheviks" (translates from Russian as "majority"). Attorney General Palmer, as head of the Justice Department, demanded that Immigration deport all such "dangerous" aliens, which actually resulted in the deportation of 556 alleged communists.

After President Wilson's term of prolabor activism, subsequent Republican presidents Warren Harding (1921–23), Calvin Coolidge (1923–29), and Herbert Hoover (1929–33) made an about-face on labor rights and urged less government and less governmental influence. During this Republican period, DOL focused on restricting immigration and deportation of undesirable aliens, while expanding Children's Bureau's activities and instituting a constitutional amendment to limit child labor. DOL also began to encourage immigrant and migrant seasonal farm workers to help with the shortage of field hands.

In 1920 the Women's Bureau, intended to promote the welfare of working women, became permanent. In 1933 Democratic President Franklin D. Roosevelt appointed Frances Perkins (1933–45) as the first woman secretary of labor and the first woman member of a presidential cabinet. Perkins had served as commissioner of labor in New York when FDR was governor of New York and worked to alleviate unemployment as the Great Depression deepened. Republicans tried to get her impeached as secretary of labor because she refused to deport alleged communist labor leader Harry Bridges, head of the International Longshoremen and Warehousemen's Union. Perkins believed the Bureau of Immigration was going too far in deporting aliens, and stopped the bureau's harassment of aliens, resulting in the Bureau of Immigration being moved to the Department of Justice in 1940.

Secretary Perkins set up the Civilian Conservation Corps (CCC) to employ young men to work on rural conservation projects for one dollar a day, and led the campaign to create Social Security as part of the New Deal, resulting in passage of the Social Security Act in 1935. DOL's headquarters building in Washington, D.C., is named for Secretary Perkins.

The Wagner-Peyser Act of 1933 ("Wagner Act" or "National Labor Relations Act") led to

Department of Labor

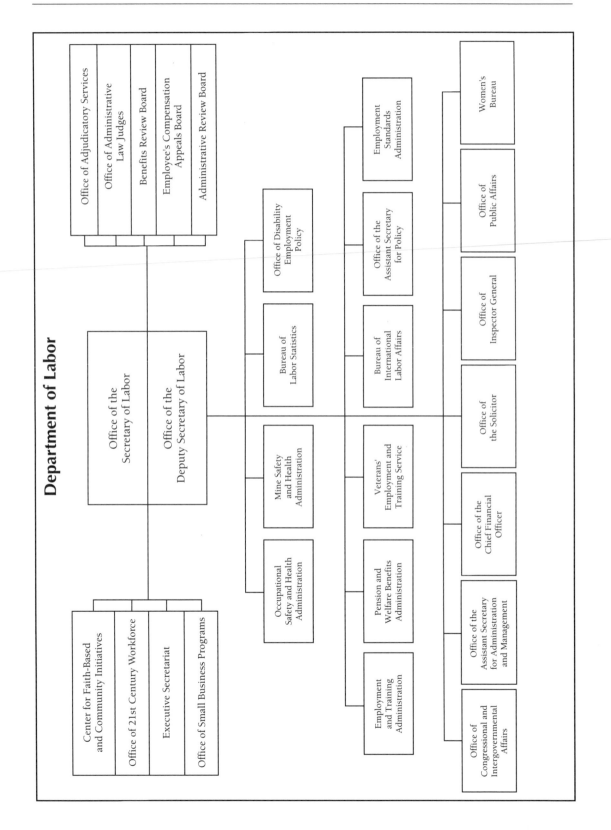

Office of the Secretary of Labor

Office of Adjudicatory Services

Office of Administrative Law Judges

Benefits Review Board

Employee's Compensation Appeals Board

Administrative Review Board

Office of the Deputy Secretary of Labor

Center for Faith-Based and Community Initiatives

Office of 21st Century Workforce

Executive Secretariat

Office of Small Business Programs

Occupational Safety and Health Administration

Mine Safety and Health Administration

Bureau of Labor Statistics

Office of Disability Employment Policy

Employment and Training Administration

Pension and Welfare Benefits Administration

Veterans' Employment and Training Service

Bureau of International Labor Affairs

Office of the Assistant Secretary for Policy

Employment Standards Administration

Office of Congressional and Intergovernmental Affairs

Office of the Assistant Secretary for Administration and Management

Office of the Chief Financial Officer

Office of the Solicitor

Office of Inspector General

Office of Public Affairs

Women's Bureau

the U.S. Employment Services and established a nationwide system of employment, placement, and recruitment. The Walsh-Healey Public Contracts Act of 1936 required that companies dealing with the government establish an eight-hour workday under safe conditions, and allowed the secretary of labor to set minimum wages based on local rates, leading eventually to the establishment of minimum wages and maximum work hours (40 per week).

When Harry Truman succeeded FDR as president in 1945, Perkins resigned, and Truman appointed Lewis B. Schwellenbach, a former federal judge and U.S. senator, as secretary of labor. Massive strikes followed, and reaction to the strikes led to the union restrictive Taft-Hartley Act of 1947 and massive budget cuts to DOL, seen as a hotbed of liberal unionism.

President John F. Kennedy appointed as secretary of labor Arthur Goldberg (1961–62), special counsel to the American Federation of Labor, who eventually became a Supreme Court justice. Under Goldberg's leadership, the Area Redevelopment Act of 1961 was passed to provide training and assistance to regions with serious unemployment, and the Manpower Development and Training Act of 1962 gave DOL responsibility to identify labor shortages, the unemployed, and sponsor manpower research.

President Lyndon B. Johnson established the Manpower Administration to coordinate training and equal opportunity employment programs. Johnson's War on Poverty established the Neighborhood Youth Corps, which helped 1.5 million poor young people work for pay while finishing high school. Passage of the Civil Rights Act of 1964 created the Office of Federal Contract Compliance Programs to fight discrimination by government contractors. The Bracero program for temporary Mexican farm labor was terminated in hopes of giving more jobs to American farmworkers.

Under presidents Richard M. Nixon and Gerald Ford, five successive secretaries of labor worked to decentralize federal labor programs.

Under Nixon, the Manpower Administration was restructured, and the Emergency Employment Act of 1971 created 170,000 temporary public service jobs. The Comprehensive Employment and Training Act of 1973 led to revenue sharing to transfer funds and decision making for training of workers to states and other local entities. Nixon also transferred Johnson's Job Corps (1969) training program for needy youths from the Office of Economic Opportunity to DOL. In 1970 the Occupational Safety and Health Administration (OSHA) was created to enforce existing safety and health rules and oversee state-run programs to eliminate workplace hazards.

When Democratic president Jimmy Carter succeeded Ford in 1977, Carter's primary domestic goal was to create jobs for the unemployed, and with his secretary of labor Ray Marshall (1977–81) stimulated 725,000 public service jobs under CETA, expanded the Job Corps, and encouraged other youth employment bills. The Targeted Jobs Tax Credit gave employers tax credits for hiring disabled people.

In 1981 Republican president Ronald Reagan's plan for economic recovery included reduced government spending and relief for business from what it regarded as burdensome rules imposed by the government, freezing rules, and lowering standards adopted during the Carter administration. OSHA's enforcement became more lax, and it encouraged voluntary rather than mandatory compliance. Other regulatory agencies followed suit as prescribed by Reagan. DOL's discretionary spending dropped a drastic 60 percent, DOL jobs were cut by 21 percent, and the Job Training and Partnership Act shifted responsibility to the states while allowing local officials to make their own policy to be approved by special private industry councils.

Under President George H. W. Bush, Secretary of Labor Elizabeth Dole (wife of then Senate Republican leader Robert Dole), undertook a "Glass Ceiling" initiative to reduce barriers to women's and minorities' salaries and promotions in corporations. Secretary Dole also made the first minimum wage increase in years, and established a Secretary's Commission on Achieving Necessary Skills to improve education and skills of American workers, specifically targeting the neediest.

President Bill Clinton's secretary of labor, Robert Reich, cut staff by more than 1,000 employees, focused on developing skills of workers, and instigated the School-to-Work Opportunities Act (1994) to help with the transition from high school to work for the 75 percent of Americans who do not graduate from college, aiming at developing skills needed by employers. Reich also oversaw enactment of the Retirement Protection Act to protect workers's retirement benefits in undefended retirement plans. Reich launched campaigns against sweatshops, unsafe workplaces, and fraudulent health insurance companies. Under his leadership DOL embarked on the Family Medical Leave Act of 1993, which gave up to 12 weeks unpaid leave for a worker to care for a new child or ill family member.

BUREAUS

ADMINISTRATIVE REVIEW BOARD

Created in April 1996 under President Bill Clinton and Secretary of Labor Robert Reich, the Administrative Review Board combines the former Board of Service Contract Appeals, the Wage Appeals Board, and the Office of Administrative Appeals. The Administrative Review Board issues final agency decisions on many federal labor laws, including nuclear, environmental, Surface Transportation Assistance Act whistle-blower cases, Office of Federal Contract Compliance Program cases, and child labor cases.

CONTACT Address: Administrative Review Board, 200 Constitution Avenue NW, Room S-4309, Washington, DC 20210; Phone: (202) 693-6200; Fax: (202) 693-6220; Website: www.dol.gov/arb.

BENEFITS REVIEW BOARD

Created by Congress in 1972, DOL's Benefits Review Board reviews and issues decisions on appeals of worker's compensation claims that qualify under the Longshore and Harbor Worker's Compensation Act and the Black Lung Benefits amendments to the Federal Coal Mine Health and Safety Act of 1969. The board functions as an appellate court in these cases, which authority was held formerly by the U.S. district courts. The board's rulings can be appealed to the U.S. COURTS OF APPEALS and to the U.S. SUPREME COURT.

CONTACT For filings and correspondence by mail: Address: Benefits Review Board, P.O. Box 37601, Washington, DC 20013-7601. For filings in person: Address: Benefits Review Board, 200 Constitution Avenue NW, Room S-5220, Washington, DC 20210. Offices of board chair, judges, and general counsel: Address: Benefits Review Board, 200 Constitution Avenue NW, Room N-5101, Washington, DC 20210; Phone: clerk of the board, (202) 693-6300; Fax: (202) 693-6310; Website: www.dol.gov/brb.

BUREAU OF INTERNATIONAL LABOR AFFAIRS (ILAB)

ILAB's mission is to help formulate international labor policies and programs that benefit U.S. workers. ILAB conducts research and formulates international economic, trade, immigration, and labor policies with other U.S. government agencies and provides technical assistance to other countries. ILAB also deals with labor and migration, publishes reports on international labor issues, represents American workers' interests in interagency policy reviews, and helps form and implement international treaties concerning labor migration, trade, and investment issues.

ILAB monitors labor developments in other countries to help create better work standards in the global economy to promote a stable, secure, and prosperous international economic system. Sometimes ILAB has to monitor American manufacturers utilizing unsafe and unfair labor shops in "countries in transition."

ILAB has five programs and offices dealing with labor issues and problems involving the United States and other countries.

CONTACT Address: Bureau of International Labor Affairs, 200 Constitution Avenue NW, Room C-4325, Washington, DC, 20210; Phone: (202) 693-4770; Fax: 693-4780; E-mail: ILAB@dol.gov; Website: www.dol.gov/ILAB/.

INTERNATIONAL CHILD LABOR PROGRAM (ICLP): Created under President Bill Clinton to investigate and report on child labor around the world, including child labor used in manufacturing, mining, and agriculture, as well as children working under forced labor conditions in either bonded or slave conditions; forced child prostitution; child labor used to produce clothing and shoes for the U.S. market; and business efforts to label products made by illegal child labor. Theoretically, the program reports on international child labor; gives grants to organizations trying to eliminate child labor and improve education for children subject to such employment; and tries to raise public awareness of child labor.

CONTACT Address: International Child Labor Program, 200 Constitution Avenue NW, Room S-5307, Washington, DC 20210; Phone: (202) 693-4843; Fax: (202) 693-4830; E-mail: Education-Initiative@dol.gov or GlobalKids@dol.gov; Website: www.dol.gov/ILAB/.

NATIONAL ADMINISTRATIVE OFFICE (NAO): Established by the North American Agreement on Labor Cooperation (NAALC), a U.S., Canada, and Mexico pact supplemental to the North American Free Trade Agreement (NAFTA). The U.S.'s NAO coordinates trilateral, tripartite cooperative activities on labor issues with Canada and Mexico; serves as the official labor review office for trilateral labor issues; and communicates with Mexico and Canada's NAOs and with the Secretariat of the Commission for Labor Cooperation and other entities.

CONTACT Address: National Administrative Office, 200 Constitution Avenue NW, Room S-5205, Washington, DC 20210; Phone: (202) 693-4900; Fax: (202) 693-4910; E-mail: USNAO@dol.gov; Website: www.dol.gov/ILAB/.

OFFICE OF FOREIGN RELATIONS (OFR): Watches international labor trends and developments and helps the secretary of labor devise special initiatives to advance U.S. international labor policy. OFR gives technical assistance to countries in transition to free market economies, as well as governments interested in improving workers' rights and conditions. OFR also looks at HIV/AIDS issues in the workplace; coordinates DOL's part of the American Labor Office Program of the U.S. Foreign Services; arranges study tours for AID-sponsored groups of foreign nationals; operates an Information Clearinghouse on U.S. workers' rights abroad; and arranges programs for foreign visitors to the United States who are interested in DOL programs and visiting as guests of other agencies.

CONTACT Address: Office of Foreign Relations, 200 Constitution Avenue NW, Room S-5303, Washington, DC 20210; Phone: (202) 693-4785; Fax: (202) 693-4784; E-mail: OFR@dol.gov; Website: www.dol.gov/ILAB.

OFFICE OF INTERNATIONAL ECONOMIC AFFAIRS (OIEA): Works to consider the impact of trade, investment, and immigration policies on U.S. workers. OIEA's Trade Policy Division gives staff support in interagency development and implementation of U.S. policy on multilateral and bilateral trade and investment issues. The International Commodities Division works on development, negotiation, and implementation of special commodity agreements. The Foreign Economic Research Division researches effects of international economic developments on U.S. workers, and the Division of Immigration Policy and Research works with the administration to form U.S. immigration policy, particularly regarding labor-market consequences of immigration proposals and legislation.

CONTACT Address: Office of International Economic Affairs, 200 Constitution Avenue NW, Room S-5317, Washington, DC 20210; Phone: (202) 693-4888; Fax: (202) 693-4851; E-mail: OIEA@dol.gov; Website: www.dol.gov/ILAB.

OFFICE OF INTERNATIONAL ORGANIZATIONS (OIO): Represents ILAB in international labor organizations, including the International Labor Organization (ILO) of the United Nations. In this role, ILO works with the DEPARTMENTS OF COMMERCE and STATE, with the AFL-CIO, and with employer representatives from the U.S. Council for International Business (USCIB). OIO also represents the United States on the Employment, Labor, and Social Affairs Committee of the Organization for Economic Cooperation and Development (OECD), which focuses on employment, training, immigration, statistics, women's issues, and social policy. OIO also works on innovations in job creation, entrepreneurship, and local development.

CONTACT Address: Office of International Organizations, 200 Constitution Avenue NW, Room S-5317, Washington, DC 20210; Phone: (202) 693-4855; Fax: (202) 693-4860; E-mail: OIO@dol.gov; Website: www.dol.gov.ILAB.

BUREAU OF LABOR STATISTICS

The Bureau of Labor Statistics (BLS) is an independent national statistical agency that collects, processes, analyzes, and disseminates statistical data to the public, the U.S. Congress, federal agencies, state and local governments, business, and labor.

BLS coordinates with the Bureau of the Census to gather statistics on the economy of the United States and works to improve their accuracy and relevance of economic measures through use of state-of-the-art statistical techniques, economic concepts, and technology. BLS is often looking for staff economists, mathematical statisticians, and computer specialists in Washington and in BLS's regional offices.

BLS's areas of research and programs it produces include studies on inflation and consumer spending; wages, earnings, and benefits; productivity; safety and health; occupations; international statistics; demographics; employment and unemployment; industries; and business costs. In addition, it keeps regional, state, national, and industry tables of statistics.

On inflation and consumer spending, BLS devises and maintains statistics of the Consumer Price Index; an Inflation Calculator; contract escalation; Producer Price Indexes; Import/Export Price Indexes; and consumer expenditures. In the field of wages, earnings, and benefits, BLS keeps track of wages by geographic area and occupation; earnings by industry; employee benefits; costs; state and county wages; national compensation data; and collective bargaining.

BLS monitors productivity and costs, multifactor productivity, and international statistical comparisons. In the labor safety and health field, it collects data on injuries, illnesses, and fatalities. On the international level, BLS produces the Import/Export Price Indexes, foreign labor statistics, and international technical cooperation.

BLS maintains labor force demographic characteristics, geographic profiles of employment and unemployment, consumer expenditures, occupational injuries and illnesses, fatalities, and longitudinal studies.

Among employment and unemployment research and statistics provided by BLS are figures on national employment and unemployment rates; state and local employment and unemployment rates; mass layoffs; employment projections; job openings and labor turnover; employment by occupation; and state and county employment.

BLS produces many publications, many of which are available on its website, and some of which come out monthly, quarterly, annually, and regionally, and include the *Occupational Outlook Handbook* and *Occupational Outlook Quarterly.*

CONTACT Address: U.S. Bureau of Labor Statistics, Postal Square Building, 2 Massachusetts Avenue NE, Washington, DC 20212-0001; Phone: (202) 691-5200; Fax: (202) 691-6325; E-mail: data question: blsdata_staff@bls.gov; Web technical questions webmaster@bls.gov; Website: www.gls.gov/. Regional offices: 61 Forsyth Street SW, Atlanta, GA 30303; John F. Kennedy Federal Building, Boston, MA 02203; 230 S. Dearborn Street, Chicago, IL 60604; 525 Griffin Square Building, Dallas, TX 75202; 3535 Market Street, Philadelphia, PA 19104; 71 Stevenson Street, San Francisco, CA 94119-3766.

CENTER FOR FAITH-BASED COMMUNITY INITIATIVES

The Center for Faith-based Initiatives, created by President George W. Bush, makes grant funds available through the DOL's Employment Training Administration to create and run skill training programs for unemployed and employed workers, with the goal of training people in high-skill and high-technology occupations. The faith-based skills training programs address high-skill technology shortages in and needs of U.S. businesses.

In conjunction with the Center for Employment Security Education and Research (CESER), DOL has created an information packet to help workforce leaders to educate faith-based and community organizations on how to work with a local "One-Stop Career Center" to help community residents with employment needs.

CONTACT Address: DOL Center for Faith-Based & Community Initiatives, 200 Constitution Avenue NW, Room S2235, Washington, DC 20210; Phone: (202) 693-6450; Website: www.dol.gov/cfbci/.

EMPLOYEE BENEFITS SECURITY ADMINISTRATION (EBSA)
(FORMERLY PENSION AND WELFARE BENEFITS ADMINISTRATION)

As redefined in the administration of President George W. Bush, EBSA attempts to inspire voluntary compliance and self-regulation by employers in making sure they deliver earned benefits to their current and former employees, although large corporations and firms that cancelled benefits increased in numbers during the Bush administration. EBSA tries to educate and help 200 million pension, health, and other employee benefit plan participants and beneficiaries and 3 million plan sponsors.

EBSA also aims to increase participants' and beneficiaries' level of knowledge so they can access and understand information and plan documents provided by DOL, either in print or on its website.

CONTACT Address: Employee Benefits Security Administration, 200 Constitution Avenue NW, Suite N-5625, Washington, DC 20210; Phones: (202) 693-8673 or (866) 275-6922, TTYL (877) 889-5627; Website: www.dol.gov/ebsa/.

EMPLOYEES' COMPENSATION APPEALS BOARD

The Employees' Compensation Appeals Board (ECAB) hears appeals from federal civilian employees on final decisions of the Office of Workers' Compensation programs. Created in 1946, ECAB considers matters of fact and law under the Federal Employees' Compensation Act (FECA), and its decisions are binding. ECAB's existence eliminated the federal government's previous immunity on employees' compensation matters.

FECA provides payment of disability compensation for wage loss or permanent physical impairment, medical care, and vocational rehabilitation for employment-related injuries incurred by federal civilian employees. Congress has amended the act to include coverage for law-enforcement officers injured or killed in the act of pursuing suspects of crimes against the United States, and to noncitizen and nonresident employees working for U.S. agencies abroad.

CONTACT Address: Employees Compensation Appeals Board, Frances Perkins Building, 200 Constitution Avenue NW, Washington, DC 20210; Phone: 866-4-USA-DOL; Website: www.dol.gov/ecab/.

EMPLOYMENT STANDARDS ADMINISTRATION (ESA)

ESA works to enhance the welfare and protect the rights of U.S. workers by overseeing employment standards such as minimum wage and overtime regulations; registration of farm labor contractors; prevailing wages paid by government contractors and subcontractors; affirmative action and nondiscrimination matters for minorities, women, veterans, and handicapped government contract and subcontract workers; compensation and benefits standards for federal and some private employers and employees; examining internal politics and financial integrity of labor unions; and certifying some protection provisions for federally sponsored transportation programs.

WAGE AND HOUR DIVISION (WHD): Strives to protect workers by enforcing several pertinent acts: the Fair Labor Standards Act's (FLSA) federal minimum wage, overtime pay, recordkeeping, and child labor requirements provisions; the Family Medical Leave Act of 1993; the Migrant and Seasonal Agricultural Worker Protection Act; the Employee Polygraph Protection Act; the Occupational Safety and Health Act's field sanitation and housing standards provisions for migrant workers; and many provisions of the Immigration and Nationality Act. WHD also enforces statute requirements for compensation under construction and goods and services produced for federal contracts.

The Federal Medical Leave Act requires private sector employers of 50 or more employees and public agencies to provide eligible employees up to 12 weeks of unpaid leave each year for the birth of a child, placement of an adopted or foster child; to care for a child, spouse, or parent with a serious health condition; or for the employee's own serious health condition. The act also requires the employer cover the employee's health benefits during that leave and restore the employee to the same or an equivalent job upon return to work.

The Migrant and Seasonal Workers Protection Act (MSPA) sets standards for housing, transportation, and wages for migrant and seasonal farmworkers, and requires that prospective migrant worker contractors register with the federal government.

The Immigration Nursing Relief Act of 1989 protects temporary alien nonimmigrant registered nurses. The Immigration Act of 1990, as amended by the Miscellaneous Technical Amendments to the Immigration and Nationality Act, applies protections for foreign students, nonimmigrant workers in "specialty occupations," and foreign crew members working as longshoremen.

The Employee Polygraph Protection Act prevents only private employers from using lie-detector tests to screen potential employees (the federal government may do it). Whistle-blower protection laws prohibit discrimination against workers who complain about safety violations in certain industries, such as nuclear, water treatment, and waste disposal plants.

OFFICE OF FEDERAL CONTRACT COMPLIANCE PROGRAMS: Works to increase equal employment opportunities for jobs with the federal government under federal contracts, and enforces equal opportunity standards and affirmative action for women, minorities, Vietnam veterans, and persons with disabilities in the

200,000 federal contracts. It enforces Executive Order 11246 amended barring discrimination in employment on the basis of race, color, religion, sex, or national origin.

CONTACT Phone: (888) 37-OFCCP.

OFFICE OF WORKERS' COMPENSATION PROGRAMS: Enforces payment to federal employees as mentioned above (see ESA), in addition to affected workers under the Longshore and Harbor Workers' Compensation Act; the Black Lung Benefits Program for coal miners; the Energy Employees Occupational Illness Compensation Program for individuals or survivors of energy (nuclear) workers for the federal government or subcontractors, who also may benefit from section five of the Radiation Exposure Compensation Act.

CONTACT Address: 200 Constitution Avenue NW, Room S-3524, Washington, DC 20210; Phone: (202) 693-0031.

OFFICE OF LABOR-MANAGEMENT STANDARDS: Works to promote union members' rights within their unions, including resolution of disputes on union officer elections; union trusteeships; general union democracy; examination of union funds and assets; and reports required of labor unions for public disclosure. The Division of Statutory Programs works to protect the rights of mass transit workers when federal money is used to acquire, improve, or operate a transit system.

CONTACT Phone: general information (202) 693-0123; information on union elections and reporting (202) 693-0124.

EMPLOYMENT AND TRAINING ADMINISTRATION (ETA)

The Employment and Training Administration (ETA)strives to make the labor market more efficient by providing high-quality job training, employment, labor market information, and income planning services by turning individuals into career entrepreneurs through state and local workforce development systems. ETA's goal is to give individuals and families guidance toward economic freedom "to achieve the American dream." ETA focuses on adults, youths, dislocated workers, workforce professionals, and trainers. ETA offers information on employer tax credits and other hiring incentives, how to find and train employees, and assistance with plant closures and downsizing.

For adults ETA plans and develops policies, legislative proposals, goals, strategies, budgets, and resources for programs such as employment and training services for welfare recipients, American Indians and Alaska Natives, migrant and seasonal farmworkers, older workers, people with disabilities, and those who have lost their jobs due to emergencies and mass layoffs. ETA also helps investigate worker petitions and prepare industry impact studies regarding trade adjustment assistance.

CONTACT Phone: (202) 693-3500.

Apprenticeship Training and Employer and Labor Services: Helps develop training for potential employees in skills needed by potential employers and unions, while focusing on enhancing opportunities for minority and female workers in need of new skills.

CONTACT Phone: (202) 693-2796.

Workforce Security: Interprets federal legislation for state unemployment compensation and employment service programs and one-stop systems. WS helps states adopt laws, regulations, and policies in conformity with federal law; develops, negotiates, and monitors reimbursable agreements with states to administer Work Opportunity and Welfare-to-Work Tax Credits Program; provides policy guidance on aliens entering the United States to find work according to the Immigration and Nationality Act; and oversees development and implementation of the U.S. labor market information system.

Youth Services: Plans, develops, and recommends policy for youth employment and training, gives policy guidance and oversight of Job Corps youth employment and training services, and does the same for the Workforce Investment Act's youth opportunity grant program.

CONTACT Phone: (202) 693-3030.

MINE SAFETY AND HEALTH ADMINISTRATION (MSHA)

The Mine Safety and Health Administration (MSHA) works to make U.S. mines safe for miners by enforcing mandatory safety and health standards. Its goals are to eliminate fatal accidents; minimize health hazards such as black lung disease; and promote improved health and safety conditions in the mines and in mineral processing operations according to the Federal Mine Safety and Health Act of 1977 (Mine Act).

MSHA holds meetings and releases publications on mine safety, emergency standards, specific disasters, mine emergencies, mine rescue teams, health hazards, and personal protection equipment. It also provides information on diesel particulate rules and hazards, finds violations, investigates accidents, assesses civil penalties, and works with states on their mining safety programs.

CONTACT Address: Mine Safety and Health Administration, 1100 Wilson Boulevard, 21st Floor, Arlington, VA 22209-3939; Phone: (703) 235-1452; Website: www.msha.gov/. *District Offices,* Mine Safety and Health Administration: 3837 So. U.S. Highway 25, Barbourville, KY 40906; Phone: (606) 546-5123. 135 Bemini Circle, Suite 213, Birmingham, AL 35209-4896; Phone: (205) 290-7300. P.O. Box 25367, Denver, CO 80225-0367; Phone: (303) 231-5458. RR 1, Box 736, Hunker, PA 15639; Phone: (724) 925-6190. 100 YMCA Drive, Madisonville, KY 42431-9019; Phone: (270) 821-4180. 5012 Mountaineer Mall, Morgantown, WV 26501; Phone: (304) 291-4277. 100 Bluestone Road, Mount Hope, WV 25880; Phone: (304) 877-3900. P.O. Box 560, Norton, VA 24273; Phone: (540) 679-0230. 100 Fae Ramsey Lane, Pikeville, KY 41501; Phone: (606) 432-0943; 2300 Old Decker Road, Suite 200, Vincennes, IN 47591; Phone: (812) 882-7617; 7 No. Wilkes-Barre Boulevard, Suite 034, Wilkes-Barre, PA 18702; Phone: (570) 826-6321. Metal/Nonmetal Mine Safety and Health in addition to the above: 547 Keystone Drive, Warrendale, PA 15086-7573; Phone: (724) 772-2333. 135 Gemini Circle, Suite 212, Birmingham, AL 35209-4896; Phone: (205) 290-7294. 515 West 1st Street, Duluth, MN 55802-1302; Phone: (205) 290-7294. 1100 Commerce Street, Room 462, Dallas, TX 75242-0499; Phone: (214) 767-8401. 2060 Peabody Road, Suite 610, Vacaville, CA 95687; Phone: (707) 447-9844.

OCCUPATIONAL SAFETY AND HEALTH ADMINISTRATION (OSHA)

OSHA sets and enforces workplace safety and health standards, and helps employers comply with the standards. OSHA's goal is to save lives, prevent injuries, and protect American workers' health, and it works with 7 million workplaces and 111 million employees. OSHA and its state partners employ 2,100 inspectors, in addition to discrimination investigators, engineers, physicians, educators, standards writers, and technical and support staff in 200 offices throughout the United States.

The Occupational Safety and Health Act of 1970 requires that each employer: (1) shall furnish to each employee a job and a place of employment free from recognized hazards that are causing or are likely to cause death or serious physical harm to the employee; and (2) shall comply with occupational safety and health standards put out under the act. Also, each employee must comply with occupational safety and health standards and all rules, regulations, and orders according to the act, as apply to the employee's own actions and conduct.

Most workers in the United States come under OSHA's authority, except for miners, transportation workers, many public employees, and the self-employed. Some professions enjoying OSHA's protections include occupational safety and health professionals, the academic community, lawyers, journalists, and personnel of government entities.

OSHA boasts that deaths on the job have been halved since OSHA was created in 1971. In 2001 OSHA consultants made 27,000 visits to small employers, collected and tested more than 5,300 air samples from the World Trade Center attack disaster, and gave safety and health training to 260,000 workers and employers.

OSHA has several new programs instigated by President George W. Bush that emphasize loosely structured, voluntary compliance instead of enforced and regulated compliance. Among those, the Alliance Program hopes for collaboration of organizations with OSHA to reach out to, educate, and lead employers and employees to cooperate. "Alliances" may include trade or professional organizations, businesses, labor organizations, educational institutions, and government agencies on a national, regional, state, or area basis. Alliance participants must define, implement, and meet their short- and long-term goals of training and education, outreach, and communication, and promote the national dialogue on workplace safety and health.

CONTACT Phone: (202) 693-2340.

OSHA's partnerships constitute voluntary and cooperative relationships with groups of employers, employees, and employee representatives to encourage, assist, and recognize efforts to eliminate serious hazards and attain worker safety and health. Most partnerships involve small businesses with 22 or fewer employees. Many focus on silica and lead exposures, serious hazards in nursing homes, food, logging, and construction industries. Other industries involved in partnerships include metal recycling, oil and gas well servicing, structural metal fabrication, grain handling, automotive radiator repair, fish processing, and janitorial contractors. Some unions partici-

pating include the Laborers, Carpenters, Roofers and Waterproofers, Operating Engineers, Plumbers and Steamfitters, Teamsters, AFGE, Iron Workers, United Food and Commercial, and Federation of Grain Millers.

Comprehensive partnerships include management and employee involvement, hazard analysis, hazard prevention and control, safety and health training, evaluation, and compliance. Comprehensive partnerships must include the following elements: situation analysis, identification of partners, partnership goals, leveraging, safety and health programs, employee involvement and rights, stakeholder involvement, a measurement system, OSHA incentives, verification process, OSHA inspections, evaluation, and termination.

Limited partnerships may require partners to establish comprehensive workplace safety and health programs, or they may just focus on eliminating a problem in a particular industry.

Voluntary Protection Programs (VPP) recognize and promote effective safety and health management through a cooperative workplace relationship between management, employees, and OSHA. VPP programs are open to a select group of facilities and workplaces with outstanding health and safety programs, and use a self-assessment checklist to measure if the program meets VPP criteria.

OSHA encourages states to develop and operate their own job safety and health programs. Twenty-six states operate OSHA programs, with those of Connecticut, New Jersey, and New York serving only state and local government employees.

EUROPEAN AGENCY FOR SAFETY AND HEALTH AT WORK (OSH): A joint project of OSHA and the European Union's European Agency for Health and Safety at work organized to promote sharing of information on current safety and health topics of common interest. The project came out of the 1998 Joint EU-US Conference on Health and Safety at work held in

Luxembourg in October 1998. Specific focuses of shared information cover construction and ergonomics.

OFFICE OF DISABILITY EMPLOYMENT (ODEP)

The Office of Disability Employment (ODEP) works to increase independence, self-determination, and employment opportunities for adults and youths with disabilities and strives to eliminate barriers to employment for them. ODEP coordinates job development opportunities for people with disabilities and their families with private employers and employees; with federal, state, and local government agencies; with educational and training institutions; with disability advocates; and with providers of services and government employees.

ODEP works with employers to increase clients' access to training, education, employment support, assistive technology, integrated employment, entrepreneurial development, and small business opportunities. To serve its clients, ODEP creates partnerships with employers and state and local agencies to inform potential employers of the benefits of hiring people with disabilities, and helps clients develop and use effective strategies to find employment and start small businesses.

ODEP programs include the Business Leadership Network; the Cultural Diversity Initiative; the Employer Assistance Referral Network; a High School/High Tech program; the Job Accommodation Network; youth leadership forums; and small business and self-employment for people with disabilities. ODEP also gives grants to research and improve development of employment opportunities and ideas for people with disabilities.

BUSINESS LEADERSHIP NETWORK (BLN): Works with government and private employers to encourage companies to hire people with disabilities, occasionally offering financial incentives. Business Steering Group members from corporations and universities throughout the United States are led by the president and CEO of the U.S. Chamber of Commerce. BLN offers websites and programs in California, Connecticut, Florida, Iowa, Kentucky, Louisiana, Maryland, Nebraska, North Dakota, Michigan, Pennsylvania, Texas, Washington, Wisconsin, and Wyoming. Among the activities state and local BLN groups focus on are a disability-friendly business program to recognized employers who are helpful; ADA (Americans With Disabilities Act) requirements and accommodation technologies; legislation on disabilities and the workplace; mental health issues in employment; how to improve attitudinal awareness; and hidden disabilities in the workplace.

CULTURAL DIVERSITY INITIATIVE: Researches and offers programs to improve employment of minority members with disabilities, whose rate of employment is lower than the average of Caucasian Americans. African Americans with disabilities have only a 36.6 percent employment rate, compared with 41.0 percent for American Indians and Alaska Natives, 44.8 percent for Hispanics, 48.1 percent for Asian/Pacific Islanders, and 52.3 percent for the overall population of people with disabilities.

ODEP works with the NAACP's High School/High Tech program, as well as with the National Urban League.

CONTACT Address: 200 Constitution Avenue NW, Washington, DC 20210; Phone: (202) 693-7880; Fax: (202) 693-7888; Website: www.dol.gov/odep.

OFFICE OF SMALL BUSINESS PROGRAMS (OSBP)

The Office of Small Business Programs (OSBP) runs DOL's efforts to procure government supplies and services from small businesses, small disadvantaged businesses, and women-owned small businesses. OSBP also provides information on small business regulatory compliance, and manages DOL's minority colleges and universities program.

CONTACT Website: www.dol.gov/osbp/.

VETERAN'S EMPLOYMENT AND TRAINING SERVICE (VETS)

Under President George W. Bush, Secretary of Labor Elaine Chao announced that "Military reservists should have confidence that while they are serving their country in active duty, their job pension and health benefits will continue for their families" in accordance with federal law. This pronouncement did not help self-employed or small business owner reservists called up to serve in Iraq. DOL also claims returning service members' rights to family and medical leave continue during their service.

VETS generally works to provide veterans with resources and services to maximize their employment opportunities, protect their employment rights, and meet labor-market demands. Special efforts are being made to rectify Vietnam veterans' experiences when they returned to the United States and no one would hire them.

Your Military Experience and Training (UMET) web site helps veterans get licenses and certifications they need to convert their military experience to civilian workforce requirements. UMET also links employers to skilled labor of the qualified pool of military veterans.

VETS collaborates with seven other service providers to develop housing for homeless veterans. Other programs provided by VETS include employment services for veterans; Transition Assistance Program; job rights for veterans and reserve component members; Homeless Veterans' Reintegration Project; Federal Contractor Pro-

gram; a veterans preference employment program; and the National Veterans' Training Institute.

The National Veterans' Training Institute (NVTI) was established in 1986 to provide specialized training and professional skills enhancement of State Employment Security Agency and other veterans' service providers' staff. Operated by the University of Colorado at Denver, NVTI's training curriculum is designed to prepare veterans to fit potential employers' needs and includes veterans' benefits, transition assistance, case management, marketing and accessing the media, management of veterans' services, veterans' re-employment rights case investigation, and grants management. Courses are accredited by the North Central Association of Colleges and Universities, and NVTI in Denver houses the Resource and Technical Assistance Center (RTAC), a resource center for veterans issues and services available to NVTI training alumni.

CONTACT Website: www.dol.gov/vets/aboutvets/contacts/main.htm.

WOMEN'S BUREAU (WB)

The Women's Bureau of DOL works to promote profitable and satisfying employment opportunities for women, empowers women by improving their skills and working conditions, and provides employers women to fill their labor needs.

Established by Congress in 1920, the Women's Bureau is the only federal agency intended to represent the needs of wage-earning women in and throughout the public policy process. WB represents women's interests by first identifying and investigating working women's issues, vigorously pioneering research and remedies, and taking action to improve women's status and conditions in the workplace. WB publishes fact sheets on the status of women workers as well as resources for addressing and correcting women's workplace concerns.

Issues that WB has worked on with great success include: conditions facing "negro women in industry" in 1922; "older women as office workers" in the 1950s; contingent workers in the 1980s; nonstandard hour child care options in the 1990s; fair wages and reasonable work hours, including inclusion of women under the Fair Labor Standards Act of 1938, setting minimum wages and maximum work hours; skills training, wider job opportunities, better pay, and better conditions for the new female workforce in World War II; worked 20 years toward passage of the Equal Pay Act of 1963; working for decades for equal pay for women and minorities, and better access to high-paying nontraditional jobs; launched effort for employer-sponsored child care in 1982 and establishment of a multimedia Work and Family Clearinghouse in 1989; and pressured for passage of the Family and Medical Leave Act of 1993.

The Women's Bureau maintains its Honor Roll program and a Business to Business Mentoring Initiative to encourage U.S. employers to make positive, concrete changes that affect millions of women and their families.

CONTACT Website: www.dol.gov/wb/.

SECRETARY'S 21ST CENTURY WORKFORCE INITIATIVE

President George W. Bush established this office to help Americans who aspire to success to have a fulfilling and financially independent life. To this end, DOL held a 21st Century Workforce summit to address the possibilities.

CONTACT Phone: (202) 693-4650 or (877) 872-5627; E-mail: 21stworkforce@dol.gov; Website: www.dol.gov/21cw/; Address: DOL, 200 Constitution Avenue NW, Washington, DC 20210; Phone: (877) USA-DOL; Website: www.dol.gov/esa/. Regional offices: 61 Forsyth Street NW, Atlanta, GA 30303; John F. Kennedy Building, Boston, MA 02203; 230 S. Dearborn Street, Chicago, IL 60604; 525 S. Griffin Street, Dallas, TX 75202; 1100 Main Street, Kansas City, MO 64105; 201 Varick Street, New York, NY 10014; 3535 Market Street, Philadelphia, PA 19104; 71 Stevenson Street, San Francisco, CA 94105; 1111 3rd Avenue, Seattle, WA 98101.

DEPARTMENT OF STATE

The Department of State is the oldest cabinet-level department. State advises the president on foreign affairs and administers numerous programs and responsibilities in developing and furthering American foreign policy. Basic foreign policy depends upon the president for direction subject to congressional support and approval, although as one-time Senate Foreign Relations chair William Fulbright stated: "The real power is located at the other end of Pennsylvania Avenue [the WHITE HOUSE]." In addition, State assists various federal agencies in regard to foreign relations and activities, including the DEPARTMENT OF COMMERCE and the Agency for International Development (AID). The department provides assistance to American citizens traveling abroad (including issuance of passports) and supervises documentation of foreigners visiting the country.

Through its many ambassadors, consulates, missions to international organizations, and staffs of experts the State Department conveys and implements American foreign policy. One of the department's key functions is conducting negotiations leading to treaties and agreements on numerous vital topics. Probably more than any other cabinet member, the secretary of state conducts personal negotiations and discussions throughout the world, providing a human face and voice to America's foreign policy. At the same time the department provides information to the American public on policies, programs, and available assistance in the international sphere.

HISTORY

State was the first department recommended by President George Washington, and he signed an act creating the "Department of Foreign Affairs" on July 27, 1789, three months after taking office on April 30, 1789. On September 15 of that year the name was changed to the Department of State. Then President Washington appointed Thomas Jefferson secretary of state on September 22, while Jefferson was winding up his duties as minister to the French government for the United States (existing under the Articles of Confederation), after five years of service. Jefferson sailed for the United States on October 22, 1789, without knowing of the appointment. On arrival in Virginia he found a letter from Washington (dated October 13) telling him of his appointment. Initially, Jefferson demurred, asking that he be reappointed to the post in France, but at Washington's urging in a letter on November 30, he agreed to serve. In his absence John Jay, chief justice of the Supreme Court, managed the routine business of the department.

Delayed by personal business and the wedding of his daughter, Martha, Jefferson arrived in the capital, New York City, on March 21, 1790, and was sworn in as secretary of state on March 22. His initial annual salary, voted by Congress, was $3,500. His entire staff consisted of five clerks or "copyists." The office was responsible for overseeing foreign affairs, which were primarily concerned with France, then in the convulsions of revolution and its "reign of terror," as well as avoiding the conflict between France and Great Britain. It also managed routine matters of domestic administration such as record keeping and certifying documents.

Jefferson was increasingly involved in a feud, both philosophical and eventually personal, with Secretary of Treasury Alexander Hamilton. He submitted a letter of resignation on July 31, 1793, to be effective on December 31. Washington had made several pleas for Jefferson to patch up his disputes with Hamilton and for Jefferson to stay on as secretary of state, all to no avail.

For the first 70 years, the office of secretary of state was considered a chief adviser to the president, a sort of vizier, and as a natural stepping-stone to the presidency. Not only Jefferson, but future Presidents James Madison (1801–09), James Monroe (1811–17), John Quincy Adams (1817–25), Martin Van Buren (1829–33), and James Buchanan (1845–49) all filled the position. Several losing presidential candidates served as secretary of state, including Henry Clay (1825–29), Lewis Cass (1857–60), James G. Blaine (1881 and 1889–92), William Jennings Bryan (1913–15), and Charles Evans Hughes (1921–25), as well as such famed congressional leaders as Daniel Webster (1841–43 and 1850–52) and John C. Calhoun (1844–45). However, in modern times, the post has lost its prime minister cachet.

Nevertheless, several secretaries of state played major roles in formulating international policies, including John Hay (1898–1905), Robert Lansing (1915–20), Henry Stimson (1929–33), George C. Marshall (1947–49), Henry Kissinger (1973–77), the first female secretary, Madeline Albright (1997–2001), and several others.

John Quincy Adams was the principal formulator of the Monroe Doctrine, which warned European powers that the Western Hemisphere was an inviolate American sphere of influence and future incursions would be resisted. Buchanan negotiated the division of Oregon territory between the United States and British Canada in 1846. William Seward (1861–69) arranged the purchase of Alaska (originally denigrated as "Seward's Folly"), and George C. Marshall (1947–49) gained eternal fame (as if commanding the U.S. Army in World War II was not enough) for the Marshall Plan, which provided assistance to rebuild Europe (including the former enemy, Germany) after World War II—a program of practical humanity.

United States Department of State

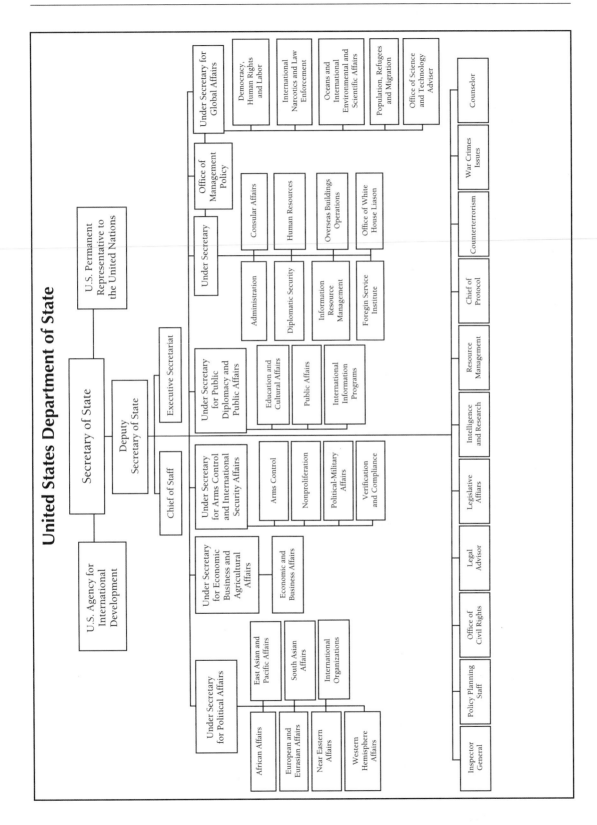

As communications improved and interrelationships of the nations of the world grew, the international role of the United States first expanded and then became dominant. Thus, the State Department as a governmental institution became increasingly significant.

The State Department has grown in importance as the United States has emerged as a world power—and now sole superpower—and due to the international focus in 20th-century geopolitics under Presidents Theodore Roosevelt, Woodrow Wilson, and Franklin D. Roosevelt. Between wars the United States was essentially isolationist, but from World War II until today, American foreign policy affects international relationships throughout the world.

Although the department's size is a far cry from Jefferson's handful of copyists, despite its key role, it is fourth from the lowest cabinet-level departments in budget, which was $9.7 billion in 2002, and fifth from lowest in number of personnel, at approximately 27,300.

CONTACT Address: 2201 C Street NW, Washington, DC 20520. United States Mission to the United Nations: 799 United Nations Plaza, New York, NY 10017; Phone: (202) 647-4000; Website: www.state.gov. Public Information Service: Phone: (202) 647-6575; Fax: (202) 647-7120.

Public use of records: The Electronic Reading Room for information access and public reference to State Department records is located in the Harry S. Truman Headquarters Building, 515 22nd Street NW, Washington, DC 20522; Phone: (202) 261-8484; Website: www.foia.state.gov.

ORGANIZATION

The *secretary of state* is appointed by the president with confirmation by the Senate required. He or she is given direct administrative support by the *secretariat* staff. Because the secretary must travel to foreign countries and organizations, one of the secretariat's special responsibilities is scheduling and advancing the preparations for trips by the secretary and various staff members and support personnel. For the benefit of the secretary and top staff, the Department's *Operations Center* operates 24 hours a day to monitor events and crises, prepares briefs, facilitates communications to the international community, and coordinates responses to foreign crises.

The *deputy secretary of state* serves not only as the chief assistant to the secretary of state but also in place of the secretary when he or she is absent and participates in development of policy, supervising and directing the department and its several elements. The exact function of the deputy secretary in part depends on the style of the secretary and the personal relationships of the secretary and deputy secretary. Policy development and administrative decisions usually involve the secretary's "cabinet" composed of the six *under secretaries,* each responsible for separate functions of the department.

Administratively connected with the Office of the Secretary are the Policy Planning Staff, the Office of Protocol, the Office of the Coordinator for Counterterrorism, certain administrative offices, and ambassadors-at-large in several foreign policy areas. An unusual office in the State Department is that of *Counselor,* who is a special adviser and assistant to the secretary of state.

The *Policy Planning Staff* develops long-term foreign policies, priorities, and objectives, and is liaison to foreign affairs think tanks and experts outside of government. This staff, established in 1947, also prepares speeches for the secretary. Its director has an equivalent rank of assistant secretary.

The *Office of Protocol,* headed by the *chief of protocol,* a presidential appointee requiring Senate conformation, advises the president and various government agencies on international protocol and directly supervises and hosts visits and ceremonial events of foreign heads of state and dignitaries. A total of 100,000 foreign officials, diplomats, their staffs, experts, and others related to foreign governments are accredited by the Office of Protocol at any one time.

This office also advises various government agencies as well as the White House on protocol, manages Blair House (the guest house for the president), and manages protocol for presidential and vice presidential trips abroad. Officiating the swearing-in of senior State Department officials and foreign service employees is another duty of the Office of Protocol. In addition, the president appoints honorary protocol officials in major cities such as New York and San Francisco to host visits of foreign dignitaries in those areas.

The *Office of the Coordinator for Counterterrorism* also operates within the office of the secretary and directs efforts to improve cooperation between the United States and other governments in regard to counterterrorism. The coordinator chairs both the Interagency Working Group on Counterterrorism and the department's task force on coordinating responses to international terrorist occurrences. To an extent, these functions are primarily intended to include the State Department in the loop on counterterrorism efforts, since some of these activities are redundant to antiterrorism efforts lodged in other agencies such as the CIA, the FBI, the DEFENSE DEPARTMENT, and DEPARTMENT OF HOMELAND SECURITY. The coordinator is the ambassador-at-large for counterterrorism, a presidential appointee confirmed by the Senate.

Also within the secretary's office are offices dealing with internal matters: *Equal Opportunity and Civil Rights Office, Civil Service Ombudsman,* and *Foreign Service Grievance Board.*

Two bureaus that operate separately from the secretary's office, but report directly to the secretary, are the *Bureau of Legislative Affairs,* responsible for liaison with Congress, and the *Bureau of Intelligence and Research,* which analyzes intelligence from varied sources on behalf of department policy makers. In addition, the bureau operates the *Geographic Learning Site* to deal with boundary issues. This bureau is partially redundant since numerous other agencies conduct intelligence gathering and analysis. Both of these bureaus are directed by *assistance secre-*

taries appointed by the president and confirmed by the Senate.

Under Secretaries

There are six under secretaries, the next step below the deputy secretary in the department's hierarchy. Each is a presidential appointee subject to Senate confirmation, and each has a specific area of responsibility, a supportive office, and in most cases with bureau offices of a specialized nature within their jurisdiction. They are the under secretary for political affairs, the under secretary for economic, business, and agricultural affairs, the under secretary for arms control and international security, the under secretary for global affairs, the under secretary for public diplomacy and public affairs, and the under secretary for management.

Most of the offices of the under secretaries are known as a "group" in State Department parlance. These groups are structured with bureaus responsible for specific functions and directed by assistant secretaries of state, who are each appointed by the president with Senate confirmation required.

UNDER SECRETARY FOR POLITICAL AFFAIRS

Denominated by the department as its "crisis manager" dealing with integrated political, economic, global, and security issues in American bilateral (one-on-one) relationships with other nations.

This office operates six bureaus broken down in geographic areas, each headed by an assistant secretary. These assistant secretaries, appointed by the president with Senate confirmation, guide the operation of diplomatic missions in their regional jurisdiction. In turn they advise the under secretary of activities in their region. They are supported by deputy assistant secretaries, country desk officers, and other staff officers.

These in turn maintain working relationships with U.S. embassies and consulates, and maintain contact with the appropriate foreign embassies located in Washington, D.C.

The geographic bureaus are: *Bureau of African Affairs, Bureau of European and Eurasian Affairs, Bureau of East Asian and Pacific Affairs, Bureau of Near Eastern Affairs, Bureau of South Asian Affairs,* and *Bureau of Western Hemisphere Affairs.*

In addition to the geographic bureaus, the under secretary for political affairs oversees the *Bureau of International Organization Affairs,* also directed by an assistant secretary, which implements American policies within various international organizations, particularly the United Nations and its affiliated agencies. Its policy areas of concern include: peacekeeping, democracy and human rights, humanitarian and refugee assistance, international trade, economic development, safe food production, transportation safety, public health, terrorism, and the environment. To effectively deal with these crucial topics, the bureau promotes effective management by international organizations with which it deals. The bureau operates through a headquarters in Washington, D.C., and field offices in New York City (home of the United Nations); Geneva, Switzerland; Vienna, Austria; Rome, Italy; Paris, France; Montreal, Canada; and Nairobi, Kenya.

This group also manages the *Bureau of Economic and Business Affairs,* which promotes American economic and business interests of all types throughout the world. Specifically, the bureau works toward regional and global stability, the securing of good jobs for Americans, enhancement of consumer choice, holding down the prices Americans pay for goods and services stemming from international trade, protection of U.S. overseas business and investors, encouraging international commercial connections, and improving global communications, efficient transportation, and energy security.

In furtherance of these goals within the bureau, the *Office of Commercial and Business Affairs* (a) coordinates advocacy for American business interests, (b) provides to American companies problem-solving assistance in regard to opening markets, maintaining a level playing field with foreign interests, and resolving trading and investment disputes in the international sphere, (c) ensures American business interests are considered in development of foreign policy, (d) develops policies and training programs to upgrade the department's support of U.S. businesses, and (e) coordinates with the Commerce Department and the Foreign Commercial Service support for trade promotion and other commercial services in places where the State Department has on-the-scene involvement.

UNDER SECRETARY FOR ECONOMIC, BUSINESS AND AGRICULTURAL AFFAIRS

The chief economic official of the Department of State advises the secretary of state in regard to international economic policy. This group office also heads the work of the department on such issues as trade, agriculture, and relations with America's economic partners around the world. The under secretary is an appointee by the president with Senate confirmation.

UNDER SECRETARY FOR ARMS CONTROL AND INTERNATIONAL SECURITY

Another presidential appointee subject to Senate confirmation. This group manages global security policy, especially in regard to nonproliferation of nuclear weaponry, arms control, arms transfers, security assistance to businesses, and regional and defense security arrangements. The legal authority for these functions include the

Foreign Assistance Act, the Arms Export Control Act, and other relevant legislation. The under secretary serves as senior principal adviser on arms control, nonproliferation, and disarmament both to the president and the secretary of state. Since it is unusual for an under secretary to advise the president directly, this reflects the importance attached to arms control.

This group manages and operates through four bureaus: Bureau of Arms Control, Bureau of Political-Military Affairs, Nonproliferation Bureau, and Bureau for Verification and Compliance, each headed by an assistant secretary appointed by the president with Senate confirmation.

BUREAU OF ARMS CONTROL: Directs U.S. negotiations for international arms control agreements covering nuclear weapons, conventional armaments, and chemical and biological potential weapons. Although the State Department reports that this bureau leads implementation of various agreements including the Anti-Ballistic Missile Treaty and the end to antipersonnel landmine transfer, this is ironic since the United States has abrogated adherence to the terms of the Anti-Ballistic Missile (ABM) Treaty and has refused to sign on to the proposed worldwide ban on landmines, which has been approved by a majority of the world's governments.

BUREAU OF POLITICAL-MILITARY AFFAIRS: Responsible for maintaining "political-military" relations among those nations cooperating with the United States. This is accomplished in part through training and assistance to the military of other nations, and attempts to maintain access by American military into other nations. The bureau promotes what it calls "responsible" defense trade, and at the same time uses export controls to protect foreign access to militarily significant technology. Despite the government policy to refuse to join in international landmine prohibitions, the bureau coordinates U.S. programs to eliminate landmines from other countries. It also is active in interagency efforts to plan

U.S. responses to potential crises caused by overseas attacks by nuclear, biological, or chemical methods, and from cyber attacks upon computer networks (including "hacking" into highly classified databases).

NONPROLIFERATION BUREAU: (a) Leads efforts to prevent the spread of weapons of mass destruction—nuclear, biological, and chemical—and missile delivery systems of such weaponry that could reach the United States or other nations; and (b) promotes transparency and "restraint" in international transfers of conventional armaments as well as dual-use (commercial and military) technology.

BUREAU FOR VERIFICATION AND COMPLIANCE: Supervises all matters of verification of and compliance by foreign parties to international agreements and commitments on arms control, nonproliferation, and disarmament. An element of these functions is the bureau's oversight of policy development, implementation, and resources dedicated to verification and compliance. The bureau is the department's liaison to the various elements of the "intelligence community," and leads Nonproliferation and Arms Control Technology Working Group, an interagency committee. It manages the Verification *Assets Fund*, prepares the president's annual report to Congress on adherence and compliance with agreements on arms control and nonproliferation, leads negotiations on these subjects with the European Union and other international organizations, and conducts bilateral meetings on solutions to problems of infrastructure protection. In addition, it operates the *Nuclear Risk Reduction Center*.

UNDER SECRETARY FOR MANAGEMENT

Principally provides support services for both domestic and overseas operations, consular affairs, personnel management, recruit training, and retirement. Within this group are numerous bureaus, offices, and other units. They are: Office of Management Policy, Chief Information Officer, Foreign Service Institute, Bureau of Human Resources, Office of Medical Services, Family Liaison Office, Bureau of Administration, Bureau of Consular Affairs, Bureau of Diplomatic Security, and Bureau of Resource Management.

OFFICE OF MANAGEMENT POLICY: Gathers and analyzes recommendations on management improvement, which it reports to the under secretary for management. It reviews drafts of presidential instructions to ambassadors, and chairs the *Permanent Coordinating Committee on Accountability Review Boards,* which review unfortunate incidents in overseas missions.

CHIEF INFORMATION OFFICER: Equivalent to an assistant secretary of state, responsible for developing, maintaining, and upgrading information technology employed by the State Department in the rapidly changing age of electronic information gathering, distribution and global communication, and other innovations.

BUREAU OF CONSULAR AFFAIRS: Directed by an assistant secretary, appointed by the president, and confirmed by the Senate, is the State Department bureau most likely to deal with individual American citizens and foreign nationals.

The *Office of Passport Services* in the bureau issues passports to Americans traveling to foreign countries, which average more than 7.5 million annually. While the applications for passports can be obtained at local post offices, they are processed at centers in Portsmouth, New Hampshire, and Charleston, South Carolina, and can be applied for at regional passport agencies. Applications are available at local post offices. Regional Passport Agencies:

CONTACT   Address: 10 Causeway Street, Boston, MA 02222; Phone: (617) 878-0900. Building 646A, 1969 Dyess Avenue, Charleston, SC 29405; Phone: (843) 308-5501. 230 South Dearborn Street, Chicago, IL 60604; Phone: (312) 341-6020. 1132 Bishop Street, Honolulu, HI 96850; Phone: (808) 522-8283. 1919 Smith Street, Suite 1400, Houston, TX 77002; Phone: (713) 751-0294. 11000 Wilshire Boulevard, Suite 1000, Los Angeles, CA 90024; Phone: (310) 575-5700. 3rd Floor, 51 SW First Avenue, Miami, FL 33130; Phone: (305) 539-3600. 305 Canal Street, New Orleans, LA 70130; Phone: (504) 412-2600. 10th Floor, 376 Hudson Street, New York, NY 10014; Phone: (212) 206-3500. 200 Chestnut Street, Room 103, Philadelphia, PA 19106; Phone: (215) 418-5937. 5th Floor, 95 Hawthorne Street, San Francisco, CA 94105; Phone: (415) 538-2700. 915 Second Avenue, Suite 992, Seattle, WA 98174; Phone: (206) 808-5700. One Landmark Square, Broad and Atlantic Streets, Stamford, CT 06901; Phone: (203) 969-9000. 1111 19th Street NW, Washington, DC 20524; Phone: (202) 647-0518. Rochester Avenue, Portsmouth, NH 03801, Phone: (603) 334-0500.

Queries about Passports (including the process of application, status of applications, emergency passports): Phone: (202) 955-0198 or the Office of Passport Policy and Advisory Services at (202) 663-2654.

Visas: Visas to hundreds of thousands of visitors to the United States are issued by consular officials at the many consulate offices around the world. While the bureau has attempted to monitor the issuance of visas, it has had difficulty in following up on the visitors and the legal length of stay—subjects of recent concern by Congress and the department in the wake of the 9/11 terrorist attacks and the recognition that there are many thousands of foreign nationals who have overstayed their visas or abused the privilege in various ways such as not attending classes although receiving a visa to pursue advanced study in the United States.

The bureau's *Office of Overseas Citizens Services* provides assistance to Americans with problems or needs while in other countries. It responds to more than 20,000 inquiries each year in regard to whereabouts and the welfare of overseas travelers, monitors cases of Americans arrested abroad, handles the cases of about 6,000 Americans who die abroad each year, and assists those caught in natural disasters, mass casualties, and hostage-taking. This office issues the *Travel Warnings* (aka Travel Advisories), which often warn against travel in countries with dangerous situations such as civil wars, violence, or epidemics. It also issues information useful to those intending to travel abroad.

Contacts: Inquiries about overseas citizens— missing persons, travel advisories, arrests, deaths and emergencies: Address: Office of American Citizens Services, Bureau of Consular Affairs, Department of State, 2201 C Street NW, Washington, DC 20520; Phone: (202) 647-5225 or 1(888) 407-4747 or from overseas (317) 472-2328; Fax: (202) 647-3732; Website: www.travel.state.gov.

Contacts for inquiries about parental child abduction or adoption of foreign children by private American citizens: Address: Office of Children's Issues, Department of State, Suite 2100, 1800 G Street NW, Washington, DC 20520; Phone: (202) 312-9700 or 1(888) 407-4747 or from overseas (317) 472-2328; Fax: (202) 312-9743; for child abduction inquiries; (202) 312-9741; Website: www.travel.state.gov.

FOREIGN SERVICE INSTITUTE: The prime training organization of the State Department, which prepares American diplomats and other foreign service professionals both overseas and at State Department headquarters. The director of the institute is a career incumbent and not a political appointee. Its *George P. Schultz National Foreign Affairs Training Center* conducts more than 500 courses. The goal is to provide training for State Department employees and their family members to make their performance more effective and improve their ability to live in foreign countries and represent the United States in a favorable manner, including courses in 60 foreign languages. More than 30,000 people annually are enrolled, including diplomats, management,

security, and medical personnel. The courses range from one day to two years, and include brief curricula at a "Transition Center" for personnel about to be sent overseas. Recently many of these courses have been made available to the general public.

CONTACT For training course information: Phone: (703) 302-7268, and for special courses on Security Seminars: Phone: (703) 302-7269; Website: www.state.gov/m/fsi.

BUREAU OF ADMINISTRATION: Gives support to the department and its embassies and consulates, including management of facilities and real property, services of procurement, transportation, and diplomatic pouch and mail services. The bureau maintains State Department records, publishes its public documents, and runs the department's libraries and language services such as translating. It sets allowance rates for family maintenance overseas, the means to educate the children of foreign service personnel, and health needs of State employees. The bureau also authenticates documents needed abroad.

In 2001 the bureau inaugurated the *Center for Administrative Innovation* with a mandate to explore techniques to improve the smooth management of the Department of State. See acaiml@state.gov.

Internal management is facilitated by *Office of Allowances,* which establishes overseas costs of living, and establishes and manages the allowances for such expenses and the benefits program of the department.

CONTACT Phone: (202) 647-5002 or 1(800) 688-9889.

The *Office of Logistics Management* facilitates the delivery of materials and goods for the Department of State and for other agencies involved in foreign affairs and overseas operations. With headquarters in Washington, D.C., there are also procurement offices in Miami, Florida, and Germany, as well as "despatch agents" located in New York, New York, Baltimore, Maryland, Miami, Florida, Brownsville, Texas, and Seattle, Washington. See Website: www.state.gov/m/a/c.

The *Office of Authentication* performs vital services for the department that are of importance to American citizens, business entities, and foreign nationals visiting the United States. Primarily these services are the authentication of legal documents so that they will be considered as legal in foreign countries. Such documents include corporate articles and bylaws, powers of attorney, diplomas, university transcripts, deeds, and adoption papers. Usually this process can be performed at the offices of the various consuls general abroad and at the Authentications Office in Washington, D.C. For use of authenticated documents in foreign countries it is recommended that the embassy or local consul general's office determine the exact authentication requirements.

CONTACT Address: Authentication Office, 518 23rd Street NW, State Annex 1, Washington, DC 20037; Phone: (202) 647-5002 or 1(800) 688-9889; E-mail: AOPROGMAUTH@STATE.GOV.

The *Office of Small and Disadvantaged Business Utilization* serves as a watchdog agency to maximize the participation of small business in contracts in which the State Department is a party. This office provides training on doing business with or through the State Department and counsels in regard to opportunities for smaller businesses to participate. See Website: www.state.gov/m/a/sdbu/.

The bureau is responsible for responding to requests under the *Freedom of Information and Privacy Acts.* These requests should be sent to the Director, Office of IRM Programs and Services, Department of State, 515 22nd Street NW, Washington, DC 20522 (indicating on the outside of the envelope if it is a Freedom of Information Act request or a Privacy Act request); Phone: (202) 261-8300.

Also the bureau manages the *electronic reading room,* where the public can inspect unclassified and declassified documents of the State Department, including historic materials. This

library is located in the Harry S. Truman Headquarters Building, 515 22nd Street NW, Washington, DC 20522; Phone: (202) 261-8484; Website: www.foia.state.gov.

When there are *overseas conferences* called by the president or the secretary of state and/or involving top White House personnel, including the president, the Bureau of Administration provides support assistance for the travel.

The newest Bureau (as of May 2001) is *Overseas Building Operations,* which runs a fast-track program of construction of infrastructure of embassies and consulates. Its activities are broken down into three sector offices: Planning and Development, Real Estate and Property Management, and Project Execution. Involved is a potential of 16,000 different properties located at 260 posts.

BUREAU OF HUMAN RESOURCES: Administers personnel matters such as setting employment standards, recruitment, assignment evaluation, promotion, discipline, career development, and retirement policies and programs for all State Department employees, both foreign and general civil service. It is headed by the *director general of the Foreign Service,* who doubles as the *director of Human Resources* and has responsibility for the *Office of Medical Services* and the *Family Liaison Office,* thus bringing related personnel matters together under one administration umbrella. The director is a presidential appointee with Senate confirmation, and has a rank equivalent to an assistant secretary.

BUREAU OF DIPLOMATIC SECURITY: Created to protect American diplomatic personnel and overseas missions. The bureau provides security advice and programs against terrorism, espionage, and criminal threats to American embassies and consular offices. This need for security came in reaction to the 1979 hostage taking, the bombings of several American embassies in Africa, the 9/11 terrorist attacks, and several assassinations or other attacks on U.S. diplomatic officials. Within the United States this bureau's agents physically protect the secretary of state and foreign dignitaries visiting the United States. They also investigate passport and visa fraud, conduct personnel security investigations (somewhat redundant with the FBI), issue security clearances to department personnel, and regulate activity of foreign missions in the United States (apparently to guarantee that these missions are not used for improper purposes such as spying).

In order to manage its domestic functions (including investigation of visa and passport fraud and protect State Department personnel and facilities, and conduct security clearances) the bureau maintains a network of domestic field offices:

77 Forsyth Street, Suite 320, Atlanta, GA 30303; Phone: (404) 331-3521. 10 Causeway Street, Suite 1001, Boston, MA 02222; Phone: (617) 565-8200. 915 Lafayette Boulevard, Room 300, Bridgeport, CT 06604; Phone: (203) 579-5701. 77 West Jackson Boulevard, Suite 2121, Chicago, IL 60604; Phone: (312) 353-6163. 1100 Commerce Street, Room 762, Dallas, TX 75242; Phone: (214) 767-0700. 755 Parfet Street, Suite 353, Lakewood, CO 80215; Phone: (303) 236-2781. 1801 Stanley Road, Suite 320, Greensboro, NC 27407; Phone: (336) 547-4292. 300 Ala Moana, Room 6-209, Honolulu, HI 96805; Phone: (808) 541-2854. 1919 Smith Street, Suite 870, Houston, TX 77002; Phone: (713) 209-3482. 255 East Temple Street, Suite 1273; Phone: (213) 894-3290. 51 SW First Avenue, Room 404; Miami, FL 33130; Phone: (305) 536-5781. 31 Rochester Avenue, Portsmouth, NH 03801; Phone: (603) 334-0519. 365 Canal Street, Suite 1130, New Orleans, LA 70130; Phone: (504) 589-2010. One Executive Drive, Suite 500, Fort Lee, NJ 07024; Phone: (201) 944-3787. 600 Arch Street, Room 3218, Philadelphia, PA 19106; Phone: (215) 861-3370. 401 West Washington Street, Suite 435, Phoenix, AZ 85003; Phone: (602) 364-7842. 555 West Beech Street, Room 222, San Diego, CA 92101; Phone: (619) 557-6194. 235 Pine Street, Suite 900, San Francisco, CA 94104; Phone: (415) 705-1176. 915 Second Avenue, Suite 3410, Seattle, WA 98174; Phone: (206) 220-7721. 2222 Gallows Road, Suite 300 (Washington Field Office), Dunn Loring, VA 22027; Phone: (571) 226-9300. 525 F. D. Roosevelt Avenue, Suite 115, Hato Ray, PR 00918; Phone: (787) 766-5704.

The bureau also manages the *Counter-terrorism Rewards Program,* chairs the *Overseas Security Advisory Council,* which works with private enterprises to give security advice to American enterprises doing business abroad, and gives technical advice to foreign governments on security issues. The office also has tackled the problem of abuses of diplomatic immunity within the United States. This immunity has been claimed to give foreign diplomatic officials immunity from prosecution for crimes committed in the United States, including vehicular manslaughter, theft, and sexual harassment.

BUREAU OF RESOURCE MANAGEMENT: Provides oversight for worldwide financial and asset management of State Department accounts and property. In addition, the bureau leads the department's strategic planning. Other responsibilities are providing pension services, developing the annual budget, monitoring adherence to the budget, and reviewing every two years the fees, royalties, rents, and other charges paid by the State Department for goods and services. It also handles payroll services such as management of foreign currency exchange, and monitoring of accounting, payroll, and fiscal records.

UNDER SECRETARY FOR GLOBAL AFFAIRS

Coordinates American foreign relations on various global matters through the Bureau for Democracy, Human Rights and Labor, Bureau for International Narcotics and Law Enforcement Affairs, Bureau of Oceans and International

Environmental and Scientific Affairs, and Bureau of Population, Refugees and Migration.

BUREAU OF DEMOCRACY, HUMAN RIGHTS AND LABOR: Responsible for ensuring that human rights and labor conditions in foreign countries are considered in the process of making American foreign policy. Its main task is to prepare and submit an annual report to Congress on human rights practices and religious freedom in all countries.

BUREAU FOR INTERNATIONAL NARCOTICS AND LAW ENFORCEMENT AFFAIRS: Mandated to reduce illegal drug importation into the United States by cooperating with foreign countries through crop control of poppies and other drug sources, and stimulating alternative development programs to replace those crops. It conducts training programs on antidrug enforcement for foreign agencies. It also provides training to fight international money laundering, fraud, public corruption, and illegal trafficking of women and children, illegal aliens, and stolen vehicles and weapons.

BUREAU OF OCEANS AND INTERNATIONAL ENVIRONMENTAL AND SCIENTIFIC AFFAIRS: Deals with environmental interrelationships of trade and biodiversity, global climate change, pollution, oceans, fisheries, marine conservation, space cooperation, technology, and health. The bureau applies traditional diplomacy to these global environmental issues.

BUREAU OF POPULATION, REFUGEES AND MIGRATION: Coordinates State Department policy on those subjects through cooperative efforts among the department, other government agencies, private voluntary entities, and international agencies in order to develop and implement a comprehensive international population policy covering a broad range of reproductive health services. The bureau also gives assistance to refugees seeking political asylum, determines the basis for admission of refugees for permanent resettlement, and develops multilateral approaches to international migration questions.

The senior coordinator for woman's issues, while independent of this group, reports directly to the under secretary. The senior coordinator deals with issues such as combating violence toward women and children and trafficking in women and children.

UNDER SECRETARY FOR PUBLIC DIPLOMACY AND PUBLIC AFFAIRS

Oversees diplomatic involvement in cultural and educational exchanges with people from other countries (public, private, governmental, and commercial). Equally important are its programs to provide information from an American point of view to the people of other countries by means of international programs that provide information on U.S. diplomacy to Americans. Cynics might call this the propaganda arm of the department.

This group functions through the Bureau of Public Affairs, the Bureau of Educational and Cultural Affairs, and the Office of International Information Programs.

BUREAU OF PUBLIC AFFAIRS: Disperses information on American foreign policy and its significance by means of press briefings, "town meetings," and conferences at various sites throughout the nation, arranging radio and television interviews with key State Department officials, and audiovisual materials and services. The *Office of the Historian* in this bureau does historical research and publishes the official documentary history of American foreign policy.

The State Department website is maintained by the Bureau of Public Affairs at http://state.gov. For public inquiries the bureau has an information line, (202) 647-6575.

BUREAU OF EDUCATIONAL AND CULTURAL AFFAIRS: Employs cultural and professional exchanges with other nations and presents programs on American history, society, art, and culture to audiences in foreign countries. These programs are usually organized through State Department embassies.

For the U.S. foreign affairs professionals the *Office of International Information Programs* develops and maintains in-house communications via the Internet, print publications, traveling and electronically transmitted speakers, and information resource services. In addition to its own officials, these media programs are intended for special international audiences, such as media, government officials, opinion leaders, and on occasion for the general public in more than 140 foreign countries.

THE FOREIGN SERVICE
United States Missions

The United States maintains diplomatic offices in more than 180 countries, which are called missions, and each is the office of the American ambassador (or the equivalent) to that country. The mission offices are generally located in the capital of the nation. In a few cases the ambassador is not resident at all times; for example, there is one ambassador for three different Caribbean island nations.

Ambassadors, pursuant to the American Constitution, are appointed by the president and must be confirmed by a vote of the United States Senate, after FBI clearances and hearings before the Foreign Relations Committee of the Senate, which must give a favorable vote to send the nomination to the floor for a vote by the full body. Occasionally, there is some objection, but in general, barring some highly adverse information, the presidential appointees are routinely approved. In the late 1990s two appointees by President Clinton were delayed at length by the chairman of the committee out of personal pique.

At the missions there are usually officers who are specialists, and sometimes officials from other government agencies such as a military attaché, the DEPARTMENT OF COMMERCE, or a local

director of the USAID program. The ambassador is known as the chief of mission, assisted by a deputy chief of mission, usually responsible for administering the support staff. In addition to Americans on the staff, many of the employees are hired from local residents who serve as office staff, translators, and other necessary support personnel. These require careful screening. In some special situations in which the United States does not have full diplomatic relations or there is a transitional situation chief of mission, there is a liaison officer known as principal officer rather than chief of mission. In the 1970s future president George H. W. Bush held that position in the People's Republic of China.

The official responsibilities of a chief of mission are: (a) explaining to the officials of the host country and its people the views of the United States, (b) reporting to the State Department the situation and current happenings in the host country, (c) coordinating and directing the staff and other American official personnel (except for the military officials) in the host country, including consular officials, (d) cooperating with Congress and the American court system to the extent necessary to keep them informed and ensuring that the conduct of the mission is consistent with American goals and the law, and (e) acting to provide security for the mission, its personnel, and their dependents.

The larger missions have various officials on the staff who are experts in particular fields. These officials may include:

Commercial officers advise businesses on trade and tariff laws of both the United States and the host country, business opportunities, and resolving trade and investments disputes.

Economic officers keep abreast of the local business climate, negotiate some trade and investment agreements, and urge the host countries to adopt trade policies favorable to American interests.

Resource officers track and report on local resources such as minerals, gas, and energy, and advise American businesses on the impact of trends in resource potential and practices.

Financial attachés analyze local financial developments and determine the host country's overall financial condition.

Agricultural officers promote the export of U.S. agricultural products to the host country, and determine issues of animal and plant health (such as hoof-and-mouth disease), and recommend protections against foreign pests and diseases stemming from the host country. These officers are also responsible for guaranteeing that U.S. imports are subject to sanitary regulations.

Political officers follow closely both the current and potential political developments in the host country and their impact on American interests both governmental and commercial, and promote (often subtly) the host country government's foreign policies that are most compatible with American aims. These officers also advise American businesses on the political situation in the host country.

Labor officers recommend to the host country labor laws on wage, working conditions, and other practices (within tolerances of conditions acceptable to American government and public opinion) that are not practices unfair to competition with American business and labor. They also monitor political activities of local labor organizations and their attitude toward American investment.

Environment, science, technology, and health officers stay current on local developments in those fields and determine the impact on American governmental and business interests.

Public affairs officers (also known as information officers and/or cultural affairs officers) have dual responsibilities: spokespersons for the mission and as administrators of official exchange programs such as Fulbright Scholars, Humphrey, and Muskie Fellows (all named for late U.S. senators), the U.S. Speakers Program, and the Worknet TV Satellite teleconferencing network, which serves more than 200 overseas posts.

Legal attachés are DEPARTMENT OF JUSTICE representatives on criminal matters, and may be sent to the post as necessary.

Information management officers direct the post's unclassified information system, the database, telecommunications, telephones, radio transmission, diplomatic pouches, and records management. When necessary, these officers confer with local authorities on communications issues, such as failure of telephone systems, interference, or lack of secure lines.

Administrative officers are responsible for the management of the post's personnel, budget, fiscal concerns, real property, other assets, motor pools, and local acquisitions, in short, the business operation of the mission.

Military attachés are often attached to American overseas missions, and at all times remain officials of the DEFENSE DEPARTMENT. Besides possible military cooperation with the host country armed forces, they may give advice on security of the post, involvement in military sales to the host country, and serve as a point of contact between U.S. military suppliers and the host country.

Visas

Usually, foreigners wishing to enter the United States, including for education, employment, or pleasure, often with specific limitations, are issued visas by the U.S. mission located in the country in which the applicant is a resident. *Inquiries:* visa cases and the application process:

CONTACT Phones: (202) 663-1225; visa cutoff dates: (202) 663-1541; J waiver status: (202) 663-1600; immigrant visa inquiries: (602) 334-0700; Website: www.travel.state.gov. A booklet, "Foreign Entry Requirements," is available for 50 cents from the Consumer Information Center, Pueblo, CO 81009.

Consulates

The Department of State maintains consulates in many of the major cities in the world, and they are directed by the *Bureau of Consular Affairs,* headed by an assistant secretary of state appointed by the president with Senate confirmation. Unlike the ambassadors who are political appointees, the consular officials, including each *Consul General,* are career incumbents in the Foreign Service.

Unlike the diplomatic missions, the consulates are primarily concerned with promoting American commercial interests, trade, and assisting individuals with problems and needs while visiting and/or doing business in a foreign country. For the people of the countries in which American consulates are located, these offices can be a source of help, information, and such routine matters as obtaining a notarization (there is a fee), replacing a lost passport, and similar matters.

Missions to International Organizations

The State Department maintains permanent missions to several international organizations, including:

UNITED STATES MISSION TO THE UNITED NATIONS

The U.S. Mission to the United Nations is headed by the *United States permanent representative to the United Nations* (commonly referred to as the U.N. ambassador). Although the representative is independent and has a cabinet-rank, he or she reports to the secretary of state. This is to ensure that the statements and votes as the American permanent representative on the Security Council of the U.N. are consistent with American foreign policy.

The equivalent rank as a cabinet-level appointee of the president with Senate approval stems from the appointment of Adlai Stevenson as U.N. ambassador by President John F. Kennedy in 1961. Stevenson, two-time Democratic nominee for president (1952 and 1956) wanted to be named secretary of state in the new administration, but Kennedy wanted someone else. At the same time Kennedy recognized Stevenson's popularity at home and respect abroad. Stevenson agreed to take the lesser post only if he would be included in the cabinet, at least nominally. Thus, the precedent was established, without formally making future ambassadors actual cabinet members.

The permanent representative serves as one of five permanent members of the U.N. Security Council out of 15 total, the United States, Russia, Great Britain, France, and the People's Republic of China. Each of these five can veto any proposal before the Security Council by merely voting No. The remaining members of the Security Council are elected on a rotating basis for two-year terms. The special powerful status of the five permanent members has its roots in the fact that they represented the five major powers that defeated the Axis—Germany, Japan, and Italy—in World War II. As a practical matter, major policy decisions would be difficult to enforce or implement without the support of all of the major powers in the world. Russia technically replaced the Soviet Union (aka Union of Soviet Socialist Republics) when that government broke into several nations that had been republics within that union, leaving Russia the major component as the natural successor. After several years of confusion and American opposition following the defeat of the Nationalist Chinese government in 1948, the People's Republic (communist) government was chosen in 1978 to take the seat of China, previously held by the Nationalist government, which had been relegated to the island of Taiwan. Taiwan is not a member of the United Nations.

HISTORY

Upon signing the United Nations Charter at the founding conference in San Francisco, California, in August 1945, the first permanent American representative, Edward R. Stettinius Jr., was appointed by President Harry S. Truman. The conference chose New York City as the future permanent headquarters, which was built on 16 acres donated by the Rockefeller family.

American permanent representatives after Stettinius died in 1946 were: Herschel V. Johnson (acting) (1946–47), Warren R. Austin (1947–53), Henry Cabot Lodge Jr. (1953–60), James J. Wadsworth (1960–61), Adlai Stevenson (1961–65), Arthur J. Goldberg (1965–68), George W. Ball (1968), James Russell Wiggins (1968–69), Charles W. Yost (1969–71), George H. W. Bush (1971–73), John A. Scali (1973–75), Daniel P. Moynihan (1975–76), William W. Scranton (1976–77), Andrew Young (1977–79), Donald McHenry (1979–81), Jeane J. Kirkpatrick (1981–85), Vernon A. Walters (1985–89), Thomas J. Pickering (1989–92), Edward J. Perkins (1992–93), Madeleine K. Albright (1993–96), Bill Richardson (1997–98), Richard C. Holbrooke (1999–2001), and John D. Negroponte (2001–   ).

Lodge was a former senator from Massachusetts, and in 1960 was the losing Republican vice presidential candidate. Stevenson played a vital role in the Cuban missile crisis with a dramatic confrontation with the Soviet representative before the Security Council in exposing the existence of missile-launching facilities in Cuba. Goldberg also served on the U.S. Supreme Court and as secretary of labor. Ball resigned in part over his disagreement with President Lyndon Johnson over increasing American involvement in Vietnam. George H. W. Bush later was elected vice president and then president of the United States. Scali was a correspondent for ABC who had played a behind-the-scenes role in defusing the Cuban missile crisis. Moynihan, who had served in both Republican and Democratic administrations, went on to a lengthy career as a senator from New York. Scranton was the former governor of Pennsylvania. Young had been an aide to Martin Luther King and was later the mayor of Atlanta, Georgia. Albright left her U.N. post to become the first female secretary of state. Richardson left to become secretary of energy and in 2002 was elected governor of New Mexico.

It was under United Nations auspices that the nation of Israel was formalized in 1947 and promptly recognized by the United States. In 1950 President Harry S. Truman sent American military forces into Korea to combat an invasion of South Korea by North Korea as a U.N.–sponsored "police action," authorized by the Security Council in 1950. A similar resolution authorized the use of American troops (as well as those of other nations) in 1991 to drive Iraqi forces out of Kuwait, which had been invaded by Iraq. This response was based on a Security Council resolution urged by U.S. president George H. W. Bush. When the Iraqis had been driven from Kuwait, a truce was negotiated by the United Nations with the acquiescence of the United States, in which the government of Iraq agreed to halt such aggressions and the means to conduct threats to other nations and to submit to inspection to guarantee that there would be no build-up or use of so-called weapons of mass destruction. In 2003, when the United States requested a Security Council resolution specifically authorizing the use of military forces to invade Iraq in search of such weapons, it became evident there were not enough votes in favor of such a resolution. Nevertheless, President George W. Bush ordered the invasion by American forces, aided by Great Britain and Australia.

ORGANIZATION

The U.N. ambassador is supported by a substantial office, which includes four presidential appointees confirmed by the Senate: *alternative representative for special political affairs, U.S. representative to the Economic and Social Council, U.S. representative for United Nations Management and Reform,* and *deputy ambassador to the United Nations.* Career incumbents include an attorney adviser and two political officers and technical experts.

There are also so-called *delegates*, prominent citizens appointed by the president, who serve on various committees and reinforce American participation. Over the years these have included

Eleanor Roosevelt and former Minnesota governor Harold Stassen.

CONTACT Address: 799 United Nations Plaza, New York, NY 10017; Phone: (212) 963-1234; Website: www.un.org.

United States Mission to the Organization of American States (OAS), Washington, D.C.;

United States Mission to International Organizations, Vienna, Austria;

United States Mission to the North Atlantic Treaty Organization (NATO), Brussels, Belgium;

United States Mission to the Organization for Economic Cooperation and Development, Paris, France;

United States Mission to the United Nations Office and Other International Organizations, Geneva, Switzerland;

United States Mission to the European Union (EU), Brussels, Belgium;

United States Mission to the International Civil Aviation Organization, Montreal, Canada;

United States Mission to the Organization for Security and Cooperation in Europe, Vienna, Austria;

United States Mission to the United Nations Agencies for Food And Agriculture, Rome, Italy;

United States Permanent Mission to the United Nations Environment Program and the United Nations Center for Human Settlements, Nairobi, Kenya.

The United States also maintains an *Observer Mission to the United Nations Educational, Scientific and Cultural Organization (UNESCO),* Paris, France, since the United States has officially withdrawn from UNESCO and refused any funding for the U.N. agency in part because UNESCO funds some birth control information and materials, and urges the use of condoms in the fight against AIDS, particularly in Africa.

The State Department also arranges American delegations to single-session international conferences on a variety of topics, including conferences sponsored by the international organizations where the United States has missions.

Ambassadors-at-Large

The State Department maintains several ambassadors-at-large who represent the United States in international organizations and discussions concerned with particular topics. Each is headquartered at the State Department offices in Washington, D.C. They are:

Ambassador-at-Large for Newly Independent States, Ambassador-at-Large for Counter-Terrorism, and *Ambassador-at-Large for War Crimes.* Each is appointed by the president with the required Senate confirmation.

DOING BUSINESS AND EMPLOYMENT

Contacts: Inquiries about contracting with the Department of State can be made through the following contacts:

CONTACT Address: Office of Acquisitions Management, Department of State, P.O. Box 9115, Arlington, VA 22219; Phone: (703) 875-6060; Fax: (703) 875-6085; for small businesses check on the Internet at www.statebuy.gov/home.

Employment: Inquiries about employment in the foreign service (not including the upper echelon and other presidential appointments) should be directed to: HR/REE/REC, Room H-518m 2401 E Street, Washington, DC 20522; Phone: (202) 261-8888; Website: www.careers.state.gov. On the Internet one might try DSRecruitment@state.gov.

DEPARTMENT OF STATE PUBLICATIONS

Some of the useful publications available from the Bureau of Consular Affairs of the Department of State, Consular Affairs, Staff, Department of State, Room 6831, Washington, DC 20520, and posted on the Internet at www.travel.state.gov are:

Travel Warning on Drugs

Travel Tips for Older Americans

Your Trip Abroad

A Safe Trip Abroad

Tips for Americans Residing Abroad (there are more than 4 million)

Tips for Travel to Canada

Tips for Travelers to the Caribbean

Tips for Travelers to Mexico

Tips for Travelers to the Middle East and Africa

Tips for Travelers to the People's Republic of China

Tips for Travelers to Russia

Tips for Travelers to South Asia

Tips for Travelers to Central and South America

Tips for Travelers to Sub-Saharan Africa

Passports: Applying for Them the Easy Way.

Some publications are free and others are as much as $1.50, which is quite a bargain. Prices and availability are posted at www.travel.state.gov.

The State Department also publishes *State Magazine* 10 times a year. Intended as an in-house magazine for department employees, it is also available to the general public by subscription. Subscriptions can be ordered through the U.S. Government Printing Office by calling toll free (866) 512-1800, or on the Web at bookstore.gpo.gov.

UNITED STATES AGENCY FOR INTERNATIONAL DEVELOPMENT (USAID)

An independent agency, USAID nevertheless is under the authority of the secretary of state, and is given basic foreign policy guidance from the secretary. In many cases the agency physically shares the facilities of the embassy post in those nations in which there are USAID offices. In the numerous countries in which the agency maintains offices, there are bilateral agreements with the host nation for providing assistance.

HISTORY

USAID was a key element of the foreign policy of President John F. Kennedy to provide mutual aid, particularly to developing countries. It was first authorized by the Foreign Assistance Act of 1961. In more than 40 years since, it has grown or retracted in part based on the foreign policy goals of the particularly administration. Its current annual budget is in the neighborhood of more than $88 billion.

CONTACT Address: 1300 Pennsylvania Avenue NW, Washington, DC 20523; Phones: (202) 712-0000, general inquiries: (202) 712-4810; media inquiries: (202) 7712-4320; Fax: (202) 216-3514; Website: www.usaid.gov.

ORGANIZATION

The agency is under the direction of the USAID administrator. The administrator, the deputy administrator, the several bureau chiefs, and the inspector general are presidential appointments with Senate confirmation. All other officials, including those heading the overseas posts, are career incumbents. Depending on the size of the post in a foreign country, there are specialists on staff.

Administrative bureaus are the *Bureau for Legislative and Public Affairs, Bureau for Policy and Program Coordination,* and *Bureau for Management.*

Program bureaus are the *Bureau for Economic Growth, Agriculture and Trade, Bureau for Global Health,* and *Bureau for Democracy, Conflict and Humanitarian Assistance.*

With a few exceptions they are all located at agency headquarters in Washington, D.C. The exceptions are an *AID Coordination Represen-*

tative based in Geneva, Switzerland; a *U.S. Representative to Development Assistance Committee* in Paris, France; and *Counselor to USAID Office for Development Cooperation* in Tokyo, Japan.

Regional bureaus supervise the work of the numerous USAID offices within the nations in each region. They are: *Bureau for Africa, Bureau for Europe and Eurasia, Bureau for Asia and the Near East, Bureau for Latin America and the Caribbean.*

Goals

There are five basic goals of the agency: population stabilization and health, enhancing economic growth in developing countries, reducing long-term threats to the environment, encouraging transition to democracy of developing nations, and humanitarian assistance. In most areas of concern, the ultimate goal is to develop local leadership, talents, and skills to make all these efforts self-sustaining.

Programs

Population and Health supports women's reproductive rights through voluntary family planning, is sensitive to local customs, training of girls and young men, and particularly child and young adult health care. *Environment* includes training to create sustainable economic growth that is environmentally sound, improving resource management practices, and reducing greenhouse gases and climate change. *Democracy* encourages democratic policies and establishing a tradition of honest elections and governmental practices. *Humanitarian Assistance* concentrates on response to disasters and assisting the local governments and business entities in preparing for or preventing disasters such as floods or epidemics.

The means used to achieve the goals and effectuate the programs include training, expert advice, loans, grants, developing cooperation, and preparing local people to establish and manage programs.

Countries with offices of USAID

Africa: Zambia, Malawi, Zimbabwe, Kenya, Uganda, Nigeria, Tanzania, Namibia, Ghana, Angola, Mozambique, Democratic Republic of Congo, Eritrea, Ethiopia, Liberia, Republic of South Africa, Guinea, Benin, Senegal, Rwanda, Madagascar, Morocco; *Europe and Eurasia:* Armenia, Georgia, Kazakhstan, Russia, Ukraine, Belarus, Kyrgyzstan, Yugoslavia, Kosovo, Croatia, Macedonia, Bosnia, Albania, Bulgaria, Romania, Hungary; *Asia and the Near East:* Egypt, Lebanon, Israel, Jordan, Nepal, Sri Lanka, India, Bangladesh, Mongolia, Cambodia, Philippines, Indonesia, *Latin America and the Caribbean:* Guyana, Bolivia, Brazil, Colombia, Dominican Republic, Ecuador, El Salvador, Guatemala, Haiti, Honduras, Mexico, Nicaragua, Panama, Paraguay, Peru, Jamaica. Egypt and Morocco, although in Africa, are under the Bureau for Asia and Near East.

For inquiries about doing business with USAID, contact the *Office of Small and Disadvantaged Business/Minority Resource Center* at (202) 712-1500. For employment, call the main USAID number or use the Internet, and ask for the Workforce Planning, Recruitment and Personnel System Division of the Office of Human Resources, USAID.

DEPARTMENT OF TRANSPORTATION

The Department of Transportation (DOT) develops, sets, and coordinates overall transportation policy with the goal of ensuring fast, safe, efficient, accessible, and convenient transportation to meet national defense interests and public needs with environmental sensitivity.

Under the Department of Transportation are 11 administrations including highway planning, development and construction; motor carrier safety; mass transit in urban areas; aviation; and railroads. DOT also oversees the safety factors of highways, oil and gas pipelines, ports, and waterways. DOT works with local and state governments on land planning, energy conservation, technical modernization, and scarce resource uses.

DOT's functioning entities include: Federal Aviation Administration, Federal Highway Administration, Federal Railroad Administration, National Highway Traffic Safety Administration, Federal Transit Administration, Saint Lawrence Seaway Development Corporation, Research and Special Programs Administration, Bureau of Transportation Statistics, Federal Motor Carrier Safety Administration, and Surface Transportation Board. Subsequent to the establishment of the Department of Homeland Security by President George W. Bush in 2002 following the attacks on the World Trade Center and the Pentagon, then secretary of transportation Norman Y. Mineta handed over civilian leadership of the United States Coast Guard and the Transportation Security Administration to Homeland Security.

CONTACT Address: Department of Transportation, 400 Seventh Street SW, Washington, DC 20590; Phone: (202) 366-4000; Website: www.dot.gov.

HISTORY

Created by congressional act, the Department of Transportation bill was signed into law by President Lyndon B. Johnson on October 15, 1966. Federal concern with transportation dates back to President Thomas Jefferson's secretary of treasury Albert Gallatin's recommendation that the federal government subsidize the National Road in 1808 to help struggling new states prosper. Before Gallatin's advocacy, the Coast Guard and Army Corps of Engineers worked to help trade and transportation. Establishment of the new department brought together several agencies dealing with transportation.

In 1965 Federal Aviation Agency administrator Najeeb Halaby suggested creation of a cabinet-level Department of Transportation to President Lyndon B. Johnson, which would absorb his independent FAA. Halaby arrived at his idea apparently because the DEFENSE DEPARTMENT of the 1960s had shut the FAA out of the decision-making process on supersonic transportation, and he concluded an overall DOT was key to form overall transportation policy. Halaby became president of Pan American Airlines, and was the father of Queen Noor of Jordan.

President Johnson became an advocate of DOT on the premise that an up-to-date transportation system is essential to a healthy economy, including employment and national defense. The new department pulled together more than 30 disparate transportation agencies and functions and 95,000 employees primarily from the Federal Aviation Agency, the Coast Guard, and the Bureau of Public Roads. In 1968 Johnson moved urban mass transportation functions from Housing and Urban Development to DOT, calling the new entity the Urban Mass Transportation Administration, now known as the Federal Transit Administration.

President Richard M. Nixon oversaw the bailout of the Penn Central Railroad, the beginning of AMTRAK, and attempts to extend federal support of supersonic transport, appointing former Massachusetts governor John A. Volpe as secretary of transportation.

The Highway Safety Act of 1970 established the National Highway Traffic Safety Administration, which separated highway administration into design, construction, and maintenance, and highway and automobile safety, a move somewhat contradictory to the original motive to bring transportation-related groups under one roof.

Secretary Volpe's high-profile tenure included airline hijackings, a sick-out of the Professional Air Traffic Controllers Organization, ending federal support for supersonic transport production, handling applications for Concorde landing locations, and the Lithuanian seaman Simas Kudirka's defection to the United States.

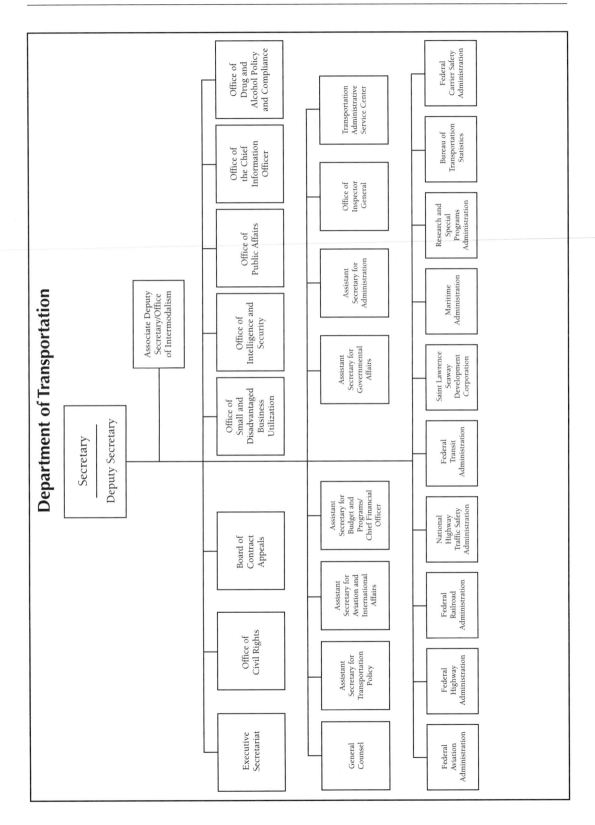

Department of Transportation

President Nixon appointed Dr. Claude S. Brinegar to succeed Volpe. A senior vice president of Union Oil Company, Brinegar had a Ph.D. in economic research and led DOT through Nixon's Watergate crisis and the 1973–74 energy crisis. He also oversaw the Northeast rail crisis, the Regional Rail Reorganization Act of 1973, and drafted the National Transportation Policy of 1974.

President Jimmy Carter appointed six-term congressman Brock Adams, a congressional transportation expert, as secretary. Adams oversaw reorganization of bankrupt northeastern railroad lines into the government backed Conrail system. Adams established the Research and Special Programs Directorate in 1977, later known as the Research and Special Programs Administration (RSPA), combining the Transportation Systems Center, the hazardous materials transportation and pipeline safety programs, and a cluster of other diverse activities that did not fit anywhere else in the bureaucracy. Adams's tenure also saw passage of the Inspectors General Act of 1978 to help department secretaries find and eliminate waste, fraud, and abuse.

Adams recommended reorganization of the Federal Highway Administration and the Urban Mass Transportation Administration into the Surface Transportation Administration before he was succeeded by Neil E. Goldschmidt, mayor of Portland, Oregon. During his tenure Goldschmidt oversaw passage of transportation deregulation in the Railroad Regulatory Act (Staggers Rail Act), the Truck Regulatory Reform Act, the International Airlines Reform Act, and the Household Goods Regulatory Reform Act.

Goldschmidt established the Office of Small and Disadvantaged Business Utilization in the secretary's office to give policy guidance for minority, women-owned, and disadvantaged businesses.

Andrew L. "Drew" Lewis, President Ronald Reagan's first secretary of transportation, brought the Maritime Administration to DOT from the COMMERCE DEPARTMENT, represented the Reagan administration in negotiations with the Professional Air Traffic Controllers Organization before their strike, and oversaw enactment of the Surface Transportation Assistance Act of 1982. Lewis also served as president of General Dynamics and Amtrak.

Reagan appointed Elizabeth Hanford Dole to succeed Lewis as secretary. Dole focused on safety-related issues, such as drunk driving, the "Dole brake light," and installation of air bags and seat belts as ordered by the Supreme Court. During her tenure the Commercial Space Launch Act of 1984 gave DOT responsibility to promote and regulate commercial space launch vehicles. The Airline Deregulation Act of 1978 and the Civil Aeronautics Board Sunset Act of 1984 sent the aviation economic fitness program, consumer protection, antitrust oversight, airline data collection, and review of international route negotiations and route awards to carriers over to DOT.

With a theme of reducing federal involvement in transportation, Dole transferred the Alaska Railroad to the state of Alaska, started the end of the Federal Railroad Administration's ownership of Conrail, and initiated establishment of the Metropolitan Washington Airports Authority, which moved administrative responsibilities for Washington National Airport and Dulles International Airport to the authority of the Federal Aviation Administration. Dole now serves as a U.S. senator from North Carolina.

President George H. W. Bush signed the Intermodal Surface Transportation Efficiency Act (ISTEA), which, in part, turned the Urban Mass Transportation Administration into the Federal Transit Administration and organized the Bureau of Transportation Statistics, and the Office of Intermodalism. Bush's first secretary of transportation, Samuel K. Skinner, became Bush's White House chief of staff, and Bush then named his deputy White House chief of staff, Andrew H. Card Jr. as secretary of transportation. Card later worked as lobbyist for the American Automobile Manufacturers Association, and now serves as President George W. Bush's White House chief of staff.

President Bill Clinton named former Denver, Colorado, mayor Federico Peña as secretary of transportation and later appointed Federal Highway administrator Rodney E. Slater to succeed Peña. Peña transferred the Office of Commercial Space Transportation from the Office of the Secretary to the Federal Aviation Administration. He also launched the Transportation Administrative Services Center (TASC) to provide fee-based services to DOT and other government agencies. Those services had been paid for by the Working Capital Fund.

During this period DOT negotiators averted an Amtrak strike and Congress demanded an Amtrak overhaul; the National Highway Traffic Safety Administration allowed consumers to turn off airbag switches; and the United States finalized an aviation agreement with Japan. Secretary Slater said transportation was about "more than concrete, asphalt, and steel" and launched several programs, including the Garett A. Morgan Technology and Transportation Futures program to help students choose careers in transportation; a "Safe Skies for Africa" initiative for improvements in aviation safety and security in Africa; and proposed ONE DOT, a unified department to increase transportation efficiency and effectiveness.

President George W. Bush appointed Democrat Norman Y. Mineta, Clinton's secretary of energy and former member of Congress, as secretary of transportation. Mineta had served as head of the Transportation Committee in Congress. Following the attacks on the World Trade Center and the Pentagon on September 11, 2001, President Bush signed into law the Aviation and Transportation Security Act to establish a new Transportation Security Administration in DOT to increase security at airports and other transportation sites. In 2002 Bush moved the Transportation Security Administration and the Coast Guard to the Department of Homeland Security.

ORGANIZATION

BUREAU OF TRANSPORTATION STATISTICS (BTS)

Created by the Intermodal Surface Transportation Efficiency Act (ISTEA) of 1991, BTS collects, analyzes, and reports data to establish cost-effective use of transportation monitoring resources for all modes of transportation. The newer Transportation Equity Act for the 21st Century (TEA-21) provided $31 million per year from 1998 to 2003 from the Highway Trust Fund, administered within the Research and Development account of the Federal Highway Administration.

BTS statistics objectively cover all modes of transportation, making it a cross-modal bureau. BTS sets standards for long-term transportation data, has statutory protections for confidentiality of its collected data, and works in statistics, economics, information technology, geographic information systems, and transportation.

BTS makes its transportation data available to decision makers in Congress, DOT, other federal agencies, state governments, metropolitan planning organizations, local governments, universities, private business, and the general public.

Office of Airline Information (OAI): Provides data on financial and market and traffic economic data on airline operations and the air transportation industry.

CONTACT Address: BTS, 400 7th Street SW, Room 3103, Washington, DC 20590; Phone: (800) 853-1351; Website: www.bts.gov/.

Commodity Flow Survey (CFS): Collects and makes available data on shipments by American manufacturers, wholesale, mining, and other industries in partnership with the U.S. Census Bureau's Economic Census.

Data Gaps Project: Works to fill gaps in information needed by planners, policy makers, managers, researchers, and other transportation data users. Gaps in statistics needed include accessibility, completeness, detail, existence, integration, quality, and timeliness of transportation. To fill these gaps, the project will seek information to determine transportation providers' number and condition of capital assets and infrastructure; assess quality of service provided; evaluate safety issues; calculate travel and transportation demand; determine attitudes and perceptions of transportation services; assess impact of technology and other changes on transportation modes; and evaluate issues of equity and fairness, i.e., who uses transportation, geography, and attitudinal information.

CONTACT Data Gaps Project; Phone: (202) 366-9934; Fax: (202) 366-3640.

Geographic Information Services (GIS): Collects and makes available transportation spatial data and transportation information.

Motor Carrier Financial and Operating Statistics (F&OS) Program: Collects data quarterly and annually from motor carriers of goods and people, including balance sheet and income statement data, as well as information on tonnage, mileage, employees, transportation equipment, and other data.

CONTACT Address: Office of Motor Carrier Information, 400 Seventh Street NW, Room 2440, K-13, Washington, DC 20590; Phone: (202) 366-4383.

THE NATIONAL TRANSPORTATION LIBRARY (NTL): Works to provide timely access to information that supports transportation policy, research, operations, and technology transfer activities. Established by the Transportation Equity Act for the 21st Century in 1998 under President Bill Clinton, NTL is the national repository for public, academic, and private business and organizations' materials, in cooperation with other federal agencies, and state and local government partners.

CONTACT Address: National Transportation Library, Information and Customer Services, 400 Seventh Street SW, Room 3430, Washington, DC 20590; Phone: (800) 853-1351; Fax: (202) 366-3676.

The *Department of Transportation Library* holds 300,000 titles, including more than 1,200 different periodicals. Subjects include the Nassif technical collection consisting of primary source materials on general transportation, surface, and water transportation. Other topics include bridges, driver studies, engineering, highways and highway safety, history of transportation, land utilization, marine engineering, mass transit, merchant marine, navigation (except air), oceanography, pipelines, railroads, ships, shipbuilding, statistics, traffic engineering, traffic surveys and forecasts, urban transportation, and waterways.

NTL has three law collections including general law and transportation law.

CONTACT Address; DOT Library, 400 Seventh Street SW, Room 2200, Washington, DC 20590; Phone: (202) 366-0746; Website: http://dotlibrary.dot.gov/.

FEDERAL AVIATION ADMINISTRATION (FAA)

Established as the Federal Aviation Agency by the Federal Aviation Act of 1958, it became part of DOT in 1997 as part of the Department of Transportation Act. Focusing on safety and the public interest, FAA assigns, maintains, and improves safety and security as its highest priority; regulates air commerce to promote safety and fulfill national defense needs; encourages and develops civil aeronautics, including new aviation technologies; through air traffic controllers controls the use of airspace and regulates both military and civil aircraft; consolidates research and development and operation of air navigation facilities and the National Airspace System; helps law-enforcement agencies enforce laws regarding controlled substances; works to develop programs to reduce aircraft and sonic boom noise and other environmental offenses; and regulates U.S. commercial transportation in space.

General activities include:

Airspace and Air Traffic Management: Operates network of airport towers, air route traffic centers, and flight service stations. It also makes air traffic rules, allocates use of airspace, and controls air traffic to meet national defense requirements.

Certification: Issues operating certificates to airports serving airplanes with more than 30 seats, protecting the public by inspecting and requiring airports to meet standards of airport design, construction, maintenance, operations, fire fighting, rescue equipment, runway and taxiway guidance signs and indicators, control of vehicles, wildlife hazards, and record keeping.

Airport Compliance Program: Enforces compliance to contractual obligations airport owners commit to when accepting federal grant funds.

Airport Environmental Program: Helps airports implement National Environmental Policy Act and other federal environmental laws and regulations through environmental review and reviews final environmental impact statements.

Financial Assistance for Airport Capital Development: Runs several financial assistance programs, including the Airport Improvement Program and the Passenger Facility Charge Program, giving millions of dollars annually for airport planning, development, noise reduction, capacity, and other projects.

Airport Planning: Sets standards and guidelines for national airport layout and system planning, including provisions of the National Plan of Integrated Airport Systems, the Military Airport Program, property transfers for airports, military base conversions, and joint-use of existing military bases.

Airport Safety: FAA issues and enforces regulations and minimum standards for manufacture, operation, and maintenance of aircraft. It also oversees maintenance of airport master records, the Airport Safety Data Program, emergency operations, vulnerability reduction, damage control at civil airports, planning for emergency management of civil airports, and direction of federal help to restore functions after attack or natural disaster.

Civil Aviation Abroad: From Washington, D.C., and through 50 officials on five continents, FAA works with its counterparts in 188 countries and with the International Civil Aviation Organization in Montreal, Quebec, Canada. The FAA and its international partners exchange aeronautical information; provide technical assistance and training; certify foreign repair shops, airmen, and mechanics; work to assure that airlines flying to the United States from other countries meet international standards, and work to standardize global standards to protect passengers.

FAA also registers aircraft and information on ownership of aircraft or their components; administers an aviation insurance program; assigns specifications for aeronautical charts; and publishes information on airways, airport services, and aeronautical technology.

Within the secretary's office, the assistant secretary for aviation and international affairs oversees domestic and international aviation and international trade, with the goal of liberalizing international air services; aims at making a deregulated, competitive domestic airline industry work; and works at expanding trade and transportation opportunities for American companies abroad.

To promote competition and deregulation internationally, the office has extended the "Open-skies" initiative and looks at issues such as foreign investment, economics of networks and their impact on prices and services, and safety surveillance of non-U.S. carriers, particularly in a post-9/11 environment.

To develop competition while deregulating in domestic aviation markets, FAA's Office of Aviation and International Affairs has a new enforcement policy regarding anticompetitive conduct, in which it defines when behavior crosses the line from competition to conduct designed to drive out new competition.

This office also oversees the Essential Air Service Program and subsidizes basic service not otherwise provided the marketplace to certain communities that were receiving certificated service when the airline industry was deregulated by President Jimmy Carter in 1978.

FAA's Office of Intelligence and Security (OIS) was established by the Aviation Security Improvement Act of 1990 (ASIA) following the terrorist attack on Pan American flight 103 over Lockerbie, Scotland. OIS develops policy and strategic planning on long-term transportation security needs. Among its duties, OIS evaluates and disseminates intelligence and security information; acts as the secretary's liaison with intelligence, law enforcement, and national defense and helps set up DOT linkages with these communities; coordinates with public and private sectors, international groups, and academia on transportation security, infrastructure protection, intermodal national transportation security issues, national defense, and drug and migrant interdiction; and helps secure movement of intermodal cargo and the infrastructure that supports such transportation.

CONTACT Address: OIS, 400 Seventh Street SW, Room 10401, Washington, DC 20590; Phone (202) 366-6525; Fax: (202) 366-7261.

CONTACT Address: General: FAA, 800 Independence Avenue SW, Washington, DC 20591; Phone: (202) 366-4000 or (202) 267-3883; Website: www.faa.gov. Regional: P.O. Box 14, 701 C Street, Anchorage, AL 99513; 801 East 12th Street, Kansas City, MO 64106; 1 Aviation Plaza, Springfield Gardens, NY 11434; 2300 East Devon Avenue, Des Plaines, IL 60018; 12 New England Executive Park, Burlington, MA 01803; 1601 Lind Avenue SW, Renton, WA, 98055; 1701 Columbia Avenue, College Park, GA 30337; 2601 Meacham Boulevard, Fort Worth, TX 76137-4298; 15000 Aviation Boulevard, Hawthorne, CA 90261; Europe, Africa, and Middle East: 15, Rue de la Loi B-1040, Brussels, Belgium; Asia-Pacific: U.S. Embassy, FAA, Singapore; Latin America-

Caribbean: 8600 NW 36th Street, Miami, FL 33166; William J. Hughes Technical Center, Atlantic City, NJ 08405; Mike Monroney Aeronautical Center, 6500 S. MacArthur, Oklahoma City, OK 73125.

OFFICE OF INTERMODALISM

The Office of Intermodalism coordinates projects, programs, and policies that involve more than one mode of transportation. Intermodalism includes the following connections: convenient, rapid, efficient, and safe transfer of people or goods from one transportation mode to another during a single journey (e.g., connection of train and bus); choices: transportation options through fair and healthy business competition between different modes of transportation; coordination and cooperation; and collaboration among transportation organizations to improve transportation services, quality, safety, and economy for all modes of transportation in an environmentally sound way.

CONTACT Address: Office of Intermodalism (S-3), U.S. Department of Transportation, 400 Seventh Street SW, Washington, DC 20590; Phone: (202) 366-5781; Fax: (202) 366-0263.

FEDERAL HIGHWAY ADMINISTRATION (FHWA)

The Department of Transportation Act established the Federal Highway Administration as an agency of DOT to administer highway transportation programs. FHWA gives out federal aid to state transportation departments, metropolitan transportation groups, local governments, and private organizations to build and maintain safe highways; gives grants toward developing statewide and metropolitan intermodal transportation plans and programs; gives technical support grants to states; works with other federal agencies to design and build roads in national forests, parks, and on Indian reservations; and works with foreign governments, including giving technical and technological assistance.

Some of the technical expertise FHWA gives to state and local partners and customers includes: roadway and bridge design, construction, and maintenance; engineering and other evaluation tools; policy and planning; highway safety; transportation systems; environmental protection and enhancement; financing; land acquisition; and research, development, and technology transfer.

FHWA provides funds to help states do emergency and permanent repairs on federal aid routes and federally owned roads damaged by natural disasters or catastrophic failures. It also works to ensure that any transportation system plans and improvements consider impacts on human and natural environments.

FHWA provides services for and on roads on or to federally owned lands and Indian reservations, including planning, locating, and designing highway projects, awarding contracts, and providing oversight at construction sites.

CONTACT Address: Federal Highway Administration, 400 Seventh Street SW, Washington, DC 20590; Phone: (202) 366-0660 or (202) 366-0650; Website: www.fhwa.dot.gov.

Federal-Aid Highway Program: Employs community planners, environmental scientists, real estate specialists, and transportation engineers in its various offices.

The Office of Infrastructure provides technical assistance; develops national policies and standards in cooperation with the states; and collects data on cost trends. Its Office of Pavement Technology develops and makes available the latest technical information for highway officials and contractors such as asphalt pavement technology, the Superpave System, and development of truly performance-based asphalt mixes, all with the goal of providing pavement smoothness and safety.

CONTACT Address: 400 7th Street SW, HIPT-1, Washington, DC 20590; Fax: (202) 493-2070.

The Office of Asset Management keeps track of pavement, bridge, and system preservation. The Intelligent Transportation Systems Joint Program Office works with other DOT offices to improve safety of the surface transportation system, including highways, transit, and rail in a truly multimodal effort.

The Office of Travel Management works on mobility, productivity, and safety of surface transportation; initiates policies and programs; serves as the FHWA advocate; and develops products, services, and technical support for integrated travel management and information systems.

Federal-Aid Highway Program's Office of Freight Management and Operations oversees truck size and weight regulations enforcement by the states; develops freight operations strategies for intermodal freight and international border clearance; works to improve freight transportation security, efficiency, and safety; works on a global intermodal freight system; develops international border architecture to improve trucking traffic across U.S. borders; and works with Canada and Mexico along with the GENERAL SERVICES ADMINISTRATION and the Immigration and Naturalization Service to improve costs, benefits, and security at border crossings.

The Freight Policy Team analyzes intermodal freight systems, attempts to forecast 2010 and 2020 freight flows, and anticipates freight capacity issues. It also develops freight metrics; collects data on and analyzes goods movement trends; conducts studies; evaluates freight financing mechanisms and looks for financing options; encourages multijurisdictional coalitions to expedite freight movement in the United States, Mexico, and Canada; and sponsors freight conferences and seminars on freight productivity, national security, financing, planning, and logistics.

OFFICE OF SAFETY: Works to reduce the number and severity of highway crashes by motorized and nonmotorized travelers on U.S. highways, streets, bicycle and pedestrian facilities, and intermodal connections. The Safety Core Business Unit (SCBU) develops and implements strategies and programs to reduce severe highway crashes. The Office of Safety is involved in advocacy; safety information and analysis; strategic planning and quality control; legislation, regulations, policy, and guidance; safety council and safety programs; technology delivery; advance product development, testing, and demonstration; monitoring and evaluation; outreach and consultation; and communication and marketing.

CONTACT Address: FHA, Safety, 400 7th Street SW, Washington, DC 20590.

The Office of Safety Design advocates road and roadside highway safety features, including parking needs of people with disabilities; develops policy and national highway safety programs; surveys safety performance goals, policy, and criteria for all public roads, and bicycle/pedestrian facilities; works on pavement skid resistance, roadway geometrics and cross-sections, and roadside safety features, traffic control devices; and highway-rail grade crossings. The *Office of Safety Programs* develops and manages programs in the above function areas, and responds to recommendations of the NATIONAL TRANSPORTATION SAFETY BOARD (NTSB).

OFFICE OF FEDERAL LANDS HIGHWAY: Administers the Federal Lands Highway Program (FLHP) by funding for 90,000 miles of public roads that serve transportation needs of federal and Indian lands that are not under state or local government responsibility. The program provides transportation engineering services for planning, design, construction, and rehabilitation of highways and bridges that provide access to federal and Indian lands, forest highway system roads, parkways and park roads, and defense access roads. It also provides training, technology, deployment, engineering services, and products to its customers. The office works in

cooperation with the National Park Service, Forest Service, Military Traffic Management Command, Fish and Wildlife Service, and the Bureau of Indian Affairs.

OFFICE OF POLICY: Advises the Federal Highway Administration administrator on international activities and on FHWA policy. Policy's Office of Highway Policy Information collects, analyzes, and distributes highway-related data from federal, state, and local sources. The Office of International Programs looks for international sources of information on road-related technologies and markets, and gives technical assistance on road transportation to interested developing countries and countries with transition economies. The Office of Legislation and Strategic Planning advocates, implements, and evaluates national studies, including conditions and performance. It leads in outreach, evaluation, and feedback. The Office of Transportation Policy Studies develops tools and data systems for policy development and studies, makes reports to Congress on highway policy issues, and monitors and forecasts economic, demographic, and personal/commercial travel trends.

CONTACT Address: Office of Policy, 400 7th Street SW, Washington, DC 20590, Routing Code: HPL, Room 3317; Fax: (202) 366-9626.

OFFICE OF RESEARCH, DEVELOPMENT AND TECHNOLOGY: Works in 40 laboratories and testing sites at the Turner-Fairbank Highway Research Center in McLean, Virginia, researching environmental and human factors; intelligent transportation systems; pavements; safety; and structures.

Office of Professional Development's National Highway Institute (NHI): Develops training and education programs by providing training, resource materials, and educational opportunities to surface transportation developers and providers in the United States and abroad.

FHWA Discretionary Programs: Through special funding FHWA solicits candidates and applications and selects projects. The kinds of programs FHWA funds, what they cover, and their descriptions follow. *Bridge:* replacement, rehabilitation, or seismic retrofit of major bridges (202-366-4675); *Corridors and Borders:* Corridor Program Improvements to high-priority and selected other corridors, and Border Program-Improvement of infrastructure and related purposes within border regions (202-366-5010); *Ferry Boats:* owned ferry boats and ferry terminal facilities that are publicly owned, majority publicly owned, or publicly operated (202-366-4658); *Innovative Bridge Research and Construction:* looks for application of innovative material technology in construction of bridges and other structures (202-493-3023); *National Historic Covered Bridges:* preserve, rehabilitate, or restore historic covered bridges or conduct research to develop ways to preserve historic bridges (202-366-4619); *Intelligent Transportation Systems Deployment Program:* looks at projects to speed integration and interoperability of ITS throughout transportation systems in metropolitan and rural areas or to improve safety and productivity of commercial vehicles and drivers with installation of Commercial Vehicle Information System and Networks (202-366-9536); *Interstate Maintenance:* resurfacing, restoring, rehabilitating, and reconstructing highways mostly on existing Interstate System routes, including projects adding travel lanes (202-366-4651); *Public Lands Highways:* all transportation projects that are eligible for funding under Title 23, U.S.C., i.e., adjacent to or providing access to federal public lands (202-366-4653); *Scenic Byways:* funding for eligible scenic byway projects along All-American roads or designated scenic byways for planning, design, and development of state scenic byway programs (202-366-4649); *Transportation and Community and System Preservation:* for planning, implementation, and research of transportation, community, and system preservation (202-366-1263); *Transportation Infrastructure Finance and Innovation Act Program:* provides

loans, lines-of-credit, and loan guarantees to some surface transportation projects deemed to be of national or regional significance (202-366-5785); *Value Pricing:* funds up to 15 pilot programs that include variable pricing component to encourage shifts in time, route, or mode of travel, and pre-implementation studies (202-366-0076).

In the planning field, the Federal Highway Administration considers census issues, economic development, freight planning, metropolitan capacity building, the national highway system, rural transportation planning, safety-conscious planning, smart growth, system management and operation, and U.S-Mexico planning. The Border Infrastructure Program grants discretionary funds for construction and improvements to the Motor Carrier Safety Inspection facilities along the U.S.-Mexican border for commercial motor vehicles. The program's goals are safer operation of Mexican commercial vehicles running in the United States, and improved traffic flow at border crossings in California, Arizona, New Mexico, and Texas. The National Corridor Planning and Development Program Coordinated Border Infrastructure Program (CORBOR Program) provides discretionary grants for planning, project development, construction, and operation of projects that serve border regions near the U.S. borders with Mexico and Canada, as well as for high-priority transportation corridors throughout the United States Grants include corridor feasibility, corridor planning, multistate coordination, environmental review, construction for metropolitan planning organizations, and for transportation and safety infrastructure improvements, operation, regulatory improvements, and coordination and safety inspection improvements in border regions.

Environmental considerations include air quality, environmental justice, highway traffic noise, and human and natural environments. The Congestion Mitigation and Air Quality (CMAQ) Improvement Program (1991) provided $6 billion for surface transportation for air quality improvements and reduction of congestion. Reauthorized in 1998 as the Transportation Equity Act for the 21st Century (TEA-21) CMAQ, the effort now is to reduce motor vehicle emissions, with the 2002 Bush administration pronouncing that the program "has value." Questions and lawsuits have arisen between the Bush administration and six states that have stricter emission control standards than the Bush administration's new reduced guidelines.

Real estate endeavors include acquisition of land, corridor and access management, outdoor advertising controls, property valuation, relocation assistance, real estate exchange, and right-of-way.

National Transportation Enhancement Clearinghouse: Works to create a national resource to provide information and Transportation Enhancements (TE) publications and improves transportation choices such as bicycle and pedestrian facilities, scenic routes, and other investments that increase recreation opportunity and access for local communities.

Transportation and Community System Preservation Pilot Program (TCSP): Gives grants to states, local governments, and metropolitan planning organizations to plan and implement strategies to improve efficiency of their transportation systems; to reduce environmental impacts of transportation; to reduce need for expensive public infrastructure investments in the future; to give efficient access to jobs, services, and centers of trade; and to examine private sector development patterns. TCSP works with the Federal Transit Administration, the Federal Rail Administration, and the U.S. Environmental Protection Agency.

Recreational Trails Program: Originally authorized by the Transportation Equity Act for the 21st Century (TEA-21) in 1998, gives money to the states to develop and maintain recreational trails and trail-related facilities for non-motorized and motorized recreational vehicles.

Other trail uses include hiking, bicycling, in-line skating, horseback riding, cross-country skiing, snowmobiling, off-road motorcycling, all-terrain vehicle riding, four-wheel driving, and use of other off-road motorized vehicles.

Under the Recreational Trails Program, funds may be used for maintenance and restoration of existing trails; development and rehabilitation of trailside and trailhead facilities and trail linkages; purchase and lease of trail construction and maintenance equipment; construction of new trails; acquisition of easements or property for trails; state administrative costs; and educational programs to promote safety and environmental protection related to trails.

States must use 30 percent of their funds for motorized trails; 30 percent for nonmotorized trails; and 40 percent for other trail uses. States decide criteria and who gets funds, and may give extra credit for projects that benefit multiple trail uses.

Safety programs include highway-rail grade crossing safety; international highway safety; intersection safety; national safety data; older driver safety; pedestrian and bicycle safety; retroreflectivity; rumble strips; roadside hardware; speed management; and work zone safety.

CONTACT Address: 400 Seventh Street SW, Washington, DC 20590; Phone: (202) 366-0650; Website: www.fhwa.dot.gov. Native American Coordination: 400 Seventh Street SW, Room 3301, Washington, DC 20590; Phone: (202) 366-2698; Website: www.fhwa.dot.gov/environment/natvamrc/htm. Field Offices: Suite 4000, 10 South Howard Street, Baltimore, MD 21201; Phone: (410) 962-0093. Suite 301, 19900 Governors Drive, Olympia Fields, IL 60461-1021; Phone: (708) 283-3510. Suite 17T26, 61 Forsyth Street SW, Atlanta, GA 30303-3104; Phones: (404) 562-3570. Suite 2100, 201 Mission Street, San Francisco, CA 94105; Phone: (415) 744-3102. Metropolitan Offices: Suite 1460, 201 North Figueroa Street, Los Angeles, CA 90012; Phone: (213) 202-3950. Room 2410, 200 W.

Adams, Chicago, IL 60606-5232; Phone: (312) 886-1616. Room 428, 1 Bowling Green, New York, NY 10004-1415; Phone: (212) 668-2206. Suite 903, 1760 Market Street, Philadelphia, PA 19103; Phone: (215) 656-7070. Federal Lands Highway Divisions: 555 Zang Street, Lakewood, CO 80228-1010; Phone: (303) 716-2000. Loudoun Tech. Center, 21400 Ridgetop Circle, Sterling, VA 20166-6511; Phone: (703) 404-6201. 610 East 5th Street, Vancouver, WA 98661-3801; Phone: (360) 696-7710.

FEDERAL MOTOR CARRIER SAFETY ADMINISTRATION

Established in the DOT on January 1, 2000, by the Motor Carrier Safety Improvement Act of 1999 under President Bill Clinton, the Federal Motor Carrier Safety Administration was once part of the Federal Highway Administration. Its primary goal is to prevent commercial motor vehicle–related fatalities and injuries, which it works to accomplish by enforcing safety regulations; targeting high-risk carriers and commercial motor vehicle drivers; improving safety information systems and commercial vehicle technologies; creating stronger operating standards for commercial motor vehicle equipment; and increasing safety awareness. FMCSA works with other federal, state, and local enforcement agencies, as well as with the motor carrier industry, labor safety interest groups, and others.

Household Goods Consumer Complaint and Safety Violation Hotline: Takes consumer complaints about household commercial moving companies. Toll free: (888) 368-7238 (DOT-SAFT). Same number available to report any commercial truck or bus safety violations.

Motor Health Safety Assistance Program: Gives grants to states for roadside inspections and other commercial motor vehicle safety programs, with the aim of detecting and correcting commercial motor vehicle safety defects, driver deficiencies, and unsafe motor carrier practices before they contribute to crashes and hazardous materials incidents. This program works toward adoption and enforcement of safety rules and regulations by the states, in accordance with standards set in the Federal Motor Carrier Safety Regulations and the Federal Hazardous Materials Regulations.

Regulatory Compliance and Enforcement: Works through Federal Motor Carrier Safety Regulations, Federal Hazardous Materials Regulations, and through the Performance and Registration Information Systems Management (PRISM) program to improve safety or remove offending high-risk carriers from American highways. PRISM reviews compliance on unsafe motor carriers and monitors and tracks their safety performance, which may lead to a Federal Operations Out-of-Service Order, or an unfit, suspension, or revocation designation.

Licensing and Insurance (L&I): Licensing and insurance for for-hire motor carriers' responsibility moved from the Interstate Commerce Commission to the Federal Motor Carrier Safety Administration in December 1995. For licensing information call (202) 366-9805. For insurance information contact Insurance Compliance Division at (202) 358-7028.

WEBSITE http://diy.dot.gov/.

Commercial Driver's License Program (CDL): Develops, issues, and evaluates standards for testing and licensing commercial motor vehicle drivers. States issue the licenses, and must comply to three-year audits of their compliance with federal standards. Noncompliance could result in loss of federal funding to states for this purpose.

Data and Analysis: Collects and disseminates data concerning safety of motor carriers in cooperation with states through roadside inspections, crashes, compliance reviews, and enforcement activities. The gathered information, combined with data from other sources, such as the National

Highway Traffic Safety Administration, helps follow trends in performance by carrier, cargo, driver demographics, and location, time, and type of incident.

Research and Technology Program: Identifies, coordinates, and administers research and development to make motor carrier operations, commercial motor vehicles, and their drivers safer.

Border and International: Works toward manageable safety requirements and procedures throughout North America in accordance with the North American Free Trade Agreement (NAFTA), including funding safety performance of motor carriers operating in border areas and state safety inspection facilities.

In 1982 Congress imposed a moratorium on granting authority for Mexican and Canadian motor carriers wanting to operate in the United States beyond a limited "commercial zone" within three to 20 miles past a city's official limit, and close to the U.S.-Mexico border. This moratorium that affected Canadian trucks was lifted in 1982 due to a bilateral agreement that gave U.S. carriers access to Canadian markets.

Signed in 1993 by President Bill Clinton, NAFTA liberalized cross-border truck and bus services, giving Mexican trucks the right to function throughout border states (1995) and then throughout the United States as of January 1, 2000. Clinton delayed NAFTA's cross-border liberalization in 1995, under great pressure to do so from Teamsters Union officials.

The Mexican government contested the Clinton administration's delay, claiming it violated NAFTA, and an international arbitration panel ruled in February 2001 the United States could prevent some Mexican carriers or trucks from operating beyond the commercial zones for safety reasons. The panel allowed the United States to treat Mexican trucks differently from Canadian and American trucks on a safety basis.

In 2002 Congress passed the Transportation Appropriations Act, including 22 separate safety conditions on opening the border with Mexico.

U.S. carriers wanting to operate in Mexico should contact (in Spanish) the Mexican Secretaria de Comunicaciones y Transportes, Calzada de las bombas No. 411, Colonia San Bartolo Coapa, Mexico, DF. 04920 Mexico; Phone: 011-5255-5684-0757; E-mail: cgonzale@sct.gob.mx.

Hazardous Materials: FMCSA enforces regulations for safe transportation of hazardous materials by highway, and enforces rules governing the manufacture and maintenance of cargo tank motor vehicles.

Safety Programs: Motor carrier safety programs aimed at reducing accidents and deaths due to or involving motor carriers include: brake safety; bus and motor coach safety; commercial driver's license; enforcement programs; fatigue; hazardous materials safety; Motor Carrier Safety Assistance Program; NAFTA; Research and Technology; Share the Road Safely Program; Skill Performance and Evaluation Certificate Program for Drivers with Missing or Impaired Arms, Hands, Fingers, Legs or Feet; and speed management.

CONTACT Address: Federal Motor Carrier Safety Administration, 400 Seventh Street SW, Washington, DC 20590; Phone: (202) 366-2519; Website: www.fmcsa.dot.gov. HOTLINE: 1-888-368-7238 or 1-888-DOT-SAFT; Information: (800) 832-5660. Field Organizations: Suite 4000, 10 S. Howard Street, Baltimore, MD 21201-2819; Phone: (410) 962-0077. Suite 17T75, 61 Forsyth Street SW, Atlanta, GA 30303-3104; Phone: (404) 562-3600. Suite 210, 1900 Governors Drive, Olympia Fields, IL 60461-1021; Phone: (708) 283-3577. Suite 2100, 201 Mission Street, San Francisco, CA 94105; Phone: (415) 744-3088.

FEDERAL RAILROAD ADMINISTRATION (FRA)

Created by the Department of Transportation Act of 1966, FRA promotes and enforces railroad safety regulations, runs financial assistance programs for railroads, researches and develops national rail transportation policy, and works to restore the Northeast Corridor rail passenger service. FRA also gives financial help to AMTRAK and financial assistance to high-speed rail technology and works to reduce grade crossing dangers in high-speed corridors, makes investments in small freight railroads and other rail projects, helps plan high-speed rail projects, and plans and utilizes magnetic levitation technology.

OFFICE OF RAILROAD SAFETY: Administers and enforces federal laws and regulations to promote railroad safety in all areas of rail safety included in the Rail Safety Act of 1970, including track maintenance, inspection and equipment standards, and record keeping. FRA also tries to educate the public on highway-railroad grade crossing safety and on the danger of trespassing on railroad property.

Railroad Safety Advisory Committee: Works with all segments of the rail community to find mutually beneficial solutions on safety and regulatory issues, such as freight power brake regulations; track safety standards; railroad communications; regulations of tourist, excursion, scenic, and historic rail services; and revisions of steam-powered locomotive inspection standards.

OFFICE OF RAILROAD DEVELOPMENT (RDV): Sponsors research and development to improve safety, security, and efficiency of U.S. railroads, and funds technology demonstration projects to foster high-speed rail. FRA defines high-speed rail as technologies that involve trains traveling at top speeds of 90 to 300 mph. FRA also works to develop all aspects of intercity passenger rail transportation and railroad safety through physical sciences and engineering, always an effort to keep railroads a viable national transportation resource.

FRA gives grants to Amtrak and to the Alaska Railroad, and smaller rail programs in line with specific congressional mandates. In the past these have included the West Virginia Railroad Development Program and the Rhode Island Freight Railroad Improvement Project.

Amtrak is a for-profit corporation that runs trains between cities in 46 states and the District of Columbia, created by the Rail Passenger Service Act of 1970, and incorporated in D.C. in 1971. Amtrak's seven-member board of directors sets corporate policy and manages Amtrak.

The Alaska Railroad was built by the United States in 1914 and run by the federal government until 1985. Congress voted to build and support the railroad to help economic development and access to mineral deposits of the then Territory of Alaska. President Harding drove the final spike to complete the railroad construction near Nenana, Alaska, in 1923.

The Alaska Railroad Transfer Act of 1982 transferred the federal government's interest in the railroad to the Alaska Railroad Corporation (ARRC), an Alaska public corporation chartered to own and operate the Alaska Railroad. ARRC provides freight and passenger service from the ice-free ports of Whittier, Seward, and Anchorage to Fairbanks, Denali National Park, and military installations. Vessel and rail barge connections link Alaska and the railroad to Seattle, Washington, and Prince Rupert, British Columbia, Canada.

CONTACT Address: FRA, 1120 Vermont Avenue NW, Washington, DC 20590; Phone: (202) 493-6000; Website: www.fra.dot.gov. Major Field Organizations: Room 1077, 55 Broadway, Cambridge, MA 02142; Phone: (617) 494-2302. Suite 550, Scott Plaza II, Philadelphia, PA 19113; Phone: (610) 521-8200. Suite 16T20, 61 Forsyth Street SW, Atlanta, GA 30303-3104; Phone: (404) 562-3800. Suite 655, 111 N. Canal Street, Chicago IL 60606; Phone: (312) 353-6203. Suite 425, 8701 Bedford Euless Road, Hurst, TX 76053; Phone: (817) 284-8142. Suite 464, 901 Loost Street, Kansas City, MO 64106; Phone: (816) 392-3840. Suite 466, 801 I Street, Sacramento, CA 95814; Phone: (916) 498-6540. Suite 650, 703 Broadway, Vancouver, WA 98660; Phone: (360) 696-7536.

FEDERAL TRANSIT ADMINISTRATION (FTA)

Formerly known as the Urban Mass Transportation Administration, the Federal Transit Administration was established in 1968. Its purposes remain the same: help develop better mass transportation equipment, facilities, and techniques in collaboration with private and public mass transportation companies; encourage research, development, and planning of area-wide mass transportation systems; help states, local governments, and authorities finance area-wide mass transit systems according to local needs; provide money to help states, local governments, and authorities to help fulfill national mobility goals required by senior citizens, individuals with disabilities, and economically disadvantaged people; and work with local communities to fund and fulfill mass transportation requirements and needs.

FTA's National Transit Library houses a vast collection of transit and transportation-related information, ranging from legislative bills to financing pamphlets, rapid transit, and the Americans with Disabilities Act.

CONTACT Address: FTA, 400 Seventh Street SW, Washington, DC 20590; Phone:(202) 366-4043; Website: www.fta.dot.gov. Field organizations: Suite 17T50, 61 Forsyth Street SW, Atlanta, GA 30303; Phone: (404) 562-3500. Suite 920, 55 Broadway, Cambridge, MA 02142; Phone: (617) 494-2055. Suite 320, 200 West Adams Street, Chicago, IL 60606; Phone: (312) 353-2789. Suite 650, 216 16th Street, Denver, CO 80202; Phone: (303) 844-3242. Suite 8A36, 619 Taylor Street, Fort Worth, TX 76102; Phone: (817) 978-0550. Suite 404, 901 Locust Street, Kansas City, MO 64106; Phone: (816) 329-3920. Suite 429, 1 Bowling Green, New York, NY 10004-1415; Phone: (212) 656-7100. Suite 500, 1760 Market Street, Philadelphia, PA 19103; Phone: (215) 656-7100. Suite 2210, 201 Mission Street, San Francisco, CA 94105; Phone: (415) 744-3133.

Suite 3142, 915 2nd Avenue, Seattle, WA 98174; Phone: (206) 220-7954. Metropolitan offices in addition to the above: Suite 1460, 210 Figueroa, Los Angeles, CA 90012; Phone: (213) 202-3950. Suite 510, 1990 K Street, Washington, DC 20006; Phone: (202) 219-3562.

Clean Fuels Formula Grant Program: Aims at making advanced bus technologies, including low-emission vehicles and clean-fuel technologies, more accessible in the mainstream of U.S. transit fleets. Grants enable transit systems to purchase or lease low-emissions buses, build alternative fueling facilities, modify existing garages to house clean fuel vehicles, and assist in utilization of biodiesel fuels.

CONTACT Phone: (202) 366-4052.

Over-the-road Bus Accessibility (Rural Transportation Accessibility Incentive Program): Provides funds for incremental capital and training expenses connected to meeting DOT's over-the-road bus accessibility rule requirements. Financial assistance is available through competitive application to private operators of intercity fixed-route services and other providers of over-the-road bus services, such as commuter buses, and charter and tour services.

CONTACT Phone: (202) 366-4020.

Urbanized Area Formula Grants: Make funds available to public bodies with designated legal authority to receive and dispense federal funds. Potential recipients are designated by governors, responsible local officials, and public transit service owners to apply for transportation management funds, usually for urbanized areas with more than 200,000 population. Monies should be used for planning, engineering design, and evaluation of transit projects and technical transportation-related studies; capital investments in bus and bus-related activities such as bus replacement; overhaul or rebuilding of buses; crime prevention and security equipment; construction of passenger and maintenance facilities; capital investments in new and existing fixed guideway systems including rolling stock, overhaul and rebuilding of vehicles, track, signals, and computer hardware and software. "Capital costs" may include preventive maintenance, or wheelchair access improvements, in line with the Americans With Disabilities Act.

CONTACT Phone: (202) 366-4020.

Non-urbanized Area Formula Grants: Make funds available to areas with 50,000 or less population to improve access to health care, shopping, education, employment, public services, and recreation; to help finance development, maintenance, improvement, and use of public transportation systems in rural and small urban areas; for improving efficient use of federal funds by coordinating programs and services; to help develop and support intercity bus transportation; and to attract private transportation providers to make transportation service available in nonurban areas. Applicants may include state and local governments, nonprofit organizations, Indian tribes and groups, and public transit operators. Entities may spend only 15 percent of allocation for administration, planning, and technical assistance.

CONTACT Phone: (202) 366-4020.

Elderly and Persons with Disabilities Grants: Fund transportation services to meet special needs of the elderly and persons with disabilities, usually for capital projects and to purchase vehicles. Some money may be available for lease arrangements and state program administration, with funds allocated by formula considering the number of elderly people and individuals with disabilities in each state. States apply for funds on behalf of local private nonprofit agencies and some public entities.

CONTACT Phone: (202) 366-4020.

Job Access and Reverse Commute: Meant to develop transit services to take workers from cities to suburban job sites, the reverse of the "normal" commute, helping welfare recipients and other low-income people get to jobs, training, and affordable child care. Besides capital and operating costs, funds include costs of promoting use of reverse commute transit by workers with nontraditional work schedules, use of tran-

sit vouchers, and promotion of use of employer-provided transportation. Vehicles that qualify in this category include bus, train, carpool, or vans.

CONTACT Phone: (202) 366-2053.

Bus and Bus-Related: Funds bus and bus-related capital projects awarded to public entities and agencies, such as transit authorities, states, municipalities, some public corporations, boards, and commissions. Funds may be used for purchase of buses for fleet and service expansion, bus maintenance and administrative facilities; transfer facilities; bus malls; transportation centers; intermodal terminals; park-and-ride stations; acquisition of replacement vehicles, rebuilding buses, preventative maintenance of buses; passenger shelters; bus stop signs; mobile radio units, supervisory vehicles, fare boxes, computers, shop and garage equipment; and costs of getting innovative financing.

CONTACT Phone: (202) 366-4020.

Fixed Guideway Modernization: Grants for modernization of fixed guideway transportation systems, which include any transit service that uses exclusive or rights-of-way or rail tracks such as heavy rail, commuter rail, trolley buses, aerial tramways, inclined planes, cable cars, automated guideway transit, ferry boats, and some bus services using high-occupancy vehicle (HOV) lanes. Eligible projects might include capital projects to improve fixed guideway systems for purchase and rehabilitation of rolling stock, track, line equipment, structures, signals and communications, power equipment and substations, passenger stations and terminals, security equipment and systems, maintenance facilities and equipment, support equipment such as computer hardware and software, system extensions, and preventive maintenance.

CONTACT Phone: (202) 366-4020.

New Starts: Gives grants for construction of new or extensions to fixed guideway systems (see above), such as light rail lines, rapid (heavy) rail lines, commuter rails, automated fixed guideway systems such as a "people mover," or a busway/high occupancy vehicle (HOV). Other projects may include transit corridor development and creation of markets and marketing to support future construction of fixed guideway systems, construction of park-and-ride parking lots, and purchase of land to protect rights-of-way.

CONTACT Phone: (202) 366-4020.

State Planning and Research: Gives funds to state departments of transportation for statewide planning and technical assistance, planning for nonurbanized areas, research, development and demonstration projects, public transportation fellowships, university research, and human resource development.

CONTACT Phone: (202) 366-4033.

National Planning & Research Programs (aka National Research & Technology Programs): Works on research, development, testing, and information transfer of innovative transit technologies and services on national problems and studies of transit safety, security, mobility, fuel efficiency, clean air, and global trade.

Priority research areas include safety and security systems for grade crossing protection, antiterrorist threats, drive-assist systems, and sharing of railroad tracks; innovations in bus transportation, such as bus rapid transit, intelligent transportation systems, clean fuels, hybrid electric, fuel-cell and battery-powered propulsion technology; infrastructure to support government capital investment to protect federally supported assets; and dissemination of new knowledge to help develop the transit industry in global markets.

Other research areas include rural transportation, quality of customer service, equal access, innovations in planning and infrastructure development, and new mobility management systems.

CONTACT Phone: (202) 366-4052

Rural Transit Assistance Program: Makes funds available for design and implementation of training and technical assistance projects to meet needs of transit operators in nonurbanized areas. The RTAP state program gives an annual allocation to each state for the above purposes.

RTAP's national program funds development of information and materials for state agencies' and local operators' use, and supports research and technical assistance projects deemed to be of national interest.

CONTACT Phone: (202) 366-4020.

Transit Cooperative Research Program (TCRP): Works to improve mobility and accessibility of the transit industry by developing and applying the latest technology and operating techniques. TCRP aims to contribute to a better transit workforce by offering new transit paradigms, transit industry best practices, new planning and management tools, forums to exchange ideas, and publishes several documents to help transit industry and agencies.

CONTACT Phone: (202) 366-4052.

National Transit Institute: Established in 1992 at Rutgers, the State University of New Jersey, the National Transit Institute offers training and education programs for the transit industry by developing and teaching new methods and techniques to improve workplace performance and productivity. Courses are conducted throughout the United States, and annual Transit Trainers Workshops bring together trainers and human resources specialists to learn and share the latest techniques in training. Future instruction topics include geographic information systems, automatic vehicle locator systems, smartcard, and other innovative technologies.

Current courses include mass transportation planning; management; environmental factors; acquisition and joint use of rights-of-way; engineering and architectural design; mass transportation procurement strategies; new technologies, including for exhaust emission reduction; ways to make mass transportation more easily accessible to individuals with disabilities and special challenges; construction, construction management, insurance, and risk management; maintenance; contract administration; inspection; innovative finance; and workplace safety.

CONTACT Phone: (202) 366-4052.

University Transportation Centers: Funded by Transit Planning and Research to universities to establish and maintain transportation centers to research and disseminate information on transportation management, and increase the numbers of highly skilled individuals entering the transportation field. Four universities are eligible for these monies: University of Minnesota, Northwestern University, Morgan State University, and North Carolina State University.

CONTACT Phone: (202) 366-4052.

International Mass Transportation Program: A new program designed to make transit products and services made in the United States competitive in the international marketplace and to create an international exchange of transit information, ideas, industry standards, and equipment and technology developments. In this pursuit FTA will sign memoranda of understanding with other government agencies, foreign governments, and transit agencies to initiate joint partnerships and collaborative research and technology projects.

Potential projects may include technical information sharing; support of U.S. transportation product industries by promoting export of U.S. goods and services; bilateral agreements to share and exchange information with underdeveloped countries and other trade partners; professional capacity building with the goal to develop and conduct innovative technology training courses in foreign countries; and training and information development of project development, construction, and management.

CONTACT Phone: (202) 366-0955.

MARITIME ADMINISTRATION (MARAD)

The Maritime Administration (MARAD) works to develop, maintain, and promote a U.S. merchant marine to carry domestic waterborne commerce and some waterborne foreign commerce. Another goal is to make this merchant marine capable of serving as a naval and military service component to assist the U.S. military in times of national emergency and war.

MARAD has four major goals: (1) to be ready as part of an intermodal service to support the military in national security situations; (2) to improve the competitive capabilities of the U.S. shipyard industry by subsidizing the building and operating of U.S. merchant-type ships; (3) to use technology and innovation to improve and integrate intermodal transportation; and (4) to increase the American merchant marine industry's involvement in foreign trade, as well as in domestic cargo and passenger trade by helping build ports and facilities.

MARAD also runs a war risk insurance program to insure shipping operators and seamen against losses cause by hostile action when commercial insurance is not available. MARAD charters government-owned ships to American operators, uses, takes, or buys private ships owned by American citizens, and assigns them to defense uses during emergencies. It also has a reserve national defense fleet of government-owned ships run by managers and general agents, including the Ready Reserve force available for quick response.

MARAD also regulates sales to foreigners and transfers of ships to foreign registry on behalf of U.S. citizens who partly or wholly own ships, and disposes of government-owned ships deemed to be unessential for national defense.

Marine Transportation System (MTS): MARAD is one of 17 agencies in MTS working to ensure safe and environmentally sound marine transportation to increase the United States's global competitiveness and improve the country's national security.

Maritime Security Program (MSP): MARAD helps maintain a privately owned, U.S. flag-flying, and American-crewed ship fleet competitive in international commerce, and available to supplement DEPARTMENT OF DEFENSE navy capabilities.

Voluntary Intermodal Sealift Agreement (VISA): Allows Department of Defense access to commercial ships to transport DOD ammunition and military cargo when needed. More than 75 percent of American merchant ships are part of VISA.

National Defense Reserve Fleet (NDRF): MARAD coordinates a source of ships that can be used for defense shipping needs during national emergencies.

Ready Reserve Force (RRF): A special group of ships that are kept in a state of readiness as part of the National Defense Reserve Fleet to be activated quickly in case of war or military deployment.

Title XI Financing: Provides government guaranteed credit for debt obligations issued by U.S. or foreign ship owners to finance or refinance U.S. flag vessels or eligible export vessels built, rebuilt, or reconditioned in American shipyards. It also offers credit to U.S. shipyards to finance cutting-edge shipbuilding technology.

CONTACT Phone: (202) 366-5737.

National Maritime Resource and Education Center (NMREC): The federal government's advocacy center to help American shipbuilders and associated industries' international competitiveness. NMREC's lobbying positions include elimination of allegedly unnecessary regulations, consensus on technical standards for the maritime industry (self-policing), and U.S. participation in national and international standards-writing.

CONTACT Phone: (202) 366-1931; Fax: (202) 366-7197.

U.S. Merchant Marine Academy (USMMA): MARAD operates the U.S. Merchant Marine Academy at Kings Point, New York, to educate young women and men to serve in the merchant marine, in the armed forces, and in the maritime part of an intermodal transportation system.

CONTACT Address: USMMA, Kings Point, NY 11024-1699; Phone: (516) 773-5000; Website: www.marad.dot.gov.

MARAD also trains people in shipboard firefighting at Earle, New Jersey, and Toledo, Ohio, and helps finance maritime academies in Vallejo,

California; Castine, Maine; Buzzards Bay, Massachusetts; Traverse City, Michigan; Fort Schuyler, New York; and Galveston, Texas.

CONTACT Address: Maritime Administration, 400 Seventh Street SW, Washington, DC 20590; Phone: (202) 366-5807; Website: www.marad.dot.gov. Field organizations: Room 1223, 501 Magazine Street, New Orleans, LA 70130-3394; Phone: (504) 589-2000. Suite 185, 2860 South River Road, Des Plaines, IL 60018-2413; Phone: (847) 298-4535. Room 418, 1 Bowling Green, New York, NY 10004-1415; Phone: (212) 668-3330. Room 211, 7737 Hampton Boulevard, Norfolk, VA 23505; Phone: (757) 441-6393. Suite 2200, 201 Mission Street, San Francisco, CA 94105-1905; Phone: (415) 744-3125. Port, intermodal, and environmental activities on ship-generated pollution: Phone: (202) 366-4721.

NATIONAL HIGHWAY TRAFFIC SAFETY ADMINISTRATION (NHTSA)

Succeeding the National Highway Safety Bureau, NHTSA was established by the Highway Safety Act of 1970. NHTSA works to reduce the number of injuries, deaths, and economic losses due to motor vehicle crashes throughout the country's highway system, and runs consumer programs according to the Motor Vehicle Information and Cost Savings Act of 1972.

To achieve these goals, NHTSA sets and enforces safety performance standards for motor vehicles and motor vehicle equipment through grants to state and local governments. It investigates safety defects in motor vehicles; sets and enforces fuel economy standards and roll-over standards; helps states and local communities reduce drunk driving and its resultant damage; promotes use of safety belts, child safety seats, and airbags; investigates odometer fraud; sets antitheft regulations; and provides motor vehicle safety information for consumers. NHTSA conducts research on how driver behavior relates to safety with the goal of new safety improvements.

NHTSA provides detailed information on air bags, child passenger safety, child car seat inspections, crash statistics, modifications for people with disabilities, driver distractions, Early Warning Reporting (EWR), school buses, Star Ratings, tire quality and safety, vehicle theft protection, and vehicle importation regulations.

NHTSA conducts studies and sets standards for aggressive and unsafe driving, alcohol and drugs, bicycles, biomechanics and trauma, motorcycles, new and old drivers, pedestrians, school buses, and traffic law enforcement.

NHTSA sets and issues federal motor vehicle safety standards prescribing safety features and vehicle standards for safety performance. It manages the New Car Assessment Program, a scheme of tests, the results of which often make news on low- and high-speed crash tests on passenger cars, light trucks, and vans.

NHTSA manages the fuel economy program that sets fleet average fuel economy standards, meaning miles per gallon achieved by passenger cars, light trucks, and vans. This program has been controversial since some consumers want higher mileage per gallon as both an economic and environmental saving, while oil companies appear to have an interest in keeping the standards low so that consumers buy more oil and gasoline products.

NHTSA works with states and local governments to develop state highway safety programs, authorized by the Transportation Equity Act for the 21st Century. State and Community Highway Safety grants provide money to states, Indian nations, and territories to develop and promote safety programs, including occupant protection, impaired driving, police traffic services, emergency medical services, traffic data records, motorcycle safety, pedestrian and bicycle safety, speed control, and improving roadway safety.

This administration maintains with varying success a national register of information on individuals whose driver licenses have been revoked, suspended, cancelled, or denied, or who have been convicted of some traffic-related violations such as driving under the influence of alcohol or drugs.

CONTACT Address: NHTSA, 400 Seventh Street SW, Washington, DC 20590; Phone: (202) 366-9550; Website: www.nhtsa.dot.gov. Regional offices: Room 17T30. 61 Forsyth Street SW, Atlanta, GA 30303-3104. Suite 6700, 10 South Howard Street, Baltimore, MD 21201. 55 Broadway, Kendall Square, Code 903, Cambridge, MA 02142. Room 8a38, 819 Taylor Street, Fort Worth, TX 76102-76177. 466 Locust Street, Kansas City, MO 64106. Room 430, 555 Zang Street, Lakewood, CO 80228. Suite 201, 19900 Governors Drive, Olympia Fields, IL 60461. Suite 2230, 201 Mission Street, San Francisco, CA 94105. 3140 Jackson Federal Building, 915 2nd Avenue, Seattle, WA 98174. Suite 204, 222 Mamaroneck Avenue, White Plains, NY 10605. Nationwide toll-free auto safety hotline: Phone: (888) DASH-2-DOT or (888) 327-4236, or (202) 366-7800.

RESEARCH AND SPECIAL PROGRAMS ADMINISTRATION (RSPA)

Established by the secretary of transportation in 1977 and formalized in 1992, RSPA is a catchall for programs that do not fit into other DOT administrations and bureaus. At first it consolidated the Materials Transportation Bureau, which regulated hazardous materials and pipeline safety; a research facility in Cambridge, Massachusetts; the Transportation Programs Bureau, which managed systems engineering, emergency transportation, university research, and cargo security, and facilitation; and the

Transportation Safety Institute. RSPA acquired responsibility for research policy and technology sharing for intermodal transportation. It now also provides preparedness guidance for civil sector transportation emergencies, and gives training and technical assistance in transportation safety.

RSPA researches solutions to create the safe, effective, and efficient transportation of people and goods throughout the world, distinguished by its focus on the transportation system as a whole. It works to make the U.S. transportation system more integrated, effective, and safe through research and recommendation of new programs to enhance quality of life, safety, and environment, especially for transportation of hazardous materials by all modes including pipelines.

OFFICE OF HAZARDOUS MATERIALS SAFETY (OHM): Works to minimize risks to life and property due to commercial transportation of hazardous materials except by outboard vessels. OHM recommends regulations changes, interprets regulations and rulings, conducts public hearings on regulatory changes, issues exemptions when deemed appropriate, and makes final decisions on registration approvals and petitions to reconsider decisions. OHM sets standards for hazmat (hazardous materials) transportation, works with international standards, and guides users on compliance and enforcement of standards. It provides scientific, engineering, radiological, and risk analysis for national and international hazardous materials transportation safety standards.

OHM's Office of Pipeline Safety runs the regulatory program to assure safe transportation of natural gas, petroleum, and other hazardous materials by pipeline, assessing risk management in design, construction, testing, operation, maintenance, and emergency response of pipeline facilities.

CONTACT Phone: (202) 366-4595; Fax: (202) 366-4566; Website: www.hazmat.dot.gov; Address: RSPA, 400 Seventh Street SW, Washington, DC 20590; Phone: (202) 366-4433; Website: www.

rspa.dot.gov. Regional offices: Suite 136, 2350 E. Devon Avenue, Des Plaines, IL 60018. Suite 306, 820 Bear Tavern Road, West Trenton, NJ 08628. Suite 520, 1701 Columbia Avenue, College Park, GA 30337. Suite 2100, 2320 LaBranch Street, Houston, TX 77004. Suite 230, 3200 Inland Empire Boulevard, Ontario, CA 91764.

JOHN A. VOLPE NATIONAL TRANSPORTATION SYSTEMS CENTER (VOLPE CENTER): Does cross-modal and cross-disciplinary research and development, engineering, and analysis of national transportation and logistics issues and problems. The Volpe Center hopes to launch innovative transportation technologies and management processes to make the whole system safer, and more effective and efficient. Named for the former Republican governor of Massachusetts and secretary of transportation, the Volpe Center brings together industry, academia, and government agencies to anticipate transportation needs and to improve the transportation system.

Issues that Volpe Center staff work on include traffic surveillance and control systems, environmental impact measurement and improvement, physical and cyber security, and advanced energy efficient transportation. The center hires out its services.

CONTACT Address: John A. Volpe National Transportation Center, 55 Broadway, Cambridge, MA 02142-1093; Phone: (617) 494-2000 or 494-2224; Website: www.volpe.dot.gov.

TRANSPORTATION SAFETY INSTITUTE (TSI): Established in 1971, develops and conducts worldwide safety, security, and environmental training products and services for hire to public and private sectors. TSI offers transit, aviation, pipeline, motor carrier, highway safety, hazardous material, and risk management training in the United States and abroad.

TSI's National Aircraft Accident Investigation School at Central Missouri State University (CMSU) trains accident investigators and aviation safety professionals to reduce death, injury, and property damage caused by aircraft accidents. Programs include classroom lectures, workshops, field activities, individual study programs, review of FAA policies, dealing with news media, accident report writing, and examining wreckage and aircraft parts. Together with the Mike Monroney Aeronautical Center's Interactive Video Teletraining Facility, CMSU offers a two-year M.S. degree in aviation safety.

The *Hazardous Materials Division* trains people responsible for compliance with and enforcement of regulations and response to hazardous materials accidents and incidents, federal and state enforcement agencies, emergency response personnel and industry shippers, carriers, and manufacturers in the complex regulations of handling hazardous materials. Students learn about regulations for highway, rail, aircraft, and vessel shipments according to the International Maritime Dangerous Goods Code. TSI also gives classes on dealing with radioactive materials, infectious substances, explosives, hazardous wastes and substances, cargo tanks, portable tanks, cylinders, and military airlift of hazardous materials.

The *Highway Safety Division* conducts training programs for highway safety officials to reduce motor vehicle crashes and their results, by giving classes on state-of-the-art enforcement of drunk driving laws; design and management of highway safety programs; delivery of emergency medical services; and use of safety belts, child safety seats, and motorcycle and bicycle helmets.

The *Coast Guard Container Inspection Training & Assistance Team* trains staff of Coast Guard and other federal agencies on the best way to conduct standardized containerized hazardous materials.

The *Transit Safety & Security Division* deputizes industry experts (associate staff) to deliver nationwide training on transit safety to government and private interests. Entities that pay for Special Programs Division's fee-for-service class programs include the Federal Aviation Administration, Transportation Security Administration, U.S. Air Force, Navy, Marines, Coast Guard,

Army Corps of Engineers, DEPARTMENT OF INTERIOR, Federal Transit Authority, Bureau of Reclamation, the motor carrier industry, the oil and gas industry, and state and local government. Special Programs will develop a special safety training program for agencies, organizations, or companies on request.

GREAT LAKES ST. LAWRENCE SEAWAY SYSTEM,
AKA SAINT LAWRENCE SEAWAY DEVELOPMENT CORPORATION (SLSDC)

Established by Saint Lawrence Seaway Act of 1954, the Saint Lawrence Seaway Corporation became part of DOT in 1966, and is a wholly owned government corporation. Working with the Saint Lawrence Seaway Management Corporation of Canada, SLSDC was originally formed to construct, operate, and maintain the part of the St. Lawrence Seaway between the Port of Montreal and Lake Erie that is in the United States. It now operates and maintains the deep-draft waterway with the Canadian corporation, and promotes use of it to develop trade.

CONTACT General: Address: Policy Headquarters, 400 Seventh Street SW, Washington, DC 20590; Phone: (800) 785-2779 or (202) 366-0091; Fax: (202) 366-7147; Operations Headquarters: 180 Andrews Street, Massena, NY 13662; Phone: (315) 764-3200; Fax: (315) 764-3235; Website: www.greatlakes-seaway.com.

SURFACE TRANSPORTATION BOARD (STB)

An independent adjudicatory body within DOT that regulates the economics of interstate surface transportation, especially railroads, within the United States to meet the needs of shippers, receivers, and consumers. Established in 1996 as part of the ICC (Interstate Commerce Commission) Termination Act of 1995, which transferred rail and nonrail function to STB, and other licensing and nonlicensing motor carrier functions to the Federal Highway Administration.

STB conducts oversight of transportation firms doing business in or carrying foreign commerce in the United States, including railroad rate and service issues; trail restructuring transactions such as mergers, line sales, line construction, and line abandonments and all connected labor matters; trucking company, moving van, and noncontiguous ocean shipping company rate matters; some intercity passenger bus company structure, financial, and operational matters; and pipeline matters not regulated by the Federal Energy Regulatory Commission.

CONTACT Address: STB, 1925 K Street NW, Washington, DC 20423-0001; Phone: (202) 565-1674.

TRANSPORTATION SECURITY ADMINISTRATION (TSA)

The Aviation and Transportation Security Act of 2001 established the Transportation Security Administration as an agency of DOT in response to the hijackings of American airplanes and their use as weapons to crash into the World Trade Center in New York and into the Pentagon in Washington, D.C., on September 11, 2001.

To protect the American people, TSA works to secure passengers' needs to travel safely while ensuring their freedom to move around. TSA's Task Force utilizes private sector leaders to devise the best practices of secure transportation for the American people.

TSA holds responsibility for civil aviation and other DOT modes of transportation security, including transportation facilities such as airports and train stations; federal security screening for passenger air transportations and intrastate air transportation (President George W. Bush's administration announced it was cutting 6,000 airport security jobs in 2003); administers laws and enforces security-related regulations and regulations in all modes of transportation; receives, assesses, coordinates, and distributes intelligence information on transportation security; identifies and undertakes research and development to improve transportation security; and coordinates domestic transportation such as aviation, rail, and other surface transportation including port security.

In a national emergency TSA oversees all transportation-related responsibilities of the federal government except for those handled by the DEPARTMENT OF DEFENSE.

TSA works with industry partners in the fields of maritime security, airport access, port security, safe commerce transport, intercity bus security, security technology, and airport screeners. It also trains commercial airline pilots to carry handguns and use them defensively to stop a terrorist or anyone else trying to hijack an airplane.

CONTACT Address: TSA, 400 Seventh Street SW, Washington, DC 20590; Phone: (202) 366-9900; Website: www.tsa.dot.gov.

DEPARTMENT OF THE TREASURY

Created by Congress on September 2, 1789, the Treasury Department has acquired many duties as the result of other acts over the years. The secretary of the treasury formulates and recommends domestic and international financial, economic, and tax policy to the president. The secretary contributes to development of fiscal and economic policy, manages the public debt, oversees Treasury's law-enforcement responsibilities, serves as financial officer of the U.S. government, and oversees production of coins and currency.

ORGANIZATION

The department is administered by the secretary of the treasury, a deputy secretary, three under secretaries, and 11 assistant secretaries, all of whom are appointed by the president and confirmed by the Senate. Within the department leadership are numerous administrators and specialists.

OFFICES AND BUREAUS

OFFICE OF DOMESTIC FINANCE

The Office of Domestic Finance advises and assists with domestic finance, banking, fiscal policy and operations, development of policies on financial institutions, consumer affairs and community policy of financial institutions, federal debt finance, financial regulation, and capital markets.

Office of Advanced Counterfeit Deterrence: Works with the U.S. Secret Service, Federal Reserve Board, and the Bureau of Engraving and Printing to reduce counterfeiting of currency, including the 1996 and 2003 features designed to be counterfeit-proof.

CONTACT   E-mail: acd@do.treas.gov; Website: www.ustreas.gov/offices/domestic-finance/acd/.

OFFICE OF FINANCIAL INSTITUTIONS: Coordinates legislation and regulation of financial institutions and securities markets, as well as financial education within the Treasury Department, helps the secretary direct the Pension Benefit Guaranty Corporation and the Community Development Financial Institutions Board, and supports the under secretary for domestic finance as director of the Securities Investor Protection Corporation.

This office develops policy for depository institutions such as commercial banks, thrift institutions, and credit unions; investment banks; financial markets; the insurance industry; and housing- and farm-related government lenders such as the Federal Home Loan Bank System, the Federal National Mortgage Association (Fannie Mae), and the Farm Credit System.

The Office of Financial Institutions also monitors the FARM CREDIT ADMINISTRATION and the Federal Agricultural Mortgage Corporation (Farmer Mac), and oversees regulations of the Office of the Comptroller of the Currency and the Office of Thrift Supervision to make sure they conform to administration policy.

Federal Financing Bank (FFB): Created as a government corporation in 1973 to centralize and reduce the cost of federal borrowing and federally assisted borrowing from the public, and to handle federal budget problems that occur due to off-budget financing flooding the government securities market with government-backed securities competing with Treasury securities. FFB also has power to purchase any obligation sold or guaranteed by a federal agency to ensure efficient financing of fully guaranteed obligations.

CONTACT   Phone: (202) 622-2470; Fax: (202) 622-0707.

OFFICE OF THE FISCAL ASSISTANT SECRETARY: Leads the *Fiscal Service,* which includes the Financial Management Service (FMS) and the Bureau of the Public Debt (BPD). It develops policy and operates the financial infrastructure of the federal government, including its payments, collections, cash management, financing, central accounting, delinquent debt collection, electronic commerce, government-wide accounting, and government investment fund management.

In managing the country's daily cash position, the office produces cash and debt forecasts that are used to predict the size and timing of the government's financing operations. It represents the secretary on the Federal Accounting Standards Advisory Board (FASAB), on the Joint Financial Management Improvement Program (JFMIP), and on the Library of Congress and National Archives Trust Fund boards. The fiscal assistant secretary sits on the Chief Financial Officers Council and is a liaison to the Federal Reserve System.

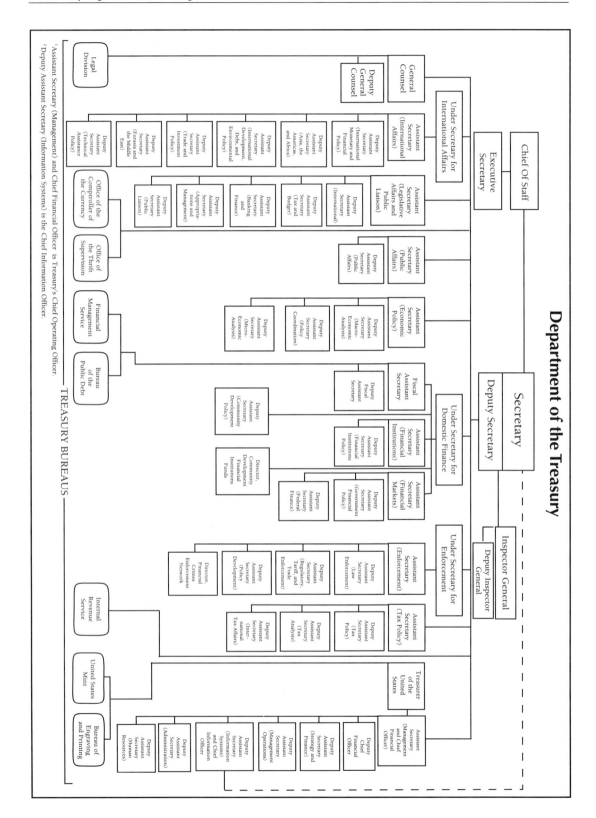

Department of the Treasury

OFFICE OF ECONOMIC POLICY

The Office of Economic Policy analyzes and reports on current and potential future developments in U.S. and international economies and financial markets and helps develop appropriate economic policies. The office works with the COUNCIL OF ECONOMIC ADVISERS and with the OFFICE OF MANAGEMENT AND BUDGET to prepare the president's budget. It also helps form and articulate public policy on microeconomic issues such as terror risk insurance, financial disclosure and auditing, stock options, parallel imports, health insurance, retirement income security, and long-term care.

CONTACT Phone: (202) 622-2200.

OFFICE OF INTERNATIONAL AFFAIRS

The Office of International Affairs works to increase economic growth and improve economic stability in developing countries, emerging market countries, and industrial countries by giving policy advice, and implementing new economic and financial programs.

Specific duties and responsibilities of International Affairs include working with economic officials in Latin America, the Caribbean, Africa, Asia, Europe, former Soviet states, and the Middle East to help improve productivity growth, reduce poverty, and prevent crises; give "on-the-ground" economic and financial technical assistance to transitional, post-conflict, emerging-market, and developing countries; lead and participate in negotiations to eradicate barriers to international trade and finance by working through the World Trade Organization, the Organization for Economic Cooperation and Development, and free trade agreements with Chile, Singapore, Mexico, and Canada; coordinate freezing of terrorist funds to combat financing terrorism; and overseeing U.S. participation in International Monetary Fund and multilateral development banks, including the World Bank, Inter-American Development Bank, African Development Bank, Asian Development Bank, and the European Bank for Reconstruction and Development.

Additionally, International Affairs works toward improving the international monetary system; monitors developments in foreign exchange and other markets and official roles in those markets; develops policy on trade financing; coordinates policy on foreign investments in the United States and its investments abroad; and analyzes the balance of payments and energy data and how basic financial and economic data affect world payment patterns and economic outlooks.

International Affairs also coordinates U.S. participation in the G-8, G-20, Western Hemisphere, and Asian-Pacific Economic Cooperation Forum and formulates and executes policies on rescheduling, swapping, or forgiving debt through the Paris Club, the Heavily Indebted Poor Country Initiative, and the Tropical Forests Conservation Act.

OFFICE OF ENFORCEMENT

The Office of Enforcement coordinates law-enforcement matters that are Treasury's responsibilities, in cooperation with other federal agencies, including domestic and international money laundering, terrorist financing and counter terrorist financing, implementation of the USA Patriot Act (2002), white-collar crime, organized crime, securities fraud, internal affairs and corruption, and trains bankers how to recognize suspicious transactions.

In George W. Bush's 2003 government restructuring (including creation of the Department of Homeland Security), the Secret Service, the

Bureau of Alcohol, Tobacco and Firearms, the Federal Law Enforcement Training Center, and the United States Customs Service were transferred from Treasury to other departments.

Office of Financial Enforcement helps enforce the Bank Secrecy Act and administers some Treasury regulations. These regulations include economic and trade sanctions and targets and blocks of financial transactions and assets of terrorists, narcotics traffickers, and foreign countries thought to pose a threat to U.S. national security and economy, according to President George W. Bush's Executive Order 13224. The National Money Laundering and Financial Crimes Strategy Act (1998) joins Treasury and the JUSTICE DEPARTMENT to combat money laundering at the federal, state, and local levels. The *Executive Office for Asset Forfeiture* (EOAF) runs the Treasury Forfeiture Fund and oversees asset taking to disrupt and dismantle criminal enterprises.

OFFICE OF TAX POLICY

The Office of Tax Policy develops and implements tax policies; estimates total government tax receipts for the president's budget, fiscal policy decisions, and cash management decisions; negotiates tax treaties for the United States and represents the United States in multilateral organization meetings concerning tax policy; and provides economic and legal analysis for domestic and international tax policy decisions. The office analyzes proposed tax legislation and tax programs; projects economic trends that might affect tax revenue; researches potential alternative taxes; produces legal advice and analysis on domestic and international tax matters; helps develop and review tax legislation and domestic and international tax regulations and rulings; and participates in international tax treaty negotiations.

The Office of Tax Policy's *Business Tax Division* develops and analyzes business tax policies, including those on corporations, partnerships and other unincorporated businesses, financial institutions and products, and energy and environment. Taxes it oversees include taxes on income, consumption, capital income, and business excise taxes, corporate tax shelters, depreciation allowances, integration of corporate and personal income taxes, and reform of business taxes.

Economic Modeling and Computer Application Division develops and runs models that simulate changes in current or proposed tax legislation, including several tax modeling systems: individual income taxes, corporate taxes, corporate panel model, depreciation, estate taxes, corporate receipts, banking, life insurance, capital gains, and estate-income tax returns.

The *Individual Taxation Division* focuses on the impact of existing and proposed individual income tax provisions on economic activity and welfare, marginal tax rates, and distribution of the tax burden among families. Policy issues this division deals with include structure of tax rates, tax treatment of different kinds of families, savings and education incentives, tax treatment of pensions and health insurance, tax-exempt bonds, and income tax compliance, payroll taxes, excise taxes, estate and gift taxes, and those of nonprofit organizations.

OFFICE OF THE TREASURER OF THE UNITED STATES

Older than the Department of the Treasury, joint treasurer positions of the United Colonies were established by the Continental Congress on July 29, 1775. First treasurers Michael Hillegas and George Clymer had to live in Philadelphia, home of the Continental Congress, and their primary job was to raise money for the Revolutionary War. Their signatures did not appear on paper money of the period, known as "continentals," while today the U.S. Treasurer's signature appears on U.S. currency. Clymer's resignation on August 6, 1776, left Hillegas as the only Continental treasurer. When the United Colonies became the United States on September 9, 1776, Hillegas continued to work with a new title, Treasurer of the United States.

During the Civil War the government took over printing money from private banks and printers to prevent counterfeiting, and its product became known as "greenbacks." Benjamin Franklin had developed the leaf design because no two leaves would ever be printed the same (an original "leaf note" remains in the SMITHSONIAN INSTITUTION). Congress authorized the U.S. government to issue paper money on July 17, 1861. Abraham Lincoln's treasurer, Frances Spinner, stirred up a rage because he hired the first female employees at Treasury, including Jennie Douglas to cut and trim paper, for which the women of New York eventually erected a statue of Treasurer Spinner in his hometown of Herkimer, New York.

Over the years the treasurer's office has grown in importance and expanded, receiving and disbursing government funds, moving to include duties such as national director of the Savings Bonds Division (1975), supervisor of the Bureau of Engraving and Printing of the U.S. Mint, and the Financial Literacy Initiative. In 1993 the Savings Bonds Division was abolished, with functions moved to the Bureau of Public Debt. Appointed in 2001, Rosario Marin became the first non-U.S. native to hold the office. Many distinguished women have held the post.

CONTACT Address: 1500 Pennsylvania Avenue NW, Washington, DC 20220; Phone: (202) 622-2000; Website: www.ustreas.gov.

OFFICE OF THE COMPTROLLER OF THE CURRENCY (OCC)

Created February 25, 1863, OCC charters, regulates, and supervises 2,200 national banks and federal branches and 56 federal branches of foreign banks in the United States. OCC's London office supervises U.S. national banks' international activities.

In 1861 Secretary of the Treasury Salmon P. Chase suggested establishment of federally chartered national banks that could issue standardized national bank notes based on U.S. bonds held by the bank. The National Currency Act of 1863 created the national banking system and gave the newly created OCC and its administrator, comptroller of the currency, the power to administer the system. Rewritten as the National Bank Act, the act authorized the comptroller of the currency to develop a staff of national bank examiners to supervise and periodically examine national banks, and to regulate lending and investment functions of national banks.

One reason the legislation created a banking system that issued money was to finance the Civil War.

The comptroller is appointed by the president for a five-year term, with the advice and consent of the Senate. The comptroller serves additionally as a director of the FEDERAL DEPOSIT INSURANCE CORPORATION (FDIC), and as a director of the Neighborhood Reinvestment Corporation.

With the goal of ensuring a stable and competitive national banking system, OCC's objectives are to ensure safety and soundness of the country's national banks; to foster competition by allowing banks to offer new products and services; to improve efficiency and effectiveness of OCC's staff and supervision; and to ensure fair and equal access to financial services for all Americans. Banks no longer issue their own money.

OCC issues rules, legal interpretations, and corporate decisions concerning banking, bank investments, banking community development efforts, trusts, and other bank operations.

OCC's 1,900 bank examiners work nationwide, conducting annual on-site reviews of national banks, perform corporate analyses, analyze a bank's loan and investment portfolios, funds management, capital, earnings, liquidity, sensitivity to and control of market risk, and compliance with consumer banking laws.

OCC has the power to examine national banks; approve or deny applications for new bank charters, branches, capital, or other changes in the corporate or banking structure; take supervisory action against banks not in compliance with laws and regulations or engaging in unsound banking practices by removing officers and directors, negotiating agreements to change banking practices, and issuing cease and desist orders and civil money penalties; and issue rules and regulations governing bank investments, lending, and other practices.

OCC is funded primarily by assessments of the national banks, which also pay for their examinations by OCC and OCC's processing of their applications. OCC also receives income from its investments, primarily in U.S. Treasury securities.

FDIC insures deposits up to $100,000 in all national banks, with individuals' deposit coverage limited to $100,000 in each bank, including all its branches.

CONTACT Address: OCC, 250 E Street SW, Washington, DC 20219; Phone: (202) 874-5000, (202) 874-4700, (800) 613-6743 for complaints; Website: www.occ.treas.gov; FDIC: (202) 898-6570; Website: www.fdic.gov.

BUREAU OF ENGRAVING AND PRINTING (BEP)

The Bureau of Engraving and Printing designs, prints, and finishes Federal Reserve notes (paper money), U.S. postage stamps, certificates, military identification cards, naturalization certificates, and hand-engraved invitations for the White House, as well as security documents for other government agencies.

From 1861 the Bureau of Engraving and Printing began with workers signing, separating, and trimming sheets of Demand Notes by hand in the Treasury Building. Within a few years, BEP was engraving and printing fractional currency, revenue stamps, government obligations, and other security documents. Beginning in 1877, BEP was the sole producer of all U.S. currency. Postage stamps became part of BEP's repertoire in 1894, making the bureau the government's official security printer.

Currently BEP prints money and other security documents in Washington, D.C., and Fort Worth, Texas, including paper money with new security features to thwart counterfeiters' use of color copiers, laser printers, and scanners. New $20, $50, and $100 bills will be produced with state-of-the-art anticounterfeiting techniques.

CONTACT Address: Bureau of Engraving & Printing, Fourteenth & C Streets SW, Washington, DC 20228; Phone: (202) 874-3019; Website: www.moneyfactory.com.

FINANCIAL MANAGEMENT SERVICES (FMS)

The Financial Management Services (FMS) manages the federal government's money and financial systems to move government cash flow efficiently. FMS serves as the government's disbursement and collection agent, accountant, reporter of financial information, and collector of debts owed to the federal government, and gives advice on cash management, credit administration, debt collection, accounting systems, investment management, and how best to take advantage of technology in financial activities.

Originally the Register of the Treasury performed account-keeping functions for the government, while each department and independent agency conducted their own disbursing functions. While the government was still small, it did not collect or spend very much money, and could maintain a rather loose system. In late 1919 after World War I, Treasury Secretary Carter Glass approved positions of commissioner of accounts and deposits and commissioner of the public debt as part of the Bureau of Accounts. In 1933 President Franklin D. Roosevelt ordered the disbursing clerks for executive departments to become part of the Division of Disbursement of the Bureau of Accounts.

Congress passed a reorganization plan in June of 1940, creating the Fiscal Service with three parts: the Bureau of Accounts, Bureau of the Public Debt, and the Office of the Treasurer of the United States. The year 1974 brought more changes, establishing the Bureau of Government Financial Operations (BGFO) bringing in all functions of the Bureau of Accounts, as well as those of the Office of the Treasurer. BGFO was renamed Financial Management Services in 1984, the beginning of the service coming into the modern age. New products and initiatives include the Electronic Funds Transfer, the Treasury Offset Program, the Electronic Federal Tax Payment System, and other electronic commerce initiatives.

FMS has about 2,100 career civil service employees, one-third of whom work in the four regional financial centers in Austin, Texas; Kansas City, Missouri; Philadelphia, Pennsylvania; San Francisco, California; and a debt collection only center in Alabama. RFC makes payments for the government by electronic funds transfers and checks, and the Debt Collection Center tries to collect debts older than 180 days for federal agencies.

FMS sends out Social Security checks, IRS tax refunds, veterans' benefits, and the "tax advance payment" by checks to U.S. taxpayers, as signed into law by President George W. Bush.

In 1996 Congress required most federal payments to be paid by Electronic Funds Transfers, and the Department of Treasury designed the Electronic Transfer Account (ETA) for people without bank accounts.

Through its Electronic Money (E-Money) Program, FMS tests new payment and collection technologies using the Internet, as well as digital signatures and biometrics. Examples of FMS's advanced technology uses include stored value cards used on military bases and in government hospitals; electronic checks; point-of-sale check truncation; and an Internet credit card collection program. As of 2000, citizens may transact business (pay fines or fees and file applications) with participating federal agencies through a federal Internet portal called www.pay.gov.

FMS is the largest collection system, taking in more than $2.3 trillion annually through more than 10,000 financial institutions, and more than $1.8 trillion of that through electronic transactions. FMS also collects individual and corporate income tax deposits, customs duties, loan repayments, fines, and proceeds from leases of federal lands. Individuals may pay federal personal and business taxes through FMS's www.eftps.gov

FMS gathers and publishes the government's financial information used by public and private sectors to keep track of the government's financial status and to establish both fiscal and monetary polities. FMS publications include "Daily Treasury Statement," "Monthly Treasury Statement," "Treasury Bulletin," "U.S. Government Annual Report," and the "Financial Report of the U.S. Government," the latter required by the Government Management and Reform Act of 1994 under President Bill Clinton.

Since President Bill Clinton signed the Debt Collection Improvement Act of 1996, FMS has collected about $15 billion in delinquent debt. In fiscal year 2002 alone, FMS included $1.4 billion in past due child support, $1.2 billion in federal nontax debt, and nearly $180 million in state and federal tax debt.

FMS's Intra-governmental Payment and Collection System (IPAC) provides a way to standardize interagency fund transfers for federal agencies, and makes more than 70,000 transfers a month.

CONTACT Address: 401 Fourteenth Street SW, Washington, DC 20227; Phone: (202) 874-6740; Website: www.fms.treas.gov. National Debt Collection Center: (800) 304-3107. Regional Financial Centers: P.O. Box 149058, Austin, TX

78741; P.O. Box 12599, Kansas City, MO 64116; P.O. Box 8676, Philadelphia, PA 19101; P.O. Box 193858, San Francisco, CA 94119.

INTERNAL REVENUE SERVICE (IRS)

The most unpopular and often feared agency in the U.S. government, the IRS is the American tax collection agency and administers the Internal Revenue Code. It is mandated to apply the tax law with integrity and fairness to all. Many citizens raise doubts about the IRS's official mission, however, because of stories of loopholes and favors being granted to the wealthy. The IRS does not enforce taxes on alcohol, tobacco, firearms, and explosives.

In 1862 President Abraham Lincoln and Congress created the commissioner of internal revenue and enacted an income tax to pay for the Civil War. Subsequently, the income tax was repealed in 1872, reestablished by Congress in 1894, and then ruled unconstitutional by the Supreme Court in 1895.

Trying again, the states ratified the 16th Amendment to the Constitution in 1913, giving Congress the authority to enact an income tax. Congress introduced the first 1040 Form and levied a 1 percent tax on net personal incomes over $3,000 and a 6 percent surtax on incomes over $500,000 that same year. Following World War I, the highest income tax rate was 77 percent in 1918. It dropped to 24 percent in 1929, and rose again during the Great Depression. Again to help pay for a war, Congress introduced payroll withholding tax and quarterly tax payments during World War II, speeding up collections and increasing taxes actually collected.

Until the 1950s, IRS workers were primarily patronage appointments. During the '50s a huge IRS reorganization replaced the patronage system with professional career employees. The name was also changed to give the image of serv-ing taxpayers when the bureau was renamed the Internal Revenue Service. IRS now employs about 100,000 people throughout the country.

In response to public outrage and complaints about IRS service and harassment by employees protected by civil service, Congress passed the IRS Restructuring and Reform Act of 1998, which included a Taxpayer Advocate Service. Reorganization of IRS created four basic operating divisions directed at types of taxpayers: Wage and Investment for taxpayers who file individual and joint tax returns; Small Business and Self-employed; Large and Mid-size Business for corporations with assets of more than $10 million; and Tax-exempt and Government Entities for employee benefit plans and tax-exempt organizations such as nonprofit charities and governmental entities. Other new divisions include Appeals, Chief Counsel, Communications and Liaison, and Criminal Investigation.

WAGE AND INVESTMENT OPERATING DIVISION: Located in Atlanta, Georgia, focuses on individual income tax payers, most of whom pay their taxes through withholdings, more than half do their own tax returns, and most of whom interact with the IRS once a year.

SMALL BUSINESS/SELF-EMPLOYED OPERATING DIVISION: At 5000 Ellin Road, New Carrolton, MD 20706 with area offices in Baltimore, Maryland; Dallas, Texas; Jacksonville, Florida; Nashville, Tennessee; Seattle, Washington; Boston, Massachusetts; Denver, Colorado; Laguna Niguel, California; Philadelphia, Pennsylvania; St. Paul, Minnesota; Chicago, Illinois; Detroit, Michigan; New York, New York; San Francisco Bay Area, California; Washington, D.C., and Puerto Rico. The Small Business Division caters to primarily self-employed people and some small businesses, who have 4–60 transactions with the IRS each year.

SB/SE offers three programs including the Taxpayer Education and Communication (TEC) organization; Customer Account Services (CAS); and Compliance. SB/SE clients include part-time or start-up small businesses; small businesses with or without employees; taxpayers with rental properties or farming businesses; individuals who invest in businesses; and corporations, s-corporations, and partnerships with assets under $10 million.

CONTACT Phone: (800) 829-1040 or (202) 622-0600; Website: www.irs.gov/.

LARGE & MID-SIZE BUSINESS OPERATING DIVISION: Serves corporations, subchapter S corporations, and partnerships with assets greater than $10 million. LMSB functions according to divisions of responsibility according to industry: communications, technology, and media; financial services; heavy manufacturing and transportation; natural resources and construction; retailers, food, pharmaceuticals, and health care; and field and specialists.

CONTACT Address: LMSB, 801 9th Street NW, 4th Floor, Washington, DC 20220; Phone: (202) 283-8710; Fax: (202) 283-8508.

TAX EXEMPT & GOVERNMENT ENTITIES OPERATING DIVISION: Serves groups that range from small local community organizations and municipalities to major universities, huge pension funds, state governments, and complex tax-exempt bond deals. Organizations this division serves may include organizations exempt from income tax, some political organizations, prepaid legal plans, and welfare benefit funds described in IRS regulations.

APPEALS DIVISION: Works to resolve tax disagreements without litigation in a way that is fair and impartial to both the government and the taxpayer, in that order. New services ordered by the Appeals Division include fast-track mediation to expedite disputes involving audits and compromise and trust fund recovery penalties. LMSB fast-track mediation works on appeals for large and mid-size businesses to resolve disputes on specific issues while the case is still being examined.

TAXPAYER ADVOCATE SERVICE: Helps taxpayers resolve problems with the IRS. This service is headquartered in Washington, D. C. (Phone (202) 622-6100; Fax (202) 622-7854), with area offices in New York; Richmond, Virginia; Fort Lauderdale, Florida; Milwaukee, Wisconsin; Dallas, Texas; Seattle, Washington; and Oakland, California.

The Taxpayer Advocate Service is now independent while within the IRS and works to help taxpayers resolve problems with the IRS and recommend changes to prevent the problems.

CONTACT Phone: (202) 622-6100; Fax: (202) 622-7854.

CRIMINAL INVESTIGATION SECTION: Has 2,900 special agents who investigate potential criminal violations of the Internal Revenue Code and other related financial crimes. Criminal Investigation also enforces laws on taxes, money laundering, and the Bank Secrecy Act. IRS tax law is based on voluntary compliance based on self-determination of what an individual owes. CI goes after individuals and corporations who deliberately do not comply with the codes. Its independent programs include Legal Source Tax Crimes; Illegal Source Financial Crimes; and Narcotics Related Financial Crimes.

CONTACT Address: Internal Revenue Service, 1111 Constitution Avenue NW, Washington, DC 20224; Phone: (202) 622-5000, (800) 829-1040; Website: www.irs.gov.

UNITED STATES MINT (U.S. MINT)

The United States Mint (U.S. Mint) produces enough coinage to supply the United States to conduct trade and commerce, and produces and sells numismatic coins, American Eagle gold and silver bullion coins, and national medals. Its Fort Knox Bullion Depository stores the country's $200 billion of silver and gold bullion.

Established as the Bureau of the Mint by congressional act on February 12, 1873, and recodified September 13, 1982, the bureau's name was changed to the United States Mint on January 9, 1984. In more recent history, this self-funded agency produces between 14 and 20 billion coins every year, and distributes coins to Federal Reserve banks and branches. The U.S. Mint produces proof and uncirculated coins, commemorative coins, and medals for sale to the general public, and receives, redeems, and processes mutilated coins.

U.S. Mint facilities include *U.S. Mint Headquarters,* Washington, D.C., formulates policy and administers the agency, does research and development, markets products, and processes orders; *Philadelphia Mint,* Pennsylvania, engraves coins and medals, produces medal and coin dies; produces coins for general circulation, regular uncirculated coin sets, commemorative coins authorized by Congress; and produces medals. Public tours available with sales center. The *Denver Mint* performs the same functions as does the Philadelphia Mint, and stores gold and silver bullion. Public tours available. *San Francisco Mint,* California, produces regular proof coin sets in clad and silver, and produces selected commemorative coins as authorized by Congress. *West Point Mint,* New York, produces all uncirculated and proof one-ounce silver bullion coins; all American Eagle gold bullion and platinum bullion coins; produces all silver, gold, platinum, and bi-metallic commemorative coins authorized by Congress; and stores silver, gold, and platinum bullion. The *U.S. Bullion Depository* at Fort Knox, Kentucky, stores gold bullion.

CONTACT Address; U.S. Mint Customer Care Center, 801 9th Street NW, Washington, DC 20220; Phone: (202) 354-7200; Website: www.usmint.gov.

BUREAU OF THE PUBLIC DEBT

The Bureau of the Public Debt borrows money needed to run the federal government; accounts for the resulting public debt; and issues and buys back Treasury securities to manage the debt. To do this the bureau sells Treasury bills, notes, bonds, and U.S. savings bonds. Bureau of the Public Debt pays interest to investors and, so far, redeems investors' securities.

The Bureau of Public Debt borrows approximately $2 trillion annually by holding about 140 auctions of bonds, as well as through ongoing sales of savings bonds ($50 and $100) at 40,000 locations throughout the United States, including Federal Reserve Banks. The Bureau also promotes sale of savings bonds through payroll savings plans and financial institutions, and makes daily or periodic reports on the size and makeup of the national debt.

Public Debt has six programs; commercial book-entry securities, direct access securities, savings securities, government securities, market regulation, and public debt accounting. It also enforces and implements regulations providing investor protection while trying to maintain a fair and liquid market for government securities.

CONTACT Address: Bureau of the Public Debt, 999 E Street NW, Washington, DC 20239-0001; Phone: (202) 219-3300; and 200 3rd Street, Parkersburg, WV 25106-1328; Website: www.publicdebt.treas.gov.

OFFICE OF THRIFT SUPERVISION (OTS)

The Office of Thrift Supervision (OTS), created by the Financial Institutions Reform, Recovery and Enforcement Act of 1989, regulates federally chartered and some state-chartered thrift (savings and loan) institutions to help meet Americans' needs for housing and other financial loans and services.

OTS examines and supervises savings and loan institutions to ensure the soundness of the industry and safety of people's money; makes sure savings and loan institutions meet consumer protection laws and regulations; makes sure policies and procedures are applied consistently throughout the U.S.; develops national thrift institution policy guidelines and implements them and new regulations; issues quarterly reports on the general condition of the thrift industry and other reports; prepares bulletins, regulations, congressional testimony, and policy documents on the condition of the thrift industry, interest rate risk, financial derivatives, and economic issues; and enforces regulations of thrift industry.

CONTACT Address: OTS, 1700 G Street NW, Washington, DC 20552; Phone: (202) 906-6000; Website: www.ots.treas.gov/.

COMMUNITY DEVELOPMENT FINANCIAL INSTITUTION (CDFI)

Created by the Riegle Community Development Improvement Act of 1994, the Community Development Financial Institution (CDFI) works to expand available credit, investment capital, and financial services to distressed urban and rural communities by stimulating new and growing diverse community development financial institutions. It also provides incentives to traditional banks and thrifts by investing in private markets, healthy local tax revenues, and empowering residents. It leverages private-sector investments from banks, foundations, and other funding sources.

CDFIs are specialized financial institutions intended to appeal to untraditional market niches and provide mortgage financing for first-time homebuyers, financing for needed community facilities, commercial loans and investments to start or expand small businesses, loans to rehabilitate rental housing, and other financial services to low-income households and local businesses. CDFI institutions include community development banks, credit unions, loan funds, venture capital funds, and microenterprise loan funds.

CDFIs also give technical assistance to small businesses and credit counseling to consumers in an effort to make sure the credit issued is used as intended and repayments are made.

Specific CDFI programs include Bank Enterprise Awards Program for innovative funding by traditional banking institutions; Financial Assistance Program for financial assistance to CDFIs to support community development in underserved markets; Native American CDFI Development Program for creating funding and technical assistance to bring services to Native American, Alaska Native, and Native Hawaiian communities; New Markets Tax Credits for giving taxpayers incentives to invest in designated Community Development Entities; and Technical Assistance programs for grants to develop technical abilities to develop a Comprehensive Business Plan to underserved markets, particularly Native American, Alaska Native, or Native Hawaiian communities.

CONTACT Address: CDFI, 601 13th Street NW, Suite 200 South, Washington, DC 20005; Phone: (202) 622-8662; Fax: (202) 622-7754; Website: www.cdfifund.gov/.

DEPARTMENT OF VETERANS AFFAIRS

The Department of Veterans Affairs is the second-largest cabinet-level department, second only to the DEPARTMENT OF DEFENSE, in both budget ($50.6 billion in 2002) and number of personnel (more than 220,000). It administers numerous veterans programs including benefits for disabilities, educational programs (GI Bill), home loan guarantees, more than 100 medical centers and 400 clinics, insurance, national cemeteries, and benefits for surviving spouses and dependents. As of 2003 about 70 million

Americans were veterans, dependents, or survivors of deceased veterans potentially eligible for VA services and/or benefits.

HISTORY

Although established as a cabinet department on March 15, 1989, by legislation that had been signed by President Ronald Reagan, the history of concern for service veterans dates back to a time long before the founding of the United States. When the Plymouth Colony Pilgrims fought the Pequot Indians in 1636, they adopted a law providing that the colony would support any disabled soldier. During the American Revolution the Continental Congress in 1776 established pensions for any soldier who was disabled in the war. During the early years of the nation several states and/or communities provided medical care, including "domiciliaries" (sanitariums/living facilities) for veterans.

The first medical facilities and a domiciliary were authorized by the federal government in 1811, as well as pensions for those disabled, which were available to their widows and dependents. In the wake of the Civil War (1861–65) at the urging of organizations of veterans of the Mexican War (1846–48) and the Grand Army of the Republic, an organization of Civil War vets, many states established "homes" for veterans in which they could live and receive medical attention for any illness or disability whether service-connected or not. These included the extensive state Veterans Home at Yountville, California, which is still in full operation.

When the United States began supplying the Allies in 1914, Congress adopted the War Risk Insurance Act to cover losses of ships, cargoes, and crews due to attacks by German submarines. In all 61 ships were lost while this program (run by the TREASURY DEPARTMENT) was in effect.

A federal system of veterans benefits was established when the United States entered World War I ("the war to end all wars") in 1917 by substantial amendment of the War Risk Insurance Act. These included disability compensation, voluntary life insurance in the maximum amount of $10,000, which was taken out by 93 percent of those in the military, and vocational rehabilitation for the disabled (including those suffering from lung complications such as tuberculosis after being exposed to chlorine and mustard gas on the western front). A growing number of veterans hospitals were constructed, reaching 54 in number by 1930. Administration of these programs was divided among the Veterans Bureau, the Bureau of Pensions (for some unknown reason located in the INTERIOR DEPARTMENT), and the National Home for Disabled Volunteer Soldiers.

All of these functions were brought together with the creation of the Veterans Administration in 1930 by legislation signed by President Herbert Hoover. President Hoover was not always so solicitous of veterans. In July 1932 he ordered the army to disperse by force—including tear gas—the so-called bonus marchers (veterans asking for immediate payment of promised bonuses to ease the poverty caused by the Great Depression) and destroy its camp of tents and shacks in Washington, D.C.

A Board of Veterans Appeals was added in 1933 to allow veterans to contest rulings on eligibility for benefits or other orders of the Veterans Administration.

With World War II raging in Europe, on October 8, 1940, the National Service Life Insurance program was added to the authority of the Veterans Administration. During the next 11 years more than 22 million policies were issued—primarily life insurance at an initial amount of $10,000—with 1.9 million still in force in 2003.

The most monumental change in veterans benefits came about through the passage of the Servicemen's Readjustment Act of 1944, by a unanimous vote of both houses of Congress, and signed by President Franklin D. Roosevelt on June 22, 1944, just a dozen days after D day, the allied invasion of France on the way to victory over Nazi Germany. This act gave birth to the so-called GI Bill for payment of tuition, expenses,

Department of Veterans Affairs

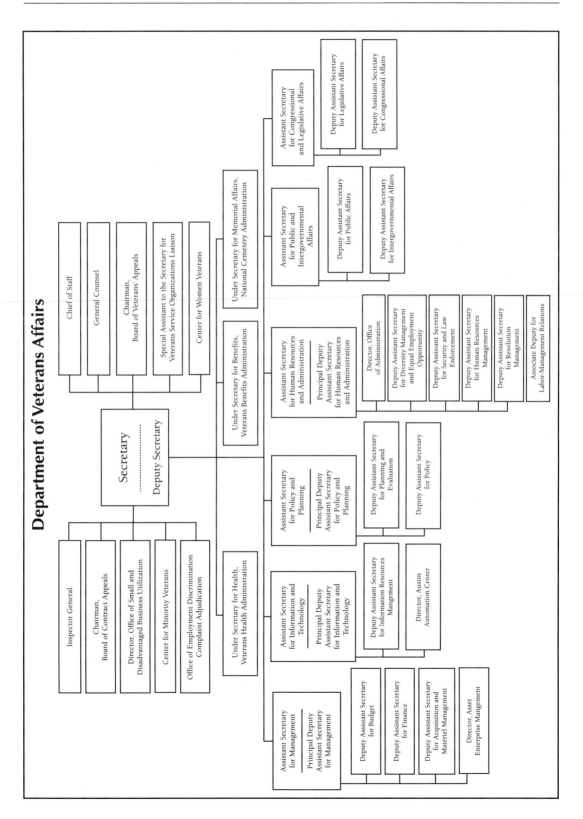

and a living stipend for advanced education, university, college, or approved vocational schooling, and below-market home loans, known as "VA Loans." Millions of young men and women were able to attend college, many the first in their family, under the GI Bill, and the VA Loans made possible purchase of homes for veterans and their families. The VA loan program had the important peripheral benefit of stimulating the home construction industry in the postwar period.

With each ensuing international conflict—Korea police action, Vietnam, Persian Gulf ("Desert Storm"), and for all military volunteers—new versions of the GI Bill have been enacted to cover veterans of those military eras.

In 1946 within the Veterans Administration, the Department of Medicine and Surgery was created, recognizing the increased medical and rehabilitation needs of the more than 15 million veterans returning from World War II (as well as the remaining survivors of World War I). That department reorganized as the Veterans Health Services and Research Administration in 1989, and was renamed the Veterans Health Administration in 1991, after the Department of Veterans Affairs was established in 1989.

Another organization reshuffle in 1953 resulted in the launching of the Department of Veterans Benefits, which became the Veterans Benefits Administration in 1988.

A major new function was added to the authority of the Veterans Administration in 1973, when the Department of the Army (within the Defense Department) transferred the entire National Cemetery System for veterans with the exception of Arlington National Cemetery. The cemetery system included a dozen established in 1862 during the Civil War. They ranged in size from the Calverton, New York, cemetery with 1,045 acres, down to the tiny Hampton, Virginia, Veterans Administration Medical Center, .03 acres.

The two most prominent of the directors of the Veterans Administration were five-star general Omar Bradley (1945–48) and Max Cleland (1977–81), who lost both legs and an arm in Vietnam and later served a term (1997–2003) as a senator from Georgia.

In 1988 the Department of Veterans Affairs Act (38 USC 201) was passed and signed by President Ronald Reagan to upgrade the Veterans Administration to cabinet-level status as the Department of Veterans Affairs, which became official on March 15, 1989. At the time of the official opening of the new department, President George H. W. Bush, a decorated Navy Air Force veteran himself, stated: "There is only one place for the veterans of America, in the Cabinet Room, at the table with the President. . . ."

ORGANIZATION

The department is headed by the secretary of veterans affairs, with a deputy secretary, three under secretaries, each responsible for administration of particular programs, and six assistant secretaries, each with specific responsibilities for an aspect of internal administration. In addition, there are the Boards of Veterans Appeals and the Contact Appeals, each with five members, including a chair who has a rank equivalent to assistant secretary.

The *secretary of veterans affairs* oversees the administration of the department and is the principal adviser to the president on veterans matters. He receives reports from the under secretaries and assistant secretaries, as well as the director of the Office of Small and Disadvantaged Business Utilization (by veterans), the Center for Minority Veterans, the Office of Employment Discrimination Complaint Adjudication, the Center for Women Veterans, and the Special Assistant to the Secretary for Veterans Organizations Liaison. The secretary's immediate staff includes a chief of staff and general counsel.

The *deputy secretary* works directly with the secretary in developing policy and facilitating programs and is responsible for oversight of the operations administered by the under securities and the assistant secretaries.

Under secretaries: The three under secretaries are the *under secretary for health* which operates the Veterans Health Administration, the *under secretary for benefits,* which directs the Veterans Benefits Administration responsible for pensions, disability and death compensation, education under the famed GI Bill (and its renewals), and a massive insurance program, and the *under secretary for memorial affairs* directing the National Cemetery Administration.

CONTACT   The headquarters of the Department of Veterans Affairs is located at 810 Vermont Avenue NW, Washington, DC 20420; Phone: (202) 273-4800; Website: www.va.gov. Office of Public Affairs for all types of information about veterans: Phone: (202) 273-5700, for media: Phone: (202) 273-6000; audiovisual material requests: Phone: (202) 273-9781, 273-9782. For public comment: Fax: (202) 273-5981; E-mail: 525.pocs@mail.va.gov.

Main phone for questions about benefits: (800) 827-1000 (used to call before submitting an e-mail application for benefits). E-mail for benefits: Veterans On Line Application (VONAPP): VONAAP@vba.va.gov (do not use if have submitted a written application). E-mail questions in regard to benefits: www.vba.va.gov/benefits/address. Education benefits: Phone: (888) 442-4551. Personnel Records Center: www.nara.gov/regional/impr; and Service Records: www.narfa.gov/regional/mprs.

For the hearing imparied: Phone: (800) 829-4833.

VETERANS BENEFITS ADMINISTRATION

The Veterans Benefits Administration administers several benefits programs through regional offices in every state, the District of Columbia, and the Philippines (see below for locations).

It pays *Pensions and Disability Compensation* to approximately 2.7 million veterans, but naturally the number is gradually diminishing each year due to the deaths of veterans far exceeding the numbers of new veterans. In addition to the veterans themselves, more than 575,000 surviving spouses, children, and even parents of deceased veterans receive benefits, including 136,000 from the Vietnam era and 286,000 World War II veterans. Amazingly, there were a couple of children of Civil War veterans, a handful from the Spanish-American war, and about 100 from World War I still receiving benefits as recently as 2002. The annual cost is currently approximately $25 billion paid out to 3.2 million persons.

Currently, the death benefits for surviving spouses of those dying while in the service, whether through combat, accident, or disease, is $935 per month, plus added benefits for each minor child and the proceeds from any veteran's life insurance program.

The VA's *Life Insurance Programs* are six in number and currently have 2.1 million policies in force with a face value of $21 billion, which were policies taken out by servicemen and women during World War II and thereafter. This is the fourth-largest insurance program in the United States, both public and private. Approximately 1.7 million policyholders are entitled to eventual dividends, which presently total a reserve of $618 million. The current maximum coverage, which most service personnel elect, is $250,000.

Also administered by the VA are two group life insurance programs: *Servicemembers' Group Life Insurance* and *Veterans' Group Life Insurance,* which currently cover about 3 million veterans, active-duty service personnel, members of the service reserves and the State and National Guards, and their families. The total coverage under these group plans is $740 billion.

GI Bill Education Benefits since 1944 have assisted almost 21 million veterans, people still on military duty, and some family members, with payments for tuition, costs of supplies, and basic housing expenses. Many would never have had the opportunity for advanced education without this program; it greatly benefited minorities, and millions were the first in their families to go to college. More than 7.8 million World War II veterans were educated with the aid of GI Bill benefits. From the Korean conflict 2.4 million veterans, and 8.2 million from the post-Korean period, including the Vietnam era (some on active duty) obtained education benefits. An additional category are those dependents such as spouses and adult children of veterans who suffered service-connected death or total disability.

The statistics for 2001 showed that the numbers benefiting from the educational program were still substantial. In that year VA educational benefits went to 291,848 veterans and men and women on active duty, 82,283 reservists and National Guardsmen, and 46,917 survivors of service personnel. Over the years $75 billion has been expended on the program, which is on-going.

Also available under the Benefits Administration is *vocational rehabilitation* for veterans needing advice, counseling, and assistance in preparing for and finding employment in decent jobs.

Under the original GI Bill the *Veterans Home Loan Guarantees* was inaugurated to provide below-market home loans to veterans, with the government guaranteeing repayment to conventional lenders who would otherwise be reluctant to make loans based on low loan to value (with low down payments) to veterans with untested or less than perfect credit ratings. By 2002 the VA Home Loans since 1944 had helped 16.6 million veterans purchase homes at a total value of $708 billion. In 2002 there were more than 3 million loans still in effect, with an amortized loan amount eventually due of $218.5 billion.

In fiscal year 2001 alone the VA guaranteed more than 252,000 new loans totaling $31.2 billion. Further, that year the VA made grants of $20 million to approximately 500 disabled veterans for housing specially adapted for their needs.

Forms: Veteran's Application for Compensation and/or Pension: 21-526; Disabled Veterans Application for Vocational Rehabilitation: 28-1900; Application for Education Benefits: 22-19909.

Assistance from Service Organizations: Veterans may appoint a recognized service organization to represent them in making claims. Information can be obtained at (800) 827-1000 or via website: www.va.gov/vso/index.

VETERANS HEALTH ADMINISTRATION

The Veterans Health Administration, headed by the under secretary for health, manages the largest health care system in the United States. It operates 163 veterans administration hospitals, more than 850 outpatient clinics, 137 nursing homes, 3 domiciliaries, and 73 home-care programs. As the veteran population ages, there has been a substantial growth in the number treated for medical, surgical, and/or rehabilitative care in recent years, jumping more than 10 percent annually by 2001, when 4.2 million persons received some form of care. These included 587,000 patients in VA hospitals or by contract in other hospitals, 87,000 in nursing homes, 45,000 in domiciliaries, and many more as outpatients, for a total 4.2 million (2001).

The annual Department of Veterans Affairs budget for health exceeds $22 billion, and employs more than 180,000 health care professionals.

Veterans are encouraged to "enroll" in its health program even before seeking treatment, but those with major disabilities, recent discharges, and those requiring treatment only for service-connected disabilities may receive treatment upon enrollment. More than 6 million are enrolled and do not require evaluation before treatment.

The Veterans Health Administration is affiliated with 107 medical schools, 55 dental schools, and more than 1,000 other educational institutions to train health professionals in VA medical centers. The annual number of trainees at any one time is more than 80,000, with the result that half the practicing physicians in the United States have had some VA training.

Recognizing the extent of the problem of emotional trauma resulting from combat and in-service mistreatment ("post-traumatic stress disorder"), a Readjustment Counseling Service was inaugurated in 1979, when veterans concerns were still under the old Veterans Administration. By 2002 there were 206 so-called vet centers to provide the counseling service. The annual usage now amounts to more than 126,000 veterans, with more than 900,000 visits from vets and their family members per year. Treatment includes counseling for those sexually assaulted while in the service—a more progressive approach than has been reported within the military itself, which has often taken a cavalier approach to claims of rape or molestation. There are also programs for alcoholics and drug addicts.

For several years after the close of the Vietnam War the armed services denied that veterans of that conflict had been harmed by the defoliant herbicide agent orange (a high-potency cocktail of acids, chemicals, and dioxin) used to spray on forest areas to make it difficult for the enemy soldiers to hide under trees and bushes, and any symptoms were said to be due to "unrelated" causes. While veterans with illnesses suspected of being related to exposure to this and other herbicides (used between January 1965 and April 1970) were treated like any veteran with an illness, the denial by the military that agent orange was the cause made the veterans ineligible for "service-connected" disability compensation.

However, the VA inaugurated the *Agent Orange Registry Program* in 1978 to identify (and possibly treat) veterans exposed to agent orange. More than 300,000 veterans were registered in the next 21 years and their records computerized. In 1979 the VA established an Advisory Committee on Health-Related Effects of Herbicides and the Veterans' Advisory Committee on Environmental Hazards. These committees provided the VA updated results of agent-orange related research.

Unfortunately, there was still considerable reluctance by the government to admit that the symptoms that the identified veterans (and in some cases, their children) suffered were a result of agent orange. In 1991 Congress passed Public Law 102-4, which directed the VA to request the National Academy of Sciences to review diseases possibly caused by herbicide exposure. The NAS research supersedes the work of the advisory committees.

The extensive and intensive study by NAS resulted in the conclusion that there was a connection between agent orange exposure and various diseases and genetic problems. As a result, various diseases were added to the VA list of "presumptive service-connected" disabilities at various times in the next decade as the NAS studies continued, including acute neuropathy, prostate cancer, spina bifida in the children of exposed veterans, chloracne, Hodgkin's disease, multiple myeloma, non-Hodgkin's lymphoma, porphyria cutanea tarda, respiratory cancers, and soft-tissue sarcoma.

In 2000 the VA asked NAS to review a report by the military that veterans who were actually spraying agent orange had a high rate of diabetes, which NAS confirmed as to type 2 diabetes, and that medical condition was added to the list of presumptive disabilities. In 2003 further evidence led to the inclusion of chronic lymphocytic leukemia in the list.

By 2003 the VA estimated that more than 178,000 veterans might qualify for disability payments based on herbicide poisoning during the Vietnam War.

More than 100,000 homeless veterans receive health care and related assistance each year—although the number of homeless vets is gradually declining. The outreach by the VA encompasses transitional (temporary) housing, transportation to government offices (including tribal), and charitable services.

Medical research is a major element in the scope of the VA health program, with annual funding exceeding $350 million directly for research, plus a share of the money used for medical care, and another combined $500 million supplied by the National Institutes of Health, various foundations, and pharmaceutical companies. The research efforts are conducted at 115 sites.

Research advancements include such areas as aging, AIDS, post-traumatic disorder, women's health issues, artificial limbs, transplants, pacemakers, and treatment for various diseases. One development was awarded the Nobel Prize.

NATIONAL CEMETERY ADMINISTRATION

The National Cemetery Administration is headed by the under secretary for memorial affairs. This function of the VA dates from the 1973 transfer from the Army Department of 82 national cemeteries to the then Veterans Affairs Administration.

Since taking on this responsibility, the number of national cemeteries has grown to 120, located in 39 states and Puerto Rico, and the number of gravesites has almost doubled. The annual internment (about one-third after cremation) rate is about 85,000 and gradually rising. The total gravesites as of 2002 were in excess of 2.4 million. There is currently undeveloped land in existing cemeteries to add another 2.4 million gravesites.

The five newest veterans cemeteries are the Saratoga National Cemetery outside Albany, New York, the Abraham Lincoln National Cemetery near Chicago, the Dallas-Fort Worth National Cemetery, the Ohio Western Reserve National Cemetery outside Cleveland, and the Fort Sill National Cemetery, Elgin, Oklahoma. Currently on the drawing board are future national cemeteries in Atlanta, Detroit, Miami, Sacramento, and Pittsburgh, aimed at providing cemeteries within 75 miles of the veterans' homes for 88 percent of deceased veterans by the target date of 2006.

The largest national cemeteries based upon existing graves are in Long Island, New York, with 241,369; Calverton, New York (142,671); Fort Snelling, Minneapolis, Minnesota (128,818); Jefferson Barracks, St. Louis, Missouri (114,781); Golden Gate, San Bruno, California (111,730); and Riverside, California (113,336). The Riverside and Calverton cemeteries are presently the busiest with new burials. Other busy cemeteries are Bushnell, Florida; Fort Snelling; Jefferson Barracks; Willamette, Portland, Oregon; Fort Sam Houston, San Antonio, Texas; Bourne, Massachusetts; San Joaquin Valley, Gustine, California; Dallas-Fort Worth; Long Island; Fort Rosencrans, San Diego, California; Tahoma, Kent, Washington; Indiantown Gap, Annville, Pennsylvania; Abraham Lincoln, Ellwood, Illinois; Bayamon, Puerto Rico; and Santa Fe, New Mexico.

Headstones and markers for veterans graves (including those outside national cemeteries) are provided by the VA. Since 1973 7.7 million headstone and markers have been provided with the current annual rate exceeding 300,000. Presidential memorial certificates are issued upon request to survivors of honorably discharged veterans at an average in excess of 300,000 per year.

In addition, the VA operates the State Cemetery Grants Program, which provides full funding for development, expansion, and improvement of veterans cemeteries run by 28 states and Guam as of 2001, with three more under construction. In that year alone 15,400 veterans and members of their families were buried in these state cemeteries. Beginning in 1980, the program has granted more than $131 million to 28 states and Guam for the development, expansion, or improvement of 54 state cemeteries.

The VA is assisted by the extensive efforts of volunteers to maintain the beauty and dignity of the cemeteries and welcome the more than 8 million people who visit the graves each year.

Assistant Secretaries

Within the VA hierarchy are six assistant secretaries of veterans affairs, who primarily perform administrative duties for the department, each working through a stable of deputy assistant secretaries handling specific functions. The assistant secretaries are:

assistant secretary for management with deputies for budget, finance, acquisition, and materiel management and the director of asset enterprise management;

assistant secretary for information and technology with deputies for information resources management and the director of the Automation Center located in Austin, Texas. Responsibilities include oversight of the operation of the VA's computer systems and telecommunication networks for medical information, benefits, life insurance, and financial management. This office is also the manager of Freedom of Information Act requests; Phone: (202) 273-8135;

assistant secretary for policy and planning with deputies for planning and evaluation, and for policy. After the September 11, 2001, terrorist attacks, the assistant secretary was assigned to direct the VA's Crisis Response Team and to create and lead a new Office of Operations, Security and Preparedness for the department;

assistant secretary for human resources and management with deputies for diversity management and equal employment opportunity, security and law enforcement, human resources management, resolution management, labor-management relations, and the director of the office of administration;

assistant secretary for public and intergovernmental affairs aided by deputies for public affairs and for intergovernmental affairs. Among the duties are consumer affairs as they relate to the department;

assistant secretary for congressional affairs and legislative affairs with deputies for both congressional and legislative liaison. The assistant secretary directly advises the secretary on the department's legislative agenda. In addition to discussions with individual members of Congress and their staffs, the assistant secretary often represents the department before House and Senate hearings on VA programs, policies, and investigations.

Appeals Boards

The *Boards of Veterans Appeals* is composed of a chair (appointed by the president and confirmed by the Senate) and about 65 board members. It employs 260 attorneys and support staff of 170. It adjudicates appeals by veterans of rulings of claims by the VA bureaucracy. The board's workload is over 35,000 cases annually. Its yearly operational budget is $40 million. Its decisions may be appealed to the U.S. COURT OF APPEALS FOR VETERANS CLAIMS.

The *Board of Contract Appeals* is headed by a chairman (who is also the chief administrative judge) and has five other administrative judges. They adjudicate disputes in which the VA is a party, generally relevant to contracts for construction, supply, and services. The board's decisions are subject to appeal to the U.S. COURT OF APPEALS FOR THE FEDERAL CIRCUIT.

Special Centers and Offices

CENTER FOR WOMEN'S VETERANS: This office advises the secretary on issues involving the particular needs of women veterans. It also evaluates VA programs, policies, and practices to guarantee they are available to and responsive to women veterans.

CENTER FOR MINORITY VETERANS: This office promotes and assesses the needs of veterans who are members of minorities. It particularly works to guarantee that minorities get full use of the various benefit programs. The recognized minorities are African Americans, Hispanics, Asian Americans, and Native Americans (Indians, native Hawaiians, and Alaskan natives).

OFFICE OF SMALL AND DISADVANTAGED BUSINESS UTILIZATION: Exists to promote the ability of smaller businesses to obtain contracts with the Veterans Administration and its components. Phone: (800) 949-8387 or (202) 565-8124. The Acquisition Resources Service and the Office of Acquisition and Materiel Management provide information for people and entities interested in doing business with the VA. Phone: (202) 273-8815. A brochure entitled *Doing Business with the Department of Veterans Affairs* is available and useful.

VA Regional Offices

Alabama: 345 Perry Hill Road, Montgomery, AL 36109

Alaska: 2925 Debarr Road, Anchorage, AK 99508

Arizona: 3225 North Central Avenue, Phoenix, AZ 85012

Arkansas: Building 65, Fort Roots (P.O. Box 1280), North Little Rock, AR 72115

California: 11000 Wilshire Boulevard, Los Angeles, CA 90024

California: Oakland Federal Building, 1301 Clay Street, Oakland CA 94612

California: 8810 Rio San Diego Drive, San Diego, CA 92108

Colorado: 155 Van Gordon Street, (P.O. 25126), Lakewood, CO 80228

Connecticut: 450 Main Street, Hartford, CT 096103

Delaware: 1601 Kirkwood Avenue, Wilmington, DE 19805

Washington, D.C.: 1120 Vermont Avenue NW, Washington, DC 20421

Florida: P.O. Box 1437, St. Petersburg, FL 33731

Georgia: 1700 Clairmont Road (P.O. Box 100026), Decatur, GA 30033

Hawaii: P.O. Box 50188, Honolulu, HI 96850

Idaho: 805 West Franklin Street, Boise, ID 83702

Illinois: 536 South Clark Street (P.O. Box 8136), Chicago, IL 83702

Indiana: 575 North Pennsylvania Street, Indianapolis, IN 46204

Iowa: 210 Walnut Street, Des Moines, IA 50309

Kansas: 5500 East Kellogg, Wichita, KS 67218

Kentucky: 545 South Third Street, Louisville, KY 40402

Louisiana: 701 Loyola Avenue, New Orleans, LA 70113

Maine: 1 VA Center, Togu, ME 04330

Maryland: 31 Hopkins Plaza, Baltimore, MD 21201

Massachusetts: John F. Kennedy Federal Building, Boston, MA 02203

Michigan: 477 Michigan Avenue, Detroit, MI 48226

Minnesota: Bishop Henry Whipple Federal Building, Ft. Snelling, St. Paul, MN 55111

Mississippi: 1600 East Woodrow Wilson Avenue, Jackson, MS, 39216

Missouri: 400 East 18th Street, St. Louis, MO 63103

Montana: Montana Health Care Center, Ft. Harrison, MT 59636

Nebraska: 5631 South 48th Street, Lincoln, NE, 68516

Nevada: 1201 Terminal Way, Reno, NV 89520

New Hampshire: 275 Chestnut Street, Manchester, NH 03101

New Jersey: 20 Washington Place, Newark, NJ 07102

New Mexico: 500 Gold Avenue SW, Albuquerque, NM 87102

New York: 111 West Huron Street, Buffalo, NY 14202

New York: 245 West Houston Street, New York City, NY 10014

North Carolina: 251 North Main Street, Winston-Salem, NC 27155

North Dakota: 655 First Avenue, Fargo, ND 58102

Ohio: 1240 East Ninth Street, Cleveland, OH 44199

Oklahoma: 125 South Main Street, Muskogee, OK 74401

Oregon: 1220 SW Third Avenue, Portland, OR 97204

Pennsylvania: 5000 Wissahickon Avenue (P.O. Box 42954), Philadelphia, PA 42954

Pennsylvania: 1000 Liberty Avenue, Pittsburgh, PA 15222

Rhode Island: 360 Westminster Mall, Providence, RI 02903

South Carolina: 1801 Assembly Street, Columbia, SC 29201

South Dakota: 25051 West 22nd Street (P.O. Box 5046), Sioux Fall, SD 57117

Tennessee: 110 Ninth Avenue South, Nashville, TN 37203

Texas: 6900 Almeda Road, Houston, TX 77030

Texas: 701 Clay Avenue, Waco, TX 76799

Utah: 125 South State Street, Salt Lake City, UT 94147

Vermont: 215 North Main Street, White River Junction, VT 05009

Virginia: 210 Franklin Road SW, Roanoke, VA 24011

Washington: 915 Second Avenue, Seattle, WA 98174

West Virginia: 640 Fourth Avenue, Huntington, WV 25701

Wisconsin: 5000 West National Avenue, Building 6, Milwaukee, WI 53295

Wyoming: 2360 East Pershing Boulevard, Cheyenne, WY 82001

Philippine Republic: 1131 Roxas Boulevard, Manila, Philippine Republic FPO 96515-1110

Puerto Rico: U.S. Courthouse and Federal Building, Carlos E. Chardon Street (G.P.O. Box 346867), San Juan, PR 00936

The *Vets Employment and Training Service (VETS)* is located within the Department of Labor, 200 Constitution Avenue NW, Washington, DC 20210, Phone: (202) 693-4700.

INDEPENDENT ENTITIES AND COMMISSIONS

The executive branch of the U.S. government includes numerous independent organizations and commissions to oversee categories of governing not covered elsewhere, or to advise executive departments. Many of these groups serve independently, but are related to a particular agency or department. As well, there are several quasi-governmental agencies explained in a subsequent chapter.

ADVISORY COUNCIL ON HISTORIC PRESERVATION (ACHP)

Promotes the preservation, enhancement, and productive use of the country's historic resources, and advises the president and Congress on national historic preservation policy.

Established in 1966 by the National Historic Preservation Act, ACHP encourages federal agencies to consider and factor historic preservation into their project requirements. It also recommends administrative and legislative changes to protect national heritage, advocates consideration of historic values in federal decision making, and works with federal, state, and local governments, Indian tribes, and the private sector to coordinate effective national preservation policies.

In 1992 Congress amended the National Historic Preservation Act to give recognized Indian tribes more responsibility for preservation of significant historic properties on tribal lands, including performing the role of a State Historic Preservation Officer on tribal land. In this function, tribes may identify and maintain inventories of culturally significant properties, nominate properties to national and tribal registers of historic places, conduct reviews of federal projects on tribal lands, and conduct educational programs on the importance of preserving historic properties.

Members are appointed by the president for four-year terms, meet four times a year, and are paid $100 per meeting.

CONTACT   Address: ACHP, 1100 Pennsylvania Avenue NW, Suite 809, Old Post Office Building, Washington, DC 20004; Phone: (202)(606) 8503, E-mail: achp@achp.gov; Website: www.achp.gov. For tribal information: NATHPO, P.O. Box 19189, Washington, DC 20036-9189; Phone: (202) 628-8476; Fax: (202) 628-2241; E-mail: bambi@nathpo.org; Website: www.nathpo.org.

AFRICAN DEVELOPMENT FOUNDATION (ADF)

A government corporation established by the African Development Foundation Act of 1980 that funds community-based, self-help initiatives to alleviate poverty and promote sustainable development in Africa, while enhancing U.S. relations with Africa. Working with in-country partner organizations, the Washington, D.C., staff of 30 has active programs in 13 sub-Saharan countries: Benin, Botswana, Cape Verde, Ghana, Guinea, Nigeria, Mali, Namibia, Niger, Senegal, Tanzania, Uganda, and Zimbabwe.

While helping advance U.S. foreign policy objectives, ADF helps local groups work toward diagnosing and solving their own problems, hoping to improve micro and small enterprises, help economic growth, provide employment, preserve Africa's rich and fragile natural resources, and strengthen basic democratic values and local institutions. ADF also promotes community-based HIV/AIDS intervention programs; builds self-supporting, sustainable, local community development agencies to provide technical assistance and support to grassroots groups; develops new models for community investment; establishes partnerships with national and local governments, donor agencies, and the local private sector to encourage grassroots development; and works with American businesses and philanthropists to raise funds for grassroots development.

ADF's seven members are appointed by the President with Senate confirmation with two with 6-year terms, and all are unpaid.

CONTACT Address: ADF, 10th Floor, 1400 I Street, Washington, DC 20005; Phone: (202) 673-3916; Website: www.adf.gov.

AMERICAN BATTLE MONUMENTS COMMISSION (ABMC)

A small executive branch independent agency designed to commemorate services of American armed forces where they have served since April 6, 1917, when the United States entered World War I; establish memorial shrines including design, construction, operation, and maintenance of American military burial grounds in foreign countries; control design and construction by U.S. citizens and public and private organizations of American military monuments and memorial markers in foreign countries; and encourage sponsors of those markers and monuments to maintain them.

Created in 1923, ABMC administers, operates, and maintains 24 permanent American burial grounds, and 37 memorials, military monuments, and markers in foreign countries, as well as five memorials in the United States, excluding the World Ward II Memorial. Approximately 125,000 Americans are buried in these cemeteries from World War I, World War II, and the Mexican War. Nearly 6,000 persons are interred at the Mexico City National Cemetery and at the Corozal American Cemetery. Nearly 95,000 missing in action or buried at sea American military service people from the two world wars, and the Korean and Vietnam wars are commemorated on stone tablets. Others who died during the Korean conflict and in the demilitarized zone after that war are kept on a computer database at the Korean War Veterans Memorial in Washington, D.C.

ABMC keeps cemeteries at the following foreign locations: Flanders Field and Henri-Chapelle, Belgium; Aisne-Marne, Brittany, Epinal, Lorraine, Meuse-Argonne, Normandy, Oise-Aisne, Rhone, Somme, St. Mihiel near Thiaucourt, and Suresnes, France; Brookwood and Cambridge, England; Luxembourg; Manila, Philippines; Mexico City; Corozal, Panama; the Netherlands; North Africa; Sicily-Romano, Italy; North Africa; Guadalcanal and Hawaii; and New Guinea.

ABMC's 11 members are appointed by the president at his/her pleasure and are unpaid

CONTACT Address: Operations, ABMC, Courthouse Plaza II, Suite 500, 2300 Clarendon Boulevard, Arlington, VA 22201; Phone: (703) 696-6897; E-mail: operations@abmc.gov; Website: www.abmc.gov/.

AMTRAK

The catchy name for the National Railroad Passenger Corporation from the words *American* and *track*. Created by the Rail Passenger Service Act of 1970, the first Amtrak train service began with 25 employees on May 1, 1971, running from New York's Penn Station to Philadelphia, followed by a schedule of 184 trains serving 314 destinations. At its inception, Amtrak inherited somewhat decrepit railroad cars from failing passenger railroads, and has constantly worked to modernize passenger cars and locomotives. The food has even improved, with linen, china, and silver dining service on some routes.

Even-numbered trains travel north and east, and uneven-numbered trains travel south and west. Exceptions to this rule include the Surfliners, which use the opposite number system, some Empire Corridor Trains, and former Santa Fe Railroad trains originally numbered by their former operator.

Amtrak employs 22,000 people and experienced an increase in passengers following the September 11, 2001, attacks on the World Trade Center and the Pentagon. While an independent government corporation incorporated under the laws of the District of Columbia, Amtrak is always threatened by the budgetary chopping block, although its value became more obvious when Americans were afraid to fly in airplanes following the 2001 attacks. Amtrak also could perform a potentially valuable service in times of war, and is considered by some to be a military asset. The appropriation for Amtrak in 2002 was about 50 percent of that for fiscal year 1978, suffering a constant decrease in federal subsidy, but reducing its dependence on government support by improving its ratio of earned revenue to total costs.

Amtrak now serves more than 540 stations in 46 states, including 22,000 route miles and excluding Alaska, Hawaii, South Dakota, and Wyoming, the latter of which is served by Amtrak Thruway Motorcoaches. Amtrak owns more than 730 route miles, which amount to about 3 percent of the nation's total, and uses tracks owned by freight railroads in most parts of the United States except for the Boston-Washington, D.C., corridor. In 2002 Amtrak's 10 busiest stations were New York's Penn Station, Philadelphia, Washington, D.C., Chicago, Newark, Boston, Trenton, Los Angeles, Princeton Junction, and Baltimore. Amtrak contracts with 14 private railroads to operate Amtrak trains on those railroads' tracks. Under the contracts, the private companies are supposed to maintain the roadbeds and coordinate the flow of train traffic, both of which occur with varied degrees of success, with deference nearly always given to the owners' freight trains. Amtrak serves about 24 million passengers a year.

By contract, Amtrak provides commuter services for another 61.1 million people annually, including state and regional authorities such as Caltrain, Metrolink, and Coasters (California); Maryland Area Regional Commuter (MARC); Massachusetts Bay Transportation Authority

(MBTA); Shoreline East (Connecticut); and Virginia Railway Express (VRE).

Amtrak boasts the unusual Amtrak Customer Advisory Committee (ACAC), made up of passionate, dedicated passengers who volunteer to communicate customers' concerns, complaints, and suggestions to Amtrak senior managers. Members of the committee gather public input while riding across the country several times a year or as daily commuters between major cities.

CONTACT Address: Amtrak, 60 Massachusetts Avenue NW, Washington, DC 20002; Phone: (202) 906-3000 or (800) USA-RAIL; Website: www.amtrak.com.

APPALACHIAN REGIONAL COMMISSION (ARC)

Advocates for and as a partner of the people of Appalachia to create opportunities for self-sustaining economic development and improved quality of life. Established by Congress in 1965 to promote economic and social development in the then-impoverished and desperate Appalachian region, the commission includes the governors of the 13 Appalachian states and a presidential appointee who represents the federal government. The nucleus of the commission began in 1960 when the region's governors formed the Conference of Appalachian Governors to work together on the problems, taking their ideas and problems to President John F. Kennedy, who had been moved by what he saw during campaign trips to West Virginia. In 1963 President Kennedy formed what became the President's Appalachian Regional Commission (PARC). President Lyndon B. Johnson used the Kennedy PARC report to develop bipartisan legislation in Congress submitted in 1964 and passed in 1965.

The governors submit their state spending plans for each year, including projects they would like funded through ARC. Grassroots people participate through local development districts, which are multicounty organizations of which elected officials, business people, and other local leaders make up the boards. The Development District Association of Appalachia (DDAA) brings together local development districts (LDDs) to communicate needs upward to the governors. Successful programs have included development of geographic information systems (GIS); innovative and creative financing of infrastructure projects; strategic planning; and financial management.

ARC goals include developing a knowledgeable and skilled population, strengthening the region's infrastructure, creating a viable economic base, working on health care initiatives to create a healthy population through education and workforce training programs, highway construction, water and sewer system construction, leadership development programs, small business start-ups and expansions, and development of health care resources.

Specific ARC programs include Economic and Human Development Activities to create jobs through education, physical infrastructure building, civic and business development, and health care projects; Distressed Counties Program funds the region's poorest counties' projects; Entrepreneurship Initiative helps communities help entrepreneurs to start and expand local businesses; Telecommunications Program works to bring the information highway into the Appalachian region; Transportation Program works to give access to jobs, markets, health care, and education through the Appalachian Development Highway System; Research and Technical Assistance Program tracks emerging issues and economic trends in the region, evaluates programs, and funds research; J-1 Visa Waiver Program helps foreign health care workers work in Appalachian areas where there are insufficient numbers of health care workers; and Business Development Revolving Loan Fund Program works to create and keep jobs by giving funds for economic development projects. Two cochairs are appointed by the president with senate confirmation, and receive fulltime pay.

CONTACT Address: ARC, 1666 Connecticut Avenue NW, Suite 700, Washington, DC 20009-1068; Phone: (202) 884-7799; E-mail: info@arc.gov; Website: www.arc.gov.

ARCHITECTURAL AND TRANSPORTATION BARRIERS COMPLIANCE BOARD (ACCESS BOARD OR ACCESS)

An independent agency dedicated to furthering the rights and access for people with disabilities. The board develops and maintains accessibility requirements for buildings, transit vehicles, sidewalks, telecommunications equipment, and electronic and information technology; provides technical assistance and training on these standards and guidelines; and enforces accessibility standards for federally funded facilities.

The acts that ARC seeks to implement include the Architectural Barriers Act (1968) requiring access to facilities designed, built, altered, or leased with federal funds; the Rehabilitation Act, which created the board in 1973; the Americans with Disabilities Act, a civil rights law that prohibits discrimination on the basis of disability; the Telecommunications Act, which requires readily achievable access to new telecommunications and customer premises equipment; and the Rehabilitation Act Amendments (1978), which amended Section 508 of the Rehabilitation Act to ensure access to electronic and information technology in the federal government; authorized the board to establish minimum accessibility guidelines under the Americans with Disabilities Act; added 11 public members to be appointed by the president to the board for four-year terms for nominal pay.

ACCESS publishes Accessibility Guidelines and Standards and several other pieces helpful to people with disabilities and those who must conform to the guidelines and standards, such as the ADAAG checklist, the ADAAG manual for buildings and facilities, a series of manuals on ADAAG for transit vehicles, technical bulletins on ADAAG sections such as visual alarms and parking; Recreation Access; a review of ADAAG; Play Facilities; Outdoor Developed Areas; Passenger Vessels; and Public Rights-of-Way. Supplemental information is available on ATMs; Detectable Warnings; State and Local Government Facilities; Building Elements Designed for Children's Use; Over-the-Road Buses; Play Facilities; and Recreation Facilities.

CONTACT Address: The Access Board, 1331 F Street NW, Suite 1000, Washington, DC 20004-1111; Phone: (202) 272-0080 or (800) 872-2253; Fax: (202) 272-0081; E-mail: info@access-board.gov; Website: www.access-board.gov.

ARCTIC RESEARCH COMMISSION

Develops and recommends national Arctic research policy and a national Arctic research plan; reviews the president's budget request and reports to Congress; facilitates and coordinates Arctic research among government agencies; works with the governor of Alaska on Arctic research; and publishes and presents its annual report to the president and to Congress. Seven members. The commission is managed by an executive director, who is a career staff officer.

CONTACT Address: 4350 N. Fairfax Drive, Suite 630, Arlington, VA 22203; Phone: (703) 525-0111; Fax: (703) 525-0114; Website: www.uaa.alaska.edu/enri/arc_web.comm1.htm.

BROADCASTING BOARD OF GOVERNORS (BBG)

An independent, autonomous entity serving as an umbrella organization to bring together all U.S. nonmilitary government and government-sponsored international broadcasting services to promote American ideas of democracy and information worldwide. BBG was created by the 1998 Foreign Affairs Reform and Restructuring Act. More than 100 million people listen to, view, or access via the Internet BBG-dispensed information. BBG information vehicles include:

Voice of America broadcasts about American society in 53 languages around the world to 91 million people each week, except in western Europe and the United States. First broadcasting on February 24, 1942, VOA now reaches audiences on shortwave and medium wave from 22 IBB stations around the world and is rebroadcast through about 900 local affiliate stations around the world. All 53 language broadcasts are available on the Internet.

Radio Sawa is a 24-hour, seven-day-a-week Arabic language network carrying Western and Arabic pop music, news and news analysis, interviews, sports, and political and social issues. Radio Sawa originates in Washington, D.C., and goes out on medium wave (AM) and FM transmitters, digital audio satellite, short wave, and Internet.

Radio Farda or Radio Tomorrow in Persian is a combined effort of Radio Free Europe, radio Liberty (RFE/RL), and Voice of America and originates from Washington, D.C., and Prague, Czech Republic. Radio Farda carries Persian and Western music, and operates 24 hours a day with news twice an hour on medium wave, digital audio satellite, and on the Internet.

Radio Free Europe/Radio Liberty broadcasts to the former Soviet Union and Eastern Europe, as well as on Radio Free Iraq and RFE/RL Persian Service in 26 languages. RFE/RL broadcasts the American view of news, analysis, and current affairs.

Radio Free Asia broadcasts U.S. views of the world in Asia, including 10 languages to China, Tibet, Burma, Vietnam, Laos, Cambodia, and North Korea via shortwave and Internet.

Office of Cuba Broadcasting (Radio Marti and TV Marti) broadcasts the U.S. view of the news of Cuba and the world to Cuba in Spanish, 24 hours a day on medium wave and shortwave.

WORLDNET Television and Film Service broadcast American views of life, news, U.S. foreign and domestic policies, and magazines features 24 hours a day via satellite, broadcast outlets, cable systems, and direct-to-home satellite receivers.

International Broadcasting Bureau (IBB) oversees administration of several of the above, as well as maintains its Office of Engineering and Technical Services and the Office of Affiliate Relations. Each program is headed by a staff director. The five-person Board of Governors are presidential appointees with senate confirmation and some pay.

CONTACT Address: Broadcasting Board of Governors, 330 Independence Avenue SW, Washington, DC 20237; Phone: (202) 401-3736; Fax: (202) 401-6605; Website: www.bbg.gov/.

CENTRAL INTELLIGENCE AGENCY (CIA)

The Central Intelligence Agency is the American federal government's organization to acquire and analyze information useful in dealing with foreign nations and forces and to conduct clandestine operations overseas. Essentially, there are two arms to the agency: information gathering and integration on the one hand, and pro-active undercover actions at the direction of the president, although this is often stated in euphemistic terms that screen the agency's "cloak and dagger" function.

By its very nature the CIA and its activities remain "highly classified" and are revealed to a handful of executives and members of Congress required to oversee intelligence operations. The number of its employees is secret, but has been estimated to be in the neighborhood of 36,000, plus various people receiving payment for ferreting out information or acting as "moles" in for-

eign organizations, both governmental and private. The budget is obfuscated by including it in an intelligence budget item that has been over $27 billion annually.

The agency was instituted by the *National Security Act of 1947* proposed by President Harry S. Truman to provide an agency to gather and coordinate information to aid in the confrontation of the increasingly belligerent Soviet Union, known to have an extensive intelligence and undercover network in much of the world. Such an umbrella intelligence agency was urged by the first secretary of defense, James Forrestal, as the World War II alliance dissolved into the cold war. As laid out in the authorizing legislation, the CIA was primarily intended for intelligence (including nonpublic, confidential information) gathering in regard to foreign countries and subsequent analysis for the use of all federal agencies.

However, the agency was also given authority to conduct overseas intervention and espionage Officially, this was added to its menu in June 1948, by *National Security Council Directive No. 10/2,* approved by President Truman, which authorized clandestine subversive operations, including secret political and paramilitary activities. This was expansively interpreted as giving the CIA responsibility to "perform such other functions and duties related to intelligence affecting the national security as the National Security Council may from time to time direct." That was a provision in the directive to the CIA's immediate predecessor agency, the Central Intelligence Group, which existed briefly in 1946 and 1947.

As structured, the CIA reports to the NATIONAL SECURITY COUNCIL, which is chaired by the president, who gives orders to the agency. The term "functions and duties" have been broadly applied to include actions that originally combated the spread of communist influence and in recent years counteracted terrorists and governments inimical to American interests. President Truman insisted that the CIA should deal only with foreign problems and not be involved in domestic spying or acting as a secret police.

The resultant missions of the CIA are: (a) providing comprehensive foreign intelligence on all matters affecting national security, and (b) conducting counterintelligence, special activities, and "other functions" directed by the president. The more pro-active counterintelligence activities are usually conducted by "planning" groups, special task forces, or "centers" within particular areas of concern. Direct support for armed forces during and prior to actual conflicts (such as the tactical support in the 2003 war against Iraq) is provided by the *Office of Military Affairs,* which often involves actual tactical military action by special teams of CIA operatives.

Starting in 1961, the agency has produced a daily intelligence report, originally called the *National Intelligence Daily,* and since 1998, the *Senior Executive Intelligence Brief,* which is early morning reading for the president and other officials.

HISTORY

The CIA owes its heritage to the wartime Office of Strategic Services (OSS), headed by William "Wild Bill" Donovan, which not only collected and analyzed intelligence about the Allies' enemies, but also served as a no-holds-barred spy and espionage network. Of the eventual 12,000 OSS employees, many were brilliant free spirits, who could crack codes, drop by parachute behind the lines, bribe, steal, or blast as well as analyze the information gathered. They included such characters as Moe Berg, the major league catcher, who spoke seven languages, and Julia Child, who would gain fame as the TV guru of French cooking. Many of the top brass of the CIA for the following three decades were former OSS officials.

In 1950 the director, former general Walter Bedell Smith, reorganized the agency into the Office of National Estimates (led by the respected analyst Sherman Kent), the Office of Research and Reports (changed to the Directorate of Intelligence in 1952), and the Office of Current Intelligence to

prepare summaries for government policy makers. Reconnaissance by photography by U-2 planes, created to fly at extreme altitudes, began in 1956. Soon followed a small office in charge of automated gathering and other computer uses (1960), the office of National Photographic Interpretation in conjunction with the DEPARTMENT OF DEFENSE (1961), and the 24-hour-a-day *CIA Operations Center* (1963). The CIA's continued growth in importance and the construction of its giant headquarters in McLean, Virginia, across the Potomac River from Washington, occurred in the 1950s under Director Allen Dulles, brother of Secretary of State John Foster Dulles.

During the following 30 years there were several reorganizations. In 1973, under Director George H. W. Bush, the Board of National Estimates was replaced by experts who coordinated among various agencies in a more "hands-on" approach. The 1980's saw the creation of the Counterterrorism Center (1986), the Counterintelligence Center (1988), and the Counternarcotics Center (1989). In the 1990s inaugurated were the Persian Gulf Task Force, the Nonproliferation Center dealing with so-called weapons of mass destruction, the Balkan Task Force in regard to Yugoslavia and Kosovo, the African Great Lakes Task Force to gain intelligence on crises in Zaire, Rwanda, and Burundi, which were involved in a bloody tribal war, the Environmental Center, and the Office of Policy Support.

To expand and revive analytic training, the *Sherman Kent School for Intelligence Analysis* was formed in 1999, and the *CIA University* was established in 2002 to upgrade agent education.

Several functions were combined in 2001 to form the *Center for Weapons Intelligence, Nonproliferation and Arms Control (WINPAC)* to better react to foreign weapons threats. In response to the September 11, 2001, terrorist attacks, the *Office of Terrorism Analysis* was set up within the Counterterrorism Center.

But all has not been smooth sailing for the CIA. Particularly in the gray area of operational activities (as distinguished from the analytical) there have been embarrassing failures, and revelations of illegal activities or judgmental errors. These include the ill-fated CIA-devised plan to help Cuban dissidents overthrow Cuban president Fidel Castro in 1961 by an invasion of Cuba at the Bay of Pigs. There were equally bizarre anti-Castro ideas and assassination plots throughout the '60s, and the unfortunate involvement of former CIA agent Howard Hunt in the break-in of the Democratic offices in the Watergate complex in 1972. Adding to the agency's public relations woes was Pulitzer Prize–winning reporter Seymour Hersh's exposé in the *New York Times* in December 1974, revealing that the CIA had conducted undercover investigations of Americans participating in the anti–Vietnam War movement (which the CIA found free of subversive influences).

It was disclosed in 1984 that the CIA was continuing to give military and financial help to the contras (anti-leftist government guerrillas) in Nicaragua long after Congress had enacted a specific statute prohibiting such aid, which came to light when a CIA-operated supply plane crashed. This was followed by the so-called Iran-contra scandal involving the use of secret profits from arms sales to Iran to help fund the contras, in which CIA personnel were among the participants.

There were other illegal or ill-executed actions by zealots in the agency in attempting to remove or undermine left-wing governments. It was later admitted that in 1970 President Richard Nixon had ordered the CIA to make sure that Chile's left-wing president-elect Salvador Allende "never take office." The chief of staff of the Chilean army was fatally wounded in a botched attempt to kidnap Allende. (This is detailed in CIA Director William Colby's book *Honorable Men, My Life in the CIA*.) A CIA-assisted revolt against President Allende in 1973 resulted in Allende's murder (or forced suicide).

Participation in the "dirty" work of this nature has been curbed. Engaging in assassinations,

directly or indirectly, was specifically prohibited in 1981 by Executive Order 12333, and any covert action (such as surveillance or wiretaps) aimed at American citizens must be for a specific authorized purpose and requires senior approval. Nevertheless, the Iran-contra scandal took place three years later.

ORGANIZATION

The Central Intelligence Agency is headed by the director of central intelligence, who is appointed by the president and confirmed by the Senate. The hierarchy includes the *deputy director,* who assists the director and on occasion sits in for him. The deputy also does double duty as Director of the *Directorate of Intelligence.* Within the purview of that directorate are the *Counterterrorist Center, Crime and Narcotics Center, Weapons, Intelligence and Nonproliferation Center* (monitoring and analyzing weapons development throughout the world) *Counterintelligence Center, Information Operations Center,* and *Offices of Asian Pacific, Latin American and African Analysis, Near East and South Asian Analysis, Russian and European Analysis, Transnational Issues, Policy Support* and *Office of Collection Strategies and Analysis.* There is also an *associate director* for *intelligence for homeland security.*

Assistant directors administer the *Directorate of Intelligence,* the *Directorate of Science and Technology,* the *Directorate of Operations,* and the *Center for the Study of Intelligence.* All these officers are presidential appointees who are confirmed by the Senate. All of these high-ranking officials and the inspector general and general counsel of the CIA are appointed by the president.

The *Directorate of Intelligence* produces and disseminates the intelligence information while the Directorate of Operations is responsible for clandestine gathering of overseas intelligence. The daily administration of the agency is managed by the *executive director* with the assistance of the *Executive Board* composed of the heads of the five mission centers along with the chief financial officer, chief information officer, Security, Human Resources and Global Support Offices. The CIA's *Office of Public Affairs* handles public relations for the director, deals with the media, the public, and internally with CIA employees.

The CIA is not a policy-making agency, but carries out orders in the complex and sometimes mysterious world of intelligence, its collection, analysis, and at times active subversion of certain foreign forces. The agency operates upon orders of the National Security Council and the president.

Congressional oversight is provided by the Senate Select Committee on Intelligence and the House Permanent Select Committee. In 2003 Congress began to question CIA's abilities and the propriety of deemphasizing on-the-ground spies in favor of high-tech "intelligence" gathering, particularly after President George W. Bush referred to content in what turned out to be forged documents in a State of the Union Address in which he erroneously asserted that Iraq had tried to buy uranium from Niger.

CONTACT Address: CIA Headquarters, Route 123, McLean, Virginia, (neighborhood: Langley, hence HQ often referred to as "Langley"). Tours of the headquarters are not possible, but people can visit the CIA Museum and the Memorial Garden. Address: Central Intelligence Agency, Office of Public Affairs, Washington, DC 20505; Phone: (703) 482-0623 (7-5 Eastern time); Fax: (7-5), return Fax number requested; E-mail: see form on website; Website: www.cia.gov.

PUBLICATIONS AND INFORMATION FOR PUBLIC USE

The CIA publishes a great deal, including much historic material. For the lengthy list check www.cia.gov/publications. The CIA also maintains the *CIA Museum* at its headquarters, which contains a wealth of artifacts and a history of U.S. intelligence.

One of the best sources of current information on world governments is created and kept up by the CIA, which includes statistics on every nation and its government officials, including cabinet members. It can be readily accessed at www.cia.gov/publications/factbook/index.

CITIZENS' STAMP ADVISORY COMMITTEE

See U.S. POSTAL SERVICE, pp. 440–441.

COMMISSION OF FINE ARTS

Established by Congress in 1910, the Commission of Fine Arts is an independent commission that advises the federal and District of Columbia governments on art and architecture, and how they affect the American capital's appearance. It assesses public building projects as well as private residences and buildings adjacent to public buildings and grounds. Any builder, developer, or private citizen wishing to build in D.C. should contact the Commission of Fine Arts staff to find out if the project is under the commission's purview.

The commission also advises the United States Mint on coin and medal design, advises the American Battle Monuments Commission on war memorial design, advises the president and Congress on art questions when requested, advises the National Capital Planning Commission on lands to be selected for the National Capital park and parkway systems, advises the army on heraldic designs, and advises various entities on statues, fountains, and monuments on public land in D.C.

The Commission of Fine Arts runs the National Capital Arts and Cultural Affairs program, which gives grants to nonprofit cultural organizations of national stature that are located in D.C., and whose primary purpose is to perform or exhibit works of art in Washington. The commission is made up of seven members appointed by the president for four-year terms without compensation.

CONTACT Address: U.S. Commission of Fine Arts, National Building Museum, 401 F Street NW, Suite 312, Washington, DC 20002-2728; Phone: (202) 504-2200; Fax: (202) 504-2195; Website: www.cfa.gov.

COMMISSION ON SECURITY AND COOPERATION IN EUROPE (CSCE OR HELSINKI COMMISSION)

CSCE became an independent U.S. government agency in 1976 to monitor and encourage compliance with the Helsinki Final Act and other Organization for Security and Cooperation in Europe (OSCE) commitments. The commission helps form U.S. policy on the OSCE and helps execute that policy, partly by sending American delegations to OSCE meetings, and by keeping in contact with parliamentarians, government officials, nongovernmental organizations, and private individuals from OSCE member states.

Members include nine U.S. senators, nine members of the U.S. House of Representatives, and one member each from the departments of STATE, DEFENSE, and COMMERCE.

CSCE holds public hearings and briefings with expert witnesses on OSCE issues, publishes public reports and a monthly digest on OSCE developments and commission activities, and sends official delegations to OSCE meetings to address and assess democratic, economic, and human rights developments.

CONTACT Address: CSCE, 234 Ford House Office Building, 3rd and D Streets SW, Wash-

ington, DC 20515; Phone: (202) 225-1901; Fax: (202) 226-4199; Website: www.csce.gov/helsinki.cfm.

COMMISSION ON THE FUTURE OF THE U.S. AEROSPACE INDUSTRY

Established in 2001, creation of the commission was part of the Floyd D. Spence National Defense Authorization Act for fiscal year 2001. The original purpose of the commission was to study the future of the U.S. aerospace industry in the global economy, particularly pertaining to national security. Vice President Cheney linked the commission and the aerospace industry to American economic security.

The commission's mission is to develop and recommend public policy reforms to allow the U.S. aerospace industry to create superior technology, excel in the global marketplace, profit from investments in human and financial capital, benefit from coordinated and integrated government decision making, assure U.S. national security, and access the most modern infrastructure. The commission looks at budgets for aerospace research, development, and procurement; adequacy of the federal acquisition process; policies, procedures, and methods for financing and payment of government contracts; statutes and regulations governing international trade and the export of technology; taxation rules, especially current tax laws and practices and how they affect the aerospace industry's international competitiveness; programs to maintain the national space launch infrastructure; and programs to support science and engineering education.

Commissioners include six industry or public members appointed by Congress and six members appointed by the president.

CONTACT Address: Commission on the Future of the United States Aerospace Industry, 1235 Jefferson Davis Highway, Suite 940, Arlington, VA

22202; Phone: (703) 602-1515; Fax: (703) 602-1532; Website: www.aerospacecommission.gov.

COMMODITY FUTURES TRADING COMMISSION (CFTC)

Created as an independent agency by Congress in the 1974 Commodity Futures Trading Commission Act to regulate commodity futures and option markets in the United States, protecting investors against manipulation, abusive trade practices, and fraud.

The five commissioners are appointed by the president with senate confirmation for five-year terms. They are paid on the executive schedule.

CFTC regulates commodity exchange members' professional activities, public brokerage houses, commission-registered futures industry salespeople, commodity trading advisers, floor brokers and floor traders, and commodity pool operators. It maintains the rules by which a commodities exchange operates, monitors enforcement of the rules, reviews terms of proposed futures contracts, and registers companies and individuals who handle customers' funds or give advice on commodities trading.

The commission hopes to protect the public by requiring that customer funds be kept in bank accounts separate from accounts maintained by the trading firms for their own use, also requiring those firms to mark customer accounts at market value at the end of each trading day.

The commission has six operating units. The new *Division of Clearing and Intermediary Oversight* oversees derivatives clearing organizations, financial integrity of registrants, customer fund protection, stock-index margin, registration and fitness of intermediaries, sales practice reviews, National Futures Association activities, and foreign market access by intermediaries. The new *Division of Market Oversight* regulates trade execution facilities, including new registered futures exchanges and derivatives transaction execution facilities. This division also regulates market surveillance, trade practice reviews and investigations, rule enforcement, and review of product-related and market-related rule changes. The *Division of Enforcement* investigates and prosecutes alleged violations of the Commodity Exchange Act and the CFTC regulations, such as improper marketing of commodity investments. The *Office of the Chief Economist* gives economics advice to the commission such as policy analysis, economic research, expert testimony, education, and training. The *Office of the General Counsel* is the commission's legal adviser, representing it in appellate litigation and some trial cases such as bankruptcy proceedings involving futures industry professionals. It also advises on application and interpretation of the Commodity Exchange Act and other statutes. The *Office of the Executive Director* manages the agency, implements policy, and formulates the agency's budget.

CONTACT Address: CFTC, Three Lafayette Square, 1155 21st Street NW, Washington, DC 20581; Phone: (202) 418-5000; Fax: (202) 418-5521; Website: www.cftc.gov/. Regional offices: 525 W. Monroe Street, Suite 1100, Chicago, IL 60661; Phone: (312) 596-0700; Fax: (312) 596-0716. 4900 Main Street, Suite 721, Kansas City, MO 64112; Phone: (816) 931-7600; Fax: (816) 931-9643. 510 Grain Exchange Building, Minneapolis, MN 55415; Phone: (612) 370-3255; Fax: (612) 370-3257. Murdock Plaza, 10900 Wilshire Boulevard, Suite 400, Los Angeles CA; Phone: (310) 443-4700; Fax: (310) 443-4745. 140 Broadway, New York, NY 10005; Phone: (646) 746-9700; Fax: (646) 746-9938.

CONSUMER PRODUCT SAFETY COMMISSION (CPSC)

Created by Congress under the Consumer Product Safety Act in 1972, CPSC is an independent federal agency that works to keep the public safe and reduce risk of injury and death allegedly caused by consumer products. To accomplish these goals, the commission develops voluntary standards with pertinent industries ("voluntary" standards were the idea of President George W. Bush); issues and enforces mandatory standards or bans products if no standard would protect the public adequately; initiates recalls of products and arranges for their repair; conducts research on potential product hazards; informs and educates the public through media, state and local governments, and private organizations; responds to public inquiries and complaints; requires manufacturers to report defects in products; collects information and data on consumer product-related injuries; and maintains the Injury Information Clearinghouse.

The president appoints all three commissioners to be confirmed by the U.S. Senate for staggered seven-year terms, and the president designates the chair. They are paid based on the executive schedule.

CONTACT Address: CPSC, East-West Towers, 4330 East-West Highway, Bethesda, MD 20814; Phone: (301) 504-0580; Website: www.cpsc.gov.

COORDINATING COUNCIL ON JUVENILE JUSTICE AND DELINQUENCY PREVENTION

An independent entity created in the Juvenile Justice and Delinquency Prevention Act to coordinate all federal juvenile delinquency prevention programs, all federal programs and activities that detain or care for unaccompanied juveniles, and all federal programs that deal with missing and exploited children. The council also reviews reasons federal agencies take juveniles into custody and recommends improvements in federal practices and facilities that hold juveniles in custody. Amendments in 1992 to the original act added responsibilities including coordination of federal programs with local and state programs. Pro-

grams have included career training for at-risk youth, focus on juveniles and the death penalty, child maltreatment and delinquency, school safety, and elimination of accidental injury and violence.

One of the council's products is the National Juvenile Justice Action Plan, which focuses on working with state and local entities to ensure immediate and appropriate sanctions and treatment services; improving public safety by prosecuting serious and violent juveniles in criminal court; decreasing juvenile criminal activity such as gang offenses, illegal firearms, and illicit drug use; breaking the cycle of domestic violence, victimization, abuse, and neglect; creating positive opportunities for children and adolescents; helping local communities communicate information to all citizens; evaluating programs and practices to see if they make a difference; and promoting public awareness of juvenile justice issues.

Members include the attorney general, nine ex-officio members, and nine nonfederal members who are juvenile justice practitioners. The ex-officio members are the attorney general; the secretaries of health and human services, labor, education, and housing and urban development; the administrator of the Office of Juvenile Justice and Delinquency Prevention; the director of the Office of National Drug Control Policy; the CEO of the Corporation for National Service; and the commissioner of the Immigration and Naturalization Service.

CONTACT Address: Office of Juvenile Justice and Delinquency Prevention, U.S. Department of Justice, 800 K Street NW, Washington, DC 20531; Phone: (202) 616-3567; Fax: (202) 307-2093; Website: http://ojjdp.ncjrs. org.

CORPORATION FOR NATIONAL AND COMMUNITY SERVICE

Consolidated by President George W. Bush as the USA Freedom Corps to coordinate volunteers in peaceful service activities in the United States and provide services the president wanted removed from the country's budget. Bush asked each volunteer to serve two years in public or community service in three organizations: the Senior Corps, Americorps, and Learn to Serve America.

The Senior Corps asks 55 and older Americans to serve in RSVP, Foster Grandparents, and Senior Companions. Retired and Senior Volunteer (RSVP) volunteers help local police departments with safety patrols, work on environmental projects, and tutor adults. Foster Grandparents serve as one-on-one tutors and mentors to young people, and Senior Companions help house-bound seniors strive for independence within their own homes.

Americorps members are specialized volunteers selected by local and national nonprofit organizations such as the American Red Cross, Habitat for Humanity, City Year, Teach for America, and Boys and Girls Clubs of America. Americorps "volunteers" receive an education award of $4,725 to go toward higher education expenses, and about half the volunteers receive a $9,300 living allowance and health benefits annually. Americorps focuses on eliminating poverty by helping those in need with the basics by building homes for low-income families, helps local groups preserve the environment, and tutors students and other people to help them have a fair chance in life. Due to President George W. Bush's tax cut and $400 billion budget deficit, he slashed Americorps' funding by about 50 percent in 2003.

Learn and Serve America gives grants to schools, colleges, and nonprofits to help get students involved in community service, as well as funds community service and service-learning to students, teachers, schools, and community groups.

Several presidents have instigated innovative volunteer service programs, including Franklin D. Roosevelt's Civilian Conservation Corps (CCC), designed to get young people to serve six to 18 months to restore parks, revitalize the economy, and support their families and them-

selves from 1933 to 1942; President John F. Kennedy established the PEACE CORPS in 1961; President Lyndon B. Johnson started VISTA (Volunteers in Service to America) and a National Teacher Corps in his war on poverty; the original Retired and Senior Volunteer Program (RSVP), Foster Grandparent Program, and the Senior Companion Program were created in the '60s; California governor Jerry Brown established the California Conservation Corps in 1976; President Jimmy Carter founded the Young Adult Conservation Corps in 1978; President George H. W. Bush founded the Office of National Service and the Thousand Points of Light Foundation to encourage volunteer service; and President Bill Clinton signed into law the National and Community Service Trust, creating AmeriCorps and the Corporation for National and Community Service. The 15 members of the board of directors are appointed by the president with senate confirmation with staggered terms and no compensation.

CONTACT Address: Corporation for National and Community Service, 1201 New York Avenue NW, Washington, DC 20525; Phone: (202) 606-5000, TTY: (202) 565-2799; Website: www.nationalservice.org/.

DEFENSE ADVANCED RESEARCH PROJECTS AGENCY (DARPA)

Established in 1958 to counteract the Soviet Union's launching of its basketball-sized satellite Sputnik, which beat the United States in the technological race. Since its inception, DARPA's focus has been on developing and using state-of-the-art technology to assure the United States leads the world in military capabilities and to prevent technological surprises by U.S. enemies.

Intended as the outside-the-box technological think tank reporting to the DEPARTMENT OF DEFENSE, DARPA now enjoys some autonomy and employs or funds top scientists and engineers in industry, universities, government laboratories, and research and development centers. All of its projects are end-specific and meant to be completed, but may be renewed as a new project.

DARPA's technical offices have an increasingly defensive orientation in the 2000s. The *Advanced Technology Office* researches and develops projects in maritime, communications, special operations, command and control, and information assurance and survivability to support military operations potentially or actually in conflict. ATO adapts commercial and emerging technologies to military use. The *Defense Sciences Office* works on medical approaches to biological warfare defense, biology, materials, and advanced mathematics. The *Information Awareness Office* develops information technologies to counter threats by developing total information awareness to be used in national security warnings and national security decision making, as well as preemptive action. The *Information Processing Technology Office* invents networking, computing, and software technologies to ensure U.S. military superiority.

DARPA's *Information Exploitation Office* develops sensor and information system technology to apply to battle space information, target technologies, command and control, information management, target perfection, and avoidance of collateral damage (killing of innocents). The *Microsystems Technology Office* works to integrate electronics, photonics, and microelectromechanical systems to protect the United States from biological, chemical, and information attacks through mobile command and control, combined manned and unmanned warfare, and adaptive military planning and execution. The *Special Projects Office* develops systems solutions to counter real and emerging threats. The *Tactical Technology Office* does advanced military research, focusing on system and subsystem approaches to aeronautic, space, and land systems development, as well as embedded processor and control systems.

CONTACT Phone: (571) 218-4323; Website: www.darpa.mil/.

DEFENSE NUCLEAR FACILITIES SAFETY BOARD

Created by Congress in 1988, the Defense Nuclear Facilities Safety Board is an independent oversight organization that gives advice to the secretary of energy to ensure protection of the public health and safety from the United States's nuclear weapons complex, which includes production, stockpile facilities, and clean ups.

During the cold war nuclear arms race, the DEPARTMENT OF ENERGY focused on design, manufacture, testing, and maintenance of U.S. nuclear weapons. Currently, the nuclear weapons "complex" is working on cleaning up sites and facilities contaminated by nuclear production and waste and dismantling nuclear weapons to achieve arms control objectives, maintaining a smaller stockpile of nuclear weapons, and storage and disposal of excess fissionable materials. The board's role may change again if the administration of President George W. Bush succeeds in getting legislation passed to design and, eventually, build small nuclear weapons.

The board is charged with reviewing and evaluating content and implementation of DOE health and safety standards as they apply to the design, construction, operation, and decommissioning of defense nuclear facilities. The board also must recommend specific changes the board believes should be implemented, review the design of new defense nuclear facilities before construction begins, review changes to older nuclear facilities, and review changes to protect the public's health and safety. The board also conducts investigations and studies, issues subpoenas, holds public hearings, gathers information, and establishes DOE reporting requirements. The five board members are appointed by the president with senate confirmation, and are paid on the executive schedule.

CONTACT   Address: Defense Nuclear Facilities Safety Board, 625 Indiana Avenue NW, Suite 700, Washington, DC 20004; Phone: (202) 694-7000 or (800) 788-4016; Website: www.dnfsb.gov.

DEFENSE SECURITY SERVICE (DSS)

Formerly known as the Defense Investigative Service (DIS), DSS conducts personnel security investigations and provides industrial security products and services throughout the United States and Puerto Rico. It also educates and trains DEPARTMENT OF DEFENSE and other agency leaders.

DSS's *Personnel Security Investigations Program* special agents do background investigations on Department of Defense military, civilian, and outside contractor personnel. The Industrial Security Program watches over already cleared contractors' facilities while doing contract work, and helps management improve their security. The *Defense Industrial Security Clearance Office* processes, issues, and maintains industrial security facility and personnel clearances from its offices in Columbus, Ohio.

The *Security, Education, and Awareness Program's Defense Security Service Academy* trains nearly 10,000 students within the Department of Defense and the defense industry each year in the nuances of core security disciplines including counterintelligence and information systems security.

Established in 1993, the DSS *Counterintelligence (CI) Office* works to spread CI information throughout the workforce, increase awareness of CI throughout DSS and the defense industry, and help its customers recognize and report possible foreign intelligence collection activities (spying) by watching for suspicious events in a "threat environment" and reporting alleged inci-

dents. DSS focuses on counterintelligence questions such as: "Who is targeting us? What is being targeted? What methods of operation are being used?"

CONTACT   Address: Defense Security Service, 601 Tenth Street, Fort Meade, MD 20755; Phone: (703) 325-9471; Website: www.dss.mil/.

DELAWARE RIVER BASIN COMMISSION (DRBC)

Created in 1961 by President John F. Kennedy and the governors of Delaware, New Jersey, Pennsylvania, and New York as a regional body with the force of law to oversee a unified approach to managing the Delaware River system over usual political boundaries. The DRBC's creation brought together 43 state agencies, 14 interstate agencies, and 19 federal agencies as equal partners in a planning, development, and regulatory agency.

DRBC engages in water quality protection, water supply allocation, regulatory review and permits, water conservation, watershed planning, drought management, flood control, and recreation. The Delaware River is the longest undammed river east of the Mississippi River, running 330 miles from the confluence of its east and west branches at Hancock, New York, to the mouth of Delaware Bay. About 17 million people rely on Delaware River Basin water for drinking and industrial use. Three reaches of the Delaware River are included in the National Wild and Scenic Rivers System. The Delaware Estuary, which includes Delaware Bay and the tidal reach of the Delaware River, is part of the National Estuary Program, a project that strives to protect nationally significant estuaries.

DRBC receives funding from the signatory parties, project review fees, water use charges, fines, and federal, state, and private grants. Members include the governors of the four basin states and one federal appointee of the president, and the governors appoint their alternates.

CONTACT Address: P.O. Box 7360, West Trenton, NJ 08628-0360; Phone: (609) 883-9500; Fax: (609) 883-9522; Website: www.state.nj.us/drbc/over.htm.

ENVIRONMENTAL PROTECTION AGENCY (EPA)

America's principal national agency charged with coordinating, promoting, and managing federal efforts to control pollution and prevent depredation of the nation's share of the planet in the modern industrial age. Subject to the political as well as physical winds, public and private pressures, and the constant growth of population and the waste people create, EPA (the common name) has struggled to keep air, water, and land cleaner, improve people's health, prevent future harm, and stimulate research in the field of environmental protection.

Tackling this daunting task are 18,000 employees, of whom more than half are engineers, scientists, and other environmental protection specialists, and numerous others are lawyers and experts in computers, finances, and public affairs. The agency operates 17 laboratories and 10 regional offices in addition to its national headquarters in Washington, D.C.

As the leading governmental agency in the field of environmental protection, EPA works with state and local governments, industries, and other federal agencies to obtain as much cooperation, coordination, and where possible either mandatory or voluntary compliance with standards of quality EPA is authorized to develop. It also encourages state and local responsibility for monitoring and enforcing compliance with national standards. If national standards should be violated, EPA can issue penalties, sanctions, and other efforts to achieve compliance.

HISTORY

EPA was established in July 1970, by an act of Congress supported by President Richard M. Nixon. This was in response to the increasing awareness that the air, water, and land were all being increasingly contaminated, which caused cumulative permanent damage to the planet and public health. It had also become obvious that the existing scattered nature of responsibilities for environmental protection, to the extent they existed, made it impossible to mount a coordinated effort.

It was anticipated that new criteria were needed to establish baseline standards for protection to develop scientific methodology to combat ecological dangers, to clean up the worst cases (by means of the "Superfund," which provides money to clean up identified sites), and to make the public, states, and industries sensitive to the depredation of the Earth. In the first three decades of its existence EPA built up a network of research facilities, regional offices, and administrative structures to fulfill the goals of the original legislation.

Despite the belief that environmental protection is universally popular, and that all citizens of the United States want clean air, clean water, limits on radiation, protection against poisons, reasonable disposal of solid waste, and scientific advances in all these areas, EPA has become highly political, subject to sharp changes in direction and philosophy with each new president. One reason for this politicization is that not only the director of EPA, but also the administrators of each subject office are appointed by the president with Senate confirmation. While the technical aspects in each area are generally managed by the associate directors, who are career specialists, the philosophic thrust is in the control of political appointees.

This was especially evident with the shift from the administration of President Bill Clinton to the administration of George W. Bush. In general President Clinton favored tougher regulations to protect the environment, to develop new methods, and to set higher standards (such as minimum percentages of pollution or contamination), although some of the most ardent conservationists occasionally complained that Clinton was too willing to compromise to reach an agreement with private enterprise. Carol Browner, EPA director in the Clinton administration, was considered a vigorous protector of the environment.

President Bush's basic position was that tough regulations or increasing the level of protection was hampering American business and the economy. Therefore, EPA was instructed to concentrate on "voluntary" compliance with environmental protections, and in many cases repeal or weaken existing regulations, such as the Marine Mammal Protection and Endangered Species Acts. In regard to polluting emissions in 2001, EPA took the position that its less stringent rules had federal preemption over tough standards set by some states. In the case of California, this led to a lawsuit by that state against EPA, challenging preemption in favor of the state's higher standards. Christine Todd Whitman, appointed EPA administrator by President George W. Bush, was an advocate of "voluntary compliance," but resisted relaxing standards on contamination of water and the atmosphere, with only limited success. She announced her resignation in May 2003.

William Reilly, EPA administrator for President George H. W. Bush (1989–93), explained the political dilemma: "The EPA has no natural constituency. It is a job where the administration antagonizes the oil industry one week, the auto industry the next, the farmers the next. Your hope is you don't antagonize more than one the same week. You don't really make political points for the president or the administration."

ORGANIZATION

EPA is directed by the *administrator* appointed by the president and confirmed by the Senate. The administrator is supported by a *deputy* *administrator,* and several *assistant administrators,* each responsible for a different subject matter office, all of whom are appointed by the president, with Senate approval. Other presidential appointees are the *chief financial officer,* the *general counsel,* and the *inspector general.*

There are also the *secretariat* (broken down into the *Office of Executive Support* and the *Office of the Executive Secretary*) staffed by career professionals directed by a *chief of staff,* and several small offices and boards with specific responsibilities who report to the administrator. Also part of the Administrator's immediate hierarchy are the *associate administrator for policy, economics and innovation,* the *associate administrator for communications, education and media relations,* and the *associate administrator for congressional intergovernmental relations.*

Administrative Offices

Administrative Offices are: *Office of Environmental Information, Administration and Resource Management,* which includes the *Office of Information Collection* and the *Office of Information Analysis and Access; Office of Enforcement and Compliance Assurance,* which is divided into the *Office of Compliance,* and the *Office of Federal Activities;* and *Office of International Activities.*

Activities Offices

The activities offices oversee and direct the programs and goals in the EPA's lengthy list of programs, and are divided into Office of Water, Office of Solid Waste and Emergency Response, Office of Air and Radiation, Office of Prevention, Pesticides and Toxic Substances, and Office of Research and Development.

OFFICE OF WATER (Phone: (202) 564-5700): Includes the *Office of Wastewater Management,* the *Office of Science and Technology,* the *Office of Wetlands, Oceans and Watersheds,* and the *Office of Ground Water and Drinking Water.* The prime task is to direct a coordinated effort to keep America's waters clean and safe for drinking, swimming, and fishing, setting water quality standards and effluent guidelines, and providing technical aid for improved water quality;

OFFICE OF SOLID WASTE AND EMERGENCY RESPONSE (Phone: (202) 260-7902): Includes the *Office of Federal Facilities Restoration and Reuse,* the *Office of Technological Innovation,* the *Office of Chemical Emergency Preparedness and Prevention,* the *Office of Solid Waste,* and the *Office of Emergency and Remedial Response.* This office sets standards and regulations for control of solid waste disposal (including underground storage tanks), manages the Superfund toxic waste cleanup program, and develops public participation in these efforts;

OFFICE OF AIR AND RADIATION (Phone: (202) 564-7400): Includes the *Office of Atmospheric Programs,* the *Office Air Quality Planning and Standards,* the *Office of Transportation and Air Quality,* and the *Office of Radiation and Indoor Air Quality.* This office establishes and maintains national standards for air quality (including emissions standards) and allowable pollution levels, as well as technical assistance and training to protect air quality by individuals, enterprises, states, and local governments;

OFFICE OF PREVENTION, PESTICIDES AND TOXIC SUBSTANCES (Phone: (202) 260-7902): Includes the *Office of Pesticide Programs* and the *Office of Pollution Prevention and Toxics.* This office establishes safe levels of pesticide residues in food, evaluates and regulates industrial chemicals and pesticides to protect public health, promotes pollution prevention, disseminates public information on toxic substances, and, ideally, develops a national strategy for control of toxics.

OFFICE OF RESEARCH AND DEVELOPMENT (Phone: (202) 564-6620): This office conducts and sponsors research on means to meet the challenge of the most serious threats to the environment and exposure to pollution. It also acts as a source of information to other government agencies and the general public on remedial

efforts in regard to pollution and environmental damage. The office manages a program entitled *Science To Achieve Results (STAR),* which awards research grants to scientists and students in environmental science.

OTHER OFFICES AND BOARDS: There are several other offices that report directly to the administrator and deputy administrator, and are directed by career officials. These are *Office of Civil Rights, Office of Cooperative Environmental Management, Office of Small and Disadvantaged Business Utilization, Office of Children's Health Protection, Office of Administrative Law Judges* (four career judges who conduct hearings on complaints of various sorts), and the *Environmental Appeals Board.*

Programs

Acid Rain Program: Responsible for reducing emissions that cause acids to be added to the atmosphere and then be included in rainfall. Acid rain knows no national boundaries and can blow across the border, particularly to and from the United States and Canada.

AirNow: Also known as the *Ozone Mapping Project,* this program provides current air pollution data (such as location and intensity of air pollution), the public health and environmental effects of air pollution, and the means to reduce such pollution and protect public health.

American Heritage Rivers: Helps communities restore and revitalize rivers and waterfronts, including coordinating federal agencies, as well as economic, environmental, and historic preservation programs in assisting the riparian towns and cities.

Antimicrobial Information Hotline: Provides direct telephonic answers on issues concerning antimicrobial pesticides, health, safety, registration of pesticides, and pesticide laws and regulations. Phone: (703) 308-0127.

Asbestos Program: Follows up on the regulation of asbestos (previously used in much construction) pursuant to the *Toxic Substances*

Control Act. Breathing of substantial amounts of asbestos can be a cause of cancer.

Beach Watch: Provides federal grants to state, local, interstate, and tribal agencies for programs to monitor and post public notices for America's beaches. This is the best source for information on beach closings and conditions such as dangers from rip tides and sharks.

Brownfields: Encourages private and local government cooperation to prevent, assess, clean up, and reuse "brownfields," which are lands that through contamination, pollution, or misuse are virtually dead. EPA maintains a home page on the topic.

Capacity Assurance: EPA works to assure there is adequate capacity to manage hazardous wastes generated in each state.

Chemical Registry System: A central system for chemical identification information, including those chemicals listed in EPA regulations, data systems, and those of interest according to other sources and publications.

Chemical Information Collection and Data Development: Gathers health and safety information on chemical substances, and requires testing and control of exposure to the chemicals.

Clean Energy: This program identifies means to produce energy with minimal detrimental effect and encourages the use of technologies that provide renewable "green" power. It provides technical assistance in developing clean air strategies. It also disseminates clean air information through networking between the government and private industry, and gives positive recognition to environmental leaders employing clean energy practices.

Clean Lakes Program: Information source on quality of various lakes, and suggested technical resources for their management, such as clean up and facilities.

Climate Leaders Partnership: A voluntary industry-government partnership to encourage businesses to develop long-term strategies to reduce the effect of climate change (global warming). This is significant because President George W. Bush has questioned the existence of global warming and suggested the issue should be studied for 10 or more years.

Coastal and Ocean Programs: Information source on ocean dumping, discharges, and efforts to remove marine debris.

Combined Heat and Power Partnership (CHP): A voluntary program to foster the generation of electric power through smaller and distributed plants, which are efficient and have low levels of pollution into the air, instead of large inefficient generators, which have a high level of emissions. Such smaller and local plants can cogenerate electricity and also heat the commercial, institutional, and industrial buildings in the neighborhood.

Combustion: This program is intended to increase the safety and reliability of the burning of hazardous wastes in incinerators, boilers, and industrial furnaces.

Corrective Action Program for Hazardous Waste Professionals: EPA has permitted about 3,700 facilities to manage corrective action in cases of accidents, spills, or activities that have released hazardous wastes into the soil, water, or air.

Design for the Environment: It provides technical advice to businesses on environmental protections to be included in the design and redesign of products, processes, technical systems, and management.

Drinking Water and Ground Water Protection: A data bank on water issues.

Endangered Species Protection: Provides protection from pesticides to endangered species.

Energy Star Programs: Helps private enterprise to develop modern energy-efficient equipment.

Environmentally Preferable Purchasing: A government-wide program that promotes purchase of "environmentally preferable" products and services by all federal agencies.

Enviroene: Maintains a website providing data bases on pollution prevention, compliance assurance, and enforcement of antipollution regulations and laws.

Fish Consumption Advisories: A data bank covering fish consumption advisories throughout the United States and Canada, including those for every state and province, tribes, and the federal governments.

Food Quality Protection Act of 1996 Implementation Program: An effort to increase the safety of America's food supply. This program does not deal with the relative value of different food products.

Great Lakes National Program: A partnership of federal, state, local, tribal, and industry entities in an integrated, ecosystem method to protect, maintain, and restore the water quality and biological integrity of the Great Lakes.

Green Chemistry: A partnership with the chemical industry to promote pollution prevention and chemical production and use that is ecologically sound.

Green Power Partnership: A voluntary program aimed at reducing environmental impact of electricity generation, particularly through increased use of renewable energy. In return for increasing the percentage of renewable energy, used by an organization—commercial, nonprofit, and public—EPA provides such a participant technical information and positive public recognition. Renewable energy includes such methods of power generation as solar power, wind, and water.

International Pesticide Activities: Acts in conjunction with other countries to improve the safety of pesticides worldwide.

Lead Programs: Provides information on the federal lead poisoning prevention program, including use of lead-based paints. The DEPARTMENT OF HOUSING AND URBAN DEVELOPMENT (HUD) has specific lead reduction and amelioration programs.

Mixed Waste: Coordinates the management of waste that contains radioactive and/or other hazardous materials.

Mobile Sources: Activities to reduce pollution from emissions by motor vehicles, including lawnmowers, boats, and railroad locomotives.

National Estuary Program: An effort to restore the ecological health of estuaries (often with standing water or with polluting tourism) while still supporting recreational and business activity.

National Pesticide Information Center: Provides information on pesticide products, pesticide poisonings, and environmental chemistry. It also lists state agencies that regulate pesticides and links to their websites.

New Chemicals: Reviews premanufacture submissions and identifies new substances that require regulatory action.

Oil Spill Program: Provides information on EPA programs intended to prevent, anticipate, and respond to oil spills that affect U.S. inland waters and coastlines.

Ozone Layer Protection: Data dissemination on the science of ozone depletion and regulations designed to protect the ozone layer.

Pay-As-You-Throw: Provides information in regard to payment for solid waste disposal computed on the amount of waste generated.

Pesticide Environmental Stewardship: A voluntary partnership with commercial pesticide users to implement pesticide pollution protection and environmental risk.

Pesticide Programs on Worker Safety: A partnership between EPA and state agencies to protect workers from pesticide poisoning risks.

Pollutant Load Allocation: An information source on EPA's limits on Total Maximum Load (TMDL) under section 303(d) of the Clean Water Act.

Pollution Prevention: Urges practices that reduce or eliminate creation of pollutants.

Product Stewardship: EPA has urged manufacturers, retailers, and users to share responsibility for and negative environmental impact of a product.

Radiation Programs: Coordinates efforts to protect public against radiation.

Recycling Non-Hazardous Waste: EPA provides information and publications about effective recycling of nonhazardous materials such as newspapers, aluminum cans, and other commonly recycled items. This will encourage and assist local agencies and/or private enterprises to develop recycling programs and cause the general public to make recycling a habit.

Screening Information Data Sets (SIDS): Makes initial assessment of the potential hazards of selected chemicals.

SmartWay Transport: A partnership with major truck and rail transportation companies with the goal of reducing pollution and greenhouse gas emissions from trucks and locomotives.

Sunwise Schools: Provides K-6 teachers with materials teaching children about the means to protect themselves from overexposure to solar radiation.

Superfund: One of the key activities of EPA, the Superfund finances the clean up of hazardous waste sites throughout the country. EPA is responsible for locating, investigating, and removing the worst hazardous waste sites. The eventual target is to do away with all dangerous hazardous waste locations. Many have been found to cause high levels of cancer, asthma, and other diseases. EPA has been criticized by the slow rate of removal of such hazardous wastes.

Toxic Release Inventory: A data bank about toxic chemicals that are being manufactured, transported, used, and/or released into the environment.

TSCA Biotechnology: Reviews new chemicals before they are introduced in the marketplace.

Underground Storage Tanks: EPA has been fairly aggressive in pressing for underground storage tanks (particularly in gas stations) that leak or otherwise pollute the surrounding area. The costs of mitigation usually fall on the property owner.

Voluntary Diesel Retrofit Program: Encourages truck fleets to install pollution-reducing devices and use cleaner-burning diesel fuel.

Volunteer Monitoring: Develops methodology for governmental agencies and members of the general public to monitor, assess, and report on the health of America's water resources, primarily through the Internet.

Waste Minimization: Works to limit the generation and release of the most persistent bioaccumulative and toxic chemicals contained in hazardous wastes.

Waste Prevention: Provides information on the efforts of municipalities to reduce their solid waste and how control of solid waste benefits society.

Wastewater Management: Includes a range of programs to use wastewater efficiently, which can be accessed.

WasteWi\$e: A voluntary program urged upon municipalities to reduce the amount of solid waste produced.

Water Efficiency: Voluntary water conservation suggested in EPA publication *Water Alliances for Voluntary Efficiency (WAVE)*. This publication is the principal effort of the water conservation program.

Water Quality Standards, Criteria and Methods: This program develops standards, criteria, guidelines, and limitations for EPA's Office of Water.

Watershed Management: Encourages solutions to water quality and ecosystem preservation at watersheds (runoff from higher levels via rivers, streams, and human-created methods)

Wetlands Program: Encourages local agencies, states, and individual owners to act to protect and restore the nation's wetlands, which are crucial to bird migration, restoring fish and mammal populations, and preventing overfill or pollution in bays, streams, rivers, lakes, and other sensitive shorelines.

Research Programs and Data Bases

Office of Research and Development: Maintains a partnership with the academic scientific community by means of research grants and fellowships.

Environmental Monitoring and Assessment Program: A research system to develop the means needed to monitor and assess the status and of national ecological resources.

Microbiology Home Page: This is a website of data on microbiology developed by EPA. It is maintained by the National Exposure Research Laboratory.

National Center for Environmental Assessment: Primarily a database of hazards to health and ecological risk assessments.

National Center for Environmental Research: An easy-access database on research funding opportunities, research programs, and projects.

National Environmental Computing Center: Operates a supercomputer for computing and communications to support major research, improved science, and educational programs.

Office of Science and Technology—Office of Water: Responsible for setting standards, criteria, guidelines, limitations, and standards required by the Clean Water Act and the Safe Drinking Water Act.

Research Offices

EPA operates research laboratories at numerous locations:

National Exposure Research Laboratory, Research Triangle Park, North Carolina; *National Exposure Research Laboratory—Ecosystems Research Division,* Athens, Georgia; *National Exposure Research Laboratory—Environmental Sciences Division,* Las Vegas, Nevada; *National Health and Environmental Effects Research Laboratories* in Research Triangle Park, North Carolina; Narragansett, Rhode Island; Gulf Breeze, Florida; Duluth, Minnesota; and Corvallis, Oregon; *National Risk Management Laboratories* in Cincinnati, Ohio; Ada, Oklahoma (Subsurface Protection and Remediation Division); Edison, New Jersey (Water Supply and Resources Division; Research Triangle Park, North Carolina (Air Pollution Prevention and Control Division);

National Vehicle and Fuel Emissions Laboratory, Ann Arbor, Michigan; *National Air and Radiation Environmental Laboratory,* Montgomery, Alabama; *Radiation and Indoor Environments National Laboratory,* Las Vegas, Nevada.

CONTACT Address: 1200 Pennsylvania Avenue NW, Washington, DC 20460-0001, and 10 regional offices (see below); Phone: (202) 260-2090; General information: (202) 564-4455; Special information: air and radiation: (202) 564-7400; water: (202) 564-5700; solid waste and emergency response: (202) 260-4610; prevention, pesticides, and toxic substances: (202) 260-2902; research and development: (202) 564-4620; Website: www.epa.gov.

Regional Offices

The first point of contact with EPA by members of the public with questions, complaints, or assistance is most commonly the nearest regional office, of which there are 10:

Region I (Massachusetts, Connecticut, Maine, New Hampshire, Vermont): One Congress Street, Suite 1100, Boston, MA 02114; Region II (New York, New Jersey, Puerto Rico, Virgin Islands): 290 Broadway, New York, NY 10007; Region III (Pennsylvania, District of Columbia, Delaware, Maryland, Virginia, West Virginia): 1650 Arch Street, Philadelphia, PA 19103; Region IV (Alabama, Florida, Georgia, Kentucky, Mississippi, North Carolina, South Carolina, Tennessee): 61 Forsyth Street SW, Atlanta, GA 30303; Region V (Illinois, Indiana, Michigan, Minnesota, Ohio, Wisconsin): 77 West Jackson Boulevard, Chicago, IL 60604; Region VI (Texas, Arkansas, Louisiana, New Mexico, Oklahoma): 1445 Ross Avenue, Suite 1200, Dallas, TX 75202; Region VII (Iowa, Kansas, Nebraska, Missouri): 901 North Fifth Street, Kansas City, KS 66101; Region VIII (Colorado, Montana, North Dakota, South Dakota, Utah, Wyoming): 999 18th Street, Denver, CO 80202; Region IX (California, Arizona, Nevada, Hawaii, Guam, American Samoa): 75 Hawthorne Street, San Francisco, CA

94105; Region X (Washington, Oregon, Idaho, Alaska): 1200 Eighth Avenue, Seattle, WA 98101.

EQUAL EMPLOYMENT OPPORTUNITY COMMISSION (EEOC)

Congress created the Equal Employment Opportunity Commission in Title VII of the Civil Rights Act of 1964, and the commission's mission has evolved through several new laws and amendments. A brief history of the commission's background includes the following significant steps:

President Franklin D. Roosevelt signed an executive order that prohibited government defense contractors from engaging in employment discrimination based on race, color, or national origin, but the order contained no enforcement authority. Roosevelt's motivation was to make sure no strikes or demonstrations would disrupt military supplies production as the country was preparing for World War II.

In July 1948, President Harry S. Truman ordered desegregation of the armed forces and required "equality of treatment and opportunity for all persons in the armed services without regard to race, color, religion or national origin." Actual integration of the armed forces was not accomplished until 1952, when the Korean conflict began.

President John F. Kennedy issued an executive order in March 1961 that prohibited federal government contractors from discriminating in employment based on race and established the President's Committee on Equal Employment Opportunity, giving the committee the authority to impose sanctions for violations of the executive order.

In June 1963, Congress passed the Equal Pay Act to counter sex-based wage discrimination by demanding that men and women doing equal work should be paid the same wage.

The Civil Rights Act of 1964 prohibited discrimination in private conduct and public accommodations, governmental services, and education. Title VII of the act prohibited employment discrimination based on race, sex, color, religion, or national origin and created the Equal Employment Opportunity Commission (EEOC). Title VII applied to private employers, labor unions, and employment agencies, and prohibited discrimination in recruitment, hiring, wages, assignment, promotions, benefits, discipline, discharge, layoffs, and every aspect of employment.

The EEOC is a five-member, bipartisan commission appointed by the president and confirmed by the Senate, of whom no more than three may be from the same political party.

President Lyndon B. Johnson issued an executive order in 1965 making nondiscrimination and affirmative action requirements to do business with the federal government. In 1967 Congress passed the Age Discrimination in Employment Act to protect people between 40 and 65 years of age from discrimination in employment.

The Equal Opportunity Act of 1972 further improved Title VII's effectiveness with several amendments as follows: gave the EEOC litigation authority, with the option of suing nongovernment respondents; made educational institutions subject to Title VII; made state and local governments, as well as the federal government and its agencies, subject to Title VII; the number of employers under Title VII was increased by moving the number of employees in a business subject to the law downward from 25 to 15; and gave complaining parties more time to file legal charges.

The Rehabilitation Act of 1973 prohibited the federal government as an employer from discriminating against qualified individuals with disabilities, and the Pregnancy Discrimination Act of 1978 made discrimination based on pregnancy unlawful. The Civil Service Reform Act of

1978 abolished the U.S. Civil Service Commission and gave its functions to the then newly established Office of Personnel, the Merit Systems Protection Board, and the EEOC, the latter of which got responsibility for enforcing antidiscrimination laws that apply to the civilian federal workforce and coordinating all federal equal employment opportunity programs.

President Jimmy Carter signed the Reorganization Plan No. 1 of 1978, which abolished the Equal Employment Opportunity Coordinating Council and transferred its responsibilities to EEOC. EEOC received the charge to develop uniform enforcement standards to apply throughout government.

In 1986 Congress approved the Age Discrimination in Employment Amendments, eliminating the upper age cap of 70 from the Age Discrimination Employment Act. President George H. W. Bush signed the Americans with Disabilities Act of 1990, the first comprehensive civil rights law for people with disabilities.

EEOC works first through conciliation, conference discussion, and persuasion, and lawsuits may follow if these efforts fail. It works also through education and technical assistance, publishes data on the employment status of minorities and women, and works with schools, unions, private industry, and government agencies to eliminate discrimination in employment.

CONTACT Address: 1801 L Street NW, Washington, DC 20507; Phone: (202) 663-4900, TTY: (202) 663-4494 or to be connected directly to the nearest of 52 field offices, call toll free (800) 669-4000 or TTY (800) 669-6820; Website: www. eeoc.gov.

EXPORT-IMPORT BANK OF THE UNITED STATES (EX-IM BANK)

An independent agency that helps arrange export financing of U.S. goods and services, theoretically not competing with private lenders. Ex-Im Bank takes credit risks and finances exports to countries that may pose economic risks to American companies where private lenders cannot or will not take those risks. Ex-Im claims to take credit risks to help American export companies compete with companies subsidized or financed by other governments.

To meet these goals, Ex-Im Bank provides working capital guarantees, export credit insurance, and loan guarantees and direct loans to finance buyers, with 85 percent of Ex-Im's transactions helping small businesses.

Recent efforts to help more small business exporters include better financing facilities and services; increased value of facilities and services to the export community; and increased dollar amounts of authorizations that help small business exports.

Ex-Im Bank partners with lenders, insurance brokers, cities and states, U.S. trade agencies, and private companies. Members include five paid directors appointed by the president with Senate confirmation. There is also a 15-member advisory committee of business people and a Sub-Sahara Africa Advisory Committee made up of people doing business in that region.

CONTACT Address: Export-Import Bank of the United States, 811 Vermont Avenue NW Washington, DC 20571; Phone: (202) 565-3946 or (800) 565-3946; E-mail: info@exim.gov, Africa eximAfrica@exim.gov, project and structured finance projectfinance@exim.gov. Regional and satellite offices: Suite 617, 5600 NW 36th Street, Miami, FL 33166; Phone: (305) 526-7425; Fax: (305) 526-7435. Suite 2440, 55 West Monroe Street, Chicago, IL 60603; Phone: (312) 353-8081; Fax: (312) 353-8098. Suite 585, 1880 S. Dairy Ashford II, Houston, TX 77077; Phone: (281) 721-0465; Fax: (281) 679-0156. Suite 1670, 1 World Trade Center, Long Beach, CA 90831; Phone: (562) 980-4580; Fax: (562) 980-4590. Room 911, 811 Vermont Avenue NW, Washington, DC 20571; Phone: (202) 565-3940; Fax:

(202) 565-3932. Satellite offices: Suite 1001, 101 Park Center Plaza, San Jose, CA 95113; Phone: (408) 271-7300; Fax: (408) 271-7307. Suite 305, 3300 Irvine Avenue, Newport Beach, CA 92660; Phone: (949) 660-1688; Fax: (949) 660-8039.

FARM CREDIT ADMINISTRATION

An independent financial regulatory agency created by President Franklin D. Roosevelt's executive order on March 27, 1933, as part of the New Deal. The agency, governed by three board members appointed by the president and confirmed by the Senate, regulates and examines banks, associations, and related entities that make up the Farm Credit System to protect the public's interest and those who borrow from Farm Credit institutions or invest in Farm Credit securities. The Farm Credit institutions the Farm Credit Administration examines include Farm Credit Banks, Agricultural Credit Bank, Production Credit Associations, Agricultural Credit Associations, and Federal Land Credit Associations, as well as organizations owned by Farm Credit lending institutions and the National Consumer Cooperative Bank (National Cooperative Bank).

The Farm Credit Association Board approves rules and regulations, examines, regulates, and oversees reporting by Farm Credit institutions, and establishes the policies that govern the Farm Credit Administration. Members include three full-time members who are appointed by the president for six-year terms with advice and consent of the Senate, and also serve as the board of the Farm Credit System Insurance Corporation. Meetings are published in the *Federal Register.*

The Farm Credit Administration manages the regulations established by the Farm Credit Act of 1971 under which Farm Credit institutions operate. The administration has the power to issue cease-and-desist orders, levy civil monetary penalties, remove Farm Credit institutions' officers and directors, and establish financial and operating reporting requirements. FCA examines all system institutions; enforces safe and sound banking practices, federal statutes, and FCA regulations; issues and amends charters for system institutions, develops regulations, reviews legal issues, and works to resolve litigation; handles borrower-related problems and complaints; and runs the fiscal, personnel, and human resources of the agency. When an institution violates regulations, the administration may become involved in that institution's management to correct an unsafe or unsound practice or when it assumes conservatorship of an institution.

The Farm Credit Administration's operating funds come from assessments collected from the institutions it regulates and examines, and not from Congress.

The Agricultural Credit Act of 1987 established the Federal Agricultural Mortgage Corporation (Farmer Mac), part of the Farm Credit System, which promotes development of a secondary market for agricultural real estate and rural housing loans, gives guarantees for payment of principal and interest on securities, and represents in obligations backed by groupings of real estate loans.

CONTACT Address: 1501 Farm Credit Drive, McLean, VA 22102-5090; Phone: (703) 883-4000; Fax: (703) 734-5784; Website: www.fca.gov.

FEDERAL ACCOUNTING STANDARDS ADVISORY BOARD (FASAB)

Publishes and distributes accounting principles for federal entities that report accounts. FASAB's publications are available in print or on their Website, www.fasb.org.

CONTACT Address: FASAB, c/o General Accounting Office, 441 G Street NW, Washington, DC 20548; Phone: (202) 512-7352.

FEDERAL COMMUNICATIONS COMMISSION (FCC)

The Federal Communications Commission (FCC) is an independent federal government agency that reports directly to Congress. Established by the Communications Act of 1934, FCC regulates interstate and international communications by radio, two-way radio, television, wire, satellite, and cable, and is responsible for development and operation of all broadcast services and rapid, efficient nationwide telephone and telegraph services, as well as international services for Americans at reasonable rates. Especially following September 11, 2001, FCC takes responsibility for use of communications to promote safety as part of the national defense.

The five commissioners are appointed by the president and confirmed by the Senate for five-year terms. Only three members may belong to the same political party, and none may have a financial interest in any commission-related business.

FCC has six bureaus and 10 staff offices that process license applications and other filings, consider and analyze complaints, conduct investigations, develop and implement regulatory programs, and take part in hearings.

ORGANIZATION

CONSUMER & GOVERNMENTAL AFFAIRS BUREAU: Educates and informs consumers on telecommunications goods and services and coordinates telecommunications policy with industry and other governmental agencies at the federal, tribal, state, and local levels; represents the commission on consumer and government committees, working groups, task forces, and at conferences; oversees the Consumer/Disability Telecommunications Federal Advisory Committee and the Local and State Government Advisory Committee; and works to resolve informal complaints through mediation.

CONTACT Phone: (888) 225-5322.

ENFORCEMENT BUREAU: Enforces the commission's rules, orders, and authorizations, as well as the Communications Act. It investigates and tries to resolve complaints of acts or omissions of common carriers (wireless, wireline, and international); acts or omissions of noncommon carriers under Title II of the Communications Act; accessibility of people with disabilities to communications services and equipment when a formal complaint is filed; noncompliance with the Emergency Alert System, lighting and marking radio transmitting towers, and pole attachment regulations; noncompliance with the children's television programming commercial limits and cable televisions; and unauthorized construction and operation of communications facilities and false distress signals.

CONTACT Phone: (888) 225-5322.

INTERNATIONAL BUREAU: Represents the commission in international and satellite matters; develops and runs procedures and programs to regulate international telecommunications facilities and services and licenses satellite operations under its jurisdiction; monitors compliance with authorizations and licenses it grants and takes action with appropriate bureaus and offices to enforce conditions; provides advice and technical assistance to U.S. trade officials on telecommunications trade agreements; and works toward international coordination of spectrum allocation and frequency and orbital assignments to minimize international radio interference that involves U.S.-held licenses.

CONTACT Phone: (202) 418-0437 or (888) 225-5322.

MEDIA BUREAU: Regulates AM and FM radio and television broadcast stations, as well as Multipoint Distribution (cable and satellite), multichannel video programming, and Instructional

Television Fixed Services. It conducts proceedings on rules and rulemaking on the legal, engineering, and economic facets of electronic media services; reviews and resolves waiver petitions, declaratory rulings and adjudications; and processes applications for authorization, assignment, transfer, renewal of media services, including AM, FM, television, and cable television service. The area of greatest significance to the public are television and radio licensing, rules of conduct, limitations on multiple ownership in market areas, and public service programming. While public benefit and potential monopolies in markets are often in conflict, and public hearings are held, the quality of programming does not always answer the 1960s criticism by early Commissioner Newton Minow that TV is a "vast wasteland."

CONTACT Phone: (202) 418-2600 or (800) 225-5322.

WIRELESS TELECOMMUNICATIONS BUREAU: Oversees PCS and cellular phones, pagers, and two-way radios, as well as radio needs of businesses, local and state governments, public safety service providers, aircraft and ship operators, and some individuals. Commercial wireless services include cellular phones, pagers, personal communications (public safety, microwave, aviation, and marine services), specialized mobile radio, air-to-ground, and exchange telecommunications services. This bureau acts for the commission occasionally in regulation and licensing of communications common carriers and ancillary operations for licensing wireless telecommunications services and facilities. It works to offer choice, opportunity, and fairness in the business of wireline communications; examines U.S. wireline telecommunications needs and promotes development and availability of wireline communications; promotes investment in wireline communications; reviews and coordinates orders, programs, and actions within other government agencies; implements law and treaties on use of radio for the safety of life and property at sea and in the air; projects the demand for existing and possible new communi-

cations requirements; and processes applications and licensing for said services.

CONTACT Phone: (202) 418-0600 or (888) 225-5322.

WIRELINE COMPETITION BUREAU: Oversees rules and policies involving telephone companies that provide interstate and some intrastate telecommunications services to the public through the use of wire-based transmission facilities (corded and cordless telephones); promotes investment in wireline telecommunications and infrastructure; and works with other bureaus and offices to ensure consistent use and regulation of wireline telecommunications.

CONTACT Phone: (202) 418-0600 or (888) 225-5322; Address: FCC, 445 Twelfth Street SW, Washington, DC 20554; Phone: (888) 225-5322; Website: www.fcc.gov.

FEDERAL DEPOSIT INSURANCE CORPORATION (FDIC)

Established by the Banking Act of 1933 in response to the many bank failures during the Great Depression in which thousands of Americans lost their life savings, the FDIC was created to insure bank and thrift deposits, currently up to the legal limit of $100,000 per account. FDIC's funding comes from insurance premiums on deposits held by insured banks and savings associations, and from interest on the required investment of the premiums in U.S. government securities. FDIC has five board members, which include an appointive director, the comptroller of the currency, the director of the Office of Thrift Supervision, and two others appointed by the president and confirmed by the Senate, with no more than three from the same political party.

FDIC actually insures about $3.2 trillion of bank and thrift deposits in the United States Banks that pay premiums to the Bank Insurance Fund while savings associations pay their premiums to the Savings Association Insurance Fund, based on each institution's level of capitalization and potential risk to its insurance fund.

FDIC examines about 5,500 state-chartered commercial savings banks that are not members of the Federal Reserve System. For deposit insurance gauging purposes, FDIC may also examine FDIC-insured institutions for safety, soundness, and compliance with regulations of the institution. Examinations are conducted on-site as well as off-site through analysis of computer data, checking compliance with consumer laws such as the Truth in Lending Act, the Home Mortgage Disclosure Act, the Equal Credit Opportunity Act, the Fair Housing Act, and the Community Reinvestment Act, as well as for safety and soundness—all on behalf of the consumer.

When a bank or savings association fails, it usually closes and FDIC becomes receiver. FDIC must resolve the closed institution in a way least costly to FDIC, which often means finding a prosperous institution to take control of the failed one. If such a takeover entity cannot be found, FDIC pays depositors the amount of their insured funds (up to $100,000), likely the business day after the closing. Depositors of funds exceeding the insured limit in a failed bank receive partial payment for their uninsured funds.

Other functions performed by FDIC regarding state nonmember banks in its insurance, supervisory, and receivership role include approval or disapproval of mergers, consolidations, and acquisitions; approval or disapproval of banks' proposals to open and operate a new branch, close a branch, or move its main office from one location to another; approve or disapprove of requests to engage as principal in activities that are not permissible for national banks; issue enforcement actions, including cease-and-desist orders, for specific violations or practices requiring corrective action; and review ownership changes or changes in the control of a bank.

CONTACT Address: FDIC, 550 Seventeenth Street NW, Washington, DC 20429; Phone: (202)

393-8400; Website: www.fdic.gov. Regional offices: Suite 1600, 1201 W. Peachtree Street NE, Atlanta, GA 30309; Phone: (404) 817-1300. Suite 3500, 500 W. Monroe Street, Chicago, IL 60661; Phone: (312) 382-7500. Suite 1900, 1910 Pacific Avenue, Dallas, TX 75201; Phone: (214) 754-0098. Suite 1200, 2345 Grand Boulevard, Kansas City, MO 64108. 4th Floor, 20 Exchange Place, New York, NY 10005; Phone: (917) 320-2500. Suite 2300, 25 Ecker Street, San Francisco, CA 94105; Phone: (415) 546-0160.

FEDERAL ELECTION COMMISSION (FEC)

Created as an independent agency by the Federal Election Campaign Act of 1971, FEC administers and enforces the Federal Election Campaign Act (FECA), which governs financing of federal elections. FEC makes campaign finance information and rules available, including limits and prohibitions of some contributions and campaign expenditures, and oversees public funding (matching funds) of presidential elections. FEC requires public disclosure of campaign finances.

The six members are appointed by the president, confirmed by the Senate, and serve six-year terms. No more than three commissioners can be from the same political party, and four votes are required for any official commission action.

FEC certifies federal campaign payments to primary candidates who qualify for funds, general election nominees, and national nominating conventions. It audits campaign funds from the federal government, and may require repayment to the U.S. Treasury if a candidate, campaign committee, or independent political advocate organization violates campaign expenditure laws and regulations.

FEC requires regular (mainly quarterly) campaign finance reports of contributions and expenditures and publishes them in public records (and the Internet) usually within 48 hours after reporting.

CONTACT Address: FEC, 999 E Street NW, Washington, DC 20463; Phone: (202) 694-1100 or (800) 424-9530, TTY: (202) 219-3336; Website: www.fec.gov.

FEDERAL LABOR RELATIONS AUTHORITY (FLRA)

An independent agency established by the Civil Service Reform Act of 1978 to establish policies and guidance to federal labor-management relations by resolving disputes under and ensuring compliance with Title VII of the Civil Service Reform Act of 1978, also known as the Federal Service Labor-Management Relations Statute. FLRA also administers the law that protects federal employees' rights to organize, engage in collective bargaining, and join labor unions and organizations of their own choosing. It also decides appropriateness of bargaining units, runs representation elections, prescribes criteria, and resolves issues on granting consultation rights to labor unions for internal agency policies and government-wide rules and regulations.

FLRA is a quasi-judicial body with three full-time members appointed for five-year terms by the president with advice and consent of the Senate. Selected by the president, the FLRA chair also serves as chair of the Foreign Service Labor Relations Board. FLRA now combines the functions of three agencies, including the authority, the Office of General Counsel, and the Federal Service Impasses Panel. FLRA also oversees the Foreign Service Impasse Disputes Panel, and the Foreign Service Labor Relations Board, both created within FLRA by the Foreign Service Act of 1980.

FLRA adjudicates disputes, decides cases concerning negotiability of collective bargaining agreement proposals, appeals of unfair labor practices and representation petitions, and some exceptions to grievance arbitration awards. The authority works with unions and government agencies to help the parties understand their rights and responsibilities according to the statute and strives to help them work better together.

FLRA's general counsel investigates allegations of unfair labor practices, and files and prosecutes unfair labor practice complaints before the authority when appropriate.

The Federal Services Impasses Panel consists of seven presidential appointees who serve part-time and strives to resolve impasses between federal agencies and members of federal employee unions in negotiations over conditions of employment under the Federal Service Labor-Management Relations Statute, the Federal Employees Flexible and Compressed Work Schedules Act, and the Panama Canal Act of 1979. The panel has authority to recommend or take action to resolve the impasse when bargaining and mediation fail.

The Foreign Service Labor Relations Board has three members appointed by the chair. The board administers the labor-management relations program for Foreign Service Employees in the U.S. Information Agency, the Agency for International Development, and the DEPARTMENT OF STATE, the DEPARTMENT OF AGRICULTURE, and the DEPARTMENT OF COMMERCE.

The Foreign Service Impasse Disputes Panel was created by the Foreign Service Act of 1980 and has five part-time members appointed by the chair of the Foreign Service Labor Relations Board, who is also the chair of the FLRA. The Disputes Panel tries to resolve impasses on conditions of employment between federal agencies and Foreign Service employees in U.S. AID, the U.S. Information Agency, Department of State, Department of Agriculture, and Department of Commerce.

CONTACT Address: 607 Fourteenth Street NW, Washington, DC 20424-0001; Phone: (202)

482-6560; Website: www.flra.gov. Regional offices: Suite 701, 285 Peachtree Center Avenue, Atlanta, GA 30303-1270; Phone: (404) 331-5212. Suite 1500, 99 Summer Street, Boston, MA 02110-1200; Phone: (617) 424-5730. Suite 1150, 55 West Monroe, Chicago, IL 60603-9729; Phone: (312) 353-6306. Suite 926, 525 Griffin Street, Dallas, TX 75202-5903; Phone: (214) 767-4996. Suite 100, 1244 Speer Boulevard, Denver, CO 80204-3581; Phone: (303) 844-5224. Suite 220, 901 Market Street, San Francisco, CA 94103-1791; Phone: (415) 356-5000. Suite 910, 800 K Street NW, Washington, DC 20001; Phone: (202) 482-6700.

FEDERAL MARITIME COMMISSION (FMC)

Established by the Reorganization Plan No. 7 of 1961, the Federal Maritime Commission regulates shipping and foreign commerce of the United States transported on water, makes sure U.S. international trade is open to all nations on fair and equitable terms, and protects the country from unauthorized activity among maritime commerce of the United States. FMC surveils steamship conferences and common carriers by water; reviews agreements subject to the Shipping Act of 1984; enforces laws and regulations against discriminatory acts and other practice by shippers, carriers, and others subject to shipping statutes; and makes sure carriers have adequate assets and insurance to handle financial responsibilities of indemnifying passengers.

FMC regulates shipping under the Shipping Act of 1984, the Merchant Marine Act (1920), the Foreign Shipping Practices Act of 1988, and the Merchant Marine Act (1930). The commission has five members appointed to five-year terms by the president with advice and consent of the Senate. Only three members may be of the same political party, and the president names one of the commissioners as chair. The chair actually serves as chief executive and administrative officer of the agency.

FMC reviews agreements under the Shipping Act of 1984's Section 5, including conference, inter-conference, cooperative working agreements among common carriers, terminal operators, and other people and entities subject to the shipping statutes. It also monitors for compliance with maritime law, rules, orders, and regulations.

The commission monitors availability and accuracy of electronic tariff publications of common carriers doing foreign commerce with the U.S., and considers special permission applications to avoid tariff requirements. It receives and reviews filings of confidential service contracts between shippers and ocean common carriers; monitors publication of essential terms of those service contracts; administers passenger indemnity provisions requiring ship owners and operators to have certificates demonstrating financial responsibility to pay judgments for personal injury or death or to refund fares if trips are cancelled; reviews potential violations of shipping statutes and rules and takes action or refers matters to other governmental agencies; conducts investigations and hearings and adjudicates formal complaints under the Administrative Procedure Act; publishes and distributes rules and regulations to interpret, enforce, and ensure compliance with shipping and other statutes by common carriers; initiates and administers programs to force compliance with shipping statutes, by such means as field investigations of shippers' activities, conferences, terminal operators, freight forwarders, passenger ship operations, rate analyses, and economic reviews of trade conditions including current and potential competition; investigates foreign government and foreign carrier practices that already or could adversely affect American shipping trade; and with the DEPARTMENT OF STATE works to eliminate discriminatory practices by foreign governments against U.S.-flag-bearing ships and to promote equal dealing between the United States and trading partners.

In investigating activities of ocean common carriers, ocean transportation intermediaries, shippers, ports and terminals, and others, the *Bureau of Enforcement* looks into alleged violations such as illegal rebating; false descriptions or false declarations of cargo; illegal or unfiled agreements; abuses of antitrust immunity; unlicensed OTI operations; carrying untariffed cargo; unbonded passenger vessel operations; and other consumer abuses including failure to carry out transportation obligations resulting in cargo delays and financial losses for shippers. Phone: (202) 523-5783, 523-5860.

The *Bureau of Consumer Complaints and Licensing* licenses ocean transportation intermediaries; sets policies and guidelines for bonding ocean transportation intermediaries; certifies owners and operators of passenger vessels in the United States market to show financial responsibility to pay off liability due to nonperformance of voyages or death or injury to passengers; responds to consumer complaints and inquiries; and oversees alternative dispute resolution program including meditation. It works to eliminate problems resulting from delay or mishandling of shipments; to recover funds wrongly collected by industry entities; to help ease problems incurred in international movement of household goods; to communicate to cruise vessel operators consumer complaints about operators' services; to adjudicate small claims; and to mediate disputes. Phone: license and bonding: (202) 523-5818, consumer complaints and conflict resolution: (202) 523-5807.

The *Bureau of Trade Analysis* monitors carrier activity and commercial conditions of U.S. liner trades, identifies and tracks competitive, commercial, and economic activity in each major U.S. trade, and reviews rates of foreign government-owned or -controlled carriers. Phone: (202) 523-5796.

CONTACT Address: 800 North Capitol Street NW, Washington, DC 20573-0001; Phone: (202) 523-5707; Website: www.fmc.gov. Area representatives: Room 320, 839 South Beacon Street, San Pedro (Los Angeles), CA 90731; Phone: (310) 514-4905; Fax: (310) 514-3931. Room 705, 909 SE First Avenue, Miami, FL 33131; Phone: (305) 536-4316; Fax: (305) 536-4317. Room 303, 4223 Canal Street, New Orleans, LA 70130; Phone: (504) 589-6662; Fax: (504) 589-6663, JFK International Airport Building 75, Room 205B, New York, NY 11430; Phone: (718) 553-2228; Fax: (718) 553-2229. Suite 100, South Nevada Street, Seattle, WA 98134; Phone: (206) 553-0221; Fax: (205) 553-0222.

FEDERAL MEDIATION AND CONCILIATION SERVICE (FMCS)

The Federal Mediation and Conciliation Service (FMCS) was created as an independent agency in 1947 as an element of the Labor-Management Relations Act of 1947, also known as the Taft-Hartley Act, to prevent or minimize labor-management disputes and their effect on the free flow of commerce by providing mediation, conciliation, and voluntary arbitration. President Harry S. Truman appointed Cyrus S. Ching as FMCS's first director in 1948.

Congress enacted the Landrum-Griffin Act (Labor Management Reporting and Disclosure Act) in 1959, establishing a bill of rights for union members to sue their union, have a voice in union affairs, and control of dues increases. The Supreme Court handed down "The Steelworker's Trilogy," giving full support to the arbitration process. President John F. Kennedy's director, William E. Simkin, pledged FMCS's full cooperation with the Association of Labor Mediation Agencies, a group of state and municipal mediation agencies.

President Richard M. Nixon's director, W.J. "Bill" Usery, created an Office of Arbitration Services, and an Arbitration Services Advisory Committee, made up of 12 labor relations experts and arbitrators, to advise on arbitration policy and procedures, as well as an Office of

Technical Services to develop techniques for dispute prevention.

In a 1975 landmark move, Congress passed Public Law 93-531 to create the Alternative Dispute Resolution Service to mediate a 100-year-old land dispute between the Hopi and Navajo Indian tribes in Arizona. Then in 1978 Congress expanded FMCS's role to mediate disputes beyond the private sector and work in the federal government as well, with further extension to the U.S. POSTAL SERVICE in 1979.

Currently FMCS's headquarters are in Washington, D.C., but most of its mediation activities are closer to the customers in field offices around the country.

DEPARTMENTS AND FUNCTIONS

Access to Neutrals: A registry of qualified private-sector mediators, lawyers, and others to resolve employment, public policy, or multiparty regulatory negotiation disputes whose résumés and qualifications can be accessed to bring these neutrals in to resolve a dispute.

Arbitration and Notice Processing: Works to resolve disagreements over interpretation of collective bargaining agreements through voluntary arbitration, resulting in a final and binding decision.

Education and Training: Develops training and education programs for employees and the labor-management community.

FMCS Institute: Offers classes in collective bargaining, conflict resolution, and arbitration.

International Dispute Resolution Services: Fill requests from friendly foreign governments' agencies and institutions for labor and nonlabor relations conflict resolution services. In these cases, FMCS provides training, systems design, and other technical assistance for collective bargaining and labor mediation to help other countries develop better labor-management relations. The International Labor Education in Action program works in Argentina, Brazil, Mexico, Panama, and Uganda currently. International

Dispute Resolution in Action works currently with Azad Kashmir, Bosnia-Herzegovina, the former Yugoslavia, Indonesia, Lithuania, Latvia, South Africa, South Korea, and Thailand. Within the *Dispute Resolution and Conflict Management* Office, departments include Collective Bargaining, which focuses on mediation assistance in contract negotiation disputes between employers and their unionized employees, sometimes through third-party neutrals; Dispute Resolution System Design, which develops customized systems for better management of conflict and resolutions; Workplace Mediation provides services to resolve disputes between employers and employees on equal employment opportunity, age discrimination, and other issues outside collective bargaining; Grievance Mediation strives to resolve workplace grievances before arbitration; and Public Policy and Negotiated Rule Making addresses mediation needs of government agencies by encouraging inclusive rule- and regulation-making processes.

Preventive Mediation: Strives to break down traditional barriers to create better working relationships through Alternative Bargaining Processes such as interest-based bargaining; Contract Administration Training, which includes translating negotiated agreements from language to practice to teach stewards and supervisors how to work together; Custom Training and Workshops and Group Facilitation conduct customer-designed dispute resolution training programs; Interpersonal Communications works on and teaches communication techniques to use in building labor-management relationships; Labor-Management Partnership Building; Organizational Development works to understand and teach awareness and understanding of the nature of both labor and management; and Repairing Broken Relationships trains labor and management in strategic planning and process to repair damaged relationships.

CONTACT Address: FMCS, 2100 K Street, Washington, DC 20427; Phone: (202) 606-8100; Website: www.fmcs.gov. Regional offices: 16th

Floor, 1 Newark Center, Newark, NJ 07102; Phone: (973) 645-2200. Suite 472, 401 West Peachtree Street NW, Atlanta, GA 30308; Phone: (404) 331-3995. Suite 100, 6161 Oak Tree Road, Independence, OH 44131; Phone: (216) 522-4800. Suite 3950, 1300 Godward Street, Minneapolis, MN 55413; Phone: (612) 370-3300. Room 550, 7677 Oakport Street, Oakland, CA 95621; Phone: (510) 273-0100.

FEDERAL MINE SAFETY AND HEALTH REVIEW COMMISSION (FMSHRC)

An independent and impartial adjudicative agency that gives administrative trial and appellate review of legal disputes under the Federal Mine Safety and Health Amendments Act of 1977, less formally known as the Mine Act. The DEPARTMENT OF LABOR regulates health and safety in U.S. mines, with federal mine inspectors of the Mine Safety and Health Administration (MSHA), enforcing DOL regulations by issuing citations and orders to mine operators. The commission deals mostly with civil penalties against mine operators and reviews whether alleged safety and health violations occurred as well as the appropriateness of proposed penalties. They also review orders to close a mine, miners' charges or complaints of safety related discrimination, and miners' requests to be paid after a mine is closed down by a closure order.

The commission has five members appointed by the president for six-year terms and confirmed by the Senate, that provide appellate review. The commission's administrative law judges decide cases at the trial level. Review by the commission of an administrative law judge's ruling requires two commissioners to vote for such a review.

CONTACT Address: FMSHRC, 601 New Jersey Avenue NW, Suite 6000, 1730 K Street NW, Washington, DC 20006-3867; Phone: (202) 434-9900; Fax: (202) 434-9944; Website: www.fmshrc.html. 1244 Speer Boulevard, Room 280, Denver, CO 80204; Phone: (303) 844-5267; Fax: (303) 844-5268.

FEDERAL RETIREMENT THRIFT INVESTMENT BOARD (FRTIB)

Established by the Federal Employees' Retirement System Act of 1986 as an independent agency to run the Thrift Savings Plan (TSP), which gives federal employees the chance to save for their retirement through the system, augmenting their Social Security and the Civil Service Retirement System's Basic Annuity. TSP is a tax-deferred contribution plan similar to 401(k) plans. The five-member board is appointed by the president and runs the agency and manages the Thrift Savings Fund's investments.

CONTACT Address: 1250 H Street NW, Washington, DC 20005; Phone: (202) 942-1600; Fax: (202) 942-1676; Website: www.frtib.gov or www.tsp.gov.

FEDERAL TRADE COMMISSION

The Federal Trade Commission was created in 1914 as part of the bipartisan progressive reform movement during the administration of President Woodrow Wilson. Its prime goals are consumer protection from unfair or deceptive business practices, and ensuring a competitive market free of monopolistic means to restrict competition. As an element of its efforts to further these goals, it makes economic analyses available to federal, state, and local governmental agencies, and conducts consumer educational programs.

FTC has substantial powers and authority to prohibit unfair trade practices and enforce laws for consumer protection. The means used include (a) investigations of complaints about alleged illegal actions brought by members of the public, competing businesses, or other governmental agencies, (b) issuing "cease-and-desist" orders against offending entities and filing legal actions for civil penalties if these orders are violated, (c) stimulating voluntary and cooperative compliance without orders or legal actions, and (d) reports to inform public and private agencies and individuals about the commission and both legal and illegal trade practices.

For an agency with a relatively modest budget ($176 million in recent years) the Federal Trade Commission is particularly aggressive in tracking down frauds and antisocial business activity and publicizing it. For example, FTA went on a crusade against so-called identity theft by publicizing the methods of bogus schemes to obtain Social Security numbers, or other private information useful for crooks to obtain credit in the consumer's name, and establishing a website (www.consumer.gov/idtheft) for continuous information to the public.

ORGANIZATION

The commission is governed by five members appointed for staggered seven-year terms by the president with Senate confirmation, provided that at no time can more than three members by registered with the same political party. The president also designates the chairperson. The administrative secretariat of career incumbents includes *directors of Policy Planning, Public Affairs, and Congressional Relations.* Also directly responsible to the commissioners is the *Office of Administrative Law Judges,* which conducts administrative hearings based on complaints of improper practices.

The *Office of Executive Director* operates three bureaus that reflect the three areas of FTC operations: *Bureau of Competition, Bureau of Consumer Protection,* and *Bureau of Economics.* Each bureau is headed by a director who is a career civil servant, and includes specialized sub-

bureaus covering particular topics (e.g., anti-competitive practices, advertising practices). The executive director is also responsible for the conduct of seven regional offices.

CONTACT Address: FTC, 600 Pennsylvania Avenue NW, Washington, DC 20580; Phone: (202) 326-2222; Website: www.ftc.gov.

Regional Offices

East Central (D.C., Delaware, Maryland, Michigan, Ohio, Pennsylvania, Virginia, West Virginia): 111 Superior Avenue, Suite 200, Cleveland, OH 44114.

Southeast (Alabama, Florida, Georgia, Mississippi, North Carolina, South Carolina, Tennessee): 225 Peachtree Street, Suite 1500, Atlanta, GA 30303.

Northeast (Connecticut, Massachusetts, Maine, New Hampshire, New Jersey, New York, Rhode Island, Vermont): One Bowling Green, Suite 318, New York, NY 10004.

Midwest (Iowa, Illinois, Indiana, Kentucky, Minnesota, Missouri, North Dakota, Nebraska): 55 Monroe Street, Suite 1860, Chicago, IL 60603.

Northwest (Alaska, Idaho, Montana, Oregon, Washington, Wyoming): 915 Second Avenue, Seattle, WA 98174.

Southwest (Arkansas, Louisiana, New Mexico, Oklahoma, Texas): 1999 Bryan Street, Suite 2150, Dallas, TX 75201.

Western (Arizona, California, Colorado, Hawaii, Nevada, Utah): 10877 Wilshire Blvd., Suite 700, Los Angeles, CA 90024, and 901 Market Street, Suite 570, San Francisco, CA 94103.

AREAS OF CONCERN AND REGULATORY ACTION

The lengthy list of areas of concern on which the Federal Trade Commission acts includes: (a) *promote competition* by preventing price-fixing agreements, mergers leading to restraints on trade, collusive combinations of supposed competitors, pricing discrimination, exclusive dealing agreements, tie-in agreements, discrimination against customers and interlocking directorates among competitors; (b) *prevent fraud and deception* by halting false and deceptive advertising, fraudulent or abusive telemarketing, Internet fraud, false labeling; (c) *protect privacy of personal financial information* by preventing illegal or unwanted use of such data, and preventing use of outdated financial information, oversight over activities of credit bureaus and bill collectors; and (d) *public education* on consumer protection. *Filing Complaints:* Individuals are encouraged to file complaints about apparent incidents of illegal activity under the jurisdiction of the FTC, either in writing or via the format laid out in the commission's website. FTC will not resolve individual complaints, but will investigate, particularly if there are many complaints about a particular business entity or a particular practice. At that point the commission may take remedial action against the violating business.

FRANKLIN DELANO ROOSEVELT MEMORIAL COMMISSION

Oversees Franklin Delano Roosevelt Memorial on 7.5 acres on West Basin Drive in Washington, D.C. The commission selected renowned landscape architect Lawrence Halprin to design the memorial in 1974. The memorial combines shade trees, waterfalls, statuary, and four outdoor galleries, each celebrating one of FDR's four terms in office.

GENERAL SERVICES ADMINISTRATION (GSA)

The General Services Administration (known familiarly throughout government as GSA) is the U.S. government's property owner, manager, purchaser, seller, and watchdog of government-wide management practices. In recent years GSA has taken the lead in development and efficient use of the Internet as early as 1996, including so-called e-government initiatives and modern data centers. It designs and constructs many federal buildings, including federal court houses—more than 160 built or renovated since 1996—and major federal buildings, such as the Ronald Reagan Building.

Annual federal spending through GSA has reached $66 billion, and the total value of its holdings is more than $500 billion. Approximately 8,300 government buildings are owned or leased and managed by GSA. An automobile fleet of more than 170,000 vehicles is maintained by GSA. Some 111 child-care centers for more than 7,600 children in federal facilities are operated by GSA.

Increasingly important are GSA reports on efficiency in government, using modern technology and techniques that save the government billions of dollars each year. Recently, it began providing this type of consumer-sensitive advice to those doing business with the government and the public in general. Since it is independent and nonpolitical, its reports are influential.

A major function is the sale of surplus or obsolete government property. At the same time it takes steps to preserve historic buildings.

GSA employs about 14,000 people and its most current annual budgets have been in the neighborhood of $16 billion. Along with the rentals to other federal agencies, GSA is almost self-supporting and requires only a relatively small appropriation, particularly in view of the amount of assets and funds within its responsibility.

HISTORY

The General Services Administration was established by the Federal Property and Administrative Services Act and signed by President Harry S. Truman on July 1, 1949. It was based on a recommendation by the Hoover Commission on government efficiency and reorganization chaired by former president Herbert Hoover.

In the more than half century since its founding, various functions have come and gone within GSA. Emergency management functions were transferred to the FEDERAL EMERGENCY MANAGEMENT AGENCY (FEMA) in 1979. NATIONAL ARCHIVES was within GSA until 1985, when it was made independent. The Strategic Stockpile was moved to the DEFENSE DEPARTMENT in 1988.

The year 1954 saw the beginning of the government motor pool by GSA, and in the late 1950s and early 1960s GSA pioneered the intergovernmental telephone system. It set up the Federal Procurement Regulation System in 1959, and a Committee on Federal Office Space in 1962 to determine obsolescence of federal buildings and to regularize replacement and renovation, and in 1972 the Federal Buildings Fund became a revolving fund to maintain, operate, and renovate federal buildings, and a fund for constructing new buildings.

Starting in 1972, GSA became a leader in electronic communications by government agency, and in 1996 was on the cutting edge of the revolution in Internet use, which is currently managed by its Federal Technology Service (originally named the Automated Data and Telecommunications Service). In 1984 GSA introduced government credit cards, now used by more than 2 million government employees.

By a series of incremental steps GSA was handed policy-making functions. The Office of Federal Management Policy was established in 1973, the Office of Acquisition Policy added in 1978, and by executive order in 1985 it was given policy oversight and guidance for management of real property. All these were merged into the Office of Governmentwide Policy as of 1995.

CONTACT Address: 1800 F Street NW, Washington, DC 20405, and 11 regional offices: Phone: (202) 708-5082; Website: www.gsa.gov. Inquiries about sales of surplus property: Phone: (202) 501-0084; public and media inquiries: Phone: (202) 501-0084. Offices dealing with the public have separate telephone numbers listed below with other information about the office. Regional offices have separate numbers, which are also listed below.

ORGANIZATION

The General Service Administration is headed by an *administrator* who is appointed by the president with Senate confirmation. This is the only GSA position appointed by the president except for the inspector general. The administrator's immediate office is lean by bureaucratic standards, with a *deputy administrator,* a chief of staff, deputy chief of staff, and some assistants as well as office staff.

The next level of operations are the following, each directed by a commissioner:

FEDERAL SUPPLY SERVICE: This service supplies government agencies worldwide, and its massive buying power results in billions of dollars in savings. Its services are operated through acquisition and distribution from different "business lines": (a) personal property and services, including office equipment, offices supplies, equipment, software, financial, environmental, and administrative services; (b) purchases and leases of vehicles; and (c) travel, transportation, and shipping, including monitoring charges. GSA maintains several large distribution centers.

CONTACT Phone: (703) 305-5600; Website: www.fss.gsa.gov.

FEDERAL TECHNOLOGY SERVICE: This service provides to governmental agencies worldwide telecommunications, including up-to-date voice, data, and video communications. It developed and maintains a system of telephonic communication for the hard-of-hearing, deaf, and with speech impediments, the *Federal Relay Service* (TTY), which can be reached at (800) 877-8339. It also provides assistance to all government agencies to protect the security of governmental data. This service also compiles the so-called blue pages of government agencies and services in all telephone directories.

CONTACT Phone: (888) FTS 6397.

PUBLIC BUILDINGS SERVICE: This service is the builder, designer, manager, and lessor or lessee of federally owned and leased properties occupied by more than a million American workers. Its management services include repairs, security, rental, and property disposal (sale).

CONTACT Phone: (202) 501-1100; Website: www.pbs.gov./pbs.

OFFICE OF GOVERNMENTWIDE POLICY: This office works with all government agencies to develop policies, training, and practices best suited for the areas of service of GSA, such as personal and real property, travel and transportation, acquisition and disposal, electronic government such as the First/Gov Website information, regulation, development, and the uses of advisory committees. Its functions are divided among the following offices: *Office of Acquisition Policy (202-501-1043);* Office of Electronic Commerce (202-501-7092), *Office of FirstGov,* which is primarily an Internet portal to more than 50 million pages of federal and state government information (202-634-0000); *Office of Information Technology* (202-501-0202); *Office of Intergovernmental Solutions* (202-501-0291), *Office of Real Property, Office of Transportation and Personal Property* (202-501-1777), *Regulatory Information Service,* which compiles and disseminates information on government regulations and primarily publishes *The United Agenda of Federal Regulatory and Deregulatory Actions* published in the *Federal Register* twice a year (202-482-7345), and *Committee Management Secretariat* has a program to increase public participation in federal decision making through federal advisory committees (202-501-8880); Website: www.gsa.gov/policy.

The administration's internal officialdom is composed of *Office of Chief Information Officer, Office of Chief Financial Officer, Office of Congressional and Intergovernmental Affairs, Office of Communications,* and *General Counsel.*

Two offices directed toward assistance to the public dealing with GSA are the uniquely named *Office of the Chief People Officer,* which provides those dealing with the General Services Administration proposed solutions to problems of workforce, workplace, and organization; and the *Office of Enterprise Development,* which concentrates on assisting small businesses doing business with GSA.

CONTACT Phone: (202) 501-1021; Website: www.gsa.gov/oed. Enterprise development also has *Small Business Centers* in each of the regional offices listed below, as well as a satellite office at 300 North Los Angeles Street, Los Angeles, CA 90012. For regional telephone numbers see regional offices.

Directly responsible to the Administrator's Office is the *Office of Civil Rights* to guarantee nondiscriminatory treatment of both employees and those dealing with GSA. The *Board of Contract Appeals* acts independently to review various contract disputes, claims, transportation rate determinations, employee expenses, and other matters. The board often uses alternative dispute resolutions for settlement without hearings. It is administered directly through the administrator's office.

REGIONAL OFFICES OF THE GENERAL SERVICES ADMINISTRATION

New England: 10 Causeway Street, Boston, MA 02222; Phone: (617) 565-5860; Small Business Center: Phone: (617) 565-8100. Northeast & Caribbean: 28 Federal Plaza, New York, NY 10178; Phone: (212) 264-2600; Small Business Center: Phone: (212) 264-1234. Mid-Atlantic: The Strawbridge Building, 20 North Eighth Street, Philadelphia, PA 19107; Phone: (215) 446-5100; Small Business Center: Phone: (215) 656-5525. Southeast Sunbelt: 77 Forsyth Street, Suite 600, Atlanta, GA 30303; Phone: (404) 331-3200; Small Business Center: Phone: (404) 331-5103. Great

Lakes: 230 South Dearborn Street, Chicago, IL 60604; Phone: (312) 353-5395; Small Business Center: Phone: (816) 926-7203. Heartland: 1500 East Bannister Road, Kansas City, MO 64131; Phone: (816) 926-7201; Small Business Center: Phone: 926-7203. Pacific Rim: 450 Golden Gate Avenue, San Francisco, CA 94102; Phone: (415) 522-3001. Small Business Centers: Phone: (415) 552-2700 and (213) 894-3210 (Los Angeles). Northwest/Arctic: 400 Fifteenth Street NW, Auburn, WA 98001; Phone: (253) 931-7000; Small Business Center: Phone: (253) 931-7956. National Capital: Seventh and D Streets SW, Washington, DC 20407; Phone (202) 708-9100; Small Business Center: Phone: (202) 708-5804.

PUBLICATIONS AND SPEAKERS

Free publications such as *U.S. Government TTY Directory, Consumer Information Catalog* may be obtained from the Federal Consumer Information Center, Pueblo, CO 81009; Phone: (888) 878-3256. Some publications can be purchased from the Government Printing Office.

Inquiries about obtaining speakers should be made to (202) 501-0705 or the nearest regional office.

HARRY S. TRUMAN SCHOLARSHIP FOUNDATION

Works to discover and select college and university juniors with exceptional leadership potential who seek careers in public service, including government, nonprofit agencies, advocacy, or education. The foundation gives approximately $30,000 for graduate study, leadership training, and community learning, at approximately $3,000 per learner.

CONTACT Address: 712 Jackson Place NW, Washington, DC 20006; Phone: (202) 395-4831; Website: www.truman.gov.

ILLINOIS & MICHIGAN CANAL NATIONAL HERITAGE CORRIDOR COMMISSION

Through the DEPARTMENT OF THE INTERIOR, manages the Illinois & Michigan Canal National Heritage Corridor. Completed in 1848, the Illinois & Michigan Canal connects the Great Lakes to the Mississippi watershed along an Indian portage route from the Chicago River near Lake Michigan to the Illinois River at Peru, Illinois. Congress created the corridor in 1984, the first National Heritage Corridor, "to retain, enhance and interpret . . . the cultural, historical, natural, recreational, and economic resources in the Corridor. . . ."

The commission has 19 members who work to provide communication and coordination between local and state government, private organizations, and the National Park Service by providing interpretive materials, cooperative agreements, loans, and funding.

CONTACT Address: 201 West 10th Street, Number 1 SE, Lockport, IL 60441; Phone: (815) 588-6040; Website: www.nps.gov/ilmi/.

THE INTER-AMERICAN FOUNDATION

An independent agency created by the Foreign Assistance Act of 1969 to give financial assistance for self-help development in Latin America and in the Caribbean. According to the act, "It shall be the purpose of the Foundation, primarily in cooperation with private regional and international organizations to: strengthen the bonds of friendship and understanding among the peoples of this hemisphere; support self-help efforts designed to enlarge the opportunities for individual development; stimulate and assist effective and ever wider participation of the people in the development process; encourage the establishment and growth of democratic institutions, private and governmental, appropriate to the requirements of the individual sovereign nations of this hemisphere." The foundation tracks progress in countries where it funds projects through its Grassroots Development Framework (GDF).

To these ends, the foundation gives funds directly to nongovernmental organizations and works to develop enterpreneurship, self-reliance, and innovation while promoting democracy. The Inter-American Foundation cancelled its fellowship program in 2000.

Of the nine-member board of directors, all of whom are appointed by the president and confirmed by the Senate, six represent the private sector, and three represent federal agencies involved in inter-American affairs.

CONTACT Address: Inter-American Foundation, 901 N. Stuart Street, 10th Floor, Arlington, VA 22203; Phone: (703) 306-4301; Fax: (703) 306-4365; E-mail: info@iaf.gov; Website: www.iaf.gov/.

J. WILLIAM FULBRIGHT FOREIGN SCHOLARSHIP BOARD

Oversees the Fulbright Program, which was established in 1946 through legislation introduced by Democratic Senator J. William Fulbright of Arkansas. Funded by the U.S. Congress and sponsored by the Bureau of Educational and Cultural Affairs in the DEPARTMENT OF STATE, the Fulbright Program gives grants to graduate students, scholars, professionals, teachers, and administrators from the United States and abroad. The program's goal is to "increase mutual understanding between the people of the United States and the people of other countries . . ." who learn and teach in each other's countries, trade ideas, and work to find joint solutions to shared issues and problems.

In 2002, the Fulbright Program managed $119 million, and foreign governments contributed $28 into the Fulbright Program. It has participants in 140 countries, 51 with which it has bi-national Fulbright Commissions and Foundations.

The 12-member board, appointed by the president, establishes policies, procedures, and selection criteria, and issues a report on the program each year.

CONTACT Address: Office of Academic Exchange Programs, Bureau of Educational and Cultural Affairs, U.S. Department of State, SA-44, 301 4th Street SW, Washington, DC 20547; Phone: (202) 619-4360; Fax: (202) 401-5914; E-mail: academic@pd.state.gov; Website: http://exchanges.state.gov/education/fulbright/.

JAMES MADISON MEMORIAL FELLOWSHIP FOUNDATION

Established as an independent agency by Congress in 1986, the James Madison Fellowship Foundation strives to improve teaching about the U.S. Constitution in secondary schools. James Madison fellows work to improve their research, writing, and analytical skills.

Junior fellowships go to students about to become full-time graduate students and have two years to complete whatever degree they seek. Senior fellowships go to experienced teachers who want to earn M.A. degrees on a part-time basis through summer and evening classes. They have five years to complete their graduate degrees including Master of Arts in American history or political science; Master of Arts in Teaching (Mat) in American Constitutional history in a history department or in American government, political institutions, and political theory in a political science department; or a Master of Education (Med) or Master of Science in Education degree in American history or American government, political institutions, and political theory. Fellows also attend a four-week six-unit Summer Institute on the Constitution at Georgetown University in Washington, D.C.

CONTACT   Address: James Madison Memorial Fellowship Foundation, 2000 K Street NW, Suite 303, Washington DC 20006-1809; Phone: (202) 653-8700; Fax: (202) 653-6045; Website: www.jamesmadison.com/.

JAPAN-UNITED STATES FRIENDSHIP COMMISSION (JUSFC)

Created by Congress in 1975 as an independent agency to give financial support to train and prepare Americans to deal with and improve U.S.-Japan relationships through Japanese studies in the United States of public affairs and education; study in Japan of the United States; and arts education and exchanges. The commission runs a trust fund originally created as post–World War II assistance to accompany return of control of U.S.-captured Japanese facilities in Okinawa to the Japanese government. The commission has 19 members, of which nine are government officials and members of the Senate and Congress.

CONTACT   Address: JUSFC, 1110 Vermont Avenue NW, Suite 800, Washington, DC 20005; Phone: (202) 418-9800; Fax: (202) 418-9802; Website: www.jusfc.gov.

MERIT SYSTEMS PROTECTION BOARD (MSPB)

Established as an independent, quasi-judicial Executive Branch agency by the Civil Service Reform Act of 1978 to protect federal employees from abuses by management, to ensure that Executive Branch agencies comply with merit systems principles, and to make sure those merit systems are conducted with no prohibited personnel practices. The board took on the employee appeals function once handled by the former Civil Service Commission.

MSPB traces its roots to President Theodore Roosevelt. As a civil service commissioner under President Benjamin Harrison, Roosevelt worked to get rid of the traditional "spoils system," in which people received jobs and got promotions based on whom they knew, and to replace it with promotion and hiring based on individual merit. However, the merit system is not perfect either, since promotions and job evaluations within that system may also depend on how well an employee gets along with superiors.

MSPB adjudicates appeals by employees of personnel actions such as removals, suspensions, furloughs, and demotions; adjudicates employee complaints filed according to the Whistleblower Protection Act, the Uniformed Services Employment & Reemployment Rights Act (USERRA), and the Veterans Employment Opportunities Act; adjudicates Special Counsel–initiated cases such as Hatch Act violations and prohibited personnel practices; adjudicates Office of Personnel Management (OPM) regulations review requests relating to a prohibited personnel practice; orders compliance with the board's final orders; and conducts and reviews federal merit systems and civil service to make sure they have no prohibited personnel practices.

MSPB's OFFICE OF THE SPECIAL COUNSEL is now an independent agency (1989) that investigates allegations of prohibited personnel practices, prosecutes violators of civil service rules and regulations, and enforces the Hatch Act.

The president appoints the Merit Systems Protection Board's three members, only two of whom may be of the same political party. Members serve for one term only of seven years.

CONTACT   Address: MSPB, 5th Floor, 1615 M Street NW, Washington, DC 20419; Phone: (202) 653-7200 or (800) 209-8960, TDD: (800) 877-8339; Fax: (202) 653-7130; E-mail: mspb@mspb.gov; Website: www.mspb.gov. Regional offices: 401 W. Peachtree Street NW, Suite 1050, Atlanta, GA 30308; Phone: (404) 730-2751; Fax: (404) 730-2767. 1800 Diagonal Road, Suite 205, Alexandria, VA 22314-2840; Phone: (703) 756-6250; Fax: (703) 756-7112. 230 South Dearborn Street, Room 3100, Chicago, IL 60604; Phone: (312) 353-2923; Fax: (312) 886-4231. U.S. Customhouse, Room 501, Second and Chestnut Streets, Philadelphia, PA 19106; Phone: (215) 597-9960; Fax: (215) 597-3456. 250 Montgomery Street, Suite 400, 4th Floor, San Francisco, CA 94104; Phone: (415) 705-2935; Fax: (415) 705-2945. Field offices: 1100 Commerce Street, Room 620, Dallas, TX 75242; Phone: (214) 767-0555; Fax: (214) 767-0102. 99 Summer Street, Suite 1810, Boston, MA 02110; Phone: (617) 424-5700; Fax: (617) 424-5708. 915 Second Avenue, Room 1840, Seattle, WA 98174; Phone: (206) 220-7975; Fax: (206) 220-7982. 165 South Union Boulevard, Suite 318, Lakewood, CO 80228; Phone: (308) 969-5101; Fax: (303) 969-5109. 26 Federal Plaza, Room 3137A, New York, NY 10278; Phone: (212) 264-9372; Fax: (212) 264-1417.

MARINE MAMMAL COMMISSION

Created September 1, 1982, to review existing laws and international conventions on marine mammals, including the International Convention for the Regulation of Whaling, the Whaling Convention Act of 1949, the Interim Convention on the Conservation of North Pacific Fur Seals, and the Fur Seal Act of 1966. The commission also oversees conditions of marine mammals, their protection and conservation, and methods of harvesting marine mammals humanely; makes recommendations on regular revisions of the endangered species and threatened species lists; and recommends ways to protect Indians, Eski-mos, and Aleuts who depend upon marine mammals for their livelihood and may be affected by marine mammal preservation.

The commission has three members, appointed by the president with the advice and consent of the Senate. Members must be knowledgeable in marine ecology and resource management and not making a profit from marine mammals, and must be approved and endorsed by the chairman of the Council on Environmental Quality, as well as by the secretary of the Smithsonian Institution, the director of the NATIONAL SCIENCE FOUNDATION, and the chair of the National Academy of Sciences. They serve one three-year term only.

CONTACT Address: Room 905, 4340 East-West Highway, Bethesda, MD 20814; Phone: (301) 504-0087, (202) 512-1530, (888) 293-6498; Fax: (202) 512-1262.

MEDICARE PAYMENT ADVISORY COMMISSION (MEDPAC)

An independent body established by the Balanced Budget Act of 1997 to advise Congress on Medicare issues such as payments to health plans in Medicare-Choice and providers of fee-for-service. MedPAC analyses access to care, quality of care, and other issues under Medicare. MedPAC seeks and receives input from congressional committee staff, health care researchers and providers, and staff of the Centers for Medicare and Medicaid Services (CMS), once known as the Health Care Financing Administration (HCFA). The commission issues reports in March and June and advises Congress on DEPARTMENT OF HEALTH AND HUMAN SERVICES regulations.

MedPAC's 17 members are appointed by the comptroller general and serve renewable three-year terms.

CONTACT Address: MedPAC, Suite 800, 1730 K Street NW, Washington, DC 20006; Phone: (202) 653-7220; Website: www.medpac.gov.

MIGRATORY BIRD CONSERVATION COMMISSION

Established in February 1929 by the Migratory Bird Conservation Act to discuss and approve land or water areas that the secretary of interior recommends for rental or purchase by the U.S. Fish and Wildlife Service with money from the Migratory Bird Conservation Fund. The commission also researches and discusses establishment of new waterfowl refuges, funds purchase or rental of migratory bird habitats, and produces an annual report of its operations. The Migratory Bird Conservation Commission raises money to establish and maintain bird habitats through funds received from selling Migratory Bird Hunting and Conservation Stamps ("Duck Stamps"), appropriations from the Wetlands Loan Act (1961), import duties on arms and ammunition, sale of refuge admission permits, and income from selling products from rights-of-way across national wildlife refuges. As of 1989, the commission approves project funding of partnerships to protect, enhance, restore, and manage wetlands and other migratory bird and wildlife habitats as prescribed in the North American Waterfowl Management Plan.

Members include the secretary of the interior as chair, the administrator of the ENVIRONMENTAL PROTECTION AGENCY, the secretary of agriculture, two U.S. senators, and two members of Congress.

CONTACT Address: 4401 N. Fairfax Drive, Mail Stop ARLSQ-622, Arlington, VA 22203-1716; Phone: (703) 358-1716; Website: http://realty.fws.gov/mbcc.html.

MISSISSIPPI RIVER PARKWAY COMMISSION (MRPC)

A multistate and province umbrella organization of states and one Canadian province along the Mississippi River in which states work collectively to preserve, promote, and enhance the scenic, historic, and recreational resources of the Mississippi River. The states are Arkansas, Illinois, Iowa, Kentucky, Louisiana, Minnesota, Mississippi, Missouri, Tennessee, Wisconsin, and Ontario, Canada.

MRPC works to obtain money for and market highway improvements, recreation trails, bikeways, scenic overlooks, and historic preservation in all pertinent states and the province. It also runs Mississippi River Country, an international marketing program.

CONTACT Address: MRPC, P.O. Box 59159, Minneapolis, MN 554-8257; Phone: (763) 212-2560; Fax: (763) 212-2533; E-mail: info@mississippiriverinfo.com; Website: www.mississippiriverinfo.com.

MORRIS K. UDALL SCHOLARSHIP AND EXCELLENCE IN NATIONAL ENVIRONMENTAL POLICY FOUNDATION

An independent national trust fund established by Congress in 1992 to promote environmental and natural resources awareness and education. The foundation and its fund honor the service of Congressman Morris K. Udall (Dem.-Arizona) and his long-range positive effect on the environment, public lands, and natural resources, as well as Udall's service to Native Americans and Alaska Natives. Nine trustees, appointed by the president with advice and consent of the Senate, run the foundation.

The foundation gives scholarships, fellowships, internships, and grants to students devoted to increasing knowledge of the importance of American natural resources and public lands and works to identify important and emerging environmental issues; establish environmental research and conflict resolution programs; train professionals in environmental and related fields; provide environmental policy outreach and education; and develop resources and programs to train Native Americans and Alaska Natives in health care and public policy. Each year the foundation awards two Ph.D. fellowships of $24,000 each for a doctoral candidate to write his or her dissertation.

The foundation also produces programs for education on environmental issues, and supports all programs at the Udall Center for Studies in Public Policy at the University of Arizona, and the Native American Congressional Summer Internship Program (since 1996).

CONTACT Address: Suite 3350, 110 South Church Avenue, Tucson, AZ 85701; Phone: (520) 670-5529; Website: www.udall.gov.

NATIONAL AERONAUTICS AND SPACE ADMINISTRATION (NASA)

NASA manages the nation's space program, as well as vital matters related to space, such as the biological effect of humans in space, a continuing study of the universe and the solar system, and earth science, which can lead to scientific predictions of climate and weather. NASA also provides educational materials on these subjects for the general public. Created in 1958 after the Soviet Union in 1957 was the first to shoot a basketball-sized science satellite (*Sputnik I*) into orbit around the Earth, NASA has one of the great scientific records in history, including the first suborbital flight of a human, the first orbit of Earth

with a human cargo, sending the first men to the Moon, and unmanned exploratory flights around and/or on to the surface of planets.

NASA also established a series of shuttle flights to a space station, and eventually joined with the Soviet Union (now Russia) in building and expanding a space station that orbited Earth for years. It also placed the high-powered Hubble telescope far enough above Earth to avoid much of the atmosphere that partially obscured images from distant parts of the universe. This alone greatly increased humankind's knowledge of outer space.

Its work was not without tragic failures. There was a fire that killed astronauts (the term for the space travelers; called cosmonauts in the Russian space program), a major tear in the surface of a spaceship on the way to the Moon, which was brought back to Earth with the crew unhurt, and two mechanical failures of shuttles in which the crews all died.

After the second loss of life in shuttle travel—when a returning shuttle lost a wing upon reentry in 2003—there was considerable debate within and outside government as to the future of the space program, its expense, and scientific value. Nevertheless, in June 2003 NASA sent an unmanned spaceship on its way to Mars to send back pictures and scientific data (particularly looking for water, the stuff of life), which landed successfully in January 2004.

HISTORY

NASA was inaugurated on October 1, 1958, by legislation spurred by the Soviet Union's successful launching of *Sputnik*, the first satellite to be rocketed into orbit around Earth. It succeeded the National Advisory Committee for Aeronautics (NACA), which had existed since 1915, with an initial budget of $5,000, as the official stimulus to aeronautical research and development. By 1958 NACA had a staff of 7,200.

NACA had built the first wind tunnel to test aircraft designs at Langley Research Center in 1920. Its concentration had been on improving conventional aircraft through design, quality of liquid fuels, and exchange of engineering information among both public and private organizations. Rocketry was outside its purview; Robert Goddard, America's principal rocket expert, a writer and experimenter, launched a small rocket as early as 1926. The first American jet aircraft was developed independently by Bell Aircraft and flew on October 1, 1942. Practical use of the helicopter was pursued by the United States Air Corps (later Force) starting in the latter days of World War II. The sound barrier was broken by test pilot Chuck Yeager, an air force veteran, in October 1947.

Trying to catch up with the Soviet space program, the army's attempt to launch a rocket capable of putting a satellite into orbit on December 6, 1957, was a public embarrassment when it blew up spectacularly a few feet from the ground with the satellite rolling around on the launch-pad, beeping meaninglessly. In early 1958 the first successful American satellite discovered the Van Allen Belt, and put into orbit a weather satellite in April 1960, a navigational satellite in June 1960, and communications and "spy" satellites in August 1960.

At the same time General James Doolittle (World War II hero who led the first bombing raid on Japan and the air war against Germany), as chairman of NACA together with NACA director Hugh H. Dryden, prepared a complete plan for an organization to conduct research, experimentation, and eventually actual space travel, which became the blueprint for NASA.

Immediately upon its formation, NASA began plans for space travel, research on space problems such as weightlessness, development of rockets and rocket fuel capable of sending rockets and their payloads into orbit and then out of the globe's gravitational pull, communications, and the centers capable of performing this work.

It gave godlike Greek names to the stages of its space program: Mercury, Gemini, and Apollo. Mercury was intended to develop powerful rockets, boosters, rocket stages, and suborbital flight, and to send useful satellites (weather and scientific research, for example) into semipermanent orbit. This was intended to lead to Gemini, which would orbit Earth with a crew aboard, provide for working in space outside of the spacecraft, and other tasks that were not known to be possible or safe. This would prepare for Apollo, which would leave Earth's atmosphere for exploratory unmanned trips around the planets and sending men first around and then to the Moon.

The United States got another jolt to its hope to regain the lead in the space race when on April 12, 1961, the Soviets sent a cosmonaut on a one-orbit trip around the world. Four weeks later, on May 6, 1961, astronaut Alan Shepard was rocketed 300 miles down the Atlantic from Florida in a 15-minute flight just below the orbiting level.

In a special message to Congress, on May 25, 1961, President John F. Kennedy gave NASA a challenge while demonstrating his confidence in its programs:

> I believe that this nation should commit itself to achieving the goal, before the decade is out, of landing a man on the moon and returning him safely to earth. . . .

Thus, NASA had the target of getting to the Moon by the end of 1969. In August 1961 the Soviets put a cosmonaut into orbit for 17 turns around Earth. On February 20, 1962, the United States responded in the space race with the Soviets when John H. Glenn Jr. was put into a three-orbit flight, after several successful experiments with the space capsules without a human aboard.

In the years 1962 through 1968 the competition between the United States and the USSR space programs continued, with the USSR always first in multiple riders, number of orbits, extra-vehicular activity, woman in space, and approach to the Moon's surface in an unmanned vehicle. During the same period, the Gemini program proved that space walks with defined tasks were possible, that an orbiting spacecraft could dock with another, that improved photography and other forms of communication and data transfer were possible, that pinpoint landings were possible, and that space trips of weeks were possible without damage to the health of the astronauts. The rockets became larger and more powerful, and the crafts themselves became larger and more comfortable.

Then on January 27, 1967, tragedy struck during a preflight simulated launch. A spark from a short circuit ignited, and fed by pure oxygen started a fire that asphyxiated three astronauts (Virgil Grissom, Edward H. White II, and Roger B. Chaffee) in the five minutes it took to open the hatch. This accident set back the program some 18 months while corrective steps were taken to avoid future fires.

The year 1968 saw renewed progress begin in January with the successful test of a module that could be released by the mother ship and land on the Moon's surface and then be propelled back up to be reconnected. On October 11 *Apollo 7* carried three astronauts into orbit. In December *Apollo 8* sent another crew of three beyond Earth's gravitational pull and on its way to swing around the Moon—seeing the far side for the first time—beamed back television images of the Moon's surface, picked suitable landing sites, then returned to Earth.

Final tests of the lunar module were made in March 1969, first from above Earth (*Apollo 9*), and in May (*Apollo 10*) while orbiting around the Moon, actually landing an unmanned module on the Moon, then ordering it to blast off the surface and redock with the command spacecraft.

Apollo 11 lifted off for the Moon on July 16, 1969, and reached orbit around the Moon on the 20th. Astronauts Neil Armstrong and Edwin E. "Buzz" Aldrin Jr. disconnected from the command ship (*Columbia*) piloted by Michael Collins and touched down. Armstrong radioed to Earth, "The Eagle has landed." Soon he stepped out on the Moon's surface, saying to Houston and the world: "One small step for man, one giant leap for mankind." A few minutes later, Aldrin joined him. They unloaded scientific instruments to be left to send back data, gathered rock samples, planted an American flag, and the next day ascended to the *Columbia,* redocked, and headed home.

NASA had met the challenge laid down by President Kennedy in 1961.

Apollos 12 through *17* were successful, except for *Apollo 13* in April 1970, which lost pressure of liquid oxygen and had to return to Earth as time and oxygen ran out. The calm voice calling earthward, "Houston. We have a problem" became an American legend.

Then NASA shelved the moon trip program and concentrated on creating a space station, *Skylab,* from mid-1973 to mid-1975, by docking orbiting satellites with the lab as it grew in size. The Soviets were concentrating on a competing program.

To service its growing space lab NASA developed and employed the shuttle program of service to *Skylab* and other functions starting April 12, 1981, and continuing until January 28, 1986. The shuttles were returnable aircraft that reached orbit and then could return to Earth, usually at Houston, Texas, or the alternative, Edwards Air Base. In this series there were 24 flights by shuttles named *Columbia, Challenger, Discovery,* and *Atlantis.* Sally Ride became the first American woman in space on a flight on June 18, 1983, and on August 30, 1983, Guion Bluford the first African American in space. The shuttle made possible many experiments.

The shuttle program was brought to a crashing halt on January 28, 1986, when the *Challenger* exploded only 73 seconds after blast-off as a worldwide television audience watched. Six astronauts and a schoolteacher passenger, Christa

McAuliffe, died. The cause was the failed O-ring on a solid fuel booster causing the fuel to explode. Questions were raised about rushing the launch without sufficient preparation and review. Later the same month the Russians launched their second and most successful space station, *Mir.*

In September 1988, NASA renewed the shuttle program, continuing without a break into 2003. In 1992 the shuttle *Endeavor* replaced the ill-fated *Challenger.* Flights became almost monthly events. Various foreign scientists were included, satellites were launched from the space lab and also retrieved, the powerful Hubble telescope was installed, and later repaired, former astronaut John Glenn (by then a 70-year-old senator) returned to space, American and Russian (the USSR had broken up into several nations, the largest of which was Russia) docking equipment were made compatible to permit serving space stations interchangeably, and in 1998 the United States, Russia, and a group of European countries began constructing the International Space Station. In 1999 from this station was launched the Chandra X-Ray laboratory, and the relaunch of a repaired Hubble telescope, which permitted a deeper and clearer look at outer space.

Then a new tragedy caused a halt in the use of the shuttle. On February 1, 2003, the venerable *Columbia,* as it began re-entry, lost a wing and broke up over three states, killing its seven astronauts. The apparent cause was foam materials from the boosters hitting the wing on liftoff with damages unknown to its doomed crew. For the time being the program was halted pending re-evaluation and study.

ORGANIZATION AND PROGRAMS

NASA is headed by an *administrator,* who is appointed by the president with Senate confirmation, as is the *deputy administrator.* The office of the administrator is composed of career professionals including *chief scientist* and *chief engi-*

neer, administrators, deputies, and a chief information officer. There are two types of offices within the NASA hierarchy: technical and administrative.

Technical offices are *Office of Space Flight, Office of Space Science, Office of Aerospace Technology, Office of Biological and Physical Research, Office of Life and Microgravity Sciences and Applications, Office of Earth Science,* and *Office of Safety and Mission Assurance.*

Administrative offices are *Office of the Chief Financial Officer, Office of the Inspector General, Office of Headquarters Operations, Office of Equal Opportunity Programs, Office the General Counsel, Office of External Relations, Office of Management Systems and Facilities, Office of Legislative Affairs, Office of Public Affairs,* and *Office of Policy and Plans.* Of these only the chief financial officer and the inspector general are appointed by the president with Senate confirmation.

OFFICE OF SPACE FLIGHT: Phone: (202-358-2015) manages the *Johnson Space Center,* the *Kennedy Space Center,* the *Marshall Space Center,* and the *Stennis Space Center.* It is responsible for the human space flight programs, the space shuttle, the international space station, as well as future exploration of space both unmanned and human. It is the leading entity in the construction of the permanently inhabited space station along with contributions by Russia, Canada, Japan, Brazil, and the 10 nations joined in the European Space Agency.

OFFICE OF SPACE SCIENCE: Phone: (202-358-1409) conducts advanced research on the origin, evolution, and structure of the solar system and the universe. A principal purpose is to improve existing space technology and develop new technology to meet needs of continued and extended space exploration. It maintains continued liaison and coordination with both private and public scientific organizations, and the Space Studies Board of the National Academy of Sciences. This office also manages NASA's participation in the Jet Propulsion Laboratory actually managed by the California Institute of Technology (CalTech) in Pasadena, California. This laboratory has developed space sensors that makes space travel functional and other research which aids solar system exploration, the Deep Space Network, space physics, and other advanced technology.

OFFICE OF AEROSPACE TECHNOLOGY Phone: (202-358-2693) principally operates the *Ames Research Center, Dryden Flight Research Center, Langley Research Center,* and *John Glenn Research Center.* It also develops commercial uses of the space technology that stems from the work of NASA, and it disseminates this technology to both the public and experts in the field.

OFFICE OF BIOLOGICAL AND PHYSICAL RESEARCH Phone: (202-358-0123) directs programs of space medicine, and biological effects on human space travelers. It establishes the standards for the human flight systems to protect, serve, and improve conditions for the astronauts.

OFFICE OF EARTH SCIENCE Phone: (202-358-2165) employs the increased knowledge of Earth systems and the changes to them by both natural and human causes in order to better predict climate, weather, and natural hazards such as earthquakes. It also manages the Goddard Flight Center.

FUNCTIONS OF CENTERS

Ames Research Center, Moffett Field, California, performs fundamental research concerning astronomical and planetary environments and their effects on humans in space and means to protect the astronauts, such as the thermal space suits.

Dryden Flight Research Center, Edwards Air Force Base, California, is the alternative landing place for the shuttle and provides landing support for the shuttle. It also conducts flight research.

Goddard Space Flight Center, Greenbelt, Maryland, performs advanced research often based on observations from space and has the prime responsibility for placing scientific instruments in space by various means including both rockets and balloons. The center manages the Wallops Flight Facility at Wallops Island, Virginia, which contains an experimental flight airport and runs a Fairmont, West Virginia, facility that evaluates software and other products used in space flights.

Lyndon B. Johnson Space Center, Houston, Texas, is the heart of the operation during space flights, managing the actual projects and developing and maintaining various programs such as the shuttle, extra-vehicular activity (EVA) commonly known as "space walks," the international space station, lunar and planetary sciences, biomedical research, space medicine, space engineering, and other scientific and engineering support for space exploration and experimentation. During flights, the contact from astronauts to ground are to the Johnson Space Center.

John F. Kennedy Space Center, Cape Canaveral, Florida, conducts the launches of all forms of space travel, including the several Moon shots, the shuttle, space station equipment and materials, and satellites delivered into orbit by multistaged rockets. It is also the landing field for returning shuttles, unless weather conditions force a landing at the backup site at Edwards Air Force Base in California.

Langley Research Center, Hampton, Virginia, does investigative research on materials, structural integrity, and innovative equipment used in space travel, and researches issues involved in launch and re-entry. It also studies the effect on Earth and the general population of atmospheric conditions and radiation useful to government and private industries. As a key function, Langley evaluates all programs, including reporting on cost effectiveness.

George C. Marshall Space Flight Center, Huntsville, Alabama, is a multitasked facility that develops space transportation system, researches microgravity, conducts optical manufacturing technology, is the leader in space propulsion research and development of increasingly powerful thrust of launching rockets, and creates the equipment for the Johnson Space Center. In all these areas the center experiments, researches, tests, designs, and creates vital elements of the space program. In addition, it runs the Chandra X-Ray Observatory program.

CONTACT Address: 300 E Street NW, Washington, DC 20546, and 10 centers for research, space, flight, and a propulsion laboratory; Phone: (202) 358-0000; E-mail: www.nasa.gov.

NATIONAL ARCHIVES AND RECORDS ADMINISTRATION (NARA)

The National Archives and Records Administration (NARA) is an independent agency and public trust that keeps the United States's records and documents and makes them accessible to the public, including the Declaration of Independence, Constitution of the United States, and the Bill of Rights, in addition to federal officials' actions. NARA also makes sure the government creates evidence, or a paper trail, of its actions, and makes historically valuable documents available on NARA website, www.nara.gov.

The National Archives Establishment was created in 1934, was merged into the GENERAL SERVICES ADMINISTRATION and renamed the National Archives and Records Service in 1949, and finally was established as an independent agency in 1984. NARA's administration is directed by the *Archivist of the United States,* who is appointed by the president, with Senate confirmation.

NARA publishes documents, such as acts of Congress in pamphlet form (slip law), and then compiles and publishes them as the *United States Statutes at Large.*

The *Federal Register* is a legal newspaper published every business day and contains proposed rules, notices of scheduled hearings, meetings, and grant applications, all current executive orders, presidential proclamations, federal agency regulations, and documents that are legally required to be published in the *Federal Register.* Established in 1935, the Office of the Federal Register coordinates all functions of the Electoral College and administers the constitutional amendment process.

All current federal regulations are published in codified form each year in the *Code of Federal Regulations.*

NARA publishes presidential speeches, news conferences, messages, press releases, and other papers released by the Office of the Press Secretary in the *Weekly Compilation of Presidential Documents* and in the *Public Papers of the President.* NARA also publishes the *United States Government Manual* as the official handbook of the federal government.

CONTACT Address: Federal Register: Phone: (202) 523-5227, TDD (202) 523-5229; Fax: (202) 523-5216; E-mail: info@fedreg.nara.gov; Website: www.nara.gov.

Since January 20, 1981, and according to the Presidential Records Act of 1978, all presidential papers and records become the property of the United States and must be given to NARA at the end of an administration for safekeeping and to stock presidential libraries. Prior to that time, presidential papers and records were thought to be personal property of the presidents.

CONTACT Phone: (301) 837-3250; Fax: (301) 837-3199.

NARA inspects agency records and management practices, conducts and records training and records management programs, and stores inactive records at the national Records Center in the Office of Records Services in Washington, D.C. It has nine regional records services facilities and a National Personnel Records Center. Regionally important historical documents are kept in regional centers. Among the documents available are bankruptcy case files, military and civilian personnel records, and information on genealogical workshops.

NATIONAL ARCHIVES TRUST FUND BOARD: Consists of the archivist of the United States, the secretary of the treasury, and the chairman of the National Endowment for the Humanities; uses money raised from sale of reproductions of historic documents and publications about its records to produce more publications. The board's funds come from sale of those reproductions and publications of some of the records.

CONTACT Phone: (301) 837-2450.

NATIONAL HISTORICAL PUBLICATIONS AND RECORDS COMMISSION: Works with State Historical Records Advisory Boards and gives grants to universities, historical societies, other nonprofits, and states to help preserve and document records collections and publish reproductions.

CONTACT Phone: (202) 501-5600; E-mail: nhprc@nara.gov; Website: www.nara.gov/nhprc.

INFORMATION SECURITY OVERSIGHT OFFICE: Oversees security classification of documents for both government and industry, following direction from the NATIONAL SECURITY COUNCIL.

CONTACT Address: NARA, 8601 Adelphi Road, College Park, MD 20740-6001; Phone: (866) 272-6272; Website: www.nara.gov.

PRESIDENTIAL LIBRARIES: NARA oversees the presidential libraries: Herbert Hoover Library, West Branch, IA 52358-0488; Phone: (319) 643-5301. Franklin D. Roosevelt Library, Hyde Park, NY 12538-1999; Phone: (914) 229-8115. Harry S. Truman Library, Independence, MO 64050-1798; Phone: (816) 833-1400. Dwight D. Eisenhower Library, Abilene, KS 67410-2900; Phone: (785) 263-4751. John F. Kennedy Library, Boston, MA 02125-5702; Phone: (617) 929-4500. Lyndon B. Johnson Library, Austin, TX 78705-5702; Phone: (512) 916-5137. Nixon Presidential Materials, College Park, MD 20740-6001; Phone: (301) 837-2550. Gerald R. Ford Library, Ann Arbor, MI 48109-2114; Phone: (616) 451-9263. Gerald R. Ford Museum, Grand Rapids, MI 49504-5353; Phone: (616) 451-9263. Jimmy Carter Library, Atlanta, GA 20207-1498; Phone: (404) 331-3042. Ronald Reagan Library, Simi Valley, CA 93065-0666; Phone: (805) 522-8444. George Bush Library, College Station, TX 77843; Phone: (979) 260-9554. William J. Clinton Presidential Materials Project, Little Rock, AR 72201; Phone: (501) 254-6866. Presidential Materials Staff, Washington, DC 20408-0001; Phone: (202) 501-5705. (The Richard M Nixon Library and Birthplace are run by the Nixon Foundation at 1800 Yorba Linda Boulevard, Yorba Linda, CA 92886; Phone: (714) 993-5075.)

REGIONAL RECORDS SERVICES FACILITIES: Northeast: 380 Trapelo Road, Waltham, MA 02514-6399; Phone: (781) 647-8745. 100 Conte Drive, Pittsfield, MA 01201-8230; Phone: (413) 445-6885. 201 Varick Street, New York, NY 10014-4811; Phone: (212) 337-1300. Mid-Atlantic: 900 Market Street, Philadelphia, PA 19107-4292; Phone: (215) 671-9027. Southeast: 1557 St. Joseph Avenue, East Point, GA 30344-2593; Phone: (404) 763-7477. Great Lakes: 7358 S. Pulaski Road, Chicago, IL 60629-5898; Phone: (773) 581-7816. 3150 Springboro Road, Dayton, OH 45439-1883; Phone: (937) 225-2852. Central Plains: 2312 E. Bannister Road, Kansas City, MO 64131-3011; Phone: (816) 926-6920. 200 Space Center Drive, Lee's Summit, MO 64064-1182; Phone: (816) 478-7089. Southwest: 501 W. Felix Street, Forth Worth, TX 76115-3405; Phone: (817) 334-5515. Rocky Mountains: Building 48, Denver Federal Center, Denver, CO 80225-0307; Phone: (303) 236-0801. Pacific: 1000 Commodore Drive, San Bruno, CA 94066; Phone: (415) 876-9009. 1st Floor, 24000 Avila Road, Laguna Niguel, CA 92607-3497; Phone: (949) 360-2618. Pacific Alaska, 6125 San Point Way NE, Seattle, WA 97115-7999; Phone: (206) 526-6501. 654 West 3rd Avenue, Anchorage, AK 99501-2145; Phone: (907) 271-2443. National Personnel Records Center: 9700 Page Avenue, St. Louis, MO 63132; Phone: (314) 538-4201.

PRESIDENT'S COUNCIL
ON BIOETHICS

Replaced the National Bioethics Advisory Commission (NBAC), an independent entity the charter of which expired October 3, 2001. The new council allows the president to have tighter control on its approach to "ageless bodies" (genetic enhancement) beyond therapy (use of biotechnology to influence the human body or mind, affecting lifespan and the mode of generating new life); cloning; drugs, children, and behavior control; early embryonic development; experimenting with human subjects; happiness and sadness; organ transplantation; property in the body; remembering and forgetting; stem cell research (embryonic stem cell research and adult stem cell research); biotechnology; sex selection; and bioethics in literature and in public policy.

The NBAC's priorities had been the "protection of the rights and welfare of human research subjects. . . . and use of genetic information, including, but not limited to human gene patenting" according to President Bill Clinton's Executive Order 12975 of October 3, 1995. The NBAC's original four criteria priorities were: "the public health or public policy urgency of the bioethical issue; the relation of the bioethical issue to the goals for federal investment in science and technology; the absence of another entity able to deliberate appropriately on the bioethical issue; and the extent of interest in the issue within the federal government."

President George W. Bush's Executive Order 13237 took a slightly more moralistic approach grounded in a new policy of limiting federal funding of stem cell research to a few existing "lines" of embryonic cells. The Executive Order provided:

a. The council shall advise the president on bioethical issues that may emerge as a consequence of advances in biomedical science and technology. In connection with its advisory role, the mission of the council includes the following functions, according to the executive order:

1. to undertake fundamental inquiry into the human and moral significance of developments in biomedical and behavioral science and technology;

2. to explore specific ethical and policy questions related to these developments;

3. to provide a forum for a national discussion of bioethical issues;

4. to facilitate a greater understanding of bioethical issues; and

5. to explore possibilities for useful international collaboration on bioethical issues.

b. In support of its mission, the council may study ethical issues connected with specific technological activities, such as embryo and stem cell research, assisted reproduction, cloning, uses of knowledge and techniques derived from human genetics or the neurosciences, and end-of-life issues. The council may also study broader ethical and social issues not tied to a specific technology, such as questions regarding the protection of human subjects in research, the appropriate uses of biomedical technologies, the moral implications of biomedical technologies, and the consequences of limiting scientific research.

c. The council shall strive to develop a deep and comprehensive understanding of the issues that it considers. In pursuit of this goal, the council shall be guided by the need to articulate fully the complex and often competing moral positions on any given issue, rather than by an overriding concern to find consensus. The council may therefore choose to proceed by offering a variety of views on a particular issue, rather than attempt to reach a single consensus position.

d. The council shall not be responsible for the review and approval of specific projects or for devising and overseeing regulations for specific government agencies.

e. In support of its mission, the council may accept suggestions of issues for consideration from the heads of other government agencies and other sources, as it deems appropriate.

f. In establishing priorities for its activities, the council shall consider the urgency and gravity of the particular issue; the need for policy guidance and public education on the particular issue; the connection of the bioethical issue to the goal of federal advancement of science and technology; and the existence of another entity available to deliberate appropriately on the bioethical issue.

Members are appointed by the president to serve renewable two-year terms and may include "not more than 18" people "who are not officers or employees of the federal government, and must be from the fields of science and medicine, law and government, philosophy and theology, and other areas of the humanities and social sciences.

CONTACT Address: President's Council on Bioethics, 1801 Pennsylvania Avenue NW, Suite 600, Washington, DC 20006; Phone: (202) 296-4669; E-mail: info@bioethics.gov; Website: www.bioethics.gov.

NATIONAL BIPARTISAN COMMISSION ON THE FUTURE OF MEDICARE

Created by Congress in the Balanced Budget Act of 1997 to examine and recommend improvements in the Medicare system so that it can cope with the financial crises coming as baby boomers (born 1946–64) retire and draw on Social Security funds, beginning in 2010. While they increase the Social Security payouts, fewer workers will be paying into the system, although baby boomers paid into the system all the time they were employed.

The commission has 17 members, divided equally (with a one-member majority) between Democrats and Republicans. All commission decisions must pass with at least 11 votes, rather than a simple majority, to avoid partisan outcomes.

CONTACT Address: Bipartisan Commission on the Future of Medicare, Adams Building, Library of Congress, 101 Independence Avenue SE, Washington, DC 20540-1998; Website: http://medicare.commission.gov or www.antiaging.com.

NATIONAL CAPITAL PLANNING COMMISSION (NCPC)

The central planning agency for the federal government. NCPC provides planning counsel for all federal land and buildings in the National Capital Region, which includes the District of Columbia; Prince George's and Montgomery Counties in Maryland; Arlington, Fairfax, Loudoun, and Prince William Counties in Virginia, and all the cities and towns bounded by these counties. The commission (five-person part-time) works to protect and enhance the historical, cultural, urban design, and natural resources of the District of Columbia.

CONTACT Address: NCPC, 401 9th Street NW, North Lobby, Suite 500, Washington, DC 20576; Phone: (202) 482-7200; Fax: (202) 482-7272; E-mail: info@ncpc.gov; Website: www.ncpc.gov.

NATIONAL COMMISSION ON LIBRARIES AND INFORMATION SCIENCE (NCLIS)

A permanent independent agency created with the 1970 enactment of Public Law 91-345. The

Museum and Library Services Act of 1996 created NCLIS for advising the director of the Institute of Museum and Library Services on its library services responsibilities.

NCLIS conducts studies and surveys, does analyses of, and coordinates plans for meeting U.S. library and information needs; promotes research and development; holds hearings and publishes documents; and provides policy advice to the director, the president, and Congress.

NCLIS consists of 14 members appointed to five-year terms by the president with advice and consent of the Senate, the librarian of Congress, and the director of the Institute of Library and Museum Services.

CONTACT Address: NCLIS, 1110 Vermont Avenue NW, Suite 820, Washington, DC 20005-3552; Phone: (202) 606-9200; Fax: (202) 606-9203; Website: www.nclis.gov.

NATIONAL COMMISSION ON TERRORIST ATTACKS UPON THE UNITED STATES

An independent commission created by Congress as part of the Intelligence Authorization Act for fiscal year 2003 to prepare an account of "circumstances surrounding" the September 11, 2001, terrorist attacks on the World Trade Center in New York and on the Pentagon in Washington, D.C. The commission looks at preparedness for and immediate response to the attacks, and will make recommendations to prevent future attacks. It is unknown whether the commission will also look at a possible lack of preparedness or into the underlying causes of the attacks. As of May 23, 2003, the commission had held two public hearings.

CONTACT Address: National Commission on Terrorist Attacks Upon the United States, 301 7th Street SW, Room 5125, Washington, DC 20407; Phone: (202) 331-4060; Fax: (202) 296-5545; E-mail: info@9-11commission.gov; Website: www.9-11commission.gov.

NATIONAL COUNCIL ON DISABILITY (NCD)

An independent agency that makes recommendations to Congress and to the president on issues that affect the United States's 54 million citizens with disabilities. The Americans with Disabilities Act was signed into law in 1990, resulting from NCD's 1986 report, "Toward Independence," that recommended that Congress enact a civil rights law for people with disabilities.

NCD's goal is to promote policies, programs, practices, and procedures to guarantee equal opportunity for all people with disabilities, and to enable people with disabilities to gain economic self-sufficiency, independent living, and acceptance and full inclusion into society. There are 15 commissioners appointed by the president and confirmed by the senate for three-year terms.

CONTACT Address: NCD, 1331 F Street NW, Suite 850, Washington, DC 20004; Phone: (202) 272-2004, TTY: (202) 272-2074; Fax: (202) 272-2022; E-mail: mquigley@ncd.gov; Website: www.ncd.gov.

NATIONAL CREDIT UNION ADMINISTRATION (NCUA)

Established in 1970 as an independent agency to regulate and insure all federal credit unions, and insure state-chartered credit unions that qualify for share insurance and apply for it. NCUA runs the Community Development Revolving Loan Fund and the Central Liquidity Facility, a government corporation that gives emergency loans to member credit unions.

NCUA conducts an investigation process and grants charters for federal credit unions to groups forming credit unions that have the common bond of occupation, profession, or other association, or to groups who have in common a well-defined neighborhood, community, or rural district. NCUA also conducts annual checks and examinations of federal credit unions to reassess the credit unions' solvency and compliance with laws and regulations, and to advise on needed improvements in management.

NCUA's "Share Insurance" program makes insurance on deposited funds available to federal credit unions, for which it is mandatory, and to those state-chartered credit unions that are required to have federal shared insurance. Not all states require shared insurance of their state-chartered credit unions. Because of NCUA insurance, depositors in NCUA-provided shared insurance credit unions have their funds insured up to $100,000. The National Credit Union Share Insurance Fund requires insured credit unions to keep 1 percent of total insured funds deposited in the fund.

NCUA has a warning system to find emerging problems in individual credit unions as well as in the system, and to keep track of operations between official examinations.

CONTACT   Address: NCUA, 1775 Duke Street, Alexandria, VA 22314-3428; Phone: (703) 518-6300; Website: www.ncua.gov. Regional offices: 9 Washington Avenue, Albany, NY 12205; Phone: (518) 862-7400; Fax: (518) 862-7420. Suite 1600, 7000 Central Parkway, Atlanta, GA 30328; Phone: (678) 443-3000; Fax: (678) 443-3020. Suite 5200, 4807 Spicewood Springs Road, Austin, TX 78759-8490; Phone: (512) 342-5600; Fax: (512) 342-5620. Suite 4206, 1775 Duke Street, Alexandria, VA 22314; Phone: (703) 519-4600; Fax: (703) 519-6674. Suite 125, 4225 Naperville Road, Lisle, IL 60532-3658; Phone: (630) 955-4100; Fax: (630) 955-4120. Suite 1350, 2300 Clayton Road, Concord, CA 94520; Phone and Fax: (925) 363-6220.

NATIONAL FOUNDATION ON THE ARTS AND THE HUMANITIES

The National Foundation on the Arts and the Humanities is an independent agency created by Congress as part of the National Foundation on the Arts and the Humanities Act of 1965 to develop national humanities and arts policies for the United States. Various administrations since then have increased or decreased funding to the arts and humanities according to their political priorities.

The foundation includes the *National Endowment for the Arts*, the *National Endowment for the Humanities*, the *Institute of Museum and Library Services*, and the *Federal Council on the Arts and the Humanities*. Each endowment has its own national council, appointed by the president and confirmed by the Senate. The National Council on the Arts includes 20 members, 14 of whom are appointed by the president, and six are members of Congress selected by House and Senate leadership and serve ex officio. The Federal Council on the Arts and the Humanities includes the chairs of both endowments, the director of Museum and Library Services, and other federal cultural officials.

NATIONAL ENDOWMENT FOR THE ARTS (NEA): An independent agency that makes grants to support "significant projects of artistic excellence," the meaning of "significant" and "excellence" subject to the political and moral inclinations of individual administrations. NEA gives national recognition and financial support to artists and arts groups, enabling many of them to exist in the 50 states, American Samoa, District of Columbia, Guam, Northern Mariana Islands, Puerto Rico, and U.S. Virgin Islands. Among NEA's better-known recipients are the PBS series *Great Performances;* design of the Vietnam Veterans Memorial; some recipients of National Book Awards, National Book Critics Circle Awards, and

Pulitzer Prizes; productions of *A Chorus Line* at the regional level; and some famous jazz artists.

NEA's chair is appointed by the president to a four-year term.

NATIONAL COUNCIL ON THE ARTS: Advises the chair of the endowment on policy, programs, and grant applications. Grants go to arts projects in the fields of dance, design, folk and traditional arts, literature, media arts such as film, television, video, radio, and audio art, music, musical theater, opera, theater, visual arts, and multidisciplinary works in the categories of grants for Arts Projects, Partnership Agreements, Leadership Initiatives, and Literature Fellowships. Occasional Lifetime Achievement fellowships in jazz, folk, and traditional arts may be awarded based on nomination processes.

Applications are welcome from nonprofit, tax-exempt American organizations such as arts organizations, arts service organizations, federally recognized tribal communities and tribes, state or local government entities, and other groups that work with goals shared with NEA. NEA also works with other funders for international exposure of American artists' work abroad, including funding appearances at international arts festivals.

NEA maintains a library, the Nancy Hanks Center in the Old Post Office Building in Washington, D.C., with 10,000 books, 200 magazine titles, and yards of files on the arts, arts management, and arts policy.

CONTACT Phone: (202) 682-5485 to arrange a visit; Address: NEA, 1100 Pennsylvania Avenue NW, Washington, DC 20506-0001; Phone: (202) 682-5400; TDD: (202) 682-5496; Website: www.nea.gov or www.arts.gov.

NATIONAL ENDOWMENT FOR THE HUMAN-ITIES: An independent agency that funds research, education, and public programs in the humanities, which the endowment defines as "language, both modern and classical, linguistics, literature, history, jurisprudence, philosophy,

archaeology, comparative religion, ethics, the history, criticism and theory of the arts, and social sciences that include historical or philosophical approaches."

NEH makes grants to individuals, groups, schools, colleges, universities, museums, public television stations, libraries, private nonprofit groups, agencies, and other groups that work in the humanities. Grant opportunities include challenge grants in which nonprofits can apply for long-term funds for educational, scholarly, preservation, and public programs in the humanities (202-606-8309); education grants and fellowships to scholars, teachers, and institutions for humanities (202-606-8500); endowment grants through the states and their possessions (202-606-8254); and grants for preservation, research, and access to the humanities through education and public programming (202-606-8570).

CONTACT Address: 1100 Pennsylvania Avenue NW, Washington, DC 20506; Phone: (202) 606-8400; Website: www.neh.gov.

INSTITUTE OF MUSEUM AND LIBRARY SERVICES: An independent agency that gives grants to support museums and libraries and created by the Museum and Library Services Act of 1996, amending the Museum Services Act. Its duties combine those of the former Institute of Museum Service and the DEPARTMENT OF EDUCATION. The director runs the institute and takes direction from the National Museum Services Board, made up of 14 members appointed by the president and the director.

IMLS gives grants to art, history, general, children's, natural history, and science and technology museums, as well as historic houses, zoos, aquariums, botanical gardens, arboretums, nature centers, and planetariums. Libraries that might be eligible include public, school, academic, research, and special libraries. IMLS also gives small grants for small libraries for tribes and Alaska Native villages, and Native Hawaiians, including technical assistance for their libraries.

Special grants are available to help museums preserve documents and objects, for technical assistance to museums, and for conservation management. IMLS also gives the National Award for Museum Service. The National Museum Services Board is advisory only and has 15 members appointed by the president and confirmed by the Senate. The National Commission on Libraries and Information Science has 14 members appointed by the president and confirmed by the Senate, and two statutory members.

CONTACT   Address: Room 510, 1100 Pennsylvania Avenue NW, Washington, DC 20506; Phone: (202) 606-8536; E-mail: imlsinfo@imls.gov; Website: www.imls.gov.

NATIONAL INVASIVE SPECIES COUNCIL

Established by President Bill Clinton's Executive Order 13112 in 1999, the council is an interdepartment council made up of the secretaries of interior, agriculture, state, defense, treasury, transportation, health and human services, and administrators of the ENVIRONMENTAL PROTECTION AGENCY and the U.S. Agency for International Development. The council works with the Invasive Species Advisory Committee, which gives advice and vital information to the council and is made up of 32 stakeholders from industry, conservation groups, scientists, state organizations, and academia. Invasive species can upset the ecology of an area or water body by multiplying and consuming native species, potentially eliminating species vital to the ecology.

CONTACT   Address: National Invasive Species Council, Department of the Interior, Office of the Secretary, 1849 C Street NW, Washington, DC 20240; Phone: (202) 513-7243; Fax: (202) 371-1751; E-mail: invasivespecies@ios.doi.gov.

NATIONAL LABOR RELATIONS BOARD (NLRB)

An independent agency established by Congress in 1935 to administer the National Labor Relations Act, which governs relations between unions and employers in the private sector, guaranteeing employees the right to organize and to bargain collectively with employers or to not bargain.

NLRB functions through secret ballot elections to determine the free democratic choice by employees whether they want to be represented by a union and which one, and to prevent and remedy unfair labor practices by employers or by employee unions. NLRB acts on unfair labor practice charges and employee election petitions that are filed with the NLRB, and does not initiate action itself. The board has 51 regional, subregional, and resident offices, which are the initial site of hearings, investigations, and rulings on issues raised under the National Labor Relations Act.

NLRB comprises five members appointed by the president to five-year terms with consent of the Senate, who sit as a quasi-judicial body in administrative proceedings including appeals from local rulings. The board's general counsel is appointed by the president to a four-year term with consent of the Senate, is independent of the board, and has duties including supervising case processing in NLRB field offices, and investigation and prosecution of unfair labor practice cases. After investigations, regional directors make the initial determination on the validity and next steps in a case within their geographic regions. Cases may be dismissed at the regional level, and may be appealed to the general counsel's office in Washington, D.C.

CONTACT   Address: NLRB, 1099 Fourteenth Street NW, Washington, DC 20570; Phone: (202) 273-1000; TDD: (202) 273-4300; Website: www.nlrb.gov.

NATIONAL MEDIATION BOARD (NMB)

Established by 1934 amendments to the Railway Labor Act of 1926 as an independent agency to facilitate labor-management relations within the railroads and airlines of the United States with the goal of minimizing work stoppages within the airline and railroad industries to avoid interruption of public service. NMB's goals include prompt and orderly resolution of disputes emanating from collective bargaining agreements; encouragement of self-organization when disputes over representation exist; and prompt and orderly resolution of disputes over application or interpretation of existing agreements.

When negotiations on revision of pay rates, rules, or working conditions fail, either party to the dispute may ask NMB to mediate. NMB usually uses mediation, interest-based problem solving, or facilitation. When disruption of essential transportation occurs, NMB may recommend that the president form a Presidential Emergency Board to prevent work stoppage or impose a lockout for up to 60 days.

NMB has responsibility to resolve peacefully union representation disputes by conducting investigations of representation applications; deciding on and certifying collective bargaining representatives of employees; and ensuring that the process proceeds and succeeds free of coercion, influence, or interference.

To attain positive change in collective bargaining and to achieve quicker dispute resolution, NMB engages in alternative dispute resolution and prevention techniques such as interest-based bargaining and facilitation; pre-dispute mediation; grievance mediation; training in facilitation process; and continuing education in communication in conflict management, consensual decision making, group problem solving, interest-based and traditional bargaining, and grievance mediation. The Board is composed of three appointees of the president and confirmed by the Senate.

CONTACT Address: NMB, 1301 K Street NW, Suite 250 East, Washington, DC 20005-7011; Phone: (202) 692-5000 or 692-5050; Website: www.nmb.gov.

NATIONAL PARK FOUNDATION (NPF)

Chartered as a nonprofit partner entity by Congress in 1967 to raise private money to support national parks and to develop a broad constituency to care about the parks. Even though it receives no federal government monies, NPF's additional goals are to give grants, create innovative partnerships to support national parks, and increase public awareness. At NPF's birth in 1967, Congress gave it a $1 million start-up grant from Laurence Rockefeller. In 2001 alone, NPF raised over $41 million, with fund-raising and administrative costs representing only 10 percent of its expenditures. Board members are appointed by secretary of interior, who serves as the foundation's chairman of the board. The director of the National Park Service serves as the secretary of the board, whose vice chairman is David Rockefeller, Jr.

NPF launched its $50 pass program in 2000 to cover for one year a person's entry into any national park that charges admission fees. Following restoration of the Washington Monument and the Edison National Historic Site with private funds, NPF started the "Proud Partner of America's National Parks" program to increase public awareness of parks and give away passes with funds from American Airlines, Discovery Communications, Inc., Ford Motor Company, Kodak, and *Time* magazine.

With Congress's passage of the National Parks Omnibus Management Act of 1998, the foundation received the charge to "design and implement a comprehensive program to assist and promote philanthropic programs of support at the individual national park unit level." Hence, NPF created five new Fund of the National Park Foundations with citizen trustees. NPF has 170 local park support organizations.

CONTACT Address: NPF, 11 Dupont Circle NW, Suite 600, Washington, DC 20036; Phone: (202) 238-4200; Fax: (202) 234-3103; Website: www.nationalparks.org.

NATIONAL SCIENCE FOUNDATION (NSF)

An independent agency created by the National Science Foundation Act of 1950 to improve U.S. scientific and engineering knowledge and research and education programs, and to improve international cooperation through science and engineering. The National Science Foundation is guided by the *National Science Board,* which has 24 members and a director who serves ex officio. Members are appointed by the president, with consent of the Senate, to six-year terms, and usually have backgrounds in science, engineering, education, research management, or public affairs (sometimes meaning partisan politics).

NSB funds long-term research in science and engineering through grants, contracts, and other agreements with universities, colleges, academic consortia, nonprofit organizations, and small businesses, encouraging cross-category cooperation and collaboration. NSB also funds undergraduate, graduate, and post-doctoral researchers, and international exchange programs, and supports national and international science and engineering interest groups such as the U.S. Antarctic Program, the Ocean Drilling Program (oil), and global geoscience studies. Administratively, the foundation operates through a

director and deputy director, both appointed by the president with senate confirmation, and directorates for biological services, computer and information science education and human resources, engineering, geosciences, mathematical and physical sciences, and social and behavioral sciences.

NSB encourages development of teaching materials, teacher preparation, college science instruments, course and curriculum development, faculty and student activities, and minority resource centers. The National Science Foundation's Commission on the Advancement of Women and Minorities in Science, Engineering, and Technology's (CAWMSET) charter term expired, and President George W. Bush did not renew it. The legislation creating CAWMSET was sponsored by Rep. Constance A. Morella (R.-Maryland), and the bill was signed in 1998 by President Bill Clinton.

NSB annually awards the Vannevar Bush Award and the Public Service Award, while the National Science Foundation presents the Alan T. Waterman Award.

CONTACT Address: National Science Board and National Science Foundation, 4201 Wilson Boulevard, Arlington, VA 22230; Phone: (703) 292-5111; Website: www.nsf.gov.

NATIONAL SKILL STANDARDS BOARD (NSSB)

Established by the National Skill Standards Act of 1994 to develop a national skill standards system of skill standards, assessment, and certification systems to help American workers compete in a global economy. NSSB's 24 members come from business, labor, and employee, education, community, and civil rights organizations.

Skill areas NSSB works on include agriculture, forestry, fishing, business and administrative services, construction, education and training, finance and insurance, health and human services, manufacturing, installation and repair, mining, public administration, legal and security services, restaurants, lodging, hospitality, tourism, recreation, retail, wholesale, real estate, scientific and technical services, telecommunications, computers, arts and entertainment, information technology, transportation, utilities, and environmental and waste management. Officials from Brazil, Chile, Germany, South Korea, Mexico, Singapore, and the United Kingdom have visited NSSB to compare notes. While this appears to be a serious national voluntary endeavor, it may be of limited effect on American workers' employment opportunities if industry continues to send jobs out of the United States as it did in 2003.

CONTACT Address: 1441 L Street NW, Suite 9000, Washington, DC 20005-3512; Phone: (202) 254-8628; Fax: (202) 254-8646; Website: www.nssb.org.

NATIONAL TECHNOLOGY TRANSFER CENTER (NTTC)

Founded in 1989 as the Robert C. Byrd National Technology Transfer Center, NTTC offers products and services to help American businesses communicate with and get information from experts and researchers in federal laboratories and agencies. Businesses can tap into this information to establish or increase their e-commerce abilities.

Activities, services, and products NTTC offers include commercialization strategy development, competitive intelligence reports, database services, donations, knowledge portals, manufacturing services, a resource center, technology evaluation and commercialization, and training services. Specialized new programs include an e-commerce center on-line for training courses, business assistance, links to e-commerce and business resources; Emergency Response Technology Program for commercializing new health- and safety-related products for emergency responders; Entrepreneurial Technology Apprenticeship Program to develop trained professionals in technology and its management; and an Environmental Technologies Program to access the ENVIRONMENTAL PROTECTION AGENCY for research, technology, and potential collaborations.

CONTACT Address: Robert C. Byrd National Technology Transfer Center, Wheeling Jesuit University, 316 Washington Avenue, Wheeling, WV 26003; Phone: (800) 678-6882; Fax: (304) 243-4388; Website: www.nttc.edu.

NATIONAL TRANSPORTATION SAFETY BOARD (NTSB)

An independent agency whose responsibility is to investigate every civil aviation accident in the United States, as well as major railroad, highway, marine, and pipeline accidents, and to issue safety recommendations to prevent future accidents.

NTSB seeks to determine the probable cause of all U.S. civil aviation accidents and some public-use aircraft accidents; some highway accidents; train accidents that involve passenger trains or any other train accident resulting in at least one death or major property damage; major marine accidents and any marine accident that involves a public vessel and nonpublic vessel; pipeline accidents with a death or substantial property damage; releases of hazardous materials in all forms of transportation; and some recurring sorts of transportation accidents.

NTSB also maintains the civil aviation accident database; conducts special studies of transportation safety issues; provides investigators for some aviation accidents in other countries that involve American aircraft or aircraft primarily made of American parts; and serves as a court of appeals for any airman, mechanic, or mariner when certificate action is taken by the Federal Aviation Administration or the U.S. Coast Guard commandant, or when civil penalties are assessed by FAA. The board also meets needs of victims and families of victims of aviation disasters by coordination with other organizations, airlines, and local and state governments.

NTSB has five board members nominated by the president and confirmed by the Senate to five-year terms, with presidential appointments to chair and vice chair two-year terms also requiring Senate confirmation.

CONTACT Address: 490 L'Enfant Plaza SW, Washington, DC 20594; Phone: (202) 314-6000; Website: www.ntsb.gov.

NEIGHBORHOOD REINVESTMENT AND NEIGHBORWORKS®

Created under Title VI of the Housing and Community Development Amendments of 1978 to expand the Urban Reinvestment Task Force's demonstration activities and "to revitalize older urban neighborhoods by mobilizing public, private, and community resources at the neighborhood level." It works to create and strengthen local partnerships of residents, businesses, and government to advance community development goals.

NeighborWorks® is a national network of 223 community-based organizations working to stimulate reinvestment in abandoned and distressed properties and to enable home ownership. The Neighborhood Reinvestment Corporation (NRC) founded the NeighborWorks® network and provides funding, training, and technical assistance. NRC offers a secondary market for

NeighborWorks® loans through the Neighborhood Housing Services of America (NHSA). Chartered organizations within the network are often known as Neighborhood Housing Services (NHS) or Mutual Housing Association (MHA), but may have other names as well. Each organization has local funding and control through a revolving loan fund to low-income people who do not qualify for conventional loans, in which as they repay their loans the money they pay back is loaned to someone else. Major social investors in this program include the Aetna Life and Casualty Company, American Express, Ahmanson Foundation, Fannie Mae and Freddie Mac, Evangelical Lutheran Church of America, Downtown Presbyterian Church of Rochester, New York, Ford Foundation, Levi Strauss Foundation, John D. and Catherine T. MacArthur Foundation, State of New Jersey, State Farm Insurance Companies, and Washington Mutual Bank.

CONTACT Address: 1325 G Street, Suite 800, Washington, DC 20005-3100; Phone: (202) 220-2300; Fax: (202) 376-2600; Website: www.nw.org/network/Home.asp.

NORTHWEST POWER PLANNING COUNCIL

Created by Congress in the Northwest Power Act of 1980 to give the citizens of Idaho, Montana, Oregon, and Washington a role in determining the future of Columbia River Basin resources, including hydroelectric power and fish and wildlife. After passage by Congress, the act was further approved by legislative vote in all four affected states. The council has eight members, two appointed by the governor of each state. The council's activities are funded by revenue made from the Bonneville Power Administration's wholesale sales of power generated by federal dams along the Columbia River.

The act's original mandates to the council were: develop a 20-year electric power plan to guarantee energy at the lowest environmental and economic cost to resources and to consumers; research and develop renewable resources such as wind, power, solar, geothermal, biomass, as well as energy conservation; develop a fish and wildlife program to protect and restore species affected and threatened by development of hydropower dams and plants in the Columbia River Basin; and work to educate and involve the public in the council's decision-making process, including state, tribal, and local governments. The plans are supposed to be updated at least every five years.

The Bonneville Power Administration, the U.S. Army Corps of Engineers, the Bureau of Reclamation, and the Federal Energy Regulatory Commission are supposed to implement the council's plans and policies.

CONTACT Address: 851 SW Sixth Avenue, Suite 1100, Portland, OR 97204; Phone: (503) 222-5161 or (800) 452-5161; Fax: (503) 820- 2370; E-mail: info@nwppc.org; Website: www.nwppc.org or www.nwcouncil.org.

(U.S.) NUCLEAR REGULATORY COMMISSION

Established by the Energy Reorganization Act of 1974, the U.S. Nuclear Regulatory Commission is mandated to regulate commercial reactors, radioactive materials, and nuclear materials waste. Many of its statutory responsibilities date back to the Atomic Energy Act of 1954. The commission is composed of five members appointed for staggered five-year terms by the president with Senate confirmation; the chair is designated by the president.

The mission of the commission is to protect the public from harm caused by nuclear materials and those nuclear reactors that generate electricity or those used for research, testing, or training workers. Nuclear reactor problems can include faulty construction, leaks, and meltdowns of radioactive elements making electricity.

The commission is responsible for ensuring that nuclear materials that generate unhealthy levels of radiation are controlled. These materials are not limited to those used by reactors, but also to those employed by industrial, medical, and educational institutions that use or produce nuclear fuel or collateral by-products.

Nuclear waste is created as a by-product of energy production by reactors, or remain after such a plant is shut down or decommissioned. The disposal of the waste (which has a half-life of more than a human lifetime) must be provided by secure storage not subject to leaks and in settings well removed from an active population, and safely transported on routes away from the danger of major leakage. These are not easy or simple issues because even nuclear waste in a lead drum dumped into the ocean has been known to seep out into the surrounding waters.

The five-member board sets basic policy and direction. The policies and decisions are administered under the direction of the *executive director of operations.* The offices of the commission are divided into two groupings, those administered by the commission, which are principally administrative, and those directed by the executive director of operations, which are concerned with programs of safety, security, regulation, and enforcement.

COMMISSION STAFF OFFICES

Appellate Adjudication, which involves appeals from administrative hearings; *Congressional Affairs,* maintaining liaison with Congress on commission activities; *General Counsel, International Programs,* involving cooperation with other governments and international nuclear regulatory organizations for control of licensing and import-export of nuclear materials and equipment; *Public Affairs,* dealing with information for the media and general public; *inspector general;* and *chief financial officer.*

EXECUTIVE DIRECTOR OF OPERATIONS OFFICES

OFFICE OF NUCLEAR MATERIAL SAFETY AND SAFEGUARDS: Responsible for all activities regulated by the commission, other than those dealing with reactors, in particular the handling of radioactive materials, in recovery, fabrication, storage and transportation of such materials used in medicine, academia, and industry. These responsibilities include safety and safeguarding of waste and dealing with accidents. This office has subdivisions of Management and Policy Development, Fuel Cycle Safety, Industrial and Medical Nuclear Safety, Materials Safety and Inspection, Rulemaking and Guidance, Waste Management, Decommissioning, Environmental and Performance Assessment, High-Level Waste, Spent Fuel Project, Licensing and Inspection, and Technical Review.

OFFICE OF NUCLEAR REACTOR REGULATION: Responsible for all the activities of nuclear reactors, and assuring that they operate according to the NRC rules, requirements, and regulations.

OFFICE OF NUCLEAR REGULATORY RESEARCH: Analyzes results of recent regulation in order to develop, recommend, and implement programs of improved regulation. This covers engineering, safety margins and systems, materials engineering, regulatory effectiveness, and risk analysis.

OFFICE OF STATE AND TRIBAL PROGRAMS: Maintains contact and information exchange between the commission and states, local governments, Native American tribal organizations, and other federal agencies.

OFFICE OF ENFORCEMENT: Takes all necessary actions to require enforcement of the rules, requirements, and regulations. This includes bringing enforcement actions before an administration law judge.

OFFICE OF INVESTIGATIONS: Conducts investigations in support of efforts to enforce regulations or prevent negligence and danger to the public from nuclear reactors. This authority extends to activities of vendors to nuclear reactors.

OFFICE OF NUCLEAR SECURITY AND INCIDENT RESPONSE: Evaluates the security systems in place at nuclear facilities and recommends means to improve them in conjunction with the DEPARTMENT OF HOMELAND SECURITY. It assesses safeguards at nuclear reactors and other facilities using radioactive materials. A key responsibility is to make sure that NRC communications are secure and there are systems in place to respond to crises such as an impending meltdown.

OFFICE OF THE CHIEF INFORMATION OFFICER: Provides information to the general public, other agencies, and the media.

OFFICE OF ADMINISTRATION: Provides means for program offices to function effectively.

FIELD OFFICES

The NRC has four field offices that conduct investigations and evaluations in meeting licensing requirements and other services and monitoring functions. They are located in Philadelphia, Atlanta, Chicago, and Dallas.

ADVISORY COMMITTEES

Advisory Committee on Reactor Safeguards: Advises the commission in regard to licensing and operations of nuclear reactors, in particular safety standards and practices. The committee also reviews standards, activities, nuclear facilities, and specific safety issues either upon request of the commission or on its own initiative. This advisory committee also advises the DEPARTMENT OF ENERGY Nuclear Facilities Safety Board on these issues. It issues an annual report that comments on the commission's Safety Research Program.

Advisory Committee on Nuclear Waste: Advises the commission in regard to nuclear waste management. It conducts studies to recommend management of radioactive materials while being transported or stored and the disposal of both low- and high-level radioactive waste, including spent nuclear fuel from reactors. The committee recommends means of decommissioning, suggests regulations, and evaluates licensing documents and rules when requested by the commission.

Both advisory committees are assisted in their work by the *Committee Support Staff,* which provides technical, management, administrative, and fiscal support.

Atomic Safety and Licensing Board Panel: Responsible for coordinating the activities of administrative law judges who conduct hearings for the commission and in other ways assists the commission in related matters such as database collection. The panel is composed of three members chaired by the chief administrative law judge, and two others, responsible for legal and technical issues, respectively. The panel is assisted in its operations by a chief counsel. It also maintains a substantial database and Digital Data Management System administered by the *Licensing Support Network Administrator* and has a support and analysis staff.

Administrative Law Judges: Both part-time and full-time, conduct hearings on nuclear facilities licensing and other issues such as adherence to safety regulations. The judges are lawyers or engineers or scientists knowledgeable in the issues involved. When three-member panels of judges are called, the presiding judge is almost always a lawyer.

CONTACT Address: One White Flint North, 11555 Rockville Pike, Rockville, MD 20852, and

Two White Flint North, 11545 Rockville Pike, Rockville, MD 20852. Mail: U.S. Nuclear Regulatory Commission, Washington, DC 20555; Phone: (301) 415-7000, 1(800) 368-5642; Public Affairs: (301) 415-8200; Freedom of Information: (301) 415-7169; E-mail: opa@nrc.gov; Website: www.nrc.gov.

OCCUPATIONAL SAFETY AND HEALTH REVIEW COMMISSION (OSHRC)

Established as an independent agency by the Occupational Safety and Health Act of 1970. OSHRC is separate from OSHA and serves as a court system that adjudicates disputes between employees and most employers in the United States and the secretary of labor when cases arise from contested workplace safety inspections.

The OSHRC's goals include reducing personal injuries, illness, and deaths among U.S. workers by requiring employers to provide a hazard-free environment and to comply with occupational safety and health standards required by the act. Policies are set by a three-person board appointed by the president, with Senate confirmation.

Employers and employees have a right to contest citations for health or safety violations or problems within 15 days following an inspection. Normally the entity receives a proposed penalty and a certain time by which to correct a hazardous situation, and employees have the right to initiate a case to challenge the time given for the entity to correct the problem. When either employer or employee formally contests a citation, OSHRC gets involved and assigns a docket number to the file, and notifies all parties to the contest. Then an administrative law judge assigns the case to a judge in Washington, D.C., Atlanta, or Denver. Each decision is subject to discretionary review by three members of the commission at the direction of any one of them within 30 days of the original decision filing. Anyone adversely affected by such a decision may ask for a review of the decision in the U.S. COURT OF APPEALS.

CONTACT Address: OSHRC, 1120 20th Street NW, Washington, DC, 20036-3419; Phone: (202) 606-5100; Website: www.oshrc.gov.

OFFICE OF COMPLIANCE

An independent agency established by the Congressional Accountability Act of 1995 to protect legislative branch and congressional employees' safety, health, and workplace rights. The office offers impartial dispute resolution processes, and works to educate legislative and congressional employees and employers on their rights and responsibilities under the Congressional Accountability Act.

CONTACT Address: Room LA 200, John Adams Building, 110 Second Street SE, Washington, DC 20540-1999; Phone: (202) 724-9250, TDD: (202) 426-1912; Fax: (202) 426-1913; Website: www. compliance.gov.

OFFICE OF GOVERNMENT ETHICS (OGE)

Originally part of the Office of Personnel Management as established by the Ethics in Government Act of 1978, it became a separate agency on October 1, 1989, as part of the Office of Government Ethics Reauthorization Act of 1988. OGE's goal is to prevent government employees from having conflicts of interest, and to resolve those that do happen.

Note: OGE's website home page informs the visitor to its website that ". . . the Government may monitor and audit the use of this system, and all persons are hereby notified that the use of this system constitutes consent to such monitoring and auditing. . . ."

OGE is run by a director who is appointed to a five-year term by the president. OGE has five offices that jointly carry out its mission. The kinds of conflicts of interest researched, investigated, and resolved include: gifts from outside sources; gifts between employees; employees who have financial interests that conflict with their government role; possible compromises of impartiality in official duties for the government; seeking other employment; misuse of one's government position; outside activities that could be prohibited or in conflict with government duties; collection of honoraria or other fees in conflict with employment; after-employment conflicts; representation or lobbying before government agencies or courts; supplementation of salary; and errors in financial disclosure, certificates of divestitures, recusals, and waivers.

CONTACT Address: OGE, Suite 500, 1201 New York Avenue NW, Washington, DC 20005-3917; Phone: (202) 208-8000; Website: www.usoge.gov.

OFFICE OF PERSONNEL MANAGEMENT (OPM)

Established by the Reorganization Plan No. 2 of 1978 pursuant to President Jimmy Carter's Executive Order 12107, OPM runs the federal government's Federal Merit Systems Standards and the "merit system" for personnel (human resources) to make sure agencies comply with personnel laws and regulations in recruiting, examining, hiring, and promoting people on the basis of their knowledge and skills (merit), without consideration of their race, religion, sex, age, political influence, or other nonmerit factors.

OPM manages federal government employees' health benefits, life insurance, and retirement benefits. It gives technical assistance for examinations for competitive positions in the civil service for General Schedule (GS) grades 1 through 15, as well as Federal Wage system positions. OPM also establishes basic qualification standards for all occupations; certifies each agency's examination units; provides employment information for competitive service positions; provides direction on policy on promotions, reassignments, reinstatements, temporary and fixed-term employment, preferences for veterans, planning and reshaping overall personnel, organizational design, career transition, appointments in excepted and competitive services, and other staffing.

OPM oversees hiring of federal government executives and gives technical support on Senior Executive Services (SES) recruitment, performance, awards, layoffs, and firings. In this role OPM reviews SES nominations and conducts orientation sessions for each agency and runs the Qualifications Review Boards that certifies candidates' qualifications. It runs the Presidential Rank Awards program, and manages three interagency development and training centers as residential training programs for incoming executives and managers.

OPM takes administrative action against health care providers who commit offenses worthy of sanctions that affect the Federal Employees' Health Benefits Program or other federal government programs.

OPM guides agency personnel managers on blue- and white-collar pay systems; special pay for geographic or neighborhood conditions; special pay considerations for jobs or locations with high turnover; allowances and other benefits, such as bonuses for signing on and relocating; allowances to keep employees in some locations; premium pay; annual, sick, and court leave; military leave; family and medical leave; excused absences; holiday work; flexible (flex time) work schedules; and compressed work schedules. OPM also works in performance management, performance pay and awards, and incentive awards for suggestions, inventions, and special acts; sets and advises on classifica-

tion policy and standards; labor-management relations such as collective bargaining, negotiation, unfair labor practices, and consultation with unions; dispute resolution systems and techniques; quality of worklife initiatives including health and fitness, work and family, AIDS, and employee assistance; and human resources development. OPM administers the Human Resources Development Council and the Government Performance and Results Act interest group, and the Training and Management Assistance program. It develops technical information systems to support personnel management, provides instructions for personnel processing and record keeping, and release of personnel data under the Freedom of Information Act and the Privacy Act. OPM also helps administrators of the Federal Prevailing Rate Advisory Committee, the Federal Salary Council, and the Presidential Advisory Committee on Expanding Training Opportunities.

Topics with which OPM works include accountability and accountability standards, civil service rules, job or GS classification and classification appeals, disabilities, family leave policies, retirement and retirement systems, veterans, and welfare-to-work programs.

As of June 1, 2002, OPM provided policy, leadership, and guidance on affirmative action and recruiting toward hiring women, minorities, people with disabilities, and veterans. However, in 2003, the Department of Justice in President George W. Bush's administration filed an amicus curiae (friend of the court) brief against the affirmative action program of student admissions at the University of Michigan; the Supreme Court ruled that the Michigan program was constitutional. OPM is supposed to promote merit and equality in recruitment, employment, training, and employee retention. It also studies and writes reports and statistical data on diversity in the federal workplace and coordinates movement of employees between federal agencies and state, local, and Indian tribal governments and education institutions.

Federal Executive Boards were created by President John F. Kennedy in November 1961 to improve management practices within the government's agencies and to encourage federal employees' participation in civic affairs outside their employment. OPM supervises the Federal Executive Boards.

CONTACT Address: OPM, 1900 E Street NW, Washington, DC 20415-0001; Phone: (202) 606-1800 and (202) 606-1200, reporting alleged violations; Website: www.opm.gov.

OFFICE OF THRIFT SUPERVISION (OTS)

Established in the DEPARTMENT OF TREASURY in 1989; regulates all federally chartered and many state-chartered thrift institutions, which include savings and loans. OTS is funded by fees assessed on the institutions it regulates.

CONTACT Address: OTS, 1700 G Street NW, Washington, DC 20552; Phone: (202) 906-6000; Website: www.ots.treas.gov.

OVERSEAS PRIVATE INVESTMENT CORPORATION (OPIC)

Established by the Foreign Affairs Reform and Restructuring Act of 1998. OPIC is now a self-sustaining development agency that helps American businesses invest in economic and social development in less developed countries and countries in transition from nonmarket economies to market economies, which would become valuable markets able to purchase goods and services from U.S. businesses. OPIC programs help U.S. businesses expand in 150 countries with an additional goal of helping improve U.S. competitiveness and strengthen and expand the American economy.

OPIC also serves as an advocate for U.S. business clients that make long-term investments in new markets abroad, including working with host country governments to develop hospitable investment climates. It helps businesses by loans and loan guarantees; private investment funds to provide equity for American companies that invest in projects in needy countries; insures investments against political risks of expropriation, currency value, and exchange problems, and against war, revolution, insurrection, or civil strife; and helps with outreach activities. Special programs include investment in minerals, oil, and gas exploration, as well as resource development and leasing operations. It also provides direct investment loans for five to 15 years to small and medium-sized businesses, usually ranging from $250,000 to $30 million.

OPIC's direct investment funds operate in East Asia, India, sub-Saharan Africa, South America, Russia, Poland, other countries in Central Europe, and Israel. Programs primarily fund work on existing plants such as expansion and modernization, or technological or other service projects that bring new benefits for host countries.

OPIC is managed by a president and CEO, executive vice president, and a board of directors all appointed by the president with Senate confirmation.

OPIC operates at no cost to taxpayers by charging U.S. businesses fees for its services, earning a profit every year it has been in operation.

CONTACT Address: OPIC, 1100 New York Avenue NW, Washington, DC 20527; Phone: (202) 336-8400; Fax: (202) 408-9859; Website: www.opic.gov.

PEACE CORPS

Established by the Peace Corps Act of 1961, the Peace Corps became an independent agency in title VI of the International Security and Development Cooperation Act of 1981. Democratic presidential candidate John F. Kennedy asked a question of 10,000 students awaiting his arrival at 2:00 A.M. on October 14, 1960 (President Dwight David Eisenhower's birthday): How many of them would be willing to serve their country and the cause of peace by living and working in the developing world? In his inauguration speech President Kennedy stated, "Ask not what your country can do for you, ask what you can do for your country." Kennedy's Peace Corps was the perfect destination for thousands of students and many others.

Sargent Shriver, husband of Eunice Kennedy Shriver, sister of the president, served as the first director of the Peace Corps, with Vice President Lyndon B. Johnson's former aide Rev. Bill Moyers as assistant director. Initially the small Peace Corps staff included daughters of senators and members of Congress, Kennedy campaign loyalists, experts, and people genuinely motivated by the Peace Corps' goal of service to others in the cause of peace and friendship.

Currently, nearly 7,000 Peace Corps volunteers serve in nearly 70 countries. More than 168,000 Americans have served in the Peace Corps, including teachers, carpenters, engineers, business people, and others such as President Jimmy Carter's mother, Lillian Carter.

Volunteers work to bring clean water, sanitation, and environment to communities, teach children and teach others to teach children, help locals start their own new businesses, help locals learn better farming skills to support themselves, and educate millions of people about HIV/AIDS, with the long-range goal of helping people control their own futures.

Nearly two-thirds of Peace Corps volunteers are female, 91 percent are single, 15 percent are minorities, the average age of volunteers is 28, and 86 percent have undergraduate college or university degrees, while 12 percent have attended graduate school or have advanced academic degrees.

Accepted Peace Corps volunteers go through training sessions of nine to 14 weeks, in which they learn the local language or dialect of the country where they are going, technical skills, and cross-cultural skills necessary to get along as a local in a new local community usually starkly different from their hometowns in the United States.

The Peace Corps also conducts its World Wise Schools Program, in which volunteers work with American schools to encourage exchanges of photos, letters, music, and artifacts.

The president appoints the director and deputy director, both requiring Senate confirmation.

CONTACT Address: 1111 Twentieth Street NW, Washington, DC 20526; Phone: (202) 692-2000 or (800) 424-8580 to volunteer; Fax: (202) 692-2231; Website: www.peacecorps.gov. Area offices: Suite 2R. 70, Building 1924, 100 Alabama Street, Atlanta, GA 30303; Phone: (404) 562-3456. Suite 450, 10 Causeway Street, Boston, MA 02222; Phone: (617) 565-5555. Suite 450, 55 W. Monroe Street, Chicago, IL 60603; Phone: (312) 353-4990. Room 527, 207 S. Houston Street, Dallas, TX 75202; Phone: (214) 767-5435. Suite 2208, 1999 Broadway, Denver, CO 80202; Phone: (303) 844-7020. Suite 8104, 11000 Wilshire Boulevard, Los Angeles, CA 90024; Phone: (310) 235-7444. Suite 420, 330 2nd Avenue, South, Minneapolis, MN 55401; Phone: (612) 348-1480. Suite 1025, 201 Varick Street, New York NY 10014; Phone: (212) 637-6498. Suite 600, 333 Market Street, San Francisco, CA 94105; Phone: (415) 977-8800. Room 1776, 2001 6th Avenue, Seattle, WA 22209; Phone: (703) 235-9191.

PENSION BENEFIT GUARANTY CORPORATION (PBGC)

A self-financing federal corporation created by Title IV of the Employee Retirement Income Security Act of 1974 to assure maintenance of defined benefit pension plans (pay specified monthly benefit at retirement) to provide uninterrupted payments of pension plan benefits to participants and beneficiaries, and keep pension insurance premiums as low as possible.

PBGC insures most private-sector defined benefit pension plans that provide benefits based on age, years of service, and salary, including two insurance programs that cover single-employer or multi-employer plans to more than 40 million workers. The maximum benefit that PBGC guarantees is set by law and adjusted yearly. In 2003 it covered up to $3,664.77 a month per retired employee.

Single-employer insurance covers payment of certain pension benefits in an insured plan that terminates without enough assets to pay the benefits it owes. Multi-employer insurance now covers plans declared insolvent and unable to pay nonforfeitable benefits, as of the Multiemployer Pension Plan Amendments Act of 1980.

PBGC supports itself by collecting insurance premiums from employers that offer insured pension plans, earning money from investments and from pension plans it takes over. The basic premium rate for single-employer plans is $19 per participant per year, and an additional $9 per $1,000 of unfunded vested benefits. The multi-employer pension plan rate per person is $2.60 for plan years beginning on September 26, 1988.

The corporation board of directors is made up of the secretaries of commerce, labor, and treasury, with the secretary of labor serving as chair. The president appoints a seven-member advisory committee representing labor (2), employers (2), and the general public (3), and advises the board on policies and procedures for PBGC investments, management, and trusteeship of terminated plans.

CONTACT Address: Pension Benefit Guaranty Corporation, 1200 K Street NW, Washington, DC 20005; Phone: (202) 326-4000 or (800) 400-4272; Website: www.pbgc.gov.

POSTAL RATE COMMISSION

Created by the Postal Reorganization Act as an independent regulatory agency that reviews the U.S. POSTAL SERVICE's requests to change domestic mail rates, fees, and mail classifications, and recommends their decisions to the board of governors of the Postal Service. Its hearings are on the record.

The Postal Rate Commission receives, researches, and conducts hearings on complaints on postage rates, postal classifications, and national problems in the Postal Service, and then recommends its decisions to the board of directors. It also serves as the appeals body that reviews Postal Service decisions to close or consolidate small post offices, and prepares an annual report.

The president appoints all five members of the Postal Rate Commission, with advice and consent of the Senate.

CONTACT Address: 1333 H Street NW, Washington, DC 20268-0001; Phone: (202) 789-6800; Fax: (202) 789-6886; Website: www.prc.gov.

PRESIDENT'S COMMISSION ON THE CELEBRATION OF WOMEN IN AMERICAN HISTORY

The commission and its website were closed in 2001 under President George W. Bush.

PRESIDENT'S COUNCIL ON INTEGRITY AND EFFICIENCY (PCIE) AND THE EXECUTIVE COUNCIL ON INTEGRITY AND EFFICIENCY (ECIE)

Both were established by President George H. W. Bush's executive order on May 11, 1992, to improve integrity, economy, and effectiveness in government agencies, and to increase professionalism and effectiveness among federal government employees. Members of both groups conduct interagency and inter-entity audits, inspections, and investigations to try to discover fraud, waste, and abuse, and to streamline efforts and improve efficiency in federal programs, and create policies, standards, and approaches to further improve the workforce.

PCIE is appointed by the president, and ECIE is appointed by agency heads, and representatives from the OFFICE OF MANAGEMENT AND BUDGET, the Federal Bureau of Investigation, the OFFICE OF GOVERNMENT ETHICS, the OFFICE OF SPECIAL COUNSEL, and the OFFICE OF PERSONNEL MANAGEMENT serve on both entities. The Office of Management and Budget's deputy director for management chairs both councils and appoints the vice chairs.

CONTACT Address: President's Council on Integrity and Efficiency, Office of Management and Budget, Room 6025, New Executive Office Building, Washington, DC 20503; Phone: (202) 395-6911; Website: www.ignet.gov.

PRESIDIO TRUST

A government agency and trust that manages the former army base at the Presidio of San Francisco, the oldest continuously operated military post in the United States. The Presidio is part of the Golden Gate National Recreation Area and is a National Historic Landmark District. It borders the largest chain of marine sanctuaries in the Northern Hemisphere, and includes buildings from every major military construction period since 1848. The Presidio is governed by a seven-member board.

CONTACT Address: Presidio of San Francisco, 34 Graham Street, P.O. Box 29052, San Francisco, CA 94129-0052; Phone: (415) 561-5300; Fax: (415) 561-5315.

SECURITIES AND EXCHANGE COMMISSION (SEC)

The Securities and Exchange Commission exists for several specific reasons: (a) to guarantee the integrity of the huge and complicated securities markets (stocks, bonds, investment trusts, and other securities) in order to protect the investing public; (b) to require complete disclosure of the financial condition of corporations of significant size; (c) to oversee all those involved in securities issuance, sales, transfer, advice-giving, and the stock markets; (d) to develop rules and regulations related to the securities industry, and the underlying securities legislation; and (e) to enforce the federal statutes and regulations related to securities.

The governing body is made up of five commissioners with five-year staggered terms ending on June 5, all appointed by the president with confirmation by the Senate, of whom no more than three can be of the same political party. The president also designates the chairperson. The commission has a staff of only 3,100, many of whom are attorneys and their support staff. Headquarters is in Washington, D.C., with 11 regional and district offices. The commissioners set policy and specifically interpret federal security laws, adopt and amend rules in response to the changing dynamics of the securities market and practices, and are responsible for enforcement of laws and regulations affecting the investment industry.

Every corporation that issues shares above a certain value level, or is involved in mergers or acquisitions, is required to file a detailed and formal registration statement and provide a detailed prospectus on the corporation with every stock offering, annual reports, and other disclosure documents. These are all subject to review and approval or disapproval by the SEC. Enforcement of security laws and SEC regulations includes numerous administrative hearings, approximately 500 legal actions annually, and referrals of severe infractions that may involve fraud to the appropriate United States attorney for prosecution.

An entire industry has grown up to service the public in the preparation of registrations, reports, and representation before the commission, its staff, administrative judges, and the courts. These are primarily attorneys, accountants, economists, and technical writers.

HISTORY

The stock market crash in October 1929 and the Great Depression that followed revealed how corrupt the U.S. securities system was. It operated without buyers having accurate information but with an abundance of disinformation, and included fraudulent and dangerous practices such as buying "on margin," which could cost the investor his or her entire investment with a small drop in the market, and "insider trading." Most investors were at the mercy of those with secret information, false advertising, and the instability of the stock exchanges.

When President Franklin D. Roosevelt took office in 1933, a prime New Deal reform was the first of a series of legislative acts to improve the operation of the stock market, to protect the investing public by requiring transparency of corporate funding through filed disclosures, and to crack down on unfair and dishonest practices.

The first two statutes enacted were the *Securities Act of 1933* (the "truth in securities" law) and the *Security Exchange Act of 1934.* The Securities Act required that companies offering securities had to be truthful about the condition of their corporation, the securities and the risks that the investor was taking that the company might not be profitable, and secondly, that people involved in the sale or trade of securities, including stockbrokers, dealers, and stock or commodities exchanges were required to conduct business to put the interests of investors first. The Security Exchange Act established the Securities Exchange Commission, and gave it powers of enforcement and broadened the scope of the original Securities Act to cover certain practices in the industry.

President Roosevelt appointed Joseph P. Kennedy as first chairman of the SEC. Kennedy, father of John F. Kennedy, was a wealthy stock trader who had added to his fortune through an understanding of the stock market, and on occasion through insider trading—taking advantage of inside knowledge of companies—selling just before corporate financial reverses became public, for example. The president's view was that the best watchdog would be such an insider, based on the aphorism "It takes one to know one." Kennedy proved to be a tough and effective top executive of the commission. In 1937 he was succeeded as chairman by a former law professor, 39-year-old William O. Douglas, a vigorous exponent of consumer protection, who served until 1939, when he was appointed to the SUPREME COURT.

New legislation incorporated within SEC jurisdiction other entities and functions. These included the *Public Utility Holding Company Act of 1935,* which brought SEC oversight to public utility companies, the *Trust Indenture Act of 1939,* covering bonds, debentures, and promissory notes offered for sale to the public, the *Investment Company Act of 1940,* which added mutual funds to SEC supervision, and the *Investment Advisers Act of 1940,* which required registration of professional investment advisers and their adherence to certain standards of conduct. In 1996 this act was amended to limit its application to investment advisers who manage more than $25 million for their clientele.

Over the years the activities of the commission have been broadened, defined, and refined by adoption of rules and regulations, and amendments to federal statutes. SEC has also joined in cooperative efforts with other government agencies and such private entities as the various stock exchanges and the National Association of Securities Dealers.

The commission's effectiveness has varied depending on the leadership of the commission and the enthusiasm—or lack thereof—of national administrations to emphasize protection of consumers. Even with supposedly strict oversight, fraudulent schemes, including manipulation of stock prices, false or exaggerated reports, and cover-ups of failures have occurred. In the case of Enron and other scandals of 2001 and beyond, there was widespread fraudulent milking of the companies, false financial statements, cover-up of losses, obscured overpayment of insider executives, and other actions the securities legislation was intended to prevent. The defrauding of investors, employees, and both federal and state governments was made possible through an unholy alliance of corporate officials, accounting firms (including the large and respected), lawyers, and stockbrokers, who lulled the investing public and government officials into believing that everything was legitimate.

ORGANIZATION

The commission itself sets basic policy, provides oversight and direction to management, and adopts and amends rules. While theoretically nonpartisan, it sets the tone of approach to security regulation and enforcement. Basic functions of the SEC are divided into four divisions:

DIVISION OF CORPORATION FINANCE: Responsible for oversight of disclosure by publicly held corporations for information about the companies, including finances, assets, and liabilities of organizers. By law the essential documents must be filed when the stock is initially issued, and periodically thereafter. The staff of the division reviews these documents, gives assistance to the corporations in order to complete and revise the documentation if found inadequate, and recommends rules to the commission in the area of corporate finance regulation.

The required documentation includes (a) registration statements upon a company's initial issue of securities (a "prospectus"), (b) annual and quarterly filings to update corporate information, (c) copies of proxy information sent to shareholders prior to each annual meeting (since the management is usually soliciting the right to vote shares in favor of its preselected slate of candidates and against any insurgent or independent candidates), (d) annual reports to stockholders, (e) documents about any "tender offer" for purchase of a large number of shares, and (f) any filings dealing with mergers of a corporation with another (often involving exchanges of stock or acquisition of another company).

These all involve reports of transactions in which the potential or actual shareholders/investors need knowledge of the corporation—particularly its financial condition—to make informed decisions. These decisions include buying, selling, or retaining shares or to approve or reject management proposals when such approval is required.

Even when the members of the public, including shareholders, may not be able to fully comprehend the strength of a corporation based on these filings, the Division of Corporation Finance requires disclosure of all information (negative as well as positive, such as pending litigation) and may require greater clarity in the reports made to the public.

Its staff gives guidance to registering corporations to assist in guaranteeing that the final version of a submission complies with the law and regulations, and may even determine that certain offerings of limited amount and scope may not require registration, or provides interpretation of regulations to prospective issuers of securities. The staff may review a proposed unprecedented financial or marketing technique, and determine whether it should be reviewed by the commission; if it determines the proposed action is apparently legal, upon request of the applicant, it will issue a letter recommending that the commission take no action against the corporation, known as a "no action" letter.

This division is also mandated to work with the commission's chief accountant to monitor the practices of accountants, through that profession's Financial Accounting Standards Board, and participate in the formulation of generally accepted accounting principles, which were so cavalierly violated in the Enron and other corporate looting scandals that emerged in 2001 and thereafter.

The division also proposes to the commission new rules in regard to matters within its sphere.

DIVISION OF MARKET REGULATION: This division regulates major participants in the security market to ensure they are fair, orderly, and efficient. These participants are: (a) stock exchanges, (b) broker-dealer firms, (c) the *National Association of Securities Dealers* (NASD), (d) the *Municipal Securities Rulemaking Board,* (e) clearing agencies, (f) transfer agents (that keep records of stocks and transfers, and actually move the documents, and (g) securities processors. Of these the exchanges, the NASD, the Municipal Securities Rulemaking Board, and the transfer agents are theoretically self-regulating, but are under oversight by the division.

The division establishes the standards for a fair, orderly, and efficient securities market, enforces regulations affecting the integrity of broker-dealers (which can be the subject of self-dealing in derogation of the interests of the investors), reviews proposed new rules and amendments to existing rules, establishes new rules, and interprets rules relevant to the securities market. It carries out an ongoing surveillance of the market to guarantee compliance. It also has oversight over the private *Securities Investor Protection Corporation,* which insures cash and securities in customer accounts against failure of stock brokerage firms.

DIVISION OF INVESTMENT MANAGEMENT: This division regulates the investment management industry, which includes all those companies and individuals managing people's investment portfolios—a total of more than $15 trillion—including investment companies, mutual funds, and investment advisers. Its oversight responsibilities include all of those entities and the utility holding companies, pursuant to the Public Utility Holding Company Act of 1935.

Its staff performs the following functions in fulfilling its regulatory responsibilities: reviews investment company and investment adviser filed documents, oversees enforcement matters affecting those entities, interprets laws and regulations in regard to the investment management industry, develops new rules and statutory amendments in this field, and makes recommendations on requests for "no action" letters and requests for exemption from any requirement.

In regard to utility holding companies, the division examines periodic reports of holding companies, participates in their audits, reviews applications, and proposes new rules.

DIVISION OF ENFORCEMENT: This division investigates and takes appropriate action to enforce the laws and regulations governing the securities industry. Its jurisdiction is civil only, resulting in administrative hearings in most matters, but more serious or continuing violations result in the filing of lawsuits in federal court, based upon the preliminary evidence. Authorization for filing either an administrative action or a lawsuit in federal court is within the prerogative of the commission. If there appears to be criminal intent, the division will refer the matter to the applicable United States attorney.

Whether to file for an administrative hearing or a suit in federal court is a decision based on several factors: the seriousness of the alleged violation, whether the violation was more technical than substantive, and the nature of the remedy desired. On occasion the commission will authorize both levels of legal action.

Regional Offices of SEC in Enforcement Division: Northeast: 233 Broadway, New York, NY 10279; Phone: (646) 428-1500. 73 Tremont Street, Suite 600, Boston, MA 02108; Phone: (217) 424-5900. 601 Walnut Street, Suite 1120 E. Philadelphia, PA 19106; Phone: (215) 597-3100. Southeast: 1401 Brickell Avenue, Suite 200, Miami, FL 33131; Phone: (305) 536-4700. 3475 Lenox Road NE, Suite 1000, Atlanta, GA 30326; Phone: (404) 842-7600. Midwest: 175 W. Jackson Boulevard, Suite 900, Chicago, IL 60604; Phone: (312) 353-7390. Central: 1801 California Street, Suite 4800, Denver, CO 80202; Phone: (303) 844-1000. 801 Cherry Street Unit 18, Suite 1900, Fort Worth, TX 76102; Phone: (817) 978-3821. 50 S.

Main Street, Suite 500, Salt Lake City, UT 84144; Phone: (801) 524-5796. Pacific: 5670 Wilshire Boulevard, 11th Floor, Los Angeles, CA 90036; Phone: (323) 965-3998. 44 Montgomery Street, Suite 1100, San Francisco, CA 94104; Phone: (415) 705-2500.

An *administrative action* is conducted by one of the *administrative law judges,* who make both findings of fact as well as legal conclusions called an "initial decision," which can be appealed to the commission in whole or in part by either side. The commission can affirm, reverse, or send it back (remand) for further hearing on particular matters. The remedies which the SEC can seek and the administrative law judge can determine are "cease and desist" orders (ordering a particular practice to cease), suspension or revocation of licenses of broker-dealers and investment advisers, public censure, being barred from the securities industry, financial penalties, and return of illegal profits ("disgorgement").

Cases brought in *federal court* can request the same sanctions as administrative action, but can also obtain affirmative relief such as orders for audits, accounting, supervision of corporate management, and can bar or suspend a person from being a corporate officer or board member. Violations of such orders can result in a finding of contempt of court, which carries potential fines and possible jail time.

ADMINISTRATIVE OFFICES: Administrative offices of the SEC are: Office of Executive Director, Office of Chief Accountant, Office of Compliance Inspections and Examinations, Office of Municipal Securities, Office of Administrative Law Judges, Office of Economic Analysis, Office of Filings and Information Services, Office of Information Technology, Office of Administration and Personnel Management, Office of Equal Employment Opportunity, Office of Comptroller, Office of General Counsel, Office of Inspector General, Office of International Affairs, Office of Investor Education and Assistance, Office of Legislative Affairs, Office of Public Affairs, Policy Evaluation and Research, and Office of the Secretary.

Executive Director: Carries out SEC management policies, formulates budget, and has oversight over the automated information systems.

Comptroller: Assists in the financial side of management functions.

Chief Accountant: Advises the commission on the conduct of audits of corporations consistent with SEC regulations. This office is involved with standard setting for auditing with government and self-regulating organizations such as the Financial Accounting Standards Board, the International Accounting Standards Board, the American Institute of Certified Public Accountants, and the Public Company Accounting Oversight Board.

Office of Compliance Inspections and Examinations: Conducts inspections of regulated organizations to stimulate compliance and uncover violations of law. In order to obtain prompt compliance of identified problems the office will issue a *"compliance letter."* If that does not result in correction, then the matter will be referred for legal action.

Office of Filings and Information Services: The receiving, managing, and storing system for all filings with the SEC. All filings commencing May 1996 are available at www.sec.gov. The *Public Reference Branch* of this office is also a prime source of information. Copies of documents can be obtained from this office for a fee.

Office of Information Technology: Operates the Electronic Data Gathering Analysis and Retrieval, known as EDGAR, processing a half million documents annually, and which are available free by public access.

Office of Investor Education and Assistance: Provides responses to questions and complaints from actual and potential security investors. It also holds investor town meetings around the country on investing (but not specific stocks) and publishes free written materials to educate investors.

CONTACT (800) 732-0330.

Office of International Affairs: Works internationally to encourage higher standards in security regulation. It also shares information and technical developments with countries with developing security markets.

Office of Economic Analysis: Staffed with economists, statisticians, analysts, and computer experts to determine the economic impacts of proposed rules and policy planning.

Office of Administration and Personnel Management: Essentially the human resources office.

Office of Equal Employment Opportunity: Promotes equal opportunities (primarily for minority employees) in recruitment, selection, training, promotion, pay, and supervision. It also manages the complaint process and acts to make certain that SEC adheres to equal opportunity regulations.

General Counsel: Performs the usual legal services for the commission, and also will intervene as amicus curiae (friend of the court) in private appellate actions when interpretation of securities laws are involved.

Office of Legislative Affairs: Handles liaison between the SEC and Congress and prepares testimony and evidence for Congressional hearings.

CONTACT Address: SEC, 450 Fifth Street NW, Washington, DC 20549; Phone: (202) 942-4150, consumer information: (800) SEC-0330, public affairs: (202) 942-00020, investor assistance or complaints: (202) 942-7040; small businesses: (202) 942-3950; Website: www.sec.gov.

SECURITIES INVESTOR PROTECTION CORPORATION (SIPC)

Created by Congress to ensure that customers of failed stock brokerage firms receive all nonnegotiable securities registered in their names or in the process of being registered. SIPC focuses on restoring funds to investors with assets in the hands of bankrupt and financially troubled brokerage firms. "Street name" securities are distributed on a pro rata basis, with SIPC's reserve funds covering customer claims up to $500,000, including a $100,000 maximum on claims for cash. Recovered funds restore SIPC's reserve.

CONTACT Address: SIPC, 805 15th Street NW, Suite 800, Washington, DC 20005-2215; Phone: (202) 371-8300; Fax: (202) 371-6728; Website: www.sipc.org/.

SELECTIVE SERVICE SYSTEM

An independent agency established in 1940 by the Military Selective Service Act to provide manpower to the armed forces in a national emergency, and to run an Alternative Service Program for men classified as conscientious objectors during a draft. The director of Selective Service is appointed by the president. Men ages 18–25 must register with Selective Service, and are often forced to register to obtain federal college tuition loans or aid. Registration takes place at U.S. post offices and at U.S. embassies and consulates outside the United States. Alternative Service Programs enable conscientious objectors to do community work or service in lieu of military service and get credit for it.

Selective Service local boards, also known as "local draft board," are made up of five local volunteers who have the power to decide which local residents will be drafted, which will receive postponements, and which will receive exemptions. Local draft boards are appointed by the director of Selective Service on the recommendation of the president, state governors, or other public officials. People interested in serving on their local draft board may submit applications. To be on a local draft board, one must be a U.S.

citizen, at least 18 years old, not a retired or active member of the armed forces or any reserve group, live in the geographic area the local draft board oversees, and be willing to spend all the time it takes to carry out necessary duties.

During peacetime Selective Service registers potential draftees, keeps track of 11,000 volunteer draft board members, and continuously trains those volunteers on procedures and how to treat and make decisions on unusual cases.

In case of a crisis in which the military needs more troops than the volunteer enlistees it already has, Congress passes legislation and the president signs the bill authorizing a draft. The "lottery," based on birth dates, determines the order in which men are selected to serve, with young men who turn 20 that year first, then those 21–25, followed by 18-year-olds about to turn 19, who would be the last to be drafted. The Selective Service System activates and orders state directors and reserve forces officers to duty. Local and appeals boards are activated, inductees accepted after evaluation receive their orders, and the draftees then have 10 days to either claim exemption, postponement, or deferment, file an appeal of the evaluation, or report to the Military Entrance Processing Station for induction. According to current rules, Selective Service is required to deliver its first soldiers within 193 days from the declaration of a crisis.

A conscription system was used during both the Civil War and World War I, and when World War I ended, the government dissolved the draft. The first peacetime conscription was advocated by President Franklin D. Roosevelt before U.S. entry into World War II. The Military Selective Service Act creating the draft system was numbered HR1776, and barely passed the House of Representatives by one vote.

At the end of World War II, the law was allowed to expire but, as a result of the cold war, Congress resurrected it, with its activity varying ever since according to the military's needs.

CONTACT Address: Selective Service System, National Headquarters, Arlington, VA 22209-2425; Phone: (703) 605-4000; Fax: (703) 605-4106; Website: www.sss.gov. Registration Information Office: Data Management Center, P.O. Box 94638, Palatine, IL 60094-4639; Phone: (847) 688-6888, TTY: (847) 688-2567. Regional Offices: Suite 276, 2834 Green Bay Road, North Chicago, IL 60064-3038; Phone: (847) 688-7990; Suite 4, 805 Walker Street, Marietta, GA 30060-2731; Phone: (770) 590-6602; Suite 1014, 333 Quebec Street, Denver, CO 80207-2323.

SMALL AGENCY COUNCIL (SAC)

Established in 1986 as a voluntary interagency management organization of about 80 sub-cabinet "small" independent federal agencies. Most agencies' principal management official represent their agency on SAC. "Small" in this case means an agency with fewer than 6,000 employees, with many members having 500 or fewer. SAC members in total have about 50,000 employees.

SAC's goals include helping develop management policies for small agencies; exchanging ideas to improve management, efficiency, and productivity; and sharing resources to strengthen internal management of each agency. SAC also represents member agencies before federal policy oversight organizations and interagency management groups.

CONTACT Phone: (202) 326-4180; Website: www.srbc.net.

SMALL BUSINESS ADMINISTRATION (SBA)

The Small Business Administration (SBA) performs several functions to assist small businesses, particularly those enterprises that have difficulty obtaining funding and technical assistance in order to expand, compete, or qualify for government contracts to become successful. SBA's basic tools are (a) guaranteed loans from conventional sources in which the small business would not qualify without the guarantee, (b) direct loans, (c) advice to the entrepreneur in organizing and managing his/her business, (d) partnership with the small business to achieve its goals, and (e) advocating for the small business with lenders and the government, and (f) providing emergency financial assistance to small businesses in response to disasters, such as fires, earthquakes, riots, and storms.

To carry out its mission hands-on, SBA is locally accessible through field offices in dozens of cities throughout the nation. SBA has more than 3,000 employees. In its first half century (1953–2003) SBA helped almost 20 million small businesses with funding that is approaching a total of $200 billion. Recently the assistance amounts to more than $12 billion annually.

HISTORY

In response to a proposal by President Dwight Eisenhower, Congress enacted the Small Business Act on July 30, 1953. However, some of its programs geared toward helping small businesses had begun with the Reconstruction Finance Corporation (RFC) formed in 1932, the Smaller War Plants Corporation created in 1942 to bring small entities into the war effort through direct loans, which dissolved after the war, followed by the Office of Small Business located in the DEPARTMENT OF COMMERCE.

The founding act spelled out SBA's mission to "aid, counsel, assist and protect, insofar as is possible, the interests of small business concerns" and help them gain favorable consideration for government contracts and purchase of surplus property. The new agency went right to work making and guaranteeing loans.

Its ability to provide a stream of investment funds was enhanced by the Investment Company Act of 1958, which permitted guarantees of investment in high-risk small business loans by privately owned venture capital firms. In 1964, as part of the so-called War on Poverty, the Equal Opportunity Loan Program guaranteed loans to people starting new businesses and who were below the poverty line, could not meet conventional credit and collateral requirements, and could show a sound business plan.

SBA also initiated outreach to minorities, veterans, and women who needed funding of start-up enterprises. Specifically, it created the *Minority Small Business Program,* microloans (useful to women with the ability to operate small stores or cottage businesses) needing only a little "seed money."

ORGANIZATION

The administrative structure of SBA is simple and direct: headed by the *administrator* assisted by the *deputy administrator,* who are appointed by the president and confirmed by the Senate, with a small secretariat, which includes a *chief of staff, chief operating officer, national ombudsman* (to hear complaints and disputes), and *counselor.*

Reporting directly to the administrator are several officers responsible for administrative matters. These are: *Office of Field Operations,* which oversees the *regional administrators* (Phone: (202) 205-6808 for information on field offices), *Office of Congressional and Legislative Affairs, Office of Hearings and Appeals, Office of Disaster Assistance, Office of Veterans Business Development, Office of Equal Employment Opportunity and Civil Rights Compliance, Office of Communications and Public Liaison,* and the offices of *general counsel, inspector general* (a presidential appointee) and *chief financial officer.*

SBA also has a unique administrative element, the *Office of Advocacy* led by the *chief counsel for advocacy,* appointed by the president with Senate confirmation, mandated by legislation to serve as an independent (and supposedly aggressive) spokesperson for small business with all government agencies, challenging them to comply with consideration of small businesses in developing and managing programs, regulations, rule making, and activities. This advocate has the authority to represent the overriding interests of small businesses with the WHITE HOUSE and Congress. It also conducts research on the performance, requirements, and importance of small businesses. The office has a staff of regional advocates who perform the same functions on the state and local levels of government and business.

Four *associate deputy administrators* are each in charge of groups of offices.

Associate deputy administrator for capital access supervises the *Office of Financial Assistance, Investment Division, Office of Surety Guarantees, Office of International Trade,* and *Office of Lender Oversight,* all dealing with different aspects of small businesses' access to financial assistance.

Associate deputy administrator for entrepreneurial development oversees the *Office of Business and Community Initiatives, Office of Small Business Centers, Office of Women's Business Ownership,* and *Office of Native American Ownership.* Each of these offices deals with a special program to provide capital, loans, and advice for a specific category of the public.

Associate deputy administrator for government contracting and minority business development fulfills the mandated responsibility to help small businesses qualified to bid on contracts with the government as well as assisting minority-owned enterprises. These offices include the *Office of Government Contracting* and the *Office of Hubzone Empowerment Contracting.*

Associate deputy administrator for management administration has oversight of management practices within the agency with two sub-offices: *administration* and the office of the *senior adviser for policy and planning* to keep SBA perpetually efficient and effective.

CONTACT Address: 409 Third Street SW, Washington, DC 20416. There are also 12 regional offices, more than 80 field offices, and four disaster area offices; Phone: (202) 205-6600, inquiries: (800) U-ASK-SBA, public affairs: (202) 205-6740; Fax: (202) 205-7064; Website:

www.sba.gov. Regional offices: 233 Peachtree Street NE, Suite 1800, Atlanta, GA 30303; Phone: (404) 331-4999. 10 Causeway Street, Suite 812, Boston, MA 02222; Phone: (617) 565-8415. 500 W. Madison Street, 1250, Chicago, IL 60661; Phone: (312) 353-4493. 4300 Amon Carter Boulevard, Suite 108, Ft. Worth, TX 76155; Phone: (817) 684-5581. 721 Nineteenth Street, Suite 400, Denver, Co 80202; Phone: (210) 844-0503. 23 W. Eighth Street, Suite 307, Kansas City, MO 64105; Phone: (816) 374-6380. 26 Federal Plaza, Room 31-08, New York, NY 10278; Phone: (212) 264-1450. 900 Market Street, 5th Floor, Philadelphia, PA 19107; Phone: (215) 580-2807. 455 Market Street, Suite S-2200, San Francisco, CA 94105. Phone: (415) 744-2118. 1200 Sixth Avenue, Suite 1805, Seattle, WA 98101; Phone: (206) 553-5676. Disaster area offices: One Baltimore Plaza, Suite 300, Atlanta, GA 30308. Phone: (404) 347-3771. 4400 Amon Carter Boulevard, Suite 102, Fort Worth, TX 76155; Phone: (817) 885-7600. 360 Rainbow Boulevard S, 3rd Floor, Niagara Falls, NY 14303; Phone: (716) 282-4612. 1825 Bell Street, Suite 208, Sacramento, CA 95825; Phone: (916) 566-7246.

SBA publications are available at the field offices.

SMITHSONIAN INSTITUTION

The Smithsonian Institution is America's most extensive cultural, artistic, and scientific depository, operating 16 museums, galleries, centers, and research facilities. Most of the principal buildings are located on both sides of the National Mall, a broad swath of lawn stretching from the Washington Monument to the Capitol in Washington, D.C. The Smithsonian's most famous operations include the National Air and Space Museum (its most popular exhibition), the National Gallery of Art, the John F. Kennedy

Center for the Performing Arts, and the original Smithsonian Building, completed in 1855.

Its museums attract more than 25 million visitors each year. Smithsonian collections total 143 million artifacts, artworks, and specimens. The Smithsonian conducts educational programs and tours, and runs research laboratories and the National Zoo. It publishes the popular *Smithsonian* magazine featuring science, art, and history. More than 2 million individuals are dues-paying members. Nevertheless, the annual federal financial support has reached $475 million as of 2004.

HISTORY

James Smithson, a childless British scientist, wrote his last will in 1826, leaving his estate in trust to his nephew, but if that relative died without heirs, then the estate would pass to "the United States of America, to found at Washington, under the name of the Smithsonian Institution, an establishment for the increase and diffusion of knowledge among men." Smithson died in 1829, and when the nephew died without heirs in 1835, the estate (valued at $500,000) was then delivered in the form of 100,000 gold sovereigns to the Philadelphia mint.

After several years of debate, Congress adopted legislation in 1845 establishing the Smithsonian Institution as a trust, managed by a board of regents. Appointed secretary and director was noted physicist Joseph Henry, who had the original Smithsonian Museum built by 1855. It still exists in its red brick splendor, nicknamed the Castle. Henry, who made several important discoveries about the nature and uses of electricity and initiated the first system of weather reports, served until his death in 1878.

Henry was succeeded by his longtime assistant, zoologist Spencer F. Baird (1878–87), who expanded the Smithsonian to match his vision of a national museum with complete collections of all North American animals, plants, and fossils.

On Baird's death, Samuel P. Langley became secretary (1887–1906). Langley, a famed self-taught professor of physics and astronomy, is best known for building the first successful, heavier-than-air unmanned plane in 1900, three years before the Wright brothers first manned flight. Langley Field near Norfolk, Virginia, is named for him. At the institution he made numerous innovations, including the "children's room" displaying specimens with common names.

The National Zoological Park was established in 1889. During the past century there have been regular additions to the institution's museums and galleries. In the cluster close to the original museum were the Freer Gallery of Art (endowed 1919), Hirshhorn Museum and Sculpture Garden (endowed 1981), National Museum of African Art, Smithsonian American Art Museum, Renwick Gallery, National Museum of American History, National Museum of the American Indian (1989), National Museum of National History, National Portrait Gallery (1962), National Postal Museum, Center for Folklife and Cultural Heritage, Arthur M. Sackler Gallery (1987), and the National Gallery of Art.

In 1971 the John F. Kennedy Center for the Performing Arts was opened nearby. The aviation wing of the original museum outgrew the premises and moved into the National Air and Space Museum just up the mall from the original building. At times, existing collections would be given to the institution, such as that of the former Museum of the American Indian in New York in 1989, which is now housed in the new building of the National Museum of the American Indian. The Woodrow Wilson International Center for Scholars was established by Congress in 1968 as a memorial to the 28th president, and supports research and scholarship.

ORGANIZATION

At the outset, Congress established a simple organization, with the *secretary* as the chief executive officer responsible to a *board of regents*. On the board are the chief justice of the Supreme Court (who serves as chancellor), the vice president, three senators, three members of the House, and seven citizen members.

Administrative support offices are Public Affairs, Visitor Information, Development, Product Development and Licensing, Equal Employment and Minority Affairs, Human Resources, Institutional Studies, Exhibits Central, Architectural History and Historic Preservation, Horticulture Services, Facilities Engineering and Operations, Imaging, Printing and Photographic Services, Chief Information Officer, Fellowships, International Relations, and Scientific Diving.

At the next tier of administration are the under secretary for science, under secretary for American museums and national programs (which has oversight of most of the museums), and the under secretary for finance and administration. The director for international art museums is responsible for the African Art Museum, Freer Gallery of Art (Asian), Arthur M. Sackler Museum (Asian), and Hirshhorn Museum and Sculpture Garden (modern art). The chief executive for Smithsonian business ventures directs such enterprises as *Smithsonian* magazine, and catalog and concession sales.

Each museum and program is headed by a director who reports to the appropriate under secretary.

The John F. Kennedy Center for the Performing Arts is administered by a separate board of trustees, which retains a president as an executive official. The Woodrow Wilson Center for International Scholars also operates under its independent board of directors, which employs a director and deputy director.

CONTACT Address: 1000 Jefferson Drive SW, Washington, DC 20560; Phone: (202) 357-2700; Website: www.si.edu. Most of the museums and galleries have their own phone number.

Visiting: Admission is free to all Smithsonian museums, except the Cooper-Hewitt National Design Museum in New York City, which is free to children under 12 and to all on Friday evenings, 5–9 P.M. Hours: The information center at the Castle opens at 9 A.M. and closes at 5:30, daily, except December 25. Other museums are usually open 10 A.M. to 5:30 P.M. daily, but closed December 25. In most museums docent tours are given several times daily.

Museums, Galleries, Programs, and Activities

JOHN F. KENNEDY CENTER FOR THE PERFORMING ARTS: The capital's only memorial to President Kennedy, the center presents a year-round program of music, dance, and drama, as well as special ceremonies and events. There are tours between 10 A.M. and 5 P.M. each weekday and between 10 A.M. and 1 P.M. on weekends. Free performances are often given at 6 P.M. Half-priced tickets are often available for those over 65, enlisted servicepeople, disabled, and low-income groups. Kennedy Center, 2700 F Street NW, Washington, D.C. 20566; Phone: (202) 467-4600 (including ticket information and requests), Research: (202) 416-8000; Website: www.kennedy-center.org.

NATIONAL GALLERY OF ART: One of the world's great collections of art, the National Gallery includes European art from the 13th century forward, paintings by French, Italian, Spanish, English, and American masters, Chinese porcelains, sculpture, bronzes, and such world-famous works as surrealist Salvador Dali's gigantic *Last Supper*. Its Micro Gallery is the nation's most comprehensive interactive multimedia system for study of art in detail, supported by a bank of 13 computers for easy access. The gallery also sells reproductions, publications, and slides. National Gallery of Art, Seventh Street and Constitution Avenue NW (also East Building at Fourth Street and Pennsylvania Avenue); Phone: (202) 737-4215, Research: (202) 842-6482, Order reproductions: (202) 842-6002, and publications: (202) 842-6691; Website: www.nga.gov.

NATIONAL AIR AND SPACE MUSEUM: Exhibits air and space artifacts, including the Wright brothers' first plane, Lindbergh's *Spirit of St. Louis,* Apollo spacecraft, Moon rocks, the Langley Imax theater, and the domed *Einstein Planetarium.* This museum is the most popular visitor site in the Smithsonian complex. At Dulles Airport is the museum's *Steven F. Udvar-Hazy Center,* which opened in 2003. Specializing in restoration of artifacts, it is home to a space shuttle and the Enola Gay B-29, which dropped the atomic bomb on Hiroshima in 1945. National Air and Space Museum, Sixth Street and Independence Avenue SW, Washington, DC 20560; Phone: (202) 357-2700, for tour information and reservations phone (202) 357-1400; Website: www.nasm.edu.

ANACOSTIA MUSEUM AND CENTER FOR AFRICAN-AMERICAN HISTORY AND CULTURE: Exhibits historic documents and educational programs on African-American history and culture. Anacostia Museum, Fort Stanton, 1901 Fort Place SE, Washington, DC 20020; Phone: (202) 357-2700; Website: www.si.edu/anacostia.

ARCHIVES OF AMERICAN ART: Contains more than 13 million documents on history of American visual arts. Archives of American Art, Smithsonian Institution, 750 Ninth Street NW, Washington, DC 20560; Phone: (202) 314-3900; Website www.artarchives.si.edu/start. Note: This building is shared with the National Portrait Gallery and the Smithsonian American Art Museum.

FREER GALLERY OF ART: Exhibits Asian art, including early Christian manuscripts up to early 20th-century artists, metal work, glass, ceramics, scrolls, sculptures, and paintings. There are also research facilities. Freer Gallery of Art, Jefferson Drive at 12th Street SW, Washington, DC, 20560; Phone: (202) 357-2700; Website: www.asia.si.edu.

NATIONAL PORTRAIT GALLERY: A collection of 18,000 depictions—paintings, photographs, and glass negatives—of Americans who contributed to the history, culture, and development of the nation. On the second floor are the Hall of Presidents, including Gilbert Stuart's portrait of George Washington, and a permanent exhibit of eminent Americans. Its extensive library is shared with the Smithsonian American Art Museum and the Archives of American Art. The gallery conducts outreach programs and tours, and is the site of special exhibits and public events in its Renaissance Great Hall. National Portrait Gallery, Eighth and F Streets NW, Washington, DC 20560; Phone: (202) 357-2700; Website: www.npg.si.edu.

HIRSHHORN MUSEUM AND SCULPTURE GARDEN: Exhibits collections of modern and contemporary art and has research facility. There are docent-led tours, lectures, films, research facilities, and a photographic and art library. Seventh Street and Independence Avenue SW, Washington, DC 20560; Phone: (202) 357-2700; Website: www.hirshhorn.si.edu.

NATIONAL MUSEUM OF AFRICAN ART: Only U.S. art museum dedicated to African art, including various media and photographic archives on African culture. Useful for research and has a specialized library. 950 Independence Avenue SW, Washington, DC 20560; Phone: (202) 357-2700; Website: www.nmafa.si.edu.

SMITHSONIAN AMERICAN ART MUSEUM: A collection of American painting, sculpture, folk art, and photography from colonial times to 1914. An extensive body of information and images can be retrieved on website www.nmaa.si.edu. There is also a research program for visiting scholars and several positions for university interns. Smithsonian American Art Museum, Eighth and G Streets NW, Washington, DC 20560; Phone: (202) 357-2700; Website: www.americanart.si.edu.

RENWICK GALLERY: Renwick collects and exhibits American crafts and decorative arts on a rotating basis from its collection. Renwick Gallery, Seventeenth Street and Pennsylvania Avenue NW, Washington, DC 20560; Phone: (202) 357-2700; Website: www.nmaa-ryder.si.edu/collections/exhibits/renwick25.

NATIONAL MUSEUM OF AMERICAN HISTORY: The exhibits provide a unique and broad view of America's past, with many actual historical artifacts such as the original Star-Spangled Banner, the first Morse telegraph, Whitney's cotton gin, gowns of presidential wives, political memorabilia, the ruby slippers from *The Wizard of Oz*, as well as science, engineering, and manufacturing equipment developed by American inventors and innovators. National Museum of American History, 14th Street and Constitution Avenue NW, Washington, DC 20560; Phone: (202) 357-2700; Website: www.americanhistory.si.edu.

NATIONAL MUSEUM OF THE AMERICAN INDIAN: Dedicated to preserving the life, languages, art, and culture of the original people of the Americas. Among its exhibits are Northwest Coast carvings, pottery and weaving of the Southwest, leather garments from the Plains, and gold jewelry of the Aztec, Maya, and Inca. Phone: (202) 2020 or (202) 357-2700; Website: www.nmai.si.edu.

NATIONAL MUSEUM OF NATURAL HISTORY: With more than 124 million specimens, this museum features permanent exhibits on human cultures, earth sciences, biology and anthropology, dinosaurs, insects, birds, mammals, marine ecosystems, and the fabled Hope Diamond. Nature films are shown in an Imax theater and research facilities (with help from staff experts). National Museum of Natural History, 10th Street and Constitution Avenue NW, Washington, DC 20560; Phone: (202) 357-2700; Website: www.mnh.si.edu.

NATIONAL POSTAL MUSEUM: Dedicated to the history of the U.S. POSTAL SERVICE, it has 13 million items covering colonial times, the Pony Express, modern automation, actual mail planes, and the largest stamp collection in the world. National Postal Museum, Two Massachusetts Avenue NE, Washington, DC 20560; Phone: (202) 357-2700; Website: www.si.edu/postal.

ARTHUR M. SACKLER GALLERY: This Asian art museum displays objects from China, Japan, Korea, Southeast Asia, and the ancient Near East, including manuscripts, paintings, ceramics, prints, textiles, sculptures, and metalwork. The original collection was a testamentary gift from Arthur M. Sackler in 1987. It is connected to the Freer Gallery by an underground hallway. Arthur M. Sackler Gallery, 1050 Independence Avenue SW, Washington, DC 20560; Phone: (202) 357-2700; Website: www.asia.si.edu.

COOPER-HEWITT NATIONAL DESIGN MUSEUM: Exhibits design collections of applied arts, industrial design, drawings, prints, glass, metalwork, wallcoverings, and trestles. Admission fee: $8 for over 12 years, children free, and free for all on Fridays, 5–9 P.M. Two East 91st Street, New York, NY 10028; Phone: (212) 860-6868; Website: www.si.edu/ndm.

NATIONAL ZOOLOGICAL PARK: Dating back to 1889, the National Zoo encompasses 163 acres next to Rock Creek Park in northwest Washington, D.C. A biopark with animals ranging from ants to giraffes, botanic gardens, aquaria, a simulated tropical rain forest, and the Reptile Discovery Center. As a major center for research on animal behavior, genetics, and reproduction the zoo is a leader in conservation studies. National Zoo, 3000 Connecticut Avenue NW, Washington, DC 20000; Phone: (202) 673-4717; E-mail: listserv@sivm.si.edu; Website:www.si.edu/natzoo.

CENTER FOR FOLKLIFE AND CULTURAL HERITAGE: Responsible for the research, documentation, and actual presentation of folk music, art, and culture, the center maintains a large inventory of documents, produces Smithsonian Folkways Recordings, creates documentary films, issues publications, and creates traveling exhibits. Free Folklife music festivals are held by the center at various locations, including Fourth of July activities on the National Mall. Center for Folklife and Cultural Heritage, 750 Ninth Street NW, Suite 4100, Washington, DC 20560; Phone: (202) 357-2700; Website: www.folklife.si.edu.

INTERNATIONAL CENTER: The center serves to bring together scholars, museum professionals, and members of the public to promote understanding of the histories, cultures, and natural environments of the various areas of the world. It organizes international conferences, workshops, and lectures. Office of International Relations, MRC 705, 1100 Jefferson Drive SW, Washington, DC 20560; Phone: (202) 357-1539.

SMITHSONIAN ENVIRONMENTAL RESEARCH CENTER: Located near Chesapeake Bay, the center measures physical, chemical, and biological impacts on the environment, and also conducts training on ecological issues and sustaining life. Smithsonian Environmental Research Center, 647 Contees Wharf Road, Edgewater, MD 21037; Phone: (410) 798-4424; Website: www.serc.si.edu.

SMITHSONIAN MARINE STATION: A laboratory to catalog and study marine biota, and research the previously unexplained causes of fish deaths. The Smithsonian Marine Station, 701 Seaway Drive, Fort Pierce, FL 34946; Phone: (561) 465-6630.

SMITHSONIAN TROPICAL RESEARCH INSTITUTE: Headquartered in the Republic of Panama, this institute maintains facilities for a group of researchers on tropical ecosystems, ranging from coral reefs to rainforests. Smithsonian Tropical Research Institute, 900 Jefferson Drive SW, MRC 555, Washington, DC 20560; Phones: (202) 786-2817, (Panama) (011) (507) 62-6022; Website: www.si.edu/stri.

WOODROW WILSON INTERNATIONAL CENTER FOR SCHOLARS: Created by Congress in 1968, the center promotes advanced scholarship in public affairs. It provides a neutral, nonpartisan forum for policy makers, journalists, businesspeople, and scholars to participate in serious dialogue. The center also encourages research in social sciences and humanities. Scholar Selection and Services Office, Woodrow Wilson Center, One Woodrow Wilson Plaza, 1300 Pennsylvania Avenue NW, Washington, DC 20004; Phone: (202) 691-4170; Research opportunities: (202) 691-4213, Internships: (202) 691-4053.

SMITHSONIAN ASTROPHYSICAL OBSERVATORY: In coordination with the Harvard College Observatory, the Smithsonian participates in the Harvard-Smithsonian Center for Astrophysics. Areas of study include atomic and molecular physics, radio and geoastronomy, high-energy astrophysics, planetary sciences, and solar and stellar physics. Its findings are published in *Center Preprint Series* and monographs. Smithsonian Astrophysical Observatory, 60 Garden Street, Cambridge, MA 02138; Phone: (617) 495-7461; Website: www.cfa-harvard.edu.

SMITHSONIAN CENTER FOR MATERIALS RESEARCH AND EDUCATION: Studies the means to preserve, protect, and analyze collection materials. Museum Support Center, Suitland, MD 20746; Phone: (301) 238-3700.

SMITHSONIAN INSTITUTION LIBRARIES: A source of information on the institution's inventory of over 1 million volumes and possibility of interlibrary loan. Smithsonian Institution Libraries, 10th Street and Constitution Avenue NW, Washington, DC 20560; Phone: (202) 357-2139; Website: www.sil.si.edu; E-mail: libhelp@sil.si.edu.

SMITHSONIAN INSTITUTION ARCHIVES: The archives preserve official records and other documents of the institution and make them available for research. Smithsonian Institution Archives, MRC 414, 900 Jefferson Drive SW, Washington, DC 20560; Phone: (202) 357-1420.

SOCIAL SECURITY ADMINISTRATION

The Social Security Administration is an independent agency that administers five programs providing security to past and present American workers.

PROGRAMS

By far the largest program is for *Old-Age and Survivors Insurance* (OASI), commonly referred to as Social Security. OASI pays monthly amounts to persons at age 70, or at earlier dates starting at age 62 or 65 (on election by the recipients, but at substantially less amounts) for the remainder of the "survivor's" life. It also provides payments to the "survivors": spouses of deceased recipients, and under-age surviving children. As of 2004 the number of old-age payment recipients was close to 40 million, and the payments to them amounted to about $417 billion annually.

The second program is for *Disability Insurance,* which provides an equivalence for Old-Age and Survivors Insurance for those people who are disabled and no longer able to work. By 2004 more than 7.7 million recipients were receiving monthly payments under the Disability Insurance program, with an annual outlay of more than $37 billion.

Both the OASI and Disability Insurance programs are funded by amounts deducted from payrolls or from self-employed workers, and so far the programs have been self-supporting. Because the number of people who will reach retirement age of 65 or 70 in the future grows, due to the increase in average lifespan and the expansion of total senior population, the amount paid out in benefits each year will begin exceeding current contributions by the employed around the year 2015 (although some calculations estimate a working balance into the 2030s) and so eventually some supplement to the contributions will be required to maintain the trust fund's future solvency.

There has been criticism that there continues to be "borrowing" from the trust fund to meet expenses of other executive agencies.

The amount of payments under these programs is based on the amounts received in the highest earnings years, and the number of qualifying "quarters" of employment. On the first of each year the amount of payments is increased by a *Cost of Living Adjustment (COLA).* Annually the administration sends benefit estimates to all those potentially eligible.

Programs financed from the general funds (as distinguished from the trust fund) are the *Supplemental Security Income (SSI),* which pro-

vides benefits for the nation's so-called neediest persons, the low-income aged, blind, and disabled, both individuals and couples, and disabled children. The numbers of recipients include more than 5.5 million blind and disabled and more than 1.1 million aged. In general the payments are less (averaging about $420 per month in 2004) than the trust fund programs, and are based on each situation, including such factors as other income, including Social Security payments, eligibility for Medicaid, and housing arrangements.

In 2000 a new SSI program was inaugurated to pay benefits to 3,000 surviving *Filipino military veterans of World War II* who had served in conjunction with the U.S. forces fighting Japan. The average monthly benefit is about $320. The state of California supplements these payments.

Costs of administration of SSA are allocated between Trust Fund and SSI financing, based on a formula of usage. The total management expense budget is only 2 percent of the total amount paid to beneficiaries. The SSA Office of the Inspector General is also paid from the administrative budget, and is vital due to the need to control fraud from false claims, misuse of Social Security numbers, and other schemes.

SSA also researches matters related to disability and other beneficiary programs, assists claimants, and makes referrals to rehabilitation services.

Through its extensive network of field offices, SSA assists in the administration of *Medicare,* which pays for much of health care for people over age 65 under the direct authority of the DEPARTMENT OF HEALTH AND HUMAN SERVICES. Medicare card numbers are the same as the Social Security number with an added "A."

HISTORY

Although the Social Security Administration was established by a reorganization act effective July 16, 1946, the administration and its main programs date from August 14, 1935, when

President Franklin D. Roosevelt signed the original Social Security Act. In addition to the federal old-age insurance, which is the heart of the program, the act included the first federal unemployment insurance, public, maternal and child health assistance, crippled children and child welfare services, and vocational rehabilitation. The original legislation also provided for direct assistance to the aged poor and the blind.

The groundwork for support for this historic legislation was laid by President Roosevelt's messages to Congress in June 1934 and January 1935 favoring legislation for economic security, followed by studies and conferences on old-age security.

Implementing the old-age security (commonly just called Social Security) took a lengthy period. Because a filibuster, led by Senator Huey Long (D.-La.), held up appropriations for Social Security, the initial expenses were paid by the DEPARTMENT OF LABOR so that the original Social Security office could open its doors. The president appointed a three-man Social Security Board with John G. Winant as chairman. During 1935 and 1936, regions were established, and cooperative agreements were reached with most states.

Congress passed legislation authorizing the deduction from payroll of payments for Social Security (originally only 1 percent, soon raised to 2 percent), and 3 million applications were distributed to employers in November 1936. However, payroll deductions were delayed by court challenges, until favorable federal court decisions ruled it was constitutional.

The assignment of Social Security numbers and Employer Identification numbers was established, and the first Social Security card applications were distributed at post offices in November 1936. By mid-March 1937, 25 million cards had been issued. On July 1, 1937, the card issuance function was transferred to the newly established Social Security field offices. The name of the old-age benefits program was amended to "Old-Age Insurance Program" to distinguish it from the direct assistance provided from the general fund.

The old-age insurance program was substantially broadened by adding benefits to dependents (underage children) and survivors (widows or widowers) in the Social Securities Amendments of 1939 signed by Roosevelt on August 10, 1939.

Starting July 1, 1939, the Social Security functions handled by the Social Security Board were given to an office within the Federal Security Agency, created that date by legislation. The Social Security Board was eventually replaced by the Social Security Administration, effective July 16, 1946. The Federal Security Agency was abolished, and the Social Security Administration came under the umbrella of the newly created Department of Health, Education and Welfare (HEW), which would later be restructured and renamed the Department of Health and Human Services.

In 1950 Congress decided to provide block grants to states for the permanently and totally disabled whose incomes were below the poverty level. Four years later, Congress enacted the so-called liability freeze, which provided that the period of disability (and probable low income) would not count against the calculation of later retirement (old-age) benefits, but the disabled person could become eligible only at age 50 or more. Theoretically, the freeze was intended to encourage rehabilitation, in cooperation with state rehab agencies, but rehabilitation of people at that age was generally illusory.

The 1954 amendments set a tough standard of "disability," which it defined as "inability to engage in any substantial gainful activity by reason of any medically determinable physical or mental impairment which can be expected to result in death or to be of long-continued and indefinite duration."

In 1956, after a spirited fight on the floor of the Senate, Congress passed legislation creating *Social Security Disability Insurance,* limited to disabled people over 50 years old, so it was really a retirement program for the disabled and was paid out of a trust fund.

Supplemental Security Income (SSI) was initiated by legislation in 1972 (effective 1974), as part of President Richard Nixon's welfare reform, and was intended to federalize programs for aid to the blind, aid to permanently and totally disabled, and aid to the needy elderly—previously left to the states through the block grants under the 1950 legislation. While originally conceived as a program to supplement the incomes of the poorest elderly who found Social Security inadequate, it turned out younger adults and an increasing number of children who were either blind or disabled became the beneficiaries of this program, and by 1994 two-thirds of the SSI case load were nonelderly adults and children.

In 1965 Congress liberalized the definition of "disabled" to those impairments expected to last more than a year. In 1967 the definition was made less liberal, since a new amendment required that the disability prevent the claimant from doing any kind of gainful employment and not just his/her prior occupation. Congress also authorized the administrator to prescribe regulations to determine criteria for determining employment availability as related to particular disabilities.

Disabled widows and widowers of deceased beneficiaries, who were over the age of 50 and were themselves sufficiently disabled to be unable medically to perform "any gainful activity," were made eligible for Supplemental Security Income.

On June 9, 1980, President Jimmy Carter signed the Social Security Disability Amendments of 1980, which (a) put a cap on total family benefits that could be received from more than one program, (b) substituted SSA regulations for agency-state agreements in determining disability when performing the evaluation function, (c) installed three-year reviews of the disability status of recipients, and (d) permitted trial periods of attempts to work that would suspend SSI payments without losing eligibility.

The 1984 Disability Benefits Reform Act, and the regulations that ensued, attempted to establish clearer criteria for finding disability and, among other matters, provided that multiple impairments that in total cause disability (inability to work) could be treated as disability, although each was not severe enough to cause disability.

SSA, previously under the Department of Health and Human Services, was made an independent agency by legislation adopted August 15, 1994, to take effect on March 31, 1995, headed by a commissioner appointed by the president for a six-year term. On July 30, 1995, public trustees with four-year terms were established for the trust funds. In 1996 the position of *chief actuary* was established.

The year 1996 was full of changes in SSA and its programs. Drug addiction and alcoholism were no longer to be allowed as permanent disabilities, effective 1997, and authority was given to SSA to pursue civil remedies for Social Security fraud (adding to criminal prosecutions). The "Welfare Reform" legislation signed August 22, 1996, authorized the removal of 500,000 noncitizens from Social Security benefits, and set tougher standards for disabilities that caused the removal of some children from benefits. Development of a counterfeit-proof Social Security card was proposed.

Three panels to review SSA operations were created in April 1998, including an eight-member bipartisan committee, a 36-member "dialogue" council, and a three-member Internet study group.

During 2000 SSA eliminated the "retirement test" for those beneficiaries 65–70 who had some earnings, since IRS filing would show the amount. For the disabled attempting to work on a trial amount, the allowable earnings were raised to $530 per month.

On May 2, 2001, President George W. Bush announced the appointment of a 16-member bipartisan commission to make recommendations about Social Security. Commissioner Kenneth S. Apfel, who had served the administration for many years, retired, and on November 13, 2001, was succeeded by Jo Anne B. Barnhart.

LOCATION 6401 Security Boulevard, Baltimore, MD 21235. SSA also maintains 1292 field offices, 38 teleservice centers, and six program service centers.

CONTACT Address: Phone: (410) 965-1234; public: inquiries; (410) 965-7700, general information: (800) 772-1213.

ORGANIZATION

Directing the Social Security Administration is a *commissioner*, appointed by the president with senate confirmation for a six-year term. The commissioner is assisted by the *deputy commissioner*, also appointed by the president with Senate approval.

Reporting directly to the commissioner and performing key functions are the *executive officer, chief of staff, Office of Executive Operations, Office of Strategic Management, chief actuary, chief information officer, Press Office, general counsel,* and *inspector general.* Serving the *Office of the Commissioner* is an extensive staff, including assistants, advisers, executive directors, secretaries, and directors of special programs.

Program Management

Program Management is divided among eight deputy commissioners, each managing a separate office and various suboffices and programs.

OFFICE DISABILITY AND INCOME SECURITY PROGRAMS: Supervises the *Office of Disability, Office of Employment Support Programs, Office of Program Benefits,* and *Office of Program Support.* This is the core of the multibillion-dollar program managed by the Social Security Administration. These include *Old-Age and Survivors Insurance (OASI)* (retirement benefits for those over 62, 65, or 70 years at the election of the employees), the disability payments for those totally disabled in lieu of the retirement benefits, and benefits to their surviving dependents and spouses. Those payments are supported by a trust fund made up of payroll deductions (or self-employment contributions) during the work years of the beneficiaries. The other principal program run by this office is the *Supplemental Security Income,* which is a needs-based program for the aged, blind, and disabled, including children. About 50 million people receive benefits as of 2004.

The other offices essentially service the program functions, assist people in dealing with the Social Security System, and inform the public.

OFFICE OF COMMUNICATIONS: Divided among *Press Officer, Office of Communications Planning and Technology,* and the *Office of External Affairs.*

OFFICE OF FINANCE ASSESSMENT AND MANAGEMENT: Oversees *Offices of Budget, Facilities Management, Publications and Logistics Management,* and *Disability Program Quality.*

OFFICE OF OPERATIONS: Supervises the *Offices of Automation Support, Central Operations, Public Service and Operations Support, Telephone Services,* and *Regional Commissioners* (10 offices around the country).

OFFICE OF POLICY: Manages the *Office of Disability and Income Assistance Policy,* and the *Office of Research, Evaluation and Statistics.*

OFFICE OF SYSTEMS: Supervises the *Offices of Information Management, Systems Design and Development, Systems Planning and Development and Systems Requirements.*

OFFICE OF HUMAN RESOURCES: Combines *Offices of Personnel* and *Training.*

Advisory Boards

Social Security Advisory Board: Created by Congress in 1994 when Congress created the Social Security Administration. The board is an independent bipartisan advisory board that advises the president, Congress, and the commissioner of Social Security on Social Security and Supplemental Security Income (SSI) programs.

The seven members of the advisory board are appointed to six-year terms, including three appointed by the president, with no more than two from one political party, and two each by the speaker of the House of Representatives and by the president pro tempore of the Senate, with no more than one from the same political party. The president appoints the chair of the advisory board for a four-year term, meant to be the same four years as the president's term. The advisory board has no authority to take any administrative actions or resolve individual claims.

Issues discussed by the advisory board include long-term financing of Social Security, safeguarding or "dipping into" public Social Security funds, disability programs, long-range research and program evaluation services it does for the Social Security Administration, development by the Social Security Administration, and increasing public awareness and understanding of Social Security and how it works.

CONTACT Address: Social Security Advisory Board, 400 Virginia Avenue SW, Suite 625, Washington, DC 20024; Phone: (202) 475-7700; Fax: (202) 475-7715; Website: www.ssab.gov. For individual claims information: SSA Office of Public Inquiries, 6401 Security Boulevard, Windsor Park Building, Baltimore, MD 21235-6401; Phone: (800) 772-1213.

Ticket-to-Work and Work Incentives Advisory Panel: 12 members, the chair and one other are appointed by the president without Senate approval, and the remaining 10 are named by Congress. The terms are two and four years, and they are paid per diem for meetings. The program is intended to encourage disabled recipients to obtain employment and eventually no longer need government assistance:

Field Offices

The more than 1,200 field officers of the Social Security Administration provide information to the public on Social Security programs, including;

a. assistance with claims for retirement, supplemental security, and other benefits;

b. assistance in claims for reimbursement of medical expenses;

c. assistance to claimants in filing appeals on benefits;

d. development and adjudication of claims;

e. referring appropriate individual cases for rehabilitation services;

f. providing information and processing assistance in regard to Medicare, lost Social Security cards, and other questions.

For information on the field offices, either find number in local telephone directory or call toll free: (800) 772-1213.

SURFACE TRANSPORTATION BOARD

See DEPARTMENT OF TRANSPORTATION, p. 323.

SUSQUEHANNA RIVER BASIN COMMISSION

An agency created by Congress in 1970 to coordinate the efforts of New York, Pennsylvania, and Maryland, through which the Susquehanna River flows, and the federal government to oversee use of the Susquehanna's water and other natural resources.

The Susquehanna River begins at Otsego Lake near Cooperstown, New York, flows through Pennsylvania, and then empties into Chesapeake Bay in Maryland. Classified as a navigable waterway, federal, state, and regional agencies have interests in the nation's 16th-largest river lying entirely within the United States and flowing into the Atlantic Ocean.

The Susquehanna River Basin Compact was adopted by Congress, as well as by the state legislatures of the three member states. Each member government is represented by its own commissioner, and the president appoints the federal representative and her/his alternate. States are usually represented either by the governors or by people whom they designate, as well as by alternates.

The commission reviews applications for projects that use water, adopts regulations, and oversees planning and management of the basin's water resources.

The commission works to improve public welfare through planning, allocation of the water supply, and sound management of water resources. Specifically, it works to reduce damages caused by floods; oversees sustained development and use of surface and groundwater in municipal, agricultural, recreational, commercial, and industrial purposes; protects and restores fisheries, wetlands, and habitats; protects stream uses and water quality; assures flows to Chesapeake Bay; and provides information to the public about the Susquehanna River Basin's water resources.

The commission directs the comprehensive plan for the management and development of the water resources of the Susquehanna Basin, and the staff puts the plan's six elements to practice.

The six areas the comprehensive plan sets out are as follows:

Flood Plain Management and Protection: Approves flood control projects within the three states along the Susquehanna; helps establish flood warning systems; helps set up community flood warning programs; advises locals on how to reduce losses due to flooding; and produces flood plain maps and other information on flood plain management.

Water Supply: Keeps track of water resources; administers interstate water resources among the three member states; decides members' storage needs and allocates water; helps plan, develop, and finance water resources projects; develops water supply storage and release plans; regulates water uses; keeps data on water flow conditions; and takes emergency actions.

Water Quality: Follows water quality programs in basin; does surface and groundwater studies; keeps track of Susquehanna River's impact on Chesapeake Bay; gives technical assistance to local, state, and federal governments and authorities; and does other monitoring throughout the basin.

Watershed Protection and Management: Works to protect the basin's wetlands; encourages sound agricultural practices; tries to help prioritize uses of sensitive lands; and reviews large-scale developments and their impact on water and wastewater systems.

Recreation, Fish, & Wildlife: Develops water-based recreational resources; promotes inclusion of recreation at water resource projects; promotes restoration of migratory fish and propagation of indigenous species; and regulates release of water to help fish renewals and recreational use.

Cultural, Visual, and Other Amenities: Guides member states to identify, designate, and classify historic and scenic areas and wildlife refuges; and looks at impact of basin water projects on local cultural values.

The commission also oversees programs on agricultural consumptive uses of water, drought coordination, flood management and protection, a sediment task force, stream signage, streamside clean up, watershed and protection, water resources management, and water storage projects.

CONTACT Address: Susquehanna River Basin Commission, 1721 N. Front Street, Harrisburg, PA 17102; Phone: (717) 238-0423; Fax: (717) 238-2436; E-mail: srbc@srbc.net; Website: www.srbc.net.

RAILROAD RETIREMENT BOARD (RRB)

Established by the Railroad Retirement Act of 1934, and given its statutory authority by the Railroad Retirement Act of 1974 and the Railroad

Unemployment Insurance Act. The board implements both of these acts and helps administer the parts of the Social Security Act and the Health Insurance for the Aged Act that affect railroad retirees. RRB administers the retirement-survivor and unemployment-sickness benefit programs for American railroad workers and their families.

The U.S. railroad system has a long history of giving retirement benefits to railroad workers, beginning with the first American industrial pension plan established in 1874 for a railroad, and the industry continued to lead other businesses in coverage in the 1930s, with the plans' imperfections exacerbated by the Great Depression. The depression revealed the national need to protect workers' retirement plans, as has the recession of the early 2000s. To take care of railroad workers while the Social Security system was developing in the early 1930s, Congress passed legislation in 1934, 1935, and 1937 to set up a railroad retirement system separate from Social Security, which are now coordinated.

Under the Railroad Retirement Act, railroad workers receive retirement and disability annuities after 10 years of service, and beginning in 2002, the same benefits are offered after five years of service if that service began after 1995. The money paid to railroad workers comes from payroll taxes paid by railroad employers and employees, as allocated by Congress.

RRB publishes annual reports and several publications and guides to railroad retirement benefits.

The three RRB members are appointed by the president with advice and consent of the Senate, with one member appointed at the recommendation of employees, one recommended by employers, and the chair representing the public and consumers.

CONTACT Address: Railroad Retirement Board, 844 North Rush Street, Chicago, IL 60611-2092; Phone: (312) 751-4500; Website: www.rrb.gov.

TENNESSEE VALLEY AUTHORITY (TVA)

A government corporation created by Congress in the TVA Act of 1933 at the request of President Franklin D. Roosevelt as part of his New Deal to bring the United States out of the Great Depression.

In the 1930s the Tennessee Valley had been sucked of its resources by longtime farming, yielding its soil no longer productive and further damaging the productivity and income potential of local farmers. TVA built dams, which provided much needed electricity, developed fertilizers to restore the earth and increase crops, helped replant forests that had been cut, and helped fight and control forest fires, while improving the fish and wildlife habitats.

During World War II, TVA developed huge hydropower construction programs to meet electricity needs for wartime production of bombs, airplanes, and aluminum.

In the 1950s TVA's 650-mile nine-foot draft navigation route extending the length of the Tennessee River had been completed. TVA was the United States's largest supplier of electricity, but could not keep up with demand. In response to political stoppage of requests for additional funding for development of coal-fired power plants, Congress passed legislation (1959) to make TVA self-supporting through sales of bonds.

TVA augmented the power supply in the revived Tennessee Valley by building nuclear power plants in the 1960s. Construction of some of the intended nuclear plants was cancelled due to the 1973 oil embargo, followed by rapidly increased fuel costs. Simultaneously in the '70s and '80s, electricity costs in the Tennessee Valley quintupled, of necessity decreasing the demand for power, and increasing construction costs. The 1990s saw the TVA cutting costs by about $800 million annually, cut its workforce by more than half, and increased the plants' productivity.

In 1998 TVA, under President Bill Clinton, invoked a clean-air strategy to reduce pollution that leads to ozone and smog, eventually reducing annual nitrogen oxide emissions from its coal-fired power plants by about 170,000 tons a year, while helping local communities and states improve air quality standards. (For more historical information, contact the New Deal Network at http://newdeal.feri.org.)

The Tennessee Valley Authority Board has three members, all of whom are appointed by the president and confirmed by the Senate and serve nine-year terms. The president appoints the chair.

TVA's system of dams on the Tennessee River helps regulate potential floods on it from Paducah, Kentucky, to Knoxville, Tennessee, as well as on the lower Ohio and Mississippi Rivers. TVA supplies wholesale electricity to 158 municipal and cooperative electric systems in seven states. Through TVA's dams, coal-fired power plants, nuclear facilities, combustion turbine installations, and hydroelectric plants, it also supplies power to federal entities and more than 60 large commercial companies that require unusually large amounts of electricity. Other local power sources include the U.S. Corps of Engineers dams in the Cumberland Valley, and the Aluminum Company of America dams, which work in conjunction with TVA.

TVA also operates an environmental research laboratory at Muscle Shoals, Alabama, which works on environmental clean up of land, air, and water resources, all focused on assisting economic growth. Programs include efforts to reduce pollution in emitted groundwater runoff, clean up of contaminated sites, research in the bioenergy field, and reduction of industrial waste.

To achieve some of these goals, TVA gives technical assistance in industrial development, potential disaster management, regional waste management, use of vanpools; to conserve fuel, and promotion of tourism.

TVA training centers also give skills training programs for potential employees.

CONTACT Address: Tennessee Valley Authority, 400 West Summit Hill Drive, Knoxville, TN 37902; Phone: (865) 632-2101; Website: www.tva.gov.

TRADE AND DEVELOPMENT AGENCY (USTDA OR TDA)

Originally created in 1980 as an organization within the International Development Cooperation Agency, USTDA became an independent agency with the Omnibus Trade and Competitiveness Act of 1988. The Jobs Through Exports Act of 1992 renamed it the Trade and Development Agency (TDA).

TDA works in more than 100 developing and middle-income countries to promote U.S. business participation in developing nations' industrial or infrastructure projects, focusing on making sure products and services used to build the projects are made in the United States. TDA funds American companies to do research and planning of projects to be developed abroad. TDA hires technical experts, all of whom are small American businesses, to evaluate grant proposals. It helps finance feasibility studies (on a share basis with the potential contractor) to evaluate the technical, financial, legal, and economic potential of a project, including advice from the U.S. embassy or consulate in the region, with the resulting information including available U.S. equipment and services. TDA then funds technical assistance to project sponsors, and sometimes funds technical assistance to foreign governments in cases in which projects will lead to increased U.S. exports.

As part of the process, TDA funds foreign procurement officials' trips to the United States to view American suppliers' products, and arranges meetings between American firms and the foreign decision makers.

TDA claims to review each project's environmental impact, and occasionally denies funding for projects that may have a negative environmental impact that local entities seem incapable or unwilling to mitigate. TDA also does not fund projects that reduce jobs in the United States. It also works with the DEPARTMENT OF COMMERCE's U.S. Foreign Commercial Service, and the State Department's commercial and economic officials.

TDA holds its trust funds in four multilateral development banks, known as MBDs: the International Finance Corporation, the Inter-American Development Bank, the Inter-American Investment Corporation, and the European Bank for Reconstruction and Development. Sometimes known as "Evergreen Funds," the accounts make funds available for project proposals or time-sensitive projects. TDA works closely with these institutions, as well as with the African Development Bank and the Asian Development Bank to identify and finance capital projects in developing countries.

TDA now has a policy requiring payment of a "success fee" to reimburse TDA for its investment in the project when U.S. firms collect payment.

CONTACT Address: Suite 200, 1621 North Kent Street, Arlington, VA 22209-2131; Phone: (703) 875-4357; Fax: (703) 875-4009; E-mail: info@tda.gov; Website: www.tda.gov.

U.S. CHEMICAL SAFETY AND HAZARD INVESTIGATION BOARD (CSB)

An independent and scientific investigatory agency created by the Clean Air Act Amendments of 1990 under President George H. W. Bush, although the Bush administration did not fund the board. CSB began operating in January 1998 under President Bill Clinton.

CSB was established to investigate accidents to find out what led to them and to identify causes to prevent similar events from occurring in the future. Intended to stimulate regulatory

functions of the ENVIRONMENTAL PROTECTION AGENCY, the DEPARTMENT OF LABOR's Occupational Safety and Health Administration, and other regulators, CSB is independent so as not to be influenced by the agencies it is intended to influence. CSB also collaborates with those agencies, particularly when they are all investigating the same accident.

CSB looks for violations of existing rules as causes of accidents, particularly at facilities to determine the facts and conditions leading to accidental releases resulting in serious injuries, deaths, or substantial property damage. It also conducts research, advises industry and labor on how to improve safety, and makes recommendations to federal, state, and local governments and agencies.

CSB has five members appointed by the president and confirmed by the Senate, with one member serving as chair and chief executive. All members serve five-year terms and may serve more than one term. Board members have to be selected "on the basis of technical qualification, professional standing, and demonstrated knowledge in the fields of accident reconstruction, safety engineering, human factors, toxicology, or air pollution regulations" according to the Clean Air Act. Members work with Congress, industry, labor, and environmental organizations, and meet with EPA, ODHA, and NTSB leaders.

CONTACT Address: U.S. Chemical Safety and Hazard Investigation Board, Suite 400, 2175 K Street NW, Washington, DC 20037-1809; Phone: (202) 261-7600; Website: www.chemsafety.gov.

U.S. COMMISSION ON CIVIL RIGHTS

Created by the Civil Rights Act of 1957, and re-created by the United States Commission on Civil Rights Act of 1983, the commission examines federal laws and the effectiveness of equal opportunity programs. It is also the ultimate source of civil rights information, and makes recommendations to the president and to Congress, often resulting in new statutes, executive orders, or regulations. The Civil Rights Commission has no enforcement power, but collects and examines information on alleged discrimination or denials of equal protection of the laws due to race, color, religion, sex, age, disability, or national origin. It is particularly interested in abuses in voting rights, enforcement of federal civil rights laws, education, employment, and housing.

CONTACT Address: U.S. Commission on Civil Rights, 624 Ninth Street NW, Washington, DC 20425; Phone: (202) 376-8177; Website: www.usccr.gov. Regional divisions: Suite 908, 400 State Avenue, Kansas City, KS 66101-2406; Phone: (913) 551-1400. Room 500, 624 Ninth Street, Washington, DC 20425; Phone: (202) 376-7533. Suite 410, 55 W. Monroe Street, Chicago, IL 60603; Phone: (3112) 353-8311. Suite 710, 1700 Broadway, Denver, CO 80290; Phone: (303) 866-1040. Suite 184OT, 61 Forsyth Street SW, Atlanta, GA 30303; Phone: (404) 562-7000. Suite 2010, 300 N. Los Angeles, Los Angeles, CA 90012; Phone: (213) 894-3437.

U.S. HOLOCAUST MEMORIAL MUSEUM

Chartered by a unanimous act of Congress in 1980, the U.S. memorial to millions of people murdered during the Holocaust and America's national institution for documentation, interpretation, and study of Holocaust history. The museum and the U.S. Holocaust Memorial Council work to increase knowledge about the Holocaust, to preserve the memory of those who suffered and survived, and to motivate visitors to reflect upon the moral and spiritual questions brought to awareness by revisiting Holocaust events, art and artifacts, and documents.

The Holocaust was a Nazi Germany state-sponsored systematic persecution, murder, and annihilation of European Jews in which Germany was aided by Hungary, Mussolini's Italy, and pro-Nazi elements from France, Norway, Holland, and Denmark from 1933 to 1945. Six million people were killed, primarily Jews. Also targeted were Gypsies, handicapped people, Poles, homosexuals, Jehovah's Witnesses, Soviet prisoners of war, and political dissidents.

As part of its unusual effort, the Holocaust Memorial Museum hosts the Holocaust Learning Center to record and make available personal histories of Holocaust survivors and their families; takes exhibitions to communities throughout the United States; and provides Holocaust survivors as volunteers who tell their own stories to visitors.

The museum's Committee on Conscience tracks and reports on countries in its "Genocide Watch" list, currently focusing on Chechnya.

The design of the museum itself functions as an exhibit of Holocaust history. The museum keeps a Survivors Registry, an Office of Survivor Affairs, a Hall of Remembrance, public programs and a media archive, and a working Task Force for International Cooperation.

CONTACT Address: U.S. Holocaust Memorial Museum, 100 Raoul Wallenberg Place SW, Washington, DC 20024-2126; Phone: (202) 488-0400, TTY: (202) 488-0406; Website: www.ushmm.org.

U.S. INTERNATIONAL TRADE COMMISSION (USITC)

Created by Congress in 1916 as the U.S. Tariff Commission, USITC is an independent, nonpartisan quasi-judicial agency that advises the executive and legislative branches of the U.S. government on tariffs on international trade and competitiveness, and on the impact of imports on U.S. companies. It also takes action against some unfair trade practices such as patent, trademark, or copyright infringement, and maintains the "Harmonized Tariff Schedule of the United States." The commission's name was updated by the Trade Act of 1974.

The main elements of USITC's operations include import injury investigations; intellectual property-based import investigations; research; trade information services; and trade policy support. Its activities include researching whether American companies are damaged by imports that benefit from pricing at less than fair value or from being subsidized; making recommendations to the president on relief for industries damaged by increasing imports; advising the president on possible interference of imported agricultural products with DEPARTMENT OF AGRICULTURE price-support programs; studying trade and tariff issues and import levels; collecting and keeping track of data on imports, exports, and American production; and establishing an international commodity code.

USITC works with the DEPARTMENT OF COMMERCE on anti-dumping investigations made possible by foreign government subsidies or by selling foreign products in the United States at below market prices. Commerce decides whether dumping is going on, and USITC decides whether American industry is materially injured by the dumping or subsidization.

USITC has six commissioners nominated by the president and confirmed by the Senate, with no more than half coming from one political party. Commissioners serve nine years, with the chair and vice chair selected by the president and coming from different political parties.

Resources include the Trade Remedy Assistance Office for public and small business members seeking help, benefits, or relief under U.S. trade laws, the National Library of International Trade, and the ITC Law Library.

CONTACT Address: U.S. International Trade Commission, 500 E Street SW, Washington, DC 20436; Phone: (202) 205-2000; Website: www.usitc.gov.

U.S. NUCLEAR WASTE TECHNICAL REVIEW BOARD (NWTRB)

Created by the Nuclear Waste Policy Amendments Act passed by Congress in 1987 to evaluate the DEPARTMENT OF ENERGY's clean up of dumped and leaked nuclear matter at Yucca Mountain, Nevada. To monitor DOE's technical and scientific clean up in the commercial nuclear waste disposal program, the board makes recommendations on scientific and technical decisions; advises DOE on its work at Yucca Mountain; and oversees coordination of private contractors and DOE on the highly scientific and technical problems faced in the clean up. NWTRB reports public concerns and reports at least twice annually to Congress on issues and problems in the clean up.

NWTRB has 11 part-time members who are selected because of their expertise and distinguished service in the fields of science or engineering involving the environmental and social sciences.

CONTACT Address: NWTRB, Suite 1300, 2300 Clarendon Boulevard, Arlington, VA 22201; Phone: (703) 235-4473; Website: www.nwtrb.gov.

UNITED STATES POSTAL SERVICE (USPS)

Created as an independent entity by the Postal Reorganization Act of 1970. A board of governors oversees U.S.P.S., and is made up of nine "governors," who are appointed by the president with advice and consent of the Senate, and who serve overlapping nine-year terms. The board of governors appoints the postmaster general, and the governors and the postmaster general appoint the deputy postmaster general, who joins them to make an 11-member board.

The Postal Service delivers the mail and handles its own real estate, planning, research, engineering, and procurement programs, while a consumer advocate represents the general public by bringing complaints and suggestions to management. Partly due to its independence, the Postal Service is the only federal agency that negotiates under collective bargaining under the National Labor Relations Act.

The Postal Service also has the power of a law enforcement agency dealing with criminal matters that might affect the mail system. Postal inspectors work to enforce more than 200 federal statutes concerning mail fraud, mail theft, mail bombs, child pornography, illegal drugs, and other postal crimes. It also tries to protect Postal Service employees.

Established in 1957, the *Citizens' Stamp Advisory Committee* evaluates all stamp proposals, many coming from the general public, and makes recommendations to the postmaster general. The committee's 15 members are appointed by the postmaster general, come from artistic, historical, professional, and other backgrounds, and meet four times a year.

CONTACT Address: United States Postal Service, 475 L'Enfant Plaza SW, Washington, DC 20260-0010; Phone: (202) 268-2000; Website: www.usps.gov. To submit artwork to be considered, write to the following address and ask for the brochure "Creating U.S. Postage Stamps," U.S Postal Service, Stamp Development, Attn.: Stamp Design, 475 L'Enfant Plaza SW, Room 5670, Washington, DC 20260-2437.

QUASI-OFFICIAL AGENCIES

LEGAL SERVICES CORPORATION (LSC)

Created by Congress in 1974 as a private, nonprofit corporation to ensure equal access to justice under the law for all Americans by making available civil legal assistance to people who cannot afford it otherwise. LSC does not provide legal services directly, but it funds about 179 independent local legal aid programs that compete for grants. Thus, legal services are made available in every county in the United States, as well as in U.S. territories, and to Native Americans and migrant farmworkers.

LSC local programs do not accept criminal cases or potentially fee-generating cases that private attorneys might accept on a contingency basis (a percentage of the recovered amount, if there is a recovery). In 1996 several other restrictions were imposed on LSC-fund recipient programs; class action lawsuits are prohibited, as are challenges to welfare reform, collection of attorneys' fees, rule making, lobbying, litigation on behalf of prisoners, drug-related housing eviction challenges, and representation of some aliens. The 2004 annual budget was $335 million, including a federal contribution.

An 11-member board of directors, appointed by the president and confirmed by the Senate, runs LSC, with no more than six members from any one political party. Local programs have their own boards of directors that set each of the organization's priorities and decide what kinds of cases to handle, within the guidelines set by Congress. Local bar associations name the majority of members of the local program, with one-third of the total board composed of client representatives. Each board hires its own executive director.

Local programs are funded by LSC grants, state and local governments, interest on lawyer trust accounts, other federal agencies, bar associations, United Way and other charitable organizations, foundations, corporations, and individual contributors. Monetary funding is also substituted with local private attorneys who represent indigent clients for free (pro bono).

CONTACT Legal Services Corporation, 3333 K Street NW, Third Floor, Washington, DC, 20007-3522; Phone: (202) 295-1500; Website: www.lsc.gov.

NATIONAL INSTITUTE OF JUSTICE (NIJ)

Created By the omnibus Crime Control and Safe Streets Act of 1968, NIJ is a research, development, and evaluation agency that researches crime control and justice issues for the U.S. DEPARTMENT OF JUSTICE, particularly at the state and local levels. Streamlined by the George W. Bush administration in 2003, NIJ merged the Office of Development and Communications into the Office of Research and Evaluation and its communications functions into the Office of the Director.

NIJ programs include the Arrestee Drug Abuse Monitoring Program (ADAM); Corrections and Law Enforcement Family Support Program; Community Mapping, Planning and Analysis for Safety Strategies (COMPASS); a Data Resources Program; a database; the Residential Substance Abuse Treatment Program (RSAT); the Violence Against Women and Family Violence Research and Evaluation Program; the National Criminal Justice Reference Service (NCJRS); the Presidential Initiative on Advancing Justice through DNA Technology program; the National Commission on the Future of DNA Evidence program; and the Breaking the Cycle program.

The National Commission on the Future of DNA Evidence makes recommendations to the attorney general on current and potential use of DNA methods, applications, and technologies for use in the criminal justice system. It looks into use of DNA in post-conviction situations;

legal concerns in DNA use; criteria for use and training of criminal justice professionals in identification, collection, and proper preservation of DNA evidence; and laboratory and emerging technologies.

The Breaking the Cycle program is a joint effort of the Office of National Drug Control Policy and the National Institute of Justice. The program's goal is to identify and evaluate defendants who were using drugs at the time of arrest, giving them individualized treatment, intensive supervision, and judicial oversight to reduce drug use and crime.

The Breaking the Cycle program consists of testing all arrestees for drugs before their initial court hearing; putting drug users in treatment and monitoring programs; pretrial and post-sentence case management; sanctions and incentives to examine and improve offender behavior; and judicial oversight to make sure arrestees comply with the program. Breaking the Cycle works with the Urban Institute in Birmingham, Alabama, Jacksonville, Florida, and Tacoma, Washington, and with the Research Triangle Institute in its other test location at Eugene, Oregon.

CONTACT Address: 810 Seventh Street NW, Washington, DC 20531; Phone: (202) 307-2942; Website: www.ojp.usdoj.gov/nij/. Birmingham, AL; Phone: (205) 917-3784, ext. 231. Jacksonville, FL; Phone: (904) 630-3632. Tacoma, WA; Phone: (253) 572-4750. Eugene, OR; Phone: (541) 682-4705.

U.S. INSTITUTE OF PEACE

An independent, nonpartisan federal institution created by Congress in 1984 to promote prevention, management, and peaceful resolution of international conflicts, and to curb violent conflict.

To achieve these goals, the institute engages in six primary activities: works to develop public knowledge of changes in international relations and the nature of conflicts through methods of conflict prevention, reconciliation, and peaceful diplomacy; supports legislative and executive branch policy makers by assembling top research talent on how to resolve international conflict by political means; facilitates peaceful resolution through dialogue within and among parties to conflicts; trains U.S. and foreign military professionals in international affairs in peaceful conflict resolution; works to equip schools from high schools on up with tools to teach peacemaking and conflict management; and uses radio, publications, Internet, and other means to educate the public on the nature of international conflict and peaceful resolution possibilities.

The first proposal for a "Peace Office" was made in 1792 by architect and publisher Benjamin Banneker and physician and educator Dr. Benjamin Rush. They asked that the Peace Office be established at the same level as the War Department (now the DEPARTMENT OF DEFENSE). Banneker and Rush were hoping for an office to promote peace within the country. Between 1935 and 1976 more than 140 bills were introduced in Congress proposing establishment of various levels of peace departments or agencies, the best known of which were proposed by Woodrow Wilson, Jennings Randolph, and Everett Dirksen.

The legislative trail to the current U.S. Institute of Peace began with a bill introduced by Sen. Vance Hartke (Dem.-Indiana) and Sen. Mark Hatfield (Rep.-Oregon) to create the George Washington Peace Academy. After several other unsuccessful attempts, a provision was tacked onto the Elementary and Secondary Education Appropriation Bill in 1979 to establish a Commission on Proposals for the National Academy of Peace and Conflict Resolution.

President Jimmy Carter appointed a nonpartisan commission made up of House and Senate leaders, eventually known as the Matsunaga Commission named for its chair, Sen. Spark Matsunaga (Dem.-Hawaii). After wide study and research, the Matsunaga Commission issued a final report in 1981 recommending creation of a national peace academy, and the bipartisan United States Institute of Peace Act finally passed and was signed by President Ronald Reagan in 1984.

The institute's board has 15 members, 12 from outside federal service, appointed by the president and confirmed by the Senate, along with the secretaries of state, defense, and president of the National Defense University, who serve ex-officio. The board oversees the institute's activities, sets the institute's long-term goals and priorities, and monitors its financial, administrative, and personnel functions. Further, it approves new programs, and selects institute grant recipients, fellows, and winners of the institute's high school National Peace Essay Contest. Members of the board must "have appropriate practical or academic experience in peace and conflict resolution" and serve a maximum of two four-year terms.

In the early 2000s, the Institute of Peace has sponsored special initiatives on the Balkans, the Muslim world, religion and peacemaking, and virtual diplomacy.

The institute's library is named the Jeannette Rankin Library in honor of the first woman elected to Congress, who also voted against World War I, voted against declaring war on Japan, and abstained on the declaration of war on Germany and Italy.

CONTACT Address; U.S. Institute of Peace, 1200 17th Street NW, Washington, DC 20036; Phone: (202) 457-1700; Website: www.usip.org.

LEGISLATIVE
BRANCH

~ CONGRESS ~

The framers of the Constitution vested all legislative powers in the Congress, which it divided into two houses, the Senate and the House of Representatives. During the debate over the provisions of the Constitution, the delegates reached what is known historically as the "Great Compromise" between the interests of the most populous states and the smaller states. The delegates decided that the number of members of the House per state would be based on population and the Senate would be composed of two senators representing each state, no matter what the population.

The representatives are elected every two years, and the number of members was fixed at 435 by statute in the early 1900s. The number of representatives in each state is recalculated every decade based on the census mandated by the Constitution, and the district lines within the states are drawn by each state government. The new districts go into effect on the year ending with a 2. The senators (currently 100) serve six-year terms, with one-third of the body elected every two years. Originally the senators were elected by state legislatures, but the Seventeenth Amendment to the Constitution adopted in 1913 provided for direct election by the people of each state.

Although the conduct of elections is governed by state laws, there are certain national requirements dictated by the Constitution, federal statutes, and federal court decisions based on constitutionality. The Twenty-fourth Amendment to the Constitution, ratified in 1964, outlawed any poll tax required for registration or voting. For almost a century these poll taxes in states of the old Confederacy resulted in suppression of the voting rights of blacks and poor whites. The series of Supreme Court decisions in the mid-1960s required that all House districts be equal in population, and district borders had to be drawn to accomplish that equality.

The Constitution sets minimum age limits for representatives at 25 years, and for the Senate 30 years. Rules of conduct, determination of vote count challenges, and the right to be seated are determined by the members of each house.

Management of each house is based on the presumption of the two-party system, with the leadership of each house in the hands of the majority party in that chamber. The leader of the majority party in the House of Representatives is the speaker of the House. The number two person of the majority party is the majority leader and the leader of the opposition is the minority leader. Both majority and minority leaders have a coterie of "whips" to urge members to vote for or against legislation as determined by their party leadership, and to count votes preliminary to voting. The speaker chairs the House, but much of the time a designated member will sit in the chair, recognizing speakers and making procedural rulings (with the aid of a staff parliamentarian).

Both parties have a caucus of members who elect their leaders, including speaker of the House (technically elected by the entire House, but based on the nomination of the majority party caucus). The chairs of House committees are named by the majority caucus, and the leading member of the minority party in each committee (known as the "ranking" committee member) is picked by his/her party caucus. A majority of each committee are of the majority party.

The president (presiding officer) of the Senate is the vice president, who cannot vote unless there is a tie in votes. Spelling the vice president in the duties as presiding officer is the president pro tempore, elected by the Senate upon nomination by the majority party caucus. Much like the House, designated senators often fill in to actually preside for periods of time. The leader of the controlling party is the majority leader and his/her counterpart for the minority is the minority leader, both chosen by their party caucus. As in the House, they are each assisted by a group of

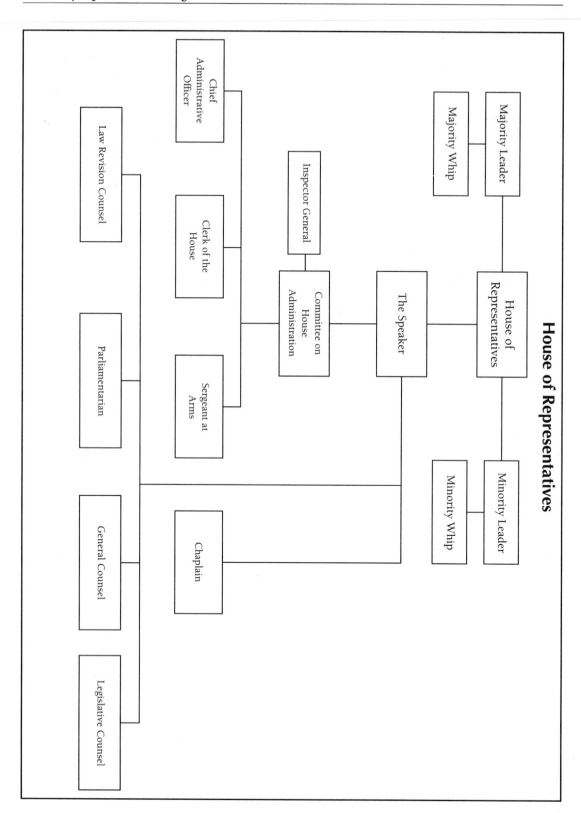

House of Representatives

whips, committee chairs, ranking members, and the membership from their party on each committee.

A major difference in the day-to-day functioning of the two houses is the control of speaking time. In the House of Representatives each speaker is given a short time to speak and is limited to the subject at hand. On the Senate side the time to speak is without limit unless 60 percent of the senators vote an end to debate (known as cloture). Thus a small number of senators (or only one) can talk a measure to death in a filibuster while blocking discussion or any action on all other matters.

The House and Senate also differ in their responsibilities. The Constitution gave the Senate the responsibility to "advise and consent" the president in regard to international treaties entered into by the president by a vote of two-thirds for approval, and by a majority vote on confirmation of appointments of SUPREME COURT justices, all federal judges, members of the cabinet, upper-level administrators and board members, and ambassadors. If the Senate does not ratify a treaty or appointment, those are rejected. Votes on such matters are preceded by committee hearings, and possibly substantial dispute by floor debate. Pursuant to the Constitution, the House of Representatives has the sole authority to initiate legislation for "raising revenue."

Possible impeachment of the president or federal judges requires a resolution passed by the House of Representatives recommending removal based on specific charges of "Treason, Bribery, or other High Crimes and Misdemeanors." If the charges are adopted by the House of Representatives, then a trial is held by the full Senate, with the chief justice of the Supreme Court sitting as presiding officer in the case of the president, and by the vice president or president pro tem in cases involving judges. A two-thirds vote is required to convict. Note: The term *impeachment* means to charge, not removal or conviction. Thus, President Andrew Johnson and Bill Clinton were "impeached" but were acquitted. The definition of "high crimes and misdemeanors" remains unclear.

If a bill passes both houses, the president may veto the legislation. If so, the Senate and House may vote to override the veto; such override requires a two-thirds vote in order to enact the law despite the veto.

One other specific responsibility of Congress is voting to fill a vacancy in the office of vice president, which is delineated by the Twenty-fifth Amendment ratified in 1967. Should the office of vice president become vacant, the president nominates a successor, who must be approved by a majority vote of both houses. This has occurred twice: on the resignation of Vice President Spiro Agnew, and on the elevation of Gerald Ford to the presidency on the resignation of President Richard Nixon.

Almost all the business of both houses passes through the committee system. There are several types of committees: standing committees, which are continuing and special committees, select committees, and joint committees (of both houses). All proposed bills are referred by the majority leadership to the appropriate committee. In the House of Representatives bills are then moved to the Rules Committee, which can hold the legislation or vote to send it to the floor for a vote by the full body. The chairs of the various committees generally have the power to withhold calling a vote on a piece of legislation and thus prevent it from being voted upon, effectively killing it for that session.

Standing committees of the House of Representatives are: agriculture, appropriations, armed services, banking and financial services, budget, commerce, education and the workforce, government reform, House administration, international relations, judiciary, resources, rules, science, small business, standards of official conduct, transportation and infrastructure, veterans' affairs, and ways and means. The House also has a select committee on intelligence.

United States Senate

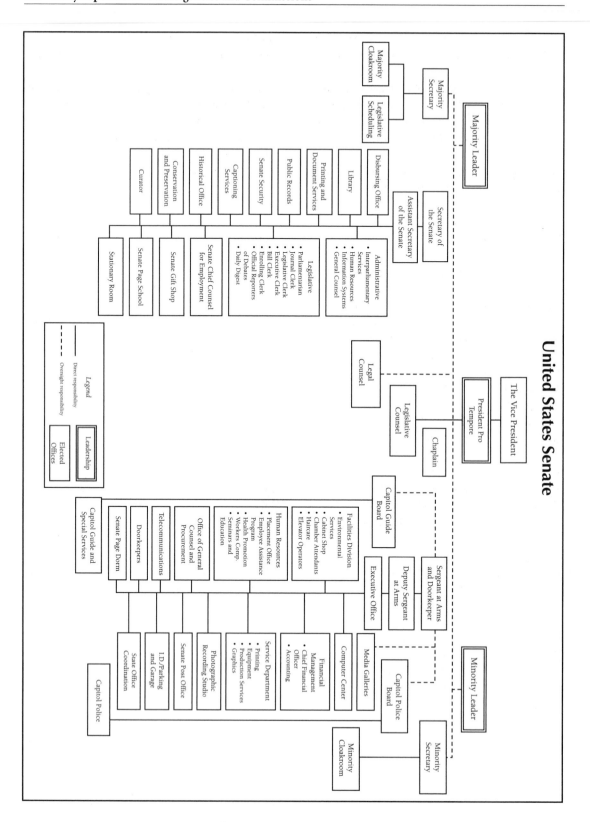

Standing committees of the Senate are: agriculture, nutrition and forestry, appropriations, armed services, banking, housing and urban affairs, budget, commerce, science and transportation, energy and natural resources, environment and public works, finance, foreign relations, governmental affairs, health, education, labor and pensions, judiciary, (with numerous subcommittees), rules and administration, small business, and veterans' affairs. In the Senate there are special committees on aging, ethics, intelligence, and Indian affairs.

Joint Committees are: economics, library, printing, and taxation.

Many of the committees have subcommittees on more narrowly focused subjects.

There are also conference committees, which are specially appointed by leaders of both parties in both houses to negotiate differences between bills passed by both houses on the same topic.

Contact: The offices of senators can be reached by telephone at (202) 224-3121; the offices of representatives can be reached by phone at (202) 225-3121; for latest listing of representatives go to www.clerk.house.gov.

The Senate office buildings are the Russell Office Building at Delaware Avenue and Constitution Avenue, the Dirksen Office Building at First Street and Constitution Avenue, and the Hart Office Building at Second Street and C Street. They are named for late senators Richard Russell, Everett Dirksen, and Phillip Hart, respectively. They are all located northeast of the Capitol and are connected by an underground tram available for senators, their staffs, and guests. The House of Representatives office buildings are the Cannon House Office Building at New Jersey Avenue and Independence Avenue, the Longworth House Office Building on Independence Avenue between South Capitol Street and New Jersey Avenue, and the Rayburn House Office Building on Independence Avenue between First Street and South Capitol Street. They are named for historic speakers of the House Joseph Cannon, Nicholas Longworth, and Sam Rayburn, respectively. They are

all south of the Capitol and are connected by an underground tram available for representatives, their staffs, and guests.

Congress supervises several governmental agencies separate from the executive branch: the General Accounting Office, Library of Congress, Congressional Budget Office, Government Printing Office, Architect of the Capitol, and United States Botanic Garden.

GENERAL ACCOUNTING OFFICE (GAO)

Created by the Budget and Accounting Act of 1921, which moved accounting, auditing, and claims functions from the TREASURY DEPARTMENT to GAO to consolidate financial management of the federal government after World War I. Since Word War I drove the national debt to new highs (at the time), Congress created GAO as an independent, nonpartisan agency to investigate how federal money is spent, dollar by dollar. The Budget and Accounting Act also required that the president prepare an annual budget for the federal government.

The more money Congress puts into government, the more extensive becomes GAO's role. After World War II, GAO worked in conjunction with the Department of the Treasury and the Bureau of the Budget (now OFFICE OF MANAGEMENT AND BUDGET-OMB) to help executive branch agencies streamline accounting and expenditures. With more spending during the cold war in the 1950s, GAO turned its focus to defense spending and private contracts. In 1952 GAO set up a network of regional offices, including opening branches in Europe and the Far East, even one in Saigon, Vietnam, to watch military expenditures and foreign aid during the Vietnam War.

GAO also took on the job of monitoring how well agencies perform their tasks, in addition and in relation to how they used money. In 1967 Congress asked GAO to evaluate President

Lyndon B. Johnson's Great Society and War on Poverty efforts, as well as energy policy, consumer protection, environment, and economy. Since the 1980s, GAO has evolved further, taking on the job of warning policy makers and the public to emerging management and financial problems throughout the federal government. Yet it took U.S. Sen. Barbara Boxer (Dem.-California) to reveal that the government was paying hundreds of dollars for toilet seats.

Currently GAO does audits and evaluations of federal government programs, usually requested by members of Congress; provides some legal services to Congress with advice from the comptroller general on legal issues that involve government programs and activities; helps draft legislation, reviews, and reports to Congress on rescissions and deferrals of federal funds; reviews bidding processes and protests; and helps government agencies interpret laws of public funds expenditures. GAO also does special investigations when auditors and evaluators find possible criminal and civil misconduct, and sometimes refers such potential infractions to the DEPARTMENT OF JUSTICE and other law enforcement agencies.

GAO publishes the *Government Auditing Standards* to guide audits, auditors, and accounting of government organizations, programs, activities, and functions. The comptroller general sits with the secretary of the treasury and the director of the Office of Management and Budget on the FEDERAL ACCOUNTING STANDARDS ADVISORY BOARD (see p. 373).

CONTACT Address: GAO, 441 G Street NW, Washington, DC 20548; Phone: (202) 512-3000; Website: www.gao.gov. For unclassified report copies: P.O. Box 37050, Washington, DC 20013; Phone: (202) 512-6000.

LIBRARY OF CONGRESS

The Library of Congress holds about 20 million volumes, meant for the use of Congress but available to all government agencies and the general public for research within the library (it is not a lending library) upon call from nearly 40 miles of shelves. The only sections of the library open to the public are some general reference books and the law library.

The collections include maps, photographs, movies, manuscripts (including presidential papers of George Washington through Calvin Coolidge), recordings (including historic speeches), music, documents, newspapers, videotapes, and the world's largest inventory of books premovable type.

HISTORY

The library was established by Congress in 1800 with an initial appropriation of $5,000 to buy "such books as may be necessary for the use of Congress." The original library was burned by British troops who invaded Washington during the War of 1812. Congress obtained the nucleus of a new library by the purchase of 6,000 books in 1815 from financially strapped former president Thomas Jefferson for the sum of $23,950.

CONTACT Address: Library of Congress, 101 Independence Avenue SE, Washington, DC 20540; Phone: (202) 707-5000; Public Affairs Office, Phone: (202) 707-2905; Website: www. loc.gov.

ORGANIZATION

Heading the Library of Congress is the librarian of Congress. Although the administration is under the umbrella of Congress, the librarian is appointed by the president with confirmation by the Senate. Not considered political in nature, the librarian of Congress also chairs the Library of Congress Trust Fund Board. The administrative staff includes the deputy librarian of Congress, a chief of staff, associate librarians for library services and human resources, the director of the Congressional Research Service, the registrar of copyrights, the law librarian, chief of the Loan Division, and the general counsel and inspector general.

FUNCTIONS

In addition to its principal role as the Congressional Research Service, in the last quarter of the 20th century Congress has given the library other management responsibilities.

CONGRESSIONAL RESEARCH SERVICES: Its original primary function, the library provides nonpartisan research and analysis for the members of Congress and their staffs. Its expert staff covers many disciplines, including law, economics, foreign affairs, physical sciences, environmental issues, public administration, political science, social sciences, and legislative histories. This often includes extensive background data and analysis. The service is available via immediate consultation by telephone or in-person to members of Congress. It also conducts seminars on various governmental topics.

CONTACT Phone: (202) 707-5700.

U.S. COPYRIGHT OFFICE: Under the Copyright Act of 1976, which processes half a million copyright applications each year, protects the rights of authors to their works, both published and unpublished. Protected copyrights include literary, musical and dramatic works, periodicals, maps, works of art, art reproductions, sculptures, technical drawings, photographs, prints, labels, movies, computer programs, architectural drawings, and other creative items. Most copyrights are valid for the life of the creator and 50 years. The Copyright Office also provides information on which publications are available in the public domain for republication without permission or a licensing fee.

CONTACT Address: Copyright Office, Library of Congress, 101 Independence Avenue SE, Washington, DC 20599 (personal visit: Room LM—401); Phone: (202) 707-3000; Forms: Phone: (202) 707-9100; Copyright Records: Phone: (202) 707-6850; Website: www.loc.gov/copyright.

AMERICAN FOLKLIFE CENTER (1976): Collects, maintains, and arranges performances of folk music and oral traditions. Created in 1976, its preservation efforts include the Federal Cylinder Project, which saves wax cylinder recordings made in the 1890s through the old 78s in the 1940s. The center maintains the Archive of Folk Culture of ethnographic material for reading, listening, and research, and a reading room. It also issues a quarterly newsletter, *Folklife Center News*.

CONTACT Phone: (202) 707-5510; Website: 1cweb.loc.gov/folklife.

CENTER OF THE BOOK (1977): Initiated in 1977, the center stimulates reading. The center has entered into cooperative agreements with educational and civic organizations, and almost every state and the District of Columbia, to develop and fund local "communities of readers, authors and local leaders." Funded by private contributions, the goal is to encourage reading and love of books.

CONTACT Phone: (202) 707-5221; E-mail: cfbooks@loc.gov.

NATIONAL FILM PRESERVATION BOARD (1996), NATIONAL SOUND RECORDING PRESERVATION BOARD (2000): Established in 1996 and 2000, respectively, both have the goal of preserving works that will be lost for all time unless gathered and provided with the technical means to guarantee they will not deteriorate.

CONTACT Film: Phone: (202) 707-5912, Recordings: Phone: (202) 707-5856. For technical information and publications: Office of the Director of Preservation, Library of Congress, Washington, DC 20540; Phone: (202) 707-1840.

Other vital services are the centralized cataloguing system of books worldwide, with Library of Congress numbers for each volume and certain basic information. Bibliographic material and for sale CD-ROMS of catalogues are available.

CONTACT Phone: (202) 707-6100; E-mail: cdsinfo@mail.loc.gov.

BOOKS FOR THE BLIND: For the blind or those with sight difficulties the library provides books in

Braille, and "talking books" (books on tape), available at 140 regional locations. Information can be obtained from most public libraries.

CONTACT National Library Service for the Blind and Physically Handicapped, Library of Congress, 1291 Taylor Street NW, Washington, DC 20542; Phone: (202) 707-5100.

RESEARCH SERVICES FOR THE PUBLIC: For determining information available from the library, contact Reference Referral Service; Phone: (202) 707-5522. For research services on technical subjects contact the Science, Technology and Business Division of the library; Phone: (202) 707-5639. For research on general topics, contact the Federal Research Division of the library; Phone: (202) 707-3909.

U.S. GOVERNMENT PRINTING OFFICE (GPO)

Authority created under Title 44 of the U.S. Code on June 23, 1860. The head of GPO is the government printer, who is appointed by the president and confirmed by the Senate. Originally created to print documents for Congress, GPO now produces official print and electronic documents for 130 federal departments and agencies, including congressional publications, federal regulations, federal reports, census and tax forms, passports, and books. It provides on-line access to more than 200,000 federal government titles, including the *Congressional Record,* the *U.S. Budget,* and the *Federal Register.* These documents are available in various formats including print, microfiche, CD-ROM, and on-line at www.gpoaccess.gov. In 2002 about 372 million government documents were downloaded from www.gpoaccess.gov.

With its main printing plant in Washington, D.C., GPO is the largest industrial employer in the capital. It also has a printing plant in Denver, Colorado, a distribution facility in Pueblo, Colorado, and a technical documentation facility in Atlantic City, New Jersey.

GPO gets its operating funds from several sources: an appropriation from Congress to cover the cost of congressional printing; one for cataloging, indexing, distribution, and on-line access to documents; and reimbursement by its government customers for the publication work GPO does. GPO gets 70 percent of its revenue from government agencies for work it farms out to private printers around the country and for products it purchases from private companies throughout the 50 states, involving 2,260 commercial concerns. GPO invites bids.

Interested persons can order government documents or other publications on-line at http://bookstore.gpo.gov.

The Federal Depository Library Program coordinates 1,200 federal depository libraries throughout the United States with free public access to government information. The superintendent of documents' programs catalog and index government information, distribute publications required by law, and provide distribution services for federal agencies. GPO also distributes U.S. government publications to nearly 70 countries under the International Exchange Program, run by the Library of Congress.

CONTACT Address: Government Printing Office, 732 North Capitol Street NW, Washington, DC 20401; Phone: (202) 512-0000; Website: www.gpo.gov, www.gpoaccess.gov, and http://bookstore.gpo.gov. Regional printing and procurement offices: Suite 110, 1888 Emery Street, Atlanta, GA 30318-2542; Phone: (404) 605-9160. 28 Court Square, Boston, MA 02108-2504; Phone: (617) 720-3680. Suite 810, 200 N. LaSalle Street, Chicago, IL 60601-1055; Phone: (312) 353-3916. Suite 112-B, 1335 Dublin Road, Columbus, OH 43215-7034; Phone: (614) 488-4616. Room 7B7, 1100 Commerce Street, Dallas, TX 75242-0395; Phone: (214) 767-0451. Room 310, 423 Canal Street, New Orleans, LA 70130-2352; Phone: (504) 589-2538. Suite 100, 3420 D Avenue, Tinker AFB, Oklahoma City, OK 73145-9188; Phone: (405) 610-4146. Suite 2, 1531 Connally Street, Lackland AFB, San Antonio, TX

78236-5514; Phone: (210) 675-1480. Room D-1010, Building 53, Denver Federal Center, Denver, CO 80225-0347; Phone: (303) 236-5292. Suite 400, 11836 Canon Boulevard, Newport News, VA 23606-2555; Phone: (757) 873-2800. Suite 110, 121501 E. Imperial Highway, Norwalk, CA 90650-3136; Phone: (562) 863-1708. Suite 109, 2221 Camino Del Rio South, San Diego, CA 92108-3609; Phone: (619) 497-6050. Room 709, 201 Varick Street, New York, NY 10014-4879; Phone: (212) 620-3321. Suite A-190, 928 Jaymore Road, Southampton, PA 18966-3820; Phone: (215) 364-6465. Room 501, 1000 Liberty Avenue, Pittsburgh, PA 15222-4000; Phone: (412) 395-4858. Room 1205, 1222 Spruce Street, St. Louis, MO 63103-2818; Phone: (314) 241-0349. Suite 1, 536 Stone Road, Benicia, CA 94510-1170; Phone: (707) 748-2970. 4735 E. Marginal Way South, Federal Center South, Seattle, WA 98134-2397; Phone: (206) 764-3726.

GPO Bookstores: Washington, DC-Main Bookstore, 710 N. Capitol Street NW; Phone: (202) 512-0132 and Retail Sales Outlet, 8660 Cherry Lane, Laurel, MD; Phone: (301) 953-7974. Suite 120, 999 Peachtree Street NE, Atlanta, GA; Phone: (404) 347-1900. Room 1653, 1240 East 9th Street, Cleveland, OH; Phone: (216) 522-4922. Room 207, 200 N. High Street, Columbus, OH; Phone: (614) 469-6956. Room 1C42, 1100 Commerce Street, Dallas, TX; Phone: (214) 767-0076. Suite 130, 1660 Wynkoop Street, Denver, CO; Phone: (303) 844-3964. Suite 160, 477 Michigan Avenue, Detroit, MI; Phone: (313) 226-7816. Suite 120, 801 Travis Street, Houston, TX; Phone: (713) 228-1187. Room 100, 100 West Bay Street, Jacksonville, FL; Phone: (904) 353-0569. 120 Bannister Mall, 5600 E. Bannister Road, Kansas City, MO; Phone: (816) 765-2256. C-Level, 505 South Flower Street, Los Angeles, CA; Phone: (213) 239-9844. Room 150-W, 310 West Wisconsin Avenue, Milwaukee, WI; Phone: (414) 297-1304. Room 2-120, 26 Federal Plaza, New York, NY; Phone: (212) 264-3825. Room 118, 1000 Liberty Avenue, Pittsburgh, PA; Phone: (412) 395-5021.

1305 SW 1st Avenue, Portland, OR; Phone: (503) 221-6217. 201 West 8th Street, Pueblo, CO; Phone: (719) 544-3142. Room 194, 915 2nd Avenue, Seattle, WA; Phone: (206) 553-4260.

CONGRESSIONAL BUDGET OFFICE

The Congressional Budget Office (CBO)was created by Congress in 1974. It has the specific function of providing an economic analysis of the impact of the federal budget at any time in any particular area of concern at the request of Congress. It was anticipated that this service would assist members of Congress in decision making on both taxing and spending.

The office's activities include economic forecasting, a biannual forecast of economic trends, and reports on the degree to which the goals set by Congress have been met through monitoring both overall results and also the impact of specific authorizations and appropriations. It gives Senate and House budget committees annual reports on the budget, assessing the impact of fiscal policy on local, state, and tribal governments. Furthermore, it monitors and reports on spending limits in various categories pursuant to the Balanced Budget and Emergency Deficit Control Act of 1985.

At times CBO's estimates and reports have proved more accurate than those of the executive branch.

ORGANIZATION

The office is headed by a director assisted by a deputy director, an executive director, and three associate directors for communications, for research and reports, and for management, business, and information services. Technical fields are managed by seven assistant directors: for microeconomic and financial studies, for long-term modeling, for budget analysis, for macroeconomic analysis, for health and human resources, for tax analysis, and for national security.

CONTACT Address: Congressional Budget Office, Second and D Streets SW, Washington, DC 20515; Phone: (202) 226-2600; Website: www.cbo.gov.

ARCHITECT OF THE CAPITOL

One of the oldest offices in American government, the first architect of the Capitol was named by Congress in 1793, at the time when President George Washington chose the site for the seat of government. The Capitol building actually was not finished until 1801, when the seat of government was moved from its temporary 10-year stay in Philadelphia.

The Office of the Architect is responsible for the Capitol building and its grounds, House and Senate office buildings, the Library of Congress buildings, the Supreme Court building, the Thurgood Marshall Federal Judiciary Building, the Capitol power plant, the Capitol police headquarters, the U.S. Botanic Gardens (for which the architect serves as director), the Robert Taft Memorial, and any new additions and improvements such as telecommunication systems.

The architect is appointed by the president with Senate confirmation for a 10-year term, but the appointment must be made from one of three recommended by a congressional commission. The staff consists of engineers, architects, landscape architects, construction experts, facilities managers and planners, and support.

Oversight is performed by the Senate Committee on Rules and Administration, the House Office Building Commission, the speaker of the House, and the Committee on House Administration.

CONTACT Address: Architect of the Capitol, U.S. Capitol Building, Washington, DC 20515; Phone: (202) 228-1793; Website: www.aoc.gov.

UNITED STATES BOTANIC GARDEN

Recently relocated and replanted, the Botanic Garden is a three-acre plot of rare botanic specimens just west of the garden's conservatory at 100 Maryland Avenue SW, Washington, DC 20024, which reopened in December 2001. The conservatory showcases a dozen exhibits and interpretative plant groupings. Plants include orchids, carnivorous plants, medicinal plants, cacti, succulents, ferns, and rare and endangered species of plants. A production facility is located at 4700 Shepherd Parkway SW, Washington, DC 20024, Phone: (202) 563-2220.

The garden's centerpiece is a 19th-century fountain created by Frédéric-Auguste Bartholdi, who designed the Statue of Liberty. The Botanic Garden was founded at the Columbian Institute for the Arts and Sciences in 1820. Briefly abandoned, it was opened as a site for botanical specimens brought from the South Seas in 1842 under the direction of the Committee of Congress on the Library and money allocated for its maintenance. From 1850 to 1933 it remained at the west end of the Capitol grounds. Then in 1934 it was moved to the Maryland Avenue location.

Since 1934 the director has been the architect of the Capitol, but an executive director handles the operation of the garden.

CONTACT Address: Office of Executive Director, 245 First Street SW, Washington, DC 20024; Phone: (202) 226-8333; plant "hotline" (202) 226-4785; Website: www.usbg.gov.

JUDICIAL BRANCH AND FEDERAL COURT SYSTEM

Authority for the federal court system is found in Article III of the Constitution, which states in Section 1: "The judicial power of the United States, shall be vested in one Supreme Court and such inferior Courts as the Congress may from time to time ordain and establish. The judges, both of the supreme and inferior courts, shall hold their offices during good behavior. . . ."

The jurisdiction of the federal courts includes cases arising out of the Constitution, actions between citizens (including corporations) of different states, disputes between states, treason, admiralty, and issues arising under federal statutes within that basic constitutional authority. The scope of constitutional authority was greatly expanded by the Fourteenth Amendment to the Constitution, which prohibits any enactment or enforcement of any law that abridges the "privileges and immunities of citizens," requires states to adhere to due process of law, and bans denial to any person of "equal protection of the laws."

The Supreme Court is the ultimate court of appeals on federal cases and state cases in which there are constitutional issues. The 1803 Supreme Court opinion in *Marbury v. Madison* confirmed its power to determine the constitutionality of statutes and government actions if brought before the court on appeal from actual cases.

All federal judgeships, including justices of the Supreme Court, are presidential appointees requiring confirmation by the Senate pursuant to its power to "advise and consent" to such appointments. All are lifetime appointments, based on good behavior.

UNITED STATES SUPREME COURT

There are nine justices of the Supreme Court, (chief justice and eight associate justices) appointed by the president, who also has the authority to name the chief justice if a vacancy occurs.

The annual term, when the court sits as a full court, begins the first week of October, and continues until the court decides to adjourn. As many as 7,000 appeals to the court are received each year, but most are not actually heard. Four of the nine justices must agree to actually hear a case, so many cases are rejected as not raising issues worth setting a new precedent, resolving conflicts among decisions of lower courts, or clarifying the law. Fewer than 200 cases are argued in front of the court annually, and an average of only 140 detailed opinions are signed each year. Certain types of orders can be issued by a single justice (procedural, reprieves, disclosure) and more than a thousand are applied for annually.

The courtroom is open to the public 9 A.M. to 4:30 P.M. each weekday, but when in session, seating may be limited. The clerk's office is open 9 A.M. to 5 P.M. weekdays unless ordered otherwise by the chief justice. The court and offices are closed on federal holidays. Its law library is open to attorneys who are members of the Supreme Court Bar, government lawyers, and members of Congress.

LOCATION United States Supreme Court Building, One First Street NE, Washington, DC 20543.

CONTACT Address: Office of the Clerk; Phone: (202) 479-3000; Website: www.supremecourtus. gov.

ADMINISTRATION

The officers of the Supreme Court are clerk of the Supreme Court, administrative assistant to the chief justice, court counsel, curator, director of budget and personnel, director of data systems, librarian, marshal, public information officer, and reporter of decisions. Each of these officials has a substantial staff.

Each justice has clerks assigned to him or her who are chosen from among recent law school graduates with outstanding academic records, who each serve for a year or more. They research the law and often write drafts of opinions under direction.

UNITED STATES COURTS OF APPEAL

There are 11 federal court circuits, each comprising several states, and each with a Court of Appeals. In addition, there is a federal circuit based in Washington, D.C., to hear customs, patent, and Court of Claims appeals, and an appeals court solely for the District of Columbia. Nationally, more than 40,000 appeals are heard each year. Each member of the Supreme Court is assigned a circuit to oversee, or to hear special matters, such as stays of execution. The term *circuit* stems from the original practice of having Supreme Court justices go on circuit to hear appeals, which was discontinued in 1891 when the Courts of Appeal were established.

Appointed for life by the president with Senate confirmation, the courts are usually three-judge panels whose written decisions can become the controlling law within the circuit. When different circuits have conflicting rulings on the same topic, the Supreme Court is likely to choose to hear an appeal on the latest case on the subject in order to have consistency.

There are also specialized federal courts: *United States Court of International Trade,* sitting in New York City; and based in Washington, D.C., the *United States Court of Federal Claims,* the *United States Tax Court,* and the *United States Court of Veterans Appeals.*

The circuits and states each encompasses are as follows: **First Circuit:** Maine, Massachusetts, New Hampshire, Rhode Island, Puerto Rico, Clerk at Boston, Massachusetts 02109; **Second Circuit:** Connecticut, New York, Vermont, Clerk at New York City, New York 10007; **Third Circuit:** Delaware, New Jersey, Pennsylvania Virgin Islands, Clerk at Philadelphia, Pennsylvania; **Fourth Circuit:** Maryland, North Carolina, South Carolina, Virginia, West Virginia, Clerk at Richmond, Virginia 23219; **Fifth Circuit:** Louisiana, Mississippi, Texas, Clerk at New Orleans, Lousiana 70103; **Sixth Circuit:** Kentucky, Michigan, Ohio, Tennessee, Clerk at Cincinnati, Ohio 45202; **Seventh Circuit:** Illinois, Indiana, Wisconsin, Clerk at Chicago, Illinois 60604; **Eighth Circuit:** Arkansas, Iowa, Minnesota, Missouri, Nebraska, North Dakota, South Dakota, Clerk at St. Louis, Missouri 63101; **Ninth Circuit:** Alaska, Arizona, California, Hawaii, Idaho, Montana, Nevada, Oregon, Washington, Guam, North Mariana Islands, Clerk at San Francisco, California 94119; **Tenth Circuit:** Colorado, Kansas, New Mexico, Oklahoma, Utah, Wyoming, Clerk at Denver, Colorado; **Eleventh Circuit:** Alabama, Florida, Georgia, Clerk at Atlanta, Georgia; **Federal Circuit:** Clerk at Washington, D.C. 20439; **District of Columbia,** Clerk at Washington, D.C. 20001.

UNITED STATES DISTRICT COURTS

The district courts are the trial courts for federal cases. About half the courts serve an entire state and the District of Columbia, but the geographically larger states have two or more district courts (California has four). In each district there is a federal prosecutor, known as the United States attorney.

There are also territorial district courts for Guam, Puerto Rico, and the Virgin Islands.

～ THE CONSTITUTION ～

The Constitution of the United States is a remarkable and unique document. It was the first charter in history that founded a nation's government completely by a single instrument. Since its adoption and ratification, the Constitution has remained the underlying basis of American governmental concepts and institutions for more than 200 years.

Starting in 1777, while the American Revolution was being fought, the United States of America formed a government pursuant to the Articles of Confederation. There was no regular executive, but a Congress, chaired by an annual president, which attempted to conduct government with the 13 states (the former colonies) acting as members of what amounted to a league of states without a head of state, no taxation system, no federal courts, and trade barriers between states. In 1787 there was a call for a national convention to revise and improve the Articles. However, many political leaders felt that an entirely new governmental structure was necessary and that the Articles should be sent to the dustbin.

The legislatures of various states responded by sending delegates who trickled in for almost a month until a quorum was able to meet in the assembly room on the second floor of Independence Hall, which was also used for the Pennsylvania legislature. The universally respected General George Washington, of Virginia, who had led the Continental Army to victory, was chosen as president of the convention. Delegates included Virginia's young James Madison, who came prepared with an outline of the separation of powers format; aged Benjamin Franklin of Pennsylvania, known as a scientist, diplomat, and publisher; brilliant Alexander Hamilton of New York; tough old Roger Sherman of Connecticut; and other leading patriots and state leaders. To a great extent these were the elite of the nation.

Thomas Jefferson and John Adams were not present since they were serving as ambassadors in Europe. Nor were patriot leaders Patrick Henry, John Hancock, and Governor George Clinton of New York, who feared surrender of states rights and powers to a powerful central government. There was genuine concern that giving the head of government too much power might lead to a monarchy, a dictatorship, or oppression of the people by the rich and powerful. But the majority believed that the success of this fragile nation required an end to the chaos and lack of cohesion. A couple of delegates stomped out in protest over certain provisions and a lack of a bill of rights. As September 1778 opened, the Pennsylvania legislature requested the convention to wrap up its business so it could begin its fall session. To ensure the support of the southern delegates, the issue of slavery was specifically put over for 20 years. In most states ratification led to strenuous debate, but eventually the document was ratified by the necessary nine states, including the key states of New York, Massachusetts, and Virginia.

In what has been called the "Miracle in Philadelphia," some of the finest political minds of the 18th century hammered out a system that produced the reality of checks and balances of three separate branches of government—legislative, executive, and judicial—and reached a compromise of the interests and powers of states both large and small by creating the House of Representatives with seats based on population and the Senate with two seats per state. The delegates literally "invented" the office of vice president, which guaranteed a smooth transition upon the death or removal of the president, and thus avoided the struggles for succession that had plagued other countries for thousands of years. The power to declare war was exclusively given to Congress as was the right to impose taxes.

Both within the language of the original Constitution and the prompt adoption of the first 10 amendments (the Bill of Rights) in 1791 are many of the protections of individual civil liberties against a government or its officials trampling on individual rights. Amendment was made purposefully difficult (passage by Congress and ratification by three-quarters of the states) so that changes are made only when there is substantial public support and apparent need.

After the first 10 amendments, which were essentially part of the original, only 17 amendments have been adopted. The Thirteenth in 1865 outlawed slavery after the Civil War. Several concerned elections and voting rights: voting separately for president and vice president (Twelfth in 1804), votes for ex-slaves (Fifteenth in 1870), election of senators by popular vote instead of the legislatures (Seventeenth in 1913), votes for women (Nineteenth in 1920), three electoral votes for the District of Columbia (Twenty-third in 1961), prohibiting the poll tax (Twenty-fourth in 1964), a national voting age of 18 (Twenty-sixth in 1971). Other amendments legalized a federal income tax (Sixteenth in 1913), shortened the period between presidential election and inauguration (Twentieth in 1933), presidential terms limited to two (Twenty-second in 1951), set up a system for filling a vacancy in the vice presidency and determining if a president was unable to perform his/her duties (Twenty-fifth in 1967). The Eighteenth (1919) and Twenty-first (1933) Amendments first estab-

lished the prohibition of the manufacture and sale of alcoholic liquor and then repealed it. The Eleventh (1798) Amendment was a technical clarification of court jurisdictions, and the most recent was the Twenty-seventh, which was passed by Congress in its first session on September 25, 1789, but was not ratified by sufficient states until this was noticed and it was then submitted to more states and ratified on May 7, 1992. It provided that Congress could not increase the salaries of members for the current term.

The Fourteenth Amendment was adopted in 1868 following the Civil War and was intended to guarantee full civil rights to ex-slaves. It included the language "that no state shall make or enforce any law which shall abridge the privileges or immunities of citizens of the United States . . . nor deny to any person . . . the equal protection of the laws." These rights to equal protection have formed the basis for applying the Bill of Rights (speech, assembly, against self-incrimination, due process, and so forth) to states and not just the federal government. The Supreme Court rulings that ended school segregation, mandated legislative districts of equal population, and the right of a criminal suspect to be advised of civil rights (the "Miranda" warnings) are all grounded in the right to "equal protection."

The American Constitution is a dynamic document that has been able to reflect changes in social attitudes, modernization, and greater democracy (a word that does not exist in the Constitution). An entire system of judicial review and interpretation of statutes and actions based on constitutional tests has arisen, which both expands and details the meaning and application of the Constitution. Nevertheless, it is essentially a conservative work embodying basic values and an essential structure that prevents dictatorial control by the government or by any of its branches. It can be looked to as the fundamental basis of government and law without bending to the winds of public opinion, political pressures, fears, or the latest social fad. By 1803 the authority of the Supreme Court to serve as the final arbiter of constitutionality (if tested in actual legal cases appealed to the court) became ingrained in the American system and completed the balance of the three branches.

Nevertheless, the Constitution is not without its critics. The president and vice president are still elected through the Electoral College, in which each state casts its electoral votes (one for each representative and senator) based on the majority—no matter how slim—cast for the candidates in that state, which has resulted in the loser in the popular vote winning the electoral vote, as in the 2000 election. The Electoral College was embodied in the Constitution when it was thought that the electors would be leading citizens chosen by the state legislatures. This indirect method has been outdated since 1828, when virtually all states chose electors by popular vote, but it persists.

Much of the criticism is directed not at the Constitution itself, but on interpretations by the Supreme Court, whether considered to be stretching the meaning of its language or narrowly out of step with modern experience. At various times the court has faced a claim that it has been politicized in the sense that appointments are made on the basis of a prospective justice's views on particular issues.

However, the American Constitution is a solid bedrock, particularly compared to the constitutions of other nations. China has adopted four different constitutions in the last half century. Mexico has amended its constitution more than 300 times since 1917. Canada put in place its Declaration of Rights only in 1982. Great Britain's constitution is in great measure a body of unwritten custom.

Like the old U.S. warship *Constitution,* it is justifiably "Old Ironsides."

THE CONSTITUTION OF THE UNITED STATES

We the people of the United States, in order to form a more perfect union, establish justice, insure domestic tranquility, provide for the common defense, promote the general welfare, and secure the blessings of liberty to ourselves and our posterity, do ordain and establish this Constitution for the United States of America.

ARTICLE I
(Legislative Department)

Section 1. All legislative powers herein granted shall be vested in a Congress of the United States, which shall consist of a Senate and House of Representatives.

Section 2. The House of Representatives shall be composed of members chosen every second year by the people of the several states, and the electors in each state shall have the qualifications requisite for electors of the most numerous branch of the state legislature.

No person shall be a Representative who shall not have attained to the age of twenty five years, and been seven years a citizen of the United States, and who shall not, when elected, be an inhabitant of that state in which he shall be chosen.

Representatives and direct taxes shall be apportioned among the several states which may be included within this union, according to their respective numbers, which shall be determined by adding to the whole number of free persons, including those bound to service for a term of years, and excluding Indians not taxed, three fifths of all other Persons. The actual Enumeration shall be made within three years after the first meeting of the Congress of the United States, and within every subsequent term of ten years, in such manner as they shall by law direct.

The number of Representatives shall not exceed one for every thirty thousand, but each state shall have at least one Representative; and until such enumeration shall be made, the state of New Hampshire shall be entitled to choose three, Massachusetts eight, Rhode Island and Providence Plantations one, Connecticut five, New York six, New Jersey four, Pennsylvania eight, Delaware one, Maryland six, Virginia ten, North Carolina five, South Carolina five, and Georgia three.

When vacancies happen in the Representation from any state, the executive authority thereof shall issue writs of election to fill such vacancies.

The House of Representatives shall choose their speaker and other officers; and shall have the sole power of impeachment.

Section 3. The Senate of the United States shall be composed of two Senators from each state, chosen by the legislature thereof, for six years; and each Senator shall have one vote. Immediately after they shall be assembled in consequence of the first election, they shall be divided as equally as may be into three classes. The seats of the Senators of the first class shall be vacated at the expiration of the second year, of the second class at the expiration of the fourth year, and the third class at the expiration of the sixth year, so that one third may be chosen every second year; and if vacancies happen by resignation, or otherwise, during the recess of the legislature of any state, the executive thereof may make temporary appointments until the next meeting of the legislature, which shall then fill such vacancies.

No person shall be a Senator who shall not have attained to the age of thirty years, and been nine years a citizen of the United States and who shall not, when elected, be an inhabitant of that state for which he shall be chosen.

The Vice President of the United States shall be President of the Senate, but shall have no vote, unless they be equally divided.

The Senate shall choose their other officers, and also a President pro tempore, in the absence of the Vice President, or when he shall exercise the office of President of the United States.

The Senate shall have the sole power to try all impeachments. When sitting for that purpose, they shall be on oath or affirmation. When the President of the United States is tried, the Chief Justice shall preside: And no person shall be convicted without the concurrence of two thirds of the members present.

Judgment in cases of impeachment shall not extend further than to removal from office, and disqualification to hold and enjoy any office of honor, trust or profit under the United States: but the party convicted shall nevertheless be liable and subject to indictment, trial, judgment and punishment, according to law.

Section 4. The times, places and manner of holding elections for Senators and Representatives, shall be prescribed in each state by the legislature thereof; but the Congress may at any time by law make or alter such regulations, except as to the places of choosing Senators.

The Congress shall assemble at least once in every year, and such meeting shall be on the first Monday in December, unless they shall by law appoint a different day.

Section 5. Each House shall be the judge of the elections, returns and qualifications of its own members, and a majority of each shall constitute a quorum to do business; but a smaller number may adjourn from day to day, and may be authorized to compel the attendance of absent members, in such manner, and under such penalties as each House may provide.

Each House may determine the rules of its proceedings, punish its members for disorderly behavior, and, with the concurrence of two thirds, expel a member.

Each House shall keep a journal of its proceedings, and from time to time publish the same, excepting such parts as may in their judgment require secrecy; and the yeas and nays of the members of either House on any question shall, at the desire of one fifth of those present, be entered on the journal.

Neither House, during the session of Congress, shall, without the consent of the other, adjourn for more than three days, nor to any other place than that in which the two Houses shall be sitting.

Section 6. The Senators and Representatives shall receive a compensation for their services, to be ascertained by law, and paid out of the treasury of the United States. They shall in all cases, except treason, felony and breach of the peace, be privileged from arrest during their attendance at the session of their respective Houses, and in going to and returning from the same; and for any speech or debate in either House, they shall not be questioned in any other place. No Senator or Representative shall, during the time for which he was elected, be appointed to any civil office under the authority of the United States, which shall have been created, or the emoluments whereof shall have been increased during such time: and no person holding any office under the United States, shall be a member of either House during his continuance in office.

Section 7. All bills for raising revenue shall originate in the House of Representatives; but the Senate may propose or concur with amendments as on other Bills.

Every bill which shall have passed the House of Representatives and the Senate, shall, before it become a law, be presented to the President of the United States; if he approve he shall sign it, but if not he shall return it, with his objections to that

House in which it shall have originated, who shall enter the objections at large on their journal, and proceed to reconsider it. If after such reconsideration two thirds of that House shall agree to pass the bill, it shall be sent, together with the objections, to the other House, by which it shall likewise be reconsidered, and if approved by two thirds of that House, it shall become a law. But in all such cases the votes of both Houses shall be determined by yeas and nays, and the names of the persons voting for and against the bill shall be entered on the journal of each House respectively. If any bill shall not be returned by the President within ten days (Sundays excepted) after it shall have been presented to him, the same shall be a law, in like manner as if he had signed it, unless the Congress by their adjournment prevent its return, in which case it shall not be a law.

Every order, resolution, or vote to which the concurrence of the Senate and House of Representatives may be necessary (except on a question of adjournment) shall be presented to the President of the United States; and be-fore the same shall take effect, shall be approved by him, or being disapproved by him, shall be repassed by two thirds of the Senate and House of Representatives, according to the rules and limitations prescribed in the case of a bill.

Section 8. The Congress shall have power to lay and collect taxes, duties, imposts and excises, to pay the debts and provide for the common defense and general welfare of the United States; but all duties, imposts and excises shall be uniform throughout the United States;

To borrow money on the credit of the United States;

To regulate commerce with foreign nations, and among the several states, and with the Indian tribes;

To establish a uniform rule of naturalization, and uniform laws on the subject of bankruptcies throughout the United States;

To coin money, regulate the value thereof, and of foreign coin, and fix the standard of weights and measures;

To provide for the punishment of counterfeiting the securities and current coin of the United States;

To establish post offices and post roads;

To promote the progress of science and useful arts, by securing for limited times to authors and inventors the exclusive right to their respective writings and discoveries;

To constitute tribunals inferior to the Supreme Court;

To define and punish piracies and felonies committed on the high seas, and offenses against the law of nations;

To declare war, grant letters of marque and reprisal, and make rules concerning captures on land and water;

To raise and support armies, but no appropriation of money to that use shall be for a longer term than two years;

To provide and maintain a navy;

To make rules for the government and regulation of the land and naval forces;

To provide for calling forth the militia to execute the laws of the union, suppress insurrections and repel invasions;

To provide for organizing, arming, and disciplining, the militia, and for governing such part of them as may be employed in the service of the United States, reserving to the states respectively, the appointment of the officers, and the authority of training the militia according to the discipline prescribed by Congress;

To exercise exclusive legislation in all cases whatsoever, over such District (not exceeding ten miles square) as may, by cession of particular states, and the acceptance of Congress, become the seat of the government of the United States, and to exercise like authority over all places purchased by the consent of the legislature of the state in which the same shall be, for the erection of forts, magazines, arsenals, dockyards, and other needful buildings;—And

To make all laws which shall be necessary and proper for carrying into execution the foregoing powers, and all other powers vested by this Constitution in the government of the United States, or in any department or officer thereof.

Section 9. The migration or importation of such persons as any of the states now existing shall think proper to admit, shall not be prohibited by the Congress prior to the year one thousand eight hundred and eight, but a tax or duty may be imposed on such importation, not exceeding ten dollars for each person.

The privilege of the writ of habeas corpus shall not be suspended, unless when in cases of rebellion or invasion the public safety may require it.

No bill of attainder or ex post facto Law shall be passed.

No capitation, or other direct, tax shall be laid, unless in proportion to the census or enumeration herein before directed to be taken.

No tax or duty shall be laid on articles exported from any state.

No preference shall be given by any regulation of commerce or revenue to the ports of one state over those of another: nor shall vessels bound to, or from, one state, be obliged to enter, clear or pay duties in another.

No money shall be drawn from the treasury, but in consequence of appropriations made by law; and a regular statement and account of receipts and expenditures of all public money shall be published from time to time.

No title of nobility shall be granted by the United States: and no person holding any office of profit or trust under them, shall, without the consent of the Congress, accept of any present, emolument, office, or title, of any kind whatever, from any king, prince, or foreign state.

Section 10. No state shall enter into any treaty, alliance, or confederation; grant letters of marque and reprisal; coin money; emit bills of credit; make anything but gold and silver coin a tender in payment of debts; pass any bill of attainder, ex post facto law, or law impairing the obligation of contracts, or grant any title of nobility.

No state shall, without the consent of the Congress, lay any imposts or duties on imports or exports, except what may be absolutely necessary for executing its inspection laws: and the net produce of all duties and imposts, laid by any state on imports or exports, shall be for the use of the treasury of the United States; and all such laws shall be subject to the revision and control of the Congress.

No state shall, without the consent of Congress, lay any duty of tonnage, keep troops, or ships of war in time of peace, enter into any agreement or compact with another state, or with a foreign power, or engage in war, unless actually invaded, or in such imminent danger as will not admit of delay.

ARTICLE II
(Executive Department)

Section 1. The executive power shall be vested in a President of the United States of America. He shall hold his office during the term of four years, and, together with the Vice President, chosen for the same term, be elected, as follows:

Each state shall appoint, in such manner as the Legislature thereof may direct, a number of electors, equal to the whole number of Senators and Representatives to which the State may be entitled in the Congress: but no Senator or Representative, or person holding an office of trust or profit under the United States, shall be appointed an elector.

The electors shall meet in their respective states, and vote by ballot for two persons, of whom one at least shall not be an inhabitant of the same state with themselves. And they shall make a list of all the persons voted for, and of the number of votes for each; which list they shall sign and certify, and transmit sealed to the seat of the government of the United States, directed to the President of the Senate. The President of the Senate shall, in the presence of the Senate and House of Representatives, open all the certificates, and the votes shall then be counted. The person having the greatest number of votes shall be the President, if such number be a majority of the whole number of electors appointed; and if there be more than one who have such majority, and have an equal number of votes, then the House of Representatives shall immediately choose by ballot one of them for President; and if no person have a majority, then from the five highest on the list the said House shall in like manner choose the President. But in choosing the President, the votes shall be taken by States, the representation from each state having one vote; A quorum for this purpose shall consist of a member or members from two thirds of the states, and a majority of all the states shall be necessary to a choice. In every case, after the choice of the President, the person having the greatest number of votes of the electors shall be the Vice President. But if there should remain two or more who have equal votes, the Senate shall choose from them by ballot the Vice President.

The Congress may determine the time of choosing the electors, and the day on which they shall give their votes; which day shall be the same throughout the United States.

No person except a natural born citizen, or a citizen of the United States, at the time of the adoption of this Constitution, shall be eligible to the office of President; neither shall any person be eligible to that office who shall not have attained to the age of thirty five years, and been fourteen Years a resident within the United States.

In case of the removal of the President from office, or of his death, resignation, or inability to discharge the powers and duties of the said office, the same shall devolve on the Vice President, and the Congress may by law provide for the case of

removal, death, resignation or inability, both of the President and Vice President, declaring what officer shall then act as President, and such officer shall act accordingly, until the disability be removed, or a President shall be elected.

The President shall, at stated times, receive for his services, a compensation, which shall neither be increased nor diminished during the period for which he shall have been elected, and he shall not receive within that period any other emolument from the United States, or any of them.

Before he enter on the execution of his office, he shall take the following oath or affirmation:—"I do solemnly swear (or affirm) that I will faithfully execute the office of President of the United States, and will to the best of my ability, preserve, protect and defend the Constitution of the United States."

Section 2. The President shall be commander in chief of the Army and Navy of the United States, and of the militia of the several states, when called into the actual service of the United States; he may require the opinion, in writing, of the principal officer in each of the executive departments, on any subject relating to the duties of their respective offices, and he shall have power to grant reprieves and pardons for offenses against the United States, except in cases of impeachment.

He shall have power, by and with the advice and consent of the Senate, to make treaties, provided two thirds of the Senators present concur; and he shall nominate, and by and with the advice and consent of the Senate, shall appoint ambassadors, other public ministers and consuls, judges of the Supreme Court, and all other officers of the United States, whose appointments are not herein otherwise provided for, and which shall be established by law: but the Congress may by law vest the appointment of such inferior officers, as they think proper, in the President alone, in the courts of law, or in the heads of departments.

The President shall have power to fill up all vacancies that may happen during the recess of the Senate, by granting commissions which shall expire at the end of their next session.

Section 3. He shall from time to time give to the Congress information of the state of the union, and recommend to their consideration such measures as he shall judge necessary and expedient; he may, on extraordinary occasions, convene both Houses, or either of them, and in case of disagreement between them, with respect to the time of adjournment, he may adjourn them to such time as he shall think proper; he shall receive ambassadors and other public ministers; he shall take care that the laws be faithfully executed, and shall commission all the officers of the United States.

Section 4. The President, Vice President and all civil officers of the United States, shall be removed from office on impeachment for, and conviction of, treason, bribery, or other high crimes and misdemeanors.

ARTICLE III
(Judicial Department)

Section 1. The judicial power of the United States, shall be vested in one Supreme Court, and in such inferior courts as the Congress may from time to time ordain and establish. The judges, both of the supreme and inferior courts, shall hold their offices during good behavior, and shall, at stated times, receive for their services, a compensation, which shall not be diminished during their continuance in office.

Section 2. The judicial power shall extend to all cases, in law and equity, arising under this Constitution, the laws of the United States, and treaties made, or which shall be made, under their authority;—to all cases affecting ambassadors, other public ministers and consuls;—to all cases of admiralty and maritime jurisdiction;—to controversies to which the United States shall be a party;—to controversies between two or more states;—between a state and citizens of another state;—between citizens of different states;—between citizens of the same state claiming lands under grants of different states, and between a state, or the citizens thereof, and foreign states, citizens or subjects.

In all cases affecting ambassadors, other public ministers and consuls, and those in which a state shall be party, the Supreme Court shall have original jurisdiction. In all the other cases before mentioned, the Supreme Court shall have appellate jurisdiction, both as to law and fact, with such exceptions, and under such regulations as the Congress shall make.

The trial of all crimes, except in cases of impeachment, shall be by jury; and such trial shall be held in the state where the said crimes shall have been committed; but when not committed within any state, the trial shall be at such place or places as the Congress may by law have directed.

Section 3. Treason against the United States, shall consist only in levying war against them, or in adhering to their enemies, giving them aid and comfort. No person shall be convicted of treason unless on the testimony of two witnesses to the same overt act, or on confession in open court.

The Congress shall have power to declare the punishment of treason, but no attainder of treason shall work corruption of blood, or forfeiture except during the life of the person attainted.

ARTICLE IV
(The States and the Federal Government)

Section 1. Full faith and credit shall be given in each state to the public acts, records, and judicial proceedings of every other state. And the Congress may by general laws prescribe the manner in which such acts, records, and proceedings shall be proved, and the effect thereof.

Section 2. The citizens of each state shall be entitled to all privileges and immunities of citizens in the several states.

A person charged in any state with treason, felony, or other crime, who shall flee from justice, and be found in another state, shall on demand of the executive authority of the state from which he fled, be delivered up, to be removed to the state having jurisdiction of the crime.

No person held to service or labor in one state, under the laws thereof, escaping into another, shall, in consequence of any law or regulation therein, be discharged from such service or labor, but shall be delivered up on claim of the party to whom such service or labor may be due.

Section 3. New states may be admitted by the Congress into this union; but no new states shall be formed or erected within the jurisdiction of any other state; nor any state be formed by the junction of two or more states, or parts of states, without the consent of the legislatures of the states concerned as well as of the Congress.

The Congress shall have power to dispose of and make all needful rules and regulations respecting the territory or other property belonging to the United States; and nothing in this Constitution shall be so construed as to prejudice any claims of the United States, or of any particular state.

Section 4. The United States shall guarantee to every state in this union a republican form of government, and shall protect each of them against invasion; and on application of the legislature, or of the executive (when the legislature cannot be convened) against domestic violence.

ARTICLE V
(Amendment)

The Congress, whenever two thirds of both houses shall deem it necessary, shall propose amendments to this Constitution, or, on the application of the legislatures of two thirds of the several states, shall call a convention for proposing amendments, which, in either case, shall be valid to all intents and purposes, as part of this Constitution, when ratified by the legislatures of three fourths of the several states, or by conventions in three fourths thereof, as the one or the other mode of ratification may be proposed by the Congress; provided that no amendment which may be made prior to the year one thousand eight hundred and eight shall in any manner affect the first and fourth clauses in the ninth section of the first article; and that no state, without its consent, shall be deprived of its equal suffrage in the Senate.

ARTICLE VI
(General Provisions)

All debts contracted and engagements entered into, before the adoption of this Constitution, shall be as valid against the United States under this Constitution, as under the Confederation.

This Constitution, and the laws of the United States which shall be made in pursuance thereof; and all treaties made, or which shall be made, under the authority of the United States, shall be the supreme law of the land; and the judges in every state shall be bound thereby, anything in the Constitution or laws of any State to the contrary notwithstanding.

The Senators and Representatives before mentioned, and the members of the several state legislatures, and all executive and judicial officers, both of the United States and of the several states, shall be bound by oath or affirmation, to support this Constitution; but no religious test shall ever be required as a qualification to any office or public trust under the United States.

ARTICLE VII
(Ratification)

The ratification of the conventions of nine states, shall be sufficient for the establishment of this Constitution between the states so ratifying the same.

Done in convention by the unanimous consent of the states present the seventeenth day of September in the year of our Lord one thousand seven hundred and eighty seven and of the independence of the United States of America the twelfth. In witness whereof We have hereunto subscribed our Names,

G. WASHINGTON: Presidt. and deputy from Virginia

New Hampshire: JOHN LANGDON, NICHOLAS GILMAN

Massachusetts: NATHANIEL GORHAM, RUFUS KING

Connecticut: WM: SAML. JOHNSON, ROGER SHERMAN

New York: ALEXANDER HAMILTON

New Jersey: WIL LIVINGSTON, DAVID BREARLY, WM. PATERSON, JONA: DAYTON

Pennsylvania: B. FRANKLIN, THOMAS MIFFLIN, ROBT. MORRIS, GEO. CLYMER, THOS. FITZSIMONS, JARED INGERSOLL, JAMES WILSON, GOUV MORRIS

Delaware: GEO: READ, GUNNING BEDFORD JUN, JOHN DICKINSON, RICHARD BASSETT, JACO: BROOM

Maryland: JAMES MCHENRY, DAN OF ST THOS. JENIFER, DANL CARROLL

Virginia: JOHN BLAIR—, JAMES MADISON JR.

North Carolina: WM. BLOUNT, RICHD. DOBBS SPAIGHT, HU WILLIAMSON

South Carolina: J. RUTLEDGE, CHARLES COTESWORTH PINCKNEY, CHARLES PINCKNEY, PIERCE BUTLER

Georgia: WILLIAM FEW, ABR BALDWIN

[The first 10 amendments, known as the *Bill of Rights,* were passed by Congress on September 25, 1789, and ratified by sufficient states on December 15, 1791.]

AMENDMENT I

Freedom of religion, speech, press, assembly, and petition

[Passed September 25, 1789, ratified by sufficient states December 15, 1791]

Congress shall make no law respecting an establishment of religion, or prohibiting the free exercise thereof; or abridging the freedom of speech, or of the press; or the right of the people peaceably to assemble, and to petition the government for a redress of grievances.

AMENDMENT II

Right of state militia to bear arms

[Passed September 25, 1789, ratified by sufficient states December 15, 1791]

A well regulated militia, being necessary to the security of a free state, the right of the people to keep and bear arms, shall not be infringed.

AMENDMENT III

Prohibition against quartering soldiers in private homes

[Passed September 25, 1789, ratified by sufficient states December 15, 1791]

No soldier shall, in time of peace be quartered in any house, without the consent of the owner, nor in time of war, but in a manner to be prescribed by law.

AMENDMENT IV

No unreasonable searches and seizures, warrants required

[Passed September 25, 1789, ratified by sufficient states December 15, 1791]

The right of the people to be secure in their persons, houses, papers, and effects, against unreasonable searches and seizures, shall not be violated, and no warrants shall issue, but upon probable cause, supported by oath or affirmation, and particularly describing the place to be searched, and the persons or things to be seized.

AMENDMENT V

Indictments required, prohibitions against double jeopardy, being a witness against oneself, or deprivation of life or property without due process; just compensation for condemnation of property

[Passed September 25, 1789, ratified by sufficient states December 15, 1791]

No person shall be held to answer for a capital, or otherwise infamous crime, unless on a presentment or indictment of a grand jury, except in cases arising in the land or naval forces, or in the militia, when in actual service in time of war or public danger; nor shall any person be subject for the same offense to be twice put in jeopardy of life or limb; nor shall be compelled in any criminal case to be a witness against himself, nor be deprived of life, liberty, or property, without due process of law; nor shall private property be taken for public use, without just compensation.

AMENDMENT VI

In criminal cases right to speedy trial, jury, informed of charges, to confront witnesses, right of defendant to subpoena witnesses, and to have attorney

[Passed September 25, 1789, ratified by sufficient states December 15, 1791]

In all criminal prosecutions, the accused shall enjoy the right to a speedy and public trial, by an impartial jury of the state and district wherein the crime shall have been committed, which district shall have been previously ascertained by law, and to be informed of the nature and cause of the accusation; to be confronted with the witnesses against him; to have compulsory process for obtaining witnesses in his favor, and to have the assistance of counsel for his defense.

AMENDMENT VII

Right to jury in civil cases

[Passed September 25, 1789, ratified by sufficient states December 15, 1791]

In suits at common law, where the value in controversy shall exceed twenty dollars, the right of trial by jury shall be preserved, and no fact tried by a jury, shall be otherwise reexamined in any court of the United States, than according to the rules of the common law.

AMENDMENT VIII

Prohibitions against excessive bail, excessive fines, and cruel and unusual punishment

[Passed September 25, 1789, ratified by sufficient states December 15, 1791]

Excessive bail shall not be required, nor excessive fines imposed, nor cruel and unusual punishments inflicted.

AMENDMENT IX

Rights not enumerated may be retained by people

[Passed September 25, 1789, ratified by sufficient states December 15, 1791]

The enumeration in the Constitution, of certain rights, shall not be construed to deny or disparage others retained by the people.

AMENDMENT X

Powers not given to federal government reserved to states or people

[Passed September 25, 1789, ratified by sufficient states December 15, 1791]

The powers not delegated to the United States by the Constitution, nor prohibited by it to the states, are reserved to the states respectively, or to the people.

AMENDMENT XI

No federal court jurisdiction over suits by citizens of one state or foreign country against a state

[Proposed by Congress March 4, 1794, ratified by sufficient states February 7, 1795, declared ratified January 8, 1798]

The judicial power of the United States shall not be construed to extend to any suit in law or equity, commenced or prosecuted against one of the United States by citizens of another state, or by citizens or subjects of any foreign state.

AMENDMENT XII

Election of president and vice president separately

[Passed by both houses of Congress December 9, 1803, signed December 12, 1803, declared ratified by sufficient states September 25, 1804]

The electors shall meet in their respective states and vote by ballot for President and Vice-President, one of whom, at least, shall not be an inhabitant of the same state with themselves; they shall name in their ballots the person voted for as President, and in distinct ballots the person voted for as Vice-President, and they shall make distinct lists of all persons voted for as President, and of all persons voted for as Vice-President, and of the number of votes for each, which lists they shall sign and certify, and transmit sealed to the seat of the government of the United States, directed to the President of the Senate;—The President of the Senate shall, in the presence of the Senate and House of Representatives, open all the certificates and the votes shall then be counted;—the person having the greatest number of votes for President, shall be the President, if such number be a majority of the whole number of electors appointed; and if no person have such majority, then from the persons having the highest numbers not exceeding three on the list of those voted for as President, the House of Representatives shall choose immediately, by ballot, the President. But in choosing the President, the votes shall be taken by states, the representation from each state having one vote; a quorum for this purpose shall consist of a member or members from two-thirds of the states, and a majority of all the states shall be necessary to a choice. And if the House of Representatives shall not choose a President whenever the right of choice shall devolve upon them, before the fourth day of March next following, then the Vice-President shall act as President, as in the case of the death or other constitutional disability of the President. The person having the greatest number of votes as Vice-President, shall be the Vice-President, if such number be a majority of the whole number of electors appointed, and if no person have a majority, then from the two highest numbers on the list, the Senate shall choose the Vice-President; a quorum for the purpose shall consist of two-thirds of the whole number of Senators, and a majority of the whole number shall be necessary to a choice. But no person constitutionally ineligible to the office of President shall be eligible to that of Vice-President of the United States.

AMENDMENT XIII

Slavery prohibited

[Proposed—declared passed by Congress—January 31, 1865, ratified by sufficient states December 6, 1865, certified December 18, 1865]

Section 1. Neither slavery nor involuntary servitude, except as a punishment for crime whereof the party shall have been duly convicted, shall exist within the United States, or any place subject to their jurisdiction.

Section 2. Congress shall have power to enforce this article by appropriate legislation.

AMENDMENT XIV

States required to apply due process, and must give all citizens equal protection; former rebels cannot hold public office until Congress decides to lift ban, neither federal nor state governments may pay debts for rebellion or loss of slaves

[Proposed by Congress June 13, 1866, ratified by sufficient number of states July 9, 1868, certified July 28, 1868]

Section 1. All persons born or naturalized in the United States, and subject to the jurisdiction thereof, are citizens of the United States and of the state wherein they reside. No state shall make or enforce any law which shall abridge the privileges or immunities of citizens of the United States; nor shall any state deprive any person of life, liberty, or property, without due process of law; nor deny to any person within its jurisdiction the equal protection of the laws.

Section 2. Representatives shall be apportioned among the several states according to their respective numbers, counting the whole number of persons in each state, excluding Indians not taxed. But when the right to vote at any election for the choice of electors for President and Vice President of the United States, Representatives in Congress, the executive and judicial officers of a state, or the members of the legislature thereof, is denied to any of the male inhabitants of such state, being twenty-one years of age, and citizens of the United States, or in any way abridged, except for participation in rebellion, or other crime, the basis of representation therein shall be reduced in the proportion which the number of such male citizens shall bear to the whole number of male citizens twenty-one years of age in such state.

Section 3. No person shall be a Senator or Representative in Congress, or elector of President and Vice President, or hold any office, civil or military, under the United States, or under any state, who, having previously taken an oath, as a member of Congress, or as an officer of the United States, or as a member of any state legislature, or as an executive or judicial officer of any state, to support the Constitution of the United States, shall have engaged in insurrection or rebellion against the same, or given aid or comfort to the enemies thereof. But Congress may by a vote of two-thirds of each House, remove such disability.

Section 4. The validity of the public debt of the United States, authorized by law, including debts incurred for payment of pensions and bounties for services in suppressing insurrection or rebellion, shall not be questioned. But neither the United States nor any state shall assume or pay any debt or obligation incurred in aid of insurrection or rebellion against the United States, or any claim for the loss or emancipation of any slave; but all such debts, obligations and claims shall be held illegal and void.

Section 5. The Congress shall have power to enforce, by appropriate legislation, the provisions of this article.

AMENDMENT XV
Right to vote cannot be denied due to race, color, or former servitude

[Proposed by Congress February 26, 1869, ratified by sufficient number of states February 3, 1870, certified March 30, 1870]

Section 1. The right of citizens of the United States to vote shall not be denied or abridged by the United States or by any state on account of race, color, or previous condition of servitude.

Section 2. The Congress shall have power to enforce this article by appropriate legislation.

AMENDMENT XVI
Income tax authorized

[Proposed by Congress July 2, 1909, ratified by sufficient number of states February 3, 1913, certified March 30, 1913]

The Congress shall have power to lay and collect taxes on incomes, from whatever source derived, without apportionment among the several states, and without regard to any census of enumeration.

AMENDMENT XVII
Direct election of senators

[Proposed by Congress, May 13, 1912, ratified by sufficient number of states April 8, 1913, certified May 31, 1913]

The Senate of the United States shall be composed of two Senators from each state, elected by the people thereof, for six years; and each Senator shall have one vote. The electors in each state shall have the qualifications requisite for electors of the most numerous branch of the state legislatures.

When vacancies happen in the representation of any state in the Senate, the executive authority of such state shall issue writs of election to fill such vacancies: Provided, that the legislature of any state may empower the executive thereof to make temporary appointments until the people fill the vacancies by election as the legislature may direct.

This amendment shall not be so construed as to affect the election or term of any Senator chosen before it becomes valid as part of the Constitution.

AMENDMENT XVIII
Prohibition of manufacture, sale, or transportation of intoxicating liquors

[Proposed by Congress December 18, 1917, ratified by sufficient number of states January 16, 1919, certified January 29, 1919, became effective January 29, 1920]

Section 1. After one year from the ratification of this article the manufacture, sale, or transportation of intoxicating liquors within, the importation thereof into, or the exportation thereof from the United States and all territory subject to the jurisdiction thereof for beverage purposes is hereby prohibited.

Section 2. The Congress and the several states shall have concurrent power to enforce this article by appropriate legislation.

Section 3. This article shall be inoperative unless it shall have been ratified as an amendment to the Constitution by the legislatures of the several states, as provided in the Constitution, within seven years from the date of the submission hereof to the states by the Congress.

AMENDMENT XIX
No restriction on right to vote because of one's sex (women's right to vote)

[Proposed by Congress June 4, 1919, ratified by sufficient number of states August 18, 1920, certified August 26, 1920]

The right of citizens of the United States to vote shall not be denied or abridged by the United States or by any state on account of sex.

Congress shall have power to enforce this article by appropriate legislation.

AMENDMENT XX
Start of presidential and congressional terms moved to January; set succession if president elect dies before taking office

[Proposed by Congress March 2, 1932, ratified by sufficient states January 23, 1933, certified February 6, 1933]

Section 1. The terms of the President and Vice President shall end at noon on the 20th day of January, and the terms of Senators and Representatives at noon on the 3d day of January, of the years in which such terms would have ended if this article had not been ratified; and the terms of their successors shall then begin.

Section 2. The Congress shall assemble at least once in every year, and such meeting shall begin at noon on the 3d day of January, unless they shall by law appoint a different day.

Section 3. If, at the time fixed for the beginning of the term of the President, the President elect shall have died, the Vice President elect shall become President. If a President shall not have been chosen before the time fixed for the beginning of his term, or if the President elect shall have failed to qualify, then the Vice President elect shall act as President until a President shall have qualified; and the Congress may by law provide for the case wherein neither a President elect nor a Vice President elect shall have qualified, declaring who shall then act as President, or the manner in which one who is to act shall be selected, and such person shall act accordingly until a President or Vice President shall have qualified.

Section 4. The Congress may by law provide for the case of the death of any of the persons from whom the House of Representatives may choose a President whenever the right of choice shall have devolved upon them, and for the case of the death of any of the persons from whom the Senate may choose a Vice President whenever the right of choice shall have devolved upon them.

Section 5. Sections 1 and 2 shall take effect on the 15th day of October following the ratification of this article.

Section 6. This article shall be inoperative unless it shall have been ratified as an amendment to the Constitution by the legislatures of three-fourths of the several states within seven years from the date of its submission.

AMENDMENT XXI
Repeal of Prohibition
[Proposed by Congress February 20, 1933, ratified by sufficient states December 5, 1933, certified December 5, 1933]

Section 1. The eighteenth article of amendment to the Constitution of the United States is hereby repealed.

Section 2. The transportation or importation into any state, territory, or possession of the United States for delivery or use therein of intoxicating liquors, in violation of the laws thereof, is hereby prohibited.

Section 3. This article shall be inoperative unless it shall have been ratified as an amendment to the Constitution by conventions in the several states, as provided in the Constitution, within seven years from the date of the submission hereof to the states by the Congress.

AMENDMENT XXII
Presidents limited to two terms
[Proposed by Congress March 24, 1947, ratified by sufficient states, February 27, 1951, certified March 1, 1951]

Section 1. No person shall be elected to the office of the President more than twice, and no person who has held the office of President, or acted as President, for more than two years of a term to which some other person was elected President shall be elected to the office of the President more than once. But this article shall not apply to any person holding the office of President when this article was proposed by the Congress, and shall not prevent any person who may be holding the office of President, or acting as President, during the term within which this article becomes operative from holding the office of President or acting as President during the remainder of such term.

Section 2. This article shall be inoperative unless it shall have been ratified as an amendment to the Constitution by the legislatures of three-fourths of the several states within seven years from the date of its submission to the states by the Congress.

AMENDMENT XXIII
District of Columbia given electoral votes

[Proposed by Congress June 16, 1960, ratified by sufficient states March 29, 1961, certified April 3, 1961]

Section 1. The District constituting the seat of government of the United States shall appoint in such manner as the Congress may direct: A number of electors of President and Vice President equal to the whole number of Senators and Representatives in Congress to which the District would be entitled if it were a state, but in no event more than the least populous state; they shall be in addition to those appointed by the states, but they shall be considered, for the purposes of the election of President and Vice President, to be electors appointed by a state; and they shall meet in the District and perform such duties as provided by the twelfth article of amendment.

Section 2. The Congress shall have power to enforce this article by appropriate legislation.

AMENDMENT XXIV
Poll taxes prohibited

[Proposed by Congress September 14, 1962, ratified by sufficient states January 23, 1964, certified February 4, 1964]

Section 1. The right of citizens of the United States to vote in any primary or other election for President or Vice President, for electors for President or Vice President, or for Senator or Representative in Congress, shall not be denied or abridged by the United States or any state by reason of failure to pay any poll tax or other tax.

Section 2. The Congress shall have power to enforce this article by appropriate legislation.

AMENDMENT XXV
Filling vacancy in vice presidency, determining presidential disability

Section 1. In case of the removal of the President from office or of his death or resignation, the Vice President shall become President.

Section 2. Whenever there is a vacancy in the office of the Vice President, the President shall nominate a Vice President who shall take office upon confirmation by a majority vote of both Houses of Congress.

Section 3. Whenever the President transmits to the President pro tempore of the Senate and the Speaker of the House of Representatives his written declaration that he is unable to discharge the powers and duties of his office, and until he transmits to them a written declaration to the contrary, such powers and duties shall be discharged by the Vice President as Acting President.

Section 4. Whenever the Vice President and a majority of either the principal officers of the executive departments or of such other body as Congress may by law provide, transmit to the President pro tempore of the Senate and the Speaker of the House of Representatives their written declaration that the President is unable to discharge the powers and duties of his office, the Vice President shall immediately assume the powers and duties of the office as Acting President.

Thereafter, when the President transmits to the President pro tempore of the Senate and the Speaker of the House of Representatives his written declaration that no inability exists, he shall resume the powers and duties of his office unless the Vice President and a majority of either the principal officers of the executive department or of such other body as Congress may by law provide, transmit within four days to the President pro tempore of the Senate and the Speaker of the House of Representatives their written declaration that the President is unable to discharge the powers and duties of his office.

Thereupon Congress shall decide the issue, assembling within forty-eight hours for that purpose if not in session. If the Congress, within twenty-one days after receipt of the latter written declaration, or, if Congress is not in session, within twenty-one days after Congress is required to assemble, determines by two-thirds vote of both Houses that the President is unable to discharge the powers and duties of his office, the Vice President shall continue to discharge the same as Acting President; otherwise, the President shall resume the powers and duties of his office.

AMENDMENT XXVI
Voting age set at 18

[Proposed by Congress March 23, 1971, ratified by sufficient states July 1, 1971, certified July 7, 1971]

Section 1. The right of citizens of the United States, who are 18 years of age or older, to vote, shall not be denied or abridged by the United States or any state on account of age.

Section 2. The Congress shall have the power to enforce this article by appropriate legislation.

AMENDMENT XXVII
Congress cannot raise its pay during current term

[Proposed by Congress, September 25, 1789, ratified by sufficient states May 7, 1992, certified, May 18, 1992. Note: Congress passed this amendment on the same day as the first 10 amendments—the Bill of Rights—but it was not ratified by the states; a historian noted it could still be submitted to the states and ratified since there was no time limit included in the amendment. So after 203 years it was ratified]

No law varying the compensation for the services of the Senators and Representatives shall take effect until an election of Representatives shall have intervened.

~ BIBLIOGRAPHY ~

Burns, James MacGregor, J. W. Peltason, Thomas E. Cronin, David B. Magleby. *Government by the People.* Upper Saddle River, N.J.: Prentice Hall, 2000.

Freedman, Leonard. *Power & Politics in America,* 7th edition. New York: Harcourt Brace, 2000.

Hill, Kathleen Thompson, and Gerald N. Hill. *Facts On File Dictionary of American Politics.* New York: Facts On File, 2002.

Jilson, Cal. *American Government Political Change and Institutional Development.* New York: Harcourt Brace, 1999.

Lowi, Theodore J., Benjamin Ginsberg, Kenneth A. Shepsle. *American Government Power and Purpose.* New York: W. W. Norton, 2002.

O'Connor, Karen, and Larry J. Sabato. *American Government Continuity and Change.* New York: Addison Wesley Longman, 2002.

Patrick, John J., Richard M. Pious, Donald A. Ritchie. *Oxford Guide to the United States Government.* New York: Oxford University Press, 2001.

Schmidt, Steffen W., Mack C. Shelley, Barbara A. Bardes. *American Government and Politics Today.* St. Paul, Minn: West/Wadsworth, 1999.

Taylor, Jim. *The Book of Presidents.* New York: Arno Press, 1972.

United States Government Manual 2000/2003, Office of the Federal Register, National Archives and Records Administration, U. S. Government Printing Office, 2002.

U.S. Senate, Committee on Governmental Affairs. *United States Government Policy and Supporting Positions ("The Plum Book").* Washington, D.C.: U.S. Government Printing Office, 2000.

Wright, John W., ed. *New York Times Almanac.* New York: Penguin Reference, 2002.

— INDEX —

Boldface page numbers refer to main entries in the encyclopedia; page numbers followed by a *t* indicate illustrations.